Significance of Mathematical Modelling and Control in Real-World Problems: New Developments and Applications

Significance of Mathematical Modelling and Control in Real-World Problems: New Developments and Applications

Editors

Mehmet Yavuz
Ioannis Dassios

Basel • Beijing • Wuhan • Barcelona • Belgrade • Novi Sad • Cluj • Manchester

Editors
Mehmet Yavuz
Necmettin Erbakan University
Konya
Türkiye

Ioannis Dassios
University College Dublin
Dublin
Ireland

Editorial Office
MDPI AG
Grosspeteranlage 5
4052 Basel, Switzerland

This is a reprint of articles from the Special Issue published online in the open access journal *Mathematical and Computational Applications* (ISSN 2297-8747) (available at: https://www.mdpi.com/journal/mca/special_issues/Model_Ctrl_Probl).

For citation purposes, cite each article independently as indicated on the article page online and as indicated below:

Lastname, A.A.; Lastname, B.B. Article Title. *Journal Name* **Year**, *Volume Number*, Page Range.

ISBN 978-3-7258-2275-1 (Hbk)
ISBN 978-3-7258-2276-8 (PDF)
doi.org/10.3390/books978-3-7258-2276-8

© 2024 by the authors. Articles in this book are Open Access and distributed under the Creative Commons Attribution (CC BY) license. The book as a whole is distributed by MDPI under the terms and conditions of the Creative Commons Attribution-NonCommercial-NoDerivs (CC BY-NC-ND) license.

Contents

About the Editors vii

Mehmet Yavuz and Ioannis Dassios
Significance of Mathematical Modeling and Control in Real-World Problems: New Developments and Applications
Reprinted from: *Math. Comput. Appl.* **2024**, *29*, 82, doi:10.3390/mca29050082 1

Dominic P. Clemence-Mkhope and Belinda G. B. Clemence-Mkhope
The Limited Validity of the Conformable Euler Finite Difference Method and an Alternate Definition of the Conformable Fractional Derivative to Justify Modification of the Method
Reprinted from: *Math. Comput. Appl.* **2021**, *26*, 66, doi:10.3390/mca26040066 5

Dominic P. Clemence-Mkhope and Gregory A. Gibson
Taming Hyperchaos with Exact Spectral Derivative Discretization Finite Difference Discretization of a Conformable Fractional Derivative Financial System with Market Confidence and Ethics Risk
Reprinted from: *Math. Comput. Appl.* **2022**, *27*, 4, doi:10.3390/mca27010004 16

Fatima Rabah, Marwan Abukhaled and Suheil A. Khuri
Solution of A Complex Nonlinear Fractional Biochemical Reaction Model
Reprinted from: *Math. Comput. Appl.* **2022**, *27*, 45, doi:10.3390/mca27030045 45

B. M. Tamilzharasan, S. Karthikeyan, Mohammed K. A. Kaabar, Mehmet Yavuz and Fatma Özköse
Magneto Mixed Convection of Williamson Nanofluid Flow through a Double Stratified Porous Medium in Attendance of Activation Energy
Reprinted from: *Math. Comput. Appl.* **2022**, *27*, 46, doi:10.3390/mca27030046 59

Sheniyappan Eswaramoorthi, S. Thamaraiselvi and Karuppusamy Loganathan
Exploration of Darcy–Forchheimer Flows of Non-Newtonian Casson and Williamson Conveying Tiny Particles Experiencing Binary Chemical Reaction and Thermal Radiation: Comparative Analysis
Reprinted from: *Math. Comput. Appl.* **2022**, *27*, 52, doi:10.3390/mca27030052 79

Gundlapally Shiva Kumar Reddy, Nilam Venkata Koteswararao, Ragoju Ravi, Kiran Kumar Paidipati and Christophe Chesneau
Dissolution-Driven Convection in a Porous Medium Due to Vertical Axis of Rotation and Magnetic Field
Reprinted from: *Math. Comput. Appl.* **2022**, *27*, 53, doi:10.3390/mca27030053 96

Chirnam Ramchandraiah, Naikoti Kishan, Gundlapally Shiva Kumar Reddy, Kiran Kumar Paidipati and Christophe Chesneau
Double-Diffusive Convection in Bidispersive Porous Medium with Coriolis Effect
Reprinted from: *Math. Comput. Appl.* **2022**, *27*, 56, doi:10.3390/mca27040056 111

Muhammad Sajjad Hossain, Muhammad Fayz-Al-Asad, Muhammad Saiful Islam Mallik, Mehmet Yavuz, Md. Abdul Alim and Kazi Md. Khairul Basher
Numerical Study of the Effect of a Heated Cylinder on Natural Convection in a Square Cavity in the Presence of a Magnetic Field
Reprinted from: *Math. Comput. Appl.* **2022**, *27*, 58, doi:10.3390/mca27040058 124

Ihtisham Ul Haq, Mehmet Yavuz, Nigar Ali and Ali Akgül
A SARS-CoV-2 Fractional-Order Mathematical Model via the Modified Euler Method
Reprinted from: *Math. Comput. Appl.* **2022**, *27*, 82, doi:10.3390/mca27050082 . . . . **141**

Amar Debbouche, Bhaskar Sundara Vadivoo, Vladimir E. Fedorov and Valery Antonov
Controllability Criteria for Nonlinear Impulsive Fractional Differential Systems with Distributed Delays in Controls
Reprinted from: *Math. Comput. Appl.* **2023**, *28*, 13, doi:10.3390/mca28010013 . . . . **157**

S. Divya, S. Eswaramoorthi and Karuppusamy Loganathan
Numerical Computation of Ag/Al_2O_3 Nanofluid over a Riga Plate with Heat Sink/Source and Non-Fourier Heat Flux Model
Reprinted from: *Math. Comput. Appl.* **2023**, *28*, 20, doi:10.3390/mca28010020 . . . . **173**

Adel M. Al-Mahdi
PreconditioningTechnique for an Image Deblurring Problem with the Total Fractional-Order Variation Model
Reprinted from: *Math. Comput. Appl.* **2023**, *28*, 97, doi:10.3390/mca28050097 . . . . **194**

Muhammad Tariq, Hijaz Ahmad, Asif Ali Shaikh, Sotiris K. Ntouyas, Evren Hınçal and Sania Qureshi
Fractional Hermite–Hadamard-Type Inequalities for Differentiable Preinvex Mappings and Applications to Modified Bessel and q-Digamma Functions
Reprinted from: *Math. Comput. Appl.* **2023**, *28*, 108, doi:10.3390/mca28060108 . . . . **223**

About the Editors

Mehmet Yavuz

Dr Mehmet Yavuz received his BSc degree (2009) from Zonguldak Bulent Ecevit University, Türkiye. He then obtained both his MSc (2012) and PhD (2016) degrees in Applied Mathematics from Balıkesir University, Türkiye. He visited the Environment and Sustainability Institute, University of Exeter, U.K., in the period 2019-2020 for postdoctoral research. He is currently an Associate Professor in the Mathematics and Computer Sciences Department at Necmettin Erbakan University, Türkiye. He has published more than 100 research papers in reputed journals and conference papers, along with 10 book chapters in international books. Moreover, he edited five international books published by esteemed publishers. He is currently concerned with fractional calculus and its applications to the different fields of science, mathematical biology, nonlinear dynamics, adaptive control, and optimal control. He has 13 years of research and teaching experience in these fields. He has also been involved in organizing and serving on scientific committees for international conferences. Yavuz has received several awards, including being listed among the world's top 2% of cited scientists since 2021 based on citations, h-index, and other metrics, as published by Elsevier & Scopus in collaboration with Stanford University. Apart from being an Associate Editor in several reputed journals and a Guest Editor for more than 10 Special Issues, he is the Editor-in-Chief of the journals *Mathematical Modelling and Numerical Simulation with Applications* (ISSN: 2791-8564) and *Bulletin of Biomathematics* (ISSN: 2980-1869).

Ioannis Dassios

Ioannis Dassios has held positions at University College Dublin, Ireland; University of Edinburgh, U.K.; University of Manchester, U.K.; and University of Limerick, Ireland. His research interests include dynamical and control systems, dynamical networks, differential and difference equations, singular systems, systems of differential equations of fractional order, optimization methods, linear algebra, and mathematical modeling of engineering problems (e.g., electrical power systems, gas networks, materials, etc.). He studied Mathematics, completed a two-year M.Sc. in Applied Mathematics, and obtained his Ph.D. degree from the University of Athens, Greece, graduating with the highest mark, "Excellent" (the top grade in the Greek system). Ioannis has published over 110 articles, two books, and three edited volumes. He has also served as a reviewer more than 1,100 times for over 100 different peer-reviewed journals. Additionally, he is a member of the editorial boards of peer-reviewed journals such as *Circuits, Systems and Signal Processing* (Springer), *Mathematics and Computers in Simulation* (Elsevier), *Applied Sciences*, *Mathematics*, *Axioms* (MDPI), *Open Physics* (DeGruyter), and *Experimental Results* (Cambridge University Press). He has also served as a Guest Editor for more than 15 Special Issues and has been involved in organizing and serving on technical committees for international conferences. Finally, Ioannis has received several awards, including being listed among the world's top 2% of cited scientists based on citations, h-index, and other metrics, as published by Elsevier & Scopus in collaboration with Stanford University. He has also been awarded grants from the UCD Output-Based Research Support Scheme (OBRSS) for the period 2016–2023, various travel support awards, and the "Top 1% Peer Reviewer in Mathematics and Engineering" award from the Web of Science Group, Clarivate Analytics, for three consecutive years.

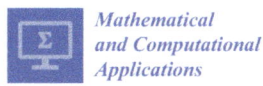

Editorial

Significance of Mathematical Modeling and Control in Real-World Problems: New Developments and Applications

Mehmet Yavuz [1,2,*] and Ioannis Dassios [3]

[1] Department of Mathematics and Computer Sciences, Faculty of Science, Necmettin Erbakan University, 42090 Konya, Türkiye
[2] Centre for Environmental Mathematics, Faculty of Environment, Science and Economy, University of Exeter, Cornwall TR10 9FE, UK
[3] School of Electrical and Electronic Engineering, University College Dublin, D04 V1W8 Dublin, Ireland; ioannis.dassios@ucd.ie
* Correspondence: m.yavuz@exeter.ac.uk

Mathematical modeling and system control are employed in many research problems, ranging from physical and chemical processes to biomathematics and life sciences. Their theoretical description is closely connected with various areas of pure and applied mathematics, including nonlinear modeling, integro-differential equations, nonlinear dynamics, pattern formation, non-Markovian processes, nonlinear and anomalous transport, time-delay equations, and so on.

The aim of this Special Issue is to collect original and high-quality contributions related to the mathematical theory of such processes and phenomena, including dynamic models, applied and computational algorithms, controller design, and mathematical methods, regarded as new and prominent for understanding the problems that arise in natural phenomena.

This Special Issue will cover new perspectives of the recent theoretical developments in mathematical modeling and/or optimal control and their illustrative applications in biology, engineering, finance, and health sciences. It aims to highlight new techniques that can be applied to the real-life problems that are modeled and to introduce new constructed effective models for the accurate prediction of infectious diseases, financial crises, etc., into the literature by adopting suitable controls/control strategies. Moreover, it aims to provide new analytical and numerical methods to propose appropriate solutions to the real-life problems of both integer- and fractional-order differential equations and to understand their complicated behaviors in nonlinear phenomena.

The Special Issue also proposes the latest developments in nonlinear dynamical modeling, optimization, and solution strategies that can be applied to prominent problems in engineering and biological systems.

Additionally, we will the reader learn new theories and new methods of nonlinear dynamical systems with regard to modeling and controlling them. It will also help the reader find new solutions to complex engineering, biological, financial, and life science problems, providing readers with new insights for novel modeling and optimization processes and underlining the relation between theory and practice. The topics of this Special Issue include, but are not limited to, the following:

- Mathematical modeling in real-world phenomena;
- Optimal control strategies in biosystems;
- New analytical and numerical methods for fractional differential equations;
- Modeling of fractional-order systems with and without nonsingular kernels;
- Deterministic and stochastic differential equations arising in science;
- Applications in bioengineering, biology, and health sciences;
- Applications in finance and economic sciences;
- Optimal control problems of a fractional order;

Citation: Yavuz, M.; Dassios, I. Significance of Mathematical Modeling and Control in Real-World Problems: New Developments and Applications. *Math. Comput. Appl.* **2024**, *29*, 82. https://doi.org/10.3390/mca29050082

Received: 9 September 2024
Accepted: 9 September 2024
Published: 18 September 2024

Copyright: © 2024 by the authors. Licensee MDPI, Basel, Switzerland. This article is an open access article distributed under the terms and conditions of the Creative Commons Attribution (CC BY) license (https://creativecommons.org/licenses/by/4.0/).

- Modeling of diffusion, heat, mass, and momentum transfer (fluid dynamics);
- Biomechanical and biomedical applications of fractional calculus;
- Impulsive systems;
- Fuzzy differential equations and their applications.

In this Special Issue, the contents of the selected studies that contributed to the topics listed above can be synthesized as follows:

- **Fractional-order approaches** used to model and investigate several real-life problems:
    - Tariq et al. [1] established new fractional identities and employed them, exploring several extensions of the fractional H-H type inequality via generalized preinvexities. Then, they discussed some applications to the q-digamma and Bessel functions via their obtained results.
    - Adel M. Al-Mahdi [2] proposed a block triangular preconditioner as using the exact triangular preconditioner leads to a preconditioned matrix with exactly two distinct eigenvalues. In the algorithm they utilized, the authors used the flexible preconditioned GMRES method for the outer iterations, the preconditioned conjugate gradient (PCG) method for the inner iterations, and the fixed point iteration (FPI) method to handle nonlinearity. Fast convergence was found in the numerical results by using the proposed preconditioners.
    - Debbouche et al. [3] set up a class of nonlinear fractional differential systems with distributed time delays in the controls and impulse effects. The controllability criteria for both linear and nonlinear systems were discussed. They also provided an illustrative example supported by graphical representations to show the validity of the obtained abstract results.
    - Haq et al. [4] developed a within-host viral kinetics model of SARS-CoV-2 under the Caputo fractional-order operator. They proved the results of the solution's existence and uniqueness by using the Banach mapping contraction principle. Moreover, they provided approximate solutions for the nonlinear fractional model using the modified Euler method (MEM).
    - Rabah et al. [5] discussed a complex nonlinear fractional model of an enzyme inhibitor reaction where reaction memory was taken into account. Analytical expressions of the concentrations of the enzyme, substrate, inhibitor, product, and other complex intermediate species were derived using Laplace decomposition and differential transformation methods.
    - Clemence-Mkhope and Gibson [6] proposed four discrete models, using the exact spectral derivative discretization finite difference (ESDDFD) method for a chaotic five-dimensional, conformable fractional derivative financial system, incorporating ethics and market confidence.
    - Clemence-Mkhope and Clemence-Mkhope [7] used the property of the conformable fractional derivative (CFD) to show the limitation of the method previously used in the literature, together with the integer definition of the derivative, as well as to derive a modified conformable Euler method for the initial value problem that was considered. A method of constructing generalized derivatives from the solution of the non-integer relaxation equation was used to motivate an alternate definition of the CFD and justify alternative generalizations of the Euler method to the CFD.
- **Heat and Fluid Dynamics**
    - Eswaramoorthi and Loganathan [8] investigated the numerical computation of Ag/Al_2O_3 nanofluid over a Riga plate with injection/suction. The energy equation was formulated using the Cattaneo–Christov heat flux, nonlinear thermal radiation, and heat sink/source.
    - Hossain et al. [9] developed a model to discover the effects of heated cylinder configurations in accordance with the magnetic field on natural convective flow within a square cavity. In the cavity, four types of configurations—left

- bottom-heated cylinder (LBC), right bottom-heated cylinder (RBC), left top-heated cylinder (LTC), and right top-heated cylinder (RTC)—were considered in the investigation.
- Eswaramoorthi et al. [10] scrutinized the Darcy–Forchheimer flow of Casson–Williamson nanofluid in a stretching surface with nonlinear thermal radiation, suction, and heat consumption. In addition, this investigation assimilated the influence of Brownian motion, thermophoresis, activation energy, and binary chemical reaction effects.

- **Convection in Porous Mediums**
  - Ramchandraiah et al. [11] analyzed the thermal instability of rotating convection in a bidispersive porous layer. Linear stability analysis was employed to examine the stability of the system.
  - Reddy et al. [12] studied the effect of vertical rotation and the magnetic field on dissolution-driven convection in a saturated porous layer with a first-order chemical reaction. The system's physical parameters depended on the Vadasz number, the Hartmann number, the Taylor number, and the Damkohler number.
  - Tamilzharasan et al. [13] developed a mathematical simulation of the steady mixed convective Darcy–Forchheimer flow of Williamson nanofluid over a linear stretchable surface. In addition, the effects of Cattaneo–Christov heat and mass flux, Brownian motion, activation energy, and thermophoresis were also studied.

Therefore, as the editors of this volume, we wish to convey our profound gratitude for the opportunity to collaborate with MDPI to publish this Special Issue. Our acknowledgment extends with sincere appreciation to the *MCA* Editorial Office, whose unwavering support was invaluable throughout this process. It was a pleasure to work under such favorable conditions, and we eagerly anticipate the prospect of future collaborations with *MCA*.

Conflicts of Interest: The authors declare no conflicts of interest.

References

1. Tariq, M.; Ahmad, H.; Shaikh, A.A.; Ntouyas, S.K.; Hınçal, E.; Qureshi, S. Fractional Hermite–Hadamard-Type Inequalities for Differentiable Preinvex Mappings and Applications to Modified Bessel and q-Digamma Functions. *Math. Comput. Appl.* **2023**, *28*, 108. [CrossRef]
2. Al-Mahdi, A.M. Preconditioning Technique for an Image Deblurring Problem with the Total Fractional-Order Variation Model. *Math. Comput. Appl.* **2023**, *28*, 97. [CrossRef]
3. Debbouche, A.; Vadivoo, B.S.; Fedorov, V.E.; Antonov, V. Controllability Criteria for Nonlinear Impulsive Fractional Differential Systems with Distributed Delays in Controls. *Math. Comput. Appl.* **2023**, *28*, 13. [CrossRef]
4. Haq, I.U.; Yavuz, M.; Ali, N.; Akgül, A. A SARS-CoV-2 Fractional-Order Mathematical Model via the Modified Euler Method. *Math. Comput. Appl.* **2022**, *27*, 82. [CrossRef]
5. Rabah, F.; Abukhaled, M.; Khuri, S.A. Solution of a Complex Nonlinear Fractional Biochemical Reaction Model. *Math. Comput. Appl.* **2022**, *27*, 45. [CrossRef]
6. Clemence-Mkhope, D.P.; Gibson, G.A. Taming Hyperchaos with Exact Spectral Derivative Discretization Finite Difference Discretization of a Conformable Fractional Derivative Financial System with Market Confidence and Ethics Risk. *Math. Comput. Appl.* **2022**, *27*, 4. [CrossRef]
7. Clemence-Mkhope, D.P.; Clemence-Mkhope, B.G.B. The Limited Validity of the Conformable Euler Finite Difference Method and an Alternate Definition of the Conformable Fractional Derivative to Justify Modification of the Method. *Math. Comput. Appl.* **2021**, *26*, 66. [CrossRef]
8. Divya, S.; Eswaramoorthi, S.; Loganathan, K. Numerical Computation of Ag/Al$_2$O$_3$ Nanofluid over a Riga Plate with Heat Sink/Source and Non-Fourier Heat Flux Model. *Math. Comput. Appl.* **2023**, *28*, 20. [CrossRef]
9. Hossain, M.S.; Fayz-Al-Asad, M.; Mallik, M.S.I.; Yavuz, M.; Alim, M.A.; Khairul Basher, K.M. Numerical Study of the Effect of a Heated Cylinder on Natural Convection in a Square Cavity in the Presence of a Magnetic Field. *Math. Comput. Appl.* **2022**, *27*, 58. [CrossRef]
10. Eswaramoorthi, S.; Thamaraiselvi, S.; Loganathan, K. Exploration of Darcy–Forchheimer Flows of Non-Newtonian Casson and Williamson Conveying Tiny Particles Experiencing Binary Chemical Reaction and Thermal Radiation: Comparative Analysis. *Math. Comput. Appl.* **2022**, *27*, 52. [CrossRef]
11. Ramchandraiah, C.; Kishan, N.; Reddy, G.S.K.; Paidipati, K.K.; Chesneau, C. Double-Diffusive Convection in Bidispersive Porous Medium with Coriolis Effect. *Math. Comput. Appl.* **2022**, *27*, 56. [CrossRef]

12. Reddy, G.S.K.; Koteswararao, N.V.; Ravi, R.; Paidipati, K.K.; Chesneau, C. Dissolution-Driven Convection in a Porous Medium Due to Vertical Axis of Rotation and Magnetic Field. *Math. Comput. Appl.* **2022**, *27*, 53. [CrossRef]
13. Tamilzharasan, B.M.; Karthikeyan, S.; Kaabar, M.K.A.; Yavuz, M.; Özköse, F. Magneto Mixed Convection of Williamson Nanofluid Flow through a Double Stratified Porous Medium in Attendance of Activation Energy. *Math. Comput. Appl.* **2022**, *27*, 46. [CrossRef]

Disclaimer/Publisher's Note: The statements, opinions and data contained in all publications are solely those of the individual author(s) and contributor(s) and not of MDPI and/or the editor(s). MDPI and/or the editor(s) disclaim responsibility for any injury to people or property resulting from any ideas, methods, instructions or products referred to in the content.

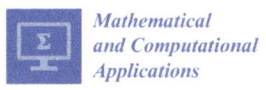

Article

The Limited Validity of the Conformable Euler Finite Difference Method and an Alternate Definition of the Conformable Fractional Derivative to Justify Modification of the Method

Dominic P. Clemence-Mkhope [1,*] **and Belinda G. B. Clemence-Mkhope** [2]

[1] Department of Mathematics and Statistics, North Carolina A&T State University, Greensboro, NC 27411, USA
[2] Office of Strategic Innovation and Effectiveness, Forsyth Technical Community College, Winston-Salem, NC 27103, USA; bbrewster-clemence@forsythtech.edu
* Correspondence: clemence@ncat.edu

Abstract: A method recently advanced as the conformable Euler method (CEM) for the finite difference discretization of fractional initial value problem $D_t^\alpha y(t) = f(t; y(t))$, $y(t_0) = y_0$, $a \leq t \leq b$, and used to describe hyperchaos in a financial market model, is shown to be valid only for $\alpha = 1$. The property of the conformable fractional derivative (CFD) used to show this limitation of the method is used, together with the integer definition of the derivative, to derive a modified conformable Euler method for the initial value problem considered. A method of constructing generalized derivatives from the solution of the non-integer relaxation equation is used to motivate an alternate definition of the CFD and justify alternative generalizations of the Euler method to the CFD. The conformable relaxation equation is used in numerical experiments to assess the performance of the CEM in comparison to that of the alternative methods.

Keywords: conformable fractional derivative (CFD); conformable Euler method (CEM); modified conformable Euler method (MCEM); difference quotient representation (DQR); generalized fractional derivative

1. Introduction

Termed the conformable Euler method (CEM), a finite difference discretization method is adopted in [1] and justified by applying the fractional power series expansion. The method is proposed to solve equations of the form

$$T_t^\alpha y(t) = f(t; y(t)), \quad y(t_0) = y_0, \quad a \leq t \leq b \quad (1)$$

where $T_t^\alpha y(t)$ denotes the conformable fractional derivative (CFD) of order α introduced in [2], since most differential equations using the CFD do not have exact analytic solutions, so that numerical approximation methods must be developed. The method has the following form:

$$\alpha \frac{y_{k+1} - y_k}{h^\alpha} = f(t_k, y_k), \quad 0 \leq k \leq N, \text{ where } h = \frac{b-a}{N}. \quad (2)$$

In [1], the method is used to solve conformable fractional differential equation systems with time delays and in [3], it is used to calculate numerical solutions for testing the hyperchaos of conformable derivative models for financial systems with market confidence and ethics risk. The purpose of the present article is to show that, while the CEM (2) clearly reduces to the ordinary Euler method, it is not valid as a generalization of the standard forward Euler method to the CFD for $0 < \alpha < 1$, and to propose alternative generalizations.

The CFD was introduced in [2] and is defined as

$$T_t^\alpha f(t) = \lim_{\varepsilon \to 0} \frac{f(t + \varepsilon t^{1-\alpha}) - f(t)}{\varepsilon}, \quad \alpha \in (0, 1]. \tag{3}$$

Among its basic properties given in [2] is that if both $T_t^\alpha f(t)$ and $\frac{d}{dt}f(t)$ exist, then the following identity holds:

$$T_t^\alpha f(t) = t^{1-\alpha} \frac{d}{dt} f(t). \tag{4}$$

As stated in [4], "there is a debate among contemporary mathematicians about what it really means by a fractional derivative ... as a consequence of introducing" the CFD. While several mathematical reasons drive this debate, the main one is the identity Equation (4), which renders questionable the fractionality of the CFD. The following titles capture the main problem with fractional derivatives and enumerate some of the arguments against the fractionality of the CFD and its generalizations: *What is a Fractional Derivative?* [5], *No violation of the Leibniz rule. No fractional derivative* [6], *Local Fractional Derivatives of Differentiable Functions are Integer-order Derivatives or Zero* [7], *No Nonlocality, No Fractional Derivative* [8], *The flaw in the conformable calculus: It is conformable because it is not fractional* [9] (see also [10–12]). This has led to the conclusion that "from mathematical point of view the introduced conformable derivatives does not provide any real improvement to the theory of fractional calculus in compare with the classical fractional derivatives. Furthermore, they bring nothing new at least as mathematical advantages in the field of the ordinary differential equations with fractional derivatives" [10].

Such debate on its nature notwithstanding, the CFD appears to have removed a hurdle for the use of fractional derivatives, that of being very complex for applications and not easy to master or use (see [13]) and spurred brisk activity in studies of previously un-explored phenomena, as is evident from the number of references in for example [12,14]. While the debate about the "mathematical fractionality" of the CFD continues, the CFD is being used in applications to arrive at conclusions about, among others, systems with time delays [1], economic models of financial systems [3], classic games [15], electrical circuits [16,17], Newtonian [18] and quantum [19] mechanics, HIV therapeutic interventions [20], general biological modeling [21], and general sub-diffusion processes [14,22]. These continued uses of the CFD, because of its ease of implementation, to describe various phenomena considered important make necessary the development of tools for its use. A method has already been devised as a generalization of the Euler method for the CFD [1] and is being applied to problems of consequence (e.g., [1,3,15]): it is important therefore that, regardless of its classification as fractional or not, all methods being developed with such use of the CFD must be properly examined and benchmarked like any other for all derivative concepts. It is in this spirit that the work presented in this article offers an assessment of the CEM and suggests alternative methods for the generalization of the standard forward Euler method to the CFD.

Motivated in part by dismissals of the CFD as referenced above and the reality that phenomena are being described with methods employing the CFD, the exact spectral derivative discretization finite difference (ESDDFD) method was introduced in [23], wherein fractionality is determined by wave type behavior of processes under study and locality is defined by the relaxation pattern as follows:

- The Euler (ordinary) exponential function $e^z \equiv \sum_{k=0}^{\infty} \frac{z^k}{k!}$ is local, whereas the Mittag-Leffler generalized exponential function $E_\alpha(z) \equiv E_{\alpha,1}(z) = \sum_{k=0}^{\infty} \frac{z^k}{\Gamma(\alpha k + 1)}$ is non-local (see, e.g., [24]).

- Debye exponential wave patterns, described by $\Phi(t) = \Phi(t_0)\exp(-ct)$ and are not fractional, whereas Kohlrausch–Williams–Watts (KWW) stretched exponential wave patterns, described by $\Phi(t) = \Phi(t_0)\exp(-c_\alpha t^\alpha)$ and $\Phi(t) = \Phi(t_0)E_\alpha(-c_\alpha t^\alpha)$ are fractional (see, e.g., [25]).

In that viewpoint, the generalized Caputo derivative can be expressed in terms of the generalized CFD, just as the Caputo derivative can be expressed in terms of the CFD (see, e.g., [26]). Further, the generalized RL derivative can be expressed in terms of the generalized Caputo derivative (which is parallel to the case for the classic Caputo and RL derivatives (see, e.g., [27]), as well as their Atangana–Baleanu extensions [28], and a parallel RL extension of the CFD can also be constructed [23]. The ESDDFD method of constructing generalized non-integer derivatives (NIDs) from the solution of the non-integer relaxation equation (NIRE), wherein fractionality is determined by wave type behavior as stated above and the CFD serves as a foundation for NIDs of both Caputo and RL types, is used in this article to motivate and justify the suggested alternatives for the generalization of the Euler method for the CFD.

The rest of this article is organized as follows. In the next section, the derivation of the CEM from [1] is recalled and it is shown that the CEM is valid only for $\alpha = 1$. In Section 3, the relationship (4) is used to describe the ordinary Euler method (OEM) for the IVP (1) and to derive a modified CEM (MCEM). Section 4 recalls the ESDDFD method, and the exact discretization of the conformable relaxation equation (CRE) is used to justify the MCEM as well as to motivate an ESDDFD Euler method (EDM). Numerical experiments are presented in Section 5 assessing the accuracy, against the analytic solution of the CRE, of the CEM, MCEM, EDM, and OEM. A discussion in Section 6 of the theoretical and experimental results presented, as well as of recommendations based on those results, conclude the article.

2. The Conformable Euler's Method

In this section, the derivation of the CEM is recalled and its validity is discussed.

2.1. Derivation of the Conformable Euler's Method

The method (2), referred to in [1,3,15] as the conformable Euler's method for (3), is obtained from truncation of a power series expansion as follows. Since $h = t_{k+1} - t_k$, it is assumed that there exist θ_k where $0 < \theta_k < 1$ is such that

$$y(t_{k+1}) - y(t_k) = \frac{1}{\alpha} h^\alpha (D_t^\alpha y)(t_k) + \frac{1}{2\alpha^2} h^{2\alpha} \left(D_t^{2\alpha} y\right)(t_k + \theta_k h). \tag{5}$$

Letting $y(t_{k+1}) - y(t_k) \longrightarrow y_{k+1} - y_k$ and substituting $(D_t^\alpha y)(t_k) = f(t_k, y_k)$ into (5) results in

$$y_{k+1} - y_k = \frac{1}{\alpha} h^\alpha f(t_k, y_k) + \frac{1}{2\alpha^2} h^{2\alpha} \left(D_t^{2\alpha} y\right)(t_k + \theta_k h),$$

or, equivalently

$$\alpha \frac{y_{k+1} - y_k}{h^\alpha} = f(t_k, y_k) + \frac{1}{2\alpha} h^\alpha \left(D_t^{2\alpha} y\right)(t_k + \theta h). \tag{6}$$

For small enough h, ignoring the second term on the right-hand side of (6) yields the conformable Euler's method (2):

$$\alpha \frac{y_{k+1} - y_k}{h^\alpha} = f(t_k, y_k), \tag{7}$$

which reduces to the usual Euler's method for $\alpha = 1$.

2.2. Validity of the Conformable Euler's Method

Since the CFD satisfies property (4), substituting $(D_t^\alpha y)(t_k) = (t_k)^{1-\alpha} \frac{dy}{dt}(t_k)$ into (5) results in

$$y_{k+1} - y_k = \frac{1}{\alpha} h^\alpha (t_k)^{1-\alpha} \frac{dy}{dt}(t_k) + \frac{1}{2\alpha^2} h^{2\alpha} \left(D_t^{2\alpha} y\right)(t_k + \theta_k h),$$

or, equivalently

$$\alpha \frac{y_{k+1} - y_k}{h^\alpha} = (t_k)^{1-\alpha} \frac{dy}{dt}(t_k) + \frac{1}{2\alpha} h^\alpha \left(D_t^{2\alpha} y \right)(t_k + \theta h). \tag{8}$$

For small enough h, ignoring the second term on the right-hand side of (8) yields

$$\alpha \frac{y_{k+1} - y_k}{h^\alpha} = (t_k)^{1-\alpha} \frac{dy}{dt}(t_k),$$

and therefore

$$\frac{\alpha}{h^{\alpha-1}} \frac{y_{k+1} - y_k}{h} = (t_k)^{1-\alpha} \frac{y_{k+1} - y_k}{h},$$

from which it follows that

$$\alpha h^{1-\alpha} = (t_k)^{1-\alpha}. \tag{9}$$

Next, let us consider separately the cases of (9) (a) $t_0 = 0$ and (b) $t_0 \neq 0$

(a) If $t_0 = 0$, then $t_k = kh$, so that

$$\alpha h^{1-\alpha} = (t_k)^{1-\alpha} = (kh)^{1-\alpha} = k^{1-\alpha} h^{1-\alpha},$$

from which we conclude that

$$\alpha = k^{1-\alpha},$$

whose only constant solution is $\alpha = 1$.

(b) If $t_0 \neq 0$, then $t_k = t_0 + kh$, so that

$$\alpha h^{1-\alpha} = (t_k)^{1-\alpha} = (t_0 + kh)^{1-\alpha} = h^{1-\alpha} \left(\frac{t_0}{h} + k \right)^{1-\alpha},$$

from which we conclude that

$$\alpha = \left(\frac{t_0}{h} + k \right)^{1-\alpha}, \tag{10}$$

whose only constant solution is $\alpha = 1$. Note that, if $\alpha < 1$ is assumed on the right-hand side of (10), then for fixed t_0, k, and writing the left-hand side as $\alpha(h)$, results in $\alpha(h) \to \infty$ as $h \to 0$, a contradiction.

Since (9) holds if, and only if, both (2) and (4) hold, we conclude therefore that both (2) and (4) hold if, and only if, $\alpha = 1$.

3. The Ordinary Euler's and Modified Conformable Euler's Methods

Next, the ordinary Euler method (OEM), obtained by re-writing the CFD in terms of the integer-order derivative, and a modified Euler method proposed in [29] are described.

3.1. The Ordinary, Integer-Order Euler's Method

As mentioned in the introduction, one of the main reasons for the dismissal of the CFD as an NID is the property (4), which may be used to re-write Equation (1) in the following form,

$$\frac{d}{dt} y(t) = t^{\alpha-1} f(t; y(t)), \quad y(t_0) = y_0, \quad a \leq t \leq b. \tag{11}$$

However, because of the singularity at $t = 0$, the re-written problem (11) is ill-posed and its ordinary Euler method (OEM) representation,

$$\frac{y_{k+1} - y_k}{h} = t_k^{\alpha-1} f(t_k, y_k), \quad (t_0, y_0), \tag{12}$$

cannot be implemented on any interval of the form $[0, b]$ without input additional to that of the given IVP (1). It can therefore be argued that the problem solved by implementing (12) with such additional information, such as

$$\frac{y_{k+1} - y_k}{h} = t_k^{\alpha-1} f(t_k, y_k), \ (t_0, y_0), \ (t_1, y_1), \tag{13}$$

which is used in Section 4, is not the same as (12).

3.2. The Modified Conformable Euler's Method

In [29], a method consistent with the definition of the CFD and property (4) is obtained by rewriting $t^{1-\alpha}$ as a derivative and then using the $\alpha = 1$ definition of the derivative as follows:

$$T_t^\alpha y(t) = t^{1-\alpha} \tfrac{d}{dt} y(t) = \left(\tfrac{d}{dt} y(t)\right) / \left(\tfrac{1}{\alpha} \tfrac{d}{dt}(t^\alpha)\right)$$
$$= \lim_{h \to 0} \left(\tfrac{y(t+h) - y(t)}{h}\right) / \left(\tfrac{1}{\alpha} \tfrac{(t+h)^\alpha - t^\alpha}{h}\right) = \alpha \lim_{h \to 0} \left(\tfrac{y(t+h) - y(t)}{(t+h)^\alpha - t^\alpha}\right). \tag{14}$$

For small enough h, therefore, and making the identifications

$$t \longrightarrow t_k, \ t + h \longrightarrow t_{k+1}, \ y(t+h) \longrightarrow y_{k+1}, \ y(t) \longrightarrow y_k \tag{15}$$

in (14) result in the following discrete representation of $_0^C T_t^\alpha y(t)$:

$$T_t^\alpha y(t) = \alpha \lim_{h \to 0} \left(\frac{y(t+h) - y(t)}{(t+h)^\alpha - t^\alpha}\right) \to \alpha \frac{y_{k+1} - y_k}{(t_{k+1})^\alpha - (t_k)^\alpha}.$$

Based on the above, it is claimed in [29] that the modified conformable Euler's method for (1) is therefore given by

$$\alpha \frac{y_{k+1} - y_k}{(t_{k+1})^\alpha - (t_k)^\alpha} = f(t_k, y_k), \tag{16}$$

valid for $0 < \alpha \leq 1$, which is also a generalization of the Euler method for $\alpha = 1$.

4. Alternative Definition of the CFD and Justification of the MCEM

4.1. An Alternative Definition of the CFD from the ESDDFD Method

The second derivation of a modified CEM is based on the exact discretization of the initial value problem for the conformable relaxation equation, obtained from the following results from [23], in which it is generally assumed that the IVP (1) is being discretized on intervals of the form $[0, b]$.

Theorem 1. *For a given definition of an NID, let* $(t, \alpha; y_0)$ *denote the analytic solution of initial value problem for the relaxation equation:*

$$D_t^\alpha y(t) = -y(t), \ y(0) = y_0, \ 0 \leq t \leq b; \ 0 < \alpha \leq 1. \tag{17}$$

Thus, a corresponding difference quotient representation (DQR) of Caputo type consistent with that derivative is

$$_0^{GC} \Delta_t^\alpha y(t) = \frac{y(t+h) - y(t)}{(1 - (t+h, \alpha; y_0)/(t, \alpha; y_0))}. \tag{18}$$

Assuming $y_0 = 1$ and using the solution of (17) for the CFD,

$$(t, \alpha) = \exp\left(-\tfrac{1}{\alpha} t^\alpha\right), \tag{19}$$

which describes behavior consistent with local, fractional, KWW wave patterns, in Equation (18) leads to the following DQR for the CFD:

$$_{0}^{CFD}\Delta_t^\alpha y(t) = \frac{y(t+h) - y(t)}{\left(1 - e^{\frac{-1}{\alpha}((t+h)^\alpha - t^\alpha)}\right)}. \tag{20}$$

Taking the limit as $h \to 0$ in Equation (20) yields the following alternative definition of the CFD:

Definition 1. *Given a real-valued function on $[0, \infty)$, the conformable fractional derivative has the following alternative definition:*

$$T_t^\alpha f(t) = {}_0^C T_t^\alpha f(t) \equiv \lim_{h \to 0} {}_0^{CFD}\Delta_t^\alpha f(t) = \alpha \lim_{h \to 0} \frac{f(t+h) - f(t)}{(t+h)^\alpha - t^\alpha},$$

where ${}_0^C T_t^\alpha f(0)$ is understood to mean ${}_0^C T_t^\alpha f(0) = \lim_{t \to 0^+} {}_0^C T_t^\alpha f(t)$.

The following result regarding the basic properties of ${}_0^C T_t^\alpha$ above has elementary proofs that follow directly from Definition 1 and are omitted here; it is the same as Theorem 2.2 of [2] and is a particular case of Theorem 2.1.6 of [23].

Theorem 2. *Let $\alpha \in (0, 1]$ and the functions f, g be α-differentiable at a point $t \in [0, \infty)$. Then, for all real-valued constants A, B, K, p, the following properties hold:*

1. ${}_0^C T_t^\alpha (Af + Bg) = A {}_0^C T_t^\alpha (f) + B {}_0^C T_t^\alpha (g)$
2. ${}_0^C T_t^\alpha (fg) = g {}_0^C T_t^\alpha (f) + f {}_0^C T_t^\alpha (g)$
3. ${}_0^C T_t^\alpha \left(\frac{f}{g}\right) = \frac{1}{g^2}(g {}_0^C T_t^\alpha (f) - f {}_0^C T_t^\alpha (g))$
4. ${}_0^C T_t^\alpha (t^p) = p t^{p-\alpha}$
5. ${}_0^C T_t^\alpha (K) = 0$
6. *If $f(t)$ is first order differentiable, then it also holds that ${}_0^C T_t^\alpha (f(t)) = t^{1-\alpha} \frac{df(t)}{dt}$*

Direct application of Definition 1 yields the following values for some common functions, which are identical to those obtained in [2], for $p, k \in \mathbb{R}$:

1. ${}_0^C T_t^\alpha (t^p) = p t^{p-\alpha}$
2. ${}_0^C T_t^\alpha (1) = 0$
3. ${}_0^C T_t^\alpha \left(e^{kt}\right) = k t^{1-\alpha} e^{kt}$
4. ${}_0^C T_t^\alpha (\sin kt) = k t^{1-\alpha} \cos kt$
5. ${}_0^C T_t^\alpha (\cos kt) = -k t^{1-\alpha} \sin kt$
6. ${}_0^C T_t^\alpha (t^\alpha) = 1$
7. ${}_0^C T_t^\alpha \left(e^{\frac{1}{\alpha} t^\alpha}\right) = e^{\frac{1}{\alpha} t^\alpha}$
8. ${}_0^C T_t^\alpha \left(\sin \frac{1}{\alpha} t^\alpha\right) = \cos \frac{1}{\alpha} t^\alpha$
9. ${}_0^C T_t^\alpha \left(\cos \frac{1}{\alpha} t^\alpha\right) = -\sin \frac{1}{\alpha} t^\alpha$

Remark 1. *Since the alternative definition of the conformable fractional derivative, Definition 1, has the same basic properties and derivative values as the conformable fractional derivative, it is the same as the CFD, that is, ${}_{t_0}^C T_t^\alpha [f(t)] = T_\alpha^{t_0}(f)(t)$, where the right-hand side uses the notation in [9]. It should therefore be noted that, as recently pointed out in [30], the alternative definition shows that the conformable derivative for differentiable functions results from the integer-order derivative with the fractional change of variable $u = (t - t_0)^\alpha / \alpha$, which can be easily seen. To see the equivalence of the CFD and this change of variable, assume f is differentiable. Then, since*

${}^C_{t_0}T^\alpha_t f(t) = T^{t_0}_\alpha f(t)(t) = (t-t_0)^{1-\alpha} \frac{d}{dt} f(t)$ and $\frac{du(t)}{dt} = (t-t_0)^{\alpha-1}$, direct substitution in identity (4) and the chain rule yield

$$\begin{aligned}
{}^C_{t_0}T^\alpha_t f(t) &= (t-t_0)^{1-\alpha} \frac{df(t)}{dt} \\
&= (t-t_0)^{1-\alpha} \frac{df(u)}{du} \frac{du(t)}{dt} \\
&= (t-t_0)^{1-\alpha} \frac{df(u)}{du} (t-t_0)^{\alpha-1} \\
&= \frac{df(u)}{du}
\end{aligned}$$

4.2. Justification of and an Alternative to the Modified Conformable Euler's Method

The identifications (15) applied in Equation (18) yield the following discretization rule for $D^\alpha_t y(t)$ as a corollary to Theorem 1.

Corollary 1. *Let $(t, \alpha; y_0)$ be as in Theorem 1. Then the following is a consistent discrete representation of $D^\alpha_t y(t)$:*

$$D^\alpha_t y(t) \longrightarrow {}^{GC}_0 \Delta^\alpha_{t_k} y_k \equiv \frac{y_{k+1} - y_k}{(1 - (t_{k+1}, \alpha; y_0)/(t_k, \alpha; y_0))}.$$

The denominator is a complex function of both the step size, $h = t_{k+1} - t_k$, and lattice point, t_k, and is described in [23] as a generalization of the nonstandard finite difference (NSFD) denominator [31]. Similarly applying the identifications (15) in Definition 1 and using (t, α) as given by Equation (19) in Corollary 1 therefore results in the following discrete representations of the CFD:

Modified Conformable Euler : ${}^C_0 T^\alpha_t y(t) = \alpha \lim_{h \to 0} \left(\frac{y(t+h) - y(t)}{(t+h)^\alpha - t^\alpha} \right) \to \alpha \frac{y_{k+1} - y_k}{(t_{k+1})^\alpha - (t_k)^\alpha}.$

NSFD Conformable EDM : ${}^C_0 T^\alpha_t y(t) = \alpha \lim_{h \to 0} \frac{y(t+h) - y(t)}{\left(1 - e^{-\frac{1}{\alpha}((t+h)^\alpha - t^\alpha)}\right)} \to \alpha \frac{y_{k+1} - y_k}{\left(1 - e^{-\frac{1}{\alpha}((t_{k+1})^\alpha - (t_k)^\alpha)}\right)}.$

A clear corollary to the foregoing are the following Euler discretization rules for the IVP (1), which provide justification of, and an alternative to, the MCEM as extensions of the Euler method to the CFD:

Corollary 2. *The following discrete representations are generalizations of the (forward) Euler method for the CFD valid for $\alpha \in (0, 1]$:*

$$\text{Modified Conformable Euler} : \alpha \frac{y_{k+1} - y_k}{(t_{k+1})^\alpha - (t_k)^\alpha} = f(t_k, y_k)$$

$$\text{ESDDFD-based Conformable Euler} : \alpha \frac{y_{k+1} - y_k}{\left(1 - e^{-\frac{1}{\alpha}((t_{k+1})^\alpha - (t_k)^\alpha)}\right)} = f(t_k, y_k).$$

5. Comparisons of Discrete Models of the Conformable Relaxation Equation

To demonstrate that the CEM is not a viable extension of the Euler method to the CFD for $\alpha \in (0, 1)$ and to validate the suggested alternatives, comparisons against the analytic solution are presented in graphical and tabular form for the following discrete representations of the CRE obtained from the conformable Euler, ordinary Euler, modified conformable Euler, and ESDDFD-based Euler methods (respectively, CEM, OEM, MCEM, and EDM):

$$\begin{aligned}
\text{CEM} &: y_{k+1} = y_k - \tfrac{1}{\alpha} h t^\alpha_k y_k, \\
\text{OEM} &: y_{k+1} = y_k - h t^{\alpha-1}_k y_k, \\
\text{MCEM} &: y_{k+1} = y_k - \tfrac{1}{\alpha}\left((t_{k+1})^\alpha - (t_k)^\alpha\right) y_k \\
\text{EDM} &: y_{k+1} = y_k - \tfrac{1}{\alpha}\left(1 - e^{-\frac{1}{\alpha}((t_{k+1})^\alpha - (t_k)^\alpha)}\right) y_k
\end{aligned}$$

5.1. Tabular Comparisons of Actual and Relative Errors

In Table 1 relative error comparisons are given for various values of α at $t_k = 1.00$.

Table 1. % error by method compared to actual value at $t_k = 1.00$.

α	Exact Value	EDM	CEM	MCEM	OEM
0.99	0.36	0.00	5.06	1.29	1.30
0.98	0.36	0.00	8.93	1.32	1.38
0.97	0.36	0.00	12.90	1.34	1.46
0.96	0.35	0.00	16.80	1.37	1.54
0.95	0.35	0.00	20.80	1.40	1.62
0.62	0.20	0.00	99.60	4.56	7.31

It is clear from Table 1 that, for this simplest example, the CEM performs poorly compared to all other methods and yields significantly incorrect approximations for $\alpha < 0.98$, with relative error reaching almost 100% at $\alpha = 0.62$. While the OEM is almost comparable to the MCEM for α close to unity, its relative error is almost double that of the MCEM for $\alpha < 0.62$. The EDM, as expected for this example, has the same values as the analytic solution.

5.2. Graphical Comparisons of Actual and Relative Errors

Comparisons are presented in terms of solution profiles as well as actual and relative errors for $\alpha = 0.95$ in Figure 1a–c and for $\alpha = 0.5$ in Figure 2a–c.

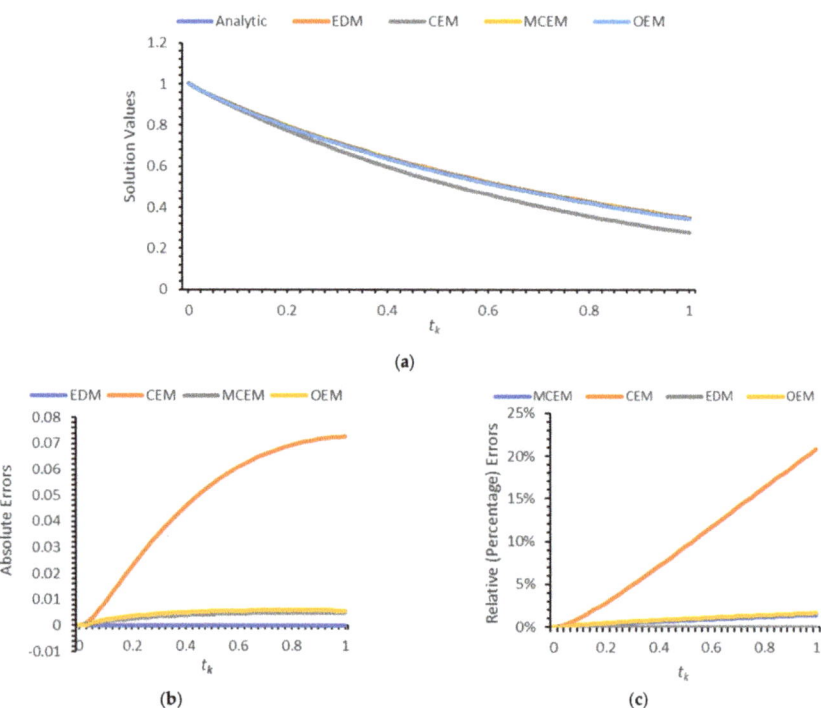

Figure 1. Analytic solution profile of (17) compared on $[0, 1]$ to approximations by the EDM, CEM, MCEM, and OEM at $\alpha = 0.95$ with $h = 0.025$: (**a**) solution values (y_k), (**b**) absolute errors ($|y(t_k) - y_k|$) and (**c**) relative (percentage) errors ($\frac{|y_k - y(t_k)|}{y(t_k)} (100)$).

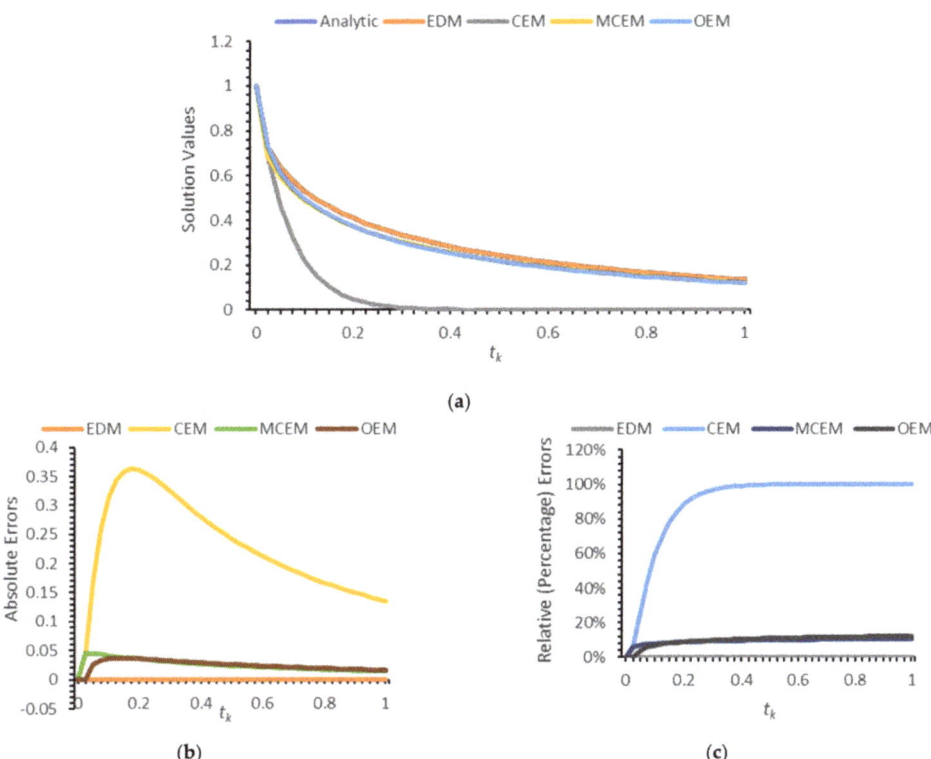

Figure 2. Analytic solution profile of (17) compared on $[0, 1]$ to approximations by the EDM, CEM, MCEM, and OEM at $\alpha = 0.5$ with $h = 0.025$: (**a**) solution values (y_k), (**b**) absolute errors ($|y(t_k) - y_k|$) and (**c**) relative (percentage) errors ($\frac{|y_k - y(t_k)|}{y(t_k)}(100)$).

6. Conclusions

A discretization method, termed the conformable Euler's method, for the fractional initial value problem with the conformable fractional derivative has been considered that extends the integer Euler method to the conformable derivative. Its justification using a fractional series expansion is recalled and it is shown that the assumption ${}_0^C T_t^\alpha(f)(t) = t^{1-\alpha}\frac{d}{dt}f(t)$ leads to the conclusion that $\alpha = 1$ in the method. The ordinary Euler method, obtained by rewriting the CFD in terms of the integer-ordered derivative, is described and its main implementation disadvantage briefly discussed. A modified conformable Euler's method is proposed that is derived from rewriting the term of the right-hand side of the equation assumed above as a derivative quotient and then using the integer definition of the derivative.

To justify the proposed modification of the CEM, the ESDDFD method, wherein fractionality is determined by wave type behavior of processes under study, of generalized difference quotient derivative representation is recalled. An alternate definition of the CFD is presented that is derived from the analytic solution of the CRE, which describes fractional KWW wave behavior, and it is shown that it has the same basic properties and returns the same derivative values as the CFD. It is observed that the alternate definition shows that the CFD is a fractional change of variable rather that a fractional operator. The MCEM follows as a limit of, and is therefore consistent with, the exact ESDDFD representation of the CRE, whereas the CEM is not.

Numerical experiments are then presented to assess the accuracy of the CEM in approximating the solution of the CRE. The CEM model of the CRE is compared with three discrete models obtained from the ordinary Euler, modified conformable Euler, and conformable NSFD (or ESDDFD) methods. Results are presented for several values of α, $0.62 \leq \alpha \leq 0.99$, showing errors for the four models relative to the analytic solution, as well as those of profile and error graphs for $\alpha = 0.95$, $\alpha = 0.5$. While comparisons are presented only for a few values of α, the results displayed are typical and conclusively show that the CEM yields incorrect approximations, with respective relative errors of 5.06%, 20.80%, and 99.60% for $\alpha = 0.99$, $\alpha = 0.95$, and $\alpha = 0.62$. In comparison, the relative errors at the same values of for the OEM and MCEM are, respectively, 1.30%, 1.62%, and 7.31% and 1.29%, 1.40%, and 4.56%; the EDM has no errors for the CRE since it is exact. Based on these numerical results, and with support of the theoretical arguments presented, it is concluded that the CEM is not a valid generalization of the standard forward Euler method to the CFD for $0 < \alpha < 1$, and that the MCEM and EDM offer more accurate alternative generalizations.

Author Contributions: Conceptualization, writing—original draft preparation, review, and editing, D.P.C.-M.; validation, visualization, writing—review and editing, B.G.B.C.-M. Both authors have read and agreed to the published version of the manuscript.

Funding: This research received no external funding.

Acknowledgments: The authors are grateful to the anonymous referees for very valuable comments and suggestions, especially for pointing out reference [30] and suggesting the Remark at the end of Section 4.1, which have greatly enhanced the paper.

Conflicts of Interest: The authors declare no conflict of interest.

Abbreviations

CFD	conformable fractional derivative
CEM	conformable Euler method
OEM	ordinary Euler method
MCEM	modified conformable Euler method
NSFD	nonstandard finite difference
ESDDFD	exact spectral derivative discretization finite difference
EDM	ESDDFD-based, NSFD Euler method, difference quotient representation
CRE	conformable relaxation equation
KWW	Kohlrausch–Williams–Watts
NID	non-integer derivatives
NIRE	non-integer relaxation equation

References

1. Mohammadnezhad, V.; Eslami, M.; Rezazadeh, H. Stability analysis of linear conformable fractional differential equations system with time delays. *Boletim Soc. Paranaense Mat.* **2020**, *38*, 159–171. [CrossRef]
2. Khalil, R.; Al Horani, M.; Yousef, A.; Sababheh, M. A new definition of fractional derivative. *J. Comput. Appl. Math.* **2014**, *264*, 65–70. [CrossRef]
3. Xin, B.; Peng, W.; Kwon, Y.; Liu, Y. Modeling, discretization, and hyperchaos detection of conformable derivative approach to a financial system with market confidence and ethics risk. *Adv. Differ. Equ.* **2019**, *2019*, 138. [CrossRef]
4. Katugampola, U.N. Correction to "What is a fractional derivative?" by Ortigueira and Machado [Journal of Computational Physics, Volume 293, 15 July 2015, Pages 4–13. Special issue on Fractional PDEs]. *J. Comput. Phys.* **2016**, *2016*, 1255–1257. [CrossRef]
5. Ortigueira, M.D.; Machado, J.T. What is a fractional derivative? *J. Comput. Phys.* **2015**, *293*, 4–13. [CrossRef]
6. Tarasov, V. No Violation of the Leibniz Rule. No Fractional Derivative. *Commun. Nonlinear Sci. Numer. Simul.* **2013**, *18*, 2945–2948. [CrossRef]
7. Tarasov, V. Local Fractional Derivatives of Differentiable Functions are Integer-order Derivatives or Zero. *Int. J. Appl. Comput. Math.* **2016**, *2*, 195–201. [CrossRef]
8. Tarasov, V.E. No nonlocality. No fractional derivative. *Commun. Nonlinear Sci. Numer. Simul.* **2018**, *62*, 157–163. [CrossRef]

9. Abdelhakim, A.A. The flaw in the conformable calculus: It is conformable because it is not fractional. *Fract. Calc. Appl. Anal.* **2019**, *22*, 242–254. [CrossRef]
10. Kiskinov, H.; Petkova, M.; Zahariev, A. Remarks about the existence of conformable derivatives and some consequences. *arXiv* **2019**, arXiv:1907.03486.
11. Kiskinov, H.; Petkova, M.; Zahariev, A. *About the Cauchy Problem for Nonlinear System with Conformable Derivatives and Variable Delays*; AIP Publishing LLC: Melville, NY, USA, 2019; Volume 3, p. 050006.
12. Kiskinov, H.; Petkova, M.; Zahariev, A.; Veselinova, M. *Some Results about Conformable Derivatives in Banach Spaces and an Application to the Partial Differential Equations*; AIP Publishing LLC: Melville, NY, USA, 2021; Volume 2333, p. 120002.
13. He, J.-H. A New Fractal Derivation. *Therm. Sci.* **2011**, *15* (Suppl. 1), S145–S147. [CrossRef]
14. Tuan, N.H.; Ngoc, T.B.; Baleanu, D.; O'Regan, D. On well-posedness of the sub-diffusion equation with conformable derivative model. *Commun. Nonlinear Sci. Numer. Simul.* **2020**, *89*, 105332. [CrossRef]
15. Xin, B.; Peng, W.; Guerrini, L. A Continuous Time Bertrand Duopoly Game With Fractional Delay and Conformable Derivative: Modeling, Discretization Process, Hopf Bifurcation, and Chaos. *Front. Phys.* **2019**, *7*, 84. [CrossRef]
16. Morales-Delgado, V.F.; Gómez-Aguilar, J.F.; Escobar-Jiménez, R.F.; Taneco-Hernández, M.A. Fractional conformable derivatives of Liouville–Caputo type with low-fractionality. *Phys. A Stat. Mech. Appl.* **2018**, *503*, 424–438. [CrossRef]
17. Martínez, L.; Rosales, J.J.; Carreño, C.A.; Lozano, J.M. Electrical circuits described by fractional conformable derivative. *Int. J. Circuit Theory Appl.* **2018**, *46*, 1091–1100. [CrossRef]
18. Chung, W.S. Fractional Newton mechanics with conformable fractional derivative. *J. Comput. Appl. Math.* **2015**, *290*, 150–158. [CrossRef]
19. Anderson, D.R.; Ulness, D.J. Properties of the Katugampola fractional derivative with potential application in quantum mechanics. *J. Math. Phys.* **2015**, *56*, 063502. [CrossRef]
20. Jajarmi, A.; Baleanu, D. A new fractional analysis on the interaction of HIV with CD4 + T-cells. *Chaos Solit. Fractals* **2018**, *113*, 221–229. [CrossRef]
21. Açan, Ö.; Al Qurashi, M.M.; Baleanu, D. New exact solution of generalized biological population model. *J. Nonlinear Sci. Appl.* **2017**, *10*, 3916–3929. [CrossRef]
22. Zhou, H.W.; Yang, S.; Zhang, S.Q. Conformable derivative approach to anomalous diffusion. *Phys. A Stat. Mech. Appl.* **2018**, *491*, 1001–1013. [CrossRef]
23. Clemence-Mkhope, D. Spectral Non-integer Derivative Representations and the Exact Spectral Derivative Discretization Finite Difference Method for the Fokker-Planck Equation. 2021. Available online: https://ui.adsabs.harvard.edu/link_gateway/2021 arXiv210602586C/arxiv:2106.02586 (accessed on 16 July 2021).
24. Gorenflo, R.; Mainardi, F.; Rogosin, S. Mittag-Leffler function: Properties and applications. In *Handbook of Fractional Calculus with Applications, Basic Theory*; De Gruyter: Berlin, Germany, 2019; Volume 1, pp. 269–296.
25. Metzler, R.; Klafter, J. The random walk's guide to anomalous diffusion: A fractional dynamics approach. *Phys. Rep.* **2000**, *339*, 1–77. [CrossRef]
26. Mainardi, F. A Note on the Equivalence of Fractional Relaxation Equations to Differential Equations with Varying Coefficients. *Mathematics* **2018**, *6*, 8. [CrossRef]
27. Abdeljawad, T. On Riemann and Caputo fractional differences. *Comput. Math. Appl.* **2011**, *62*, 1602–1611. [CrossRef]
28. Atangana, A.; Baleanu, D. New Fractional Derivatives with Nonlocal and Non-Singular Kernel: Theory and Application to Heat Transfer Model. *Therm. Sci.* **2016**, *20*, 763–769. [CrossRef]
29. Clemence-Mkhope, D. A Comment on the Conformable Euler's Finite Difference Method. *arXiv* **2021**, arXiv:2105.10385.
30. Anderson, D.R.; Camrud, E.; Ulness, D.J. On the nature of the conformable derivative and its applications to physics. *J. Fract. Calc. Appl.* **2019**, *10*, 92–135.
31. Mickens, R.E. *Nonstandard Finite Difference Schemes: Methodology And Applications*; World Scientific Publishing Company: Singapore, 2020.

Mathematical and Computational Applications

Article

Taming Hyperchaos with Exact Spectral Derivative Discretization Finite Difference Discretization of a Conformable Fractional Derivative Financial System with Market Confidence and Ethics Risk

Dominic P. Clemence-Mkhope * and Gregory A. Gibson

Department of Mathematics and Statistics, North Carolina A&T State University, Greensboro, NC 27411, USA; gagibson@ncat.edu
* Correspondence: clemence@ncat.edu

Abstract: Four discrete models, using the exact spectral derivative discretization finite difference (ESDDFD) method, are proposed for a chaotic five-dimensional, conformable fractional derivative financial system incorporating ethics and market confidence. Since the system considered was recently studied using the conformable Euler finite difference (CEFD) method and found to be hyperchaotic, and the CEFD method was recently shown to be valid only at fractional index $\alpha = 1$, the source of the hyperchaos is in question. Through numerical experiments, illustration is presented that the hyperchaos previously detected is, in part, an artifact of the CEFD method, as it is absent from the ESDDFD models.

Keywords: conformable calculus; fractional-order financial system; ESDDFD and NSFD methods; hyperchaotic attractor; market confidence; ethics risk

Citation: Clemence-Mkhope, D.P.; Gibson, G.A. Taming Hyperchaos with Exact Spectral Derivative Discretization Finite Difference Discretization of a Conformable Fractional Derivative Financial System with Market Confidence and Ethics Risk. *Math. Comput. Appl.* **2022**, *27*, 4. https://doi.org/10.3390/mca27010004

Academic Editor: Paweł Olejnik

Received: 27 November 2021
Accepted: 31 December 2021
Published: 10 January 2022

Publisher's Note: MDPI stays neutral with regard to jurisdictional claims in published maps and institutional affiliations.

Copyright: © 2022 by the authors. Licensee MDPI, Basel, Switzerland. This article is an open access article distributed under the terms and conditions of the Creative Commons Attribution (CC BY) license (https://creativecommons.org/licenses/by/4.0/).

1. Introduction

Hyperchaotic systems [1,2]—typically defined as systems with at least two positive Lyapunov exponents [3–5]—of a fractional-order have been investigated in many contexts, such as systems of Rössler [6] or Lorenz [7] type, those with flux controlled memristors [8] or realized in circuits [9–11], those arising from cellular neural networks [12], and financial systems [13]. As recounted in [13], a nonlinear financial system depicting the relationship among interest rates, investments, prices, and savings was first introduced by Huang and Li [14]. It was extended to fractional-order in Chen [15], to uncertain fractional-order form in Wang et al. [16], to delayed form in Mircea et al. [17], and to discrete form in Xin et al. [18]. The average profit margin was added as a variable in Yu et al. [19], while investment incentive and market confidence were introduced in Xin et al. [20,21]. Xin and Zhang [21] updated the 3-dimensional Huang and Li [8] model to a 4-dimensional one by accounting for market confidence and [13] incorporated ethics risk to obtain a 5-dimensional system, which was then fractionalized to obtain the following fractional-order financial system considered in [13]:

$$
\begin{aligned}
T_t^{\alpha_1} x &= z + (y-a)x + k(w-pu) \\
T_t^{\alpha_2} y &= 1 - by - x^2 + k(w-pu) \\
T_t^{\alpha_3} z &= -x - cz + k(w-pu) \\
T_t^{\alpha_4} w &= -dxyz \\
T_t^{\alpha_5} u &= k(w-pu)
\end{aligned}
\qquad (1)
$$

where $\alpha = (\alpha_1, \alpha_2, \alpha_3, \alpha_4, \alpha_5)$ is subject to $\alpha_1, \alpha_2, \alpha_3, \alpha_4, \alpha_5 \in (0,1)$, and $T_t^{\alpha_i}, 1 \leq i \leq 5$, denotes the conformable fractional derivative of order α_i. The variables x, y, z, w, and

u are the interest rate, investment demand, price index, market confidence, and ethics risk, respectively; the parameters a, b, and c are the saving amount, cost per investment, and demand elasticity of commercial markets, respectively, and $a, b, c \geq 0$; k, p, d are impact factors associated with ethics risk.

Since analytic solutions do not exist, suitable numerical schemes to obtain solutions of the conformable derivative financial system are needed. Though there are several methods to solve a conformable derivative system [22–47], these are too complex for many people. Inspired by the discretization process for the Caputo derivative for Ricatti equations [45] and Chua systems [46], the conformable Euler's finite difference (CEFD) method [47] for the 5-dimensional fractional-order financial system is proposed in [13]. Numerical experiments with the resulting discrete model were conducted to detect a hyperchaotic attractor of the system. However, the standard Euler discretization of integer-order systems, such as studied in [13], is known to induce (see, e.g., [48,49]) numerical instabilities and spurious behavior where none exist in the continuous system. Moreover, the CEFD method has recently been shown [50] to be valid only for $\alpha = 1$ and is, therefore, not a valid fractional method. Nonstandard finite difference (NSFD) models have extensively [48] been shown to eliminate induced chaos; the exact spectral derivative discretization finite difference (ESDDFD) methodology is a novel extension, developed in the context of advection–reaction–diffusion equations [51], of the NSFD method to non-integer derivatives [52].

It is, therefore, natural to ask whether some of the hyperchaotic behavior detected in the fractional financial system is an artifact of the method and whether ESDDFD models can be constructed to eliminate such induced hyperchaos. The purpose of the present study is to investigate this question—in particular, the effects of the discretization of the derivative and that of non-linear terms. To this end, the following four discrete models using the ESDDFD method are constructed for the system (1) and the bifurcation experiments of [13] are repeated with the new models.

$$\begin{aligned}
\frac{x_{k+1}-x_k}{\phi_j(h,\alpha_1)} &= F_i^x(x_k, y_k, z_k, u_k, w_k) \\
\frac{y_{k+1}-y_k}{\phi_j(h,\alpha_2)} &= F_i^y(x_k, y_k, z_k, u_k, w_k) \\
\frac{z_{k+1}-z_k}{\phi_j(h,\alpha_3)} &= -x_k - cz_k + k(w_k - pu_k) \\
\frac{u_{k+1}-u_k}{\phi_j(h,\alpha_5)} &= k(w_k - pu_k) \\
\frac{w_{k+1}-w_k}{\phi_j(h,\alpha_4)} &= F_i^w(x_k, y_k, z_k, z_k)
\end{aligned} \quad (2)$$

$i = 1, 2$ and $j = 1, 2$, where:

$$\begin{aligned}
F_1^x(x_k, y_k, z_k, u_k, w_k) &= z_k + (y_{k+1} - a)x_k + k(w_k - pu_k) \\
F_1^y(x_k, y_k, z_k, u_k, w_k) &= 1 - by_k - x_k x_k + k(w_k - pu_k) \\
F_1^w(x_k, y_k, z_k, z_k) &= -\frac{d}{2} x_k y_k (z_k + z_k) \\
F_2^x &= F_1^x(x_k, y_{k+1}, z_k, u_k, w_k) \\
F_2^y &= F_1^y(x_k, y_{k+1}, z_k, u_k, w_k) \\
F_2^w &= F_1^w(x_k, y_{k+1}, z_k, z_{k+1})
\end{aligned}$$

The remainder of this article is organized as follows. In Section 2, the ESDDFD fundamentals, a description of the model (1), and the CEFD model from [3] are presented. Section 3 presents the construction of the denominator functions, $\phi_j(h, \alpha_m), 1 \leq m \leq 5$, for the ESDDFD model (2) and compares sub-models of (2) with corresponding CEFD sub-models. In Section 4, experimental results of hyperchaotic attractor detection from the proposed financial system using both methods are presented. Concluding remarks in Section 5 close the paper.

2. Preliminaries

2.1. The Conformable Derivative ESDDFD Discrete Model Construction Fundamentals

While the Riemann–Liouville, Caputo, Atangana–Baleanu, and Grünwald–Letnikov fractional derivatives [53–60] are widely used in various applications, their definitions lack the chain rule, a classical derivative property satisfied by the conformable fractional derivative (CFD) [61–63] and its various extensions (see e.g., [64]). A financial system with a market confidence and ethics risk model was recently [13] added to the many existing applications of the CFD in various scientific fields [22,65–74].

2.2. The Conformable Derivative Hyperchaotic Financial System and Its CEFD Model

The conformable fractional derivative financial system model (1) is based on a successive addition of various factors, starting with the Huang and Li [8] nonlinear financial system model:

$$\begin{aligned} x' &= z + (y - a)x \\ y' &= 1 - by - x^2 \\ z' &= -x - cz \end{aligned} \quad (3)$$

modeling the interaction of interest rate (x), investment demand (y), and price index (z); the variables and parameters are the same as in (1). Model (3) was extended, by Xin and Zhang [15], to account for market confidence:

$$\begin{aligned} x' &= z + (y - a)x + m_1 w \\ y' &= 1 - by - x^2 + m_2 w \\ z' &= -x - cz + m_3 w \\ w' &= -dxyz \end{aligned} \quad (4)$$

where m_1, m_2, m_3 are the impact factors associated with market confidence (w); the remaining variables and parameters are the same as in (3). Model (1) is the fractionalization, predicated on the practice that fractional-order economic systems [15,75–79] can generalize their integer-order forms [14,80,81], of the following extension of (4) in [13] to account for both market confidence and ethics risk (u):

$$\begin{aligned} x' &= z + (y - a)x + k(w - pu) \\ y' &= 1 - by - x^2 + k(w - pu) \\ z' &= -x - cz + k(w - pu) \\ w' &= -dxyz \\ u' &= k(w - pu) \end{aligned} \quad (5)$$

When $\alpha = (1, 1, 1, 1, 1)$, system (1) degenerates to system (5); in the absence of ethics risk, (5) reduces to (4); in the absence of market confidence, (4) reduces to (3). In these three cases, therefore, any discrete method developed for (1) must reduce to that of the three respective reduced systems. Chaotic behavior for both the CEFD and ESDDFD models will be numerically investigated in Section 4 for (1) as well as the reduced fractional counterpart of system (3).

The following discrete model was obtained in [13] from the CEFD method and used to numerically investigate hyperchaos of the system (1):

$$\begin{aligned} x_{k+1} &= x_k + \frac{h^{\alpha_1}}{\alpha_1}(z_k + (y_k - a)x_k + k(w_k - pu_k)) \\ y_{k+1} &= y_k + \frac{h^{\alpha_2}}{\alpha_2}(1 - by_k - x_k x_k + k(w_k - pu_k)) \\ z_{k+1} &= z_k - \frac{h^{\alpha_3}}{\alpha_3}(x_k + cz_k - k(w_k - pu_k)) \\ u_{k+1} &= u_k + \frac{h^{\alpha_5}}{\alpha_5}k(w_k - pu_k) \\ w_{k+1} &= w_k - \frac{h^{\alpha_4}}{\alpha_4}dx_k y_k z_k \end{aligned} \quad (6)$$

3. ESDDFD Discretization of the Conformable Derivative System and Its Reductions

In the ESDDFD and NSFD discretization methodologies, the first step is to consider a linear sub-system whose exact or best scheme can be constructed. Such a sub-system, in this case, is the following:

$$\begin{aligned} T_t^{\alpha_1} x &= -ax, \\ T_t^{\alpha_2} y &= -by, \\ T_t^{\alpha_3} z &= -cz, \\ T_t^{\alpha_4} w &= 0, \\ T_t^{\alpha_5} u &= -kpu, \end{aligned} \quad (7)$$

which has only positive solutions for any positive initial data. The exact discretization of (7), which has a solution identical to that of (7), is as follows:

$$\begin{aligned} \frac{x_{k+1} - x_k}{\phi_1(h, \alpha_1)} &= -ax_k, \\ \frac{y_{k+1} - y_k}{\phi_1(h, \alpha_2)} &= -by_k, \\ \frac{z_{k+1} - z_k}{\phi_1(h, \alpha_3)} &= -cz_k, \\ \frac{w_{k+1} - w_k}{\phi_1(h, \alpha_4)} &= 0, \\ \frac{u_{k+1} - u_k}{\phi_1(h, \alpha_5)} &= -kpu_k, \end{aligned} \quad (8)$$

where the nonstandard denominators $\phi_1(h, \alpha_i), 1 \leq i \leq 5$, are given by:

$$\phi_1(h, \alpha_i) = \frac{1}{Q_i}\left(1 - e^{-\frac{Q_i}{\alpha_i}[(t+h)^{\alpha_i} - t^{\alpha_i}]}\right),$$

with $Q_1 = a$, $Q_2 = b$, $Q_3 = c$, $Q_4 = 0$, $Q_5 = kp$.

Since (1) reduces to (7), any valid discrete model for (1) must be reducible to one consistent with its exact discretization—that is, (8). By comparison, a reduction of the CEFD model (6) to the sub-system (7) yields the following discrete sub-system:

$$\begin{aligned} x_{k+1} &= x_k - \frac{h^{\alpha_1}}{\alpha_1} a x_k, \\ y_{k+1} &= y_k - \frac{h^{\alpha_2}}{\alpha_2} b y_k, \\ z_{k+1} &= z_k - \frac{h^{\alpha_3}}{\alpha_3} c z_k, \\ w_{k+1} &= w_k + Q_4 \frac{h^{\alpha_4}}{\alpha_4} w_k, \\ u_{k+1} &= u_k - \frac{h^{\alpha_5}}{\alpha_5} kpu_k, \end{aligned} \quad (9)$$

which is positive only if the following condition is satisfied: $\left(1 - \frac{h^{\alpha_i}}{\alpha_i} Q_i\right) \geq 0$, $1 \leq i \leq 5$, with the Q_i as in (8); such conditional positivity is known to induce chaotic behavior. All of the sub-Equations (8) are of the form:

$$T_t^{\alpha} P = -\lambda P,$$

whose CEFD scheme is:

$$P_{k+1} = P_k - \frac{h^{\alpha}}{\alpha} \lambda P_k,$$

which has been conclusively shown in [50] to be valid only for $\alpha = 1$.

It is shown in [50] that a modified CEFD (MCEFD) may be obtained from the following alternate CFD definition, which is equivalent to the fractional change of variables in the integer-valued derivative (see also [82]):

Definition 1. *Given a real-valued function on $[0, \infty)$, the conformable fractional derivative has the following alternative definition:*

$$_0^C T_t^\alpha [f(t)] \equiv \lim_{h \to 0} {}^{CFD}\Delta_t^\alpha [f(t)] = \alpha \lim_{h \to 0} \frac{f(t+h) - f(t)}{[(t+h)^\alpha - t^\alpha]},$$

where $_0^C T_t^\alpha [f(0)]$ is understood to mean $_0^C T_t^\alpha [f(0)] = \lim_{t \to 0^+} {}_0^C T_t^\alpha [f(t)]$.

Therefore, the Euler scheme, resulting from the MCFED, is the same as that given in Equation (8), only with the denominator of:

$$\phi_1(h, \alpha_i) = \frac{1}{Q_i} \left(1 - e^{-\frac{Q_i}{\alpha_i}[(t+h)^{\alpha_i} - t^{\alpha_i}]} \right)$$

replaced by:

$$\phi_2(h, \alpha_i) = \frac{1}{\alpha_i} \left[(t+h)^{\alpha_i} - t^{\alpha_i} \right], \ 1 \leq i \leq 5,$$

which is equivalent to replacing h^{α_i} by $\alpha_i \phi_2(h, \alpha_i)$ in the CEFD scheme (9).

To enable the assessment of the effect of the denominators $\phi_j(h, \alpha_i)$, $j = 1, 2$, the following schemes are compared:

$$\begin{aligned}
\frac{x_{k+1} - x_k}{\phi_j(h, \alpha_1)} &= z_k + (y_k - a) x_k, \\
\frac{y_{k+1} - y_k}{\phi_j(h, \alpha_2)} &= 1 - b y_k - (x_k)^2, \\
\frac{z_{k+1} - z_k}{\phi_j(h, \alpha_3)} &= -x_k - c z_k, \ j = 1, 2.
\end{aligned} \quad (10)$$

To enable the assessment of the effect of the non-local discretization of nonlinear terms, the following schemes are compared:

$$\begin{aligned}
\frac{x_{k+1} - x_k}{\phi_j(h, \alpha_1)} &= z_k + (y_{k+1} - a) x_k, \\
\frac{y_{k+1} - y_k}{\phi_j(h, \alpha_2)} &= 1 - b y_k - x_{k+1} x_k, \\
\frac{z_{k+1} - z_k}{\phi_j(h, \alpha_3)} &= -x_k - c z_k, \ j = 1, 2.
\end{aligned} \quad (11)$$

The terms $(y - a)x$, and x^2 are discretized non-locally as, respectively, $(y_{k+1} - a)x_k$ and $x_{k+1} x_k$, while discretization of the terms z (in the first Equation of (10)) and x (in the third as z_k and x_k) ensures respective consistency with the terms cz in the third and ax in the first Equation of (11) in the cases where $c = 1$ and $a = 1$.

By comparison, the scheme obtained through a reduction of the CEFD model (6) to its 3-dimensional sub-system (3) yields the following discrete sub-system:

$$\begin{aligned}
x_{k+1} &= x_k + \frac{h^{\alpha_1}}{\alpha_1} (z_k + (y_k - a) x_k) \\
y_{k+1} &= y_k + \frac{h^{\alpha_2}}{\alpha_2} (1 - b y_k - x_k x_k) \\
z_{k+1} &= z_k + \frac{h^{\alpha_3}}{\alpha_3} (-x_k - c z_k).
\end{aligned} \quad (12)$$

Since system (12) reduces to the $x - y - z$ sub-system of (9), which suffers from induced chaos, it is to be expected that it too suffers the same, which will be numerically investigated in the next section.

The ESDDFD models (2) are then obtained by discretizing $k(w - pu)$ as $k(w_k - pu_k)$ to ensure consistency with (8) and then discretizing xyz non-locally as either $\frac{1}{2}x_k y_k(z_k + z_k)$ or $\frac{1}{2}x_k y_{k+1}(z_k + z_{k+1})$, where the form $x_k y_{k+1}$ is used to match the xy term in the x-equation.

$$\frac{x_{k+1} - x_k}{\phi_j(h, \alpha_1)} = z_k + (y_k - a)x_k + k(w_k - pu_k)$$

$$\frac{y_{k+1} - y_k}{\phi_j(h, \alpha_2)} = 1 - by_k - (x_k)^2 + k(w_k - pu_k)$$

$$\frac{z_{k+1} - z_k}{\phi_j(h, \alpha_3)} = -x_k - cz_k + k(w_k - pu_k) \tag{13}$$

$$\frac{u_{k+1} - u_k}{\phi_j(h, \alpha_5)} = k(w_k - pu_k)$$

$$\frac{w_{k+1} - w_k}{\phi_j(h, \alpha_4)} = -\frac{d}{2}x_k y_k(z_k + z_k), \quad j = 1, 2.$$

and

$$\frac{x_{k+1} - x_k}{\phi_j(h, \alpha_1)} = z_k + (y_{k+1} - a)x_k + k(w_k - pu_k)$$

$$\frac{y_{k+1} - y_k}{\phi_j(h, \alpha_2)} = 1 - by_k - x_{k+1}x_k + k(w_k - pu_k)$$

$$\frac{z_{k+1} - z_k}{\phi_j(h, \alpha_3)} = -x_k - cz_k + k(w_k - pu_k) \tag{14}$$

$$\frac{u_{k+1} - u_k}{\phi_j(h, \alpha_5)} = k(w_k - pu_k)$$

$$\frac{w_{k+1} - w_k}{\phi_j(h, \alpha_4)} = -\frac{d}{2}x_k y_{k+1}(z_k + z_{k+1}), \quad j = 1, 2.$$

The schemes (13) are explicit and can be explicitly solved for each $j = 1, 2$, in the order $x_{k+1}, y_{k+1}, z_{k+1}, u_{k+1}, w_{k+1}$ to obtain the following:

$$x_{k+1} = x_k + \phi_j(h, \alpha_1)[z_k + (y_k - a)x_k + k(w_k - pu_k)]$$

$$y_{k+1} = y_k + \phi_j(h, \alpha_2)\left[1 - by_k - (x_k)^2 + k(w_k - pu_k)\right]$$

$$z_{k+1} = z_k - \phi_j(h, \alpha_3)[x_k + cz_k - k(w_k - pu_k)] \tag{15}$$

$$u_{k+1} = u_k + \phi_j(h, \alpha_5)[k(w_k - pu_k)]$$

$$w_{k+1} = w_k - \frac{d}{2}\phi_j(h, \alpha_4)x_k y_k(z_k + z_k), \quad j = 1, 2.$$

While implicit, the schemes (14) can be explicitly solved for each $j = 1, 2$ in the order $u_{k+1}, z_{k+1}, x_{k+1}, y_{k+1}, w_{k+1}$ to obtain the following:

$$u_{k+1} = u_k + \phi_j(h, \alpha_5)[k(w_k - pu_k)]$$

$$z_{k+1} = z_k - \phi_j(h, \alpha_3)[x_k + cz_k - k(w_k - pu_k)]$$

$$x_{k+1} = \frac{1}{[1 + \phi_j(h, \alpha_1)x_k \phi_j(h, \alpha_2)x_k]}(x_k + \phi_j(h, \alpha_1)x_k\{y_k + \phi_j(h, \alpha_2)[1 - by_k + k(w_k - pu_k)]\})$$

$$+ \frac{1}{[1 + \phi(h, \alpha_1)x_k \phi(h, \alpha_2)x_k]}\phi_j(h, \alpha_1)[z_k - ax_k + k(w_k - pu_k)]$$

$$w_{k+1} = w_k - \phi_j(h, \alpha_4)\frac{d}{2}x_k y_{k+1}(z_k + z_{k+1})$$

4. Numerical Experiments

In this section, hyperchaos detection experiments are conducted, parallel to those of [13], by varying the parameters related to ethics risk, such as α_5, the confidence factor k, and the risk factor p, in the CEFD and ESDDFD models and their reductions. The following parameters and initial point values are fixed following [1]: $h = 0.002$, $a = 0.8$, $b = 0.6$, $c = 1$, $d = 2$, $\alpha_1 = 0.3$, $\alpha_2 = 0.5$, $\alpha_3 = 0.6$, $\alpha_4 = 0.24$, $x_0 = 0.4$, $y_0 = 0.6$, $z_0 = 0.8$, $w_0 = 0.3$, $u_0 = 0.4$.

4.1. Three-Dimensional Systems Comparison

There were no experiments performed in [13] for this case. Simulations for both the ESDDFD model (11) and the CEFD model (12) are performed with the same parameters. The following models (16)–(19), obtained through the ESDDFD method,

$$\frac{x_{k+1}-x_k}{\frac{1}{0.8}\left[1-e^{\frac{-0.8}{0.3}[(t+h)^{0.3}-t^{0.3}]}\right]} = z_k + (y_k - 0.8)x_k,$$
$$\frac{y_{k+1}-y_k}{\frac{1}{0.6}\left[1-e^{\frac{-0.6}{0.5}[(t+h)^{0.5}-t^{0.5}]}\right]} = 1 - 0.6y_k - (x_k)^2, \quad (16)$$
$$\frac{z_{k+1}-z_k}{\left[1-e^{\frac{-1}{0.6}[(t+h)^{0.6}-t^{0.6}]}\right]} = -x_k - z_k,$$

$$\frac{x_{k+1}-x_k}{\frac{1}{0.3}\left[(t+h)^{0.3}-t^{0.3}\right]} = z_k + (y_k - 0.8)x_k,$$
$$\frac{y_{k+1}-y_k}{\frac{1}{0.5}\left[(t+h)^{0.5}-t^{0.5}\right]} = 1 - 0.6y_k - (x_k)^2, \quad (17)$$
$$\frac{z_{k+1}-z_k}{\frac{1}{0.6}\left[(t+h)^{0.6}-t^{0.6}\right]} = -x_k - z_k,$$

$$\frac{x_{k+1}-x_k}{\frac{1}{0.8}\left[1-e^{\frac{-0.8}{0.3}[(t+h)^{0.3}-t^{0.3}]}\right]} = z_k + (y_{k+1} - 0.8)x_k,$$
$$\frac{y_{k+1}-y_k}{\frac{1}{0.6}\left[1-e^{\frac{-0.6}{0.5}[(t+h)^{0.5}-t^{0.5}]}\right]} = 1 - 0.6y_k - x_{k+1}x_k, \quad (18)$$
$$\frac{z_{k+1}-z_k}{\left[1-e^{\frac{-1}{0.6}[(t+h)^{0.6}-t^{0.6}]}\right]} = -x_k - z_k,$$

$$\frac{x_{k+1}-x_k}{\frac{1}{0.3}\left[(t+h)^{0.3}-t^{0.3}\right]} = z_k + (y_{k+1} - 0.8)x_k,$$
$$\frac{y_{k+1}-y_k}{\frac{1}{0.5}\left[(t+h)^{0.5}-t^{0.5}\right]} = 1 - 0.6y_k - x_{k+1}x_k, \quad (19)$$
$$\frac{z_{k+1}-z_k}{\frac{1}{0.6}\left[(t+h)^{0.6}-t^{0.6}\right]} = -x_k$$

are compared to (20), obtained through the CEFD method:

$$x_{k+1} = x_k + \frac{h^{0.3}}{0.3}(z_k + (y_k - 0.8)x_k),$$
$$y_{k+1} = y_k + \frac{h^{0.5}}{0.5}(1 - 0.6y_k - x_k x_k), \quad (20)$$
$$z_{k+1} = z_k + \frac{h^{0.6}}{0.6}(x_k - z_k).$$

While bifurcations can be seen in Figure 1a for the CEFD model, they are absent from the results of the ESDDFD models, Figure 1b–e.

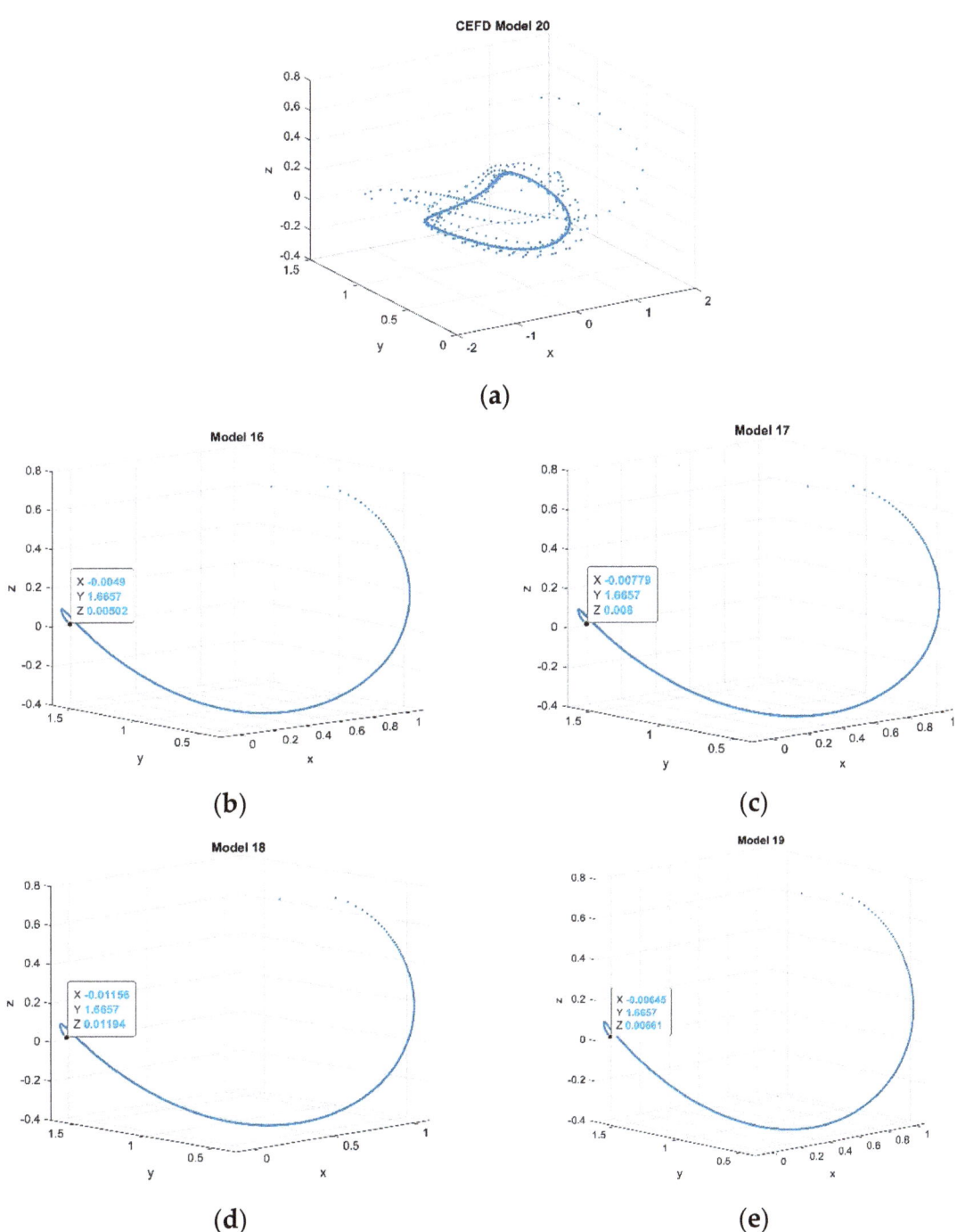

Figure 1. Phase portraits (**a**) CEFD model (20) (**b**) MCEFD model (16) (**c**) Model 17 (**d**) Model 18 (**e**) model (19).

4.2. Five-Dimensional Systems Comparison: Varying α_5, k, and p

For this case, experiments performed in [13] are performed with the same parameters for models obtained through the ESDDFD method, for the various cases and values of (α_5, k, p) used in [13]. Model (21) from the CEFD method,

$$\begin{aligned}
x_{k+1} &= x_k + \frac{h^{0.3}}{0.3}(z_k + (y_k - 0.8)x_k + k(w_k - pu_k)) \\
y_{k+1} &= y_k + \frac{h^{0.5}}{05}(1 - 0.6y_k - x_kx_k + k(w_k - pu_k)) \\
z_{k+1} &= z_k - \frac{h^{0.6}}{0.6}(x_k + z_k - k(w_k - pu_k)) \\
w_{k+1} &= w_k - \frac{h^{0.24}}{0.24}2x_ky_kz_k \\
u_{k+1} &= u_k + \frac{h^{\alpha_5}}{\alpha_5}k(w_k - pu_k)
\end{aligned} \qquad (21)$$

is compared to the following four models—respectively, MCEFD (22), ESDDFD1 (23), ESDDFD2 (24), ESDDFD3 (25)—obtained through the ESDDFD and NSFD methods:

$$\begin{aligned}
\frac{x_{k+1}-x_k}{\frac{1}{0.3}\left[(t+h)^{0.3}-t^{0.3}\right]} &= z_k + (y_k - 0.8)x_k + k(w_k - pu_k) \\
\frac{y_{k+1}-y_k}{\frac{1}{0.5}\left[(t+h)^{0.5}-t^{0.5}\right]} &= 1 - 0.6y_k - x_kx_k + k(w_k - pu_k) \\
\frac{z_{k+1}-z_k}{\frac{1}{0.6}\left[(t+h)^{0.6}-t^{0.6}\right]} &= -x_k - z_k + k(w_k - pu_k) \\
\frac{w_{k+1}-w_k}{\frac{1}{0.24}\left[(t+h)^{0.24}-t^{0.24}\right]} &= -x_ky_k(z_k + z_k) \\
\frac{u_{k+1}-u_k}{\frac{1}{\alpha_5}\left[(t+h)^{\alpha_5}-t^{\alpha_5}\right]} &= k(w_k - pu_k)
\end{aligned} \qquad (22)$$

$$\begin{aligned}
\frac{x_{k+1}-x_k}{\frac{1}{0.8}\left[1-e^{\frac{-0.8}{0.3}[(t+h)^{0.3}-t^{0.3}]}\right]} &= z_k + (y_k - 0.8)x_k + k(w_k - pu_k) \\
\frac{y_{k+1}-y_k}{\frac{1}{0.6}\left[1-e^{\frac{-0.6}{0.5}[(t+h)^{0.5}-t^{0.5}]}\right]} &= 1 - 0.6y_k - x_kx_k + k(w_k - pu_k) \\
\frac{z_{k+1}-z_k}{\left[1-e^{\frac{-1}{0.6}[(t+h)^{0.6}-t^{0.6}]}\right]} &= -x_k - z_k + k(w_k - pu_k) \\
\frac{w_{k+1}-w_k}{\left[1-e^{\frac{-1}{0.24}[(t+h)^{0.24}-t^{0.24}]}\right]} &= -x_ky_k(z_k + z_k) \\
\frac{u_{k+1}-u_k}{\frac{1}{kp}\left[1-e^{\frac{-kp}{\alpha_5}[(t+h)^{\alpha_5}-t^{\alpha_5}]}\right]} &= k(w_k - pu_k)
\end{aligned} \qquad (23)$$

$$\begin{aligned}
\frac{x_{k+1}-x_k}{\frac{1}{0.3}\left[(t+h)^{0.3}-t^{0.3}\right]} &= z_k + (y_{k+1} - 0.8)x_k + k(w_k - pu_k) \\
\frac{y_{k+1}-y_k}{\frac{1}{0.5}\left[(t+h)^{0.5}-t^{0.5}\right]} &= 1 - 0.6y_k - x_{k+1}x_k + k(w_k - pu_k) \\
\frac{z_{k+1}-z_k}{\frac{1}{0.6}\left[(t+h)^{0.6}-t^{0.6}\right]} &= -x_k - z_k + k(w_k - pu_k) \\
\frac{w_{k+1}-w_k}{\frac{1}{0.24}\left[(t+h)^{0.24}-t^{0.24}\right]} &= -x_ky_{k+1}(z_k + z_{k+1}) \\
\frac{u_{k+1}-u_k}{\frac{1}{\alpha_5}\left[(t+h)^{\alpha_5}-t^{\alpha_5}\right]} &= k(w_k - pu_k)
\end{aligned} \qquad (24)$$

$$\frac{x_{k+1}-x_k}{\frac{1}{0.8}\left[1-e^{\frac{-0.8}{0.3}[(t+h)^{0.3}-t^{0.3}]}\right]} = z_k + (y_{k+1} - 0.8)x_k + k(w_k - pu_k)$$

$$\frac{y_{k+1}-y_k}{\frac{1}{0.6}\left[1-e^{\frac{-0.6}{0.5}[(t+h)^{0.5}-t^{0.5}]}\right]} = 1 - 0.6y_k - x_{k+1}x_k + k(w_k - pu_k)$$

$$\frac{z_{k+1}-z_k}{\left[1-e^{\frac{-1}{0.6}[(t+h)^{0.6}-t^{0.6}]}\right]} = -x_k - z_k + k(w_k - pu_k) \quad (25)$$

$$\frac{w_{k+1}-w_k}{\left[1-e^{\frac{-1}{0.24}[(t+h)^{0.24}-t^{0.24}]}\right]} = -x_k y_{k+1}(z_k + z_{k+1})$$

$$\frac{u_{k+1}-u_k}{\frac{1}{kp}\left[1-e^{\frac{-kp}{\alpha_5}[(t+h)^{\alpha_5}-t^{\alpha_5}]}\right]} = k(w_k - pu_k)$$

4.2.1. Varying α_5 with Fixed $k = 2$ and $p = 1$ and $\alpha_5 \in [0.232, 0.328]$

In this case, Ref. [13] concluded that system (6) is hyperchaotic with $\alpha_5 \in [0.232, 0.328]$; fixing $\alpha_5 = 0.24$, a set of two positive Lyapunov exponents and three negative Lyapunov exponents were found. Profiles for x, y, z, w and u, when $\alpha_5 = 0.232$ for model (21), are given below. Chaos can be clearly seen in Figure 2 which gives the phase portraits for the CEFD model. For each model (22) through (25). Figure 3 shows phase portraits using the same step size and parameter values. These models produce identical graphs, which differ significantly from the graphs for model (21). The bifurcation tests for the ESDDFD model are performed with the same parameters. The bifurcation diagrams for x, z and u for model (21) are in Figure 4. These again show clear signs of chaos while the bifurcation diagrams for models (22) through (25), which are given in Figures 5–8, do not.

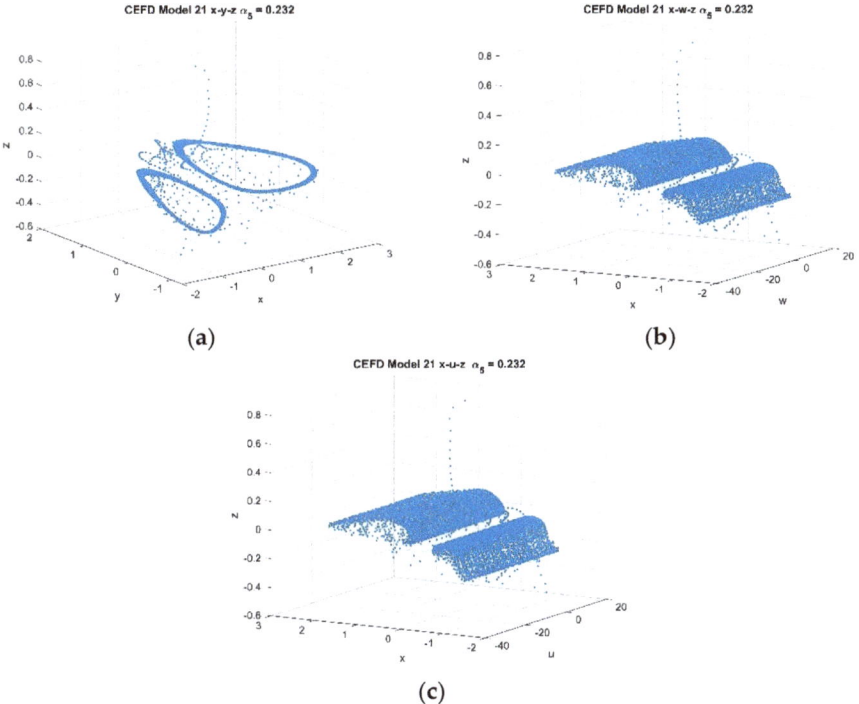

Figure 2. CEFD model (21) profiles of (**a**) $x - y - z$, (**b**) $x - u - z$, (**c**) $x - w - z$, at $h = 0.002$, $k = 2, p = 1, \alpha_5 = 0.232$.

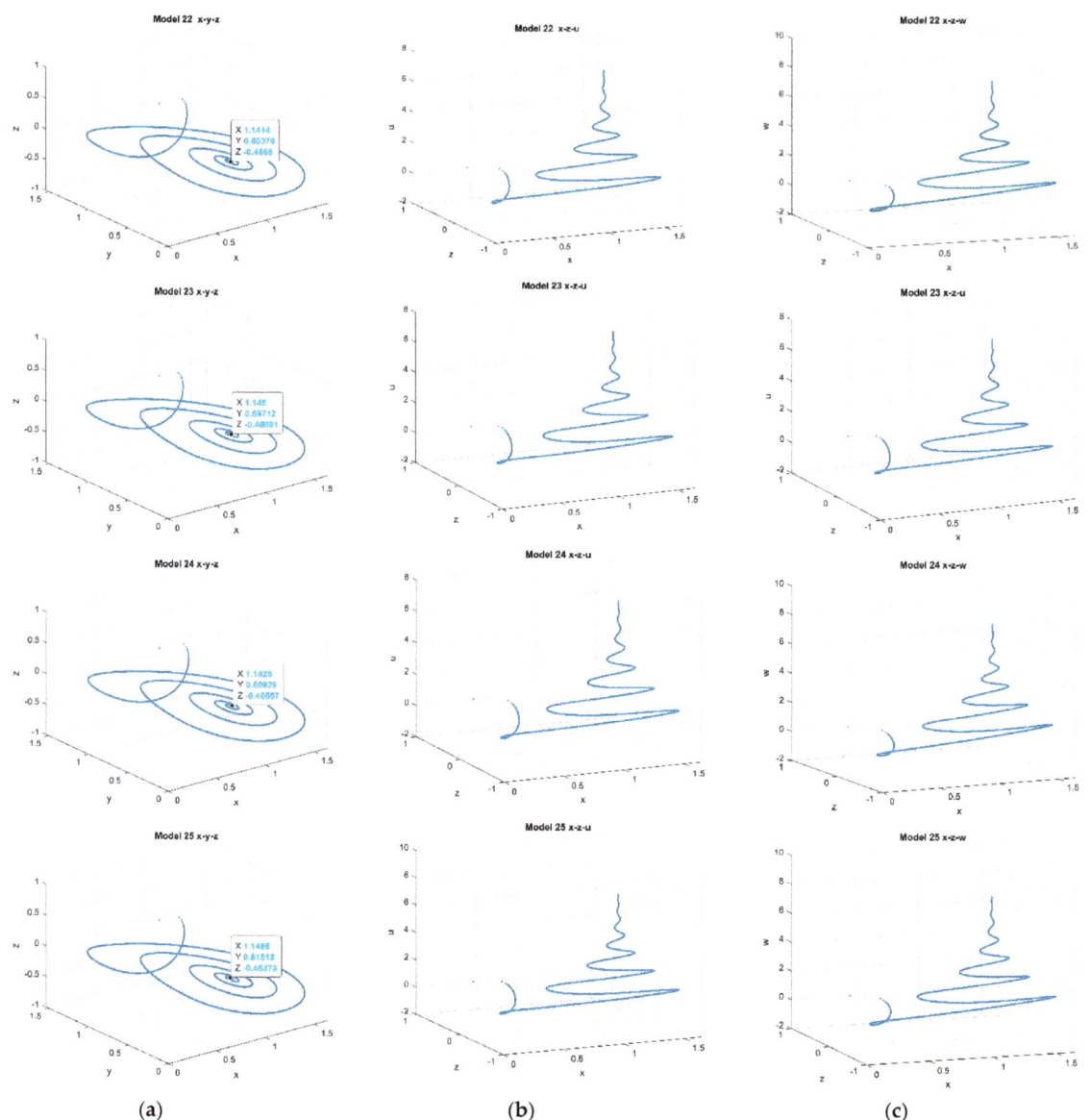

Figure 3. Phase portraits (**a**) $x - y - z$, (**b**) $x - u - z$, (**c**) $x - z - w$, at $h = 0.002$, $k = 2$, $p = 1$, $\alpha_5 = 0.232$ for models (22) through (25).

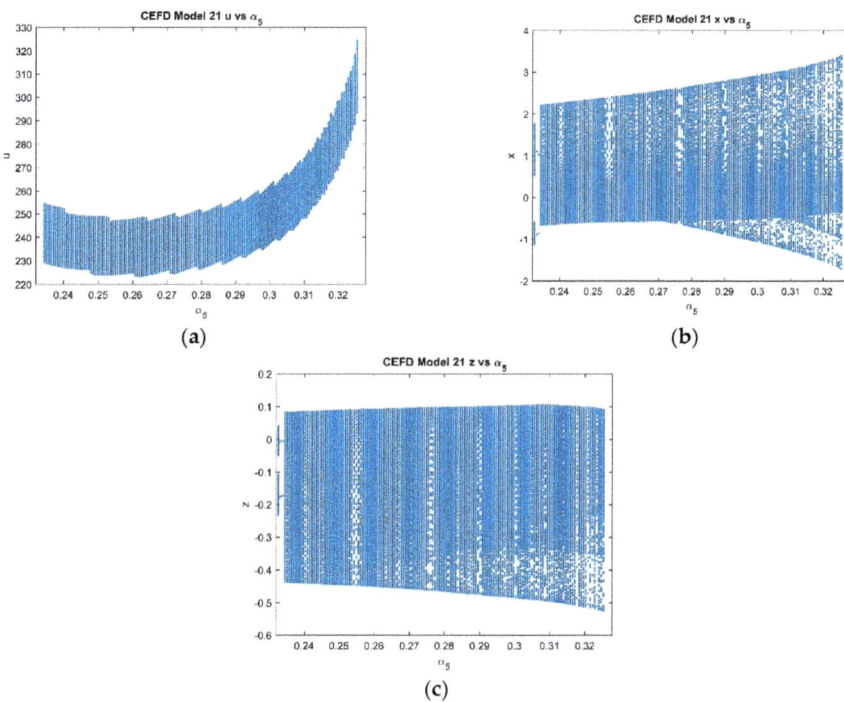

Figure 4. CEFD model (21); bifurcation of (**a**) u (**b**) x (**c**) z versus α_5 for $h = 0.002$.

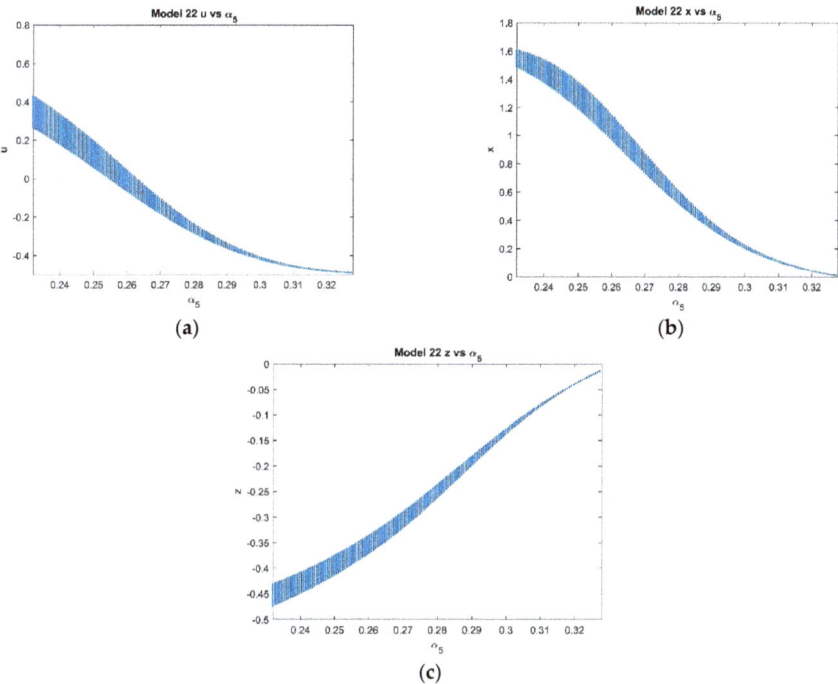

Figure 5. MCEFD Model (22); (**a**) u vs. α_5, (**b**) x vs. α_5, (**c**) z vs. α_5, at $k = 2$, $p = 1$, $\alpha_5 \in [0.232, 0.328]$.

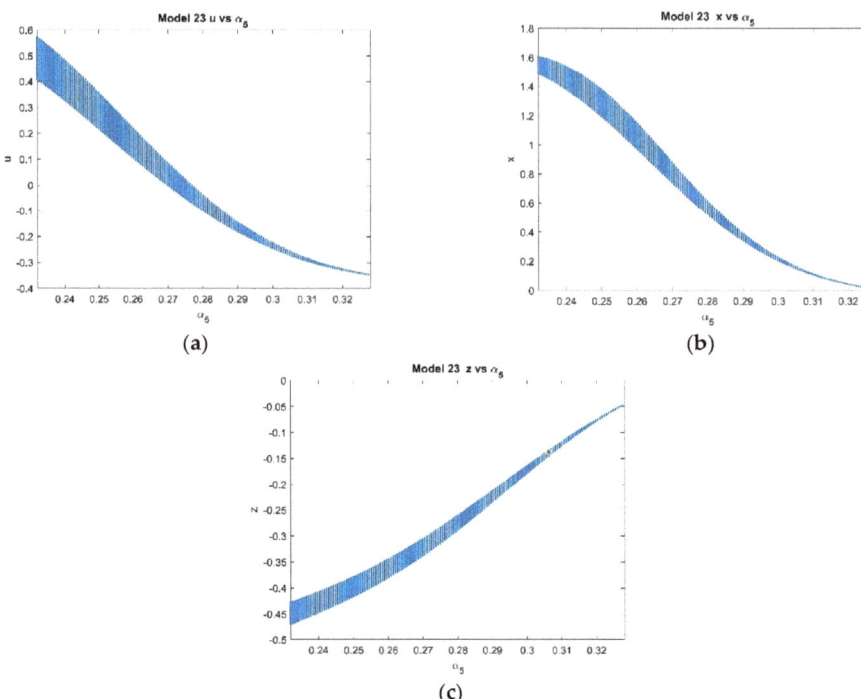

Figure 6. ESDDFD model (23); (**a**) u vs. α_5, (**b**) x vs. α_5, (**c**) z vs. α_5, at $k = 2$, $p = 1$, $\alpha_5 \in [0.232, 0.328]$.

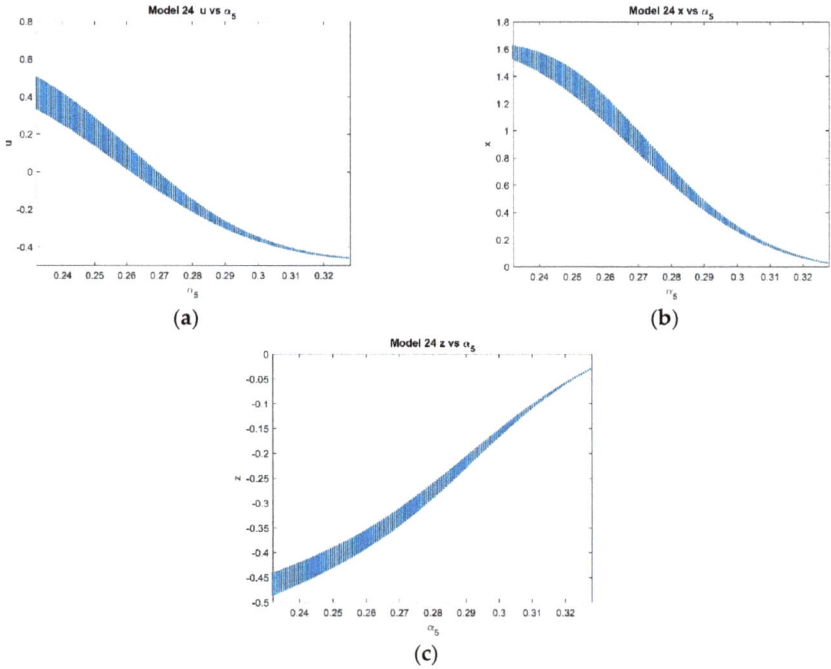

Figure 7. ESDDFD model (24); (**a**) u vs. α_5, (**b**) x vs. α_5, (**c**) z vs. α_5, at $k = 2$, $p = 1$, $\alpha_5 \in [0.232, 0.328]$.

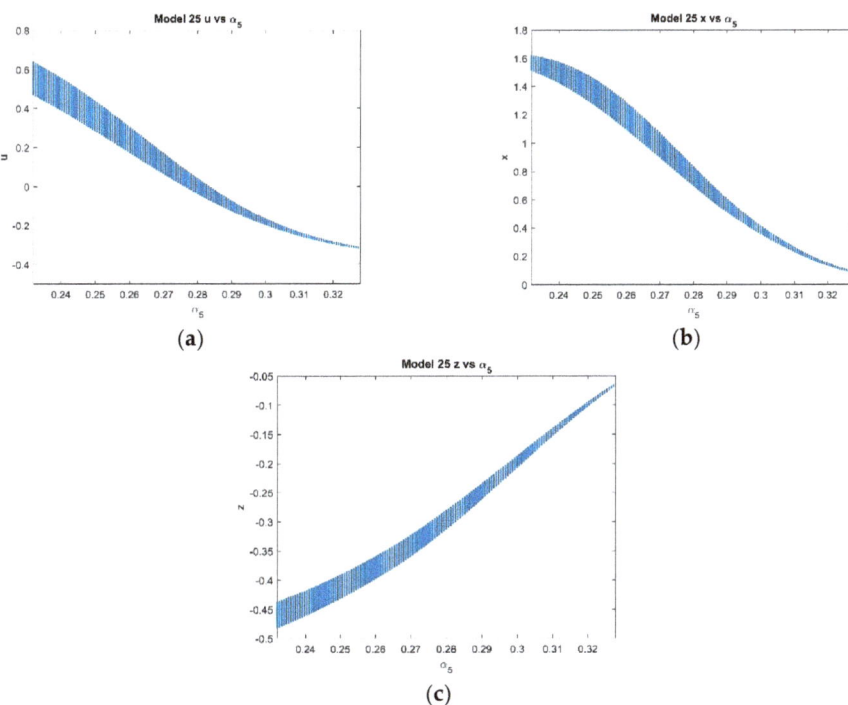

Figure 8. ESDDFD model (25); (**a**) u vs. α_5, (**b**) x vs. α_5, (**c**) z vs. α_5, at $k = 2$, $p = 1$, $\alpha_5 \in [0.232, 0.328]$.

For step sizes above 0.003, CEFD, (21), fails. MCEFD, (22) fails for step sizes above 0.573. The graphs in Figure 9 were produced using the same parameter values as before, except $h = 0.1$. The graphs in Figure 10 were done with $h = 1.0$. These show the effect of larger step sizes on methods (23), (24), and (25). The ESDDFD methods preserve the end behavior at much larger step sizes than CEFD and MCEFD. Note the differences in the early behavior between the methods, especially when compared with $h = 0.002$.

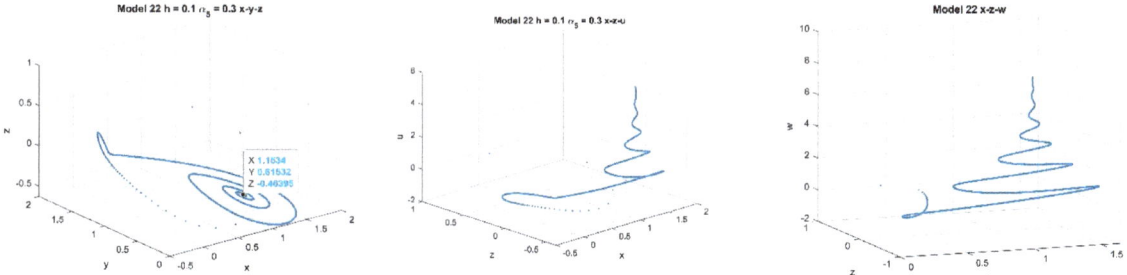

Figure 9. Cont.

(a) (b) (c)

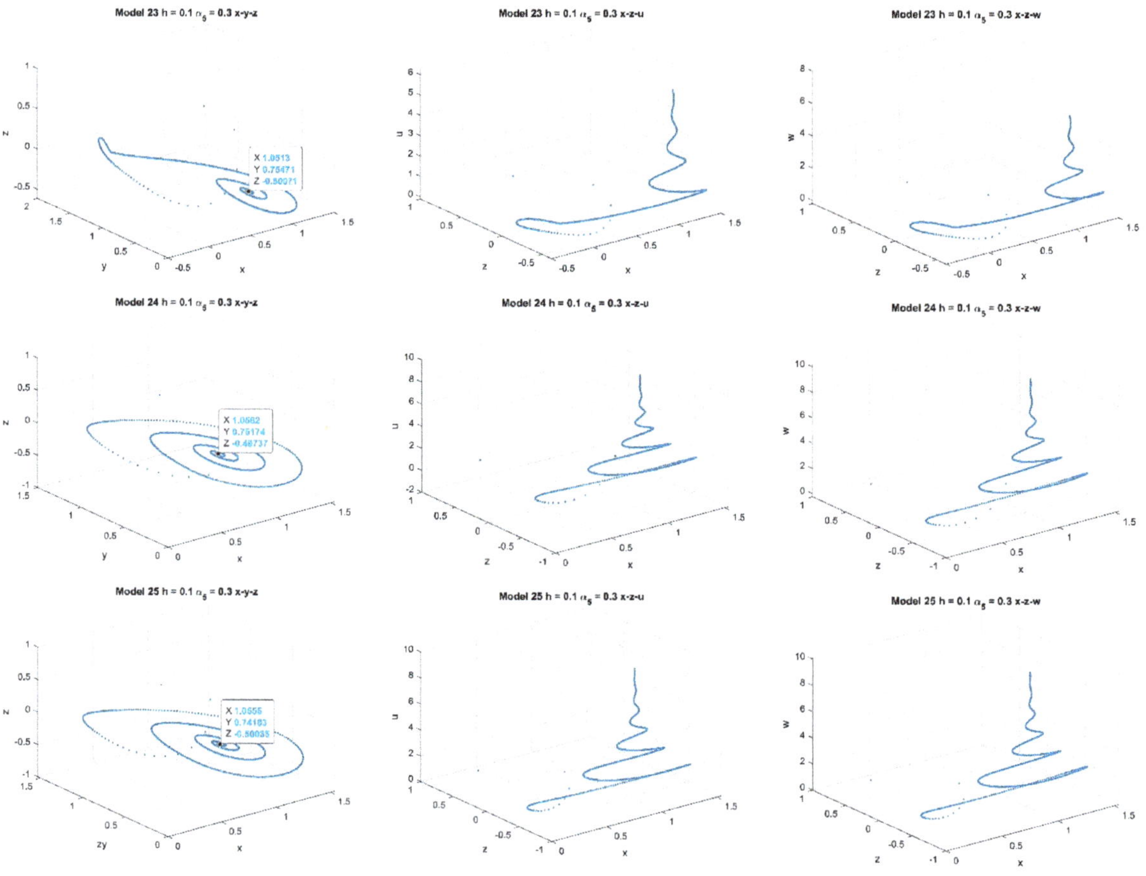

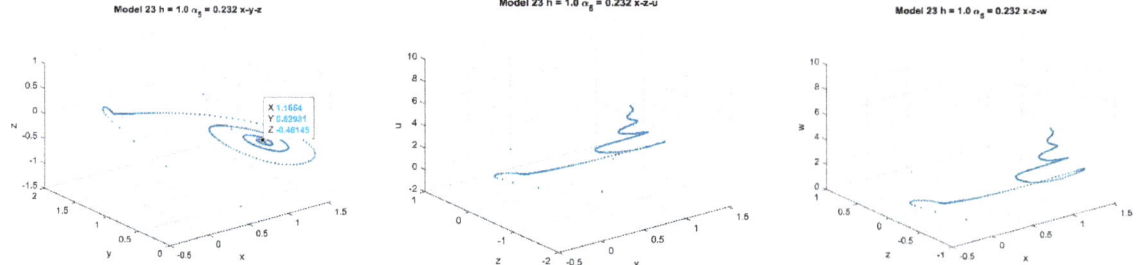

Figure 9. Phase portraits (**a**) $x - y - z$, (**b**) $x - u - z$, (**c**) $x - z - w$, at $h = 0.1,\ k = 2,\ p = 1,\ \alpha_5 = 0.232$ for models (22) through (25).

Figure 10. *Cont.*

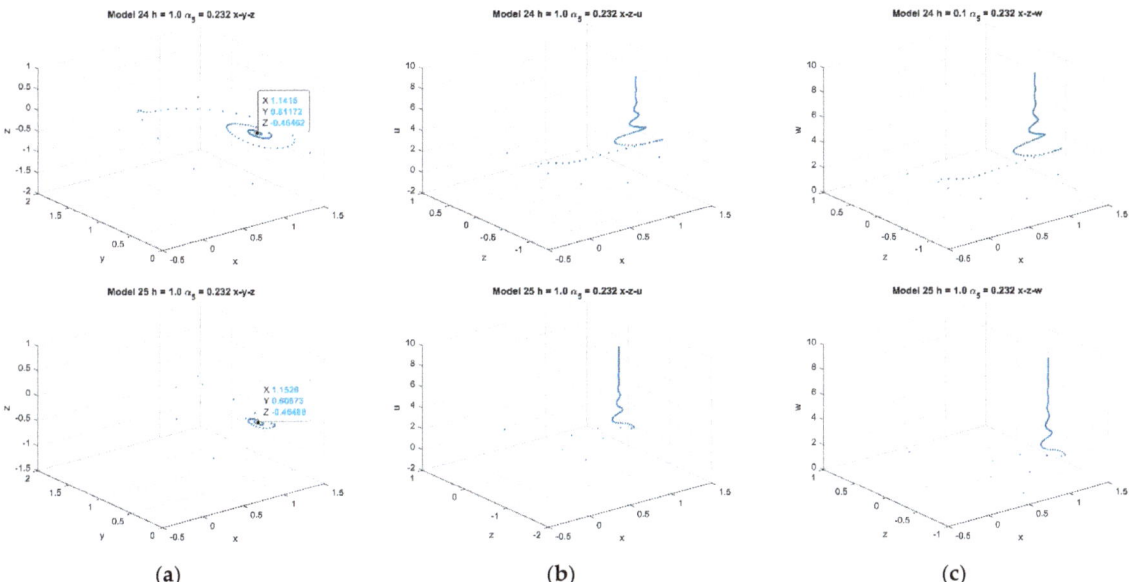

Figure 10. Phase portraits (**a**) $x - y - z$, (**b**) $x - u - z$, (**c**) $x - z - w$, at $h = 1.0$, $k = 2$, $p = 1$, $\alpha_5 = 0.232$ for models (22) through (25). $h = 1.0$, $\alpha_5 = 0.232$ for (23) through (25).

4.2.2. Varying p with Fixed $k = 2$, $\alpha_5 = 0.3$, and $p \in [1, 2]$

In this case, Ref. [13] concluded that system 6 is hyperchaotic with $p \in [1, 2]$. Fixing $p = 1$, a set of two positive Lyapunov exponents and three negative Lyapunov exponents was determined. Bifurcation tests for the ESDDFD models are performed with the same parameters for the full discrete model (2). Figure 11 shows the bifurcation diagrams for u, x and z for the CEFD model (21). Figures 12–15 show the bifurcation diagrams for the models (22) through (25). As in Section 4.2.1, the CEFD diagrams show evidence of chaos while the other models do not.

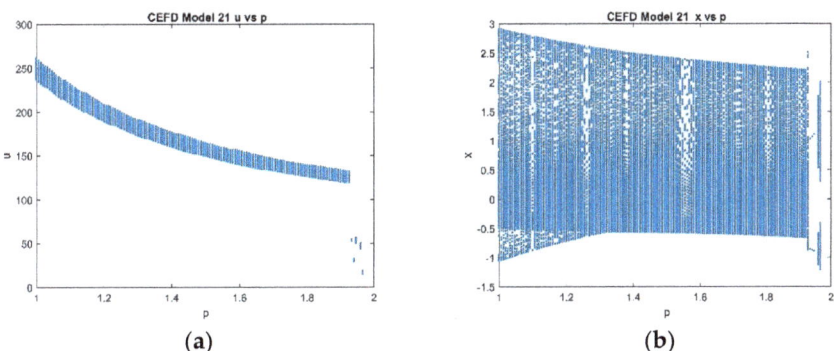

Figure 11. *Cont.*

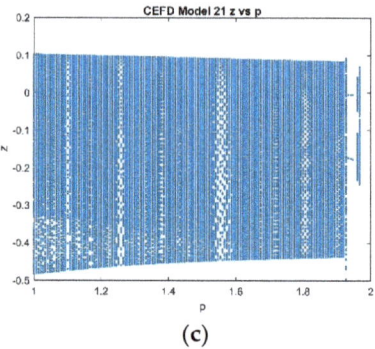

(c)

Figure 11. CEFD model (21); (**a**) u vs. p, (**b**) x vs. p, (**c**) z vs. p, at $k=2$, $\alpha_5 = 0.3$, $p \in [1, 2]$.

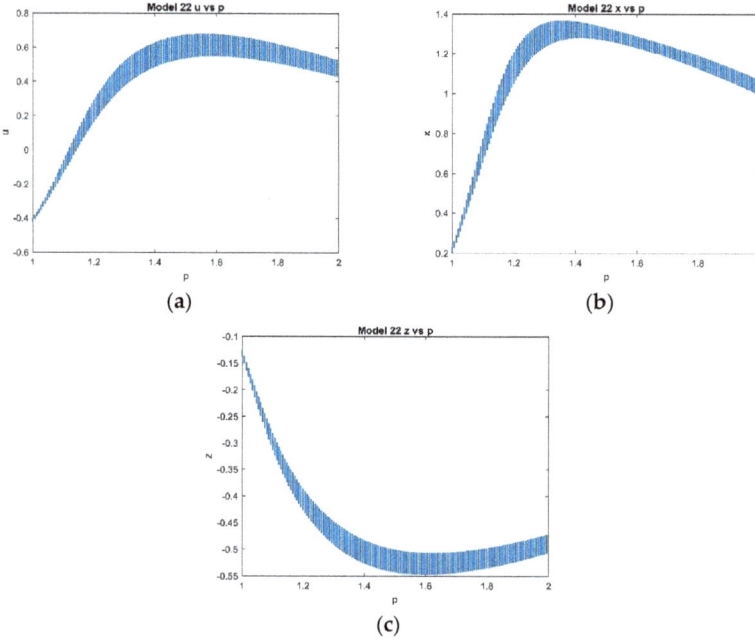

Figure 12. MCEFD model (22); (**a**) u vs. p, (**b**) x vs. p, (**c**) z vs. p, at $k=2$, $\alpha_5 = 0.3$, $p \in [1, 2]$.

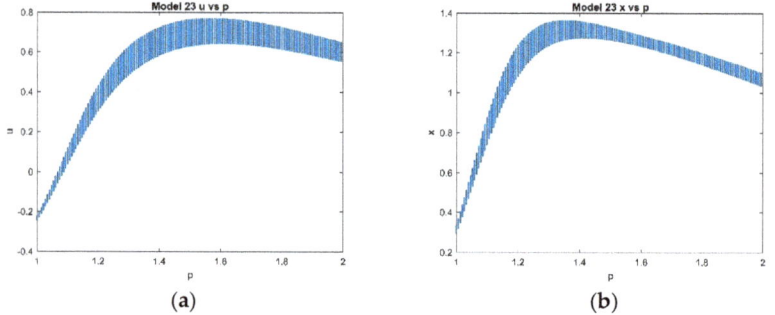

Figure 13. *Cont.*

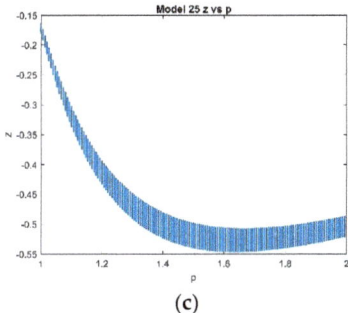

(c)

Figure 13. ESDDFD1 model (23); (**a**) u vs. p, (**b**) x vs. p, (**c**) z vs. p, at $k = 2$, $\alpha_5 = 0.3$, $p \in [1, 2]$.

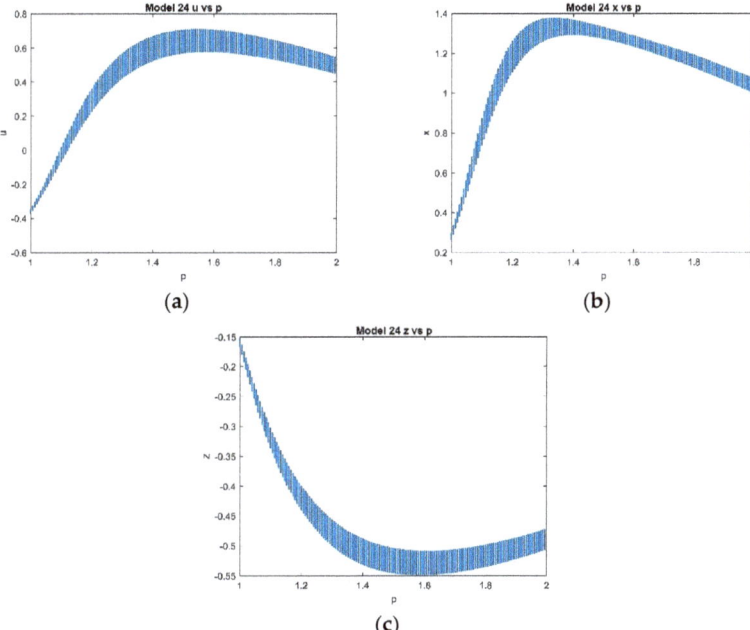

Figure 14. ESDDFD2 model (24); (**a**) u vs. p, (**b**) x vs. p, (**c**) z vs. p, at $k = 2$, $\alpha_5 = 0.3$, $p \in [1, 2]$.

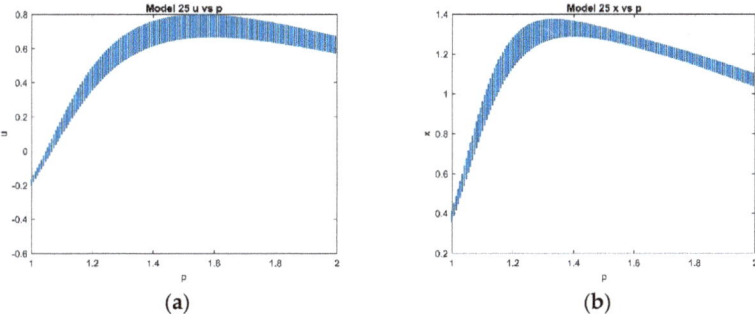

Figure 15. *Cont.*

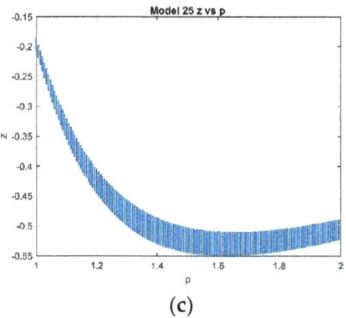

(c)

Figure 15. ESDDFD2 model (25); (**a**) u vs. p, (**b**) x vs. p, (**c**) z vs. p, at $k=2$, $\alpha_5 = 0.3$, $p \in [1, 2]$.

Setting $p = 1.94$, phase portraits are given for models (22) through (25) in Figure 16. Figure 17 shows the phase portraits for model (21). There are clear signs of chaos in the phase portraits for model (21) and no chaos in those for the other models.

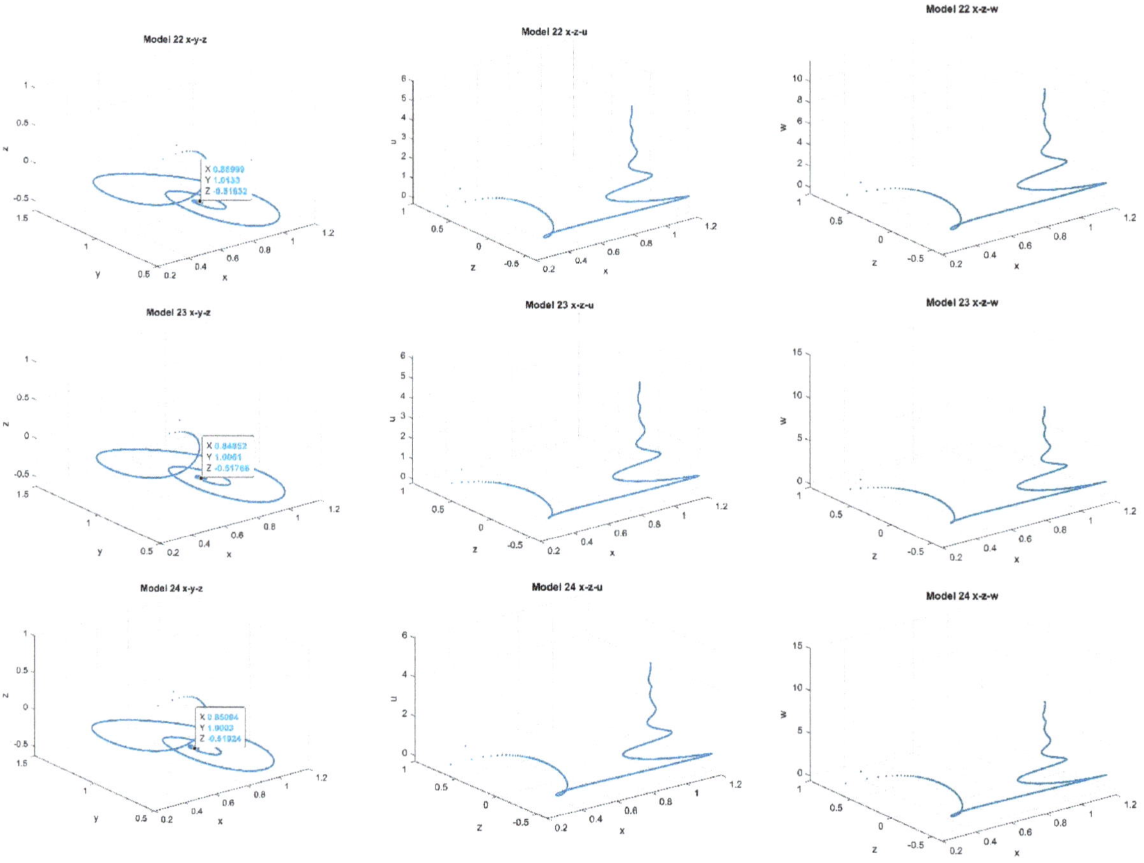

Figure 16. *Cont.*

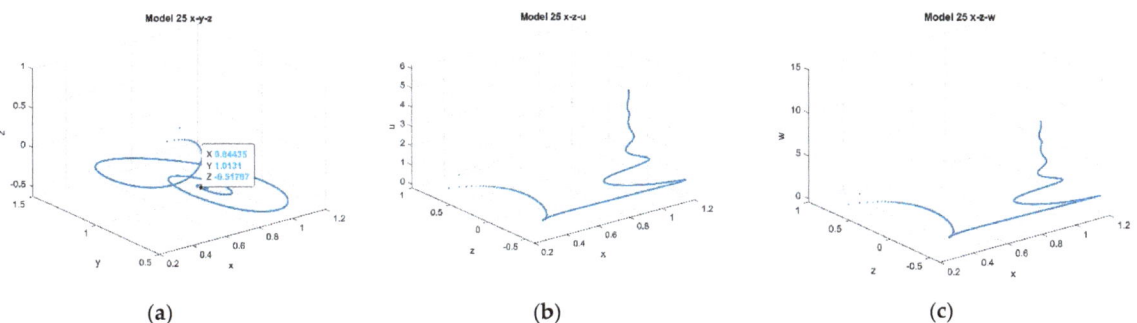

Figure 16. Phase portraits (a) $x - y - z$, (b) $x - u - z$, (c) $x - z - w$, at $h = 0.002$, $k = 2$, $p = 1.94$, $\alpha_5 = 0.3$ for models (22) through (25).

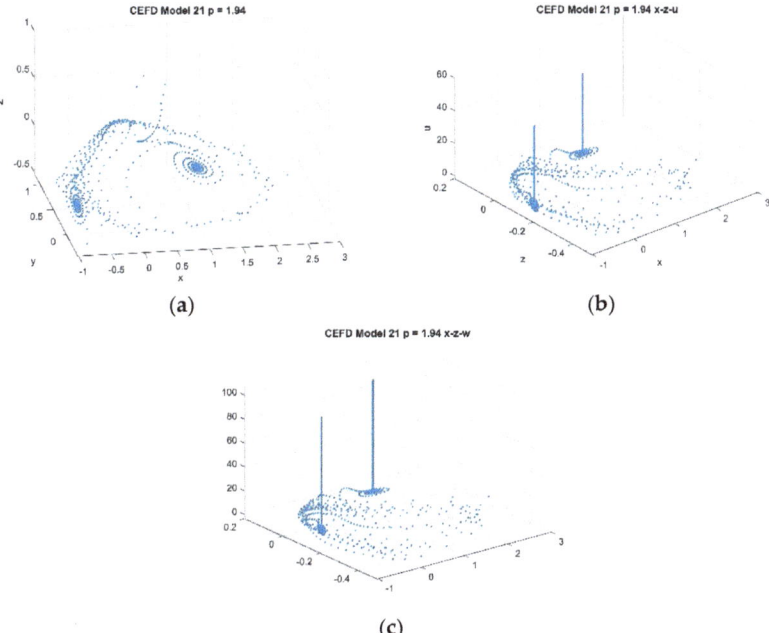

Figure 17. Model (21) phase portraits (a) $x - y - z$, (b) $x - z - u$, and (c) $x - z - w$ at $k = 2$, $p = 1.94$, $\alpha_5 = 0.3$.

4.2.3. Varying k with Fixed $p = 1$ and $\alpha_5 = 0.3$, with $k \in [1.5, 2.5]$

In this case, Ref. [13] concluded that system (6) is hyperchaotic with $k \in [1.5, 2.5]$. Fixing $k = 1.5$, a set of two positive Lyapunov exponents and three negative Lyapunov exponents were determined. Bifurcation tests for the ESDDFD models are performed with the same parameters for the full discrete model (2). Figure 18 gives the bifurcation diagrams for CEFD, model (21). Figures 19–22 give the bifurcation diagrams for x, u and z, for models (22) through (25). Once again there is chaos evident in the CEFD diagrams but no chaos in the diagrams for the other models.

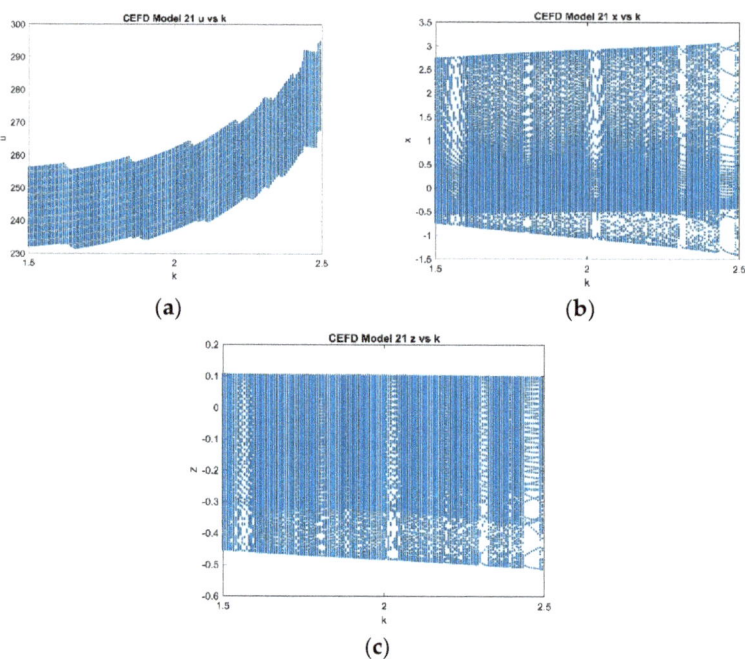

Figure 18. CEFD model (21); (**a**) u vs. k, (**b**) x vs. k, (**c**) z vs. k, at $p = 1$, $\alpha_5 = 0.3$, $k \in [1.5, 2.5]$.

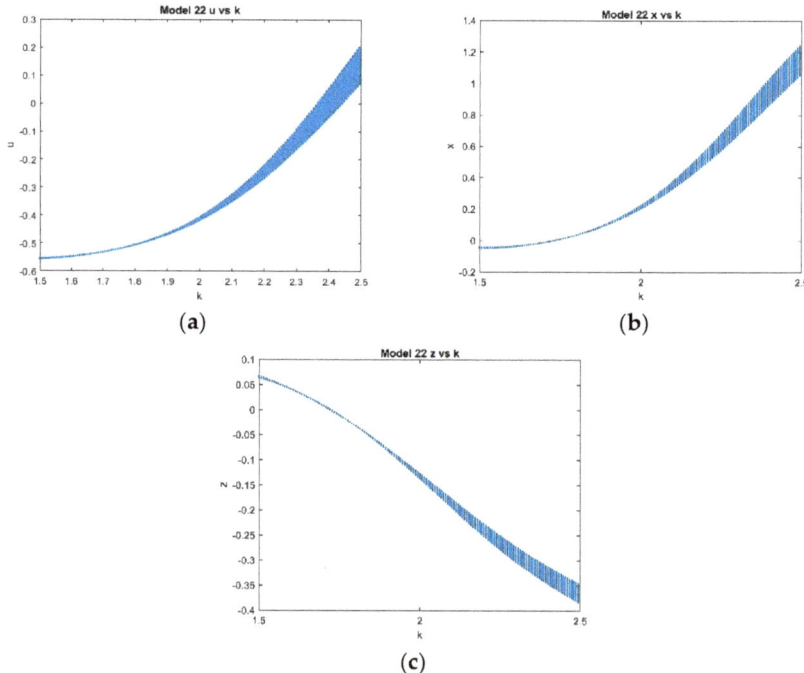

Figure 19. MCEFD model (22); (**a**) u vs. k, (**b**) x vs. k, (**c**) z vs. k, at $p = 1$, $\alpha_5 = 0.3$, $k \in [1.5, 2.5]$.

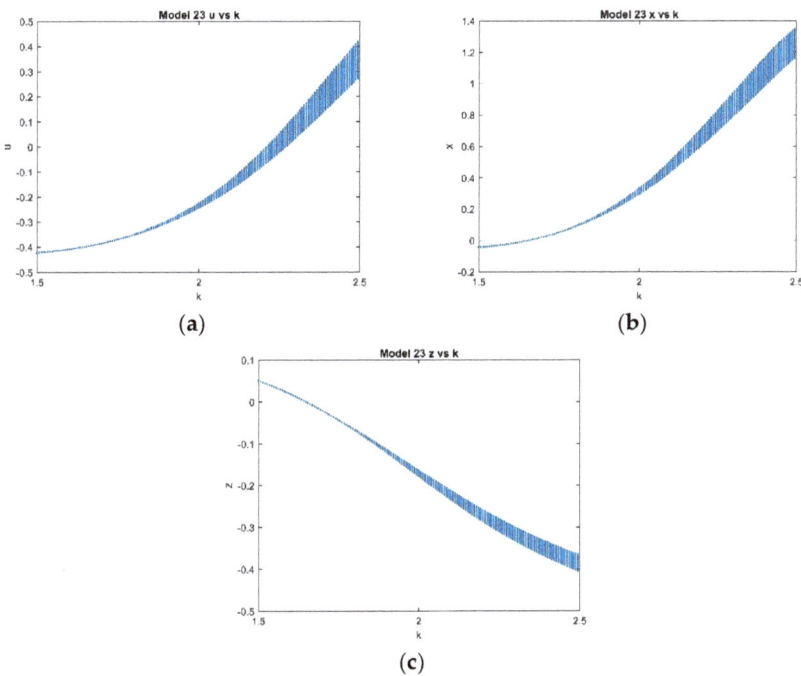

Figure 20. ESDDFD1 model (23); (**a**) u vs. k, (**b**) x vs. k, (**c**) z vs. k, at $p = 1$, $\alpha_5 = 0.3$, $k \in [1.5, 2.5]$.

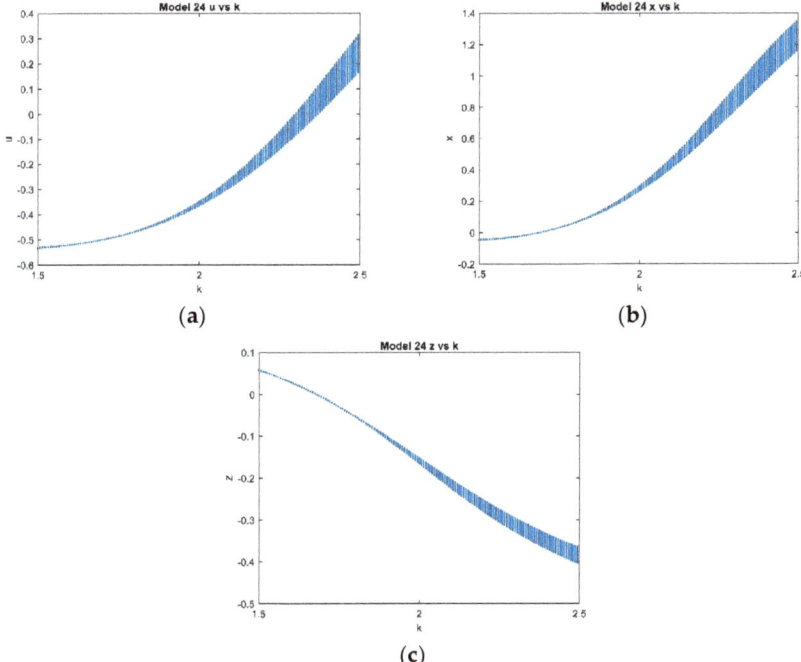

Figure 21. ESDDFD2 model (24); (**a**) u vs. k, (**b**) x vs. k, (**c**) z vs. k, at $p = 1$, $\alpha_5 = 0.3$, $k \in [1.5, 2.5]$.

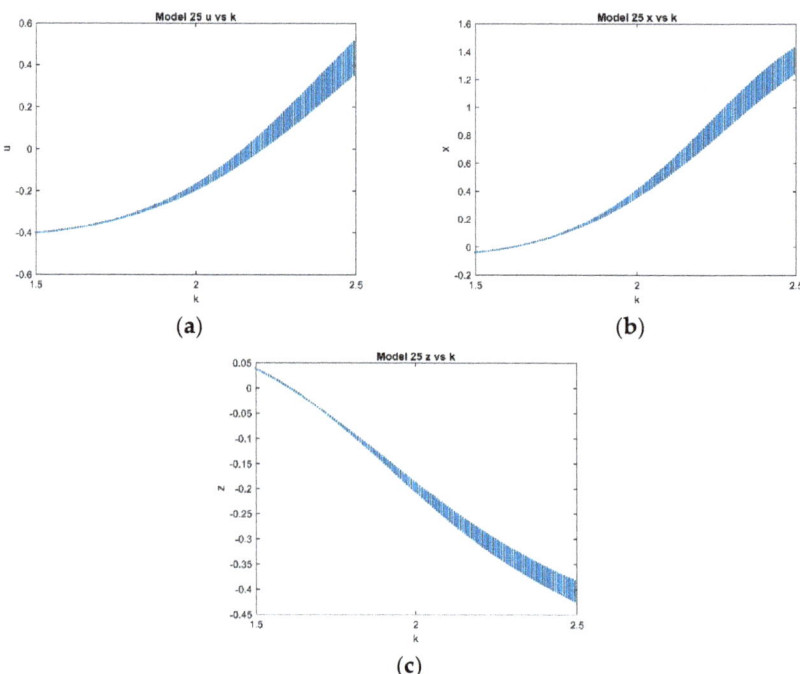

Figure 22. ESDDFD2 model (25); (**a**) u vs. k, (**b**) x vs. k, (**c**) z vs. k, at $p = 1$, $\alpha_5 = 0.3$, $k \in [1.5, 2.5]$.

Setting $k = 2.45$, phase portraits are given for models (22) through (25) in Figure 23. The phase portraits for CEFD, model (21), are given in Figure 24. Again, while the phase portraits for CEFD show chaos, it is lacking in the phase portraits for models (22) through (25).

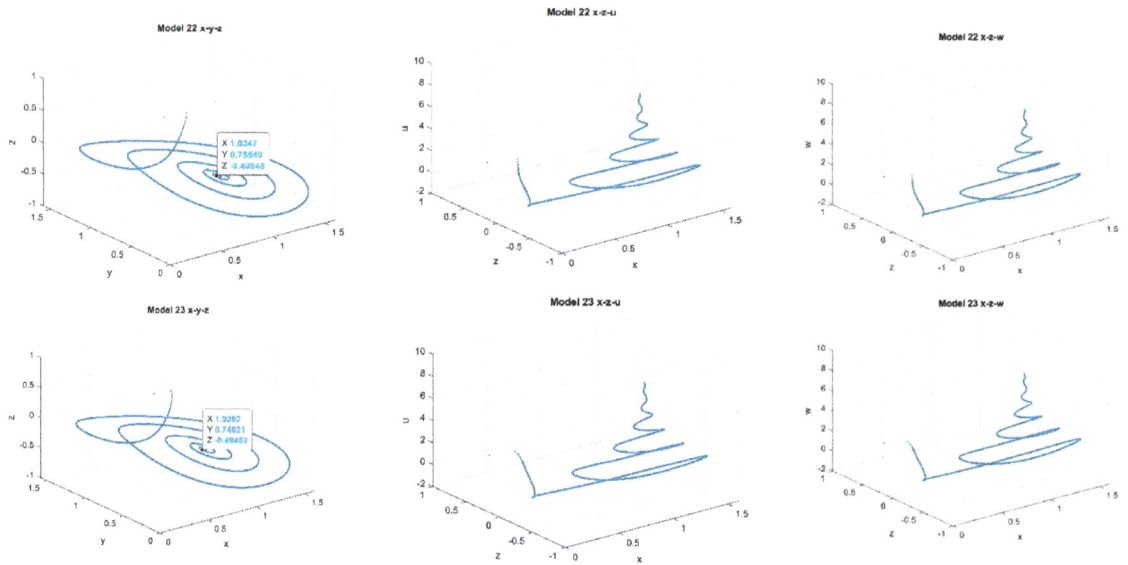

Figure 23. *Cont.*

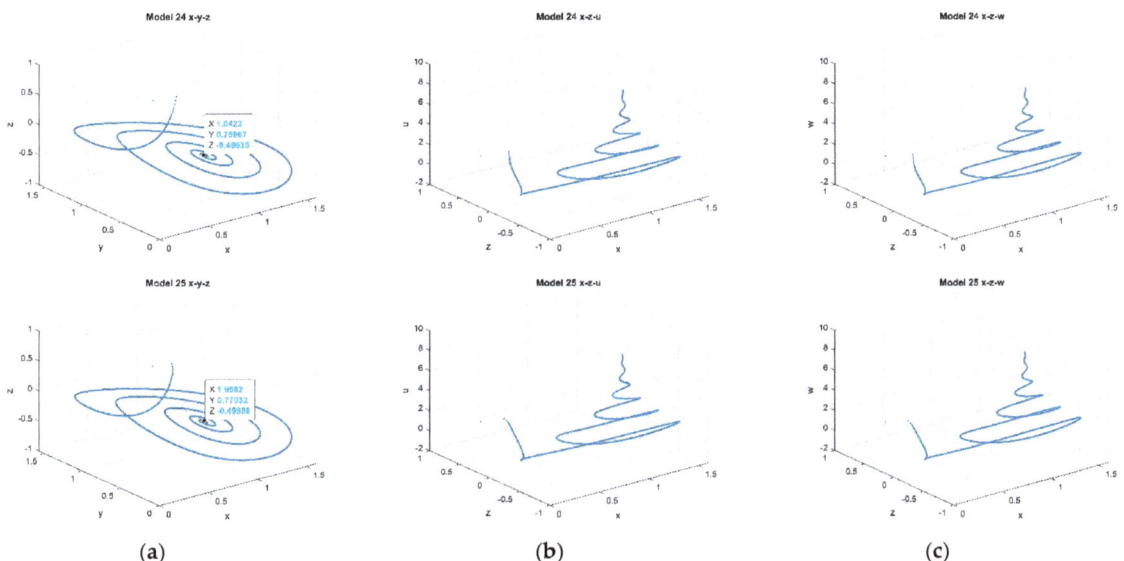

Figure 23. Phase portraits (**a**) $x - y - z$, (**b**) $x - u - z$, (**c**) $x - z - w$, at $h = 0.1$, $k = 2.45$, $p = 1$, $\alpha_5 = 0.3$ for models (22) through (25).

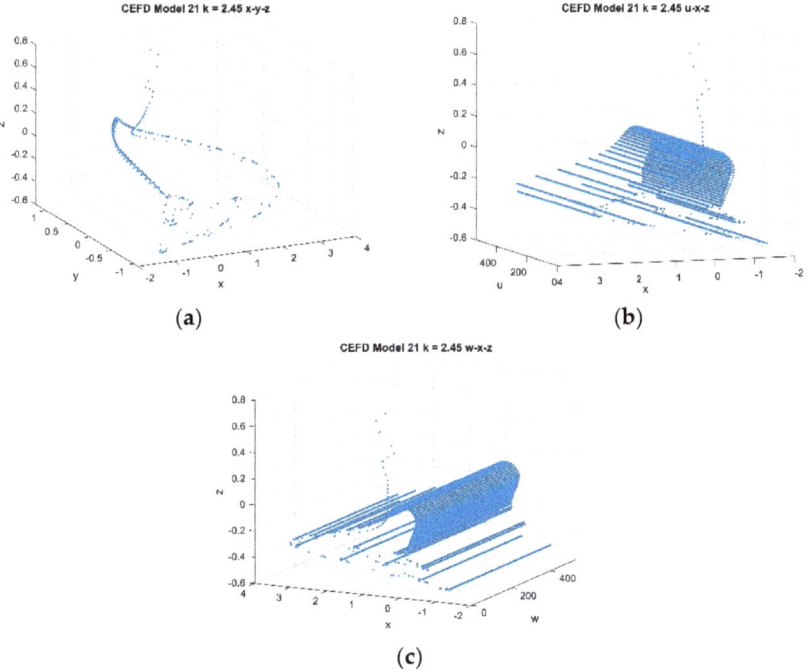

Figure 24. Model (21) phase portraits; (**a**) $x - y - z$, (**b**) $x - z - u$, and (**c**) $x - z - w$ at $k = 2.45$, $p = 1$, $\alpha_5 = 0.3$.

4.2.4. With Fixed $k = 2$, $p = 1$ and $\alpha_5 = 0.24$

In this case, Ref. [13] concluded that system (6) has a hyperchaotic attractor in the $y - z - u$ and $x - y - w$ planes. Two phase portraits for model (21) are given in Figure 25 while the corresponding phase portraits for models (22) through (25) are given in Figure 26. While the results for model (21) show chaos, the results for models (22) through (25) do not.

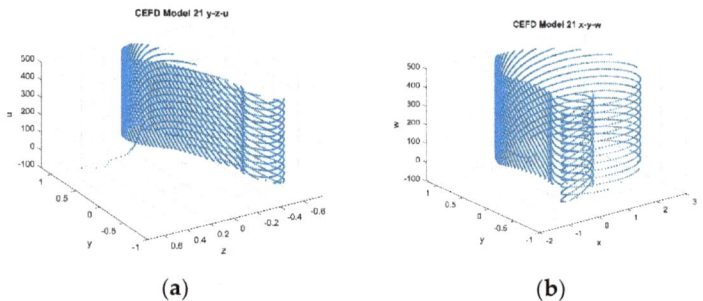

Figure 25. Phase portraits (**a**) $y - z - u$, (**b**) $x - y - w$, at $h = 0.002$, $k = 2$, $p = 1$, $\alpha_5 = 0.24$ for model (21) CEFD.

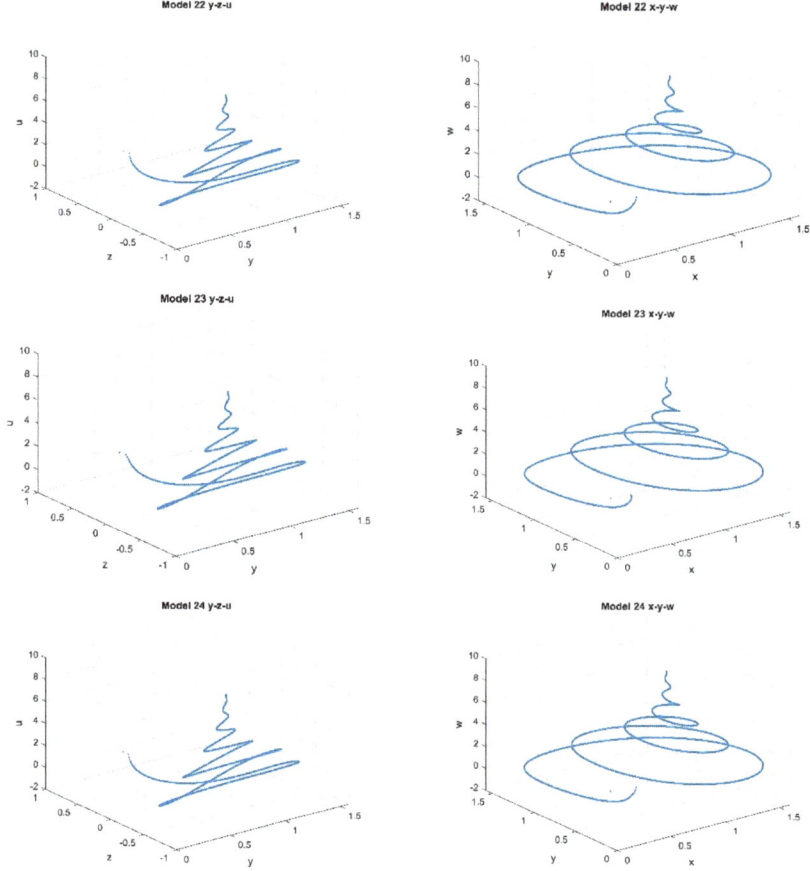

Figure 26. *Cont.*

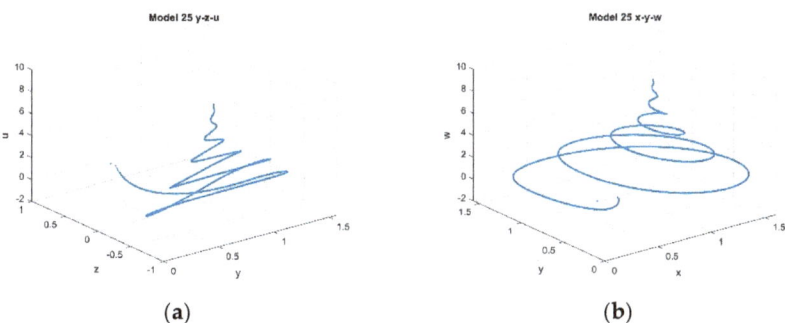

Figure 26. Phase portraits (**a**) $y - z - u$, (**b**) $x - y - w$, at $h = 0.002$, $k = 2$, $p = 1$, $\alpha_5 = 0.24$ for models (22) through (25).

5. Discussion

A discrete model using the conformable Euler finite difference (CEFD) model, (6), was constructed in [13] and used to detect hyperchaotic behavior of the system (1). In this paper, a discrete model (2) has been constructed for the system (1), and the parameters from [13] were used to study hyperchaos using bifurcation techniques. The discrete model (2) is constructed using the exact spectral derivative discretization finite difference (ESDDFD) method, a universal extension of the nonstandard finite difference method to fractional derivatives, which is designed to eliminate contrived chaos. Various cases are considered in parallel to those considered in [13] as well as for sub-systems relevant to the construction of the discrete model (2). While the proposed ESDDFD models produce similar results to each other, those results are significantly different from those obtained in [13] and exhibit no hyperchaotic behavior.

In view of the results obtained, it is reasonable to question the validity of the conclusions of hyperchaotic behavior previously reported for related models, which the authors intend to pursue in the future. While the conformable derivative is a local derivative and has neither memory nor nonlocality, it is a multiple of the Caputo FD [83], and therefore related to those with these properties. It will, therefore, be interesting to explore what, if any, properties of the conformable system are inherited by the Caputo and Riemann–Liouville FDs through these relationships. Further, as suggested in [13], studies incorporating real economic data with parameter estimation for the financial system with market confidence and ethics for all these derivatives are also necessary. Finally, as can be easily seen from Theorem 4.1 of [50], the discretization methods presented here for CFD systems are easy to implement and are equally applicable to all Caputo type derivatives, and hence, to Riemann–Liouville derivatives through their relationship; hence, they have potential to impact a wide range of fractional derivative applications.

Author Contributions: Conceptualization, D.P.C.-M. and G.A.G.; methodology, D.P.C.-M.; software, G.A.G.; validation, G.A.G.; formal analysis, D.P.C.-M.; writing—original draft preparation, D.P.C.-M.; writing—review and editing, D.P.C.-M. and G.A.G.; visualization, G.A.G. All authors have read and agreed to the published version of the manuscript.

Funding: This research received no external funding.

Conflicts of Interest: The authors declare no conflict of interest.

References

1. Zhang, L.; Sun, K.; He, S.; Wang, H.; Xu, Y. Solution and dynamics of a fractional-order 5-D hyperchaotic system with four wings. *Eur. Phys. J. Plus* **2017**, *132*, 31. [CrossRef]
2. Wang, S.; Wu, R. Dynamic analysis of a 5D fractional-order hyperchaotic system. *Int. J. Control Autom. Syst.* **2017**, *15*, 1003–1010. [CrossRef]
3. Liu, Y.; Li, J.; Wei, Z.; Moroz, I. Bifurcation analysis and integrability in the segmented disc dynamo with mechanical friction. *Adv. Differ. Equ.* **2018**, *2018*, 210. [CrossRef]

4. Wei, Z.; Moroz, I.; Sprott, J.C.; Akgul, A.; Zhang, W. Hidden hyperchaos and electronic circuit application in a 5D self-exciting homopolar disc dynamo. *Chaos Interdiscip. J. Nonlinear Sci.* **2017**, *27*, 033101. [CrossRef] [PubMed]
5. Wei, Z.; Rajagopal, K.; Zhang, W.; Kingni, S.T.; Akgül, A. Synchronisation, electronic circuit implementation, and fractional-order analysis of 5D ordinary differential equations with hidden hyperchaotic attractors. *Pramana* **2018**, *90*, 50. [CrossRef]
6. Li, C.; Chen, G. Chaos and hyperchaos in the fractional-order Rössler equations. *Phys. A Stat. Mech. Appl.* **2004**, *341*, 55–61. [CrossRef]
7. Wang, Y.; He, S.; Wang, H.; Sun, K. Bifurcations and Synchronization of the Fractional-Order Simplified Lorenz Hyperchaotic System. *J. Appl. Anal. Comput.* **2015**, *5*, 210–219. [CrossRef]
8. Rajagopal, K.; Karthikeyan, A.; Duraisamy, P. Hyperchaotic Chameleon: Fractional Order FPGA Implementation. *Complexity* **2017**, *2017*, 8979408. [CrossRef]
9. El-Sayed, A.M.A.; Nour, H.M.; Elsaid, A.; Matouk, A.E.; Elsonbaty, A. Dynamical behaviors, circuit realization, chaos control, and synchronization of a new fractional-order hyperchaotic system. *Appl. Math. Model.* **2016**, *40*, 3516–3534. [CrossRef]
10. El-Sayed, A.; Elsonbaty, A.; Elsadany, A.; Matouk, A. Dynamical Analysis and Circuit Simulation of a New Fractional-Order Hyperchaotic System and Its Discretization. *Int. J. Bifurc. Chaos* **2016**, *26*, 1650222. [CrossRef]
11. Mou, J.; Sun, K.; Wang, H.; Ruan, J. Characteristic Analysis of Fractional-Order 4D Hyperchaotic Memristive Circuit. *Math. Probl. Eng.* **2017**, *2017*, 2313768. [CrossRef]
12. Huang, X.; Zhao, Z.; Wang, Z.; Li, Y. Chaos and hyperchaos in fractional-order cellular neural networks. *Neurocomputing* **2012**, *94*, 13–21. [CrossRef]
13. Xin, B.; Peng, W.; Kwon, Y.; Liu, Y. Modeling, discretization, and hyperchaos detection of conformable derivative approach to a financial system with market confidence and ethics risk. *Adv. Differ. Equ.* **2019**, *2019*, 138. [CrossRef]
14. Huang, D.; Li, H. *Theory and Method of the Nonlinear Economics*; Sichuan University Press: Chengdu, China, 1993.
15. Chen, W.-C. Nonlinear dynamics and chaos in a fractional-order financial system. *Chaos Solitons Fractals* **2008**, *36*, 1305–1314. [CrossRef]
16. Wang, Z.; Huang, X.; Shen, H. Control of an uncertain fractional order economic system via adaptive sliding mode. *Neurocomputing* **2012**, *83*, 83–88. [CrossRef]
17. Mircea, G.; Neamţu, M.; Bundău, O.; Opriş, D. Uncertain and Stochastic Financial Models with Multiple Delays. *Int. J. Bifurc. Chaos* **2012**, *22*, 1250131. [CrossRef]
18. Xin, B.; Chen, T.; Ma, J. Neimark–Sacker Bifurcation in a Discrete-Time Financial System. *Discret. Dyn. Nat. Soc.* **2010**, *2010*, 405639. [CrossRef]
19. Yu, H.; Cai, G.; Li, Y. Dynamic analysis and control of a new hyperchaotic finance system. *Nonlinear Dyn.* **2011**, *67*, 2171–2182. [CrossRef]
20. Xin, B.; Li, Y. 0-1 Test for Chaos in a Fractional Order Financial System with Investment Incentive. *Abstr. Appl. Anal.* **2013**, *2013*, 876298. [CrossRef]
21. Xin, B.; Zhang, J. Finite-time stabilizing a fractional-order chaotic financial system with market confidence. *Nonlinear Dyn.* **2015**, *79*, 1399–1409. [CrossRef]
22. Pérez, J.E.S.; Gómez-Aguilar, J.F.; Baleanu, D.; Tchier, F. Chaotic Attractors with Fractional Conformable Derivatives in the Liouville–Caputo Sense and Its Dynamical Behaviors. *Entropy* **2018**, *20*, 384. [CrossRef]
23. Eslami, M.; Rezazadeh, H. The first integral method for Wu–Zhang system with conformable time-fractional derivative. *Calcolo* **2016**, *53*, 475–485. [CrossRef]
24. Ilie, M.; Biazar, J.; Ayati, Z. The first integral method for solving some conformable fractional differential equations. *Opt. Quantum Electron.* **2018**, *50*, 55. [CrossRef]
25. Hosseini, K.; Bekir, A.; Ansari, R. New exact solutions of the conformable time-fractional Cahn–Allen and Cahn–Hilliard equations using the modified Kudryashov method. *Optik* **2017**, *132*, 203–209. [CrossRef]
26. Ünal, E.; Gökdoğan, A. Solution of conformable fractional ordinary differential equations via differential transform method. *Optik* **2017**, *128*, 264–273. [CrossRef]
27. Kumar, D.; Seadawy, A.R.; Joardar, A.K. Modified Kudryashov method via new exact solutions for some conformable fractional differential equations arising in mathematical biology. *Chin. J. Phys.* **2018**, *56*, 75–85. [CrossRef]
28. Srivastava, H.; Gunerhan, H. Analytical and approximate solutions of fractional-order susceptible-infected-recovered epidemic model of childhood disease. *Math. Methods Appl. Sci.* **2019**, *42*, 935–941. [CrossRef]
29. Kaplan, M. Applications of two reliable methods for solving a nonlinear conformable time-fractional equation. *Opt. Quantum Electron.* **2017**, *49*, 312. [CrossRef]
30. Yavuz, M.; Özdemir, N. A different approach to the European option pricing model with new fractional operator. *Math. Model. Nat. Phenom.* **2018**, *13*, 12. [CrossRef]
31. Kartal, S.; Gurcan, F. Discretization of conformable fractional differential equations by a piecewise constant approximation. *Int. J. Comput. Math.* **2018**, *96*, 1849–1860. [CrossRef]
32. Iyiola, O.; Tasbozan, O.; Kurt, A.; Cenesiz, Y. On the analytical solutions of the system of conformable time-fractional Robertson equations with 1-D diffusion. *Chaos Solitons Fractals* **2017**, *94*, 1–7. [CrossRef]
33. Ruan, J.; Sun, K.; Mou, J.; He, S.; Zhang, L. Fractional-order simplest memristor-based chaotic circuit with new derivative. *Eur. Phys. J. Plus* **2018**, *133*, 3. [CrossRef]

34. He, S.; Sun, K.; Mei, X.; Yan, B.; Xu, S. Numerical analysis of a fractional-order chaotic system based on conformable fractional-order derivative. *Eur. Phys. J. Plus* **2017**, *132*, 36. [CrossRef]
35. Yokus, A. Comparison of Caputo and conformable derivatives for time-fractional Korteweg-de Vries equation via the finite differencemethod. *Int. J. Mod. Phys. B* **2018**, *32*, 1850365. [CrossRef]
36. Rezazadeh, H.; Ziabarya, B. Sub-equation method for the conformable fractional generalized Kuramoto–Sivashinsky equation. *Comput. Res. Prog. App. Sci. Eng.* **2016**, *2*, 106–109.
37. Zhong, W.; Wang, L. Basic theory of initial value problems of conformable fractional differential equations. *Adv. Differ. Equ.* **2018**, *2018*, 321. [CrossRef]
38. Tayyan, B.A.; Sakka, A.H. Lie symmetry analysis of some conformable fractional partial differential equations. *Arab. J. Math.* **2018**, *9*, 201–212. [CrossRef]
39. Yaslan, H. Numerical solution of the conformable space-time fractional wave equation. *Chin. J. Phys.* **2018**, *56*, 2916–2925. [CrossRef]
40. Kurt, A.; Çenesiz, Y.; Tasbozan, O. On the Solution of Burgers' Equation with the New Fractional Derivative. *Open Phys.* **2015**, *13*, 355–360. [CrossRef]
41. Khalil, R.; Abu-Shaab, H. Solution of some conformable fractional differential equations. *Int. J. Pure Appl. Math.* **2015**, *103*, 667–673. [CrossRef]
42. Unal, E.; Gokdogan, A.; Celik, E. Solutions of sequential conformable fractional differential equations around an ordinary point and conformable fractional Hermite differential equation. *arXiv* **2015**, arXiv:1503.05407.
43. Liu, S.; Wang, H.; Li, X.; Li, H. The extremal iteration solution to a coupled system of nonlinear conformable fractional differential equations. *J. Nonlinear Sci. Appl.* **2017**, *10*, 5082–5089. [CrossRef]
44. Çenesiz, Y.; Kurt, A. The solutions of time and space conformable fractional heat equations with conformable Fourier transform. *Acta Univ. Sapientiae Math.* **2015**, *7*, 130–140. [CrossRef]
45. El-Sayed, A.; Salman, S. On a discretization process of fractional-order Riccati differential equation. *J. Fract. Calc. Appl.* **2013**, *4*, 251–259.
46. Agarwal, R.; El-Sayed, A.; Salman, S. Fractional-order Chua's system: Discretization, bifurcation and chaos. *Adv. Differ. Equ.* **2013**, *1*, 320. [CrossRef]
47. Mohammadnezhad, V.; Eslami, M.; Rezazadeh, H. Stability analysis of linear conformable fractional differential equations system with time delays. *Bol. Soc. Parana. Mat.* **2020**, *38*, 159–171. [CrossRef]
48. Micken, R.E. *Nonstandard Finite Difference Schemes: Methodology and Applications*; World Scientific Publishing Company: Singapore, 2020.
49. Garba, S.; Gumel, A.; Lubuma, J. Dynamically-consistent non-standard finite difference method for an epidemic model. *Math. Comput. Model.* **2011**, *53*, 131–150. [CrossRef]
50. Clemence-Mkhope, D.P.; Clemence-Mkhope, B.G.B. The Limited Validity of the Conformable Euler Finite Difference Method and an Alternate Definition of the Conformable Fractional Derivative to Justify Modification of the Method. *Math. Comput. Appl.* **2021**, *26*, 66. [CrossRef]
51. Clemence-Mkhope, D.P. The Exact Spectral Derivative Discretization Finite Difference (ESDDFD) Method for Wave Models. *arXiv* **2021**, arXiv:2106.07609.
52. Clemence-Mkhope, D.P. Spectral Non-integer Derivative Representations and the Exact Spectral Derivative Discretization Finite Difference Method for the Fokker–Planck Equation. *arXiv* **2021**, arXiv:2106.02586.
53. Zheng, R.; Jiang, X. Spectral methods for the time-fractional Navier-Stokes equation. *Appl. Math. Lett.* **2019**, *91*, 194–200. [CrossRef]
54. Xu, H.; Jiang, X. Creep constitutive models for viscoelastic materials based on fractional derivatives. *Comput. Math. Appl.* **2017**, *73*, 1377–1384. [CrossRef]
55. Fan, W.; Qi, H. An efficient finite element method for the two-dimensional nonlinear time–space fractional Schrödinger equation on an irregular convex domain. *Appl. Math. Lett.* **2018**, *86*, 103–110. [CrossRef]
56. Yang, X.; Qi, H.; Jiang, X. Numerical analysis for electroosmotic flow of fractional Maxwell fluids. *Appl. Math. Lett.* **2018**, *78*, 1–8. [CrossRef]
57. Gao, X.; Chen, D.; Yan, D.; Xu, B.; Wang, X. Dynamic evolution characteristics of a fractional order hydropower station system. *Mod. Phys. Lett. B* **2018**, *32*, 1750363. [CrossRef]
58. Wang, F.; Chen, D.; Zhang, X.; Wu, Y. Finite-time stability of a class of nonlinear fractional-order system with the discrete time delay. *Int. J. Syst. Sci.* **2017**, *48*, 984–993. [CrossRef]
59. Wu, G.-C.; Baleanu, D.; Huang, L.-L. Novel Mittag–Leffler stability of linear fractional delay difference equations with impulse. *Appl. Math. Lett.* **2018**, *82*, 71–78. [CrossRef]
60. Wu, G.-C.; Baleanu, D.; Luo, W.-H. Analysis of fractional non-linear diffusion behaviors based on Adomian polynomials. *Therm. Sci.* **2017**, *21*, 813–817. [CrossRef]
61. Khalil, R.; Al Horani, M.; Yousef, A.; Sababheh, M. A new definition of fractional derivative. *J. Comput. Appl. Math.* **2014**, *264*, 65–70. [CrossRef]
62. Abdeljawad, T. On conformable fractional calculus. *J. Comput. Appl. Math.* **2015**, *279*, 57–66. [CrossRef]
63. Abdeljawad, T.; Al-Mdallal, Q.; Jarad, F. Fractional logistic models in the frame of fractional operators generated by conformable derivatives. *Chaos Solitons Fractals* **2019**, *119*, 94–101. [CrossRef]

64. Imbert Alberto, F. Contributions to Conformable and Non-Conformable Calculus. Ph.D. Thesis, Universidad Carlos III de Madrid, Madrid, Spain, 2019. Available online: https://www.researchgate.net/publication/342654962_Contributions_to_Conformable_and_non-Conformable_Calculus (accessed on 28 May 2021).
65. Acan, O.; Firat, O.; Keskin, Y. Conformable variational iteration method, conformable fractional reduced differential transform method and conformable homotopy analysis method for non-linear fractional partial differential equations. *Waves Random Complex Media* **2018**, *8*, 1–19. [CrossRef]
66. Attia, R.A.M.; Lu, D.; Khater, M.M.A. Chaos and Relativistic Energy-Momentum of the Nonlinear Time Fractional Duffing Equation. *Math. Comput. Appl.* **2019**, *24*, 10. [CrossRef]
67. Bohner, M.; Hatipoğlu, V.F. Dynamic cobweb models with conformable fractional derivatives. *Nonlinear Anal. Hybrid Syst.* **2018**, *32*, 157–167. [CrossRef]
68. Tarasov, V. No nonlocality. No fractional derivative. *Commun. Nonlinear Sci. Numer. Simul.* **2018**, *62*, 157–163. [CrossRef]
69. Rosales, J.; Godínez, F.; Banda, V.; Valencia, G. Analysis of the Drude model in view of the conformable derivative. *Optik* **2018**, *178*, 1010–1015. [CrossRef]
70. Akbulut, A.; Melike, K. Auxiliary equation method for time-fractional differential equations with conformable derivative. *Comput. Math. Appl.* **2018**, *75*, 876–882. [CrossRef]
71. Martínez, L.; Rosales, J.; Carreño, C.; Lozano, J. Electrical circuits described by fractional conformable derivative. *Int. J. Circuit Theory Appl.* **2018**, *46*, 1091–1100. [CrossRef]
72. Rezazadeh, H.; Khodadad, F.; Manafian, J. New structure for exact solutions of nonlinear time fractional Sharma–Tasso–Olver equation via conformable fractional derivative. *Appl. Appl. Math.* **2017**, *12*, 13–21.
73. Korkmaz, A. Explicit exact solutions to some one-dimensional conformable time fractional equations. *Waves Random Complex Media* **2017**, *29*, 124–137. [CrossRef]
74. He, S.; Banerjee, S.; Yan, B. Chaos and Symbol Complexity in a Conformable Fractional-Order Memcapacitor System. *Complexity* **2018**, *2018*, 4140762. [CrossRef]
75. Xin, B.; Chen, T.; Liu, Y. Synchronization of chaotic fractional-order WINDMI systems via linear state error feedback control. *Math. Probl. Eng.* **2010**, *2010*, 859685. [CrossRef]
76. Yavuz, M.; Özdemir, N. European Vanilla Option Pricing Model of Fractional Order without Singular Kernel. *Fractal Fract.* **2018**, *2*, 3. [CrossRef]
77. Baskonus, H.M.; Mekkaoui, T.; Hammouch, Z.; Bulut, H. Active Control of a Chaotic Fractional Order Economic System. *Entropy* **2015**, *17*, 5771–5783. [CrossRef]
78. Ma, J.; Ren, W. Complexity and Hopf Bifurcation Analysis on a Kind of Fractional-Order IS-LM Macroeconomic System. *Int. J. Bifurc. Chaos* **2016**, *26*, 1650181. [CrossRef]
79. Huang, Y.; Wang, N.; Zhang, J.; Guo, F. Controlling and synchronizing a fractional-order chaotic system using stability theory of a time-varying fractional-order system. *PLoS ONE* **2018**, *13*, e0194112. [CrossRef] [PubMed]
80. Xin, B.; Chen, T.; Liu, Y. Projective synchronization of chaotic fractional-order energy resources demand–supply systems via linear control. *Commun. Nonlinear Sci. Numer. Simul.* **2011**, *16*, 4479–4486. [CrossRef]
81. Almeida, R.; Malinowska, A.B.; Monteiro, T. Fractional differential equations with a Caputo derivative with respect to a Kernel function and their applications. *Math. Methods Appl. Sci.* **2017**, *41*, 336–352. [CrossRef]
82. Anderson, D.R.; Camrud, E.; Ulness, D.J. On the nature of the conformable derivative and its applications to physics. *J. Fract. Calc. Appl.* **2019**, *10*, 92–135.
83. Mainardi, F. A Note on the Equivalence of Fractional Relaxation Equations to Differential Equations with Varying Coefficients. *Mathematics* **2018**, *6*, 8. [CrossRef]

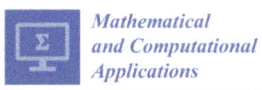

Article

Solution of A Complex Nonlinear Fractional Biochemical Reaction Model

Fatima Rabah, Marwan Abukhaled * and Suheil A. Khuri

Department of Mathematics and Statistics, American University of Sharjah, Sharjah P.O. Box 26666, United Arab Emirates; g00049347@alumni.aus.edu (F.R.); skhoury@aus.edu (S.A.K.)
* Correspondence: mabukhaled@aus.edu

Abstract: This paper discusses a complex nonlinear fractional model of enzyme inhibitor reaction where reaction memory is taken into account. Analytical expressions of the concentrations of enzyme, substrate, inhibitor, product, and other complex intermediate species are derived using Laplace decomposition and differential transformation methods. Since different rate constants, large initial concentrations, and large time domains are unavoidable in biochemical reactions, different dynamics will result; hence, the convergence of the approximate concentrations may be lost. In this case, the proposed analytical methods will be coupled with Padé approximation. The validity and accuracy of the derived analytical solutions will be established by direct comparison with numerical simulations.

Keywords: enzyme inhibitor; biochemical reaction; fractional differential system; Laplace transformation; semi-analytic

Citation: Rabah, F.; Abukhaled, M.; Khuri, S.A. Solution of A Complex Nonlinear Fractional Biochemical Reaction Model. *Math. Comput. Appl.* **2022**, *27*, 45. https://doi.org/10.3390/mca27030045

Academic Editors: Mehmet Yavuz and Ioannis Dassios

Received: 18 April 2022
Accepted: 20 May 2022
Published: 26 May 2022

Publisher's Note: MDPI stays neutral with regard to jurisdictional claims in published maps and institutional affiliations.

Copyright: © 2022 by the authors. Licensee MDPI, Basel, Switzerland. This article is an open access article distributed under the terms and conditions of the Creative Commons Attribution (CC BY) license (https://creativecommons.org/licenses/by/4.0/).

1. Introduction

Data gathering and experimental analysis do not generally provide rigorous tools for understanding the kinetics of modern complex physical, biological, and biochemical research. Therefore, researchers have increasingly employed mathematical modeling, where theoretical analysis would lead to new insights and pave the way for better designs and controlled systems [1–6].

A desired feature of fractional operators is their essential multiscale nature. Consequently, time-fractional operators empower memory effects. In other words, the response of a system is dependent on its previous history. In contrast, space-fractional operators enable nonlocal and scale effects [7]. This nonlocal property of fractional derivatives gives insight into a system's future state features from the previous and present states. Therefore, fractional models are more suitable for simulating physical phenomena and hence more accurate for biochemical reactions. Moreover, fractal geometries that model nonlocal transport, which arises in complex microstructural systems, are often seen in fractional derivative models [8].

Recent research has affirmed that modeling natural phenomena arising in biology, chemistry, and physics with fractional differential equations is more suitable for describing memory and hereditary properties of various materials and processes. For example, Ionescu et al. detailed, in a comprehensive review, the latest developments in fractional calculus applications in biological systems [9]. Rihan discussed some fractional-order differential models of biological systems with memory, such as dynamics of tumor-immune system and dynamics of HIV infection [10]. Other examples of fractional models covering various fields of sciences and engineering can be found in fluid flow [11], electrical networks [12], viscoelasticity [13], and control theory [14]. The reader is encouraged to see the recently published survey-cum-expository review article [15], and the following articles, which shed more light on the discussion on and applications of fractional models [16–21].

Nonetheless, exact solutions to most nonlinear fractional-order differential equations cannot be found. Therefore, many semi-analytical and numerical methods have been developed in recent years to find approximate solutions instead. Most classical numerical methods used for ordinary differential equations have been successfully modified for fractional differential equations such as implicit Euler scheme [10], spectral collocation methods [22], Adams–Bashforth methods [23], and Runge–Kutta methods [24]. Some of the newly developed numerical methods include a new predictor-corrector formula, Legendre spectral method, discretization of Riemann–Liouville, and a modified Adams–Bashforth method [25–28].

Although numerical solutions can be accurate and efficiently obtained, they have some drawbacks that make them less appealing than analytical solutions. Numerical stability and adjusting parameters to match the numerical data can be exceptionally challenging [29]. As with numerical methods, most analytical schemes that have been initially developed for integer-order differential systems have been modified for fractional differential systems [30–36].

This paper studies a nonlinear fractional model of enzyme inhibitor reactions subject to two different sets of initial conditions and kinetic parameters. Modified Laplace decomposition and differential transformation methods are applied to derive simple analytical expressions for the concentrations of species. The obtained expressions converge and stabilize over a prescribed small time domain. However, with possible divergent solutions over large intervals, these methods are coupled with Padé approximation to maintain convergent series solutions for larger reaction times [37]. The used methods are accessible to the broader research community and can be adapted to solve other models that arise in chemistry and chemical engineering.

2. A Model of Complex Enzyme Inhibitor Reactions

Consider the complex chemical reaction network for mixed enzymatic inhibition as shown in Figure 1.

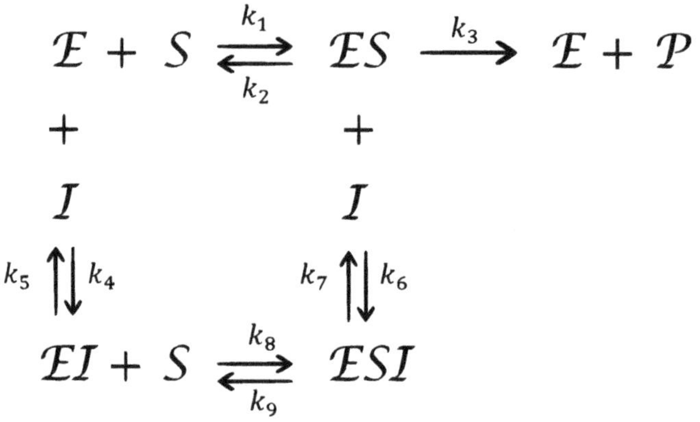

$$\mathcal{E} + S \underset{k_2}{\overset{k_1}{\rightleftarrows}} \mathcal{ES} \xrightarrow{k_3} \mathcal{E} + \mathcal{P}$$

$$+ \qquad\qquad +$$

$$I \qquad\qquad I$$

$$k_5 \updownarrow k_4 \qquad\qquad k_7 \updownarrow k_6$$

$$\mathcal{EI} + S \underset{k_9}{\overset{k_8}{\rightleftarrows}} \mathcal{ESI}$$

Figure 1. A complex chemical reaction for a mixed enzymatic inhibition.

Where $\mathcal{E}, S, \mathcal{P}$, and $\mathcal{I}$ represent enzyme, substrate, product, and inhibitor, respectively. $\mathcal{ES}, \mathcal{EI}$, and $\mathcal{ESI}$ represent the complex intermediate species. The parameters $k_1, \cdots, k_9$ represent the rate constants. If we express the concentrations of $\mathcal{E}, S, \mathcal{P}, \mathcal{I}, \mathcal{ES}, \mathcal{EI}$, and $\mathcal{ESI}$ by E, S, P, I, C_1, C_2, and C_3, respectively, then the mass action law leads to the following nonlinear fractional differential model, which is a modification of the integer-derivative model discussed by Akgül et al. [38]:

$$\begin{aligned}
D_t^\alpha E &= -k_1 ES + (k_2 + k_3)C_1 - k_4 EI + k_5 C_2 S, \\
D_t^\alpha S &= -k_1 ES + k_2 C_1 + k_4 EI - (k_5 + k_8)C_2 S + k_9 C_3, \\
D_t^\alpha I &= -k_4 EI + k_5 C_2 S - k_6 C_1 I + k_7 C_3, \\
D_t^\alpha P &= k_3 C_1, \\
D_t^\alpha C_1 &= k_1 ES - (k_2 + k_3)C_1 - k_6 C_1 I + k_7 C_3, \\
D_t^\alpha C_2 &= k_4 EI - (k_5 + k_8)C_2 S + k_9 C_3, \\
D_t^\alpha C_3 &= k_6 C_1 I - (k_7 + k_9)C_3 + k_8 C_2 S,
\end{aligned} \qquad (1)$$

where $0 < \alpha \leq 1$. D_t^α is the Caputo fractional derivative defined by

$$D_{x_0}^\alpha f(x) = {}^{RL}D_{x_0}^\alpha \left(f(x) - \sum_{k=0}^{m-1} \frac{f^{(k)}(x_0)}{k!}(x - x_0)^k \right), \qquad (2)$$

where ${}^{RL}D_{x_0}^\alpha f(x) = D^m \left(J_{x_0}^{m-\alpha} f(x) \right)$, $m - 1 < \alpha \leq m$, and $m \in \mathbb{N}$, and $J_{x_0}^\alpha f(x)$ is the Riemann–Liouville fractional integration of order α for a real-valued function $f : \mathbb{R}^+ \to \mathbb{R}$ defined by

$$J_{x_0}^\alpha f(x) = \frac{1}{\Gamma(\alpha)} \int_{x_0}^x (x - s)^{\alpha - 1} f(t) dt, \quad \alpha > 0, x > 0. \qquad (3)$$

3. Analytical Expressions for the Concentrations

Consider the nonlinear fractional reaction system (1) subject to the following set of initial concentrations:

$$E(0) = e_0,\ S(0) = s_0,\ I(0) = i_0,\ P(0) = p_0,\ C_1(0) = c_{1_0},\ C_2(0) = c_{2_0},\ C_3(0) = c_{3_0}. \qquad (4)$$

We will derive two approximate analytical expressions of the concentrations of enzyme, substrate, product, inhibition, and the complex intermediate species using modified Laplace decomposition (LDM) and differential transformation (DTM) methods.

The difference between Riemann–Louivelle and Caputo fractional derivatives, which is just in the order of operators, makes Caputo definition closer to the traditional integer-derivative operator and hence more used than Riemann–Louivelle.

3.1. Laplace Decomposition Approach

We begin with the following lemma whose proof follows immediately from (2) and (3) [39].

Lemma 1. *The Laplace transform of the Caputo fractional derivative of order α is given by*

$$\mathcal{L}\{D^\alpha f(x)\} = \frac{s^m F(s) - \sum_{i=1}^m s^{m-i} f^{(i-1)}(0)}{s^{m-\alpha}}, \qquad (5)$$

where $m \in \mathbb{N}$ and $m - 1 < \alpha \leq m$.

Applying Laplace transform to each equation in the reaction system (1) gives

$$\begin{aligned}
\mathcal{L}\{E(t)\} &= \tfrac{e_0}{s} + \tfrac{1}{s^\alpha}\mathcal{L}\{-k_1 ES + (k_2 + k_3)C_1 - k_4 EI + k_5 C_2 S\}, \\
\mathcal{L}\{S(t)\} &= \tfrac{s_0}{s} + \tfrac{1}{s^\alpha}\mathcal{L}\{-k_1 ES + k_2 C_1 + k_4 EI - (k_5 + k_8)C_2 S + k_9 C_3\}, \\
\mathcal{L}\{I(t)\} &= \tfrac{i_0}{s} + \tfrac{1}{s^\alpha}\mathcal{L}\{-k_4 EI + k_5 C_2 S - k_6 C_1 I + k_7 C_3\}, \\
\mathcal{L}\{P(t)\} &= \tfrac{p_0}{s} + \tfrac{1}{s^\alpha}\mathcal{L}\{k_3 C_1\}, \\
\mathcal{L}\{C_1(t)\} &= \tfrac{c_{1_0}}{s} + \tfrac{1}{s^\alpha}\mathcal{L}\{k_1 ES - (k_2 + k_3)C_1 - k_6 C_1 I + k_7 C_3\}, \\
\mathcal{L}\{C_2(t)\} &= \tfrac{c_{2_0}}{s} + \tfrac{1}{s^\alpha}\mathcal{L}\{k_4 EI - (k_5 + k_8)C_2 S + k_9 C_3\}, \\
\mathcal{L}\{C_3(t)\} &= \tfrac{c_{3_0}}{s} + \tfrac{1}{s^\alpha}\mathcal{L}\{k_6 C_1 I - (k_7 + k_9)C_3 + k_8 C_2 S\}.
\end{aligned} \qquad (6)$$

We seek an approximate solution to system (6) and hence a solution to the fractional system (1) in the form of a power series about $t = 0$, that is

$$E(t) = \sum_{n=0}^{\infty} E_n(t), \quad S(t) = \sum_{n=0}^{\infty} S_n(t), \quad I(t) = \sum_{n=0}^{\infty} I_n(t), \quad P(t) = \sum_{n=0}^{\infty} P_n(t),$$
$$C_1(t) = \sum_{n=0}^{\infty} C_{1_n}(t), \quad C_2(t) = \sum_{n=0}^{\infty} C_{2_n}(t), \quad C_3(t) = \sum_{n=0}^{\infty} C_{3_n}(t). \tag{7}$$

The nonlinear terms in system (6) are expressed in terms of Adomian polynomials as follows:

$$ES = \sum_{n=0}^{\infty} A_{1n} = \frac{1}{n!} \left(\frac{d}{d\lambda}\right)^n \left(\sum_{k=0}^{n} \lambda^k E_k \sum_{k=0}^{n} \lambda^k S_k\right)\bigg|_{\lambda=0},$$

$$EI = \sum_{n=0}^{\infty} A_{2n} = \frac{1}{n!} \left(\frac{d}{d\lambda}\right)^n \left(\sum_{k=0}^{n} \lambda^k E_k \sum_{k=0}^{n} \lambda^k I_k\right)\bigg|_{\lambda=0},$$

$$C_1 I = \sum_{n=0}^{\infty} A_{3n} = \frac{1}{n!} \left(\frac{d}{d\lambda}\right)^n \left(\sum_{k=0}^{n} \lambda^k (C_1)_k \sum_{k=0}^{n} \lambda^k I_k\right)\bigg|_{\lambda=0},$$

$$C_2 S = \sum_{n=0}^{\infty} A_{4n} = \frac{1}{n!} \left(\frac{d}{d\lambda}\right)^n \left(\sum_{k=0}^{n} \lambda^k (C_2)_k \sum_{k=0}^{n} \lambda^k S_k\right)\bigg|_{\lambda=0}. \tag{8}$$

Substituting (7) and (8) recursively in (6) and then applying the inverse Laplace transforms lead to the analytical expressions of all concentrations expressed in series forms. The first two terms of each of these series are given below

$$E_0 = e_0, \; S_0 = s_0, \; I_0 = i_0, \; P_0 = p_0, \; C_{1_0} = c_{1_0}, \; C_{2_0} = c_{2_0}, \; C_{3_0} = c_{3_0},$$

$$E_1 = (s_0 c_{2_0} k_5 - s_0 e_0 k_1 + c_{1_0} k_2 + c_{1_0} k_3 - i_0 e_0 k_4) \frac{t^\alpha}{\Gamma(\alpha+1)},$$

$$S_1 = (-s_0 c_{2_0} k_5 - s_0 c_{2_0} k_8 - s_0 e_0 k_1 + c_{1_0} k_2 - c_{3_0} k_9 + i_0 e_0 k_4) \frac{t^\alpha}{\Gamma(\alpha+1)},$$

$$I_1 = (s_0 c_{2_0} k_5 - i_0 c_{1_0} k_6 + c_{3_0} k_7 - i_0 e_0 k_4) \frac{t^\alpha}{\Gamma(\alpha+1)},$$

$$P_1 = (c_{1_0} k_3) \frac{t^\alpha}{\Gamma(\alpha+1)}, \tag{9}$$

$$C_{11} = (-s_0 e_0 k_1 - c_{1_0} k_2 - c_{1_0} k_3 - i_0 c_{1_0} k_6 + c_{3_0} k_7) \frac{t^\alpha}{\Gamma(\alpha+1)},$$

$$C_{21} = (-s_0 c_{2_0} k_5 - s_0 c_{2_0} k_8 + c_{3_0} k_9 + i_0 e_0 k_4) \frac{t^\alpha}{\Gamma(\alpha+1)},$$

$$C_{31} = (s_0 c_{2_0} k_8 + i_0 c_{1_0} k_6 - c_{3_0} k_7 - c_{3_0} k_9) \frac{t^\alpha}{\Gamma(\alpha+1)}.$$

3.2. Differential Transformation Method

First proposed by Zhou [40], the differential transformation method (DTM) is an iterative approach for obtaining a Taylor series solution of a differential equation without the need for the tedious computing of symbolic higher derivatives. Arikoglu and Ozkol [41] modified the original version of the DTM to make it applicable to solve fractional differential equations. In this section, we derive a series solution of system (1) using the fractional DTM [42].

The fractional power series expansion of the continuous analytical function $f(x)$ is given by

$$f(t) = \sum_{k=0}^{\infty} F(k)(t - t_0)^{k/\alpha}, \tag{10}$$

where $F(k)$ is the fractional differential transformation of $f(t)$ defined by

$$F(k) = \begin{cases} \frac{1}{(k/\alpha)!} D^{k/\alpha} \Big|_{t=t_0}, & \text{if } k/\alpha \in Z^+, k = 0, 1, 2, \ldots, (q\alpha - 1) \\ 0, & \text{if } k/\alpha \notin Z^+ \end{cases}. \quad (11)$$

For a fractional-order q, the Caputo fractional derivative is given by

$$D_{t_0}^q f(t) = \frac{1}{\Gamma(m-q)} D^m \left\{ \int_{t_0}^t \frac{\left[f(t) - \sum_{k=0}^{m-1} (1/k!)(t-t_0)^k f^{(k)}(t_0) \right]}{(t-x)^{1+q-m}} dt \right\}. \quad (12)$$

The following properties of fractional differential transformations are needed in the derivation of the analytical solution of system (1) [42].

Theorem 1. *If $f(x) = g_1(x) \pm g_2(x) \pm \cdots \pm g_n(x)$, then $F(k) = G_1(k) \pm G_2(k) \pm \cdots \pm G_n(k)$.*

Theorem 2. *If $f(x) = \prod_{j=1}^n g_j(x)$, then*

$$F(k) = \sum_{k_{n-1}=0}^k \sum_{k_{n-2}=0}^{k_{n-1}} \cdots \sum_{k_2=0}^{k_3} \sum_{k_1=0}^{k_2} G_1(k_1) G_2(k_2 - k_1) \ldots G_{n-1}(k_{n-1} - k_{n-2}) G_n(k - k_{n-1}).$$

Theorem 3. *If $f(x) = (x - x_0)^p$, then $F(k) = \delta(k - \alpha p)$, where*
$$\delta(k) = \begin{cases} 1 & \text{if } k = 0 \\ 0 & \text{if } k \neq 0 \end{cases}.$$

Theorem 4. *If $f(x) = D_{x_0}^q[g(x)]$, then $F(k) = \frac{\Gamma(q + 1 + k/\alpha)}{T(1 + k/\alpha)} G(k + \alpha q)$.*

By applying the fractional operator in (12) to system (1), we obtain the same series solution given in (10) for the integer case. For fractional order derivatives, the variations between the LDM and DTM were very small, and will be discussed in the Results and Discussion section.

3.3. Padé Approximation

It is known that the convergence of the truncated series solutions obtained by Laplace decomposition and differential transformation methods are guaranteed only over small domains. The divergence of the series solution obtained by the LDM or DTM may also result for large initial conditions. In this case, LDM and DTM methods can be coupled with Padé approximation to insure convergence. The Padé approximant of the function $f(x)$, which is a convergent ratio of two polynomials constructed from its Taylor series expansion, gives a better approximation of the function, especially when there are poles. When the function $f(x)$ is expressed as a power series, the $[L/M]$ Padé approximant is given by

$$f(x) = \frac{P_L(x)}{Q_M(x)} = \frac{p_0 + p_1 x + p_2 x^2 + p_3 x^3 + \cdots + p_L x^L}{1 + q_1 x + q_2 x^2 + q_3 x^3 + \cdots + q_M x^M}. \quad (13)$$

4. Results and Discussion

In this section, two study cases are presented. In each case, the nonlinear reaction system (1) is solved for a different set of parameters and a different set of initial concentrations.

Example 1. *To verify the accuracy of the proposed approaches, we first solve the underlined system for the integer-derivative, $\alpha = 1$, subject to the following initial conditions (4).*

$$e_0 = 0.1, \ s_0 = 0.2, \ i_0 = 0.01, \ p_0 = c_{10} = c_{20} = c_{30} = 0, \quad (14)$$

and the following constant rates

$$k_1 = 0.1, \ k_2 = 0.2, \ k_3 = 0.4, \ k_4 = 0.9, \ k_5 = 1, \ k_6 = 0.4, \ k_7 = 0.9, \ k_8 = 0.2, \ k_9 = 0.5. \quad (15)$$

The LDM and DTM solutions were identical for all seven species. For example, the identical five-term series solution obtained by the LDM and the DTM representing the concentration of enzyme is given by

$$E(t) = 0.1 - 0.0029 \, t + 0.000778 \, t^2 - 0.000152 \, t^3 + 0.0000242 \, t^4. \quad (16)$$

The analytical expressions of the concentrations of all other species are provided in the Supporting Information. Figure 2a–g shows that for the integer case ($\alpha = 1$), the derived analytical concentration curves obtained by the LDM and the DTM are identical and strongly agree with the fourth-order Runge–Kutta numerical curves. Figure 2 also reflects the temporal dependence of relative concentrations of enzyme reaction components. It is noticed that concentrations of enzyme, substrate, and product decrease as time increases, whereas the concentrations of inhibitor, enzyme–substrate, enzyme–inhibitor, and enzyme–substrate–inhibitor increase with time.

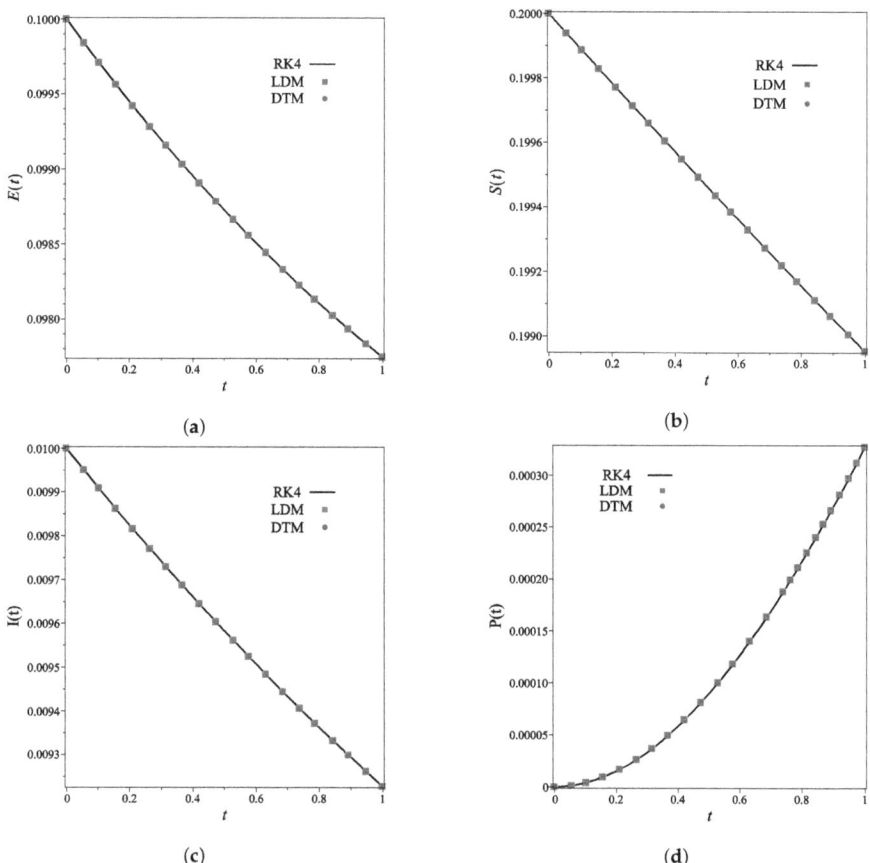

Figure 2. Cont.

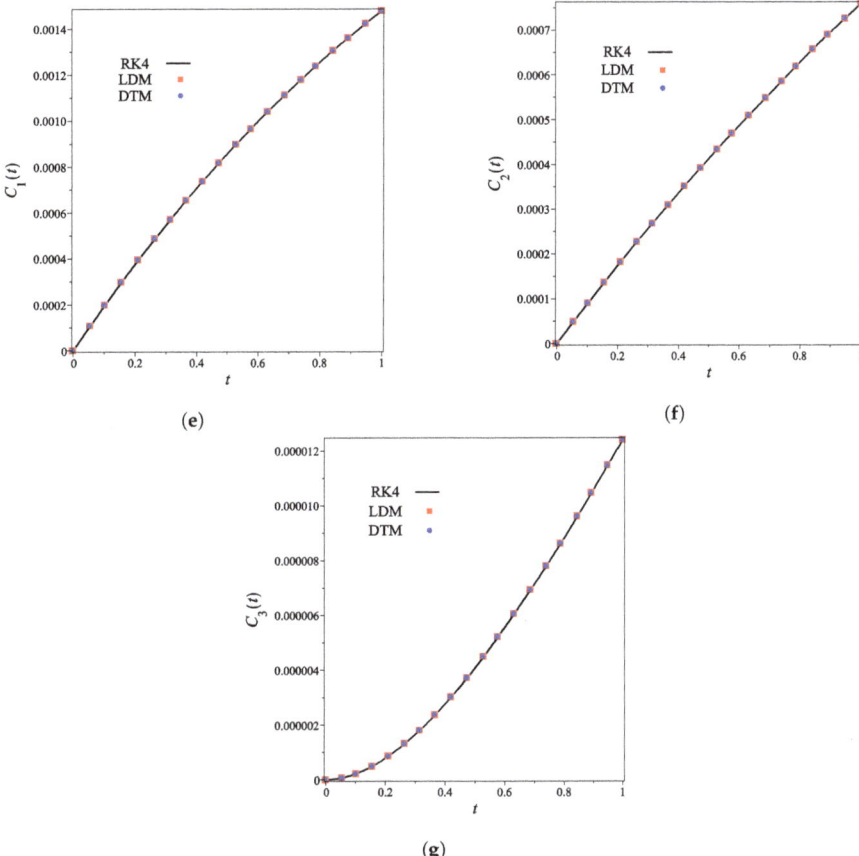

Figure 2. Analytical and numerical concentration curves for reaction system (1) for the integer-derivative case ($\alpha = 1$) with initial concentrations (14) and rate constants (15). (**a**) Enzyme. (**b**) Substrate. (**c**) Product. (**d**) Inhibitor. (**e**) Intermediate species ES. (**f**) Intermediate species EI. (**g**) Intermediate species ESI.

The nonlinear fractional reaction system (1) is also solved for the fractional derivatives $\alpha = 0.9$, and $\alpha = 0.8$. Figure 3a–g shows strong agreements between LDM and DTM concentration curves of enzyme, substrate, product, inhibition and all complex intermediate species. In this Figure, the fractional derivative α is an index of memory, where it is noticed that the concentrations of the enzyme components depend on the fractional order. Figure 3 clearly shows that as α increases, the fractional concentration curve gets closer to the curve representing the concentration for the integer case ($\alpha = 1$).

Figure 3a–c confirms that the enzyme, substrate, and inhibitor concentrations increase as the fractional power increases and decrease as time increases. In contrast, Figure 3d–g portrays that the product and intermediate species concentrations increase and reach their maximum with the rise of time and decrease of the fractional power.

Tables 1 and 2 assert that the actual variations between the LDM and DTM for the fractional cases are smaller than what they appear in Figure 3. This can also be inferred from the very small y-axis increments in Figure 3.

Table 1. Maximum variation between LDM and DTM computed concentrations when $\alpha = 0.9$.

Concentration	Maximum Difference	Occurred at x
Enzyme	0.0000424	1.000
Substrate	0.0000024	0.007
Inhibition	0.0000103	1.000
Production	0.0000205	0.925
Complex ES	0.0000323	0.925
Complex EI	0.0000105	1.000
Complex ESI	0.0000004	0.525

Table 2. Maximum variation between LDM and DTM computed concentrations when $\alpha = 0.8$.

Concentration	Maximum Difference	Occurred at x
Enzyme	0.0000843	0.850
Substrate	0.0000049	0.600
Inhibition	0.0000206	1.000
Production	0.0000408	0.825
Complex ES	0.0000643	0.825
Complex EI	0.0000208	1.950
Complex ESI	0.0000009	0.450

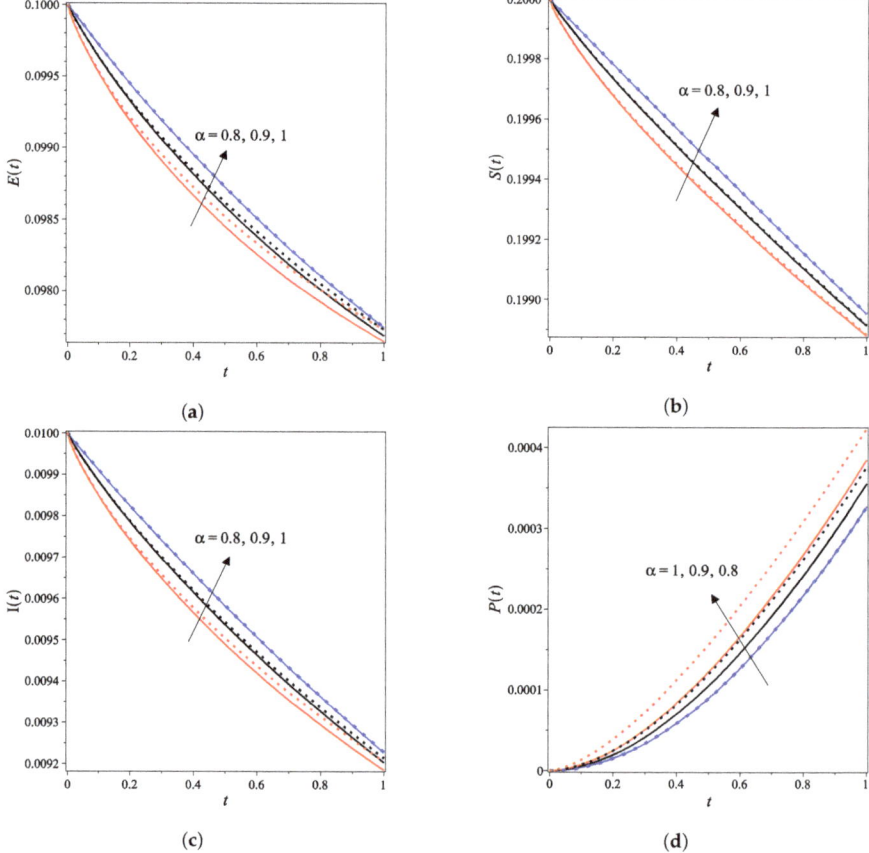

Figure 3. *Cont.*

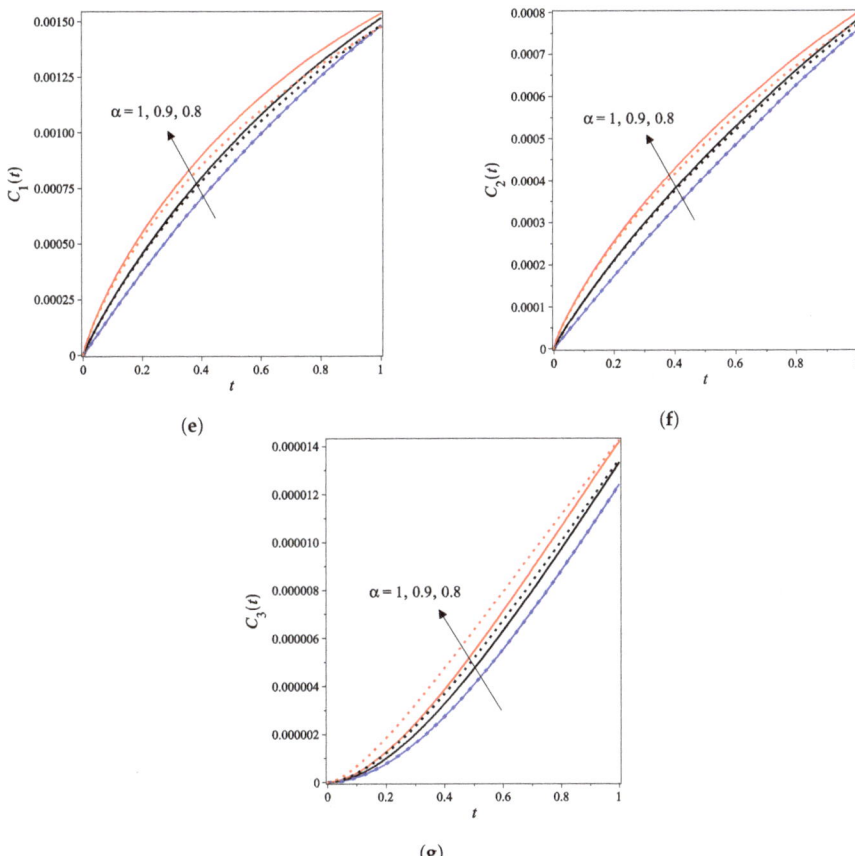

(g)

Figure 3. Analytical concentration curves for fractional reaction system (1) with initial concentrations (14) and rate constants (15) for the integer-derivative case $\alpha = 1$ and the fractional-derivative cases $\alpha = 0.9$ and 0.8. Solid and dotted curves represent the LDM and the DTM solutions, respectively. (**a**) Enzyme. (**b**) Substrate. (**c**) Product. (**d**) Inhibitor. (**e**) Intermediate species ES. (**f**) Intermediate species EI. (**g**) Intermediate species ESI.

Example 2. *Consider the nonlinear fractional reaction system (1) subject to the following set of relatively large initial concentrations:*

$$e_0 = 12,\ s_0 = 5,\ i_0 = 2,\ p_0 = c_{10} = c_{20} = c_{30} = 0, \tag{17}$$

and the following set of constant rates

$$k_1 = 0.01,\ k_2 = 0.2,\ k_3 = 0.04,\ k_4 = 0.19,\ k_5 = 0.1,\ k_6 = 0.4,\ k_7 = 0.09,\ k_8 = 0.22,\ k_9 = 0.05. \tag{18}$$

For the integer case, $\alpha = 1$, the obtained LDM, and DTM truncated series solutions (concentrations) were identical but diverged rapidly over a small domain. This divergence was controlled by using a $[4/4]$ Padé approximant for each analytical derived expression. In Figure 4a, the divergent enzyme concentration curves obtained by the LDM and DTM are depicted against time. In contrast, Figure 4b shows how the use of Padé approximation overcomes this obstacle. Figure 5 is similar to Figure 4 but for the substrate concentration. All concentration curves for the case $\alpha = 1$ and their $[4/4]$ corresponding Padé approximations are provided in the Supporting Information.

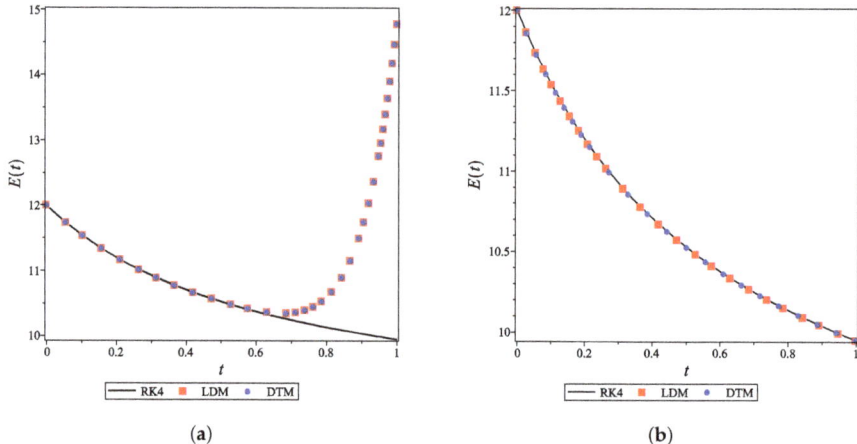

Figure 4. Analytical and numerical concentration curves of Enzyme ($E(t)$) for the integer-derivative system (1) with $\alpha = 1$, initial conditions (17), and parameters (18). (**a**) Divergent analytical concentration curve. (**b**) Convergent analytical concentration curve.

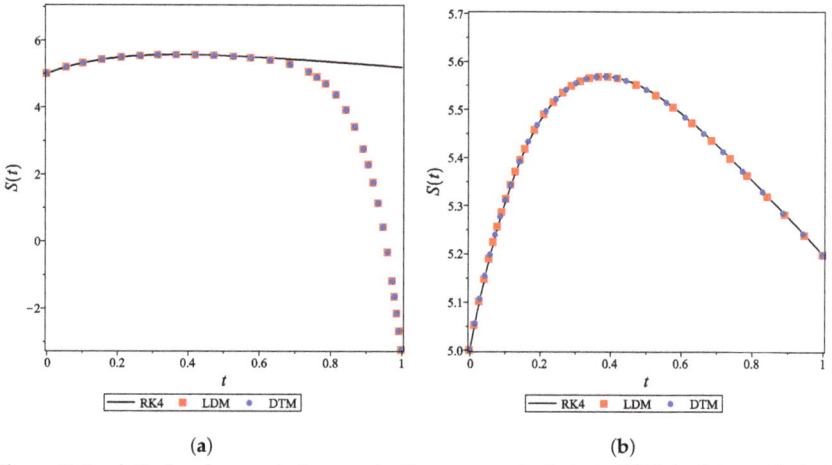

Figure 5. Analytical and numerical concentration curves of substrate ($S(t)$) for integer-derivative system (1) with $\alpha = 1$, initial conditions (17), and parameters (18). (**a**) Divergent analytical concentration curve. (**b**) Convergent analytical concentration curve.

The DTM was employed to derive analytical expressions for the concentration curves of all species for fractional values of α ($\alpha = 0.9, 0.8$). All the obtained curves of more than 10-term truncated series (provided in the Supporting Information) diverged over a relatively small domain. Therefore, large order Padé approximations were needed to obtain the convergent series solutions, as shown in Figure 6. A single command using Maple or MATLAB can be used to generate Padé approximations (given in supplementary material).

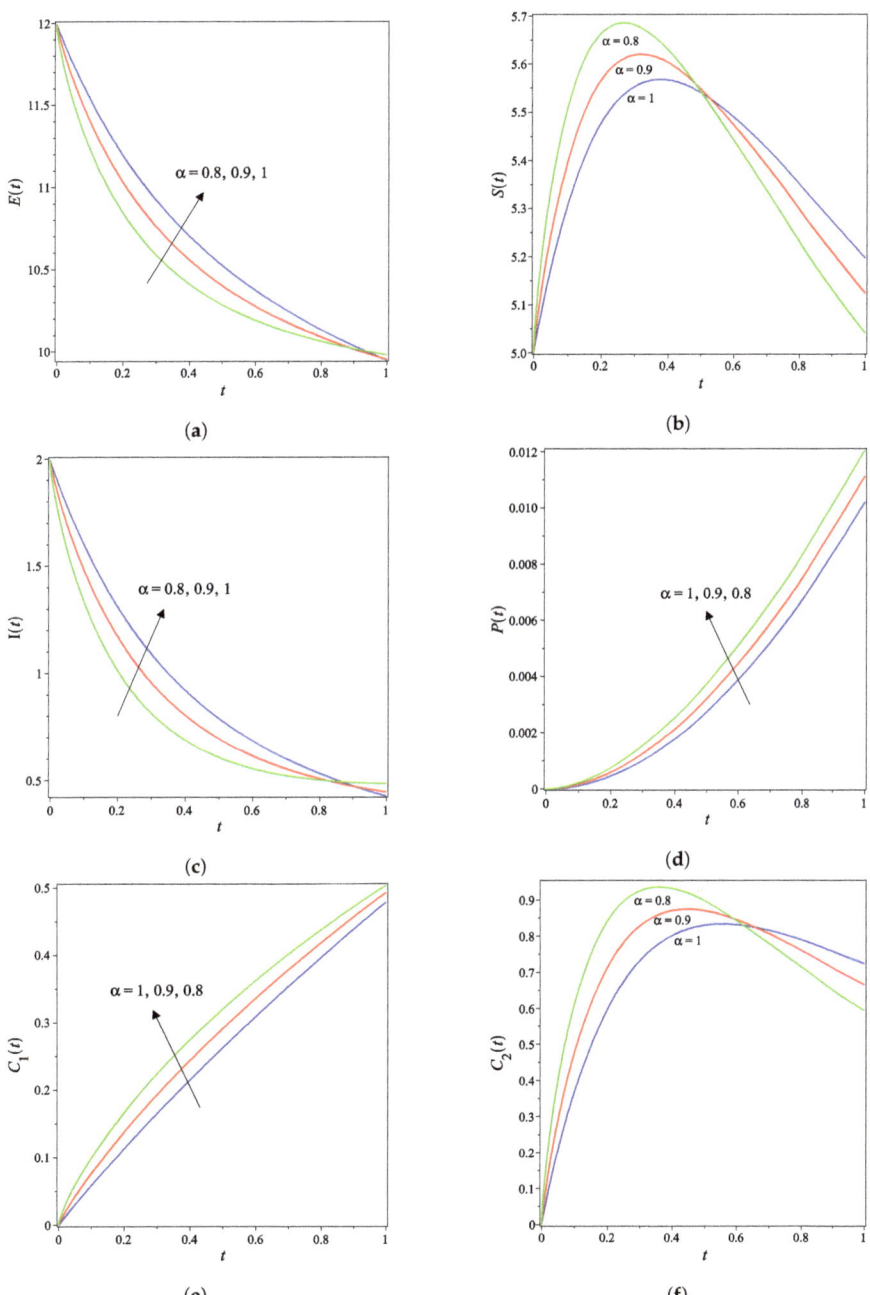

Figure 6. Cont.

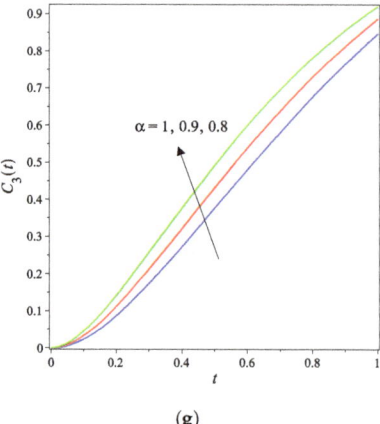

(g)

Figure 6. Analytical LDM concentration curves of E, S, I, P, ES, EI and ESI for system (1) with initial conditions (17) and parameters (18). (**a**) Enzyme. (**b**) Substrate. (**c**) Product. (**d**) Inhibitor. (**e**) Intermediate species ES. (**f**) Intermediate species EI. (**g**) Intermediate species ESI.

5. Conclusions

This paper discussed a complex nonlinear fractional model of enzyme inhibitor reactions subject to two different sets of initial concentrations, each with a different set of reaction rates. The simple, efficient, and reliable Laplace decomposition (LDM) and differential transformation (DTM) methods were utilized to solve the nonlinear fractional biochemical reaction system. The LDM was implemented by using Laplace transform of Caputo fractional derivative to convert the nonlinear fractional-derivative system (1) into an algebraic system, where the nonlinear terms are expressed in the form of Adomian polynomials. Then, the solution is obtained by employing the linearity of the Laplace and the inverse Laplace transforms. The fractional differential transformation method was implemented by directly applying Equations (10) and (11), and Theorem 2. The derived solution of system (1) represent the analytic expressions for the concentrations of enzyme, inhibitor, substrate, product, and the complex intermediate species: enzyme–substrate, enzyme–inhibitor, and enzyme–inhibitor–substrate were derived and discussed. From this study, it was concluded that different rate constants and initial concentrations produce different dynamics. Furthermore, it was shown that a Padé approximation of the series solution obtained by LDM and DTM would preserve convergence and stability when large initial concentrations or large rate constants are assumed. The derived LDM and DTM concentration expressions for the enzyme inhibitor reaction model were shown to be very close to the fourth-order Runge–Kutta method when the results were compared for the integer-derivative case.

The derived fractional analytical concentration curves would play a significant role in predicting the future state of the biochemical reaction model. In addition, the derived analytical expressions would be essential in investigating the effects of various reaction rates to reach better designs and controlled systems. The used methods are accessible to the broader research community. They can be extended to solve various fractional models to obtain a better insight into dynamical behavior for biological or chemical systems with possible hereditary properties.

Supplementary Materials: The following are available at https://www.mdpi.com/article/10.3390/mca27030045/s1.

Author Contributions: Conceptualization and methodology, M.A. and S.A.K.; software F.R.; validation, M.A., S.A.K. and F.R.; formal analysis, F.R. and S.A.K.; investigation, F.R.; writing—original draft preparation, F.R.; writing—review and editing, M.A.; visualization, S.A.K.; funding acquisition, M.A. All authors have read and agreed to the published version of the manuscript.

Funding: This work was partially supported by the American University of Sharjah Award #OAPCAS-1110-C00016. However, this paper represents the author's opinions and does not mean to represent the position or opinions of the American University of Sharjah.

Conflicts of Interest: The authors declare no conflict of interest.

References

1. Saravanakumar, R.; Pirabaharan, P.; Abukhaled, M.; Rajendran, L. Theoretical analysis of voltammetry at a rotating disk electrode in the absence of supporting electrolyte. *J. Phys. Chem. B* **2020**, *124*, 443–450. [CrossRef] [PubMed]
2. Abukhaled, M.; Guessoum, N.; Alsaeed, N. Mathematical modeling of light curves of RHESSI and AGILE terrestrial gamma-ray flashes. *Astrophys. Space Sci.* **2019**, *364*, 120. [CrossRef]
3. Saravanakumar, S.; Eswari, A.; Rajendran, L.; Abukhaled, M. A mathematical model of risk factors in HIV/AIDS transmission Dynamics: Observational study of female sexual network in India. *Appl. Math. Inf. Sci.* **2020**, *14*, 967–976.
4. Devi, M.C.; Pirabaharan, P.; Abukhaled, M.; Rajendran, L. Analysis of the steady-state behavior of pseudo-first-order EC-catalytic mechanism at a rotating disk electrode. *Electrochim. Acta* **2020**, *345*, 136175. [CrossRef]
5. Abukhaled, M.; Khuri, S. An efficient semi-analytical solution of a one-dimensional curvature equation that describes the human corneal shape. *Math. Comput. Appl.* **2019**, *24*, 8. [CrossRef]
6. Selvi, M.S.M.; Rajendran, L.; Abukhaled, M. Estimation of Rolling Motion of Ship in Random Beam Seas by Efficient Analytical and Numerical Approaches. *J. Mar. Sci. Appl.* **2021**, *20*, 55–66. [CrossRef]
7. Patnaik, S.; Hollkamp, J.P.; Semperlotti, F. Applications of variable-order fractional operators: A review. *Proc. R. Soc. A* **2020**, *476*, 20190498. [CrossRef]
8. Flores-Tlacuahuac, A; Biegler, L. Optimization of Fractional Order Dynamic Chemical Processing Systems. *Ind. Eng. Chem. Res.* **2014**, *53*, 5110–5127. [CrossRef]
9. Ionescu, C.; Lopes, A.; Copot, D.; Machado, J.; Bates, J. The role of fractional calculus in modeling biological phenomena: A review. *Commun. Nonlinear. Sci. Numer. Simulat.* **2017**, *51*, 141–159. [CrossRef]
10. Rihan, F.A. Numerical modeling of fractional-order biological systems. *Abstr. Appl. Anal.* **2013**, *2013*, 816803. [CrossRef]
11. Lazopoulos, K.A.; Lazopoulos, A.K. Fractional vector calculus and fluid mechanics. *J. Mech. Behav. Biomed. Mater.* **2017**, *26*, 43–54. [CrossRef]
12. Gomez-Aguilar, J.F. Cordova-Fraga, T.; Escalante- Martínez, J.E.; Calderon-Ram, C.; Escobar-Jimenez, R.F. Electrical circuits described by a fractional derivative with regular Kernel. *Rev. Mex. De Fis.* **2016**, *62*, 144–154.
13. Meral, F.C.; Royston, T.J.; Magin, R. Fractional calculus in viscoelasticity: An experimental study. *Ommun. Nonlinear. Sci. Numer. Simulat.* **2010**, *15*, 939–945. [CrossRef]
14. Matušu, R. Application of fractional order calculus to control theory. *Math Model. Methods Appl. Sci.* **2011**, *5*, 1162–1169.
15. Srivastava, H.M. Fractional-order derivatives and integrals: Introductory overview and recent developments. *Kyungpook Math. J.* **2020**, *60*, 73–116.
16. Dubey, V.P.; Kumar, R.; Kumar, D. Approximate analytical solution of fractional order biochemical reaction model and its stability analysis. *Int. J. Biomath.* **2019**, *12*, 1950059. [CrossRef]
17. Dulf, E.-H.; Vodnar, D.C.; Danku, A.; Muresan, C.; Crisan, O. Fractional-Order Models for Biochemical Processes. *Fractal Fract.* **2020**, *4*, 12. [CrossRef]
18. Iyiola, O.; Tasbozan, O.; Kurt, A.; Çenesiz, Y. On the analytical solutions of the system of conformable time-fractional Robertson equations with 1-D diffusion. *Chaos Solitons Fractals* **2017**, *94*, 1–7. [CrossRef]
19. Arafa, A. Different approach for conformable fractional biochemical reaction diffusion models. *Appl. Math. J. Chin. Univ.* **2020**, *35*, 452. [CrossRef]
20. Baeumer, B.; Kovacs, M.; Meerschaert, M. Numerical solutions for fractional reaction diffusion equations. *Comput. Math. Appl.* **2008**, *55*, 2212. [CrossRef]
21. Atangana, A. Modeling the Enzyme Kinetic Reaction. *Acta Biotheor* **2015**, *63*, 239. [CrossRef] [PubMed]
22. Bhrawy, A.; Zaky, M. Numerical simulation for two-dimensional variable-order fractional nonlinear cable equation. *Nonlinear Dyn.* **2015**, *80*, 101–116. [CrossRef]
23. Atangana, A.; Owolabi, K.M. New numerical approach for fractional differential equations. *Math. Model. Nat. Phenom.* **2018**, *13*, 3. [CrossRef]
24. Milici, C.; Machado, J.T. Draganescu, G. Application of the Euler and Runge–Kutta Generalized Methods for FDE and Symbolic Packages in the Analysis of Some Fractional Attractors. *Int. J. Nonlinear Sci. Numer. Simul.* **2020**, *21*, 159–170. [CrossRef]
25. Jhinga, A.; Daftardar-Gejji, V. A new numerical method for solving fractional delay differential equations. *Comput. Appl. Math.* **2019**, *38*, 166. [CrossRef]
26. Kumar, S.;Baleanu, D. A new numerical method for time fractional non-linear sharma-tasso-oliver equation and klein-gordon equation with exponential kernel law. *Front. Phys.* **2020**, *8*, 136. [CrossRef]
27. Ali, U.; Khan, M.A.; Khater, M.M.A.; Mousa, A.A.; Attia, R.A.M. A new numerical approach for solving 1D fractional diffusion-wave equation. *J. Funct. Spaces* **2021**, *2021*, 1–7. [CrossRef]

28. Toufik, M.; Atangana, A. New numerical approximation of fractional derivative with non-local and non-singular kernel: Application to chaotic models. *Eur. Phys. J. Plus* **2017**, *132*, 444. [CrossRef]
29. Devi, M.C.; Pirabaharan, P.; Rajendran, L.; Abukhaled, M. An efficient method for finding analytical expressions of substrate concentrations for different particles in an immobilized enzyme system. *Reac. Kinet. Mech. Cat.* **2020**, *130*, 35–53. [CrossRef]
30. Javeed, S.; Baleanu, D.; Waheed, A.; Shaukat, K.M.; Affan, H. Analysis of Homotopy Perturbation Method for Solving Fractional Order Differential Equations. *Mathematics* **2019**, *7*, 40. [CrossRef]
31. Zurigat, M.; Momani, S.; Odibat, Z.; Alawneh, A. The homotopy analysis method for handling systems of fractional differential equations. *Appl. Math. Model.* **2010**, *34*, 24–35. [CrossRef]
32. Mohammed, O.; Salim, H. Computational methods based laplace decomposition for solving nonlinear system of fractional order differential equations. *Alex. Eng. J.* **2018**, *57*, 3549–3557. [CrossRef]
33. He, C.-H.; Shen, Y.; Ji, F.-Y.; He, J.-H. Taylor series solution for fractal Bratu-type equation arising in electrospinning process. *Fractals* **2020**, *28*, 2050011. [CrossRef]
34. Hadid, S.; Khuri, S.A.; Sayfy, A. A Green's function iterative approach for the solution of a class of fractional BVPs arising in physical models. *Int. J. Appl. Comput. Math.* **2020**, *6*, 91. [CrossRef]
35. Morales-Delgado, V.F.; Gomez-Aguilar, J.F.; Saad, K.; Khan, M.; Agarwal, P. Analytic solution for oxygen diffusion from capillary to tissues involving external force effects: A fractional calculus approach. *Phys. A: Stat. Mech. Appl.* **2019**, *523*, 48–65. [CrossRef]
36. Abukhaled, M.; Khuri, S.; Rabah, F. Solution of a nonlinear fractional COVID-19 model. *Int. J. Numer. Methods Heat Fluid Flow* **2022**, ahead-of-print. [CrossRef]
37. Ganjefar, S.; Rezaei, S. Modified homotopy perturbation method for optimal control problems using the Padé approximant. *Appl. Math. Model.* **2016**, *40*, 7062–7081. [CrossRef]
38. Akgül, A.; Khoshnaw, S.H. Application of fractional derivative on non-linear biochemical reaction models. *Int. J. Intell. Netw.* **2020**, *1*, 52–58. [CrossRef]
39. Alchikh, R.; Khuri, S.A. Numerical solution of a fractional differential equation arising in optics. *Optik* **2020**, *208*, 163911. [CrossRef]
40. Zhou, J.K. *Differential Transformation and Its Applications for Electrical Circuits*; Huazhong University Press: Wuhan, China, 1986.
41. Arikoglu, A.; Ozkol, I. Solution of fractional differential equations by using differential transform method. *Chaos Solitons Fractals* **2007**, *34*, 1473–1481. [CrossRef]
42. Ertürk, V.S.; Momani, S. Solving systems of fractional differential equations using differential transform method. *J. Comput. Appl. Math.* **2008**, *215*, 142–151. [CrossRef]

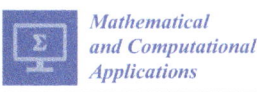

Article

Magneto Mixed Convection of Williamson Nanofluid Flow through a Double Stratified Porous Medium in Attendance of Activation Energy

B. M. Tamilzharasan [1], S. Karthikeyan [1], Mohammed K. A. Kaabar [2], Mehmet Yavuz [3,4,*] and Fatma Özköse [5]

1. Department of Mathematics, Erode Arts and Science College, Erode 638009, Tamil Nadu, India; mathsmaran365@gmail.com (B.M.T.); skarthi.eac@gmail.com (S.K.)
2. Institute of Mathematical Sciences, Faculty of Science, University of Malaya, Kuala Lumpur 50603, Malaysia; mohammed.kaabar@wsu.edu
3. Department of Mathematics and Computer Sciences, Faculty of Science, Necmettin Erbakan University, Konya 42090, Turkey
4. Department of Mathematics, College of Engineering, Mathematics and Physical Sciences, University of Exeter, Cornwall TR11 2LD, UK
5. Department of Mathematics, Faculty of Science, Erciyes University, Kayseri 38280, Turkey; fpeker@erciyes.edu.tr
* Correspondence: m.yavuz@exeter.ac.uk or mehmetyavuz@erbakan.edu.tr

Abstract: This article aims to develop a mathematical simulation of the steady mixed convective Darcy–Forchheimer flow of Williamson nanofluid over a linear stretchable surface. In addition, the effects of Cattaneo–Christov heat and mass flux, Brownian motion, activation energy, and thermophoresis are also studied. The novel aspect of this study is that it incorporates thermal radiation to investigate the physical effects of thermal and solutal stratification on mixed convection flow and heat transfer. First, the profiles of velocity and energy equations were transformed toward the ordinary differential equation using the appropriate similarity transformation. Then, the system of equations was modified by first-order ODEs in MATLAB and solved using the bvp4c approach. Graphs and tables imply the impact of physical parameters on concentration, temperature, velocity, skin friction coefficient, mass, and heat transfer rate. The outcomes show that the nanofluid temperature and concentration are reduced with the more significant thermal and mass stratification parameters estimation.

Keywords: Williamson nanofluid; thermal stratification; solutal stratification; mixed convection; Darcy–Forchheimer flow; activation energy

1. Introduction

Nanotechnology is the technique of analyzing and separating or adding an object's atoms and molecules that need to be made very small. Over the last thirty years, nanotechnology has significantly impacted vast applications in the petroleum industry, food production, medicine, nuclear energy, cooling of the reactor, and the polymer industry. Primarily, in 1995, Choi and Eastman [1] "coined the term nanofluid by incorporating the substance of nanoparticles into base fluids and theoretically demonstrated their efficiency". Based on their findings, they noticed a considerable increase in the thermal conduction of the base liquid. Buongiorno [2] demonstrated the role of Brownian motion and thermophoresis in a nanofluid. The seven slip mechanisms were studied by Buongiorno and Buongiorno's concepts: inertia, thermophoresis, gravity, Magnus effects, fluid drainage, Brownian diffusion, and diffusionphoresis.

Williamson [3] developed "the flow of Pseudo-plastic equation" and analyzed the properties of the pseudo-plastic flow holding three constants. These are the viscous constant, plasticity constant, and the ratio between the viscous constant and the plasticity constant.

Nadeem et al. [4] tested the Williamson fluid model for 2D flows through a stretching sheet. The role of radiation and heat absorption on an incompressible pseudo-plastic Williamson fluid over the unsteady flow of the boundary layer via a porous stretched surface was explored by Hayat et al. [5] and Karthikeyan et al. [6], and they discovered that increasing the Weissenberg number decreases the skin friction coefficient. According to Zeeshan et al. [7], water- and engine oil-based CNTs flowed through a porous medium. On the other hand, the MHD Williamson fluid flow through a nonlinear curved surface in convective homogeneous and heterogeneous reactions was implemented by K. Ahmed et al. [8]. H. Waqas et al. [9] presented a numerical result for the Carreau–Yasuda nanofluid in a porous medium with bioconvective microorganisms. Nasir Shehzad et al. [10] determined that the suction/injection parameter was generated due to a constant and porous medium in the presence of a heat source, and a chemical reaction was observed. The cutting-edge reports in Williamson nanofluid flow with thermal radiation and heat generation are seen in [11–19].

Cattaneo [20] suggested a modified Fourier's law that included a relaxation time element to overcome the paradox of Fourier's law and heat conduction. Christov [21] extended Cattaneo's theory by including Oldroyd derivatives, and it was named the Cattaneo–Christov model theory. Eswaramoorthi et al. [22] expressed the impact of a Williamson fluid flow of two-dimensional Darcy–Forchheimer on a Riga plate. Dual stratification and a double Catteneo–Christov flux were established for the energy equations. The contribution of Jeffery fluid flow to the non-Fourier heat flux model on a nonlinear stretched surface with double stratification was studied by Hayat et al. [23] and Shankar Goud [24]. Ali et al. [25] used the Cattaneo–Christov dual diffusion model to discuss the 3D incompressible unsteady effect of magneto-hydrodynamics on the transient rotating flow of Maxwell viscous nanofluid. The relation between thermal boundary layer and thermal relaxation time was observed in Abu-hamdeh et al. [26]. Rashid et al. [27] examined the thermal radiation effects of Darcy–Forchheimer Maxwell fluid flow along an exponentially stretching surface with activation energy. Shafiq et al. [28] "reported the influence of convective boundary conditions, thermal radiation and chemical reaction on the three-dimensional flow of Darcy Forchheimer nanofluid across a rotating surface with Arrhenius activation energy". "Entropy formation, activation energy, and binary chemical reaction effects on the Darcy Forchheimer flow of Williamson nanofluid through a nonlinear stretchable flat surface were deliberated" by Ghulam Rasool et al. [29] and Hayat et al. [30].

The activation energy is the smallest quantity of energy forced to trigger a chemical reaction in a system. Energy exists in two types: kinetic and potential. A reaction among molecules could be incomplete due to kinetic energy loss or an inadequate collision. At this point, only the minimum amount of energy is required to initiate the chemical reaction. Bestman [31] was the first to investigate the impact of activation energy on natural action in a permeable boundary layer. Dawar et al. [32] addressed nonlinear stretching plates in magnetohydrodynamics pseudo-plastic nanofluid flow with activation energy. The method of homotopy analysis was performed by Alsaadi et al. [33] to examine the Arrhenius energy equation in the nanomaterial of magneto-Williamson flow. The influence of the activation energy, slip, porosity parameter, and entropy approach on the mixed convective flow of Darcy–Forchheimer along a stretched curved surface was noticed by Muhammad et al. [34]. Danook et al. [35] investigated the mixed convective heat transfer in a turbulent flow of nanofluid. Wasim Jamshed et al. [36] worked on the unsteady flow of a non-Newtonian Casson nanofluid with solar radiation using the Keller box method. The significance of MHD mixed convective flows Casson nanofluids over an elongating irregular surface immersed vertically in a Darcy–Brinkman porous medium was exploited by Alghamdi et al. [37]. Currently, investigators are analyzing the Arrhenius activation energy [38–48]. Other related studies have been conducted in [49–55].

For heat and mass transfer concepts, stratification is an essential component. Due to temperature differences, concentration variations, and differing fluid densities, it happens in inflow distribution. Heat and mass transport occur at the same time in the dual stratification process. Natural and mixed convection in a dual stratification medium are essential to study because of their applications. Groundwater reservoirs, industrial food, and regulating hydrogen and oxygen levels in the atmosphere are just a few examples of stratification. Sreelakshmi et al. [56] examined the steady flow of Maxwell fluid Darcy–Forchheimer over a stretching surface with thermal and solutal stratification. Darcy–Forchhemer MHD viscoelastic flow of nanofluid through a nonlinear stretching surface with dual stratification effects was deliberated by Hayat et al. [57]. Eswaramoorthi et al. [58] tested the impact of dual stratification and double non-Fourier heat flux model on the mathematical modeling of a Williamson fluid flow on a Darcy–Forchheimer over a Riga plate. Williamson fluid flow over a stretching in a linear surface was examined by Ahmed et al. [59] Some recent thermal and solutal stratification articles were found in [43–48,56–70].

The vast majority of researchers collaborate on the mixed convective Darcy–Forchheimer flow with the non-Fourier heat flux model via the prescribed boundary layer but have not handled a dual stratified porous medium in Williamson nanofluid. Here, the gap was filled by the Williamson nanofluid on the double Cattaneo–Christov theory, radiation, dual stratification, and the impact of activation energy. The numerical findings were produced using the MATLAB bvp4c approach. Finally, in Williamson nanofluid flow, all the physical parameters were represented by a graphical process. This process is widely used in chemical and thermal engineering fields.

2. Development of the Flow Analysis

Assume a Williamson nanofluid's steady flow through a linearly stretching surface in a Darcy–Forchheimer porous material. The Cattaneo–Christov theory, Arrhenius energy, thermal radiation, and magnetic field are studied. The flow process is revealed by thermal and solutal stratification. Throughout this work, the x and y directions represent velocity components of u and v, respectively (see Figure 1). The surface velocity is presumed to be $u_w = ax$, where $a > 0$ denotes the stretching surface rate. The flow equation [69] is as follows:

$$\frac{\partial u}{\partial x} + \frac{\partial v}{\partial y} = 0 \qquad (1)$$

$$u\frac{\partial u}{\partial x} + v\frac{\partial v}{\partial y} = \vartheta \frac{\partial^2 u}{\partial y^2} + \vartheta\sqrt{2}\wedge \frac{\partial u}{\partial y}\frac{\partial^2 u}{\partial y^2} + \frac{\vartheta}{k_f}u + \frac{C_B}{x\sqrt{k_f}}u^2 - \frac{\sigma B_0^2}{\rho_f}u \\ + \frac{1}{\rho_f}\left\{ \begin{array}{c} (1-c_\infty)g\rho_{f\infty}\Lambda_1(T-T_\infty) \\ -g\left(\rho_p - \rho_{f\infty}\right)(C-C_\infty) \end{array} \right\} \qquad (2)$$

$$u\frac{\partial T}{\partial x} + v\frac{\partial T}{\partial y} + \Gamma_T\left(u^2\frac{\partial^2 T}{\partial x^2} + v^2\frac{\partial^2 T}{\partial y^2} + \left(u\frac{\partial u}{\partial x}\frac{\partial T}{\partial x} + v\frac{\partial u}{\partial y}\frac{\partial T}{\partial x}\right) + 2uv\frac{\partial T^2}{\partial x \partial y}\right) \\ +u\frac{\partial v}{\partial x}\frac{\partial T}{\partial y} + v\frac{\partial v}{\partial y}\frac{\partial T}{\partial y} \\ = \frac{k_f}{(\rho c)_f}\frac{\partial^2 T}{\partial y^2} + \frac{1}{(\rho c)_f}\frac{16\sigma^* T_\infty^3}{3k_p}\frac{\partial^2 T}{\partial y^2} + \frac{Q_1}{\rho_f C_p}(T-T_\infty) \\ +\tau\left(D_m\left(\frac{\partial T}{\partial y}\right)\left(\frac{\partial C}{\partial y}\right) + \frac{D_n}{T_\infty}\left(\frac{\partial T}{\partial y}\right)^2\right) \qquad (3)$$

$$u\frac{\partial C}{\partial x} + v\frac{\partial C}{\partial y} + \Gamma_C\left[u^2\frac{\partial^2 C}{\partial x^2} + v^2\frac{\partial^2 C}{\partial y^2} + \left(u\frac{\partial u}{\partial x}\frac{\partial C}{\partial x} + v\frac{\partial u}{\partial y}\frac{\partial C}{\partial x}\right) + 2uv\frac{\partial^2 C}{\partial x \partial y} + u\frac{\partial v}{\partial x}\frac{\partial C}{\partial y}\right. \\ \left. +v\frac{\partial v}{\partial y}\frac{\partial C}{\partial y}\right] = D_m\frac{\partial^2 C}{\partial y^2} + \frac{D_n}{T_\infty}\frac{\partial^2 T}{\partial y^2} - k_r^2(C-C_\infty)\left(\frac{T}{T_\infty}\right)^n exp\left(-\frac{E_A}{kT}\right) \qquad (4)$$

The boundary conditions are

$$u = U_w(x) = ax, v = -V_w(x), T = T_w(x) = T_0 + bx, C = C_w(x) = C_0 + c_1 x \text{ at } y = 0, \\ u \to 0, \frac{\partial u}{\partial y} \to 0, T \to T_\infty = T_0 + b_1 x, C \to C_\infty = C_0 + c_2 x \text{ at } y \to \infty \qquad (5)$$

Consider
$$\eta = \sqrt{\frac{a}{\vartheta}}y,\ u = ax f'(\eta), v = -\sqrt{a\vartheta}\ f(\eta)\ \theta(\eta) = \frac{T - T_\infty}{T_w - T_0},\ \phi(\eta) = \frac{C - C_\infty}{C_w - C_o} \quad (6)$$

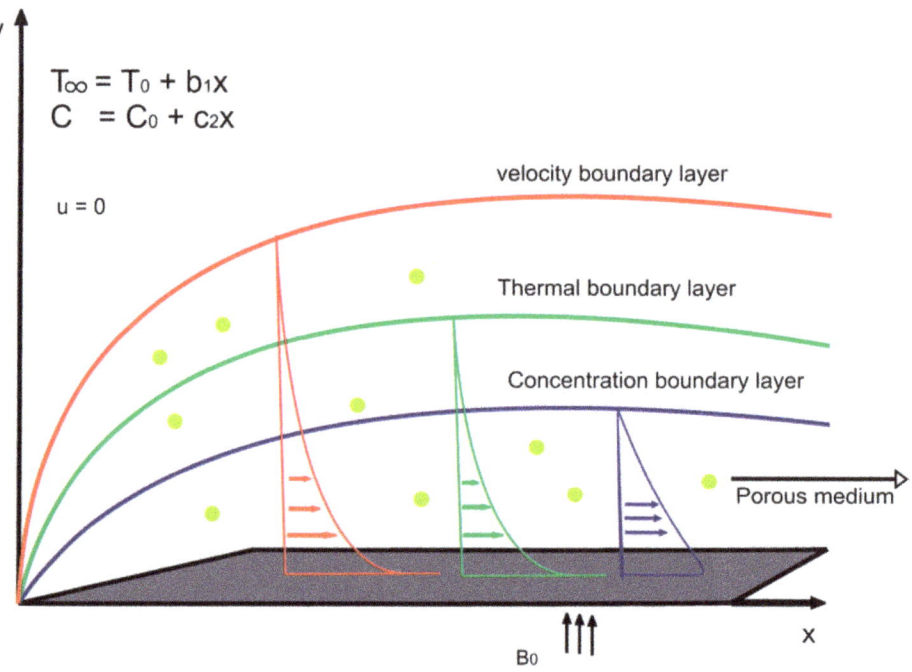

Figure 1. The geometry of the physical model.

Equations (2)–(4) can be modified as follows by using (6):

$$f''' + ff'' - f'^2 + Wif''f''' - Kf' + \lambda(\theta - B_N\phi) - Fcf'^2 - Mf' = 0 \quad (7)$$

$$\frac{1}{Pr}\left(1 + \frac{4}{3}Rd\right)\theta'' - \omega_\theta\left(f^2\theta'' + \theta f'^2 + f'^2 S_\theta - ff'\theta' - ff''\theta - ff''S_\theta\right) \\ + N_B\phi'\theta' + N_T\theta'^2 + H_A\theta - f'\theta + f\theta' - S_\theta f' = 0 \quad (8)$$

$$\frac{1}{SC}\phi'' + f\phi' - \omega_\phi\left(f^2\phi'' - ff''S_\phi - ff''\phi + f'^2\phi + f'^2 S_\phi - ff'\phi'\right) - f'\phi + f'S_\phi + \frac{N_T}{SCN_B}\theta'' \\ -\sigma_o\phi(1 + \theta\delta_o)^n \exp\left(\frac{-E}{1+\theta\delta_o}\right) = 0 \quad (9)$$

The boundary conditions are

$$\eta \to 0,\ f(0) = fw;\ f'(0) = 1;\ \theta(0) = 1 - S_\theta;\ \phi(0) = 1 - S_\phi \\ \eta \to \infty,\ f'(\infty) = 0;\ \theta(\infty) = 0;\ \phi(\infty) = 0 \quad (10)$$

$$E = \frac{E_A}{kT_\infty},\ Fc = \frac{C_B}{\sqrt{k_f}},\ Gr = \left(\frac{(g\beta(1-C_\infty)(T_w - T_\infty)x^3)}{\vartheta^2}\right),\ H_A = \frac{Q_1}{\rho_f C_p a},\ fw = -\frac{V_w}{\sqrt{a\vartheta}},\ M = \frac{\sigma B_0^2}{\rho_f a},$$

$$Sc = \frac{\vartheta}{D_B},\ N_B = \frac{\tau D_B C_\infty}{\vartheta},\ B_N = \left(\frac{(\rho_p - \rho_{f\infty})C_\infty}{\rho_{f\infty}\wedge_1(1-C_\infty)(T_w - T_0))}\right),\ Pr = \frac{k_f}{(\rho c)_f},\ Re_x = \frac{U_w x}{\vartheta},$$

$Wi = \Lambda x \sqrt{\frac{2a^3}{\theta}}$, $\lambda = \left(\frac{Gr}{Re_x^2}\right) = \left(\frac{(g\Lambda_1(1-C_\infty)(T_w-T_\infty))}{a^2 x}\right)$, $N_T = \left(\frac{\tau D_T(T_w-T_0)}{T_\infty \theta}\right)$, $R = \frac{4\sigma^* T_\infty^3}{k_p k_f}$,
$\delta = \left(\frac{(T_w-T_0)}{T_\infty}\right)$.

Physical quantities for skin friction, Nusselt, and Sherwood number are obtained as follows:

$$C_f = \frac{2\tau_\omega}{\rho U_\omega^2}, \quad Nu = \frac{xq_\omega}{k_f(T_w - T_0)}, \quad Sh_x = \frac{xj_\omega}{D_m(C_w - C_0)} \quad (11)$$

where

$$\tau_\omega = \mu\left(\frac{\partial u}{\partial y}\left[1 + \Lambda\sqrt{\frac{1}{2}\frac{\partial u}{\partial y}}\right]\right)$$
$$q_\omega = -\left(k_f \frac{\partial T}{\partial y} + \frac{16\sigma^* T_\infty^3}{3k_p}\frac{\partial T}{\partial y}\right)$$
$$j_\omega = -D_m \frac{\partial C}{\partial y}$$

The following are the dimensionless parts of local skin friction, heat, and mass transfer rates.

$$\frac{1}{2}C_f Re^{\frac{1}{2}} = f''(0) + \frac{Wi}{2}f''(0)^2,$$
$$Re^{-\frac{1}{2}}Nu = -\left(1 + \frac{4}{3}Rd\right)\theta'(0), \quad (12)$$
$$Re^{-\frac{1}{2}}Sh_x = -\phi'(0).$$

3. The Solution Methodology

A system of nonlinear ODEs (7)–(9) with boundary conditions (10) is solved via the MATLAB bvp4c code. The problems are converted into first-order ODEs using the mathematical algorithm described below (Figure 2).

Let $f = y(1), f' = y(2), f'' = y(3), \theta = y(4), \theta' = y(5), \phi = y(6)$, and $\phi' = y(7)$. The following is a list of first-order ODEs:

$y'(1) = y(2)$,
$y'(2) = y(3)$,
$y'(3) = yy1 = \left(\frac{1}{1+Wi\, y(3)}\right)$
$\quad * \left(-y(1)y(3) + y(2)^2 + K\, y(2) + Fc\, y(2)^2 + M\, y(2)\right.$
$\quad \left. -\lambda\, (y(4) - B_N\, y(6)))\right)$,
$y'(4) = y(5)$,
$y'(5) = yy2 = \left(\frac{1}{1+(\frac{4}{3})Rd} - Pr\, \omega_\theta\, y(1)^2\right)$
$\quad * (-Pr\, y(1)\, y(5) + Pr\, y(2)y(4) + Pr\, S_\theta\, y(2)$
$\quad + Pr\, \omega_\theta\left(y(4)\, y(2)^2 + y(2)^2\, S_\theta - y(1)\, y(2)\, y(5) - y(1)\, y(3)\, y(4)\right.$
$\quad \left. -y(1)\, y(3)\, S_\theta\right) - Pr\, H_A\, y(4) - Pr\, N_B\, y(7)\, y(5) - Pr\, N_T\, y(5)^2)$,
$y'(6) = y(7)$,
$y'(7) = yy3 = \left(1/\left(1 - Sc\, \omega_\phi\, y(1)^2\right)\right) * (-Sc\, y(1)\, y(7) + Sc\, y(2)\, y(6) + Sc\, S_\phi\, y(2)$
$\quad + Sc\, \omega_\phi\, (y(6)\, y(2)^2 + y(2)^2 S_\phi - y(1)\, y(2)\, y(7) - y(1)\, y(3)\, y(6)$
$\quad -y(1)\, y(3)S_\phi) - (N_T/N_B) * yy2$
$\quad + Sc\, \sigma_0 (1 + \delta_o\, y(4))^n\, y(6)\, \exp(-E/(1 + \delta_o\, y(4))))$

with boundary condition

$$y0(1) = fw, \quad y0(2) = 1, \quad y0(4) = (1 - S_\theta), \quad y0(6) = (1 - S_\phi),$$
$$yinf(2) = 0, \quad yinf(4) = 0, \quad yinf(6) = 0$$

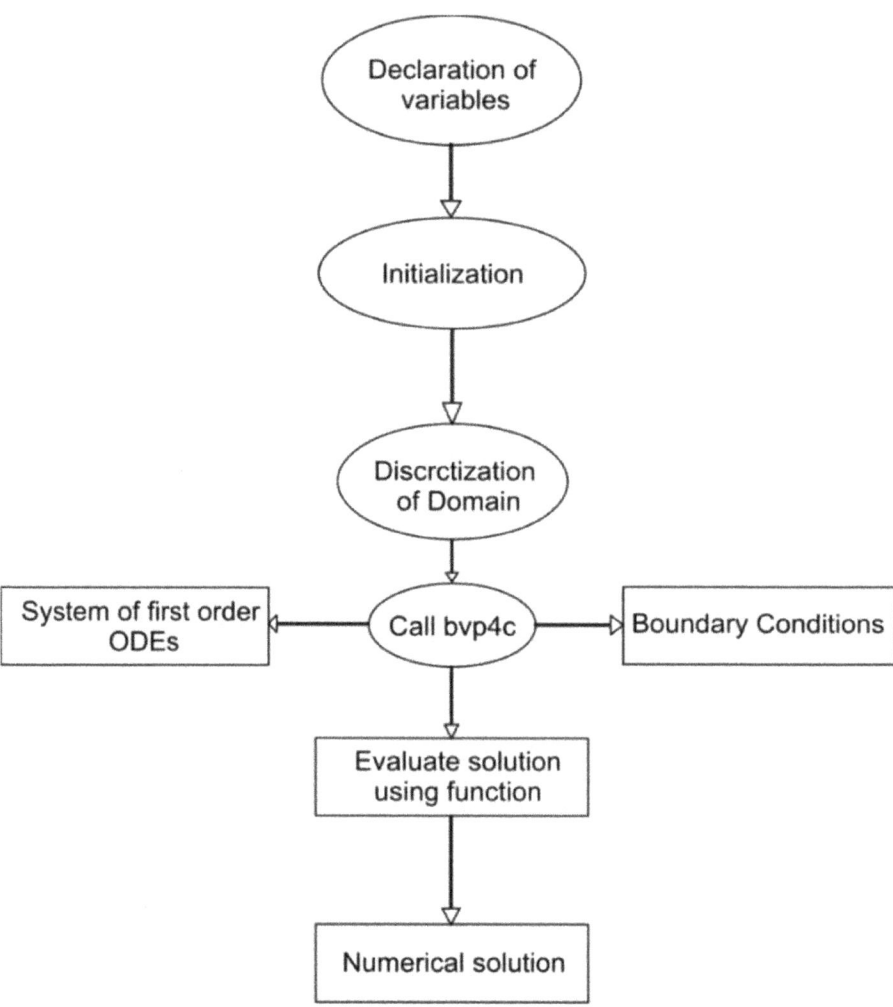

Figure 2. BVP4C computation flowchart.

4. Results and Discussion

Table 1 shows the association between Nusselt numbers taken from Mustafa et al.'s results and our results. We were able to match our results identically to Mustafa's results. The quantitative data of the skin friction drag force ($1/2C_f Re^{1/2}$), heat transfer rate ($NuRe^{-1/2}$), and Sherwood number ($Sh_x Re^{1/2}$) for the several values of Richardson number λ, Weissenberg number Wi, Forchheimer number Fc, Magnetic parameter M, and suction/injection parameter fw were presented in Table 2. Moreover, it was discovered that as Wi and λ values grow, the skin friction coefficient also increases, whereas it was significantly decreased when Fc, fw, and M increased. Tables 3 and 4 incorporated the effects of the embedded parameters Radiation R, Thermal relaxation time parameter ω_θ, Thermal stratification S_θ, Thermophoresis parameter N_T, Mass relaxation parameter ω_ϕ, Mass stratification S_ϕ, and Schmidt number Sc on heat and mass diffusion rates. The higher variation of ω_θ, S_θ, N_T, and S_ϕ was related to the reduced mass and heat transfer rates. It was also accelerated as the thermal radiation, Schmidt number, and mass relaxation time were increased.

Table 1. Correlation of Nusselt number $\left(NuRe^{-\frac{1}{2}}\right)$ when $Wi = Fc = K = R = \omega_\theta = H_A = \omega_\phi = 0$, $M = B_N = N_B = 0.5$, $Sc = 5$, and $\delta_0 = 1$.

Pr	N_T	E	σ_0	n	λ	$NuRe^{-1/2}$ Mustafa et al. [69]	Present
2	0.5	1	1	0.5	0.5	0.706605	0.706604
4	0.5	1	1	0.5	0.5	0.935952	0.935955
7	0.5	1	1	0.5	0.5	1.132787	1.132788
10	0.5	1	1	0.5	0.5	1.257476	1.257482
5	0.1	1	1	0.5	0.5	1.426267	1.426269
5	0.5	1	1	0.5	0.5	1.013939	1.013938
5	0.7	1	1	0.5	0.5	0.846943	0.846928
5	1.0	1	1	0.5	0.5	0.649940	0.649939
5	0.5	0	1	0.5	0.5	0.941201	0.941209
5	0.5	1	1	0.5	0.5	1.013939	1.013943
5	0.5	2	1	0.5	0.5	1.064551	1.064563
5	0.5	4	1	0.5	0.5	1.114549	1.114191
5	0.5	1	0	0.5	0.5	1.145304	1.145301
5	0.5	1	1	0.5	0.5	1.013939	1.013938
5	0.5	1	2	0.5	0.5	0.926282	0.926281
5	0.5	1	5	0.5	0.5	0.798671	0.798669
5	0.5	1	2	−1	0.5	1.030805	1.030804
5	0.5	1	2	−0.5	0.5	0.999470	0.999468
5	0.5	1	2	0	0.5	0.964286	0.964285
10	0.5	1	2	1	0.5	0.886830	0.886830
10	0.5	1	2	0.5	0	1.032281	1.032280
10	0.5	1	2	0.5	0.5	1.056704	1.056706
10	0.5	1	2	0.5	3	1.154539	1.154538
10	0.5	1	2	0.5	5	1.215937	1.215938

Table 2. Numerical analysis of $1/2C_f Re^{1/2}$, $NuRe^{-1/2}$, and $Sh_x Re^{1/2}$ for different parameters Wi, Fc, λ, M, and fw.

Wi	Fc	λ	M	fw	$1/2C_f Re^{1/2}$	$NuRe^{-1/2}$	$Sh_x Re^{-1/2}$
0	0.4	0.5	0.5	0.3	−1.493123	1.667677	0.688683
0.1	0.4	0.5	0.5	0.3	−1.455877	1.661396	0.681731
0.2	0.4	0.5	0.5	0.3	−1.41351	1.653626	0.673835
0.3	0.4	0.5	0.5	0.3	−1.362763	1.643289	0.664469
0.2	0	0.5	0.5	0.3	−1.329383	1.662128	0.682787
0.2	0.2	0.5	0.5	0.3	−1.372209	1.657807	0.678189
0.2	0.4	0.5	0.5	0.3	−1.41351	1.653626	0.673835
0.2	0.6	0.5	0.5	0.3	−1.45342	1.649575	0.669706
0.2	0.4	0	0.5	0.3	−1.470747	1.646644	0.666783
0.2	0.4	0.2	0.5	0.3	−1.44786	1.64946	0.669584
0.2	0.4	0.4	0.5	0.3	−1.424968	1.652245	0.672411

Table 2. Cont.

Wi	Fc	λ	M	fw	$1/2C_f Re^{1/2}$	$NuRe^{-1/2}$	$Sh_x Re^{-1/2}$
0.2	0.4	0.6	0.5	0.3	−1.402068	1.655	0.675269
0.2	0.4	0.5	0	0.3	−1.167756	1.642785	0.789742
0.2	0.4	0.5	0.5	0.3	−1.41351	1.653626	0.673835
0.2	0.4	0.5	1	0.3	−1.56368	1.632112	0.646948
0.2	0.4	0.5	1.5	0.3	−1.696232	1.612796	0.626083
0.2	0.4	0.5	0.5	−0.3	−1.13794	1.366538	0.605637
0.2	0.4	0.5	0.5	−0.1	−1.22469	1.476979	0.612521
0.2	0.4	0.5	0.5	0.1	−1.316926	1.576889	0.632016
0.2	0.4	0.5	0.5	0.3	−1.41351	1.653626	0.673835

Table 3. Numerical study of $NuRe^{-1/2}$ for various parameters R, ω_θ, and S_θ.

R	ω_θ	S_θ	$NuRe^{-1/2}$
0	0.1	0.2	1.292138
0.5	0.1	0.2	1.653626
1	0.1	0.2	1.877266
1.5	0.1	0.2	1.926091
0.5	−0.1	0.2	1.64429
0.5	0	0.2	1.662016
0.5	0.1	0.2	1.653626
0.5	0.2	0.2	1.561214
0.5	0.1	0	1.849146
0.5	0.1	0.1	1.753203
0.5	0.1	0.2	1.653626
0.5	0.1	0.3	1.550338

Table 4. Numerical results of $Sh_x Re^{1/2}$ for different parameters Sc, N_T, ω_ϕ, and S_ϕ.

Sc	N_T	ω_ϕ	S_ϕ	$Sh_x Re^{-1/2}$
0.5	0.5	0.1	0.2	0.015548
1	0.5	0.1	0.2	0.673835
1.5	0.5	0.1	0.2	1.186802
2	0.5	0.1	0.2	1.628294
1	0.2	0.1	0.2	1.038076
1	0.3	0.1	0.2	0.911577
1	0.4	0.1	0.2	0.790267
1	0.5	0.1	0.2	0.673835
1	0.5	0	0.2	0.591323
1	0.5	0.1	0.2	0.673835
1	0.5	0.2	0.2	0.759523
1	0.5	0.3	0.2	0.848478
1	0.5	0.1	0	0.899109

Table 4. Cont.

Sc	N_T	ω_ϕ	S_ϕ	$Sh_x Re^{-1/2}$
1	0.5	0.1	0.1	0.786382
1	0.5	0.1	0.2	0.673835
1	0.5	0.1	0.3	0.561474

The embedded parameters with fixed values $Wi = 0.2, \delta_o = \omega_\theta = 0.1, \omega_\phi = 0.1$, $Pr = 2, Fc = 0.4, K = 0.2, \sigma_o = 1, B_N = 0.5, R = 0.5, H_A = -0.5, N_B = 0.5$, $N_T = 0.5, n = 0.5, fw = 0.3, S_\theta = 0.2, Sc = 1.0, M = 0.5, \lambda = 0.5, E = 1$ and $S_\phi = 0.2$ are existence in velocity f', temperature θ and concentration ϕ profiles. Specifications of the suction/injection parameter fw on velocity field f with the range of $0 \leq \eta \leq 4$ the fluid velocity profile of the nanofluid while comparing the values of Fc and K were noted in Figure 3. In the graph flow between Fc and K, then values of fw varied from $fw = -0.3$ to $+0.3$ increase, and the velocity profile f' of the graph automatically decreases. The influence of mixed convection parameters λ on the velocity field for various values of the parameters is shown in Figure 4. As shown in Figure 4, the velocity field decays with raising values of $\lambda = 0$ to 0.6. Supporting flow is represented on a warm surface by λ values greater than zero, whereas resisting flow is shown on a cold surface by λ values less than zero. The influence of the Forchheimer number Fc on the velocity profile is seen in Figure 5 for varied $Wi = 0.0$ and 0.4 values. It is determined that the velocity field diminishes when the Forchheimer number rises. The effect of the Weissenberg number Wi on velocity flow is seen in Figure 6 for both magnetic field parameter scenarios. Figure 6 shows that increasing Wi depreciates the velocity field. The relaxation time is prolonged, which restricts fluid motion. The Weissenberg number is used in physical studies of viscoelastic flows to test the impact of elastic to viscous forces. As a result of lowering the velocity of the boundary layer, the Forchheimer number Fc and the porous medium K have different parameter values. In Figures 7 and 8, we present the variation of the Weissenberg number Wi and the magnetic field M of the base flow of the velocity profile. Figures 7 and 8 show that increasing Wi and M lowers the velocity distribution. The Lorentz force is formed when the magnetic field is strengthened. This force aids in reducing the velocity distribution as well as Wi.

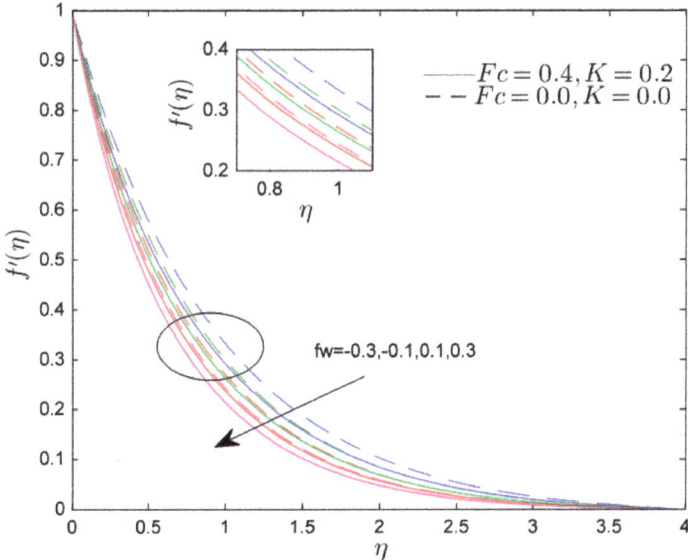

Figure 3. Effect of Suction/Injection parameter (fw) on $f'(\eta)$.

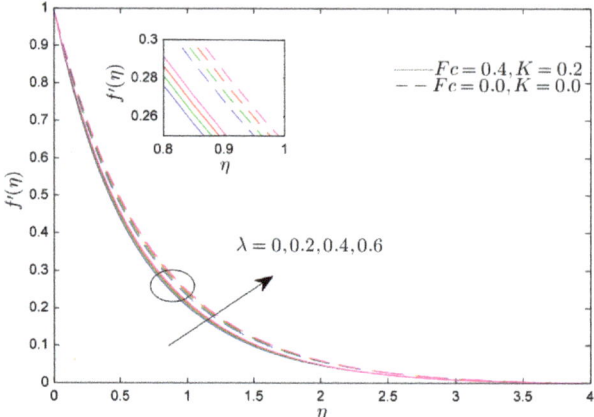

Figure 4. Effect of Richardson number (λ) on $f'(\eta)$.

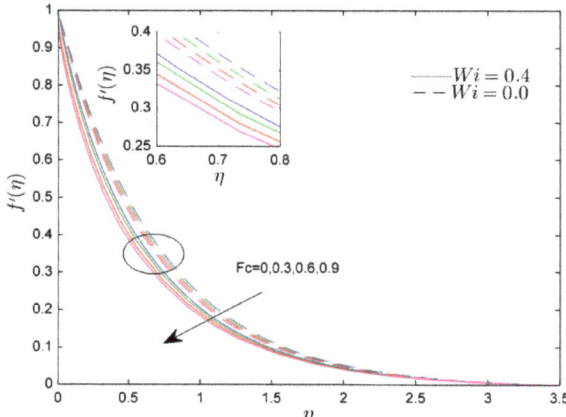

Figure 5. Effect of Forchheimer number (Fc) on $f'(\eta)$.

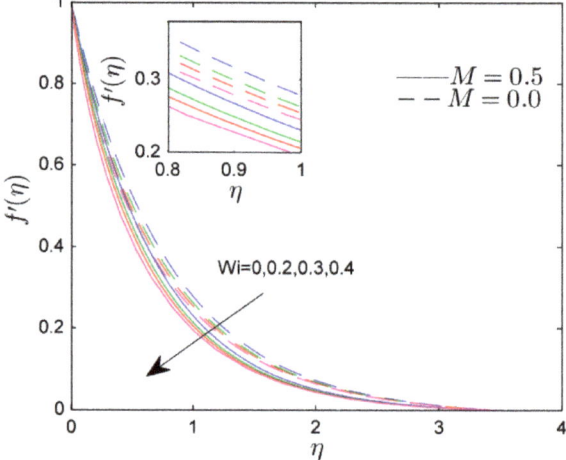

Figure 6. Effect of Weissenberg number (Wi) on $f'(\eta)$ when $M = 0, 0.5$.

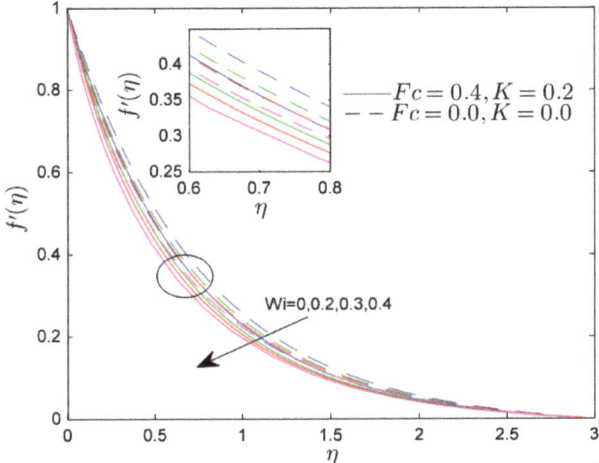

Figure 7. Effect of Weissenberg number (Wi) on $f'(\eta)$ when $Fc = 0$, 0.4 and $K = 0$, 0.4.

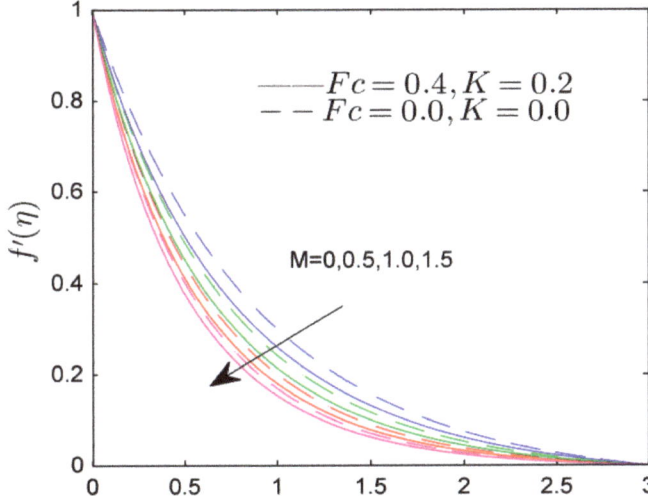

Figure 8. Effect of a Magnetic parameter (M) on $f'(\eta)$.

Specifications of the heat absorption H_A on temperature profile θ within the range of $0 \leq \eta \leq 8$ were established in Figure 9. In the graph, the flow depends on thermal radiation values. When the values of H_A increase, the temperature field also increases. Figure 10 demonstrates the impact of the suction/injection parameter on temperature for different parameters of the Forchheimer number Fc. The temperature field reduces for higher values of fw. Figure 11 reveals the influence of the radiation parameter R on the temperature profile. In these cases, the temperature profile was increased for various values of the thermal radiation grown by varying the thermal relaxation time parameters ω_θ. For various Brownian motion and chemical reaction parameters, Figures 12 and 13 indicate the performance of growing levels of thermal and solutal stratification parameters. The stratification parameter is the ratio of free stream temperature to fluid surface temperature. A significantly larger stratification parameter causes a rise in free stream temperature or a decrease in a nanofluid stream, whereas the concentration profile exhibits the inverse correlation. Temperature and concentration distribution within the boundary layer and the ambient fluid were reduced as the S_θ and S_ϕ values increased. The profiles of non-dimensional temperature and concentration against thermal relaxation time ω_θ and mass relaxation time parameter ω_ϕ were plotted in Figures 14 and 15. The temperature field shrinks for $N_T = 0.0$ and 0.5 as ω_θ increases. For $E = 0.0, 0.5$, an upsurge in ω_ϕ decreases the concentration gradient. Figure 16 shows the effect of Sc on the concentration profile with the range of $0 \leq \eta \leq 8$ when $N_T = 0.0$. It was discovered that concentration decreased as Sc increased. Because of this, the Schmidt number has an opposite relation with mass diffusivity. The characteristics of the thermophoresis parameter N_T on the profile of concentration were observed in Figure 17 for $S_\phi = 0.0$ and 0.2. The concentration here rises as a function of S_ϕ. The presence of a high value of N_T helps reduce the concentration boundary layer.

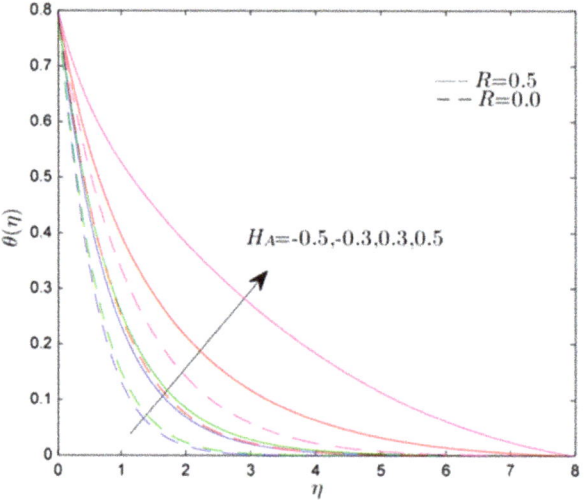

Figure 9. Effect of heat generation parameter (H_A) on $\theta(\eta)$.

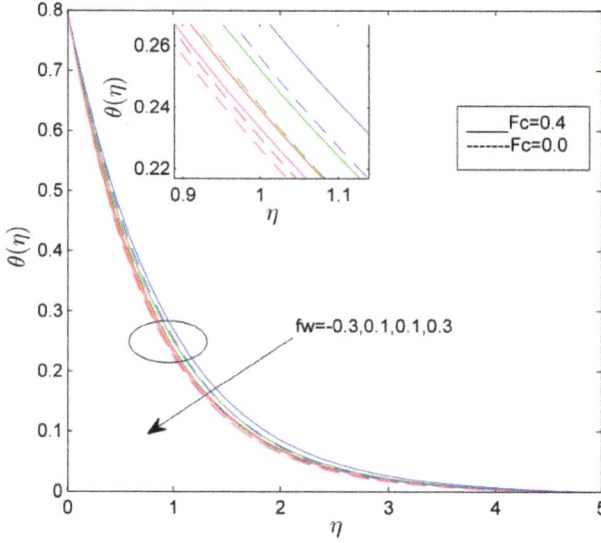

Figure 10. Effect of suction/injection parameter (fw) on $\theta(\eta)$.

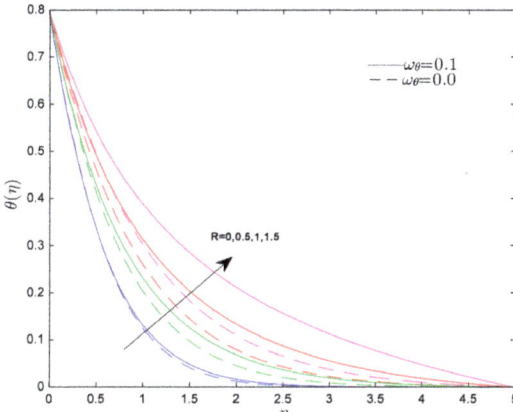

Figure 11. Effect of thermal radiation parameter (R) on $\theta(\eta)$.

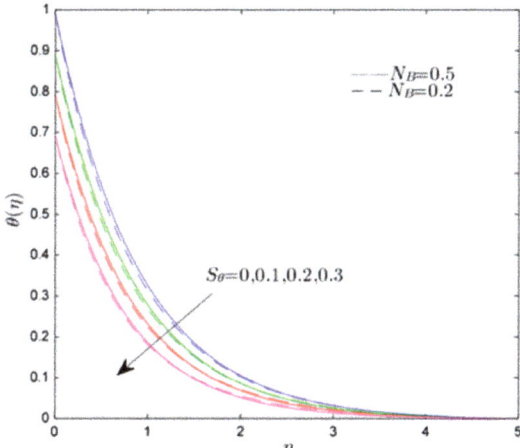

Figure 12. Effect of thermal stratification parameter (S_θ) on $\theta(\eta)$.

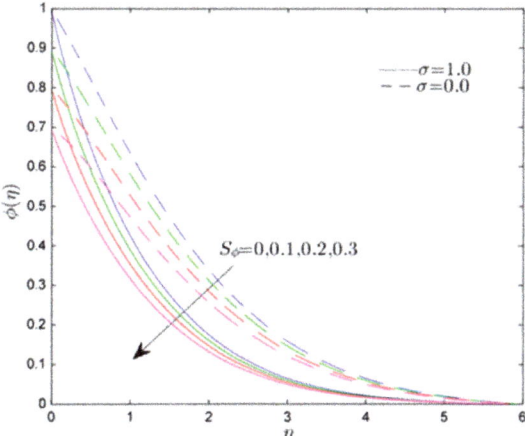

Figure 13. Effect of Solutal stratification (S_ϕ) on $\phi(\eta)$.

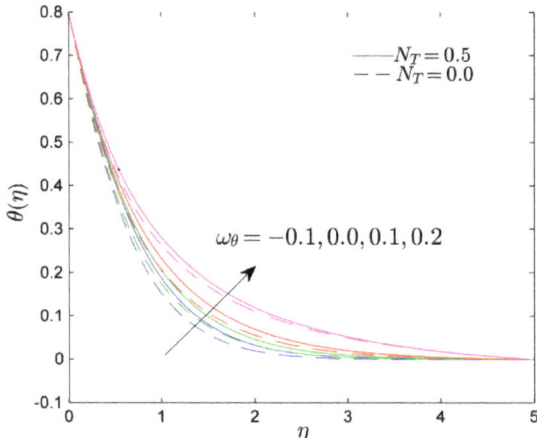

Figure 14. Effect of thermal relaxation time parameter (ω_θ) on $\theta(\eta)$.

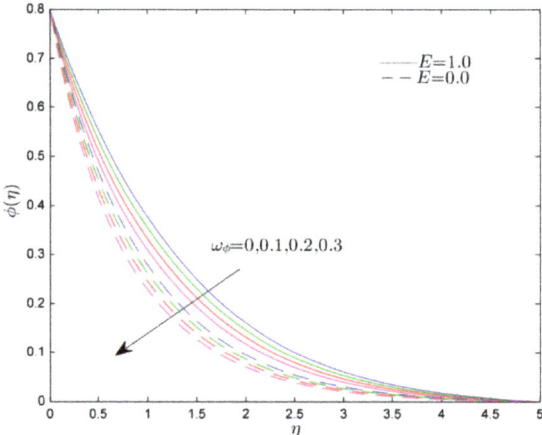

Figure 15. Effect of Mass relaxation parameter (ω_ϕ) on $\phi(\eta)$.

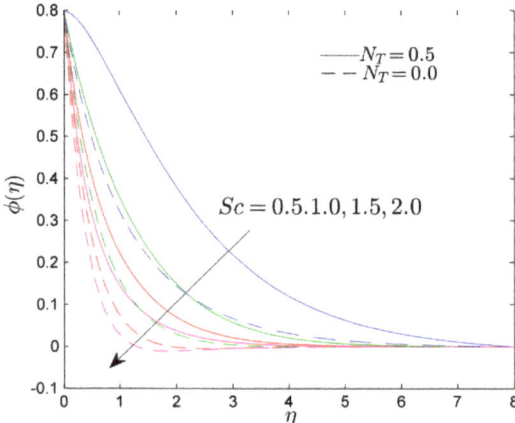

Figure 16. Effect of Schmidt number (Sc) on $\phi(\eta)$.

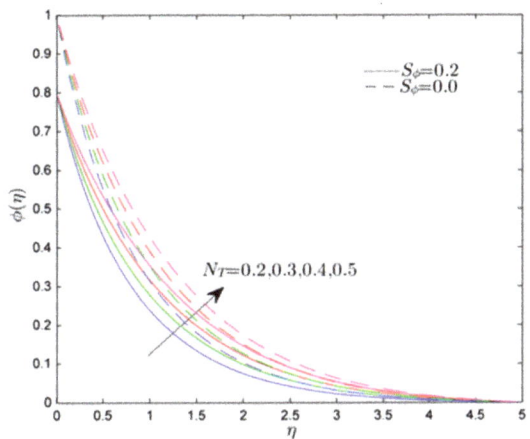

Figure 17. Effect of Thermophoresis parameter (N_T) on $\phi(\eta)$.

Figures 18–20 show the role of numerous parameters on skin friction coefficients and heat and mass transfer rates. We concluded from Figure 18a,b that the skin friction coefficient rises at fw and Wi while also increasing in Ri and Wi. Figure 19a,b display a lower Nusselt number due to a lower R and ω_θ as well as diminished N_T and S_θ. Figure 20a,b depict the mass diffusion rate for various estimates of fw and S_ϕ. The mass diffusion rate increased in this case as the values of fw and S_ϕ increased, and Sc and ω_ϕ also increased.

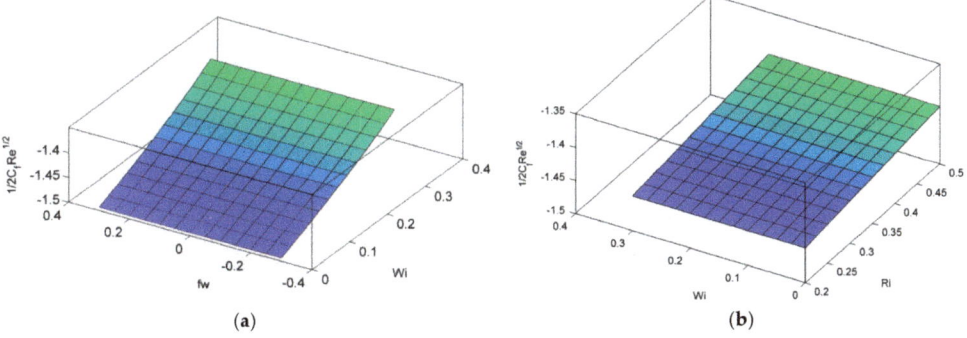

Figure 18. Three-dimensional plots of skin friction for (**a**) fw and Wi, (**b**) Ri, and Wi.

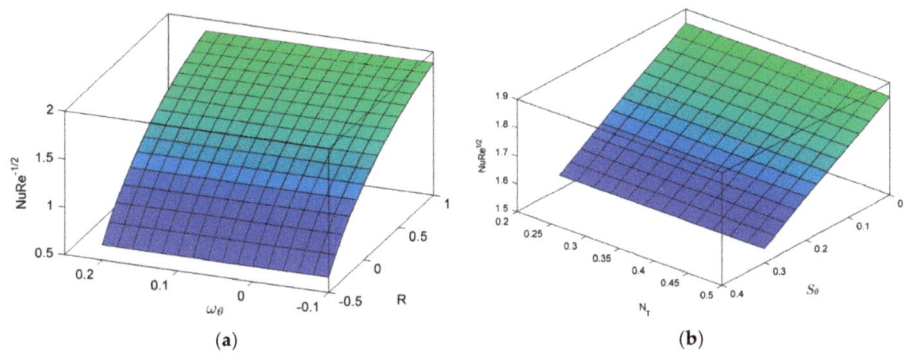

Figure 19. 3D plot of Nusselt number for (**a**) R and ω_θ, (**b**) N_T and S_θ.

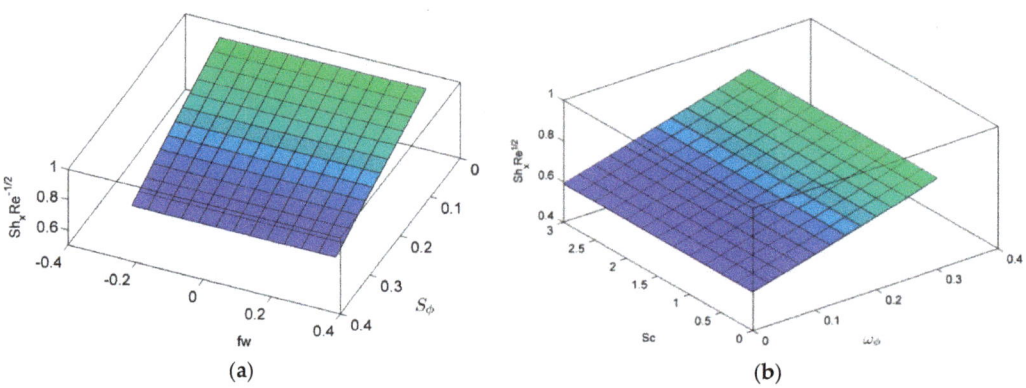

Figure 20. The 3D plot of Sherwood number for (**a**) fw and S_ϕ, (**b**) Sc and ω_ϕ.

5. Conclusions

The numerical and analytical results of the Darcy–Forchheimer Williamson nanofluid flow through a linear stretched surface were observed in this paper. In addition, the effects of thermal and solutal stratification, activation energy, and the Cattaneo–Christov dual flux were all considered. The following are the outcomes of this work.

i. The velocity profile was reduced by the Weissenberg number and Forchheimer number, while the mixed convective parameter shows the increasing tendency in velocity profile.
ii. The temperature distribution was raised with a high thermal relaxation time and radiation values.
iii. For higher estimations of Schmidt number and mass relaxation time, the concentration profile diminished.
iv. Increases in the thermal and mass stratification parameters reduce the temperature and concentration profile.
v. Heat and mass transfer rates were declined for large values of thermal radiation, thermal relaxation time, mass stratification, and suction parameter.

The findings discussed in this work should benefit scientists and engineers in various chemical and thermal engineering applications such as nuclear reactors, cooling systems, and hybrid power systems.

Author Contributions: Conceptualization, B.M.T. and S.K.; methodology, B.M.T. and M.K.A.K.; software, B.M.T.; validation, B.M.T., M.Y. and F.Ö.; formal analysis, S.K. and M.Y.; investigation, S.K. and M.K.A.K.; resources, M.Y. and F.Ö.; data curation, S.K.; writing—original draft, B.M.T.; writing—review and editing, B.M.T. and S.K.; visualization, M.Y. and F.Ö.; supervision, S.K. and M.K.A.K.; project administration, M.Y. and F.Ö.; funding acquisition, M.Y., M.K.A.K. and F.Ö. All authors have read and agreed to the published version of the manuscript.

Funding: This research received no external funding.

Acknowledgments: The authors are grateful to "Research and Development Wing, Live4Research, Tiruppur, Tamilnadu, India" for the valuable support throughout this project work. Fatma Özköse was supported by Research Fund of the Erciyes University. Project number: FDS-2021-11059.

Conflicts of Interest: The authors declare no conflict of interest.

Abbreviations

List of Symbols

Symbol	Description	Units
a	Stretching rate	(s^{-1})
C_B	Drag coefficient	
C_p	Specific heat	$(Jkg^{-1}k^{-1})$
B_0	Magnetic field	$(kgs^{-2}A^{-1})$
C_w	Surface concentration	(kgm^{-3})
$1g$	Acceleration due to gravity	(ms^{-2})
C_∞	Ambient fluid concentration	(kgm^{-3})
$1D_B$	Mass diffusivity	(m^2s^{-1})
C	Fluid concentration	(kgm^{-3})
D_T	Thermophoretic diffusion coefficient	(m^2s^{-1})
$E = (E_A/kT_\infty)$	Activation energy	Dimensionless
$Fc = (C_B/\sqrt{k_f})$	Forchheimer number	Dimensionless
$Gr = \left(\frac{g\beta(1-C_\infty)(T_w-T_\infty)x^3}{\vartheta^2}\right)$	Local Grashof number	Dimensionless
$H_A = (Q_1/\rho_f C_p a)$	Heat generation parameter	Dimensionless
k	Thermal conductivity	$(Wm^{-1}k^{-1})$
k_f	Permeability of porous medium	Dimensionless
$fw = -(V_w/\sqrt{a\vartheta})$	Suction/injection parameter	Dimensionless
k_p	Mean absorption coefficient	Dimensionless
k_r	Reaction rate	Dimensionless
$M = (\sigma B_0^2/\rho_f a)$	Magnetic parameter	Dimensionless
n	Fitted rate	Dimensionless
$N_B = (\tau D_B C_\infty/\vartheta)$	Brownian diffusion parameter	Dimensionless
$B_N = \left(\frac{(\rho_p-\rho_{f\infty})C_\infty}{\rho_{f\infty}\wedge_1(1-C_\infty)(T_w-T_0)}\right)$	Buoyancy ratio parameter	Dimensionless
$Pr = (k_f/(\rho c)_f)$	Prandtl number	Dimensionless
$Re_x = (U_w x/\vartheta)$	Local Reynolds number	Dimensionless
$\lambda = \left(\frac{Gr}{Re_x^2}\right) = \left(\frac{(g\wedge_1(1-C_\infty)(T_w-T_\infty))}{a^2 x}\right)$	Richardson number	Dimensionless
$Sc = (\vartheta/D_B)$	Schmidt number	Dimensionless
T	Fluid temperature	(K)
$Wi = (\wedge x\sqrt{2a^3/\vartheta})$	Weissenberg number	Dimensionless
T_∞	Ambient temperature	(K)
u and v	Velocity components	(ms^{-1})
U_w	Stretching surface velocity	(ms^{-1})
S_θ	Thermal stratification	Dimensionless
x and y	Direction coordinates	(m)
S_ϕ	Solutal stratification	Dimensionless
T_w	Wall temperature	(K)
$N_T = \left(\frac{\tau D_T(T_w-T_0)}{T_\infty \vartheta}\right)$	Thermophoresis parameter	Dimensionless
$R = (4\sigma^* T_\infty^3/k_p k_f)$	Thermal Radiation	Dimensionless
$\rho_f C_p$	Heat capacity	$(Jk^{-1}m^{-3})$

Greek Symbols

Symbol	Description	Units
$\omega_\theta = (a\Gamma_T)$	Thermal relaxation time parameter	Dimensionless
$\delta = \left(\frac{T_w-T_0}{T_\infty}\right)$	Temperature difference parameter	Dimensionless
$\omega_\phi = (a\Gamma_C)$	Mass relaxation parameter	Dimensionless
ρ_f	Fluid density	(kgm^{-3})
α	Thermal diffusivity	(m^2s^{-1})
$\wedge$	Williamson parameter	Dimensionless
θ	Non dimensional temperature	Dimensionless
ϕ	Non dimensional concentration	Dimensionless
σ_0	Dimensionless reaction rate	Dimensionless

References

1. Choi, S. Enhancing thermal conductivity of fluids with nanoparticles. In Proceedings of the ASME International Mechanical Engineering Congress & Exposition, San Francisco, CA, USA, 12–17 November 1995; pp. 99–105.
2. Buongiorno, J. Convective transport in nanofluids. *J. Heat Transf.* **2006**, *128*, 240–250. [CrossRef]
3. Williamson, R.V. The Flow of Pseudoplastic Materials. *Ind. Eng. Chem.* **1929**, *21*, 1108–1111. [CrossRef]
4. Nadeem, S.; Hussain, S.T.; Lee, C. Flow of a Williamson fluid over a stretching sheet. *Braz. J. Chem. Eng.* **2013**, *30*, 619–625. [CrossRef]
5. Hayat, T.; Shafiq, A.; Alsaedi, A. Hydromagnetic boundary layer flow of Williamson fluid in the presence of thermal radiation and Ohmic dissipation. *Alex. Eng. J.* **2016**, *55*, 2229–2240. [CrossRef]
6. Karthikeyan, S.; Bhuvaneswari, M.; Sivasankaran, S.; Rajan, S. Cross diffusion, radiation and chemical reaction effects on MHD combined convective flow towards a stagnation-point upon vertical plate with heat generation. *IOP Conf. Ser. Mater. Sci. Eng.* **2018**, *390*, 012088. [CrossRef]
7. Zeeshan, A.; Shehzad, N.; Atif, M.; Ellahi, R. SS symmetry Electromagnetic Flow of SWCNT/MWCNT Suspensions in Two Immiscible Water- and Engine-Oil-Based Newtonian Fluids through Porous Media. *Symmetry* **2022**, *14*, 406. [CrossRef]
8. Ahmed, K.; Akbar, T.; Muhammad, T. Physical Aspects of Homogeneous–Heterogeneous Reactions on MHD Williamson Fluid Flow across a Nonlinear Stretching Curved Surface Together with Convective Boundary Conditions. *Math. Probl. Eng.* **2021**, *2021*, 7016961. [CrossRef]
9. Waqas, H.; Farooq, U.; Ali, S.; Hashim, K.; Marjan, M.A. Numerical analysis of dual variable of conductivity in bioconvection flow of Carreau–Yasuda nanofluid containing gyrotactic motile microorganisms over a porous medium. *J. Therm. Anal. Calorim.* **2021**, *145*, 2033–2044. [CrossRef]
10. Shehzad, N.; Zeeshan, A.; Shakeel, M.; Ellahi, R.; Sait, S.M. Effects of Magnetohydrodynamics Flow on Multilayer Coatings of Newtonian and Non-Newtonian Fluids through Porous Inclined Rotating Channel. *Coatings* **2022**, *12*, 430. [CrossRef]
11. Loganathan, K.; Mohana, K.; Mohanraj, M.; Sakthivel, P.; Rajan, S. Impact of third-grade nanofluid flow across a convective surface in the presence of inclined Lorentz force: An approach to entropy optimization. *J. Therm. Anal. Calorim.* **2020**, *144*, 1935–1947. [CrossRef]
12. Yusuf, T.A.; Mabood, F.; Prasannakumara, B.C.; Sarris, I.E. Magneto-bioconvection flow of Williamson nanofluid over an inclined plate with gyrotactic microorganisms and entropy generation. *Fluids* **2021**, *6*, 109. [CrossRef]
13. Qureshi, M.A. Numerical simulation of heat transfer flow subject to MHD of Williamson nanofluid with thermal radiation. *Symmetry* **2021**, *13*, 10. [CrossRef]
14. Salahuddin, T.; Malik, M.Y.; Hussain, A.; Bilal, S.; Awais, M. MHD flow of Cattaneo–Christov heat flux model for Williamson fluid over a stretching sheet with variable thickness: Using numerical approach. *J. Magn. Magn. Mater.* **2016**, *401*, 991–997. [CrossRef]
15. Qayyum, S.; Khan, M.I.; Hayat, T.; Alsaedi, A.; Tamoor, M. Entropy generation in dissipative flow of Williamson fluid between two rotating disks. *Int. J. Heat Mass Transf.* **2018**, *127*, 933–942. [CrossRef]
16. Hayat, T.; Qayyum, A.; Alsaedi, A. Three-dimensional mixed convection squeezing flow. *Appl. Math. Mech.* **2015**, *36*, 47–60. [CrossRef]
17. Ibrahim, W.; Negara, M. Viscous dissipation effect on mixed convective heat transfer of MHD flow of Williamson nanofluid over a stretching cylinder in the presence of variable thermal conductivity and chemical reaction. *Heat Transf.* **2021**, *50*, 2427–2453. [CrossRef]
18. Khan, W.A.; Khan, M.; Alshomrani, A.S.; Ahmad, L. Numerical investigation of generalized Fourier's and Fick's laws for Sisko fluid flow. *J. Mol. Liq.* **2016**, *224*, 1016–1021. [CrossRef]
19. Eswaramoorthi, S.; Loganathan, K.; Jain, R.; Gyeltshen, S. Darcy-Forchheimer 3D Flow of Glycerin-Based Carbon Nanotubes on a Riga Plate with Nonlinear Thermal Radiation and Cattaneo–Christov Heat Flux. *J. Nanomater.* **2022**, *2022*, 5286921. [CrossRef]
20. Conduzionedelcalore, C.C.S. Atti del Seminario Matematico e Fisico dell'Universita di Modena e Reggio Emilia. *Modena by Seminario matematico e fisico Università di Modena* **1948**, *3*, 83–101.
21. Christov, C.I. On frame indifferent formulation of the Maxwell–Cattaneo model of finite-speed heat conduction. *Mech. Res. Commun.* **2009**, *36*, 481–486. [CrossRef]
22. Eswaramoorthi, S.; Alessa, N.; Sangeethavaanee, M.; Namgyel, N. Numerical and Analytical Investigation for Darcy-Forchheimer Flow of a Williamson fluid over a Riga Plate with Double Stratification and Cattaneo–Christov Dual Flux. *Adv. Math. Phys.* **2021**, *2021*, 1867824. [CrossRef]
23. Hayat, T.; Khan, M.I.; Farooq, M.; Alsaedi, A.; Waqas, M.; Yasmeen, T. Impact of Cattaneo–Christov heat flux model inflow of variable thermal conductivity fluid over a variable thicked surface. *Int. J. Heat Mass Transf.* **2016**, *99*, 702–710. [CrossRef]
24. Shankar, B. Goud Heat generation/absorption influence on steady stretched permeable surface on MHD flow of a micropolar fluid through a porous medium in the presence of variable suction/injection. *Int. J. Thermofluids* **2020**, *7–8*, 100044. [CrossRef]
25. Ali, B.; Nie, Y.; Hussain, S.; Manan, A.; Sadiq, M.T. Unsteady magneto-hydrodynamic transport of rotating Maxwell nanofluid flow on a stretching sheet with Cattaneo–Christov double diffusion and activation energy. *Therm. Sci. Eng. Prog.* **2020**, *20*, 100720. [CrossRef]
26. Abu-Hamden, N.H.; Alsulami, R.A.; Rawa, M.J.H.; Alazwari, M.A.; Goodarzi, M.; Safaei, M.R. A Significant Solar Energy Note on Powell-Eyring Nanofluid with Thermal Jump Conditions: Implementing Cattaneo–Christov Heat Flux Model. *Mathematics* **2021**, *9*, 669. [CrossRef]

27. Rashid, S.; Khan, M.I.; Hayat, T.; Ayub, M.; Alsaedi, A. Darcy–Forchheimer flow of Maxwell fluid with activation energy and thermal radiation over an exponential surface. *Appl. Nanosci.* **2020**, *10*, 2965–2975. [CrossRef]
28. Shafiq, A.; Rasool, G.; Khalique, C.M. Significance of thermal slip and convective boundary conditions in three dimensional rotating darcy-forchheimer nanofluid flow. *Symmetry* **2020**, *12*, 741. [CrossRef]
29. Rasool, G.; Zhang, T.; Chamkha, A.J.; Shafiq, A.; Tlili, I.; Shahzadi, G. Entropy generation and consequences of binary chemical reaction on mhd darcy-forchheimer Williamson nanofluid flow over non-linearly stretching surface. *Entropy* **2020**, *22*, 18. [CrossRef]
30. Hayat, T.; Aziz, A.; Muhammad, T.; Alsaedi, A. Darcy–Forchheimer Three-Dimensional Flow of Williamson Nanofluid over a Convectively Heated Nonlinear Stretching Surface. *Commun. Theor. Phys.* **2017**, *68*, 387–394. [CrossRef]
31. Bestman, A.R. Natural convection boundary layer with suction mass transfer in a porous medium. *Int. J. Energy Res.* **1990**, *14*, 389–396. [CrossRef]
32. Dawar, A.; Shah, Z.; Islam, S. Mathematical modeling and study of MHD flow of Williamson nanofluid over a nonlinear stretching plate with activation energy. *Heat Transf.* **2021**, *50*, 2558–2570. [CrossRef]
33. Alsaadi, F.E.; Hayat, T.; Khan, M.I.; Alsaadi, F.E. Heat transport and entropy optimization inflow of magneto-Williamson nanomaterial with Arrhenius activation energy. *Comput. Methods Programs Biomed.* **2020**, *183*, 105051. [CrossRef]
34. Muhammad, R.; Khan, M.I.; Jameel, M.; Khan, N.B. Fully developed Darcy-Forchheimer mixed convective flow over a curved surface with activation energy and entropy generation. *Comput. Methods Programs Biomed.* **2020**, *188*, 105298. [CrossRef] [PubMed]
35. Danook, S.H.; Jasim, Q.K.; Hussein, A.M. Nanofluid Convective Heat Transfer Enhancement Elliptical Tube inside Circular Tube under Turbulent Flow. *Math. Comput. Appl.* **2018**, *23*, 78. [CrossRef]
36. Jamshed, W.; Goodarzi, M.; Prakash, M.; Nisar, K.S.; Zakarya, M.; Abdel-Aty, A.H. Evaluating the unsteady Casson nanofluid over a stretching sheet with solar thermal radiation: An optimal case study. *Case Stud. Therm. Eng.* **2021**, *26*, 101160. [CrossRef]
37. Alghamdi, M.; Wakif, A.; Thumma, T.; Khan, U. Case Studies in Thermal Engineering Significance of variability in magnetic field strength and heat source on the radiative-convective motion of sodium alginate-based nanofluid within a Darcy-Brinkman porous structure bounded vertically by an irregular slender surface. *Case Stud. Therm. Eng.* **2021**, *28*, 101428. [CrossRef]
38. Loganathan, K.; Rajan, S. An entropy approach of Williamson nanofluid flow with Joule heating and zero nanoparticle mass flux. *J. Therm. Anal. Calorim.* **2020**, *141*, 2599–2612. [CrossRef]
39. Ibrahim, W.; Negara, M. The Investigation of MHD Williamson Nanofluid over Stretching Cylinder with the Effect of Activation Energy. *Adv. Math. Phys.* **2020**, *2020*, 9523630. [CrossRef]
40. Sajid, T.; Tanveer, S.; Sabir, Z.; Guirao, J.L.G. Impact of Activation Energy and Temperature-Dependent Heat Source/Sink on Maxwell-Sutterby Fluid. *Math. Probl. Eng.* **2020**, *2020*, 5251804. [CrossRef]
41. Zaib, A.; Abelman, S.; Chamkha, A.J.; Rashidi, M.M. Entropy Generation of Williamson Nanofluid near a Stagnation Point over a Moving Plate with Binary Chemical Reaction and Activation Energy. *Heat Transf. Res.* **2018**, *49*, 1131–1149. [CrossRef]
42. Hayat, T.; Aziz, A.; Muhammad, T.; Alsaedi, A. Effects of binary chemical reaction and Arrhenius activation energy in Darcy–Forchheimer three-dimensional flow of nanofluid subject to rotating frame. *J. Therm. Anal. Calorim.* **2019**, *136*, 1769–1779. [CrossRef]
43. Ibrahim, W.; Negara, M. Viscous dissipation effect on Williamson nanofluid over stretching/ shrinking wedge with thermal radiation and chemical reaction. *J. Phys. Commun.* **2020**, *4*, 045015. [CrossRef]
44. Ramzan, M.; Gul, H.; Kadry, S.; Chu, Y.M. Role of bioconvection in a three dimensional tangent hyperbolic partially ionized magnetized nanofluid flow with Cattaneo–Christov heat flux and activation energy. *Int. Commun. Heat Mass Transf.* **2021**, *120*, 104994. [CrossRef]
45. Kumar, R.; Sood, S.; Shehzad, S.A.; Sheikholeslami, M. Radiative heat transfer study for flow of non-Newtonian nanofluid past a Riga plate with variable thickness. *J. Mol. Liq.* **2017**, *248*, 143–152. [CrossRef]
46. Khan, W.A.; Khan, M.; Alshomrani, A.S. Impact of chemical processes on 3D Burgers fluid utilizing Cattaneo–Christov double-diffusion: Applications of non-Fourier's heat and non-Fick's mass flux models. *J. Mol. Liq.* **2016**, *223*, 1039–1047. [CrossRef]
47. Hayat, T.; Muhammad, K.; Farooq, M.; Alsaedi, A. Squeezed flow subject to Cattaneo–Christov heat flux and rotating frame. *J. Mol. Liq.* **2016**, *220*, 216–222. [CrossRef]
48. Loganathan, K.; Alessa, N.; Kayikci, S. Heat Transfer Analysis of 3-D Viscoelastic Nano-fluid Flow Over a Convectively Heated Porous Riga Plate with Cattaneo–Christov Double Flux. *Front. Phys.* **2021**, *9*, 1–12. [CrossRef]
49. Karthik, T.S.; Loganathan, K.; Shankar, A.N.; Carmichael, M.J.; Mohan, A.; Kaabar, M.K.A.; Kayikci, S. Zero and Nonzero Mass Flux Effects of Bioconvective Viscoelastic Nanofluid over a 3D Riga Surface with the Swimming of Gyrotactic Microorganisms. *Adv. Math. Phys.* **2021**, *2021*, 9914134. [CrossRef]
50. Ahmad, A.G.; Kaabar, M.K.A.; Rashid, S.; Abid, M. A Novel Numerical Treatment of Nonlinear and Nonequilibrium Model of Gradient Elution Chromatography considering Core-Shell Particles in the Column. *Math. Probl. Eng.* **2022**, *2022*, 1619702. [CrossRef]
51. Yavuz, M.; Sene, N.; Yıldız, M. Analysis of the Influences of Parameters in the Fractional Second-Grade Fluid Dynamics. *Mathematics* **2022**, *10*, 1125. [CrossRef]
52. Islam, T.; Yavuz, M.; Parveen, N.; Fayz-Al-Asad, M. Impact of Non-Uniform Periodic Magnetic Field on Unsteady Natural Convection Flow of Nanofluids in Square Enclosure. *Fractal Fract.* **2022**, *6*, 101. [CrossRef]

53. Fayz-Al-Asad, M.; Yavuz, M.; Alam, M.; Sarker, M.; Alam, M.; Bazighifan, O. Influence of fin length on magneto-combined convection heat transfer performance in a lid-driven wavy cavity. *Fractal Fract.* **2021**, *5*, 107. [CrossRef]
54. Sene, N. Second-grade fluid with Newtonian heating under Caputo fractional derivative: Analytical investigations via Laplace transforms. *Math. Model. Numer. Simul. Appl.* **2022**, *2*, 13–25. [CrossRef]
55. Khan, A.; Khan, A.; Sinan, M. Ion temperature gradient modes driven soliton and shock by reduction perturbation method for electron-ion magneto-plasma. *Math. Model. Numer. Simul. Appl.* **2022**, *2*, 1–12. [CrossRef]
56. Sreelakshmi, K.; Sarojamma, G.; Makinde, O.D. Dual stratification on the Darcy–Forchheimer flow of a maxwell nanofluid over a stretching surface. In *Defect and Diffusion Forum*; Trans Tech Publications Ltd.: Freienbach, Switzerland, 2018; Volume 387, pp. 207–217. [CrossRef]
57. Hayat, T.; Shah, F.; Hussain, Z.; Alsaedi, A. Outcomes of double stratification in Darcy–Forchheimer MHD flow of viscoelastic nanofluid. *J. Brazilian Soc. Mech. Sci. Eng.* **2018**, *40*, 145. [CrossRef]
58. Eswaramoorthi, S.; Alessa, N.; Sangeethavaanee, M.; Kayikci, S.; Namgyel, N. Mixed Convection and Thermally Radiative Flow of MHD Williamson Nanofluid with Arrhenius Activation Energy and Cattaneo–Christov Heat-Mass Flux. *J. Math.* **2021**, *2021*, 2490524. [CrossRef]
59. Ahmed, K.; Khan, W.A.; Akbar, T.; Rasool, G.; Alharbi, S.O.; Khan, I. Numerical Investigation of Mixed Convective Williamson Fluid Flow Over an Exponentially Stretching Permeable Curved Surface. *Fluids* **2021**, *6*, 260. [CrossRef]
60. Ramzan, M.; Gul, H.; Darcy-Forchheimer, M.Z. 3D Williamson nanofluid flow with generalized Fourier and Fick's laws in a stratified medium. *Bull. Polish Acad. Sci. Technol. Sci.* **2020**, *68*, 327–335. [CrossRef]
61. Haider, F.; Hayat, T.; Alsaedi, A. Flow of hybrid nanofluid through Darcy-Forchheimer porous space with variable characteristics. *Alex. Eng. J.* **2021**, *60*, 3047–3056. [CrossRef]
62. Irfan, M.; Khan, M. Simultaneous impact of nonlinear radiative heat flux and Arrhenius activation energy inflow of chemically reacting Carreau nanofluid. *Appl. Nanosci.* **2020**, *10*, 2977–2988. [CrossRef]
63. Hayat, T.; Naz, S.; Waqas, M.; Alsaedi, A. Effectiveness of Darcy-Forchheimer and nonlinear mixed convection aspects in stratified Maxwell nanomaterial flow induced by convectively heated surface. *Appl. Math. Mech.* **2018**, *39*, 1373–1384. [CrossRef]
64. Kumar, K.A.; Reddy, J.V.R.; Sugunamma, V.; Sandeep, N. MHD Carreau fluid flow past a melting surface with Cattaneo–Christov heat flux. In *Applied Mathematics and Scientific Computing*; Trends in Mathematics; Birkhäuser: Cham, Switzerland, 2019; pp. 325–336. [CrossRef]
65. Hayat, T.; Muhammad, T.; Shehzad, S.A.; Alsaedi, A.; Al-Solamy, F. Radiative Three-Dimensional Flow with Chemical Reaction. *Int. J. Chem. React. Eng.* **2016**, *14*, 79–91. [CrossRef]
66. Sahoo, A.; Nandkeolyar, R. Entropy generation in convective radiative flow of a Casson nanofluid in non-Darcy porous medium with Hall current and activation energy: The multiple regression model. *Appl. Math. Comput.* **2021**, *402*, 125923. [CrossRef]
67. Chu, Y.M.; Nazeer, M.; Khan, M.I.; Ali, W.; Zafar, Z.; Kadry, S.; Abdelmalek, Z. Entropy analysis in the Rabinowitsch fluid model through inclined Wavy Channel: Constant and variable properties. *Int. Commun. Heat Mass Transf.* **2020**, *119*, 104980. [CrossRef]
68. Hayat, T.; Javed, M.; Imtiaz, M.; Alsaedi, A. Double stratification in the MHD flow of a nanofluid due to a rotating disk with variable thickness. *Eur. Phys. J. Plus* **2017**, *132*, 146. [CrossRef]
69. Mustafa, M.; Khan, J.A.; Hayat, T.; Alsaedi, A. Buoyancy Effects on the MHD nanofluid flow past a vertical surface with chemical reaction and activation energy. *Int. J. Heat Mass Transf.* **2017**, *108*, 1340–1346. [CrossRef]
70. Loganathan, K.; Alessa, N.; Namgyel, N.; Karthik, T.S. MHD Flow of Thermally Radiative Maxwell Fluid Past a Heated Stretching Sheet with Cattaneo—Christov Dual Diffusion. *J. Math.* **2021**, *2021*, 5562667. [CrossRef]

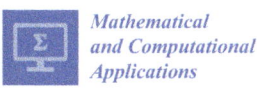

Article

Exploration of Darcy–Forchheimer Flows of Non-Newtonian Casson and Williamson Conveying Tiny Particles Experiencing Binary Chemical Reaction and Thermal Radiation: Comparative Analysis

Sheniyappan Eswaramoorthi [1], S. Thamaraiselvi [1] and Karuppusamy Loganathan [2,3,*]

[1] Department of Mathematics, Dr. N.G.P. Arts and Science College, Coimbatore 641035, India; eswaramoorthi@drngpasc.ac.in (S.E.); 202ma022@drngpasc.ac.in (S.T.)
[2] Department of Mathematics and Statistics, Manipal University Jaipur, Jaipur 303007, India
[3] Research and Development Wing, Live4Research, Tiruppur 638106, India
* Correspondence: loganathankaruppusamy304@gmail.com

Abstract: This discussion intends to scrutinize the Darcy–Forchheimer flow of Casson–Williamson nanofluid in a stretching surface with non-linear thermal radiation, suction and heat consumption. In addition, this investigation assimilates the influence of the Brownian motion, thermophoresis, activation energy and binary chemical reaction effects. Cattaneo–Christov heat-mass flux theory is used to frame the energy and nanoparticle concentration equations. The suitable transformation is used to remodel the governing PDE model into an ODE model. The remodeled flow problems are numerically solved via the BVP4C scheme. The effects of various material characteristics on nanofluid velocity, nanofluid temperature and nanofluid concentration, as well as connected engineering aspects such as drag force, heat, and mass transfer gradients, are also calculated and displayed through tables, charts and figures. It is noticed that the nanofluid velocity upsurges when improving the quantity of Richardson number, and it downfalls for larger magnitudes of magnetic field and porosity parameters. The nanofluid temperature grows when enhancing the radiation parameter and Eckert number. The nanoparticle concentration upgrades for larger values of activation energy parameter while it slumps against the reaction rate parameter. The surface shear stress for the Williamson nanofluid is greater than the Casson nanofluid. There are more heat transfer gradient losses the greater the heat generation/absorption parameter and Eckert number. In addition, the local Sherwood number grows when strengthening the Forchheimer number and fitted rate parameter.

Keywords: Casson and Williamson fluid; MHD; Cattaneo–Christov dual flux; non-linear thermal radiation; binary chemical reaction

Citation: Eswaramoorthi, S.; Thamaraiselvi, S.; Loganathan, K. Exploration of Darcy–Forchheimer Flows of Non-Newtonian Casson and Williamson Conveying Tiny Particles Experiencing Binary Chemical Reaction and Thermal Radiation: Comparative Analysis. *Math. Comput. Appl.* **2022**, *27*, 52. https://doi.org/10.3390/mca27030052

Academic Editors: Mehmet Yavuz and Ioannis Dassios

Received: 23 May 2022
Accepted: 17 June 2022
Published: 20 June 2022

Publisher's Note: MDPI stays neutral with regard to jurisdictional claims in published maps and institutional affiliations.

Copyright: © 2022 by the authors. Licensee MDPI, Basel, Switzerland. This article is an open access article distributed under the terms and conditions of the Creative Commons Attribution (CC BY) license (https://creativecommons.org/licenses/by/4.0/).

1. Introduction

Nowadays, heat transfer enrichment is a fascinating topic because of its numerous applications in engineering and industry. In many industrial processes, regular fluids (water, oil and ethylene glycol) are often employed. However, these fluids have a low heat transfer phenomenon because of their low thermal conductivity. To address this shortcoming, the nanometer-sized particle was mixed with regular fluids and enriches the regular fluid thermal conductivity; see [1–3]. This is the way of preparing the nanofluid, and this fluid has played an essential role in many fields such as solar water heating, heat exchangers, transformer cooling, cancer therapy, etc. Choi [4] was the first to publish the characteristics of nanoparticles, which were coupled with experimental evidence data. The nanofluid flow over a cylinder with suction was explored by Sheikholeslami [5]. It was uncovered that the local Nusselt number elevates when mounting the nanoparticle volume fraction values. Ramana Reddy et al. [6] addressed the time-dependent MHD flow of nanofluid past a slendering surface. It was detected that the fluid temperature progressed when enhancing the Brownian motion parameter. Makinde et al. [7] employed the impact of Brownian motion and thermophoresis effects of MHD flow of nanofluid past a heated surface. It was noted that the heat transfer rate decays when upturning the quantity of the Brownian motion parameter. The consequences of Brownian motion and thermophoresis of stagnation point flow of nanofluid past a non-uniform cylinder were presented by Shafey et al. [8]. It was noticed that the heat transfer gradient slumps when rising the thermophoresis quantity. Rasheed et al. [9] addressed the MHD flow of water-based nanofluids with convective heating conditions. It was seen that the thermophoretic parameter improves the thickness of the thermal boundary layer.

The non-Newtonian fluid has stimulated various scientists to investigate the events of heat-mass transport because of its necessary part in industrial and engineering processes, such as drilling muds, polymer extrusion, optical fibers, polymer production, etc. The non-Newtonian fluid defies the Newton's viscosity law. To deal with the huge nature of the rheological behavior of such fluids, several non-Newtonian models have been devised. Casson fluid is one of the non-Newtonian type models, and at the infinite non-linear shear rate, the fluid material's yield stress does not push flow, and it has zero viscosity. The MHD flow of Casson nanofluid past a heated surface with viscous dissipation was analyzed by Alotaibi et al. [10]. It was found that the drag force coefficient decays when strengthening the Casson parameter. Nayak et al. [11] provide the impact of the triple diffusive bioconvective flow of Casson nanofluid past a sheet. It was observed that the wall motile micro-organism decimates when developing the Casson parameter. Entropy optimization of MHD flow of Casson nanofluid over a stretching surface with convective heating and mass conditions was illustrated by Butt et al. [12]. It was proved that the Casson fluid parameter leads to a slow down of the entropy production. Ibrahim et al. [13] discovered the chemically reactive MHD flow of Casson nanofluid past a stretching surface with viscous dissipation. It was noticed that the nanoparticle concentration profile decreases when raising the Casson parameter. The multiple slip effects of a Casson nanofluid on a stretching surface were numerically performed by Afify [14], and he proved that the mass transfer gradient enriches when enhancing the Casson parameter. Varun Kumar et al. [15] scrutinized the MHD chemically reactive flow of Casson nanoliquid past a curved stretching sheet. It was noted that liquid velocity depresses when enhancing the Casson parameter. The 2D flow of Casson nanofluid on a thin moving needle was examined by Naveen Kumar et al. [16], and they proved that the thermophoresis parameter improves the mass transfer rate. Gohar et al. [17] studied the Darcy–Forchheimer flow of Casson hybrid nanofluid on a curved surface. It was detected that the Casson parameter suppresses the hybrid nanofluid motion.

Williamson fluid is also the non-Newtonian division model, which exhibits the shear thinning property; that is, the fluid viscosity decays when rising the shear stress rate. Waqas et al. [18] examined the MHD flow of Williamson nanofluid past a heated wedge. It was revealed that the wall shear stress downfalls when mounting the Weissenberg number. The MHD flow of Williamson nanofluid past a porous stretching surface with suction was presented by Li et al. [19]. It was noted that the Williamson parameter leads to depromoting the friction drag. Ahmed et al. [20] presented the consequences of MHD Williamson nanofluid flow on an exponentially porous stretching surface. It was uncovered that the fluid speed depresses when escalating the Williamson parameter. The 2D flow of Williamson fluid over a cylinder was addressed by Iqbal et al. [21], and it was acknowledged that the skin friction coefficient decreases as the Weissenberg number increases. Gorla and Gireesha [22] demonstrated the convective heat transport analysis of a Williamson nanofluid past the stretching surface. It was noticed that the nanofluid volume fraction intensifies when heightening the Williamson parameter. The MHD flow of Williamson nanofluid past a heated stretching surface was examined by Srinivasulu and Goud [23]. It was concluded that the heat transfer gradient downfalls when promoting the quantity of the Williamson parameter.

In the last few decades, many researchers have focused on studying the thermal radiation effect because the consequences of thermal radiation in flow structures are helpful in atomic reactors, spacecraft, ship compressors, and solar radiation. Most of the investigation is based on linearized Rosseland approximation; however, this concept is applicative when the temperature distinction between ambient and fluid is small. However, on many industrial occasions, this difference is enormous. So, a non-linearized Rosseland approximation is introduced to overcome this restriction. MHD Casson nanofluid in a bi-directional heated stretching surface with non-linear radiation was deliberated by Mahanta et al. [24]. It was detected that the temperature ratio parameter leads to enriching the entropy generation profile. Humane et al. [25] scrutinized the thermally radiative MHD Casson–Williamson nanofluid flow on a porous stretching surface with a chemical reaction. MHD heat-generating Casson nanofluid through a thin needle with non-linear thermal radiation was examined by Akinshilo et al. [26]. Ghasemi et al.[27] numerically solved the non-linear thermal radiative flow of nanofluid with a magnetic field via the spectral relaxation method. It was noted that the nanofluid concentration upsurges when enhancing the thermal radiation parameter. The bio-convective flow of Carreau nanofluid with non-linear thermal radiation with a magnetic dipole was presented by Imran et al. [28]. It was shown that the thermal boundary layer thickens when the temperature ratio parameter is large. Bhatti et al. [29] demonstrated the impact of MHD flow of Williamson nanofluid through a shrinking porous sheet. The problem of non-linear radiative flow of nanofluid with the inclined magnetic field was numerically solved via the finite difference method by Mahanthesh and Thriveni [30]. Their results clearly explain that the fluid temperature ascends when upgrading the quantity of the thermal radiation parameter. Cao et al. [31] investigated the non-linear thermal radiative flow of a ternary-hybrid nanofluid with partial slip. The 3D radiative flow of Cu/Ag-water-based nanofluid with entropy optimization was illustrated by Eswaramoorthi et al. [32], and they detected that the Bejan number rises as the radiation parameter enhances.

The smallest amount of energy necessary to start a chemical reaction is known as activation energy. This conception was initiated by Arrhenius in 1889, and this incident has plentiful appliances in geothermal engineering, water emulsions, oil emulsion and food processing. Shah et al. [33] addressed the chemically reactive flow of Casson nanofluid with activation energy and radiation, and they found that activation energy leads to magnifying the nanoparticle concentration. The 3D time-dependent flow of Williamson nanofluid with heat generation and the activation energy was inspected by Aziz et al. [34]. Their findings show that the higher chemical reaction parameter suppresses the nanofluid concentration. Kalaivanan et al. [35] discussed the Arrhenius activation energy and non-linear thermal impacts of second-grade nanofluid past a stretching surface. It was exposed that the heat transfer gradient weakens when strengthening the exponential fitted rate. The MHD flow of Casson nanofluid over a stretching cylinder with Arrhenius activation energy was examined by Zeeshan et al. [36]. It was seen that the nanoparticle concentration enhances for strengthening the activation energy parameter. Tayyab et al. [37] securitized the consequences of Darcy–Forchheimer flow of 3D nanofluid on a sheet with activation energy. The 3D Darcy–Forchheimer flow past a porous space with the presence of Arrhenius activation energy was presented by Rashid et al. [38]. It was revealed that the reaction rate leads to a decline in the nanoparticle concentration profile. Alsaadi et al. [39] elucidated the flow of MHD WNF with the influence of Arrhenius activation energy. The impact of activation energy of a second-grade nanofluid on a surface with heat source/sink was analyzed by Punith Gowda et al. [40]. Varun Kumar et al. [41] studied the impact of Arrhenius activation energy on a hybrid nanofluid past a curved surface. It was proved that the nanofluid concentration improves when escalating the activation energy parameter. The MHD flow of Williamson nanofluid with activation energy was investigated by Tamilzharasan et al. [42], and they found that the activation energy parameter improves the heat transfer rate.

In light of the above analysis, no research articles provide the impact of the non-linear thermal radiative flow of Casson–Williamson nanofluid over a heated stretchy plate with activation energy. In addition, zero nanoparticle mass flux and Cattaneo–Christov heat-mass flux conditions are included in our study. This research has implications for thermal sciences, food processing, chemical engineering, polymer extrusion, and many other fields in which heat conduction and convection are improved. In the limiting scenarios, the calculated values derived from specified parameters are consistent with existing findings in the literature, while tables and graphs have been built and explained to spread the responses of dimensionless quantities. This type of flow model is used in food processing, heavy mechanical apparatus, enzymes, ceramic processing, heating/cooling processes, etc.

2. Mathematical Formulation

Let us consider the chemically reactive 2D Darcy–Forchheimer flow of Casson–Williamson nanofluid past a stretchy plate. The x-axis is in the stretching direction and the y-axis is perpendicular to it. The uniform magnetic field of strength B_0 is applied in the y-direction, and the induced magnetic effect is neglected because of the small quantity of Reynolds number. Moreover, the flow is disclosed under the consequences of Arrhenius activation energy; suction/injection, viscous dissipation and non-linear thermal radiation are all taken into our account. The zero nanoparticle mass flux condition is assumed on the surface of the sheet. Let T_w and C_w represent the temperature and nanoparticle concentration, which are higher than the free-stream temperature (T_∞) and nanoparticle concentration (C_∞), see Figure 1.

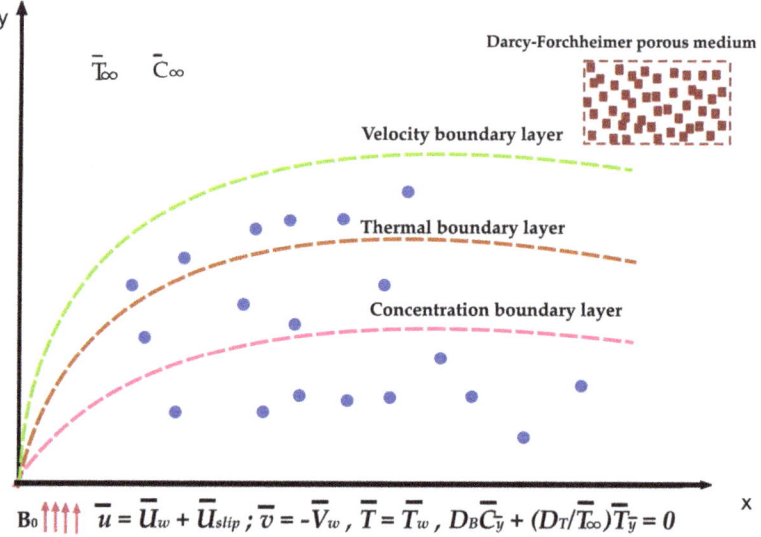

Figure 1. Physical model of flow.

The Cauchy stress tensor of Williamson fluid is expressed as $S = -pI + \tau_1$, where $\tau_1 = \left[\mu_\infty + \frac{(\mu_0 - \mu_\infty)}{1 - \Gamma_1 \gamma_1^*}\right] A_1$; here, τ_1 is the extra stress tensor, μ_0 is the limiting viscosity at zero shear rate, μ_∞ is the limiting viscosity at infinity shear rate, $\Gamma_1 > 0$ is the time constant and A_1 is the Rivlin–Ericson tensor. The simplified form of the extra stress tensor is $\tau_1 = \left[+\frac{\mu_0}{1-\Gamma_1 \gamma_1^*}\right] A_1$; see [43].

Similarly, Casson fluid flow is

$$\tau_{ij} = \begin{cases} 2\left(\mu_{nf} + \dfrac{Q_y}{\sqrt{2\pi}}\right)k_{ij}, & \pi > \pi_c \\ 2\left(\mu_{nf} + \dfrac{Q_y}{\sqrt{2\pi_c}}\right)k_{ij}, & \pi < \pi_c \end{cases}$$

here, Q_y is the yield stress of fluid, k_{ij} is the (i,j)th laceration direction component rate, $\pi = k_{ij}k_{ij}$ is the product of the component of rate of deformation with itself and π_c is the critical value of the product of the component of the strain tensor rate with itself; see [44].

The flow model may be described as follows using the given assumptions; see Mustafa et al. [45].

$$\overline{u}_{\overline{x}} + \overline{v}_{\overline{y}} = 0 \tag{1}$$

$$\overline{u}\overline{u}_{\overline{x}} + \overline{v}\overline{u}_{\overline{y}} = \nu\left(1 + \frac{1}{\beta}\right)\overline{u}_{\overline{y}\overline{y}} + \sqrt{2}\Gamma\nu\overline{u}_{\overline{y}}\overline{u}_{\overline{y}\overline{y}} - \frac{\nu}{k_1}\overline{u} - \frac{C_b}{\overline{x}\sqrt{k_1}}\overline{u}^2 - \frac{\sigma B_0^2 \overline{u}}{\rho_f}$$

$$+ \frac{1}{\rho_f}\left[(1 - \overline{C}_\infty)\rho_{f\infty}\beta(\overline{T} - \overline{T}_\infty) - (\rho_p - \rho_{f\infty})(\overline{C} - \overline{C}_\infty)\right]g, \tag{2}$$

$$\overline{u}\overline{T}_{\overline{x}} + \overline{v}\overline{T}_{\overline{y}} + \lambda_T \Omega_T = \alpha \overline{T}_{\overline{y}\overline{y}}$$

$$+ \frac{1}{\rho C_p}\frac{16\sigma^*}{3k^*}\frac{\partial}{\partial \overline{y}}\left(\overline{T}^3 \overline{T}_{\overline{y}}\right) + \frac{Q}{\rho_f C_p}(\overline{T} - \overline{T}_\infty) + \tau\left[D_B \overline{T}_{\overline{y}}\overline{C}_{\overline{y}} + \frac{D_T}{\overline{T}_\infty}\overline{T}_{\overline{y}}^2\right] + \frac{\mu}{\rho C_p}\left(1 + \frac{1}{\beta}\right)\overline{u}_{\overline{y}}^2 \tag{3}$$

$$\overline{u}\overline{C}_{\overline{x}} + \overline{v}\overline{C}_{\overline{y}} + \lambda_C \Omega_C = D_B \overline{C}_{\overline{y}\overline{y}} + \frac{D_T}{\overline{T}_\infty}\overline{C}_{\overline{y}\overline{y}} - k_r^2(\overline{C} - \overline{C}_\infty)\left(\frac{\overline{T}}{\overline{T}_\infty}\right)^n \exp\left(\frac{-E_a}{\kappa \overline{T}}\right) \tag{4}$$

where

$$\Omega_T = \overline{u}\overline{u}_{\overline{x}}\overline{T}_{\overline{x}} + \overline{v}\overline{v}_{\overline{y}}\overline{T}_{\overline{y}} + \overline{u}^2 \overline{T}_{\overline{x}\overline{x}} + \overline{v}^2 \overline{T}_{\overline{y}\overline{y}} + 2\overline{u}\overline{v}\overline{T}_{\overline{x}\overline{y}} + \overline{u}\overline{v}_{\overline{x}}\overline{T}_{\overline{y}} + \overline{v}\overline{u}_{\overline{y}}\overline{T}_{\overline{x}}$$

$$\Omega_C = \overline{u}\overline{u}_{\overline{x}}\overline{C}_{\overline{x}} + \overline{v}\overline{v}_{\overline{y}}\overline{C}_{\overline{y}} + \overline{u}^2 \overline{C}_{\overline{x}\overline{x}} + \overline{v}^2 \overline{C}_{\overline{y}\overline{y}} + 2\overline{u}\overline{v}\overline{C}_{\overline{x}\overline{y}} + \overline{u}\overline{v}_{\overline{x}}\overline{C}_{\overline{y}} + \overline{v}\overline{u}_{\overline{y}}\overline{C}_{\overline{x}}$$

The boundary conditions are

$$\overline{u} = \overline{U}_\omega + L\left(1 + \frac{1}{\beta} + \Gamma \overline{u}_{\overline{y}}\right)\overline{u}_{\overline{y}}; \overline{v} = -\overline{V}_\omega \overline{T} = \overline{T}_\omega, D_B \overline{C}_{\overline{y}} + \frac{D_T}{\overline{T}_\infty}\overline{T}_{\overline{y}} = 0 \text{ as } \overline{y} = 0$$

$$\overline{u} \to 0, \overline{T} \to \overline{T}_\infty, \overline{C} \to \overline{C}_\infty \text{ as } \overline{y} \to \infty \tag{5}$$

From the above Equations (Equations (2) and (5)), $\beta \to \infty$ & $\Gamma \neq 0$ is treated as a Williamson fluid model and $\beta \neq \infty$ & $\Gamma = 0$ is treated as a Casson fluid model.

The dimensionless parameters are

$$\varpi = \sqrt{\frac{a}{\nu}}\overline{y}; \overline{u} = a\overline{x}v_1'; \overline{v} = -\sqrt{a\nu}v_1(\varpi)$$

$$v_2(\varpi) = \frac{\overline{T} - \overline{T}_\infty}{\overline{T}_\omega - \overline{T}_\infty}; v_3(\varpi) = \frac{\overline{C} - \overline{C}_\infty}{\overline{C}_\infty} \tag{6}$$

Substituting Equation (6) into Equations (2)–(4), we obtain

$$\left(1+\frac{1}{\beta}\right)v_1'''(\varpi) - v_1'^2(\varpi) + v_1(\varpi)v_1''(\varpi) + We v_1''(\varpi)v_1'''(\varpi) - \lambda v_1'(\varpi) - Fr v_1'^2(\varpi) - M v_1'(\varpi)$$
$$+ Ri(v_2(\varpi) - Nr v_3(\varpi)) = 0 \quad (7)$$

$$\frac{1}{Pr}v_2''(\varpi) + \frac{1}{Pr}\frac{4}{3}R[(\theta_w - 1)^3\{v_2''(\varpi)v_2^3(\varpi) + 3v_2^2(\varpi)v_2'^2(\varpi)\} + 3(\theta_w - 1)^2\{v_2''(\varpi)v_2^2(\varpi)$$
$$+ 2v_2(\varpi)v_2'(\varpi)^2\} + 3(\theta_w - 1)\{v_2''(\varpi)v_2(\varpi) + v_2'^2(\varpi)\} + v_2''(\varpi)] + v_1(\varpi)v_2'(\varpi)$$
$$-\Gamma_T\{v_1(\varpi)v_1'(\varpi)v_2'(\varpi) + v_1^2(\varpi)v_2''(\varpi)\} + Hg v_2 + \left(1 + \frac{1}{\beta}\right)Ec v_1''^2 + Nb v_2' v_3' + Nt v_2'^2 = 0 \quad (8)$$

$$\frac{1}{Sc}v_3''(\varpi) + v_1(\varpi)v_3'(\varpi) - \Gamma_C\{v_1(\varpi)v_1'(\varpi)v_3'(\varpi) + v_1^2(\varpi)v_3''(\varpi)\} + \frac{1}{Sc}\left(\frac{Nt}{Nb}\right)v_2''(\varpi)$$
$$-\sigma^{**}(1 + \delta v_2(\varpi))^n v_3(\varpi) \exp\left(\frac{-E}{1 + \delta v_2(\varpi)}\right) = 0 \quad (9)$$

The covered boundary conditions are

$$v_1(0) = fw, v_1'(0) = 1 + K\left[1 + \frac{1}{\beta} + \frac{We}{\sqrt{2}}v_1''(0)\right]v_1''(0), v_2(0) = 1, Nb v_3'(0) + Nt v_2'(0) = 0$$
$$v_1'(\infty) \to 0, v_2(\infty) \to 0, v_3(\infty) \to 0 \quad (10)$$

The non-dimensional form of skin friction coefficient, local Nusselt number and local Sherwood number are expressed as

$$\frac{1}{2}Cf\sqrt{Re} = -\left[\left(1 + \frac{1}{\beta}\right)v_1''(0) + \frac{We}{2}v_1''^2(0)\right]; \frac{Nu}{\sqrt{Re}} = -\left[1 + \frac{4}{3}R\{1 + (\theta_w - 1)v_2(0)\}^3\right]v_2'(0)$$
$$\frac{Sh}{\sqrt{Re}} = \frac{Nb}{Nt}v_2'(0)$$

3. Numerical Solution

The derived ODE models (7)–(9) along with the conditions (10) are numerically solved by applying the MATLAB bvp4c scheme. Initially, the higher-order terms are converted into first-order terms, see [46,47].

Let $v_1 = y_1, v_1' = y_2, v_1'' = y_3, v_1''' = y_3', v_2 = y_4, v_2' = y_5, v_2'' = y_5', v_3 = y_6, v_3' = y_7, v_3'' = y_7'$.

$$y_1' = y_2$$
$$y_2' = y_3$$
$$y_3' = \frac{y_2^2 - y_1 y_3 + \lambda y_2 + Fr y_2^2 + M y_2 - Ri[y_4 - Nr y_6]}{(1 + \frac{1}{\beta}) + We y_3}$$
$$y_4' = y_5$$
$$A = -y_1 y_5 + \Gamma_T y_1 y_2 y_5 - \frac{1}{Pr}\frac{4}{3}R[(3\theta_n - 1)^3 y_4^2 y_5^2 + 6(\theta_n - 1)^2 y_4 y_5^2 + 3(\theta_n - 1)y_5^2]$$

$$B = -Hgy_4 - Nby_5y_7 - Nty_5^2 - \left(1 + \frac{1}{\beta}\right)Ecy_3^2$$

$$y_5' = \frac{A + B}{\frac{1}{Pr}[1 + \frac{4}{3}R[1 + (\theta_n - 1)^3 y_4^3 + 3(\theta_n - 1)^2 y_4^2 + 3(\theta_n - 1)y_4]] - \Gamma_T y_1^2}$$

$$y_6' = y_7$$

$$C = -y_1 y_5 + \Gamma_T y_1 y_2 y_5 - \frac{1}{Pr}\frac{4}{3}R[(3\theta_n - 1)^3 y_4^2 y_5^2 + 6(\theta_n - 1)^2 y_4 y_5^2 + 3(\theta_n - 1)y_5^2]$$

$$D = -Hgy_4 - Nby_5y_7 - Nty_5^2 - \left(1 + \frac{1}{\beta}\right)Ecy_3^2$$

$$E = \frac{1}{Pr}[1 + \frac{4}{3}R[1 + (\theta_n - 1)^3 y_4^3 + 3(\theta_n - 1)^2 y_4^2 + 3(\theta_n - 1)y_4]] - \Gamma_T y_1^2$$

$$y_7' = \frac{-y_1 y_7 + \Gamma_C y_1 y_2 y_7 - \left(\frac{1}{Sc}\right)\left(\frac{Nt}{Nb}\right)\left(\frac{C+D}{E}\right) + \sigma^{**}(1 + \delta y_4)^n y_6 exp\left(\frac{-E}{1+\delta y_4}\right)}{\frac{1}{Sc} - \Gamma_C y_1^2}$$

With the conditions

$$y_1(0) = fw, \ y_2(0) = 1 + K\left[1 + \frac{1}{\beta} + \frac{We}{\sqrt{2}} y_3(0)\right] y_3(0), \ y_2(\infty) = 0,$$

$$y_4(0) = 1, \ Nby_7(0) + Nty_5(0) = 0, \ y_4(\infty) = 0, \ y_6(\infty) = 0 \quad (11)$$

We implemented the MATLAB bvp4c scheme to find the numerical solution for the above problem with maximum error is 10^5 and step size is 0.05.

4. Results and Discussion

This segment provides the details about the changes of velocity, temperature, naofluid concentration, skin friction coefficient (SFC), local Nusselt number (LNN) and local Sherwood number (LSN) for different flow parameters through graphs and tables. The consequences of fw, λ, Fr, M, Ri and Nr (Table 1), R, Hg, Ec, Γ_T, Nb, Nt and θ_n (Table 2) and Γ_c, σ^{**}, δ, n and E (Table 3) on SFC, LNN and LSN for Casson–Williamson nanofluid are deliberated in Tables 1–3. Table 4 provides the comparison of our numerical results to Mustafa et al. [45] and found excellent agreement. It is detected that there is SFC shrinkage when boosting the fw, λ, Fr, M, Nr, Γ_T, Nt Γ_C and E, and it upturns when enriching the Ri R, Hg, Ec, Nb, θ_n, σ^{**}, δ and n. The heat transfer gradient (HTG) loses when strengthening the quantity of λ, Fr, M, Nr, Hg, Ec, Nt, Γ_C, δ, n and E, and it upturns when enhancing the amount of fw, Ri, R, Γ_T, Nb, θ_n and σ^{**}. The LSN proliferate when mounting the quantity of λ, Fr, M, Nr, R, Hg, Nb, θ_n, Γ_c and δ. The quite opposite trend is obtained when changing the presence of fw, Ri, Ec, Γ_T, Nt, σ^{**}, n and E.

Table 1. The skin friction coefficient, local Nusselt number and local Sherwood number for fw, λ, Fr, M, Ri and Nr for both fluids.

fw	λ	Fr	M	Ri	Nr	$\frac{1}{2}Cf\sqrt{Re}$		$Nu/\sqrt{Re}$		$Sh/\sqrt{Re}$	
						Casson	Williamson	Casson	Williamson	Casson	Williamson
−0.6	0.2	0.4	0.5	0.5	0.5	−0.509450	−0.391709	0.579321	0.583070	−0.325537	−0.327817
−0.3						−0.540008	−0.427964	0.641809	0.642974	−0.363858	−0.364580
0.0						−0.571635	−0.468255	0.708673	0.706679	−0.405644	−0.404386
0.3						−0.603205	−0.511666	0.779139	0.773945	−0.450585	−0.447240
0.6						−0.633606	−0.556634	0.852262	0.844421	−0.498239	−0.493078
0.4	0.0	0.4	0.5	0.5	0.5	−0.594642	−0.508055	0.806499	0.800459	−0.468292	−0.464370
	0.4					−0.629919	−0.543188	0.800562	0.794198	−0.464437	−0.460312
	0.8					−0.657162	−0.571883	0.796283	0.789413	−0.461663	−0.457217
	1.2					−0.679033	−0.595949	0.793056	0.785643	−0.459573	−0.454781
0.4	0.2	0.0	0.5	0.5	0.5	−0.603953	−0.514606	0.804272	0.798227	−0.466845	−0.462923

Table 1. Cont.

fw	λ	Fr	M	Ri	Nr	$\frac{1}{2}Cf\sqrt{Re}$ Casson	$\frac{1}{2}Cf\sqrt{Re}$ Williamson	$Nu/\sqrt{Re}$ Casson	$Nu/\sqrt{Re}$ Williamson	$Sh/\sqrt{Re}$ Casson	$Sh/\sqrt{Re}$ Williamson
		0.6				−0.617898	−0.532082	0.802808	0.796584	−0.465894	−0.461858
		1.2				−0.629722	−0.547022	0.801560	0.795165	−0.465084	−0.460939
		1.8				−0.639957	−0.560048	0.800480	0.737920	−0.464384	−0.460133
0.4	0.2	0.4	0.0	0.5	0.5	−0.560068	−0.475720	0.812721	0.806599	−0.472339	−0.468357
			0.5			−0.613519	−0.526577	0.803268	0.797104	−0.466193	−0.462195
			1.0			−0.650934	−0.565199	0.797237	0.790500	−0.462281	−0.457920
			1.5			−0.679033	−0.595949	0.793786	0.785643	−0.459573	−0.454781
0.4	0.2	0.4	0.5	0.0	0.5	−0.660336	−0.580349	0.798424	0.788312	−0.463051	−0.456505
				0.4		−0.622571	−0.536848	0.802412	0.795557	−0.465637	−0.461193
				0.7		−0.595805	−0.506627	0.804836	0.799939	−0.467212	−0.464033
				1.0		−0.570084	−0.477980	0.806865	0.803636	−0.468530	−0.466432
0.4	0.2	0.4	0.5	0.5	−1.0	−0.606275	−0.522759	0.808362	0.804310	−0.469503	−0.466870
					−0.5	−0.608591	−0.523896	0.806752	0.802074	−0.468456	−0.465418
					0.0	−0.611002	−0.525165	0.805055	0.799680	−0.467353	−0.463865
					0.5	−0.613519	−0.526577	0.803268	0.797104	−0.466193	−0.462195
					1.0	−0.616151	−0.528155	0.801381	0.794318	−0.464969	−0.460390

Table 2. The skin friction coefficient, local Nusselt number and local Sherwood number for R, Hg, Ec, Γ_T, Nb, Nt and θ_n for both fluids.

R	Hg	Ec	Γ_T	Nb	Nt	θ_n	$\frac{1}{2}Cf\sqrt{Re}$ Casson	$\frac{1}{2}Cf\sqrt{Re}$ Williamson	$Nu/\sqrt{Re}$ Casson	$Nu/\sqrt{Re}$ Williamson	$Sh/\sqrt{Re}$ Casson	$Sh/\sqrt{Re}$ Williamson
0.0	−0.5	0.4	0.1	0.5	0.5	1.2	−0.629685	−0.5443759	0.552386	0.545982	−0.552386	−0.545982
0.4							−0.613519	−0.526577	0.803268	0.797104	−0.466193	−0.462195
0.8							−0.600650	−0.513580	1.023377	1.017386	−0.411036	−0.408267
1.2							−0.590235	−0.503470	1.221039	1.215175	−0.372078	−0.370007
0.4	−0.4	0.4	0.1	0.5	0.5	1.2	−0.609973	−0.522867	0.776546	0.770393	−0.448914	−0.444955
	−0.2						−0.600663	−0.513212	0.708901	0.702637	−0.405788	−0.401838
	0.0						−0.586188	−0.498333	0.608328	0.600989	−0.343240	−0.338747
	0.2						−0.560224	−0.471686	0.431109	0.417147	−0.237329	−0.229206
	0.4						−0.548398	−0.443644	0.248746	0.158094	−0.133635	−0.083938
0.4	−0.5	0.0	0.1	0.5	0.5	1.2	−0.616797	−0.530165	0.828958	0.830200	−0.482937	−0.483750
		0.5					−0.612698	−0.525686	0.796834	0.788861	−0.462020	−0.456860
		1.0					−0.608584	−0.521271	0.764598	0.747832	−0.441233	−0.430502
		1.5					−0.604457	−0.516918	0.732266	0.707121	−0.420586	−0.404665
0.4	−0.5	0.4	0.0	0.5	0.5	1.2	−0.612511	−0.525620	0.799275	0.793245	−0.463602	−0.459696
			0.2				−0.614542	−0.527555	0.807356	0.801051	−0.468849	−0.464754
			0.4				−0.616637	−0.529576	0.815834	0.809232	−0.474367	−0.470068
			0.6				−0.618798	−0.531690	0.824758	0.817834	−0.480190	−0.475670
0.4	−0.5	0.4	0.1	0.1	0.5	1.2	−0.624871	−0.534266	0.795002	0.784238	−2.304167	−2.269369
				0.5			−0.613519	−0.526577	0.803268	0.797104	−0.466193	−0.462195
				1.0			−0.612246	−0.525851	0.804174	0.798416	−0.233391	−0.231523
				1.5			−0.611828	−0.525618	0.804470	0.798843	−0.155658	−0.154441

Table 2. Cont.

R	Hg	Ec	Γ_T	Nb	Nt	θ_n	$\frac{1}{2}Cf\sqrt{Re}$		$Nu/\sqrt{Re}$		$Sh/\sqrt{Re}$	
							Casson	Williamson	Casson	Williamson	Casson	Williamson
0.4	−0.5	0.4	0.1	0.5	0.5	1.2	−0.613519	−0.526577	0.803268	0.797104	−0.466193	−0.46295
						1.0	−0.614246	−0.526134	0.790345	0.783132	−0.915639	−0.906320
						1.5	−0.614786	−0.525509	0.777196	0.768887	−1.347998	−1.331962
						2.0	−0.615136	−0.524713	0.763870	0.754421	−1.763066	−1.738850
0.4	−0.5	0.4	0.1	0.5	0.5	1.0	−0.617049	−0.530398	0.748078	0.741525	−0.487877	−0.483603
						1.2	−0.613519	−0.526577	0.803268	0.797104	−0.466193	−0.462195
						1.4	−0.609177	−0.521923	0.871668	0.865948	−0.440864	−0.437192
						1.6	−0.603889	−0.516328	0.956034	0.950777	−0.412023	−0.408740

Table 3. The skin friction coefficient, local Nusselt number and local Sherwood number for Γ_c, σ^{**}, δ, n and E for both fluids.

Γ_C	σ^{**}	δ	n	E	$\frac{1}{2}Cf\sqrt{Re}$		$Nu/\sqrt{Re}$		$Sh/\sqrt{Re}$	
					Casson	Williamson	Casson	Williamson	Casson	Williamson
0.0	1.0	1.0	0.5	1.0	−0.613044	−0.526039	0.803508	0.797397	−0.466349	−0.462385
0.1					−0.613519	−0.526577	0.803268	0.797104	−0.466193	−0.462195
0.2					−0.613985	−0.527112	0.803024	0.796807	−0.466035	−0.462003
0.3					−0.614443	−0.528172	0.802775	0.796199	−0.465873	−0.461608
0.1	0.0	1.0	0.5	1.0	−0.621718	−0.537316	0.802043	0.793644	−0.465398	−0.459954
	0.4				−0.616422	−0.529896	0.803344	0.796616	−0.466243	−0.461879
	0.8				−0.614204	−0.527324	0.803393	0.797110	−0.466274	−0.462199
	1.2				−0.612990	−0.526016	0.803097	0.797019	−0.466082	−0.462140
0.1	1.0	0.0	0.5	1.0	−0.613684	−0.526784	0.803713	0.797484	−0.466482	−0.462441
		0.3			−0.613634	−0.526719	0.803572	0.797365	−0.466391	−0.462364
		0.6			−0.613585	−0.526657	0.803438	0.797250	−0.466303	−0.462290
		1.0			−0.613519	−0.526577	0.803268	0.797104	−0.466193	−0.462195
0.1	1.0	1.0	0.0	1.0	−0.613558	−0.526629	0.803468	0.797283	−0.466323	−0.462311
			0.5		−0.613519	−0.526577	0.803268	0.797104	−0.466193	−0.462195
			1.0		−0.613492	−0.526540	0.803029	0.796883	−0.466038	−0.462052
			1.5		−0.613478	−0.526520	0.802745	0.796615	−0.465854	−0.461878
0.1	1.0	1.0	0.5	0.0	−0.611041	−0.524071	0.802264	0.796452	−0.465541	−0.461773
				1.0	−0.613519	−0.526577	0.803268	0.797104	−0.466193	−0.462195
				2.0	−0.616499	−0.529962	0.803240	0.796521	−0.466175	−0.461817
				3.0	−0.618951	−0.533118	0.802802	0.795459	−0.465891	−0.461129

Table 4. Comparison of local Nusselt number when $We = \lambda = Fr = R = \Gamma_T = Hg = \Gamma_C = 0$ and $M = Nr = 0:5, Sc = 5$ and $\delta = 1$ with Mustafa et al. [45].

Pr	Nt	E	σ^{**}	n	Ri	$Nu/\sqrt{Re}$	
						Ref. [45]	Present
2.0	0.5	1.0	1.0	0.5	0.5	0.706605	0.706604
4.0						0.935952	0.935955
7.0						1.132787	1.132788
10.0						1.257476	1.257482
5.0	0.1	1.0	1.0	0.5	0.5	1.426267	1.426269
	0.5					1.013939	1.013938
	0.7					0.846943	0.846928
	1.0					0.649940	0.649939
5.0	0.5	0.0	1.0	0.5	0.5	0.941201	0.941209
		1.0				1.013939	1.013943
		2.0				1.064551	1.064563
		4.0				1.114549	1.114191

Table 4. Cont.

Pr	Nt	E	σ^{**}	n	Ri	$Nu/\sqrt{Re}$ Ref. [45]	$Nu/\sqrt{Re}$ Present
5.0	0.5	1.0	0.0	0.5	0.5	1.145304	1.145301
			1.0			1.013939	1.013938
			2.0			0.926282	0.926281
			5.0			0.798671	0.798669
5.0	0.5	1.0	2.0	−1.0	0.5	1.030805	1.030804
				−0.5		0.999470	0.999468
				0.0		0.964286	0.964285
				1.0		0.886830	0.886830
10.0	0.5	1.0	2.0	0.5	0.0	1.032281	1.032280
					0.5	1.056704	1.056706
					3.0	1.154539	1.154538
					5.0	1.215937	1.215938

Figure 2a–d display the variances of fluid velocity versus Ri(a), fw(b), λ(c) and M (d). It is clearly shown that the fluid speed enhances when heightening the quantity of Ri and it depresses when mounting the quantity of fw, λ and M for both fluids. In addition, the velocity of the Casson nanofluid is low near the plate and high away from the plate compared to Williamson nanofluid. Physically, a larger quantity of M generates a drag force named the Lorentz force. This force leads to suppressing the fluid movement on a plate surface, and this causes a decline in the fluid speed and thinner momentum boundary layer. The fluid temperature variations on R(a), Hg(b), Γ_T(c) and Ec(d) for both fluids are illustrated in Figure 3a–d. It is acknowledged that the fluid warmness escalates when enhancing the R and Hg values, and it suppresses when the Γ_T and Ec values are rising. Physically, the presence of a radiation parameter has enriched the fluid thermal state, thereby strengthening the fluid warmness and thicker thermal boundary layer thickness. In addition, the greater availability of Eckert number creates a more robust viscous dissipation effect, which enriches the fluid warmness. Figure 4a–d show the consequences of σ^{**}(a), fw(b), E(c) and Nt(d) on nanoparticle concentration profile. It is seen that the nanoparticle concentration reduces when raising the values σ^{**}. A opposite behavior occurs for varying the values of fw, E and Nt. The skin friction coefficient for a distinct combination of M, λ and fw is presented in Figure 5a–d. It is found that the surface shear stress decays when enhancing the magnetic field and porosity parameter for both fw values. In addition, the Williamson nanofluid has a greater skin friction coefficient value than the Casson nanofluid. Figure 6a–d portrayed the changes of local Nusselt number for a distinct combination of values of M, λ and fw. It is concluded that the heat transfer gradient slowly depresses when increasing the magnetic field and porosity parameters for both fw values. The local Sherwood number for various combination of values of M, λ and fw is shown in Figure 7a–d. It is seen from these figures that the local Sherwood number slowly depresses when increasing the magnetic field and porosity parameters for both fw values.

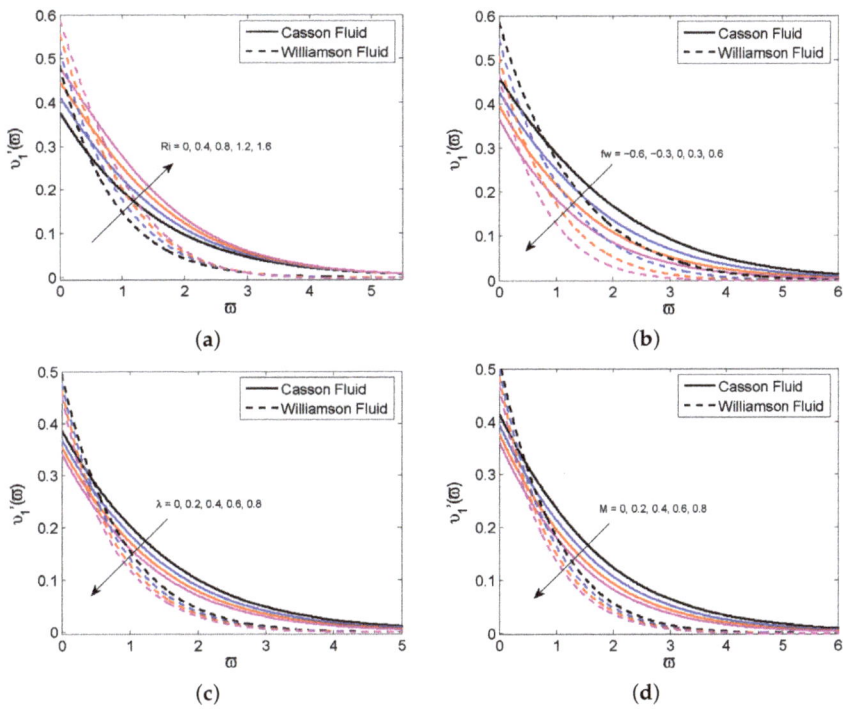

Figure 2. The nanofluid velocity for various values Ri (**a**), fw (**b**), λ (**c**) and M (**d**).

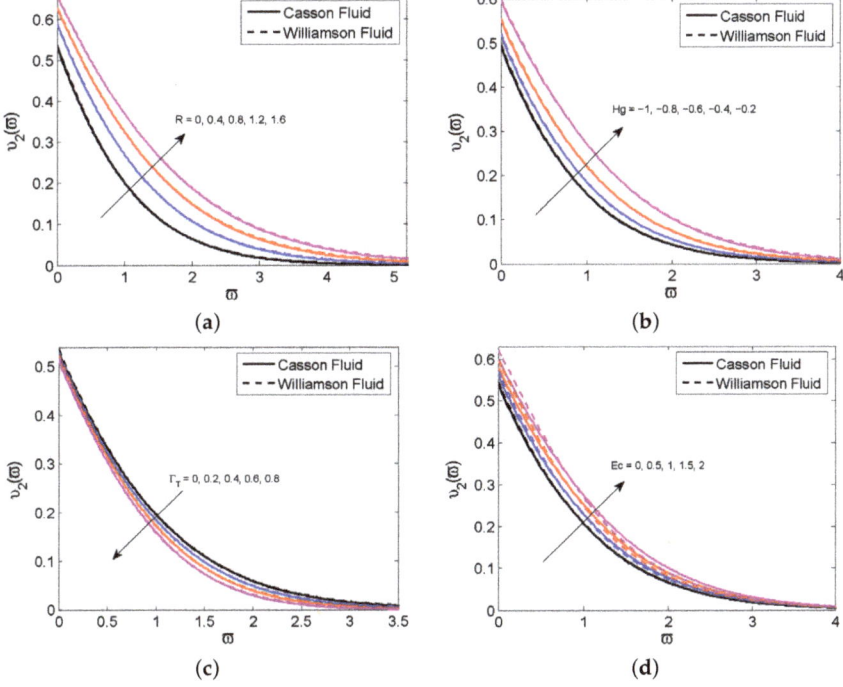

Figure 3. The nanofluid temperature profile for various vales of R (**a**), Hg (**b**), Γ_T (**c**) and Ec (**d**).

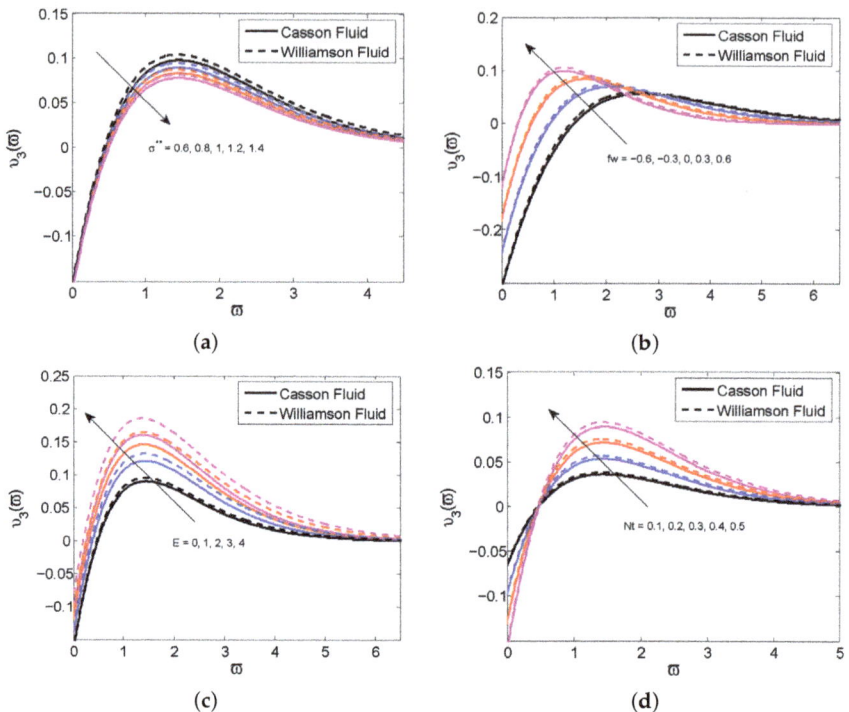

Figure 4. The nanoparticle concentration for various values of σ^{**} (**a**), fw (**b**), E (**c**) and Nt (**d**).

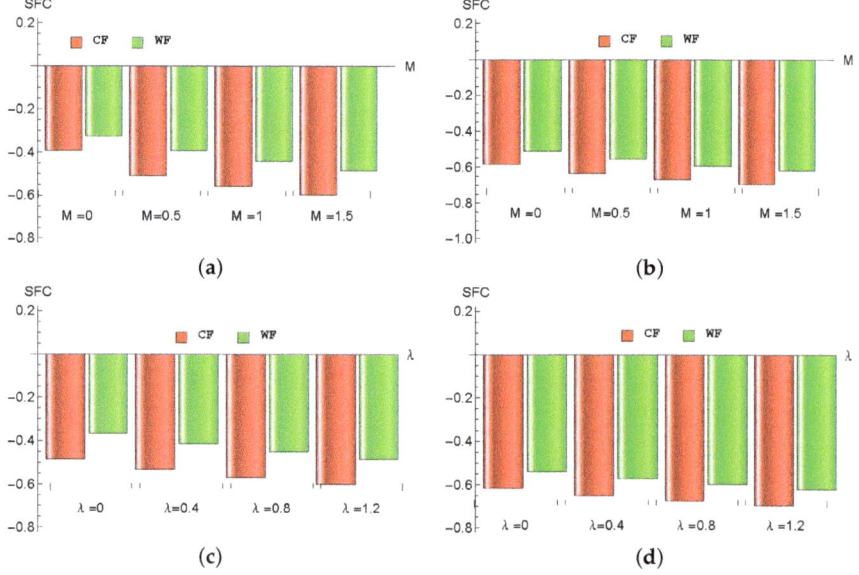

Figure 5. The skin friction coefficient (SFC) for different values of M with $fw = -0.6$ (**a**), M with $fw = 0.6$ (**b**), λ with $fw = -0.6$ (**c**) and λ with $fw = 0.6$ (**d**) for Casson nanofluid (CF) and Williamson nanofluid (WF).

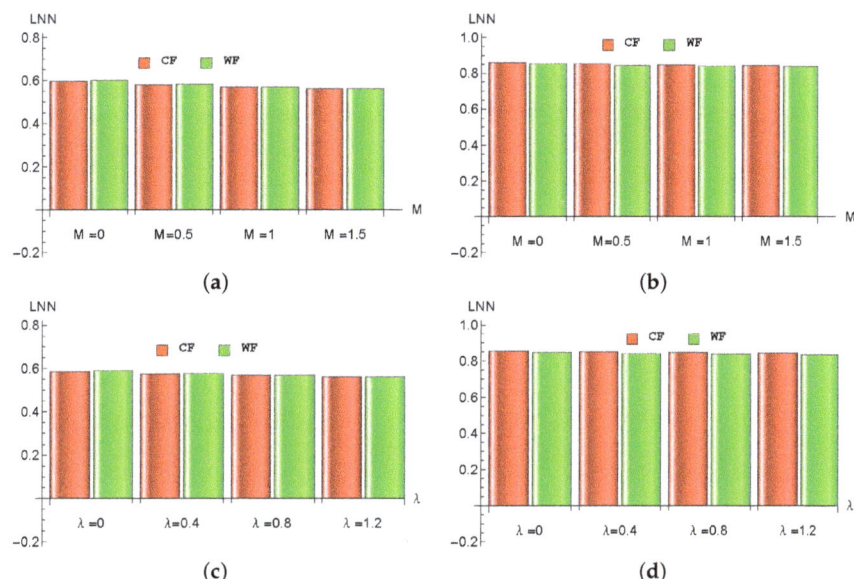

Figure 6. The local Nusselt number (LNN) for different values of M with $fw = -0.6$ (**a**), M with $fw = 0.6$ (**b**), λ with $fw = -0.6$ (**c**) and λ with $fw = 0.6$ (**d**) for Casson nanofluid (CF) and Williamson nanofluid (WF).

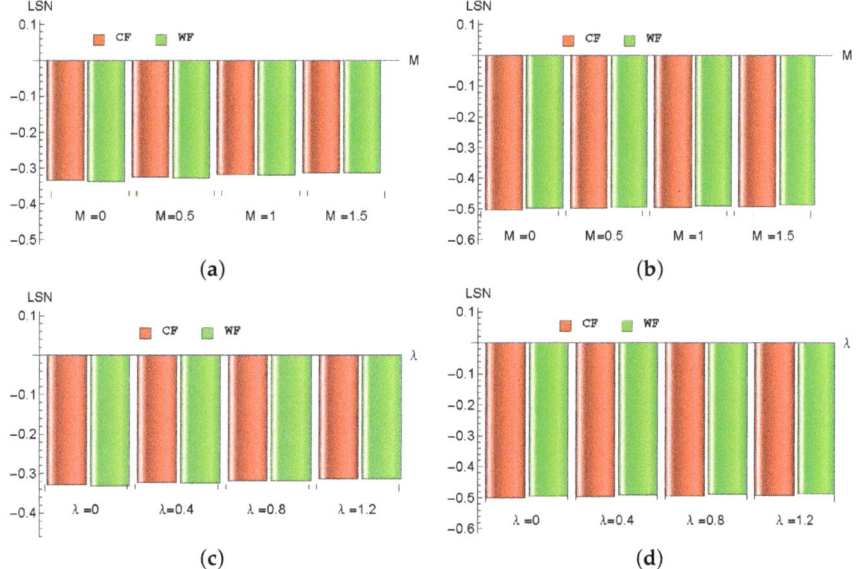

Figure 7. The local Sherwood number (LSN) for different values of M with $fw = -0.6$ (**a**), M with $fw = 0.6$ (**b**), λ with $fw = -0.6$ (**c**) and λ with $fw = 0.6$ (**d**) for Casson nanofluid (CF) and Williamson nanofluid (WF).

5. Conclusions

Here, Brownian motion and the thermophoresis impact of the non-linear radiative flow of C-WNF in a Darcy–Forchheimer porous space with suction and heat consumption is investigated. The present investigation includes the consequences of activation energy and binary chemical reaction. The governing mathematical models are numerically solved by the bvp4c algorithm with MATLAB. The main outcomes of our discussion are as follows:

- The fluid speed enhances for Richardson number but it slows against porosity, suction/injection and magnetic field parameters.
- The fluid becomes more warmed as the radiation, heat generation parameters and Eckert number increase.
- The nanoparticle concentration enhances upon strengthening the suction/injection and thermophoresis parameters and it downfalls upon escalating the reaction rate.
- The skin friction reduces after enriching the Forchheimer number, porosity and magnetic field parameters.
- The heat transfer gradient increases when escalating the values of radiation parameter and it downturns against radiation and heat generation parameters.
- The mass transfer gradient enhances upon heightening the Brownian motion parameter and it weakens against the thermophoresis parameter.
- In the future, we extend this flow model through the Riga plate with the convective heating condition.

Author Contributions: Data curation, S.E.; Formal analysis, K.L.; Investigation, S.T.; Methodology, S.E. and S.T. All authors have read and agreed to the published version of the manuscript.

Funding: This research received no external funding.

Conflicts of Interest: The authors declare no conflict of interest.

Abbreviations

The following abbreviations are used in this manuscript:

Nomenclature

Symbols	Description
a, b	Positive constants
B_0	Magnetic field strength (T)
C	Fluid concentration ($mol\ L^{-1}$)
C_b	Drag coefficient
C_p	Specific heat ($Jkg^{-1}K^{-1}$)
C_∞	Ambient fluid concentration
D_B	Brownian diffusion coefficient (m^2s^{-1})
D_T	Thermophoretic diffusion coefficient
$E(=Ea/kT_\infty)$	Activation energy parameter
Ea	Activation energy
$Fr(=C_b/\sqrt{k_1})$	Forchheimer number
f	Dimensionless velocity
g	Acceleration due to gravity (ms^{-2})
$Gr_x(=(g\beta(1-C_\infty)(T_w-T_\infty)x^3/\nu^2)$	Local Grashof number
$Hg(=\frac{Q}{\rho_f C_p a})$	Heat generation/absorption parameter
k	Thermal conductive ($Wm^{-1}K^{-1}$)
k_1	Permeability of porous medium (m^2)
k^*	Mean absorption coefficient
kr	Reaction rate
$M(=\frac{\sigma B_0^2}{\rho_f a})$	Magnetic parameter
n	Fitted rate or stretching sheet index parameter
Ec	Eckert number
$Nb(=\frac{\tau D_B(C_w-C_\infty)}{\nu})$	Brownian diffusion parameter
$Nt(=\frac{\tau D_T(T_w-T_\infty)}{T_\infty \nu})$	Thermophoresis parameter
$Pr(=\frac{\nu}{\alpha}=\frac{m^2s^{-1}}{m^2s^{-1}}=1)$	Prandtl number
Q	Heat generation/absorption coefficient ($JM^{-1}m^{-3}s^{-1}$)

$R(=\frac{4\sigma^* T_\infty^3}{kk^*})$	Thermal radiation
$Re_x(=\frac{U_\omega x}{\nu})$	Local Reynolds number
$Ri(=\frac{Gr_x}{Re_x^2}=\frac{g\beta(1-C_\infty)(T_\omega-T_\infty)}{a^2 x})$	Richardson number
$Sc(=\frac{\nu}{D_B})$	Schmith number
T	Fluid temperature (K)
T_∞	Ambient temperature (K)
u, v	Velocity components (ms^{-1})
U_ω	Stretching surface velocity (ms^{-1})
$We(=\Gamma x\sqrt{2a^3/\nu})=sm\sqrt{\frac{2s-3}{m^2 s-1}}=\text{constant}$	Weissenberg number
x, y	Direction coordinates (m)
Greek Symbols	**Description**
α	Thermal diffusivity $(m^2 s^{-1})$
β	Casson parameter
$\delta(=\frac{T_\omega-T_\infty}{T_\infty})$	Temperature difference parameter
Γ	Williamson parameter or time constant
$\Gamma_T(=a\lambda_T)$	Thermal relaxation parameter
$\Gamma_C(=a\lambda_C)$	Solute relaxation parameter
λ	Local porosity parameter
λ_C	Relaxation time of mass flux
λ_T	Relaxation time of heat flux
ν	Kinetic viscosity $(m^2 s^{-1})$
ϕ	Non-dimensional nanofluid concentration
ρ_f	Fluid density (kgm^{-2})
σ	Electrical conductivity (Sm^{-1})
σ^*	Stefan–Boltzmann constant $(Wm^{-2}K^{-4})$
$\sigma^{**}(=\frac{kr^2}{a})$	Dimensionless reaction rate
τ	Heat capacity ratio
θ	Non-dimensional temperature
θ_n	Temperature ratio parameter
η	Similarity variable
μ	Dynamic viscosity $(Kgm^{-1}s^{-1})$
p	Dust phase
∞	Fluid properties at ambient condition

References

1. Elnaqeeb, T.; Animasaun, I.L.; Shah, N.A. Ternary-hybrid nanofluids: significance of suction and dual-stretching on three-dimensional flow of water conveying nanoparticles with various shapes and densities. *Z. Naturforsch. A* **2021**, *76*, 231–243. [CrossRef]
2. Islam, T.; Yavuz, M.; Parveen, N.; Fayz-Al-Asad, M. Impact of non-uniform periodic magnetic field on unsteady natural convection flow of nanofluids in square enclosure. *Fractal Fract* **2022**, *6*, 101. [CrossRef]
3. Saleem, S.; Animasaun, I.L; Yook, S.J.; Al-Mdallal, Q.M.; Shah, N.A.; Faisal, M. Insight into the motion of water conveying three kinds of nanoparticles shapes on a horizontal surface: Significance of thermo-migration and Brownian motion. *Surf. Interfaces* **2022**, *30*, 101854. [CrossRef]
4. Choi, S.U.S. Enhancing thermal conductivity of fluids with nanoparticles. *ASME-Publications-Fed* **1995**, *231*, 99–106.
5. Sheikholeslami, M. Effect of uniform suction on nanofluid flow and heat transfer over a cylinder. *J. Braz. Soc. Mech. Sci. Eng.* **2015**, *37*, 1623–1633. [CrossRef]
6. Ramana Reddy, J.V.; Sugunamma, V.; Sandeep, N. Thermophoresis and Brownian motion effects on unsteady MHD nanofluid flow over a slendering stretching surface with slip effects. *Alex. Eng. J.* **2018**, *57*, 2465–2473. [CrossRef]
7. Makinde, O.D.; Mabood, F.; Khan, W.A.; Tshehla, M.S.; MHD flow of a variable viscosity nanofluid over a radially stretching convective surface with radiative heat. *J. Mol. Liq.* **2016**, *219*, 624–630. [CrossRef]
8. Shafey, A.M.E.; Alharbi, F.M.; Javed, A.; Abbas, N.; ALrafai, H.A.; Nadeem, S.; Issakhov, A. Theoretical analysis of Brownian and thermophoresis motion effects for Newtonian fluid flow over nonlinear stretching cylinder. *Case Stud. Therm. Eng.* **2021**, *28*, 101369. [CrossRef]
9. Rasheed, H.U.; Islam, S.; Khan, Z.; Khan, J.; Mashwani, W.K.; Abbas, T.; Shah, Q. Computational analysis of hydromagnetic boundary layer stagnation point flow of nano liquid by a stretched heated surface with convective conditions and radiation effect. *Adv. Mech. Eng.* **2021**, *13*, 16878140211053142. [CrossRef]

10. Alotaibi, H.; Althubiti, S.; Eid, M.R.; Mahny, K.L. Numerical treatment of MHD flow of Casson nanofluid via convectively heated non-linear extending surface with viscous dissipation and suction/injection effects. *Comput. Mater. Continua* **2021**, *66*, 229–245. [CrossRef]
11. Nayak, M.K; Prakash, J.; Tripathi, D.; Pandey, V.S; Shaw S. 3D Bioconvective multiple slip flow of chemically reactive Casson nanofluid with gyrotactic microorganisms. *Heat Transf. Res.* **2020**, *49*, 135–153. [CrossRef]
12. Butt, A.S.; Maqbool, K.; Imran, S.M.; Ahmad, B. Entropy generation effects in MHD Casson nanofluid past a permeable stretching surface. *Int. J. Exergy* **2020**, *31*, 150–171. [CrossRef]
13. Ibrahim, S.M.; Lorenzini, G.; Vijaya Kumar, P.; Raju, C.S.K. Influence of chemical reaction and heat source on dissipative MHD mixed convection flow of a Casson nanofluid over a nonlinear permeable stretching sheet. *Int. J. Heat Mass Transf.* **2017**, *111*, 346–355. [CrossRef]
14. Afify, A.A. The influence of slip boundary condition on Casson nanofluid flow over a stretching sheet in the presence of viscous dissipation and chemical reaction. *Math. Probl. Eng.* **2017**, *2017*, 3804751. [CrossRef]
15. Varun Kumar, R.S.; Dhananjaya, P.G.; Naveen Kumar, R.; Punith Gowda, R.J.; Prasannakumara, B.C. Modeling and theoretical investigation on Casson nanofluid flow over a curved stretching surface with the influence of magnetic field and chemical reaction. *Int. J. Comput. Methods Eng. Sci. Mech.* **2022**, *23*, 12–19. [CrossRef]
16. Naveen Kumar, R.; Punith Gowda, R.J.; Madhukesh, J.K.; Prasannakumara, B.C.; Ramesh, G.K. Impact of thermophoretic particle deposition on heat and mass transfer across the dynamics of Casson fluid flow over a moving thin needle. *Phys. Scr.* **2021**, *96*, 075210. [CrossRef]
17. Khan, T.S.; Sene, N.; Mouldi, A.; Brahmia, A. Heat and mass transfer of the Darcy–Forchheimer Casson hybrid nanofluid flow due to an extending curved surface. *J. Nanomat.* **2022**, *2022*, 3979168. [CrossRef]
18. Waqas, S.H.; Khan, S.U.; Imran, M.; Bhatti, M.M. Thermally developed Falkner–Skan bioconvection flow of a magnetized nanofluid in the presence of a motile gyrotactic microorganism: Buongiorno's nanofluid model. *Phys. Scr.* **2019**, *94*, 115304. [CrossRef]
19. Li, Y.X.; Alshbool, M.H.; Lv, Y.P.; Khan, I.; Khan, M.R.; Issakhov, A. Heat and mass transfer in MHD Williamson nanofluid flow over an exponentially porous stretching surface. *Case Stud. Therm. Eng.* **2021**, *26*, 100975. [CrossRef]
20. Ahmed, K.; Akbar, T. Numerical investigation of magnetohydrodynamics Williamson nanofluid flow over an exponentially stretching surface. *Adv. Mech. Eng.* **2021**, *13*, 168781402110198. [CrossRef]
21. Iqbal, W.; Naeem, M.N.; Jalil, M. Numerical analysis of Williamson fluid flow along an exponentially stretching cylinder. *AIP Adv.* **2019**, *9*, 055118. [CrossRef]
22. Gorla, R.S.R.; Gireesha, B.J. Dual solutions for stagnation-point flow and convective heat transfer of a Williamson nanofluid past a stretching/shrinking sheet. *Heat Mass Transf.* **2016**, *52*, 1153–1162. [CrossRef]
23. Srinivasulu, T.; Goud, B.S. Effect of inclined magnetic field on flow, heat and mass transfer of Williamson nanofluid over a stretching sheet. *Case Stud. Therm. Eng.* **2021**, *23*, 100819. [CrossRef]
24. Mahanta, G.; Das, M.; Nayak, M.K.; Shaw, S. Irreversibility Analysis of 3D Magnetohydrodynamic Casson Nanofluid Flow Past Through Two Bi-Directional Stretching Surfaces with Nonlinear Radiation. *J. Nanofluids* **2021**, *10*, 316–326. [CrossRef]
25. Humane, P.P.; Patil, V.S.; Patil, A.B. Chemical reaction and thermal radiation effects on magnetohydrodynamics flow of Casson–Williamson nanofluid over a porous stretching surface. *Proc. Inst. Mech. Eng. E: J. Process Mech. Eng.* **2021**, *235*, 2008–2018. [CrossRef]
26. Akinshilo, A.T.; Mabood, F.; Ilegbusi, A.O. Heat generation and nonlinear radiation effects on MHD Casson nanofluids over a thin needle embedded in porous medium. *Int. Commun. Heat Mass Transf.* **2021**, *127*, 105547. [CrossRef]
27. Ghasemi, S.E.; Mohsenian, S.; Gouran, S.; Zolfagharian, A. A novel spectral relaxation approach for nanofluid flow past a stretching surface in presence of magnetic field and nonlinear radiation. *Results Phys.* **2022**, *32*, 105141. [CrossRef]
28. Imran, M.; Farooq, U.; Muhammad, T.; Khan, S.U.; Waqas, H. Bioconvection transport of Carreau nanofluid with magnetic dipole and nonlinear thermal radiation. *Case Stud. Therm. Eng.* **2021**, *26*, 101129. [CrossRef]
29. Bhatti, M.M.; Abbas, T.; Rashidi, M.M. Numerical study of entropy generation with nonlinear thermal radiation on magnetohydrodynamics non-Newtonian nanofluid through a porous shrinking sheet. *J. Magn.* **2016**, *21*, 468–475. [CrossRef]
30. Mahanthesh, B.; Thriveni, K. Significance of inclined magnetic field on nano-bioconvection with nonlinear thermal radiation and exponential space based heat source: A sensitivity analysis. *Eur. Phys. J. Spec. Top.* **2021**, *230*, 1487–1501. [CrossRef]
31. Cao, W.; Animasaun, I.L.; Yook, S.J.; Oladipupo, V.A.; Ji, X. Simulation of the dynamics of colloidal mixture of water with various nanoparticles at different levels of partial slip: Ternary-hybrid nanofluid. *Int. Commun. Heat Mass Transf* **2022**, *135*, 106069. [CrossRef]
32. Eswaramoorthi, S.; Divya, S.; Faisal, M.; Namgyel, N. Entropy and heat transfer analysis for MHD flow of-water-based nanofluid on a heated 3D plate with nonlinear radiation. *Math. Probl. Eng.* **2022**, *2022*, 7319988. [CrossRef]
33. Shah, Z.; Kumam, P.; Deebani, W. Radiative MHD Casson Nanofluid Flow with Activation energy and chemical reaction over past nonlinearly stretching surface through Entropy generation. *Sci. Rep.* **2020**, *10*, 4402. [CrossRef] [PubMed]
34. Aziz, S.; Ahmad, I.; Khan, S.U.; Ali, N. A three-dimensional bioconvection Williamson nanofluid flow over bidirectional accelerated surface with activation energy and heat generation. *Int. J. Mod. Phys. B* **2021**, *35*, 2150132. [CrossRef]
35. Kalaivanan, R.; Vishnu Ganesh, N.; Al-Mdallal, Q.M. An investigation on Arrhenius activation energy of second grade nanofluid flow with active and passive control of nanomaterials. *Case Stud. Therm. Eng.* **2020**, *22*, 100774. [CrossRef]

36. Zeeshan, A.; Mehmood, O.U.; Mabood, F.; Alzahrani, F. Numerical analysis of hydromagnetic transport of Casson nanofluid over permeable linearly stretched cylinder with Arrhenius activation energy. *Int. Commun. Heat Mass Transf.* **2022** *130*, 105736. [CrossRef]
37. Tayyab, M.; Siddique, I.; Jarad, F.; Ashraf, M.K.; Ali, B. Numerical solution of 3D rotating nanofluid flow subject to Darcy–Forchheimer law, bio-convection and activation energy. *S. Afr. J. Chem. Eng.* **2022**, *40*, 48–56. [CrossRef]
38. Rashid, S.; Hayat, T.; Qayyum, S.; Ayub, M.; Alsaedi, A. Three dimensional rotating Darcy–Forchheimer flow with activation energy. *Int. J. Numer. Methods Heat Fluid Flow* **2018**, *29*, 935–948. [CrossRef]
39. Alsaadi, F.E.; Hayat, T.; Khan, M.I.; Alsaadi, F.E. Heat transport and entropy optimization in flow of magneto-Williamson nanomaterial with Arrhenius activation energy. *Comput. Methods Progr. Biomed.* **2020**, *183*, 105051. [CrossRef]
40. Punith Gowda, R.J.; Naveen Kumar, R.; Jyothi, A.M.; Prasannakumara, B.C.; Sarris, I.E. Impact of binary chemical reaction and activation energy on heat and mass transfer of marangoni driven boundary layer flow of a non-Newtonian nanofluid. *Processes* **2021**, *9*, 702. [CrossRef]
41. Varun Kumar, R.S.; Alhadhrami, A.; Punith Gowda, R.J.; Naveen Kumar, R.; Prasannakumara, B.C. Exploration of Arrhenius activation energy on hybrid nanofluid flow over a curved stretchable surface. *ZAMM-J. Appl. Math. Mech./Z. Angew. Math. Mech.* **2021**, *101*, e202100035. [CrossRef]
42. Tamilzharasan, B.M.; Karthikeyan, S.; Kaabar, M.K.; Yavuz, M.; Özköse, F. Magneto Mixed Convection of Williamson Nanofluid Flow through a Double Stratified Porous Medium in Attendance of Activation Energy. *Math. Comput. Appl.* **2022**, *27*, 46. [CrossRef]
43. Nadeem, S.; Hussain, S.T. Flow and heat transfer analysis of Williamson nanofluid. *Appl. Nanosci.* **2014**, *4*, 1005–1012. [CrossRef]
44. Raju, C.S.K; Sandeep, N.; Ali, M.E.; Nuhait, A.O. Heat and mass transfer in 3-D MHD Williamson–Casson fluids flow over a stretching surface with non-uniform heat source/sink. *Therm. Sci.* **2019**, *23*, 281–293. [CrossRef]
45. Mustafa, M.; Khan, J.A.; Hayat, T.; Alsaedi, A. Buoyancy effects on the MHD nanofluid flow past a vertical surface with chemical reaction and activation energy. *Int. J. Heat Mass Transf.* **2017**, *108*, 1340–1346. [CrossRef]
46. Ali, F.; Loganathan, K.; Eswaramoorthi, S.; Prabu, K.; Zaib, A.; Chaudhary, D.K. Heat transfer analysis on Carboxymethyl cellulose water-based cross hybrid nanofluid flow with entropy generation. *J. Nanomater.* **2022**, *2022*, 5252918. [CrossRef]
47. Eswaramoorthi, S.; Loganathan, K.; Jain, R.; Gyeltshen, S. Darcy–Forchheimer 3D flow of glycerin-based carbon nanotubes on a Riga plate with nonlinear thermal radiation and Cattaneo–Christov heat flux. *J. Nanomater.* **2022**, *2022*, 5286921. [CrossRef]

Article

Dissolution-Driven Convection in a Porous Medium Due to Vertical Axis of Rotation and Magnetic Field

Gundlapally Shiva Kumar Reddy [1], Nilam Venkata Koteswararao [2], Ragoju Ravi [1], Kiran Kumar Paidipati [3] and Christophe Chesneau [4,*]

[1] Department of Applied Sciences, National Institute of Technology Goa, Ponda 403401, India; gshivakumarreddy913@nitgoa.ac.in (G.S.K.R.); ravi@nitgoa.ac.in (R.R.)
[2] The School of Advanced Sciences and Languages, VIT Bhopal University, Sehore 466114, India; nilam.venkatakoteswararao@vitbhopal.ac.in
[3] Area of Decision Sciences, Indian Institute of Management Sirmaur, Sirmaur 173025, India; kkpaidipati@iimsirmaur.ac.in
[4] Laboratoire de Mathématiques Nicolas Oresme (LMNO), Université de Caen Normandie, Campus II, Science 3, 14032 Caen, France
* Correspondence: christophe.chesneau@unicaen.fr

Abstract: This article aims to study the effect of the vertical rotation and magnetic field on the dissolution-driven convection in a saturated porous layer with a first-order chemical reaction. The system's physical parameters depend on the Vadasz number, the Hartmann number, the Taylor number, and the Damkohler number. We analyze them in an in-depth manner. On the other hand, based on an artificial neural network (ANN) technique, the Levenberg–Marquardt backpropagation algorithm is adopted to predict the distribution of the critical Rayleigh number and for the linear stability analysis. The simulated critical Rayleigh numbers obtained by the numerical study and the predicted critical Rayleigh numbers by the ANN are compared and are in good agreement. The system becomes more stable by increasing the Damkohler and Taylor numbers.

Keywords: linear stability; magnetic field; porous layer; chemical reaction; Levenberg–Marquardt backpropagation algorithm

1. Introduction

Dissolution-driven convection occurs in the host phase of a partially miscible system when a buoyantly unstable density stratification develops upon dissolution. The onset of convection in a porous layer has received considerable interest in science, engineering, and technology, such as food engineering, oil recovery, chemical reactor design, and plastic processing. Dissolution-driven convection in porous media has received recent interest in the context of the long-term geological storage of carbon dioxide in the underground, natural, brine-filled caverns, often referred to as saline aquifers, in the production of mineral deposits, and a variety of other applications. Following injection into the saline aquifer, dissolution of supercritical carbon dioxide in the host brine causes a local density increase, leading to gravitational instability of the diffusive boundary layer and the formation of convective fingers [1–6]. In addition, Benard and chemical instabilities were studied for the dissociation of a horizontal layer of Navier–Stokes fluid due to the Boussinesq approximation. Dissolution-driven convection of a binary fluid in a reactive porous layer was foremost studied [7,8], then secondary instabilities [9], and constant temperatures and chemical equilibrium in binary fluid at the boundary surfaces while the solubility of the dissolved issue relies upon temperature [10–18]. The diffusive boundary layer becomes unstable in anisotropic porous media where both the capillary transition zone and dispersion are considered, even if the geochemical reaction is significantly large. While the reaction enhances stability by consuming the solute, porous media anisotropy, hydrodynamic dispersion, and capillary transition zone destabilize the diffusive boundary layer that is unstably formed in a gravitational field [19–21]. Stability techniques that look at and broaden the way the solute's dissolution influences the thermal convection and prolongs this evaluation by the use of an asymptotic energy method, Galerkin and spectral techniques, are expecting the structure of the preliminary bifurcation. Darcy, Darcy Brinkmann, and Darcy Lapwood Brinkmann's models were used to study porous, anisotropic porous, and sparsely packed porous medium over multiple diffusive convection [22–25].

Exhausting the magnetic field is an adequate method to regulate a thermally induced flow. The magnetic field will propagate a Lorentz force to permeate the convective flow. The penetration effect depends on the strength of the applied magnetic field and its assimilation into the convective flow direction. The magnetic field is significant for engineering applications such as magnetohydrodynamics, cooling of nuclear reactors, micropump electronic packages, and microelectronic devices. The density can be enhanced or reduced depending on the magnetic field and electrode configuration. The magnetic field effect on formally charged transfer-controlled active dissolution and the Lorentz force reduces the field gradient force, which boosts active dissolution. The convective cavities of various aspect ratios in the magnetohydrodynamics of fluids are broadly studied [26–38]. Due to the simultaneous action of buoyancy and induced magnetic forces, heat transfer to liquid metals may be significantly affected by the presence of a magnetic field, but very small effects are experienced by other fluids. The Coriolis and centrifugal buoyancy forces arising from rotation have a remarkable influence on the local heat transfer when compared with the nonrotating results. A series of interferograms, stream functions, and isotherm plots demonstrated the strong effect of rotation on the flow field and heat transfer. A correlation of the Nusselt number as a function of Taylor and Rayleigh numbers is presented [15,19,39–42].

Various machine learning techniques, in particular artificial neural networks (ANN), have been widely used in different research areas for predicting data. Recently, many researchers have used ANN to predict the data and compare them with their results. Neural networks are used to solve different types of large data-related problems and solve the Navier–Stokes equations for turbulence by using the Bayesian cluster. The combination of ANN and gene expression programming compares the local Nusselt number with their numerical results [43–45]. The investigation of bifurcating fluid phenomena using a reduced-order modeling setting was aided by artificial neural networks, ANNs, to study the flow and thermal fields of the onset of convection in a rectangular channel. From their results, they found that the ANN can precisely predict the Nusselt number with less computational time and cost compared to the DNS [46–51].

The purpose of this article is to explore the magnetic effect, the Coriolis effect, and chemical reaction effects on the onset of convection in a porous medium. To the best of our knowledge, linear stability theory and ANN prediction of threshold Rayleigh number for the onset of magneto-rotating convection in a porous medium with first-order chemical reaction have not been studied so far. The plan for this article is as follows: Section 2 describes the mathematical modeling under consideration, Section 3 presents the ANN methodology, and Section 4 discusses the results. The paper ends with a conclusion in Section 5.

2. Mathematical Modeling

2.1. Basic Equations

Consider an electrically conducting fluid-saturated porous layer of thickness d that is salted from below and confined between two parallel horizontal planes at $z = 0$ and $z = d$. The horizontal coordinate x and vertical coordinate z increase upwards in a Cartesian coordinate with the origin at the bottom of the porous medium. The surfaces are extended infinitely in x and y directions and a constant salinity gradient C is maintained across the porous layer. Let $\Omega = \Omega \hat{e}_z$ be the constant angular velocity of the layer. To make the Boussinesq approximation valid, the physical properties of the fluid are assumed to be constant, except for density in the buoyancy term. The porous medium is considered homogeneous and isotropic. Based on [15,19,39,40], with the physical configuration recalled in Figure 1, the governing equations are

$$\nabla \cdot \mathbf{u} = 0, \tag{1}$$

$$\rho_0 Ca \frac{\partial u}{\partial t} + \frac{\mu}{K}\mathbf{u} = -\nabla p + \rho_0 g \beta_c (C - C_0)\hat{e}_z + \sigma_1(\mathbf{u} \times B_0 \hat{e}_z) \times B_0 \hat{e}_z - \frac{2\rho_0 \Omega}{\delta}\hat{e}_z \times \mathbf{u}, \tag{2}$$

$$\epsilon \frac{\partial C}{\partial t} + (\mathbf{u} \cdot \nabla)C = \epsilon D_v \nabla^2 C - \beta C, \tag{3}$$

subject to the following boundary conditions

$$\mathbf{u} = 0, \ C = C + \Delta C \text{ on } z = 0,$$
$$\mathbf{u} = 0, \ C = C_0, \text{ on } z = d. \tag{4}$$

Here, Ca, μ, K, p, ρ, β_c, g, t, ϵ, D_v, and β are the acceleration coefficient, dynamic viscosity, permeability, dynamic pressure, reference density, solute expansion coefficient, gravity acceleration, time, porosity, solute diffusion coefficient, and reaction rate of the solute, respectively. The dimensionless quantities are given as follows:

$$x = x^*d, \qquad y = y^*d, \qquad z = z^*d,$$
$$u = \frac{\phi D_v}{d}u^*, \qquad v = \frac{\phi D_v}{d}v^*, \qquad w = \frac{\phi D_v}{d}w^*,$$
$$t = \frac{d^2}{D_v}t^*, \qquad C = C_0 C^*, \tag{5}$$

as well as the non-dimensional quantities

$$Ra = \frac{g\rho_0 \beta_c \Delta C K d^n}{\phi^n \mu D_v^n}, \qquad Dm = \frac{\beta d^2}{\phi D_v}, \qquad Ha = \frac{\sigma_1 B_0^2 K}{\mu},$$
$$Ta = \frac{2\rho_0 \Omega \kappa_f}{\mu \phi}, \qquad Va = \frac{\mu d^2}{\rho_F C_a K D_v}, \tag{6}$$

where Ra, Ta, Ha, Dm, and Va are the Rayleigh number, Taylor number, Hartmann number, Damkohler number, and Vadasz number, respectively. The non-dimensional form of the governing Equations (1)–(3) and the corresponding boundary conditions (4) are given by

$$\nabla \cdot \mathbf{u} = 0, \tag{7}$$

$$\frac{1}{Va}\frac{\partial \mathbf{u}}{\partial t} + \mathbf{u} = -\nabla p + RaC\hat{e}_z + Ha^2[(\mathbf{u} \times \hat{e}_z) \times \hat{e}_z] - Ta\hat{e}_z \times \mathbf{u}, \tag{8}$$

$$\frac{\partial C}{\partial t} + (\mathbf{u}.\nabla)C = \nabla^2 C - DmC, \tag{9}$$

subject to the boundary conditions

$$\mathbf{u} = 0, \ C = 1 \text{ on } z = 0,$$
$$\mathbf{u} = 0, \ C = 0 \text{ on } z = 1. \tag{10}$$

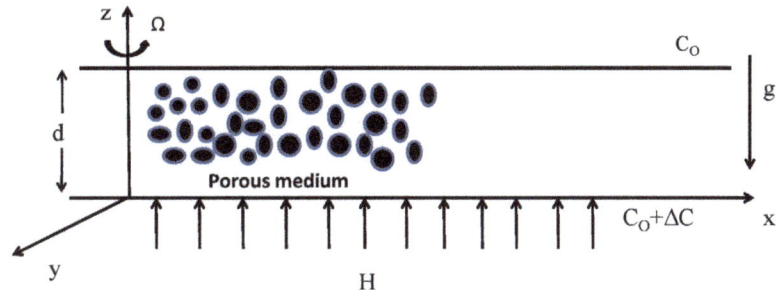

Figure 1. Physical configuration.

2.2. Basic Flow

The basic stationary flow of Equations (7)–(10) is as follows:

$$u_b = 0, \qquad (11)$$

$$C_b = 1 - z. \qquad (12)$$

2.3. Linear Stability Analysis

The perturbation of the basic state for the Equations (7)–(10) is

$$\mathbf{u} = u_b + U', \; C = C_b + C', \; p = P_b + P'. \qquad (13)$$

By substituting Equation (13) into Equations (7)–(10), one obtains

$$\nabla U' = 0 \qquad (14)$$

$$\frac{1}{Va}\frac{\partial U'}{\partial t} + U' = -\nabla P' + RaC'\hat{e}_z + Ha^2[(U' \times \hat{e}_z) \times \hat{e}_z] - Ta\hat{e}_z \times U', \qquad (15)$$

$$\frac{\partial C'}{\partial t} = w' + \nabla^2 C' - DmC', \qquad (16)$$

subject to the boundary conditions

$$U' = 0, \; C' = 0 \text{ on } z = 0,$$
$$U' = 0, \; C' = 0 \text{ on } z = 1. \qquad (17)$$

By taking the third component of the curl of Equation (15) and curl of curl of Equation (15), one obtains

$$\left(1 + \frac{1}{Va}\frac{\partial}{\partial t} - Ha^2\right)w_z - Ta^{1/2}\frac{\partial w'}{\partial z} = 0, \qquad (18)$$

$$\left(\frac{1}{Va}\nabla^2\frac{\partial}{\partial t} + \nabla^2 + Ha^2\frac{\partial^2}{\partial z^2}\right) - Ra\nabla_h^2 C' + Ta^{1/2}\frac{\partial w_z}{\partial z} = 0. \qquad (19)$$

From Equations (16), (18) and (19), we obtain

$$\left[D_2\left(D_1 D_3 + Ta\frac{\partial^2}{\partial z^2}\right) - Ra\nabla_h^2 D_1\right] w' = 0, \qquad (20)$$

where

$$D_1 = 1 + \frac{1}{Va}\frac{\partial}{\partial t} - Ha^2, \tag{21}$$

$$D_2 = \frac{\partial}{\partial t} - \nabla^2 + Dm, \tag{22}$$

$$D_3 = \frac{1}{Va}\nabla^2\frac{\partial}{\partial t} + \nabla^2 + Ha^2\frac{\partial^2}{\partial z^2}. \tag{23}$$

Let us introduce the normal mode by writing that the perturbation is in the form of

$$w' = e^{i(lx+my)+\sigma t}\sin(\pi z), \tag{24}$$

where l and m are the wave numbers along x and y directions and σ is a complex parameter. Substituting Equation (24) into Equation (20), one obtains

$$Ra = \frac{\sigma + \delta^2 + Dm}{q^2}\left(\frac{1}{Va}\sigma\delta^2 + \delta^2 + Ha^2\pi^2\right) + \frac{Ta\pi^2(\sigma + \delta^2 + Dm)}{q^2\left(1 + \frac{\sigma}{Va} - Ha^2\right)}, \tag{25}$$

where $q^2 = l^2 + m^2$ and $\delta^2 = \pi^2 + q^2$.

2.4. Stationary Mode

To study the stationary stability, take $\sigma = 0$ in the Rayleigh number for the exchange of the stabilities at the onset of stationary convection, say Ra_{sc}. It is given as

$$Ra_{sc} = \frac{\delta^2 + Dm}{q^2}\left(\delta^2 + Ha^2\pi^2\right) + \frac{Ta\pi^2(\delta^2 + Dm)}{q^2(1 - Ha^2)}. \tag{26}$$

The critical Rayleigh number at the onset of stationary convection Ra_c^{sc} is

$$Ra_c^{sc} = Dm + 2\pi\sqrt{\frac{(Dm + \pi^2)(-1 + Ha^4 - Ta)}{Ha^2 - 1}} + \frac{\pi(-2 + Ha^2 + Ha^4 - Ta)}{Ha^2 - 1}. \tag{27}$$

The above stationary Rayleigh number reduces to $Ra_{sc} = \frac{\delta^4}{q^2}$ with the critical values $Ra_c^{sc} = 4\pi^2$, $q_c^{sc} = \pi$ in the absence of a magnetic field, Coriolis effect, and chemical reaction effect, which agrees with the results of Horton and Rogers [41] and Lapwood [42] for the onset of convection in a porous layer.

2.5. Oscillatory Mode

To study the oscillatory stability, take $\sigma = i\omega$. The Rayleigh number at the onset of oscillatory convection is

$$Ra_{oc} = \frac{\delta^4\omega^4 + \alpha_1\omega^2 + \alpha_2}{q^2Va[(-1 + Ha^2)^2Va^2 + \omega^2]}, \tag{28}$$

where

$$\alpha_1 = Va\pi^2(DmHa^2 + TaVa) + (Dm + Ha^2\pi^2)\delta^2 - (-1 + Ha^2)^2Va\delta^4, \tag{29}$$

$$\alpha_2 = -Da^4 + (-1 + Ha^2)(Dm + Ha^2\pi^2) - \pi^2Ta)\delta^2 +$$
$$(-1 + Ha^2)Va^3\left[Dm\pi^2(-Ha^2 + Ha^4 - Ta)\right]\delta^4 + -\delta^6, \tag{30}$$

$$\omega^2 = -(-1 + Ha^2)^2Va^2 + \frac{\pi^2Ta\left[Dm + (-1 + Ha^2)Va + \delta^2\right]}{Ha^2\pi^2Va + \delta^2(Dm + Va + \delta^2)}. \tag{31}$$

3. Artificial Neural Network Modeling

Let us now present some basis for the ANN modeling. An ANN is a computing system based on biological neural networks (which are interconnected) that resemble a brain. In general, ANN can be used to predict data. In this study, we used a network with three layers: input, hidden, and output, as well as other components, such as feed-forward propagation, an optimal number of neurons, and backpropagation (update weights and biases) (see Figures 2 and 3). To train the suggested network, we use the Levenberg–Marquardt backpropagation algorithm, as proposed by Yu and Wilamowski [46]. To prepare the organization, data are first divided into three groups. A total of 650 datasets were utilized to train, test, and validate the ANN model, with 70%, 15%, and 15% of the data being randomly allocated for preparing and assessing. The optimal number of neurons (Nn) for the best performing artificial neural network architecture is determined by examining three different statistical values: coefficient of determination (R^2), root mean square error ($RMSE$), and root mean relative error ($RMRE$), which are defined by

$$R^2 = 1 - \frac{\sum_i^N (Ra_{c,s} - Ra_{c,a})^2}{\sum_i^N (Ra_{c,s} - \overline{Ra_{c,a}})^2},$$

$$RMSE = \sqrt{\frac{\sum_i^N (Ra_{c,s} - Ra_{c,a})^2}{N}}$$

$$RMRE = \sqrt{\frac{1}{N}\sum_i^N \left|\frac{(Ra_{c,s} - Ra_{c,a})}{Ra_{c,s}}\right|}. \tag{32}$$

Here, $Ra_{c,s}$ is the simulated critical Rayleigh number, $Ra_{c,a}$ is the ANN critical Rayleigh number, the index i refers to the i-th experiment, bar denotes average value, and N is data size or number. See Seo et al. [45] for further details on these measures. The regression plots of training, testing, and validation for these three different sets are illustrated in Figure 4. The values of R^2, $RMSE$, and $RMRE$ for different values of Va, Ha, Ta, and Dm are illustrated in Tables 1 and 2. From these tables, it is clear that the present ANN model can predict the critical Ra for linear stability analysis for different Va, Ha, Ta, and Dm.

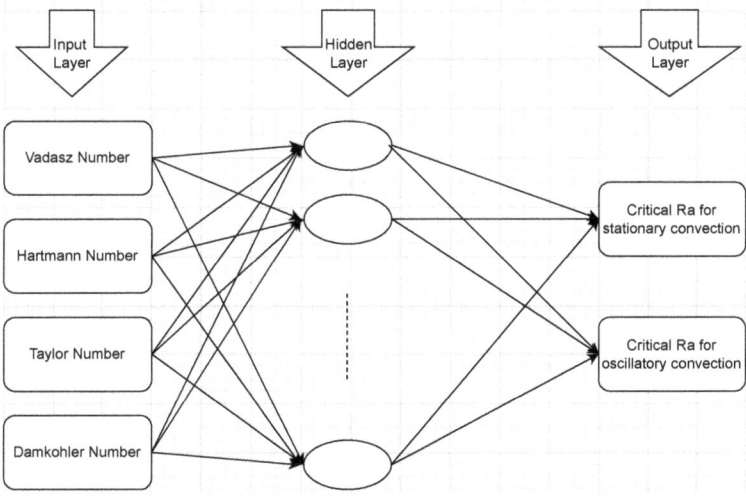

Figure 2. Schematic representation of a multilayer feed-forward network consisting of two inputs, one hidden layer, and two outputs.

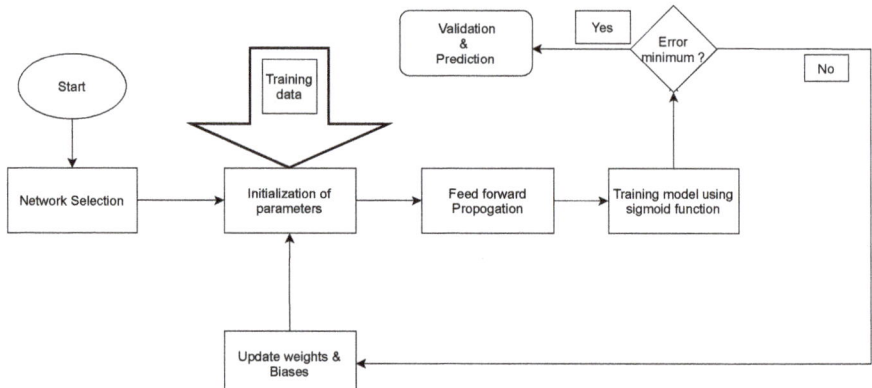

Figure 3. Flow chart of the artificial neural network.

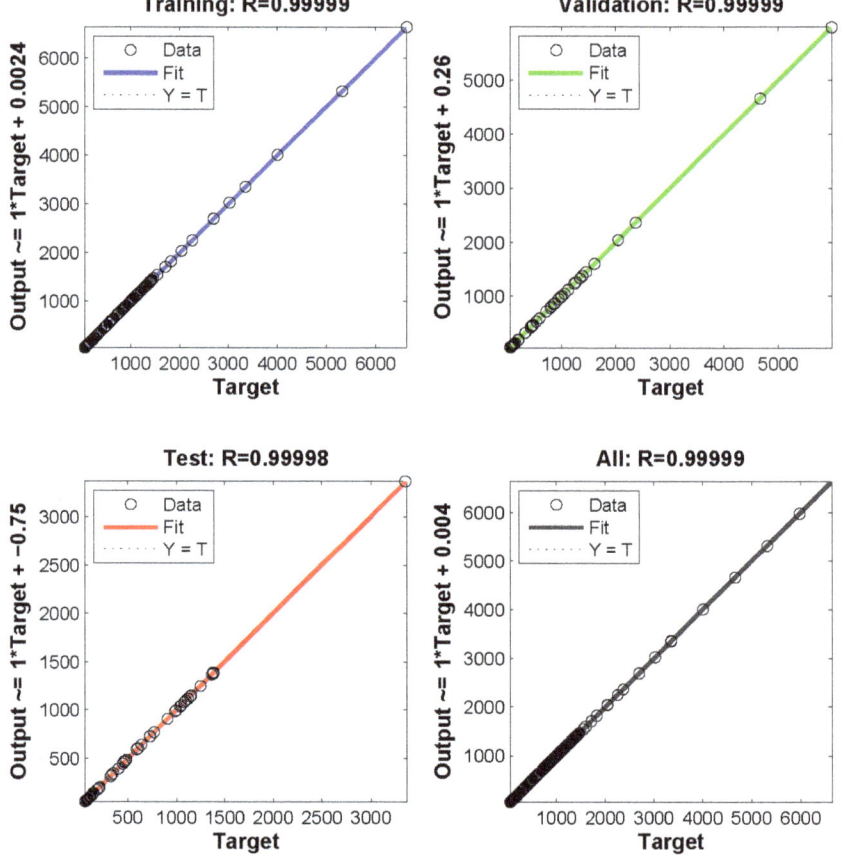

Figure 4. Regression plots for training, validation, and testing; the targets are simulated data and the outputs are ANN-predicted data.

Table 1. Calculated stationary values of R^2, $RMSE$, and $RMRE$ at various values of Ta, Dm, and Ha.

Values		Stationary		
		R^2	$RMSE$	$RMRE$
$Ta = 0, 5, 10, \ldots, 50$	$Va = 0.5, Ha = 0.5, Dm = 2$	0.999992	0.301510	0.549099
$Dm = 0.5, 1, 1.5, \ldots, 5$	$Va = 0.5, Ha = 0.5, Ta = 20$	0.999991	0.316226	0.562340
$Ha = 0.1, 0.2, 0.3, \ldots, 0.9$	$Va = 0.5, Dm = 2, Ta = 20$	0.999996	0.333332	0.5773497

Table 2. Calculated oscillatory values of R^2, $RMSE$, and $RMRE$ at various values of Ta, Dm, and Ha.

Values		Oscillatory		
		R^2	$RMSE$	$RMRE$
$Ta = 0, 5, 10, \ldots, 50$	$Va = 0.5, Ha = 0.5, Dm = 2$	0.999999	0.447213	0.668740
$Dm = 0.5, 1, 1.5, \ldots, 5$	$Va = 0.5, Ha = 0.5, Ta = 20$	0.999994	0.316226	0.562340
$Ha = 0.1, 0.2, 0.3, \ldots, 0.9$	$Va = 0.5, Dm = 2, Ta = 20$	0.999966	0.333327	0.577345

4. Discussion

The numerical results and discussion are presented in this section. In this results part, we evaluated a numerical study of the effect of the magnetic field and rotation on the onset of dissolution-driven convection saturated porous layer with ANN prediction. The critical Rayleigh number at the onset of stationary (Ra_c^{sc}) and oscillatory (Ra_c^{oc}) convection is obtained for the prescribed values of the other parameters. The investigations are performed for various values of the Hartmann number, Taylor number, Vadasz number, and Damkohler number. In Figures 5–10, solid and dotted lines represent the stationary and oscillatory convection, respectively. The following physically realistic range of these parameters is considered: $0 \leq Va \leq 20$ [37], $0 \leq Ta \leq 50$ [22], $0 \leq Ha \leq 0.9$ [40], and $0 \leq Dm \leq 20$ [23].

First, we shall discuss the theory of bifurcation points in Figures 5–7, the results obtained numerically by linear and weakly nonlinear stability analysis. Takens–Bogdanov and codimension two bifurcation points are identified in these figures. Takens–Bogdanov bifurcation point is the point at which the oscillatory neutral curve intersects the stationary neutral curve and approaches zero as the intersection point is approached. At the Takens–Bogdanov bifurcation point, we have

$$R_s(q_s) = R_o(q_o) \text{ and } q_s = q_o. \tag{33}$$

The codimension two bifurcation point is the intersection between a Hopf and Pitchfork bifurcation with distinct wave numbers. At the codimension two bifurcation point, we have

$$R_s(q_s) = R_o(q_o) \text{ and } q_s \neq q_o. \tag{34}$$

The effect of the Vadasz number Va on the neutral curves is presented in Figure 8. We find that the Ra_c^{sc} is independent of the Vadasz number Va, whereas the Ra_c^{oc} decreases with a decrease in the value of the Vadasz number Va. This reports the porosity effects on driven convection in a Newtonian-fluid-saturated porous layer. Furthermore, from this figure, one can notice that for $Va = 1$, there exists a threshold $Ta^* \in (1.9, 2)$ such that for $Ta < Ta^*$, stationary convection sets in, while for $Ta^* \in (1.9, 2)$, there is a switch from stationary to oscillatory convection. Similar behavior can be observed for the other values of Va.

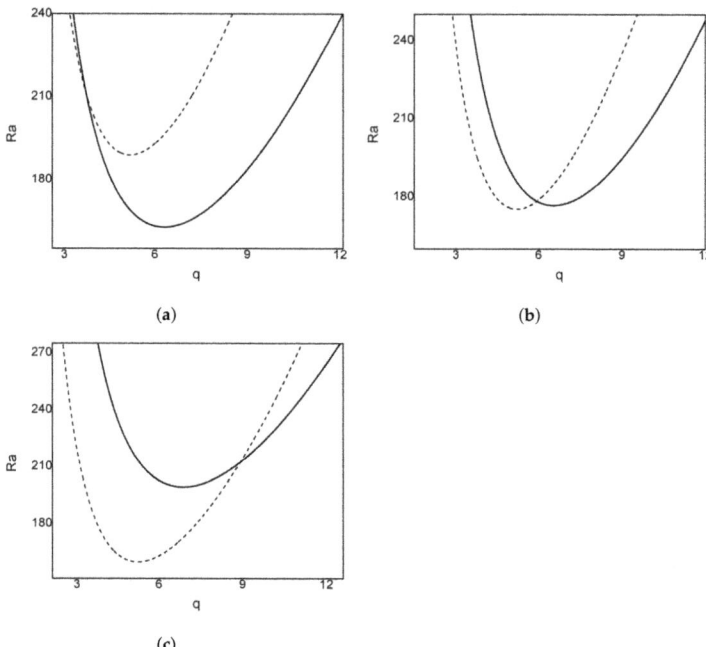

Figure 5. Neutral curves (solid lines represent the stationary convection and dotted lines represent the oscillatory convection) for $Dm = 20$, $Ta = 3.1$, $Va = 20$: (**a**) $Ha = 0.5$, (**b**) $Ha = 0.6$, (**c**) $Ha = 0.7$.

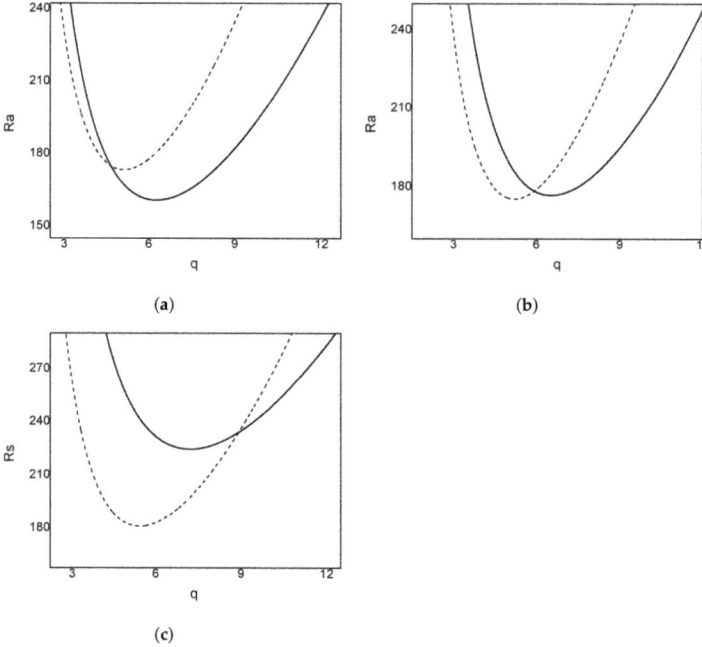

Figure 6. Neutral curves (solid lines represent the stationary convection and dotted lines represent the oscillatory convection) for $Dm = 20$, $Ha = 0.6$, $Va = 20$: (**a**) $Ta = 2.5$, (**b**) $Ta = 3.1$, (**c**) $Ta = 5$.

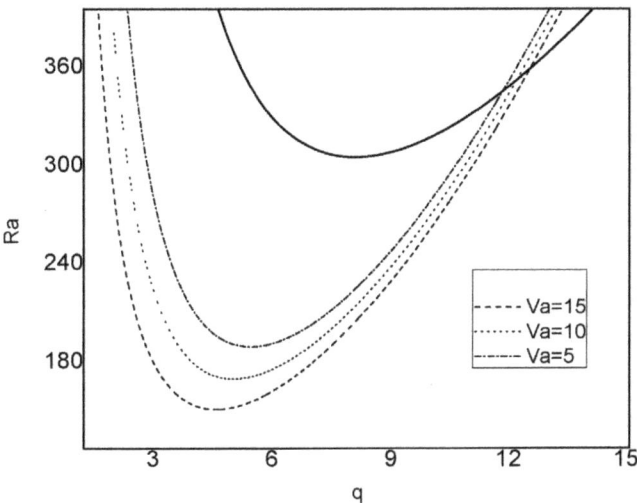

Figure 7. Neutral curves (solid lines represent the stationary convection and dotted lines represent the oscillatory convection) for $Dm = 20$, $Ha = 0.5$, $Ta = 10$.

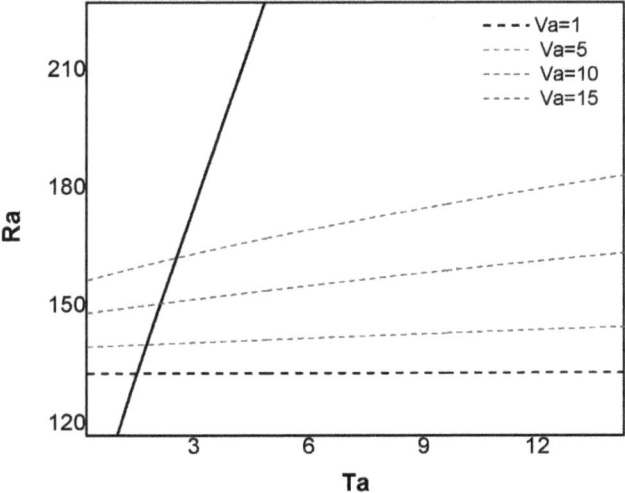

Figure 8. Plots of the critical Ra as the function of Ta for $Va = 1, 5, 10, 15$.

Figure 9 illustrates the effect of the magnetic field on the onset of convection. From this figure, one can observe that the Hartmann number has a stabilizing effect on stationary convection. On the contrary, the Hartmann number has a stabilizing effect on oscillatory convection. We find that the minimum value of the stationary Rayleigh number for stationary mode increases with increasing Hartmann number Ha. On the other hand, the minimum value of the oscillatory Rayleigh number decreases with an increase in the value of the Hartmann number Ha. Thus, Ha has a contrasting effect on the stability of the system in the case of stationary and oscillatory modes. From this figure, we notice that for $Ha = 0.2$, there exists a threshold $Ta^* \in (1.9, 2)$ such that for $Ta < Ta^*$, oscillatory convection sets in, while for $Ta^* \in (1.9, 2)$, there is a switch from oscillatory to stationary convection. Similar behavior can be observed for the other values of Va.

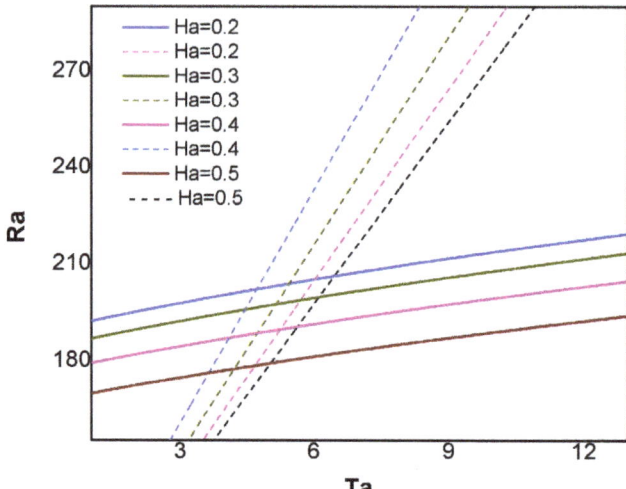

Figure 9. Plots of critical Ra as the function of Ta for $Dm = 5$, $Va = 5$, $Ha = 0.2, 0.3, 0.4, 0.5$.

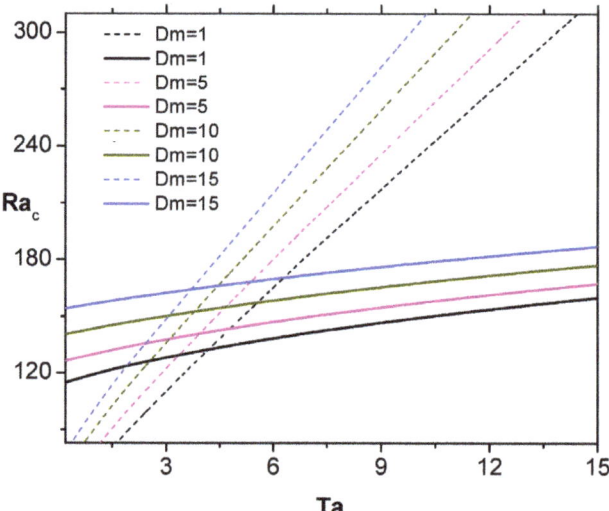

Figure 10. Plots of critical Ra as the function of Ta for $Va = 15$, $Ha = 0.5$, $Dm = 1, 5, 10, 15$.

Similarly, Figure 10 depicts the effect of Dm on the system. From this figure, we see that the effect of increasing Dm is to increase the Ra_c^{sc} and Ra_c^{oc}, implying that Dm has a stabilizing effect on the onset of dissolution-driven convection in a porous medium. This can be explained as follows. An increase in the value of Dm promotes the dissolution reaction to absorb some of the heat energy, causing the surrounding environment to feel cold. Hence, a larger solute gradient is required for the onset of convection so that the system is stabilized. We find that for fixed values of other physical parameters, there exists a critical Taylor number Ta_c such that when $Ta < Ta_c$, convection begins as an oscillatory type, and when $Ta > Ta_c$, the convection switches to stationary. Further, when $Ta = Ta_c$, the stationary and oscillatory modes occur simultaneously.

Furthermore, Figures 8–10 demonstrate the Coriolis effect on the onset of convection. All of these figures show that the Ra_c^{sc} and Ra_c^{oc} increase as the Taylor number increases. Hence, the Taylor number has a stabilizing effect on the system. This can be explained as follows: in the fluid, the rotation creates vorticity. As a result, the fluid has a faster velocity in horizontal planes. Hence, the perpendicular velocity of the fluid decreases. Therefore, the convection does not start right away.

The comparison of numerical and predicted ANN data of the critical Ra with different values of Va, Ha, Ta, and Dm is shown in Figures 11 and 12. From all these figures, it is obvious to see that the trained predictive ANN model holds well with the numerical results.

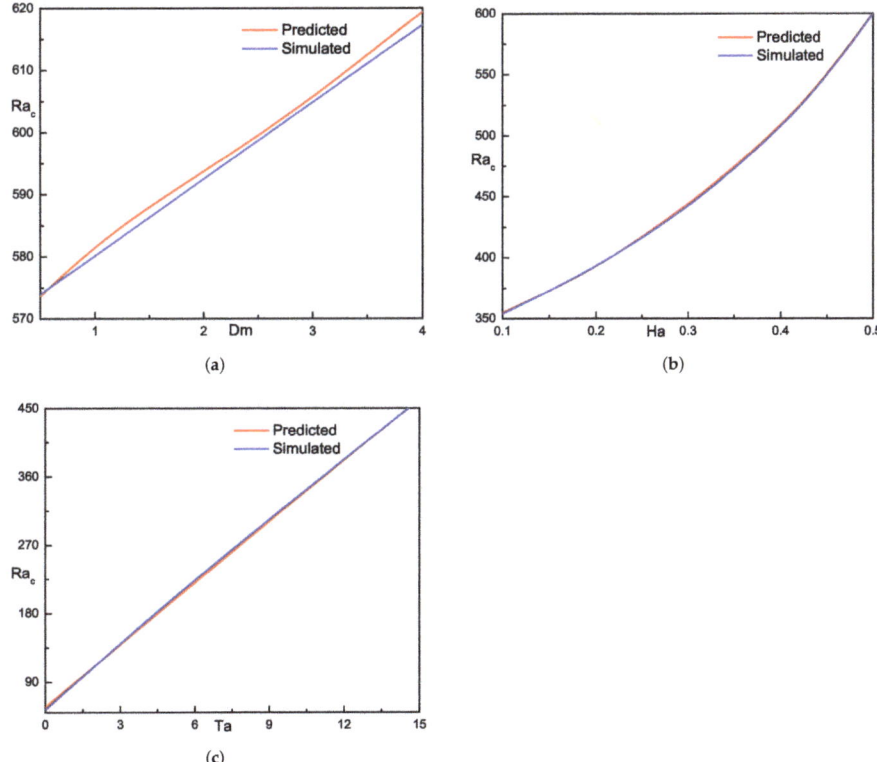

Figure 11. Comparison of the simulated and ANN-predicted critical Rayleigh number values for (**a**) Dm, (**b**) Ha, and (**c**) Ta.

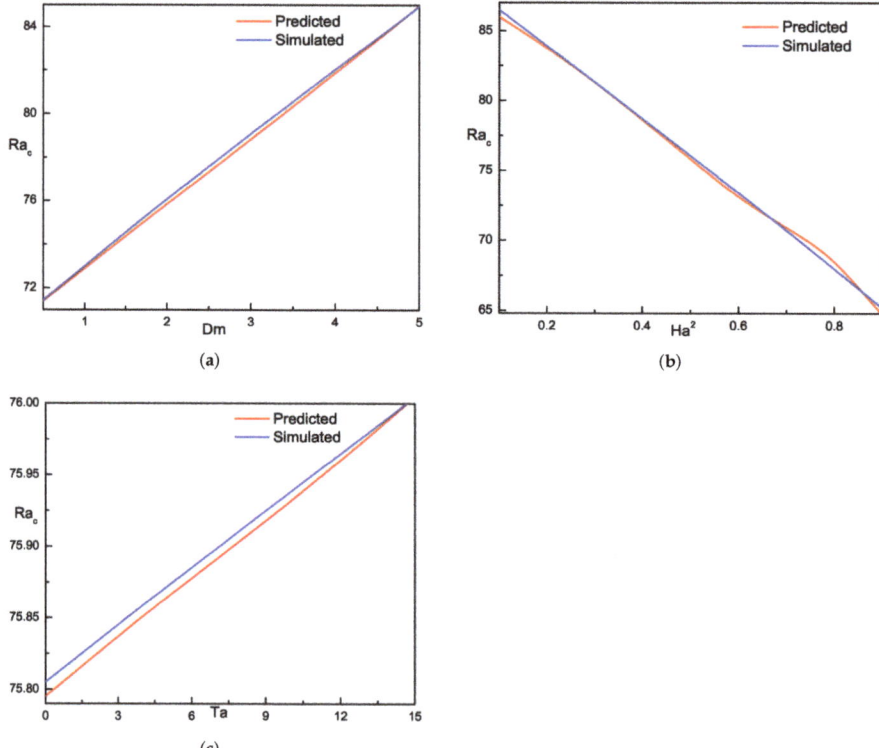

Figure 12. Comparison of the simulated and ANN-predicted critical Rayleigh number values for (**a**) Dm, (**b**) Ha, and (**c**) Ta.

5. Conclusions

In the present analysis, the onset of dissolution-driven convection in a porous layer with the effect of the magnetic field and rotation is studied. The behavior of various physical parameters is investigated. The results can be summarized as follows: Takens–Bogdanov and codimension two bifurcation points are identified. The Vadasz number does not show any effect on stationary convection, whereas it has a destabilizing effect on oscillatory convection. The Hartmann number has destabilizing and stabilizing effects on stationary and oscillatory convection, respectively. The Damkohler number has a stabilizing effect on the system. Furthermore, an artificial neural network (ANN) is used to model and predict the critical Rayleigh numbers. The simulated and predicted values of the proposed ANN model were found to be highly close, indicating that the expected critical Rayleigh number and the observed critical Rayleigh number are quite similar.

In future work, we plan to study linear instability and nonlinear stability. Another interesting problem is to investigate the stationary or oscillatory convection at the onset of instability using Brinkmann's law.

Author Contributions: Conceptualization, G.S.K.R. and N.V.K.; methodology, G.S.K.R., N.V.K., R.R., K.K.P. and C.C.; software, G.S.K.R., N.V.K., R.R., K.K.P. and C.C.; validation, G.S.K.R., N.V.K., R.R., K.K.P. and C.C.; formal analysis, G.S.K.R., N.V.K., R.R., K.K.P. and C.C.; investigation, G.S.K.R., N.V.K., R.R., K.K.P. and C.C.; resources, G.S.K.R., N.V.K., R.R., K.K.P. and C.C.; data curation, G.S.K.R., N.V.K., R.R., K.K.P. and C.C.; writing—original draft preparation, G.S.K.R., N.V.K., R.R., K.K.P. and C.C.; writing—review and editing, G.S.K.R., N.V.K., R.R., K.K.P. and C.C.; visualization, G.S.K.R., N.V.K., R.R., K.K.P. and C.C. All authors have read and agreed to the published version of the manuscript.

Funding: This research received no external funding.

Conflicts of Interest: The authors declare no conflict of interest.

References

1. Ghoshal, P.; Kim, M.C.; Cardoso, S.S. Reactive–convective dissolution in a porous medium: the storage of carbon dioxide in saline aquifers. *Phys. Chem. Chem. Phys.* **2017**, *19*, 644–655. [CrossRef] [PubMed]
2. Ilya, A.; Ashraf, M.; Ali, A.; Shah, Z.; Kumam, P.; Thounthong, P. Heat source and sink effects on periodic mixed convection flow along the electrically conducting cone inserted in porous medium. *PLoS ONE* **2021**, *16*, e0260845. [CrossRef] [PubMed]
3. Alshehri, A.; Shah, Z. Computational analysis of viscous dissipation and Darcy-Forchheimer porous medium on radioactive hybrid nanofluid. *Case Stud. Therm. Eng.* **2022**, *30*, 101728. [CrossRef]
4. Vo, D.D.; Shah, Z.; Sheikholeslami, M.; Shafee, A.; Nguyen, T.K. Numerical investigation of MHD nanomaterial convective migration and heat transfer within a sinusoidal porous cavity. *Phys. Scr.* **2019**, *94*, 115225. [CrossRef]
5. Jamshed, W.; Şirin, C.; Selimefendigil, F.; Shamshuddin, M.D.; Altowairqi, Y.; Eid, M.R. Thermal Characterization of Coolant Maxwell Type Nanofluid Flowing in Parabolic Trough Solar Collector (PTSC) Used Inside Solar Powered Ship Application. *Coatings* **2021**, *11*, 1552. [CrossRef]
6. Mahabaleshwar, U.S.; Rekha, M.B.; Kumar, P.N.V.; Selimefendigil, F.; Sakanaka, P.H.; Lorenzini, G.; Nayakar, S.N.R. Mass transfer characteristics of MHD casson fluid flow past stretching/shrinking sheet. *J. Eng. Thermophys.* **2020**, *29*, 285–302. [CrossRef]
7. Steinberg, V.; Brand, H. Convective instabilities of binary mixtures with fast chemical reaction in a porous medium. *J. Chem. Phys.* **1983**, *78*, 2655–2660. [CrossRef]
8. Steinberg, V.; Brand, H.R. Amplitude equations for the onset of convection in a reactive mixture in a porous medium. *J. Chem. Phys.* **1984**, *80*, 431–435. [CrossRef]
9. Gatica, J.E.; Viljoen, H.J.; Hlavacek, V. Interaction between chemical reaction and natural convection in porous media. *Chem. Eng. Sci.* **1989**, *44*, 1853–1870. [CrossRef]
10. Pritchard, D.; Richardson, C.N. The effect of temperature-dependent solubility on the onset of thermosolutal convection in a horizontal porous layer. *J. Fluid Mech.* **2007**, *571*, 59–95. [CrossRef]
11. Rees, D.A.S.; Selim, A.; Ennis-King, J. *The Instability of Unsteady Boundary Layers in Porous Media*; Springer: Berlin/Heidelberg, Germany, 2008.
12. Slim, A.C.; Ramakrishnan, T. Onset and cessation of time-dependent, dissolution-driven convection in porous media. *Phys. Fluids* **2010**, *22*, 124103. [CrossRef]
13. Bestehorn, M.; Firoozabadi, A. Effect of fluctuations on the onset of density-driven convection in porous media. *Phys. Fluids* **2012**, *24*, 114102. [CrossRef]
14. Kim, M.C.; Choi, C.K. Effect of first-order chemical reaction on gravitational instability in a porous medium. *Phys. Rev. E* **2014**, *90*, 053016. [CrossRef] [PubMed]
15. Hill, A.A.; Morad, M.R. Convective stability of carbon sequestration in anisotropic porous media. *Proc. R. Soc. Math. Phys. Eng. Sci.* **2014**, *470*, 20140373. [CrossRef]
16. Al-Sulaimi, B. The energy stability of Darcy thermosolutal convection with reaction. *Int. J. Heat Mass Transf.* **2015**, *86*, 369–376. [CrossRef]
17. Emami-Meybodi, H. Stability analysis of dissolution-driven convection in porous media. *Phys. Fluids* **2017**, *29*, 014102. [CrossRef]
18. Salibindla, A.K.; Subedi, R.; Shen, V.C.; Masuk, A.U.; Ni, R. Dissolution-driven convection in a heterogeneous porous medium. *J. Fluid Mech.* **2018**, *857*, 61–79. [CrossRef]
19. Gautam, K.; Narayana, P.A.L. On the stability of carbon sequestration in an anisotropic horizontal porous layer with a first-order chemical reaction. *Proc. R. Soc. A* **2019**, *475*, 20180365. [CrossRef]
20. Babu, A.B.; Koteswararao, N.V.; Reddy, G.S. Instability conditions in a porous medium due to horizontal magnetic field. In *Numerical Heat Transfer and Fluid Flow*; Springer: Singapore, 2019; pp. 621–628.
21. Babu, A.B.; Rao, N.; Tagare, S.G. Weakly nonlinear thermohaline convection in a sparsely packed porous medium due to horizontal magnetic field. *Eur. Phys. J. Plus* **2021**, *136*, 795. [CrossRef]
22. Babu, A.B.; Anilkumar, D.; Rao, N.V.K. Weakly nonlinear thermohaline rotating convection in a sparsely packed porous medium. *Int. J. Heat Mass Transf.* **2022**, *188*, 122602. [CrossRef]
23. Reddy, G.S.K.; Ragoju, R. Thermal instability of a Maxwell fluid saturated porous layer with chemical reaction. *Spec. Top. Rev. Porous Media Int. J.* **2022**, *13*, 33–47. [CrossRef]
24. Yin, Y.; Qu, Z.; Zhu, C.; Zhang, J. Visualizing gas diffusion behaviors in three-dimensional nanoporous media. *Energy Fuels* **2021**, *35*, 2075–2086. [CrossRef]
25. Yin, Y.; Qu, Z.; Prodanović, M.; Landry, C.J. Identifying the dominant transport mechanism in single nanoscale pores and 3D nanoporous media. *Fundam. Res.* **2022**. [CrossRef]
26. Utech, H.P.; Flemmings, M.C. Elimination of solute banding in indium antimonide crystals by growth in a magnetic field. *J. Appl. Phys.* **1966**, *37*, 2021–2024. [CrossRef]
27. Vives, C.; Perry, C. Effects of magnetically damped convection during the controlled solidification of metals and alloys. *Int. J. Heat Mass Transf.* **1987**, *30*, 479–496. [CrossRef]

28. Garandet, J.P.; Alboussiere, T.; Moreau, R. Buoyancy driven convection in a rectangular enclosure with a transverse magnetic field. *Int. J. Heat Mass Transf.* **1992**, *35*, 741–748. [CrossRef]
29. Alboussiere, T.; Garandet, J.P. Buoyancy-driven convection with a uniform magnetic field. Part 1. Asymptotic analysis. *J. Fluid Mech.* **1993**, *253*, 545–563. [CrossRef]
30. Rudraiah, N.; Venkatachalappa, M.; Subbaraya, C.K. Combined surface tension and buoyancy-driven convection in a rectangular open cavity in the presence of a magnetic field. *Int. J. Non-Linear Mech.* **1995**, *30*, 759–770. [CrossRef]
31. Davoust, L.; Cowley, M.D.; Moreau, R.; Bolcato, R. Buoyancy-driven convection with a uniform magnetic field. Part 2. Experimental investigation. *J. Fluid Mech.* **1999**, *400*, 59–90. [CrossRef]
32. Priede, J.; Gerbeth, G. Hydrothermal wave instability of thermocapillary-driven convection in a transverse magnetic field. *J. Fluid Mech.* **2000**, *404*, 211–250. [CrossRef]
33. Pirmohammadi, M.; Ghassemi, M.; Sheikhzadeh, G.A. The effect of a magnetic field on buoyancy-driven convection in differentially heated square cavity. In Proceedings of the 2008 14th Symposium on Electromagnetic Launch Technology, Victoria, BC, Canada, 10–13 June 2008; pp. 1–6.
34. Sankar, M.; Venkatachalappa, M.; Do, Y. Effect of magnetic field on the buoyancy and thermocapillary driven convection of an electrically conducting fluid in an annular enclosure. *Int. J. Heat Fluid Flow* **2011**, *32*, 402–412. [CrossRef]
35. Erglis, K.; Tatulcenkov, A.; Kitenbergs, G.; Petrichenko, O.; Ergin, F.G.; Watz, B.B.; Cbers, A. Magnetic field driven microconvection in the Hele–Shaw cell. *J. Fluid Mech.* **2013**, *714*, 612–633. [CrossRef]
36. Babu, A.B.; Reddy, G.S.K.; Tagare, S.G. Nonlinear magneto convection due to horizontal magnetic field and vertical axis of rotation due to thermal and compositional buoyancy. *Results Phys.* **2019**, *12*, 2078–2090. [CrossRef]
37. Govender, S.; Vadasz, P. The effect of mechanical and thermal anisotropy on the stability of gravity driven convection in rotating porous media in the presence of thermal non-equilibrium. *Transp. Porous Media* **2007**, *69*, 55–66. [CrossRef]
38. Babu, A.B.; Reddy, G.S.K.; Tagare, S.G. Nonlinear magnetoconvection in a rotating fluid due to thermal and compositional buoyancy with anisotropic diffusivities. *Heat Transf. Asian Res.* **2020**, *49*, 335–355. [CrossRef]
39. Wang, S.; Wenchang, T. The onset of Darcy–Brinkman thermosolutal convection in a horizontal porous media. *Phys. Lett. A* **2009**, *373*, 776–780. [CrossRef]
40. Deepika, N.; Murthy, P.V.S.N.; Narayana, P.A.L. The effect of magnetic field on the stability of double-diffusive convection in a porous layer with horizontal mass throughflow. *Transp. Porous Media* **2020**, *134*, 435–452. [CrossRef]
41. Horton, C.W.; Rogers, F.T. Convection currents in a porous medium. *J. Appl. Phys.* **1945**, *16*, 367–370. [CrossRef]
42. Lapwood, E.R. Convection of a fluid in a porous medium. *Math. Proc. Camb. Philos. Soc.* **1948**, *44*, 508–521. [CrossRef]
43. Dey, P.; Abhijit, S.; Das, A.K. Development of GEP and ANN model to predict the unsteady forced convection over a cylinder. *Neural Comput. Appl.* **2016**, *27*, 2537–2549. [CrossRef]
44. Rana, P.; Gupta, V.; Kumar, L. LTNE magneto-thermal stability analysis on rough surfaces utilizing hybrid nanoparticles and heat source with artificial neural network prediction. *Appl. Nanosci.* **2021**. [CrossRef]
45. Seo, Y.M.; Pandey, S.; Lee, H.U.; Choi, C.; Park, Y.G.; Ha, M.Y. Prediction of heat transfer distribution induced by the variation in vertical location of circular cylinder on Rayleigh-Bénard convection using artificial neural network. *Int. J. Mech. Sci.* **2021**, *209*, 106701. [CrossRef]
46. Yu, H.; Wilamowski, B.M. Levenberg–Marquardt training. In *Intelligent Systems*; CRC Press: Boca Raton, FL, USA, 2018; Chapter 12, pp. 1–16.
47. Seo, Y.M.; Luo, K.; Ha, M.Y.; Park, Y.G. Direct numerical simulation and artificial neural network modeling of heat transfer characteristics on natural convection with a sinusoidal cylinder in a long rectangular enclosure. *Int. J. Heat Mass Transf.* **2020**, *152*, 119564. [CrossRef]
48. Khosravi, R.; Rabiei, S.; Bahiraei, M.; Teymourtash, A.R. Predicting entropy generation of a hybrid nanofluid containing graphene–platinum nanoparticles through a microchannel liquid block using neural networks. *Int. Commun. Heat Mass Transf.* **2019**, *109*, 104351. [CrossRef]
49. Amani, M.; Amani, P.; Bahiraei, M.; Wongwises, S. Prediction of hydrothermal behavior of a non-Newtonian nanofluid in a square channel by modeling of thermophysical properties using neural network. *J. Therm. Anal. Calorim.* **2019**, *135*, 901–910. [CrossRef]
50. Bahiraei, M.; Heshmatian, S.; Keshavarzi, M. Multi-criterion optimization of thermohydraulic performance of a mini pin fin heat sink operated with ecofriendly graphene nanoplatelets nanofluid considering geometrical characteristics. *J. Mol. Liq.* **2019**, *276*, 653–666. [CrossRef]
51. Bahiraei, M.; Mazaheri, N.; Hosseini, S. Neural network modeling of thermo-hydraulic attributes and entropy generation of an ecofriendly nanofluid flow inside tubes equipped with novel rotary coaxial double-twisted tape. *Powder Technol.* **2020**, *369*, 162–175. [CrossRef]

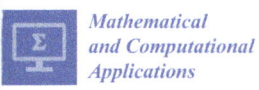

Article

Double-Diffusive Convection in Bidispersive Porous Medium with Coriolis Effect

Chirnam Ramchandraiah [1], Naikoti Kishan [1], Gundlapally Shiva Kumar Reddy [2], Kiran Kumar Paidipati [3] and Christophe Chesneau [4,*]

1. Department of Mathematics, Osmania University, Hyderabad 500007, India; ramchandaryadav567@gmail.com (C.R.); kishan_n@osmania.ac.in (N.K.)
2. Department of Applied Sciences, National Institute of Technology Goa, Ponda 403401, India; gshivakumarreddy913@nitgoa.ac.in
3. Area of Decision Sciences, Indian Institute of Management Sirmaur, Sirmaur 173025, India; kkpaidipati@iimsirmaur.ac.in
4. Department of Mathematics, LMNO, CNRS-Université de Caen, Campus II, Science 3, CEDEX, 14032 Caen, France
* Correspondence: christophe.chesneau@gmail.com

Abstract: In this paper, the thermal instability of rotating convection in a bidispersive porous layer is analyzed. The linear stability analysis is employed to examine the stability of the system. The neutral curves for different values of the physical parameters are shown graphically. The critical Rayleigh number is evaluated for appropriate values of the other governing parameters. Among the obtained results, we find: the Taylor number has a stabilizing effect on the onset of convection; the Soret number does not show any effect on oscillatory convection, as the oscillatory Rayleigh number is independent of the Soret number; there exists a threshold, $R_c^* \in (0.45, 0.46)$, for the solute Rayleigh number, such that, if $R_c > R_c^*$, then the convection arises via an oscillatory mode; and the oscillatory convection sets in and as soon as the value of the Soret number reaches a critical value, ($\in (0.6, 0.7)$), and the convection arises via stationary convection.

Keywords: bidispersive porous media; thermal convection; linear stability analysis

1. Introduction

In recent years, great attention has been devoted to the thermal instability in bidispersive porous medium (BDPM). A BDPM is an extension of a regular porous medium. In general, it is considered a regular porous medium where the solid phase is replaced by another porous medium. A BDPM is composed of clusters of large particles that are agglomerations of small particles [1,2]. The voids between the clusters are known as macropores, and the voids within the clusters are known as micropores. In other words, a BDPM is a porous medium in which fractures or tunnels have been introduced. In the present model, the f-phase and p-phase are represented by 'fracture phase' and 'porous phase', respectively. Understanding convection in a BDPM is of considerable interest for geophysical applications [3,4]. The theory of thermal convection in a BDPM was developed by Nield and Kuznetsov [5–11], Kuznestsov and Nield [12], and Sraughan [13,14]. All these authors considered two different velocities and two different temperatures in the macro and micro pores. In their analysis, they found that, in a BDPM, the critical values of Rayleigh numbers are much larger than those in the regular porous medium. Later, much research made an effort to investigate the convective instability in a BDPM.

Very recently, Falsaperla et al. [15] and Gentile and Straughan [16,17] studied the same problem by using a single equation for temperature. In particular, Gentile and Straughan [16,17] analyzed the non-linear stability theory for the problem of thermal convection in a BDPM. They proved that the linear and non-linear stability thresholds coincide. Very recently, Capone et al. [18] have shown that the linear instability and non-linear stability thresholds for the problem of thermal instability in a rotating BDPM are different. Later, Capone and De Luca [19] extended their work by considering inertia terms, and they showed that the effect of the Vadasz number can give rise to an oscillatory mode at the loss of stability of a thermal motionless state.

On the other hand, double-diffusive instability in porous media is an interesting subject of research due to its applications in different industries, such as the migration of solutes in watersaturated soils, the spread of pollutants, drying processes, evaporative cooling of high-temperature systems, and solar ponds [8]. The study of thermosolutal convection of a fluidsaturated porous medium has attracted the attention of many researchers [20–28]. In addition, Straughan [29] developed a model for double-diffusive convection in a BDPM. Later, Straughan [30] extended this work by considering the effect of inertia. He showed that the inertia term had a very strong effect on the double-diffusive convection in a BDPM. Badday and Harfash [31] have studied the double-diffusive convection in BDPM with chemical reaction and magnetic field effects.

In this paper, the coriolis effect on thermosolutal convection in a rotating bidispersive porous layer is studied. We reconsider the problem investigated in [18] in light of the Soret effect. The plan of the article is as follows. Section 2 describes the mathematical problem. In Section 3, we describe the linear stability analysis. The critical values of Rayleigh numbers at the onset of stationary and oscillatory convection are determined. The results and discussions are presented in Section 4, which contains a table to provide some examples in which stationary or oscillatory instability sets in, and figures showing the neutral stability curves for steady and oscillatory instability. The paper ends with a conclusion part in Section 5.

2. Mathematical Formulation

Let us consider a horizontal fluid saturated bidisperse porous layer confined between $z = 0$ and $z = d$. In this setting, let V_i^f and V_i^p be the velocity of the fluid in the macro pores and the velocity of the fluid in the micro pores, respectively. The fixed temperatures at $z = 0$ and at $z = d$ are $T_L^0 C$ and $T_U^0 C$, respectively, with $T_L > T_U > 0$. It is rotating at a constant rate Ω. The axis of rotation is parallel to z-axis. The Boussinesq approximation is used to account for the density variations.

The hydrodynamic model representing flow behavior in bidisperse porous layer differs from the classical porous layer theory by exhibiting two different pressures in the pores, following the multiporosity model. The flow within each type of pores is determined by its own pressure gradient through Darcy's law. Hence, four additional equations corresponding to the micro-pores are considered to make the relevant equations for mass and momentum balances closed. The governing equations consist of the momentum and continuity equations (see the references [18,31], and the visual representation in Figure 1). By adopting the Boussinesq approximation in the macro and micro pores, these equations can be written as

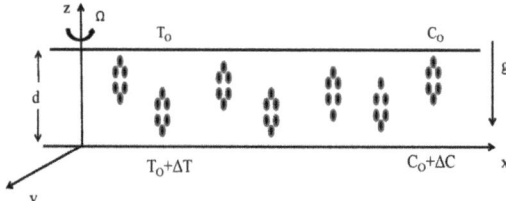

Figure 1. Physical Configuration.

$$\nabla \cdot \mathbf{V}^f = 0, \nabla \cdot \mathbf{V}^p = 0, \tag{1}$$

$$-\frac{\mu}{\kappa_f}\mathbf{V}^f - \delta\left(\mathbf{V}^f - \mathbf{V}^p\right) - \nabla P^f - \rho g \hat{e}_z - \frac{2\rho_0 \Omega}{\delta}\hat{e}_z \times \mathbf{V}^f = 0, \tag{2}$$

$$-\frac{\mu}{\kappa_p}\mathbf{V}^p - \delta\left(\mathbf{V}^p - \mathbf{V}^f\right) - \nabla P^p - \rho g \hat{e}_z - \frac{2\rho_0 \Omega}{\epsilon}\hat{e}_z \times \mathbf{V}^p = 0. \tag{3}$$

Then, we consider a linear relation for the density of form

$$\rho = \rho_0[1 - \alpha(T - T_0) + \alpha_c(C - C_0)]. \tag{4}$$

The equation of the energy balance can be written as

$$(\rho c)_m \frac{\partial T}{\partial t} + (\rho c)_f \left(\mathbf{V}^f + \mathbf{V}^p\right) \cdot \nabla T = k_m \nabla^2 T, \tag{5}$$

where c is the specific heat in the porous medium. The coefficients $(\rho c)_m$ and k_m are given by

$$(\rho c)_m = (1 - \epsilon)(1 - \delta)(\rho c)_s + [\delta + \epsilon(1 - \delta)](\rho c)_f, \tag{6}$$

$$k_m = (1 - \epsilon)(1 - \delta)k_s + [\delta + \epsilon(1 - \delta)]k_f. \tag{7}$$

The equation for the concentration field taking into account the Soret effect on the diffusion coefficient can be written as

$$\varepsilon_1 \frac{\partial C}{\partial t} + \left(\mathbf{V}^f + \mathbf{V}^p\right) \cdot \nabla C = \varepsilon_2 \nabla^2 C + \hat{S}\nabla^2 T, \tag{8}$$

where

$$\varepsilon_1 = \delta + \epsilon(1 - \delta), \tag{9}$$

$$\varepsilon_2 = \delta k_c^f + \epsilon(1 - \delta)k_c^p, \tag{10}$$

$$\hat{S} = \phi S_T^f + \epsilon(1 - \phi)S_T^p, \tag{11}$$

subject to the boundary conditions

$$\mathbf{V}^f \cdot \hat{e}_z = \mathbf{V}^p \cdot \hat{e}_z = 0, \text{ on } z = 0, d, \tag{12}$$

$$T(x, y, 0, t) = T_L, \ T(x, y, d, t) = T_U \ (T_L > T_U), \tag{13}$$

$$C(x, y, 0, t) = C_L, \ C(x, y, d, t) = C_U (C_L > C_U). \tag{14}$$

The basic state solution is then

$$\mathbf{V}_b^f = 0, \ \mathbf{V}_b^p = 0, \ T_b = T_L - \beta z, \ C_b = C_L - \beta_c z, \tag{15}$$

where $\beta = \frac{T_L - T_U}{d}$ and $\beta_c = \frac{C_L - C_U}{d}$.

Let $\mathbf{V}^f, \mathbf{V}^p, P^f, P^p, T,$ and C be a perturbation to the steady Equation (15).

The perturbations are non-dimensional, with length scale d, velocity scale V, time scale τ, temperature scale $T*$, and concentration scale $C*$, where

$$\tau = \frac{(\rho c)_m d^2}{k_m}, \qquad V = \frac{k_m}{(\rho c)_f d},$$

$$T* = \frac{\beta V (\rho c)_f d^2}{k_m}, \qquad C* = \frac{\beta_c V d^2}{\varepsilon_2}.$$

Define the quantities $\gamma, \kappa_r, A, \eta, R, R_C, Ta, Le$, and S by

$$\gamma = \frac{\delta \kappa_f}{\mu}, \quad \kappa_r = \frac{\kappa_f}{\kappa_p}, \quad \varpi = \frac{(\rho c)_m}{(\rho c)_f},$$

$$Ta = \frac{2\rho_0 \Omega \kappa_f}{\mu \phi}, \quad R = \frac{\rho_0 \beta g \alpha d^2 (\rho c)_f \kappa_f}{\mu k_m}, \quad R_C = \frac{\rho_0 \beta_c g \alpha_c d^2 \kappa_f}{\mu \varepsilon_2},$$

$$Le = \frac{k_m}{(\rho c)_m \varepsilon_2}, \quad S = \frac{\hat{S} T_*}{\varepsilon_2 C_*}.$$

All these quantities have been explained in the nomenclature. The non-dimensional equations (after omitting the asterisks) governing the system are

$$\nabla \cdot \mathbf{V}^f = 0, \nabla \cdot \mathbf{V}^p = 0, \tag{16}$$

$$-\mathbf{V}^f - \gamma \left(\mathbf{V}^f - \mathbf{V}^p \right) - \nabla P^f + (R\theta - R_C \phi) \hat{e}_z - Ta \hat{e}_z \times \mathbf{V}^f = 0, \tag{17}$$

$$-\kappa_r \mathbf{V}^p - \gamma \left(\mathbf{V}^p - \mathbf{V}^f \right) - \nabla P^p + (R\theta - R_C \phi) \hat{e}_z - \eta Ta \hat{e}_z \times \mathbf{V}^p = 0, \tag{18}$$

$$\frac{\partial \theta}{\partial t} + \left(\mathbf{V}^f + \mathbf{V}^p \right) \cdot \nabla \theta = \left(\mathbf{w}^f + \mathbf{w}^p \right) + \nabla^2 \theta, \tag{19}$$

$$\varepsilon_1 Le \frac{\partial \phi}{\partial t} + ALe \left(\mathbf{V}^f + \mathbf{V}^p \right) \cdot \nabla \phi = \left(\mathbf{w}^f + \mathbf{w}^p \right) + \nabla^2 \phi + S \nabla^2 \theta, \tag{20}$$

$$\mathbf{w}^f = \mathbf{w}^p = \theta = \phi = 0 \text{ on } z = 0, 1. \tag{21}$$

By taking the third component of curl of Equations (17) and (18), one obtains

$$\mathbf{w}_3^f + \gamma \left(\mathbf{w}_3^f - \mathbf{w}_3^p \right) - Ta \frac{\partial \mathbf{w}^f}{\partial z} = 0, \tag{22}$$

$$\kappa_r \mathbf{w}_3^p + \gamma (\mathbf{w}_3^p - \mathbf{w}_3^f) - \eta Ta \frac{\partial \mathbf{w}^p}{\partial z} = 0, \tag{23}$$

where $D = \frac{\partial}{\partial t}$, $\mathbf{w}_3^f = \frac{\partial v^f}{\partial x} - \frac{\partial u^f}{\partial y}$.

By taking the third component of double curl of Equations (17) and (18), one has

$$\nabla^2 \mathbf{w}^f + \gamma \left(\nabla^2 \mathbf{w}^f - \nabla^2 \mathbf{w}^p \right) - R \nabla_h^2 \theta + R_C \nabla_h^2 \phi + Ta \frac{\partial \mathbf{w}_3^f}{\partial z} = 0, \tag{24}$$

$$\kappa_r \nabla^2 \mathbf{w}^p + \gamma \left(\nabla^2 \mathbf{w}^p - \nabla^2 \mathbf{w}^f \right) - R \nabla_h^2 \theta + R_C \nabla_h^2 \phi + \eta Ta \frac{\partial \mathbf{w}_3^p}{\partial z} = 0, \tag{25}$$

where

$$\nabla_h^2 = \frac{\partial^2}{\partial x^2} + \frac{\partial^2}{\partial y^2}$$

and

$$\nabla^2 = \frac{\partial^2}{\partial x^2} + \frac{\partial^2}{\partial y^2} + \frac{\partial^2}{\partial z^2}.$$

Solving Equations (22) and (23) with respect to $\mathbf{w}_3^f$ and $\mathbf{w}_3^p$, respectively, one has

$$\mathbf{w}_3^f = \frac{Ta(\gamma + \kappa_r) \mathbf{w}_z^f + \eta Ta \gamma \mathbf{w}_z^p}{\gamma + \kappa_r + \gamma \kappa_r}, \tag{26}$$

$$\mathbf{w}_3^p = \frac{Ta \left(\gamma \mathbf{w}_z^f \right) + \eta Ta (1 + \gamma) \mathbf{w}_z^p}{\gamma + \kappa_r + \gamma \kappa_r}. \tag{27}$$

Substituting Equations (26) and (27) into Equations (24) and (25), respectively, one obtains

$$\nabla^2 \mathbf{w}^f + \gamma\left(\nabla^2 \mathbf{w}^f - \nabla^2 \mathbf{w}^p\right) - R\nabla_h^2 \theta + R_C \nabla_h^2 \phi + \frac{Ta^2(\gamma + \kappa_r)\mathbf{w}_{zz}^f + \eta Ta^2 \gamma \mathbf{w}_{zz}^p}{\gamma + \kappa_r + \gamma \kappa_r} = 0, \quad (28)$$

$$\kappa_r \nabla^2 \mathbf{w}^p + \gamma\left(\nabla^2 \mathbf{w}^p - \nabla^2 \mathbf{w}^f\right) - R\nabla_h^2 \theta + R_C \nabla_h^2 \phi + \frac{\eta Ta^2 \gamma \mathbf{w}_{zz}^f + \eta^2 Ta^2(1+\gamma)\mathbf{w}_{zz}^p}{\gamma + \kappa_r + \gamma \kappa_r} = 0. \quad (29)$$

Hence, considering Equations (19), (20), (28) and (29), we see the following problem in $\mathbf{w}^f, \mathbf{w}^p, \theta$, and ϕ:

$$\nabla^2 \mathbf{w}^f + \gamma\left(\nabla^2 \mathbf{w}^f - \nabla^2 \mathbf{w}^p\right) - R\nabla_h^2 \theta + R_C \nabla_h^2 \phi + \frac{Ta^2(\gamma + \kappa_r)\mathbf{w}_{zz}^f + \eta Ta^2 \gamma \mathbf{w}_{zz}^p}{\gamma + \kappa_r + \gamma \kappa_r} = 0, \quad (30)$$

$$\kappa_r \nabla^2 \mathbf{w}^p + \gamma\left(\nabla^2 \mathbf{w}^p - \nabla^2 \mathbf{w}^f\right) - R\nabla_h^2 \theta + R_C \nabla_h^2 \phi + \frac{\eta Ta^2 \gamma \mathbf{w}_{zz}^f + \eta^2 Ta^2(1+\gamma)\mathbf{w}_{zz}^p}{\gamma + \kappa_r + \gamma \kappa_r} = 0, \quad (31)$$

$$\frac{\partial \theta}{\partial t} = \mathbf{w}^f + \mathbf{w}^p + \nabla^2 \theta, \quad (32)$$

$$\varepsilon_1 Le \frac{\partial \phi}{\partial t} = \mathbf{w}^f + \mathbf{w}^p + \nabla^2 \phi + S\nabla^2 \theta. \quad (33)$$

3. Linear Stability Analysis

Let us consider the normal mode solutions in the form of

$$\left(\mathbf{w}^f, \mathbf{w}^p, \theta, \phi\right) = \left(w^f, w^p, \theta, \phi\right) \sin(n\pi z) e^{i(lx+my)+\sigma t}. \quad (34)$$

Substituting the above normal mode solution into the Equations (30)–(33), we find

$$[A\Lambda(1+\gamma) + n^2 \pi^2 Ta^2 B] w^f + [\eta \gamma n^2 \pi^2 Ta^2 - \gamma \Lambda A] w^p - a^2 R A \theta + a^2 R_C A \phi = 0, \quad (35)$$

$$[\eta \gamma n^2 \pi^2 Ta^2 - \gamma \Lambda A] w^f + [\Lambda A B + \eta^2 n^2 \pi^2 Ta^2 (1+\gamma)] w^p - a^2 R A \theta + a^2 R_C A \phi = 0, \quad (36)$$

$$w^f + w^p + [\sigma - \Lambda]\theta = 0, \quad (37)$$

$$w^f + w^p - S\Lambda\theta - [\varepsilon_1 Le\sigma + \Lambda]\phi = 0, \quad (38)$$

where

$$\begin{cases} a^2 = l^2 + m^2 \text{ is the wave number,} \\ \sigma = \iota\omega, \\ A = \gamma + \kappa_r + \gamma\kappa_r, \\ B = \gamma + \kappa_r, \\ \Lambda = \pi^2 + a^2. \end{cases}$$

Requiring zero determinant of the above system, one has

$$R = \frac{\xi_1 + \omega^2 \xi_2 + \iota(\xi_3 + \omega^2 \xi_4)}{\xi_5}, \quad (39)$$

with

$$\begin{cases} \xi_1 = \Lambda^2[-a^2\Lambda R_C(S-1)(x_1 + A\Lambda(1+B+3\gamma)) + \Lambda(x_2 + x_3\Lambda + x_4\Lambda^2)], \\ \xi_2 = x[a^2AR_C(x_1 + A\Lambda(1+B+3\gamma)) + x\Lambda(x_2 + x_3\Lambda + x_4\Lambda^2)], \\ \xi_3 = a^2A\Lambda R_C(1-x+Sx)[x_1 + A\Lambda(1+B+3\gamma)] + \Lambda^2[x_2 + x_3\Lambda + x_4\Lambda^2], \\ \xi_4 = x^2(x_2 + x_3\Lambda + x_4\Lambda^2), \\ \xi_5 = a^2A(\omega^2x^2 + \Lambda^2)[\pi^2Ta^2(B + \eta(\gamma\eta - 2\gamma + \eta)) + A\Lambda(1+B+3\gamma)], \\ x_1 = \pi^2Ta^2(B + \eta^2 + \eta^2\gamma - 2\eta\gamma), \\ x_2 = \pi^4Ta^4(B + B\gamma - \gamma^2)\eta^2, \\ x_3 = A\pi^2Ta^2(B^2 + 2\eta\gamma^2 + (1+\gamma^2)\eta^2), \\ x_4 = A^2(B + B\gamma - \gamma^2), \\ x = Le\varepsilon_1. \end{cases}$$

3.1. Stationary Convection:

Substituting $\omega = 0$ in Equation (39), one obtains

$$R_{T_{sc}} = \frac{\xi_6 + \xi_7\Lambda + \xi_8\Lambda^2 + \xi_9\Lambda^3}{\xi_{10} + \xi_{11}\Lambda}, \quad (40)$$

where

$$\begin{cases} \xi_6 = a^2\pi^2Rc(1-S)Ta^2(\kappa_r + \gamma(-1+\eta)^2 + \eta^2), \\ \xi_7 = a^2ARc(1-S)(1+k+4\gamma) + \pi^4Ta^4\eta^2, \\ \xi_8 = \pi^2Ta^2((\kappa_r + \gamma)^2 + 2\eta\gamma^2 + (1+\gamma)^2\eta^2), \\ \xi_9 = A^2, \\ \xi_{10} = a^2\pi^2Ta^2(\kappa_r + \gamma(-1+\eta)^2 + \eta^2), \\ \xi_{11} = a^2A(1+k+4\gamma). \end{cases}$$

In the absence of rotation and the Soret effect, the above-stationary Rayleigh number reduces to

$$Ra_{sc} = \frac{\delta^4(\gamma + \kappa_r + \gamma\kappa_r)}{q^2(1 + \kappa_r + 4\gamma)}, \quad (41)$$

which, on comparison, satisfies [16] (Equation (31)).

The case of a monodispersive porous layer rotating about a vertical axis with the Darcy model has been considered in Capone and Rionero [32]. As $\kappa_r \to \infty$, $\gamma \to 0$ $Rc \to 0$, and $\eta \to \infty$ in Equation (40), we find

$$Ra_{sc} = \frac{\delta^2(\pi^2Ta^2 + \delta^2)}{q^2}. \quad (42)$$

After some calculations, we find

$$Ra_{scl} = \pi^2(1 + \sqrt{1 + Ta^2})^2, \quad (43)$$

which is in good agreement with [32] (Equation (4.24), p. 195).

3.2. Oscillatory Convection

To study the oscillatory stability, we consider the real and imaginary parts of R. The Rayleigh number at the onset of oscillatory convection is

$$R_{T_{oc}} = \frac{\xi_{12} + \xi_{13}\Lambda + \xi_{14}\Lambda^2 + \xi_{15}\Lambda^3}{\xi_{16} + \xi_{17}\Lambda}, \quad (44)$$

where

$$\begin{cases}
\xi_{12} = a^2\pi^2 RcTa^2(\kappa_r + \gamma(-1+\eta)^2 + \eta^2), \\
\xi_{13} = a^2 ARc(1+k+4\gamma) + \pi^4 Ta^4(1+x)\eta^2, \\
\xi_{14} = \pi^2 Ta^2(1+x)((\kappa_r+\gamma)^2 + 2\eta\gamma^2 + (1+\gamma)^2\eta^2), \\
\xi_{15} = (1+x)A^2, \\
\xi_{16} = xa^2\pi^2 Ta^2(\kappa_r + \gamma(-1+\eta)^2 + \eta^2), \\
\xi_{17} = xa^2 A(1+k+4\gamma).
\end{cases}$$

4. Discussion

The numerical results and discussions are presented in this section. The critical Rayleigh number at the onset of stationary convection, $Ra^c_{T_{SC}}$; at the onset of oscillatory convection, $Ra^c_{T_{OC}}$; the critical wave number at the onset of stationary convection, q^c_{sc}; and at the onset of oscillatory convection, q^c_{oc}, are obtained for the prescribed values of other parameters. Figures 2–8 show the neutral curves in the parametric plane (q, R_T) with different values of the Ta, S, R_C, and κ_r.

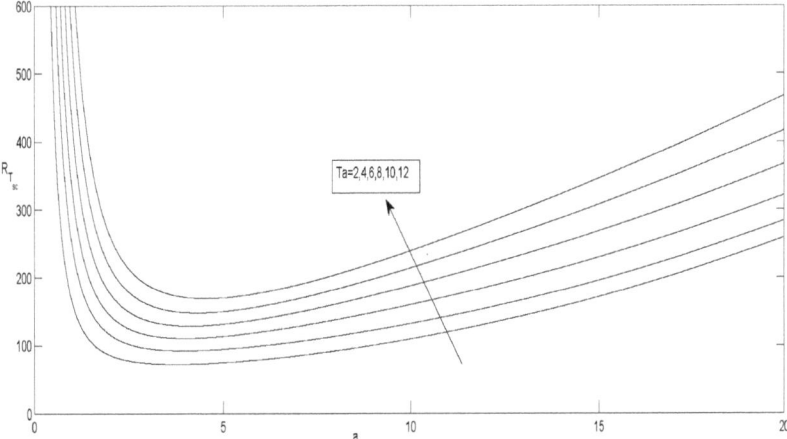

Figure 2. Neutral curves for the different values of Ta and for the fixed values of $\gamma = 0.5, \eta = 0.2, \kappa_r = 1$, $R_C = 50$, and $S = 0.5$ for the stationary mode.

In the stationary mode, the neutral curves are displayed in Figures 2–5. Figure 2 shows the neutral curves in the parametric plane (q, R_T) with different values of the Taylor number. From this figure, one can observe that, as Ta increases, the curves shift upward, indicating a delay in the onset of instability. This can be explained as follows: Vorticity is introduced into the fluid when it rotates. As a result, the fluid travels faster in horizontal planes. The velocity of the fluid perpendicular to the planes decreases as a result of this motion, therefore $Ra^c_{T_{SC}}$ rises with Ta.

The effect of the Soret parameter on the onset of instability is shown in Figure 3. In it, we see that $R^c_{T_{sc}}$ decreases with the Soret parameter, which means that the Soret parameter destabilizes the system. For various values of solute Rayleigh number, with changing values of wave number and then Rayleigh numbers, the neutral curves are obtained in Figure 4. We can see from this figure that $R^c_{T_{sc}}$ increases as R_c increases, indicating that the presence of R_c suppresses the onset of convection.

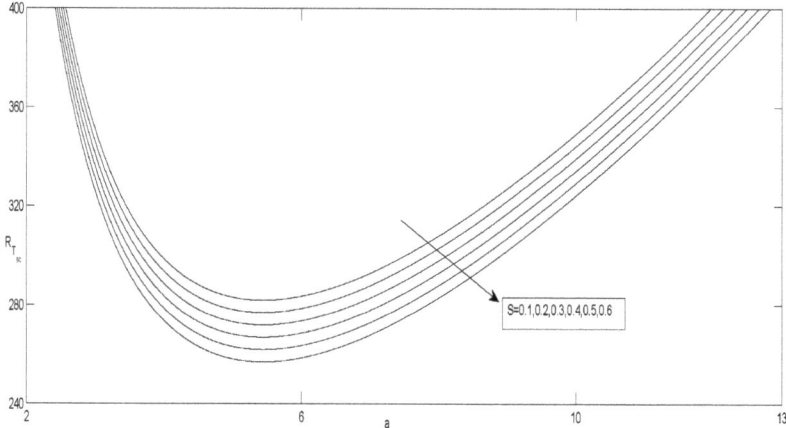

Figure 3. Neutral curves for the different values of S and for the fixed values of $\gamma = 0.5$, $\eta = 0.2$, $\kappa_r = 1$, $R_C = 50$, and $Ta = 20$ for the stationary mode.

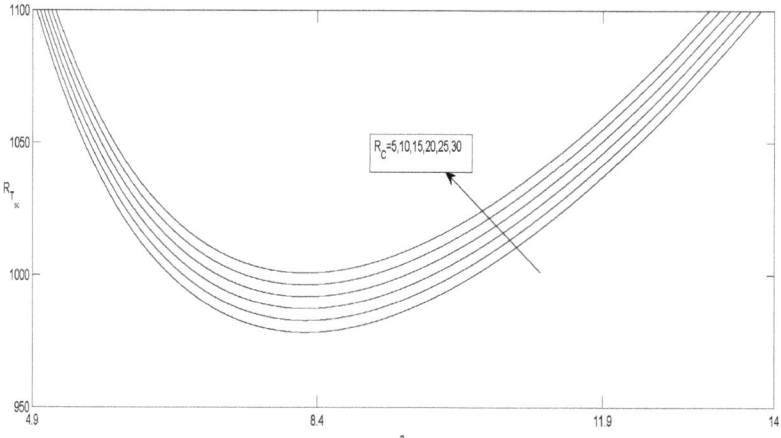

Figure 4. Neutral curves for the different values of R_C and for the fixed values of $\gamma = 0.5$, $\eta = 0.2$, $\kappa_r = 1$, $S = 0.2$, and $Ta = 50$ for the stationary mode.

Figure 5 depicts the neutral curves at the onset of stationary convection for various values of κ_r. According to this figure, $R^c_{T_{sc}}$ decreases as κ_r increases, indicating that the presence of a solute Rayleigh number advances the onset of convection. The neutral curves at the onset of oscillatory convection are displayed in Figures 6–8. Figure 6 displays the neutral curves for different values of Ta. According to this figure, increasing Ta causes $R^c_{T_{oc}}$ to increase, indicating that Ta has the effect of stabilizing the system.

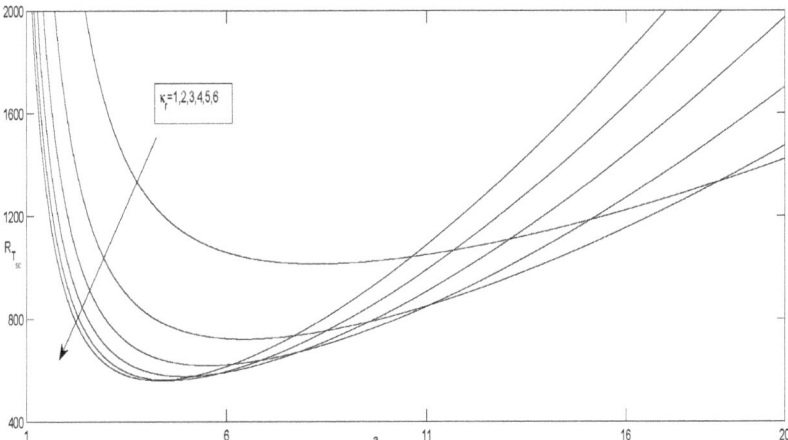

Figure 5. Neutral curves for the different values of κ_r and for the fixed values of $\gamma = 0.5, \eta = 0.2$, $R_C = 50, S = 0.2$, and $Ta = 50$ for the stationary mode.

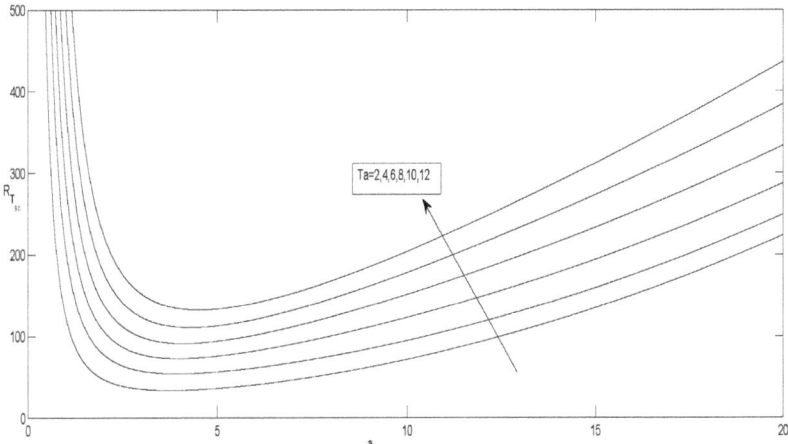

Figure 6. Neutral curves for the different values of Ta and for the fixed values of $\gamma = 0.5, \eta = 0.2$, $R_C = 50$, and $\kappa_r = 1$ for the oscillatory mode.

Figure 7 depicts the neutral curves for different values of R_C at the onset of oscillatory convection, and it is found that the neutral curves move upward with an increase in the value of R_C, thus R_C stabilizes the oscillatory convection.

Figure 8 shows the effect of κ_r. In particular, we observe that the effect of κ_r advances the onset of convection. This can be understandable, mathematically, because $\kappa_r = \frac{\kappa_f}{\kappa_p}$, κ_r increases as κ_p decreases (κ_f is assumed to be fixed here). In other words, as micropermeability declines, fluid movement in micropores becomes more difficult. As a result, convective motions become more difficult, yielding more stability to the system.

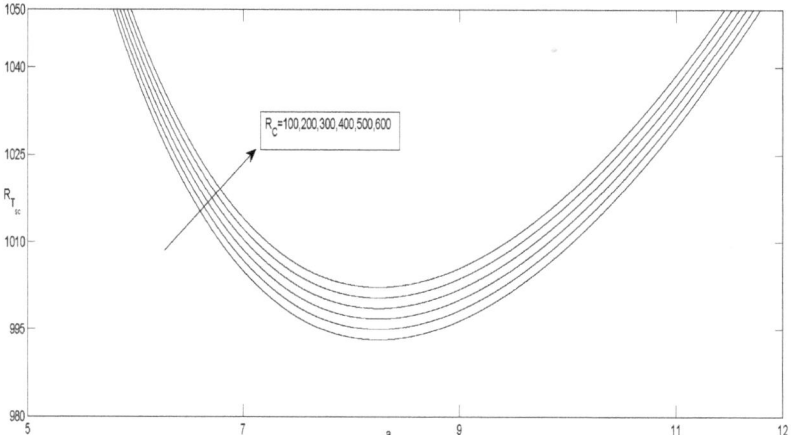

Figure 7. Neutral curves for the different values of R_C and for the fixed values of $\gamma = 0.5, \eta = 0.2$, $Ta = 50$, and $\kappa_r = 1$ for the oscillatory mode.

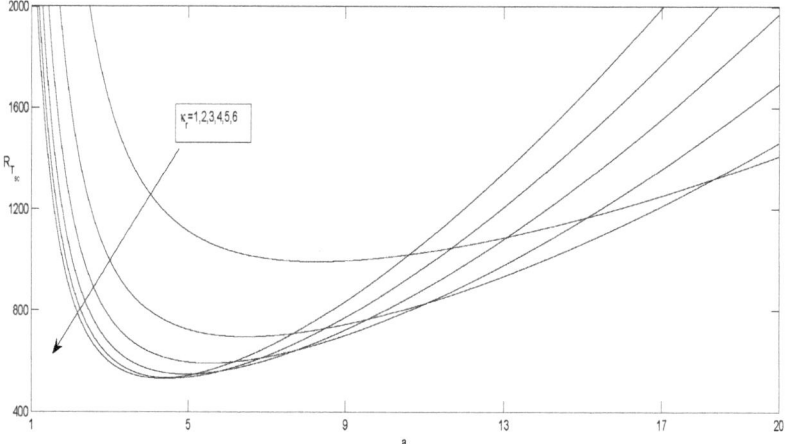

Figure 8. Neutral curves for the different values of κ_r, and for the fixed values of $\gamma = 0.5, \eta = 0.2, Ta = 50$ and $R_C = 100$ for the oscillatory mode.

In Tables 1–3, we present some examples in which steady or oscillatory instability sets in for the constant values of physical parameters. According to Table 1, there is a threshold $R_c^*(\in 0.45, 0.46)$ for the solute Rayleigh number, such that, if $R_c > R_c^*$, then the convection arises via an oscillatory mode. According to Table 2, oscillatory convection occurs initially, and as soon as the value of S reaches a critical value ($\in (0.6, 0.7)$), the convection ceases to be oscillatory, and stationary convection occurs as the first bifurcation. Table 3 shows that, as the value of κ_r increases, convection always occurs via stationary mode.

Table 1. Critical stationary and oscillatory Rayleigh numbers for different values of Rc and the fixed values of $\kappa_r = 1$, $Ta = 5$, and $S = 0.5$.

Rc	Stationary R	Stationary a	Oscillatory R	Oscillatory a	Instability
0	61.6464	3.9578	62.7612	3.9578	Stationary
1	62.1464	3.9578	62.7793	3.9578	Stationary
2	62.6464	3.9578	62.7973	3.9578	Stationary
3	63.1464	3.9578	62.8154	3.9578	Oscillatory
4	63.6464	3.9578	62.8335	3.9578	Oscillatory
5	64.1464	3.9578	62.8516	3.9578	Oscillatory

Table 2. Critical stationary and oscillatory Rayleigh numbers for the different values of S and the fixed values of $\kappa_r = 1$, $Ta = 50$, and $Rc = 50$.

S	Stationary R	Stationary a	Oscillatory R	Oscillatory a	Instability
0.1	1018.7706	8.2527	992.2842	8.2527	Oscillatory
0.2	1013.7706	8.2527	992.2842	8.2527	Oscillatory
0.3	1008.7706	8.2527	992.2842	8.2527	Oscillatory
0.4	1003.7706	8.2527	992.2842	8.2527	Oscillatory
0.5	998.7706	8.2527	992.2842	8.2527	Oscillatory
0.6	993.7706	8.2527	992.2842	8.2527	Oscillatory
0.7	988.7706	8.2527	992.2842	8.2527	Stationary
0.8	983.7706	8.2527	992.2842	8.2527	Stationary
0.9	978.7706	8.2527	992.2842	8.2527	Stationary

Table 3. Critical stationary and oscillatory Rayleigh numbers for the different values of κ_r and the fixed values of $S = 0.8$, $Ta = 50$, and $Rc = 50$.

κ_r	Stationary R	Stationary a	Oscillatory R	Oscillatory a	Instability
1	983.7706	8.2540	992.2842	8.2540	Stationary
2	691.3454	6.4421	694.5709	6.4421	Stationary
3	588.8136	5.5171	590.1849	5.5171	Stationary
4	546.4455	4.9469	547.0506	4.9469	Stationary
5	531.2631	4.5668	531.5936	4.5668	Stationary

5. Conclusions

In this study, we investigated the onset of rotating convection in a horizontal bidispersive porous layer that is uniformly heated and salted from below. The behaviour of various parameters, such as the $Ta, S, R_C,$ and κ_r, has been analysed. The results can be summarized as follows:

- $R^c_{T_{sc}}$ and $R^c_{T_{oc}}$ increase as the Taylor number increases, indicating that Ta has a stabilizing effect on the onset of convection.
- $R^c_{T_{sc}}$ and $R^c_{T_{oc}}$ are increasing functions of R_c and decreasing functions of κ_r.
- S does not show any effect on $R^c_{T_{oc}}$, as $R^c_{T_{oc}}$ is independent of S.
- There exists a threshold $R^*_c \in (0.45, 0.46)$ for the solute Rayleigh number such that, if $R_c > R^*_c$, then the convection arises via an oscillatory mode.
- The oscillatory convection sets in and, as soon as the value of S attains a critical value ($\in (0.6, 0.7)$), the convection ceases to be oscillatory, and stationary convection occurs as the first bifurcation.

Author Contributions: Conceptualization, C.R. and G.S.K.R.; methodology, C.R.; software, C.R.; validation, C.R., N.K., G.S.K.R., K.K.P. and C.C.; formal analysis, C.R.; investigation, C.R.; data curation, C.R.; writing—original draft preparation, C.R.; writing—review and editing, C.R., N.K., G.S.K.R., K.K.P. and C.C.; visualization, C.R.; supervision, G.S.K.R., N.K., K.K.P. and C.C. All authors have read and agreed to the published version of the manuscript.

Funding: This research received no external funding.

Acknowledgments: The authors would like to thank the reviewers for their insightful comments on the paper.

Conflicts of Interest: The authors declare no conflict of interest.

Nomenclature

C_a	Acceleration coefficient
κ_f	Permeability in macro pores
κ_p	Permeability in micro pores
ζ	Interaction coefficient
μ	Fluid viscosity
g	Gravity
α	Coefficient of thermal expansion
α_c	Density coefficient for salinity
σ	Heat capacity ratio
ϵ	Macro porosity
δ	Micro porosity
ρ	Density
k_s	Thermal conductivity of the solid
k_f	Thermal conductivity of the fluid
$(\rho c)_s$	Product of density and specific heat in the solid skeleton
$(\rho c)_f$	Product of density and specific heat in the pores
ρ_0	Reference density
k_m	Thermal conductivity
p^f	Pressure in macro pores
p^p	Pressure in micro pores
T	Temperature
C	Salt concentration field
R	Rayleigh number
R_C	Solutal Rayleigh number
Ta	Taylor number
Le	Lewis number
S	Soret number
d	Length
Superscripts	
$\prime$	Perturbated quantity
c	Critical value
Subscripts	
b	Base state
0	Reference valve

References

1. Chen, Z.Q.; Cheng, P.; Hsu, C.T. A theoretical and experimental study on stagnant thermal conductivity of bi-dispersed porous media. *Int. Commun. Heat Mass Transf.* **2000**, *27*, 601–610. [CrossRef]
2. Chen, Z.Q.; Cheng, P.; Zhao, T.S. An experimental study of two phase flow and boiling heat transfer in bi-disperse porous channels. *Int. Commun. Heat Mass Transf.* **2000**, *27*, 293–302. [CrossRef]
3. Gérard, A.; Genter, A.; Kohl, T.; Lutz, P.; Rose, P.; Rummel, F. The deep EGS (Enhanced Geothermal System) project at Soultz-sous-Forêts (Alsace, France). *Geothermics* **2006**, *35*, 473–483. [CrossRef]
4. Nie, R.S.; Meng, Y.F.; Jia, Y.L.; Zhang, F.X.; Yang, X.T.; Niu, X.N. Dual porosity and dual permeability modeling of horizontal well in naturally fractured reservoir. *Transp. Porous Med.* **2012**, *92*, 213–235. [CrossRef]
5. Nield, D.; Kuznetsov, A. Forced convection in a bidisperse porous medium channel: A conjugate problem. *Int. J. Heat Mass Transf.* **2004**, *47*, 53755380. [CrossRef]
6. Nield, D.; Kuznetsov, A. A twovelocity twotemperature model for a bidispersed porous medium: Forced convection in a channel. *Transp. Porous Media* **2005**, *59*, 325339. [CrossRef]
7. Nield, D.A.; Kuznetsov, A.V. The onset of convection in a bidispersive porous medium. *Int. J. Heat Mass Transf.* **2006**, *49*, 3068–3074. [CrossRef]

8. Nield, D.; Kuznetsov, A. A note on modeling high speed flow in a bidisperse porous medium. *Transp. Porous Media* **2013**, *96*, 495499. [CrossRef]
9. Nield, D.; Kuznetsov, A. The effect of combined vertical and horizontal heterogeneity on the onset of convection in a bidisperse porous medium. *Int. J. Heat Mass Transf.* **2007**, *50*, 33293339. [CrossRef]
10. Nield, D.; Kuznetsov, A. Natural convection about a vertical plate embedded in a bidisperse porous medium. *Int. J. Heat Mass Transf.* **2008**, *51*, 16581664. [CrossRef]
11. Nield, D.; Kuznetsov, A. Forced convection in a channel partly occupied by a bidisperse porous medium: Symmetric case. *J. Heat Transf.* **2011**, *133*, 072601. [CrossRef]
12. Kuznetsov, A.V.; Nield, D. Thermally developing forced convection in a bidisperse porous medium. *J. Porous Media* **2006**, *9*, 393402.
13. Straughan, B. On the NieldKuznetsov theory for convection in bidispersive porous media. *Transp. Porous Media* **2009**, *77*, 159168 [CrossRef]
14. Straughan, B. *Convection with Local Thermal NonEquilibrium and Microfluidic Effects*; Springer: Berlin/Heidelberg, Germany, 2015.
15. Falsaperla, P.; Mulone, G.; Straughan, B. Bidispersiveinclined convection. *Proc. R. Soc. A* **2016**, *472*, 20160480. [CrossRef] [PubMed]
16. Gentile, M.; Straughan, B. Bidispersive thermal convection. *Int. J. Heat Mass Transf.* **2017**, *114*, 837840. [CrossRef]
17. Gentile, M.; Straughan, B. Bidispersive vertical convection. *Proc. R. Soc. A* **2017**, *473*, 20170481. [CrossRef]
18. Capone, F.; De Luca, R.; Gentile, M. Coriolis effect on thermal convection in a rotating bidispersive porous layer. *Proc. R. Soc. A* **2020**, *476*, 20190875. [CrossRef]
19. Capone, F.; De Luca, R. The Effect of the Vadasz Number on the Onset of Thermal Convection in Rotating Bidispersive Porous Media. *Fluids* **2020**, *5*, 173. [CrossRef]
20. Rionero, S. Onset of convection in porous layers salted from above and below. *Note Mat.* **2012**, *32*, 159173.
21. Rionero, S. Global nonlinear stability for a triply diffusive convection in a porous layer. *Contin. Mech. Thermodyn.* **2012**, *24*, 629641. [CrossRef]
22. Rionero, S. Triple diffusive convection in porous media. *Acta Mech.* **2013**, *224*, 447458. [CrossRef]
23. Iasiello, M.; Vafai, K.; Andreozzi, A.; Bianco, N. Hypo- and hyperthermia effects on LDL deposition in a curved artery. *Comput. Therm. Sci. Int. J.* **2019**, *11*, 95–103. [CrossRef]
24. Iasiello, M.; Vafai, K.; Andreozzi, A.; Bianco, N. Low-density lipoprotein transport through an arterial wall under hyperthermia and hypertension conditions—An analytical solution. *J. Biomech.* **2016**, *49*, 193–204. [CrossRef] [PubMed]
25. Maiti, S.; Shaw, S.; Shit, G.C. Fractional order model for thermochemical flow of blood with Dufour and Soret effects under magnetic and vibration environment. *Colloids Surf. Biointerfaces* **2021**, *197*, 111395. [CrossRef] [PubMed]
26. Reddy, G.S.K.; Ragoju, R. Thermal instability of a Maxwell fluid saturated porous layer with chemical reaction. *Spec. Top. Rev. Porous Media Int. J.* **2022**, *13*, 33–47. [CrossRef]
27. Babu, A.B.; Reddy, G.S.K.; Tagare, S.G. Nonlinear magneto convection due to horizontal magnetic field and vertical axis of rotation due to thermal and compositional buoyancy. *Results Phys.* **2019**, *12*, 2078–2090. [CrossRef]
28. Benerji, Babu, A.; Reddy, G.S.K.; Tagare, S.G. Nonlinear magnetoconvection in a rotating fluid due to thermal and compositional buoyancy with anisotropic diffusivities. *Heat Transf. Asian Res.* **2020**, *49*, 335–355. [CrossRef]
29. Straughan, B. Bidispersive double diffusive convection. *Int. J. Heat Mass Transf.* **2018**, *126*, 504–508. [CrossRef]
30. Straughan, B. Effect of inertia on double diffusive bidispersive convection. *Int. J. Heat Mass Transf.* **2019**, *129*, 389–396. [CrossRef]
31. Badday, A.J.; Harfash, A.J. Double-diffusive convection in bidispersive porous medium with chemical reaction and magnetic field effects. *Transp. Porous Media* **2021**, *139*, 45–66. [CrossRef]
32. Capone, F.; Rionero, S. Inertia effect on the onset of convection in rotating porous layers via the auxiliary system method. *Int. J. Nonlinear Mech.* **2013**, *57*, 192–200. [CrossRef]

Article

Numerical Study of the Effect of a Heated Cylinder on Natural Convection in a Square Cavity in the Presence of a Magnetic Field

Muhammad Sajjad Hossain [1,*], Muhammad Fayz-Al-Asad [2], Muhammad Saiful Islam Mallik [1], Mehmet Yavuz [3,*], Md. Abdul Alim [2] and Kazi Md. Khairul Basher [4]

[1] Department of Arts and Sciences, Faculty of Engineering, Ahsanullah University of Science and Technology (AUST), Dhaka 1208, Bangladesh; saiful_math.as@aust.edu
[2] Department of Mathematics, Bangladesh University of Engineering and Technology (BUET), Dhaka 1000, Bangladesh; fayzmath.buet@gmail.com (M.F.-A.-A.); maalim@math.buet.ac.bd (M.A.A.)
[3] Department of Mathematics and Computer Sciences, Faculty of Science, Necmettin Erbakan University, Konya 42090, Türkiye
[4] e-Math Info Ltd., Dhaka1000, Bangladesh; cmcmath2015@gmail.com
* Correspondence: msh80edu@gmail.com (M.S.H.); mehmetyavuz@erbakan.edu.tr (M.Y.)

Abstract: The present research was developed to find out the effect of heated cylinder configurations in accordance with the magnetic field on the natural convective flow within a square cavity. In the cavity, four types of configurations—left bottom heated cylinder (LBC), right bottom heated cylinder (RBC), left top heated cylinder (LTC) and right top heated cylinder (RTC)—were considered in the investigation. The current mathematical problem was formulated using the non-linear governing equations and then solved by engaging the process of Galerkin weighted residuals based on the finite element scheme (FES). The investigation of the present problem was conducted using numerous parameters: the Rayleigh number ($Ra = 10^3$–10^5), the Hartmann number ($Ha = 0$–200) at $Pr = 0.71$ on the flow field, thermal pattern and the variation of heat inside the enclosure. The clarifications of the numerical result were exhibited in the form of streamlines, isotherms, velocity profiles and temperature profiles, local and mean Nusselt number, along with heated cylinder configurations. From the obtained outcomes, it was observed that the rate of heat transport, as well as the local Nusselt number, decreased for the LBC and LTC configurations, but increased for the RBC and RTC configurations with the increase of the Hartmann number within the square cavity. In addition, the mean Nusselt number for the LBC, RBC, LTC and RTC configurations increased when the Hartmann number was absent, but decreased when the Hartmann number increased in the cavity. The computational results were verified in relation to a published work and were found to be in good agreement.

Keywords: natural convection; magnetic field; FES; heated cylinder; square cavity

1. Introduction

As a mechanism of heat transfer, the natural convective electrical conduction flow of fluid, in accordance with the effect of magnetic field in cavities, has been thoroughly studied by researchers due to its technical importance in engineering applications. The extensive studies of various applications include electronic device cooling, ventilation of rooms, reactor insulation, solar ponds, fire prevention and crystal growth in liquids [1]. By considering this importance, many researchers have conducted many numerical and experimental studies inside the cavities with and without obstacles to research the flow and heat transfer behaviors. Krakov and Nikiforov [2] studied the influence of the vertical magnetic field on thermo-magnetic convection in a square cavity. They showed that the convective flow can have either a one-cell or two-cell structure in the cavity. Steady-state natural convection in a square cavity using a fully compact higher-order computational method was performed by Kalita et al. [3]. Conjugate gradient and hybrid bi-conjugate gradient are used to find good convergence at higher Rayleigh numbers by solving the symmetrical and non-symmetrical algebraic systems. Natural convection in a square enclosure was performed by Shu and Wee [4] using the SIMPLE-generalized differential quadrature method and produced accurate numerical results only for a few grid points. Basak and Roy [5] examined the thermal effects of natural convection flows within a square cavity. They found that the power law correlations played a vital role between the average Nusselt number and Rayleigh numbers for convection-dominated regimes. Natural convection fluid flow and heat transfer using discrete source–sink pairs in square cavities were studied by Deng [6]. The result showed that total heat transmission is directly proportional to the amount of eddies in the enclosure. Pirmohammadi et al. [7] investigated buoyancy-driven convection and the influence of magnetic field within a differentially heated square cavity. The result indicated that the magnetic field reduces the rate of convective heat transfer. Magneto convection and partially active vertical walls in a square cavity were studied by Nithyadevi et al. [8].

With the increase in the Hartmann number, the average Nusselt number decreased, but the Prandtl number and Grashof number increased. The porous layer on the flow structure and heat transfer within a square was examined by Hamimid et al. [9] to find out the velocity pressure formulation. Jani et al. [10] studied MHD free convection in a square cavity with a hot bottom wall and cooled side walls. It was found that the magnetic field reduced free convection strength as well as flow velocity and at higher Rayleigh numbers. Natural convection with an inner circular cylinder through square enclosure was investigated by Lee et al. [11]. It was found that the size of the local heating zone influenced the production and dissolution of vortices. Hussein et al. [12] studied transient natural convection flow in the enclosures and obtained heat transfer properties of three-dimensional impacts of transitory natural convection. Natural convection in a square cavity was examined by Park et al. [13], where two inner circular cylinders were positioned in the cavity. Hossain et al. [14] performed a trapezoidal cavity, including the effect of the magnetic field as well as non-uniformly heated bottom wall. It was demonstrated that the average and local Nusselt number with the non-uniform heating of the cavity's bottom wall depended on dimensionless parameters, as well as tilt angles. The effect of a perpendicular magnetic field on free convection in a rectangular cavity to solve the resulting boundary value problem was examined by Singh et al. [15]. Park et al. [16] studied natural convection in a square enclosure with four circular cylinders to locate various rectangular positions of the cylinders on the flow and thermal fields. Hossain et al. [17] analyzed magneto-natural convection within trapezoidal cavity and utilized circular block in the cavity and observed that the conduction-dominant region had changed for different angles of Φs. Seo et al. [18,19] investigated flow instability on natural convection in a square enclosure with the aid of four inner cylinders. The effects of the rectangular array cylinder positions in a square enclosure on heat transfer characteristics were highlighted. The effect of buoyancy force by using bottom heating in a square cavity was analyzed by Siddiki et al. [20]. An analysis of the flow of natural convection was conducted by Hossain et al. [21] in a trapezoidal cavity, in which a non-uniformly heated triangular block was used inside the cavity. They observed that the heat transfer rates were significantly affected by tilt angles and heated triangular blocks. Feldman [22] studied the oscillatory instability flow of natural convection in a square enclosure, incorporating a tandem of vertically aligned cylinders.

Hossain et al. [23] demonstrated natural convection in a trapezoidal cavity and also utilized magnetic fields and cold triangular obstacles. They observed that streamlines, isotherms and average Nusselt numbers were affected by rotations of the cold triangular obstruction. Magneto-hydrodynamic free convection through a square enclosure Lattice Boltzmann simulation was studied by Laouer and Djeghiour [24]. It was seen that the heat transfer rate fell as the Ha increased, but it increased when the Ra increased. Furthermore, for high Rayleigh numbers and a wide range of Hartmann numbers, the magnetic field direction had a significant impact on the heat transfer and fluid movement inside the enclosure. Fayz-Al-Asad et al. [25] analyzed natural convection in a wavy cavity to obtain the result of the fin length and its location. They found that there was a significant impact on the flow structure and temperature for the fin lengths and their locations. Magneto-hydrodynamic natural convection flow was studied by Hossain et al. [26]. They used heated triangular obstacles in accordance with a porous trapezoidal cavity. They showed that local and average Nusselt numbers were highly influenced by a variety of aspect ratios of heat source obstacles within the cavity. Liao and Li [27] presented an empirical correlation of natural convection with the effect of a magnetic field in a square enclosure to anticipate the heat transfer transition for various values of Ha and Ra. Shahid et al. [28] studied a lid-driven rectangular cavity using a multi-relaxation time Lattice Boltzmann simulation. They analyzed the aspect ratio of the cavity, as well as the sizes of the heated obstacles on fluid flow. Natural convection flow in a trapezoidal cavity was studied by Khan et al. [29]. They used a porous matrix within the cavity, along with heated cylindrical barriers. They showed that the average Nusselt number showed a dominant boost for both the fluid and solid phases. Fayz-Al-Asad et al. [30,31] studied a vertically wavy enclosure. They used magneto conditions to find out the effect of undulation in the cavity. They observed that, due to the increase in the number of undulations, the evolution of heat transport increased. The study of a rectangular heating source of natural convective flow within a triangular cavity was conducted by Fayz-Al-Asad et al. [32]. They confirmed that the rate of heat variation increased as the Rayleigh number increased in the cavity. Fayz-Al-Asad et al. [33] analyzed the magneto-combined convection in a lid-driven wavy cavity. They found that variations of lengths of the fin surface had a significant impact on the flow building and heat line sketch. Mixed convection flow in a lid-driven cavity was performed by Xiong et al. [34] for different obstacles. The results showed that the intensity of maximum convection was achieved for a higher Grashof number. Recently, Alshare et al. [35] conducted a hydrothermal and entropy critique of nanofluid natural convection inside an elliptical shape in the concentric irregular cavity. They observed that a single increase in undulation increased the Nusselt number by an average of 9.5% within the examined range (N = 1 to 4). Furthermore, doubling the nanoparticle volume fraction increased the Nusselt number by nearly 8%. In addition, the finite element method, magnetic field and natural convection were found to be more detailed [36–39].

To the best knowledge of the scientist, it was noted that no inquiry has been conducted on the effect of heated cylinders in accordance with magnetic-natural convection flow in a square cavity in which the geometrical result for the heat transport characteristics is necessary in order to know the industrial functions. The flow field has been characterized by the streamlines whereas the thermal area is defined by the isotherms, local and average Nusselt numbers. For computation, the Prandtl number (Pr = 0.71) is considered for the airflow in the cavity. The present research study was conducted for the assorted configurations of heated cylinders for the range of Ha and Ra on flow, as well as thermal field through square enclosure.

2. Problem Definition

The physical configuration for the current investigation is shown in Figure 1. A steady, two-dimensional square cavity with various heated cylinders (LBC, RBC, LTC and RTC) embedded inside, along with magnetic field (B_0) with the y-axis, was used in the present model. The dimension of the cavity was defined by its height (H) and length (L). The gravitational force (g) always worked in the vertically downward direction. The left and right walls of the cavity were thermally insulated (T_i). The base wall of the cavity was considered to be at a uniform hot temperature (T_h) and the top wall was maintained at a cold temperature (T_c), where $T_h > T_c$. Furthermore, a heated cylinder of a diameter D was placed in various positions within the square cavity. The diameter of the cylinder was made to be one third of the cavity's height. The electrically conductive fluid with

$Pr = 0.71$ [10] was placed in the square cavity and the flow of fluid was thought to be Newtonian and laminar. In addition, stable fluid properties were seen, and the boundary walls of the cavity were no-slip.

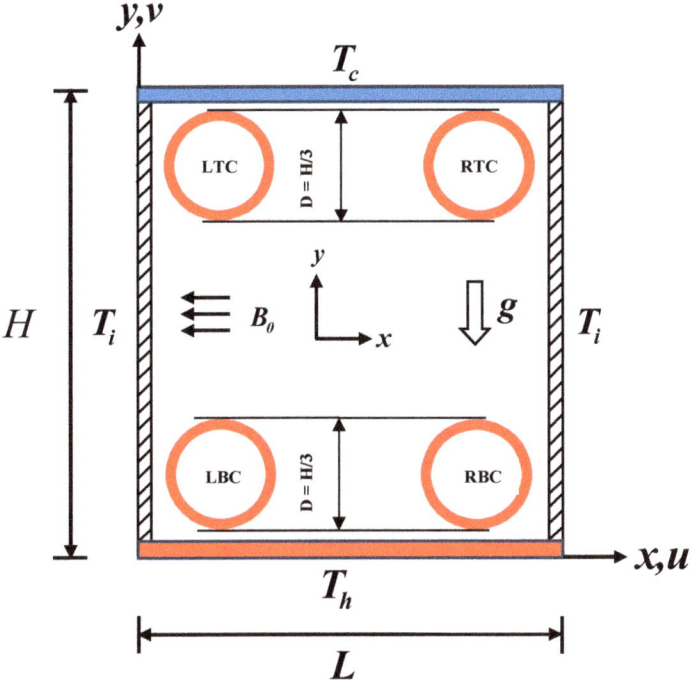

Figure 1. Schematic model of the present study.

3. Mathematical Modeling

The flow of fluid was steady, viscous and incompressible in the present study. The electrically conducting flow of fluid was also invariant, excluding density variation. Furthermore, Boussinesq approximation was used to report the variation of density as a function of temperature and, in this way, connect the temperature field to the flow field for the treatment of buoyancy term in the momentum equation. In addition, viscous dissipation, the effect of radiation, the low-magnetic Reynolds number model for Lorentz force and Joule heating were neglected in this study. The two-dimensional conservations equations of mass, momentum and energy for the present study in dimensionless form were as follows [10,14,17,23,26,40,41]:

$$\frac{\partial U}{\partial X} + \frac{\partial V}{\partial Y} = 0, \tag{1}$$

$$U\frac{\partial U}{\partial X} + V\frac{\partial U}{\partial Y} = -\frac{\partial P}{\partial X} + \Pr\left(\frac{\partial^2 U}{\partial X^2} + \frac{\partial^2 U}{\partial Y^2}\right), \tag{2}$$

$$U\frac{\partial V}{\partial X} + V\frac{\partial V}{\partial Y} = -\frac{\partial P}{\partial Y} + \Pr\left(\frac{\partial^2 V}{\partial X^2} + \frac{\partial^2 V}{\partial Y^2}\right) + RaPr\theta - Ha^2 PrV, \tag{3}$$

$$U\frac{\partial \theta}{\partial X} + V\frac{\partial \theta}{\partial Y} = \left(\frac{\partial^2 \theta}{\partial X^2} + \frac{\partial^2 \theta}{\partial Y^2}\right). \tag{4}$$

Using the following variables in the present study, Equations (1)–(4) were non-dimensionalized:

$$X = \frac{x}{L},\ Y = \frac{y}{L},\ U = \frac{uL}{\alpha},\ V = \frac{vL}{\alpha},\ P = \frac{pL^2}{\rho\alpha^2},\ \theta = \frac{T-T_c}{T_h-T_c},$$

$$Ha = B_0 L\sqrt{\frac{\sigma}{\mu}},\ Pr = \frac{v}{\alpha},\ Ra = \frac{g\beta(T_h-T_c)L^3}{\alpha v},$$

where X and Y both are non-dimensional coordinates alongside horizontal and vertical directions, respectively; U and V are non-dimensional velocity components in X and Y directions, respectively; θ and P are the non-dimensional temperature and pressure; and Ra, Pr and Ha, are the Rayleigh number, the Prandtl number and the Hartmann number, respectively. Thermal diffusivity, volumetric thermal expansion coefficient, kinematic viscosity, density, specific heat, acceleration due to gravity and dimensional temperature difference of the fluid are represented, respectively, by the symbols α, β, v, ρ, c_p, g, and ΔT.

The related boundary conditions for Equations (1)–(4) take the following forms:
on the left and right (side) walls: $U = 0$, $V = 0$, $\frac{\partial \theta}{\partial n} = 0$;
on the top wall: $U = 0$, $V = 0$, $\theta = 0$;
on the bottom wall: $U = 0$, $V = 0$, $\theta = 1$;
on the insider elliptic obstacle: $U = 0$, $V = 0$, $\theta = 1$.

The heat transfer co-efficient, as well as the local Nusselt number (Nu_{local}) and mean Nusselt number (Nu_{av}) on the heated part of the cavity, were determined as follows:

$$Nu_{local} = -\frac{\partial \theta}{\partial Y} \text{ and } Nu_{av} = \int_0^1 Nu_{local}\, dX$$

4. Numerical Details

The computational technique was employed to simulate the flow dynamics within the cavity for the problem presented in this paper, with the help of the Galerkin weighted residual finite element technique. Using this technique, the solution domain was discretized into finite element meshes composed of non-uniform triangular elements. Then, the nonlinear governing partial differential equations (i.e., mass, momentum and energy equations) were transferred into a system of integral equations by applying this technique. The Galerkin weighted residual finite element technique (as shown in the works of Taylor and Hood [42], Zienkiewicz [43] and Dechaumphai [44]) was applied to Equations (1)–(4) for the evaluation of finite element equations as:

$$\int_A N_\alpha \left(\frac{\partial U}{\partial X} + \frac{\partial V}{\partial Y}\right) dA = 0, \tag{5}$$

$$\int_A N_\alpha \left(U\frac{\partial U}{\partial X} + V\frac{\partial U}{\partial Y}\right) dA = -\int_A H_\lambda \left(\frac{\partial P}{\partial X}\right) dA + Pr\int_A N_\alpha \left(\frac{\partial^2 U}{\partial X^2} + \frac{\partial^2 U}{\partial Y^2}\right) dA, \tag{6}$$

$$\int_A N_\alpha \left(U\frac{\partial V}{\partial X} + V\frac{\partial V}{\partial Y}\right) dA = -\int_A H_\lambda \left(\frac{\partial P}{\partial Y}\right) dA + Pr\int_A N_\alpha \left(\frac{\partial^2 V}{\partial X^2} + \frac{\partial^2 V}{\partial Y^2}\right) dA + RaPr\int_A N_\alpha \theta\, dA - Ha^2 \int_A N_\alpha V\, dA, \tag{7}$$

$$\int_A N_\alpha \left(U\frac{\partial \theta}{\partial X} + V\frac{\partial \theta}{\partial Y}\right) dA = \int_A N_\alpha \left(\frac{\partial^2 \theta}{\partial X^2} + \frac{\partial^2 \theta}{\partial Y^2}\right) dA, \tag{8}$$

where A is the element section; N_α refers to functions of element interpolation for velocity and temperature and $\alpha = 1, 2, \ldots, 6$; H_λ refers to functions of element exclamation for pressure; and $\lambda = 1, 2, 3$.

Gauss's theorem with appropriate boundary integral terms, in accordance with heat flux and surface tractions, was applied to Equations (6)–(8), then becoming

$$\int_A N_\alpha \left(U \frac{\partial U}{\partial X} + V \frac{\partial U}{\partial Y} \right) dA + \int_A H_\lambda \left(\frac{\partial P}{\partial X} \right) dA \\ + Pr \int_A \left(\frac{\partial N_\alpha}{\partial X} \frac{\partial U}{\partial X} + \frac{\partial N_\alpha}{\partial Y} \frac{\partial U}{\partial Y} \right) dA = \int_{S_0} N_\alpha S_x dS_0, \quad (9)$$

$$\int_A N_\alpha \left(U \frac{\partial V}{\partial X} + V \frac{\partial V}{\partial Y} \right) dA + \int_A H_\lambda \left(\frac{\partial P}{\partial Y} \right) dA \\ + Pr \int_A \left(\frac{\partial N_\alpha}{\partial X} \frac{\partial V}{\partial X} + \frac{\partial N_\alpha}{\partial Y} \frac{\partial V}{\partial Y} \right) - RaPr \int_\alpha N_\alpha \theta dA + Ha^2 \int_\alpha N_\alpha V dA = \int_{s_0} N_\alpha S_y dS_0, \quad (10)$$

$$\int_\alpha N_\alpha \left(U \frac{\partial \theta}{\partial X} + V \frac{\partial \theta}{\partial Y} \right) dA + \int_\alpha \left(\frac{\partial N_\alpha}{\partial X} \frac{\partial \theta}{\partial X} + \frac{\partial N_\alpha}{\partial Y} \frac{\partial \theta}{\partial Y} \right) dA = \int_{S_w} N_\alpha q_{lw} dS_w, \quad (11)$$

where (9)–(10) specify the surface tractions (S_x, S_y) alongside the outflow boundary S_0 and (11) specifies the components of velocity and heat flux (q_w), which flows into or out from field alongside S_w.

Now, the basic unidentified elements for the major partial differential equations are velocity distributions components U and V; the temperature distribution θ; and the pressure distribution P. These distributions, by their uppermost derivative orders, were then applied to Equations (5)–(8):

$$U(X,Y) = N_\beta U_\beta, \ V(X,Y) = N_\beta V_\beta, \ \theta(X,Y) = N_\beta \theta_\beta, \ P(X,Y) = H_\lambda P_\lambda, \quad (12)$$

where $\beta = 1, 2, \ldots, 6$; $\lambda = 1, 2, 3$.

The finite element equations, by substituting Equation (12), are as follows:

$$K_{\alpha\beta x} U_\beta + K_{\alpha\beta y} V_\beta = 0, \quad (13)$$

$$K_{\alpha\beta\gamma x} U_\beta U_\gamma + K_{\alpha\beta\gamma y} V_\gamma U_\gamma + M_{\alpha\mu x} P_\mu + Pr \left(S_{\alpha\beta xx} + S_{\alpha\beta yy} \right) U_\beta = Q_{\alpha u}, \quad (14)$$

$$K_{\alpha\beta\gamma x} U_\beta V_\gamma + K_{\alpha\beta\gamma y} V_\gamma V_\gamma + M_{\alpha\mu y} P_\mu + Pr \left(S_{\alpha\beta xx} + S_{\alpha\beta yy} \right) + Ha^2 K_{\alpha\beta} V_\beta - RaPr K_{\alpha\beta} \theta_\beta = Q_{\alpha v}, \quad (15)$$

$$K_{\alpha\beta\gamma x} U_\beta \theta_\gamma + K_{\alpha\beta\gamma y} V_\beta \theta_\gamma + \left(S_{\alpha\beta xx} + S_{\alpha\beta yy} \right) \theta_\beta = Q_{\alpha \theta}, \quad (16)$$

where element matrices coefficients are in the shape of the integrals in the element region and alongside the element edges S_0 and S_w as:

$$K_{\alpha\beta x} = \int_A N_\alpha N_{\beta,x} dA, \ K_{\alpha\beta y} = \int_A N_\alpha N_{\beta,y} dA, \ K_{\alpha\beta\gamma x} = \int_A N_\alpha N_\beta N_{\gamma,x} dA,$$
$$K_{\alpha\beta\gamma y} = \int_A N_\alpha N_\beta N_{\gamma,y} dA, \ K_{\alpha\beta} = \int_A N_\alpha N_\beta dA, \ S_{\alpha\beta xx} = \int_A N_{\alpha,x} N_{\beta,x} dA \ S_{\alpha\beta yy} = \int_A N_{\alpha,y} N_{\beta,y} dA,$$
$$M_{\alpha\mu x} = \int_A H_\alpha H_{\mu,x} dA, \ M_{\alpha\mu y} = \int_A H_\alpha H_{\mu,y} dA,$$
$$Q_{\alpha u} = \int_{S_0} N_\alpha S_x dS_0, \ Q_{\alpha v} = \int_{S_0} N_\alpha S_y dS_0, \ Q_{\alpha \theta} = \int_{S_w} N_\alpha q_{1w} dS_w, Q_{\alpha \theta s} = \int_{S_w} N_\alpha q_{2w} dS_w.$$

The non-linear resulting finite element Equations (13)–(16) are algebraic. Finally, the process of Newton–Raphson, as well as the integration technique, was used to iteratively determine the equations of residuals. A convergence of the procedure of computation is put aside once the convergence criteria or the condition is determined as $\left| \frac{\Psi^{n+1} - \Psi^n}{\Psi^{n+1}} \right| < 10^{-6}$, where n refers to the iterative number, $\psi = \psi(U, V, \theta)$.

As the code validation is necessary for the accurateness of the numerical technique, the present problem is considered with $Pr = 0.71$, $Ha = 50$ and $Ra = 10^5$, which had been solved for streamlines (stream function) and isotherms for 2D magneto-hydrodynamic free convection flow through the square cavity. The result was checked for streamlines and isotherms and then the present work was compared with the reported reference of Jani et al. [10] and presented in Figure 2. From the above comparisons of the figures, we found a good agreement between the present work and Jani et al. [10], which is displayed in Figure 2. Furthermore, mesh configuration is a technique in which a large domain is subdivided into a set of sub domains called finite elements, control volume and so on. A lot of boundary value problems of several engineering fields have been solved with the aid of irregular geometry via a set of finite elements. The answer for the current geometry for the specific non-dimensional parameters was computed at discrete locations called numerical grids. The mesh structure for the current problem is provided in Figure 3.

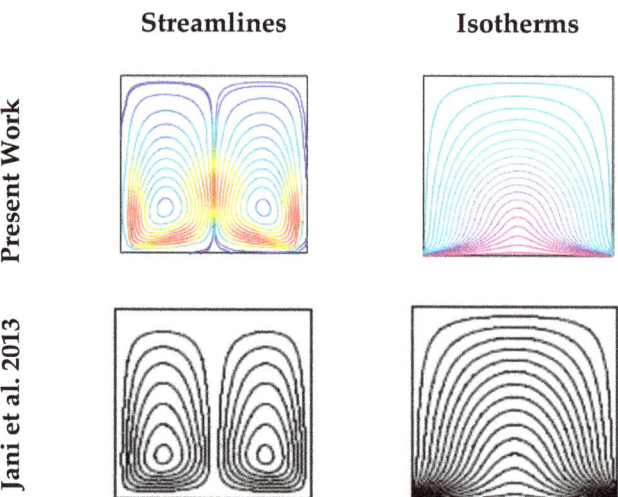

Figure 2. Comparison of streamlines and isotherms of by Jani et al. [10] and the present work with $Pr = 0.71$, $Ha = 50$ and $Ra = 10^5$.

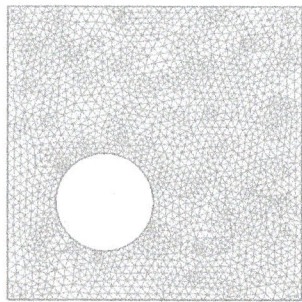

Figure 3. Mesh configuration for the cavity.

In addition, to select a proper grid size, in the present study, a particular grid sensitivity selecting procedure was performed for the square cavity along with various heated cylinders for $Pr = 0.71$, $Ha = 100$ and $Ra = 10^5$, considering assorted size of mesh. The manifest meshing is shown in Table 1 and Figure 4, where the average Nusselt number is calculated. It was found that further increments of Nu_{av} have insignificant transform. Throughout the study, for 23,780 nodes and 3568 elements, the mesh configuration was chosen for accurate simulation to find the optimized, desired result in the present study.

Table 1. Grid sensitivity tests at $Pr = 0.71$, $Ha = 100$ and $Ra = 10^5$.

Nodes	16,030	19,099	21,560	23,780	32,945	37,682
Elements	2408	2878	3258	3568	4978	5696
Nu_{av}	0.130212	0.130203	0.137988	0.141502	0.141502	0.1415
Time (s)	15.913	19.308	22.568	26.879	36.5135	38.495

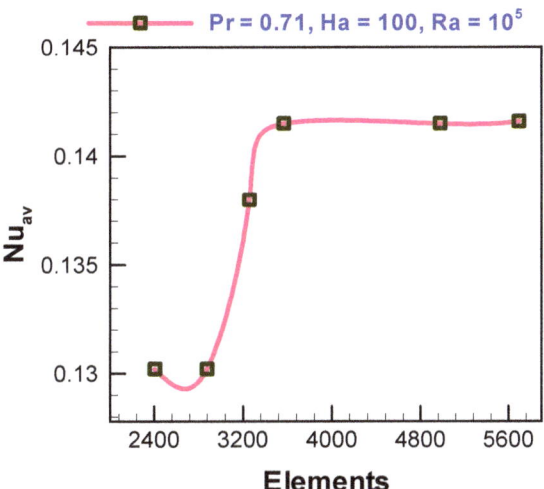

Figure 4. Grid sensitivity tests for $Pr = 0.71$, $Ha = 100$ and $Ra = 10^5$.

5. Results and Discussion

In the present study, the effect of a heated cylinder for different configurations, LBC, RBC, LTC and RTC, in accordance with the magnetic field for the fluid flow on the natural convection in a square cavity numerically, was studied. The results of the square cavity with an insider heated cylinder were presumed for electrically conductive fluid with the Prandtl number ($Pr = 0.71$) and a confined airflow. The wide range of governing parameters were the Rayleigh number ($10^3 \leq Ra \leq 10^5$) and the Hartmann number ($0 \leq Ha \leq 200$), studied here in order to find the computational results. The results were analyzed in the form of streamlines and isotherms, velocity profiles, temperature profiles, heat transfer rates and local and mean Nusselt numbers, alongside the heated wall of the cavity.

5.1. Effect of Cylinder Position and Magnetic Field on Streamlines and Isotherms

Streamlines and isotherms for assorted heated cylinder configurations along with different parameters Ha, Pr and Ra were shown in Figures 5–8. As the beneath wall of the cavity and cylindrical block were heated, the flow of hot fluids creates eddy circulation cells, rotating along the cold walls inside the cavity from the heating wall for all parameters: Pr, Ha and Ra. To find the variations of streamlines and isotherms on various configurations of heated cylinders (LBC, RBC, LTC and RTC), a numerical study was performed with $Pr = 0.71$, $Ha = 0$–200 and $Ra = 10^3$–10^4, correspondingly, for flow and thermal field in Figures 5 and 6. The impact of the presence of a magnetic field for streamlines and isotherms is also demonstrated in Figures 5a and 6, respectively, for cavity configuration (LBC). Figure 5a shows that one eddy circulation cell formed inside the cavity. The flow strength decreases and streamlines close to the heated cylinder configurations due to the enhancement of the Hartmann number, which is shown in Figure 5b–d. The effect of the Hartmann number ($Ha = 0$–200) on the distributions of the velocity and temperature contours for right bottom configuration (RBC), while $Ra = 10^3$ and $Pr = 0.71$ is also shown in Figure 5. A tiny recirculation cell appeared in the center of the square of the cavity and the recirculation cell was smaller, owing to the increase in the Hartmann number, which is shown in Figure 5. Figure 5 also illustrates the streamlines for the left top heated cylinder configurations (LTC), along with variations of the Hartmann number ($Ha = 0$–200), when $Ra = 10^3$ and $Pr = 0.71$. Figure 5 shows in the LTC configuration that one cell was created inside the center of the square cavity in the absence of magnetic field. In addition to this, one large vortex also formed in the left bottom side of the cavity. The cell became bigger and oval shaped in the cavity with the increase of the Hartmann number and also, a tiny vortex was found in the left top side of the cavity. The variation of the Hartmann number for the right top cylindrical heat source (RTC) configuration is shown in Figure 5 for the square cavity. It can be seen that the smaller cell was formed in the square cavity due to both the absence and presence of Ha, compared with the LTC. Figure 6 shows that the isotherms for the left bottom heated cylinder configuration (LBC) are likely linear, as well as nonlinear close to the upper wall and base wall, correspondingly, with the increase in the Hartmann number when $Ra = 10^3$ and $Pr = 0.71$ (see Figure 6a–d). Furthermore, Figure 6a–d shows the thermal increases, owing to the increase of the magnetic field parameter: the Hartmann number (Ha). The temperature distributions for the right bottom cylindrical heat source configuration (RBC) with magnetic field's effect on the parameter Hartmann number ($Ha = 0$–200) is shown in Figure 6a–d for fixed $Ra = 10^3$ and $Pr = 0.71$. The isotherms were parallel to the upper wall of the cavity. On the other hand, a nonlinearity effect was found near to the base wall of the cavity. The isotherms for LTC shown in Figure 6 were almost as linear as those near to the top wall. However, bend isotherms could be seen near the base wall through the effect of the Hartmann number. By increasing the Hartmann number, it could be seen that the isotherms in the RTC transform slightly in the cavity, as shown in Figure 6. When the Rayleigh number increased, that is, for higher $Ra = 10^5$, streamlines and isotherms were analyzed, as shown in Figures 7 and 8 for various configurations of heated cylinders (LBC, RBC, LTC and RTC) within the square cavity for $Ha = 0$–200 and $Pr = 0.71$. As shown in Figure 7, by analyzing all configurations of the heated cylinders (LBC, RBC, LTC and RTC), it can be understood that one primary larger eddy circulation cell was created inside the cavity when $Ha = 0$. However, due to the increase in the Hartmann number ($0 \leq Ha \leq 200$), the velocity flow strength dwindled. Therefore, likely larger secondary recirculation cells with tiny vortices were created inside the square cavity. At higher $Ra = 10^5$–10^3 and when $Pr = 0.71$, it is shown in Figure 8 that isotherms for every arrangement of heated cylinders (LBC, RBC, LTC and RTC) looked parallel and non-parallel, respectively, near to the upper and beneath wall of the cavity for the impact of magnetic field $Ha = 0$–200. However, due to the increased Hartmann number and strength of flow of convection, more compacted and non-parallel isotherm lines were seen in the cavity. In addition to this, fewer bond isotherm lines were also observed near the side walls of the cavity.

5.2. Velocity and Temperature Profiles

Figure 9 displays the effects of the Hartmann number (Ha) on velocity pro-files with distances for different cylinder configurations (LBC, RBC, LTC and RTC) adjacent to the line X = 0.3. As shown in Figure 9, the velocity decreased for each cylinder configuration (LBC, RBC, LTC and RTC) and with the increasing value of the Hartmann number below the central portion of the cavity. On the other hand, the velocity increased with the decrease in the Hartmann number. Due to the counterclockwise and clockwise flow directions, the maximum and minimum velocities were found in the absence of a magnetic field. The temperature fields with the distance X are plotted in Figure 10 for different cylinder heat source configurations (LBC, RBC, LTC and RTC). Figure 10 shows, for LBC, RBC, LTC and RTC, that when the Hartmann number was absent, the maximum and minimum temperatures were found in the cavity. The temperature field lessened due to the increase in the Hartmann number. For LBC and LTC, the temperature field transformed slightly with the increase in the Hartmann number to X < 0.2, but transformed significantly when the Hartmann number was X > 0.2. An inverse result was observed for RBC and RTC. It was observed that the change in the temperature field was insignificant when the Hartmann number increased to X < 0.4, but the change was significant when the Hartmann number was X > 0.4.

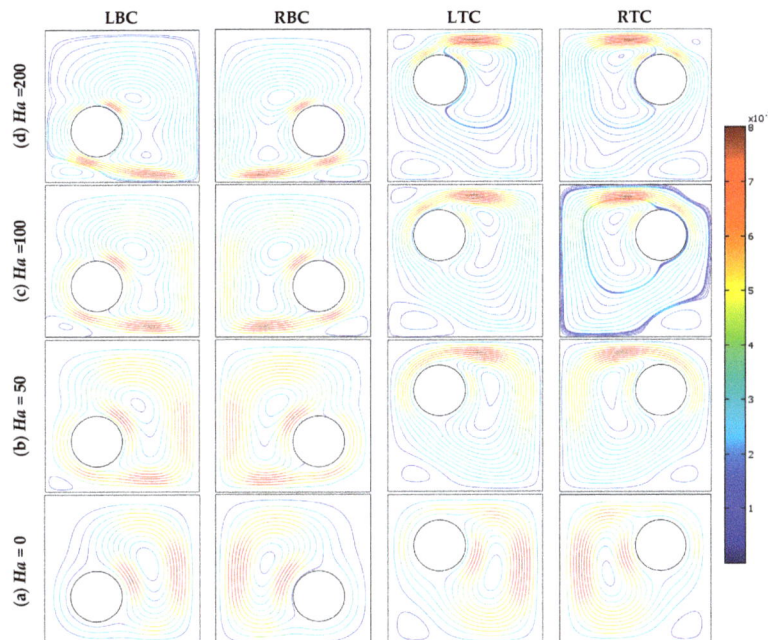

Figure 5. Streamlines for different orientations of heated cylinders for Ha = 0–200, $Ra = 10^3$ and $Pr = 0.71$.

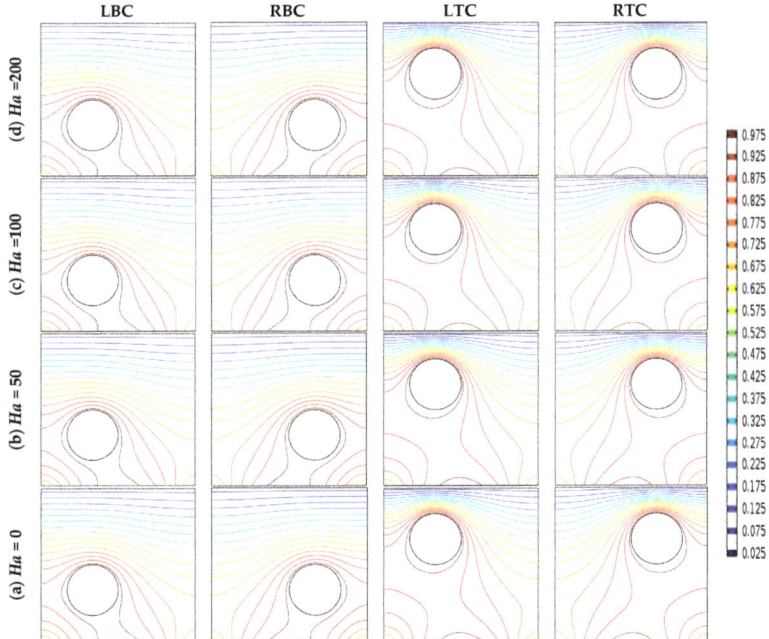

Figure 6. Isotherms for different orientations of heated cylinders for Ha = 0–200, $Ra = 10^3$ and $Pr = 0.71$.

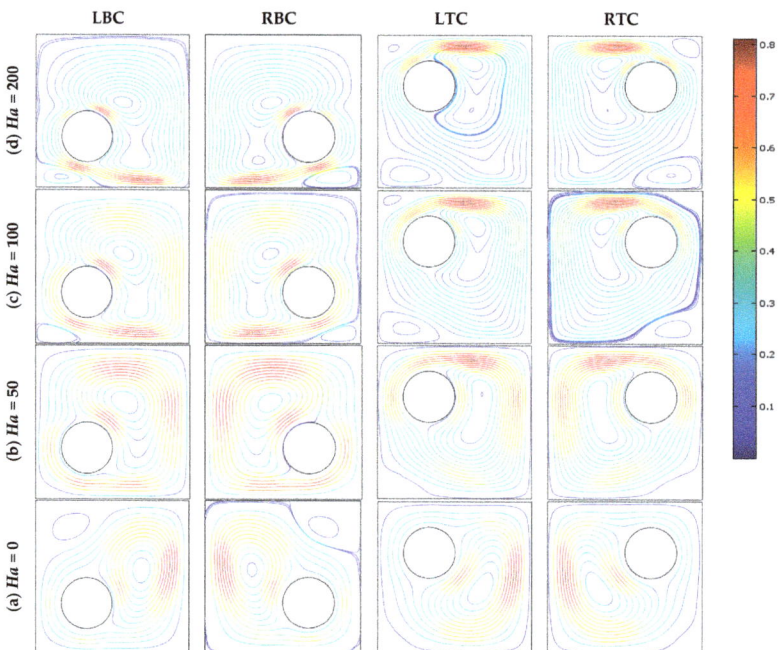

Figure 7. Streamlines for different orientations of heated cylinders for $Ha = 0\text{–}200$, $Ra = 10^5$ and $Pr = 0.71$.

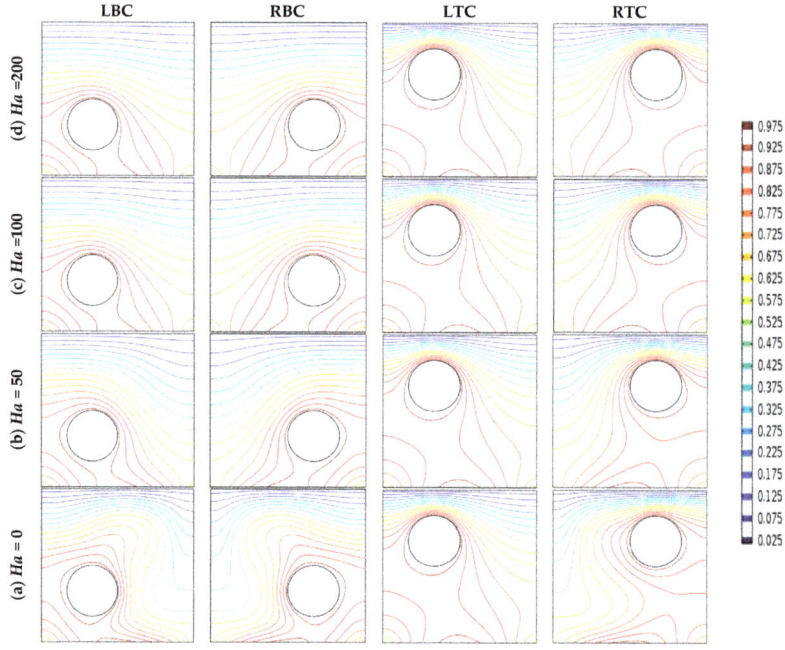

Figure 8. Isotherms for different orientations of heated cylinders for $Ha = 0\text{–}200$, $Ra = 10^5$ and $Pr = 0.71$.

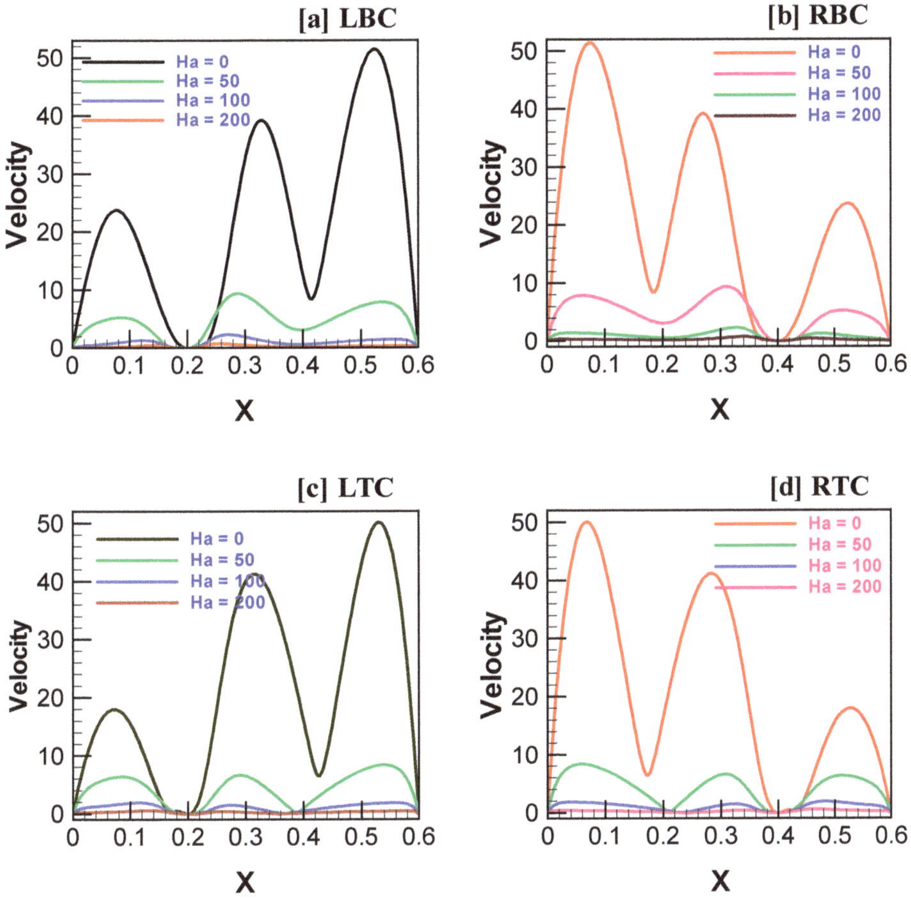

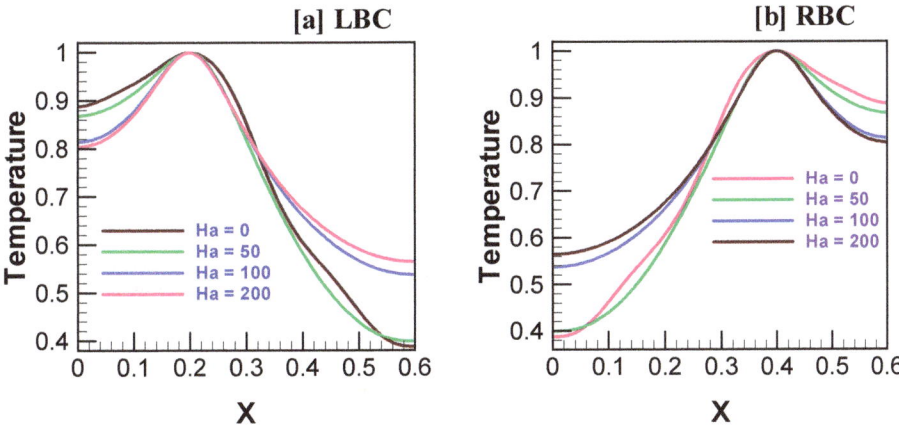

Figure 9. Variations of velocity vs. distance for different orientations of heated cylinders for $Ha = 0$–200, $Ra = 10^5$ and $Pr = 0.71$.

Figure 10. *Cont.*

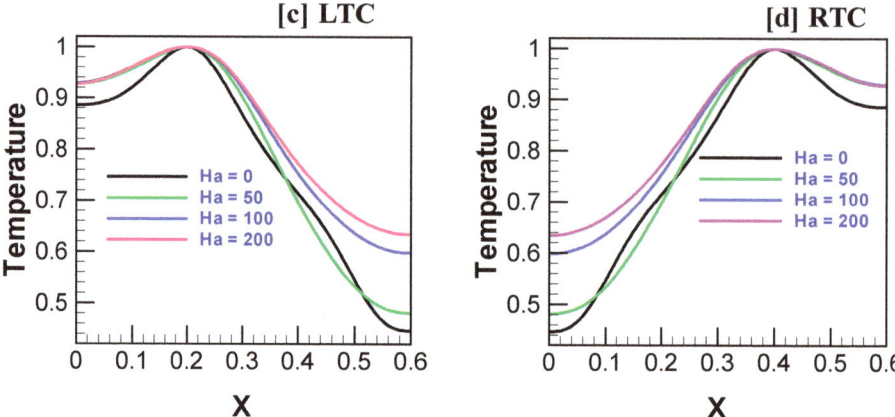

Figure 10. Variations of temperature with distance for different orientations of heated cylinders for $Ha = 0$–200, $Ra = 10^5$ and $Pr = 0.71$.

5.3. Heat Transfer

The heat transfer rates, as well as the local Nusselt number with the distance wall for different configurations (LBC, RBC, LTC and RTC) are presented in Figure 11 for the variations of the Hartmann number. Regarding the LBC and LTC configurations, Figure 11 shows that the local Nusselt number decreased with the increase in the Hartmann number, but for the RBC and RTC configurations, it was observed that the local Nusselt number increases due to the increasing Hartmann number. The heat transfer rates, as well as the mean Nusselt number for different configurations (LBC, RBC, LTC and RTC) are presented in Figure 12 against the variations of the Hartmann number. Figure 12 shows, for all configurations, that the mean Nusselt number increases due to the absence of the Hartmann number, but the mean Nusselt number decreases due to the increase in the Hartmann number.

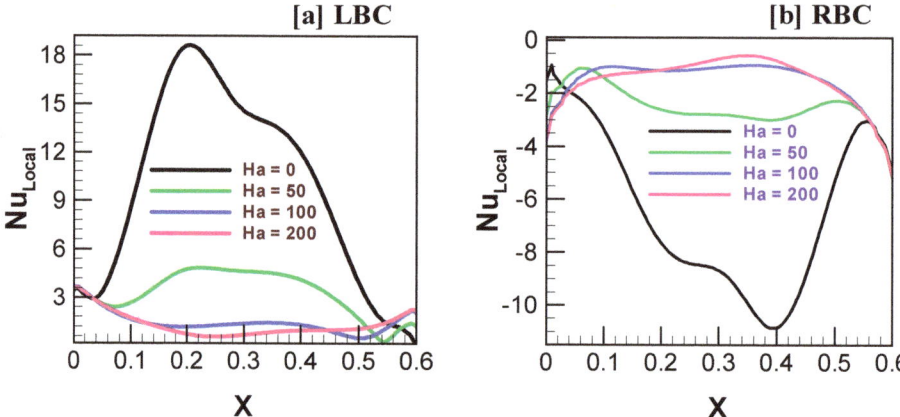

Figure 11. *Cont.*

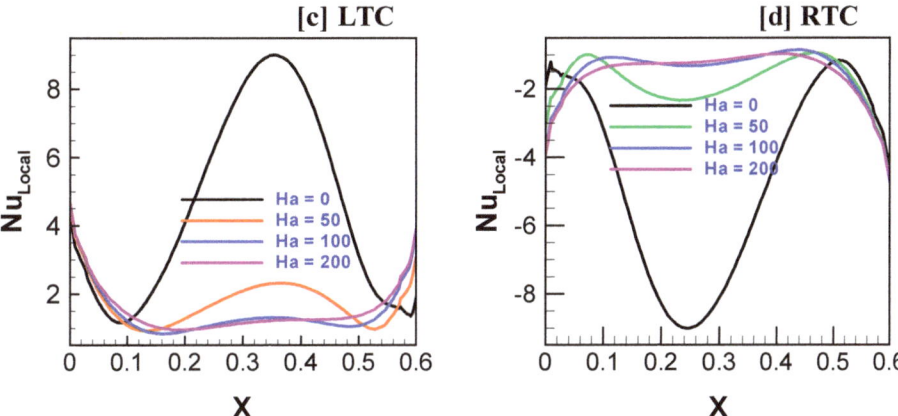

Figure 11. Variations of local Nusselt number with distance for different orientations of heated cylinders for $Ha = 0–200$, $Ra = 10^5$ and $Pr = 0.71$.

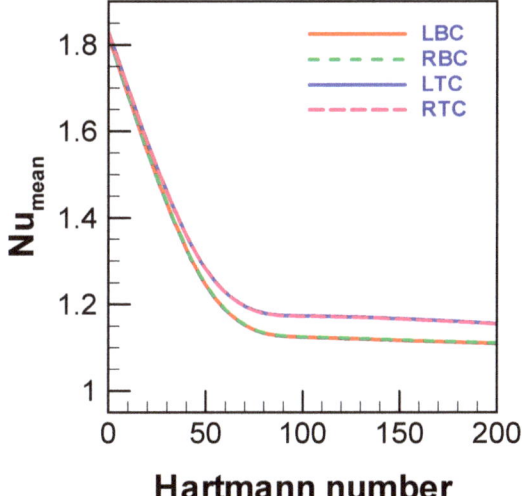

Figure 12. Variations of average Nusselt number with the Hartmann number for different orientations of heated cylinders for $Ha = 0–200$, $Ra = 10^5$ and $Pr = 0.71$.

6. Conclusions

A 2D computational framework was generated to analyze the fluid dynamic performance in a square cavity in order to find the effect of heating cylinders in line with a magnetic field using natural convection by applying the free triangular grid-established finite element technique through the use of an easy algorithm. The numerical work within a square cavity for various cylindrical heat source configurations (LBC, RBC, LTC and RTC) when $Pr = 0.7$, $0 \leq Ha \leq 200$ and $10^3 \leq Ra \leq 10^5$ was studied in this work by employing the Galerkin weighted residual method of finite element formulation. The results are displayed for assorted cylinder configurations in the phase of streamlines, isotherms, velocity profiles, temperatures and heat transfers rates, as well as the local and mean Nusselt number for the bottom wall of the cavity. The concise summary is as follows:

- ■ The distributions of flow field and isotherm patterns, velocity and temperature profiles, rate of heat transport for various cylinder configurations within the cavity fully

depended on the Prandlt number (*Pr*), the Rayleigh number (*Ra*) and the Hartmann number (*Ha*) and the heated bottom wall of the cavity.
- The number of vortices increased within the streamlines for various configurations of the cavity due to enhance of the Hartmann number.
- The bonding of isotherm lines reduced close to the side walls of the cavity.
- The bend isotherm lines were observed adjacent to the base wall of the cavity.
- The velocity decreased for each heated cylinder configurations (LBC, RBC, LTC and RTC), as well as for the increasing value of the Hartmann number below the central portion of the cavity, but the velocity increased with the decrease in the Hartmann number.
- For the LBC and LTC configurations, the local Nusselt number decreased with the increase of the Hartmann number, but for the RBC and RTC configurations, the local Nusselt number increased with the increase in the Hartmann number.
- The mean Nusselt number for the LBC, RBC, LTC and RTC configurations increased due to the absence of the Hartmann number, but the mean Nusselt number decreased due to the increase in the Hartmann number.

Author Contributions: Conceptualization, visualization, software implementation, methodology, investigation, writing—original draft and editing: M.S.H.; writing—review, methodology, administration and supervision: M.A.A. and M.Y.; writing—review and editing: M.F.-A.-A. and M.S.I.M.; formal analysis: M.S.H. and M.F.-A.-A.; visualization: K.M.K.B. All authors have read and agreed to the published version of the manuscript.

Funding: This research received no external funding.

Acknowledgments: All authors want to express thankfulness to everyone for contribution to accomplish this research work.

Conflicts of Interest: The authors declare no conflict of interest.

Nomenclature

B_0	Magnetic field
Cp	Specific heat at constant pressure (J/kg·K)
g	Gravitational acceleration (m/s^2)
h	Convective heat transfer coefficient (W/m^2·K)
Ha	Hartmann number
k	Thermal conductivity of fluid (W/m·K)
K	Thermal conductivity ratio fluid
N	Non-dimensional distance
Nu_{av}	Mean Nusselt number
Nu_{local}	Local Nusselt number
P	Non-dimensional pressure
p	Pressure
Pr	Prandtl number
Ra	Rayleigh number
T	Non-dimensional temperature
U	Dimensionless horizontal velocity
u	Velocity in x-direction (m/s)
V	Dimensionless vertical velocity
v	Velocity in y-direction (m/s)
x, y	Cartesian coordinates
X, Y	Dimensionless Cartesian coordinates
Greek symbols	
α	Thermal diffusivity (m^2/s)
β	Coefficient of thermal expansion (K^{-1})
θ	Temperature of fluid
$\Delta\theta$	Discrepancy of temperature

μ	Dynamic viscosity of the fluid (Pa·s)
ν	Kinematic viscosity of the fluid (m^2/s)
r	Fluid density (kg/m^3)
σ	Fluid electrical conductivity (Ω^{-1}m^{-1})

Abbreviations

LBC	Left bottom heated cylinder
LTC	Left top heated cylinder
RTC	Right top heated cylinder
RBC	Right bottom heated cylinder

References

1. Ostrach, S. Natural convection in enclosure. *ASME J. Heat Transf.* **1988**, *110*, 1175–1190. [CrossRef]
2. Krakov, M.S.; Nikiforov, I.V. Influence of vertical uniform outer magnetic field on thermomagnetic convection in square cavity. *Magnetohydrodynamics* **2001**, *21*, 125–145. [CrossRef]
3. Kalita, J.C.; Dalal, D.C.; Dass, A.K. Fully Compact Higher-Order Computation of Steady-State Natural Convection in a Square Cavity. *Phys. Rev. E* **2001**, *64*, 066703. [CrossRef] [PubMed]
4. Shu, C.; Wee, K.H.A. Numerical Simulation of Natural Convection in a Square Cavity by SIMPLE-Generalized Differential Quadrature Method. *Comput. Fluids* **2002**, *31*, 209–226. [CrossRef]
5. Basak, T.; Roy, S.; Balakrishnan, A.R. Effects of thermal boundary conditions on natural convection flows within a square cavity. *Int. J. Heat Mass Transf.* **2006**, *49*, 4525–4535. [CrossRef]
6. Deng, Q. Fluid flow and heat transfer characteristics of natural convection in square cavities due to discrete source–sink pairs. *Int. J. Heat Mass Transf.* **2008**, *51*, 5949–5957. [CrossRef]
7. Pirmohammadi, M.; Ghassemi, M.; Sheikhzadeh, G.A. Effect of a Magnetic Field on Buoyancy-Driven Convection in Differentially Heated Square Cavity. *IEEE Trans. Magn.* **2009**, *45*, 407–411. [CrossRef]
8. Nithyadevi, N.; Kandaswamy, P.; Sundari, S.M. Magnetoconvection in a square cavity with partially active vertical walls: Time periodic boundary condition. *Int. J. Heat Mass Transf.* **2009**, *52*, 1945–1953. [CrossRef]
9. Hamimid, S.; Guellal, M.; Amroune, A.; Zeraibi, N. Effect of a Porous Layer on the Flow Structure and Heat Transfer in a Square Cavity. *Fluid Dyn. Mater. Process.* **2012**, *8*, 69–90. [CrossRef]
10. Jani, S.; Mahmoodi, M.; Amini, M. Magnetohydrodynamic Free Convection in a Square Cavity Heated from Below and Cooled from Other Walls. *Int. J. Mech. Ind. Sci. Eng.* **2013**, *7*, 750–755. [CrossRef]
11. Lee, H.; Doo, J.; Ha, M.; Yoon, H. Effects of thermal boundary conditions on natural convection in a square enclosure with an inner circular cylinder locally heated from the bottom wall. *Int. J. Heat Mass Transf.* **2013**, *65*, 435–450. [CrossRef]
12. Hussein, A.K.; Awad, M.M.; Kolsi, L.; Fathinia, F.; Adegun, I.K. A comprehensive review of transient natural convection flow in enclosures. *J. Basic Appl. Sci. Res.* **2014**, *11*, 17–27.
13. Park, Y.; Ha, M.; Choi, C.; Park, J. Natural convection in a square enclosure with two inner circular cylinders positioned at different vertical locations. *Int. J. Heat Mass Transf.* **2014**, *77*, 501–518. [CrossRef]
14. Hossain, M.S.; Alim, M.A. MHD free convection within trapezoidal cavity with non-uniformly heated bottom wall. *Int. J. Heat Mass Transf.* **2014**, *69*, 327–336. [CrossRef]
15. Singh, A.K.; Chandran, P.; Sacheti, N.C. Effect of perpendicular magnetic field on free convection in a rectangular cavity. *Sultan Qaboos Univ. J. Sci.* **2015**, *20*, 49–59. [CrossRef]
16. Park, Y.G.; Ha, M.Y.; Park, J. Natural convection in a square enclosure with four circular cylinders positioned at different rectangular locations. *Int. J. Heat Mass Transf.* **2015**, *81*, 490–511. [CrossRef]
17. Hossain, M.S.; Alim, M.A.; Kabir, K.H. Numerical Analysis on MHD Natural Convection within Trapezoidal Cavity Having Circular Block. *Am. J. Appl. Math. Stat.* **2016**, *4*, 161–168. [CrossRef]
18. Seo, Y.M.; Park, Y.G.; Kim, M.; Yoon, H.S.; Ha, M.Y. Two-dimensional flow instability induced by natural convection in a square enclosure with four inner cylinders. part i: Effect of horizontal position of inner cylinders. *Int. J. Heat Mass Transf.* **2017**, *113*, 1306–1318. [CrossRef]
19. Seo, Y.M.; Mun, G.S.; Park, Y.G.; Ha, M.Y. Two-dimensional flow instability induced by natural convection in a square enclosure with four inner cylinders. part ii: Effect of various positions of inner cylinders. *Int. J. Heat Mass Transf.* **2017**, *113*, 1319–1331. [CrossRef]
20. Siddiki, M.N.A.A.; Habiba, F.; Chowdhury, R. Effect of Buoyancy Force on the Flow Field in a Square Cavity with Heated from Below. *Int. J. Discret. Math.* **2017**, *2*, 43–47. [CrossRef]
21. Hossain, M.S.; Alim, M.A.; Andallah, L.S. Numerical Investigation of Natural Convection Flow in a Trapezoidal Cavity with Non-uniformly Heated Triangular Block Embedded Inside. *J. Adv. Math. Comput. Sci.* **2018**, *28*, 1–30. [CrossRef]
22. Feldman, Y. Oscillatory instability of 2D natural convection flow in a square enclosure with a tandem of vertically aligned cylinders. *Fluid Dyn.* **2018**, *50*, 51–410. [CrossRef]
23. Hossain, M.S.; Alim, M.A.; Andallah, L.S. A comprehensive analysis of natural convection in a trapezoidal cavity with magnetic field and cooled triangular obstacle of different orientations. *AIP Conf. Proc.* **2019**, *2121*, 030003. [CrossRef]

24. Laouer, A.; Djeghiour, R. Lattice Boltzmann Simulation of Magnetohydrodynamic Free Convection in a Square Enclosure with Non-uniform Heating of the Bottom Wall. *J. Adv. Res. Fluid Mech. Therm. Sci.* **2019**, *59*, 13–28.
25. Fayz-Al-Asad, M.; Munshi, M.J.H.; Sarker, M.M.A. Effect of fin length and location on natural convection heat transfer in a wavy cavity. *Int. J. Sci. Tech.* **2020**, *7*, 070303. [CrossRef]
26. Hossain, M.S.; Alim, M.A.; Andallah, L.S. Numerical Simulation of MHD Natural Convection Flow Within Porous Trapezoidal Cavity With Heated Triangular Obstacle. *Int. J. Appl. Comput. Math.* **2020**, *6*, 166. [CrossRef]
27. Liao, C.; Li, W. Assessment of the magnetic field influence on heat transfer transition of natural convection within a square cavity. *Case Stud. Therm. Eng.* **2021**, *28*, 101638. [CrossRef]
28. Shahid, H.; Yaqoob, I.; Khan, W.A.; Aslam, M. Multi relaxation time Lattice Boltzmann analysis of lid-driven rectangular cavity subject to various obstacle configurations. *Int. Commun. Heat Mass Transf.* **2021**, *129*, 105658. [CrossRef]
29. Khan, Z.H.; Hamid, M.; Khan, W.A.; Sun, L.; Liu, H. Thermal non-equilibrium natural convection in a trapezoidal porous cavity with heated cylindrical obstacles. *Int. Commun. Heat Mass Transf.* **2021**, *126*, 105460. [CrossRef]
30. Fayz-Al-Asad, M.; Alam, M.N.; Rashad, A.M.; Sarker, M.M.A. Impact of undulation on magneto-free convective heat transport in an enclosure having vertical wavy sides. *Int. Commun. Heat Mass Transf.* **2021**, *127*, 105579. [CrossRef]
31. Fayz-Al-Asad, M.; Alam, M.N.; Tunç, C.; Sarker, M.M.A. Heat transport exploration of free convection flow inside enclosure having vertical wavy walls. *J. Appl. Comput.* **2021**, *7*, 520–527. [CrossRef]
32. Fayz-Al-Asad, M.; Alam, M.N.; Ahmad, H.; Sarker, M.M.A.; Alsulami, M.D.; Gepreel, K.A. Impact of a closed space rectangular heat source on natural convective flow through triangular cavity. *Results Phys.* **2021**, *23*, 104011. [CrossRef]
33. Fayz-Al-Asad, M.; Yavuz, M.; Alam, M.N.; Sarker, M.M.A.; Bazighifan, O. Influence of Fin Length on Magneto-Combined Convection Heat Transfer Performance in a Lid-Driven Wavy Cavity. *Fractal Fract.* **2021**, *5*, 107. [CrossRef]
34. Xiong, P.Y.; Hamid, A.; Iqbal, K.; Irfan, M. Numerical simulation of mixed convection flow and heat transfer in the lid-driven triangular cavity with different obstacle configurations. *Int. Commun. Heat Mass Transf.* **2021**, *123*, 105202. [CrossRef]
35. Alshare, A.; Abderrahmane, A.; Guedri, K.; Younis, O.M.; AliH, M.; Al-Kouz, W. Hydrothermal and Entropy Investigation of Nanofluid Natural Convection in a Lid-Driven Cavity Concentric with an Elliptical Cavity with a Wavy Boundary Heated from Below. *Nanomaterials* **2022**, *12*, 1392. [CrossRef]
36. Asad, M.F.A.; Hosssain, A.; Sarker, M.M.A. Numerical investigation of MHD mixed convection heat transfer having vertical fin in a lid-driven square cavity. *AIP Conf. Proc.* **2019**, *2121*, 030023. [CrossRef]
37. Versaci, M.; Jannelli, A.; Morabito, F.C.; Angiulli, G. A semi-linear elliptic model for a circular membrane MEMS device considering the effect of the fringing field. *Sensors* **2021**, *21*, 5237. [CrossRef]
38. Islam, T.; Yavuz, M.; Parveen, N.; Fayz-Al-Asad, M. Impact of Non-Uniform Periodic Magnetic Field on Unsteady Natural Convection Flow of Nanofluids in Square Enclosure. *Fractal Fract.* **2022**, *6*, 101. [CrossRef]
39. Fayz-Al-Asad, M.; Sarker, M.M.A.; Munshi, M.J.H. Numerical investigation of natural convection flow in a hexagonal enclosure having vertical fin. *J. Sci. Res.* **2019**, *11*, 173–183. [CrossRef]
40. Sene, N. Second-grade fluid with Newtonian heating under Caputo fractional derivative: Analytical investigations via Laplace transforms. *Math. Model. Numer. Simul. Appl.* **2022**, *2*, 13–25. [CrossRef]
41. Yavuz, M.; Sene, N.; Yıldız, M. Analysis of the influences of parameters in the fractional second-grade fluid dynamics. *Mathematics* **2022**, *10*, 1125. [CrossRef]
42. Taylor, C.; Hood, P. A numerical Solution of the Navier-Stokes Equations Using Finite Element Technique. *Comput. Fluids* **1973**, *1*, 73–100. [CrossRef]
43. Zienkiewicz, O.C.; Taylor, R.L. *The Finite Element Method*, 4th ed.; McGraw-Hill: New York, NY, USA, 1991.
44. Dechaumphai, P. *Finite Element Method in Engineering*, 2nd ed.; Chulalongkorn University Press: Bangkok, Thailand, 1999.

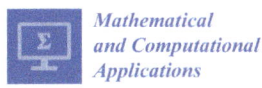

Article

A SARS-CoV-2 Fractional-Order Mathematical Model via the Modified Euler Method

Ihtisham Ul Haq [1], Mehmet Yavuz [2,*], Nigar Ali [1] and Ali Akgül [3,4]

1 Department of Mathematics, University of Malakand, Chakdara 18000, Khyber Pakhtunkhwa, Pakistan
2 Department of Mathematics and Computer Sciences, Faculty of Science, Necmettin Erbakan University, Konya 42090, Türkiye
3 Department of Mathematics, Art and Science Faculty, Siirt University, Siirt 56100, Türkiye
4 Mathematics Research Center, Department of Mathematics, Near East University, North Cyprus, Mersin 10, Nicosia 99138, Türkiye
* Correspondence: mehmetyavuz@erbakan.edu.tr

Abstract: This article develops a within-host viral kinetics model of SARS-CoV-2 under the Caputo fractional-order operator. We prove the results of the solution's existence and uniqueness by using the Banach mapping contraction principle. Using the next-generation matrix method, we obtain the basic reproduction number. We analyze the model's endemic and disease-free equilibrium points for local and global stability. Furthermore, we find approximate solutions for the non-linear fractional model using the Modified Euler Method (MEM). To support analytical findings, numerical simulations are carried out.

Keywords: SARS-CoV-2; Banach mapping contraction principle; local stability; global stability; Modified Euler Method

Citation: Haq, I.U.; Yavuz, M.; Ali, N.; Akgül, A. A SARS-CoV-2 Fractional-Order Mathematical Model via the Modified Euler Method. *Math. Comput. Appl.* **2022**, 27, 82. https://doi.org/10.3390/mca27050082

Academic Editor: Cristiana João Soares da Silva

Received: 20 July 2022
Accepted: 22 September 2022
Published: 26 September 2022

Publisher's Note: MDPI stays neutral with regard to jurisdictional claims in published maps and institutional affiliations.

Copyright: © 2022 by the authors. Licensee MDPI, Basel, Switzerland. This article is an open access article distributed under the terms and conditions of the Creative Commons Attribution (CC BY) license (https://creativecommons.org/licenses/by/4.0/).

1. Introduction

COVID-19 caused by SARS-CoV-2 is a highly transmissible and pathogenic coronavirus that appeared in late 2019 and has posed a danger to both human health and public safety [1,2]. The World Health Organization (WHO) declared it an endemic because it killed and affected many worldwide, particularly in the USA and Europe, in a short period of time [3]. Clinical research has not yet produced a remedy that can completely eradicate the virus from the human body. However, the research remains ongoing. Many therapies (such as vaccination, monoclonal antibody therapy, and plasma therapy) have been developed by researchers who successfully treat early-stage diseases, including MERS-CoV, SARS-CoV, Ebola, HIV, and influenza-like viral diseases. Additionally, our body's immune system responds well to infections or disorders. Throughout this uncontrollable condition, nearly all virus-infected regions were locked down, social gatherings were banned, and strict social distancing measures in all situations were implemented to control virus spread. Research worked to control the spread of this virus from different points of analysis such as microbiology [4,5], pathology [6,7], and applied mathematics [8].

In addition to biological and medical research, theoretical studies based on mathematical models may also be crucial to this anti-pandemic effort in analyzing the behavior of the outbreak that made it an epidemic, making decisions about how to stop its spread, and in comprehending patterns of virus transmission within hosts. Several mathematical models for COVID-19 have been formulated at an epidemiological level [6,9–21]. The replication cycle of the SARS-CoV-2 virus and its interactions with the innate and adaptive immune systems are only limited by research done at the within-host level [5,22,23]. Susceptible, infected, and removed (SIR) models are generally used for measles, rubella, and other infectious diseases to investigate the quick spread behavior of these infectious diseases [24]. A susceptible, exposed, infected, and removed (SEIR) model is comparable to the SIR model. The classes S, I, and R represent the number of populations in each partition at a specific point in time [25,26]. However, the incubation period is used in the SEIR model, so a specific incubation period for infectious diseases is more applicable [26,27]. The incubation period of SARS-CoV-2 is 1–14 days [28–31]. Different models have been developed to study the mechanism behind the spread of COVID-19 [32–34].

At the time of SARS-CoV-2 infection, macrophages are first targeted by SARS-CoV-2, and SARS-CoV-2 propagates to T cells afterwards. At this stage of the virus route, T cells are activated and further involve differentiation. In addition, T cells produce cytokines (INF-α), IL-6, and IL-10) associated with the different types of a T cell. A large amount of cytokines provides a greater activation of the immune response to fight against the virus. Particularly, T cells, $CD4^+$ T cells, and $CD8^+$ T cells have been playing a significant antiviral role in the fight against pathogens. There is also a risk of mounting autoimmunity or devastating inflammation. $CD4^+$ T cells help the immune system of the body by generating virus-specific antibodies with the activation of T-dependent B cells. However, $CD8^+$ T cells can kill virally infected cells, as they are cytotoxic. In general, many $CD8^+$ T cells in the infected SARS-CoV-2 body are found in nearly 80% of the total infiltrative inflammatory cells in the interstitial pulmonary tract, which play a significant role in clearing CoVs. The loss of $CD4^+$ T cells is correlated with the reduced conscription of lymphocytes and neutralizing the production of antibodies and cytokines, resulting in severe immune-mediated interstitial pneumonitis and delayed SARS-CoV-2 lung clearance [34–37].

Researchers have shown that a long-lasting and persistent response of T cells to S and other structural proteins (including the proteins M and N), which provides the sufficient knowledge to draft the SARS vaccine by combining viral structural proteins. These vaccines may provide a robust, efficient, and long-term response to the virus by memory cells [36]. Clinical trials also show that a monoclinic antibody therapy is an effective treatment tool that responds well to SARS-CoV-2 [34].

Fractional calculus is often employed for epidemic models [38–44]. It has been shown that the fractional-order model outperforms the integer-order model in handling the modeling process since it has many other desirable characteristics, such as excellent fitting with real data. Furthermore, memory and heredity characteristics make it more effective in modeling and analyzing real-world problems. Numerous definitions or operators in the fractional calculus, such as Caputo, Riemann-Liouville, Atangana-Baleanu, and Caputo-Fabrizio derivative [45,46], are helpful in modeling epidemic diseases.

In our paper, we study a model of in-host viral kinetics that describes the response of SARS-CoV-2 to epithelial cells. Section 2 presents the formulation of the model, Section 3 describes preliminaries, Section 4 presents the uniqueness and existence of the solution to the proposed model, Section 5 presents the steady state points and the derivation of the primary reproduction ratio, Sections 6 and 7 present local and global stability analyses, respectively, Section 8 presents the numerical solution algorithm, Section 9 shows graphical representations to support the logical result, and Section 10 concludes.

2. Mathematical Model

We consider the mathematical model [5,47] used to analyze the fractional model of the within-host viral kinetics of SARS-CoV-2.

$$\begin{aligned} \mathbb{E}_p'(t) &= \delta(\mathbb{E}_p(0) - \mathbb{E}_p(t)) - \gamma \mathbb{E}_p(t) \mathbb{F}(t) \\ \mathbb{I}_p'(t) &= \gamma \mathbb{E}_p(t) \mathbb{F}(t) - \beta \mathbb{I}_p(t) \\ \mathbb{F}'(t) &= \rho \mathbb{I}_p(t) - \omega \mathbb{F}(t), \end{aligned} \qquad (1)$$

with initial conditions

$$\mathbb{E}_p(0) > 0, \mathbb{I}_p(0) \geq 0, \text{and}, \mathbb{F}(0) \geq 0. \qquad (2)$$

Here, the whole population is divided into three compartments: virus-free pulmonary epithelial cells, represented by $\mathbb{E}_p(t)$, virus-free cells, represented by $\mathbb{F}(t)$, and virus-infected pulmonary epithelial cells, denoted by $\mathbb{I}_p(t)$. Here δ, β, and ω denote the death rate of uninfected pulmonary epithelial cells, infected pulmonary epithelial cells, and the virus, respectively. The production rate of the virus is denoted by ρ. In the model, the term $\mathbb{E}_p(0)$ denotes the initial number of uninfected cells at time zero, and $\delta \mathbb{E}_p(0)$ shows a constant regeneration of uninfected epithelial cells.

Several researchers have taken into account fractional-order derivative (FOD) for modelling the infectious diseases [48–50]. We used FOD in the Caputo sense, because it gives better results than the classical order. Several FOD operators were developed, but the Caputo and the Riemann–Liouville FD operators are the most generally used due to their simplicity and similarities [38,39,51]. Other derivatives include Katugampola, Hadamard, Atangana-Baleanu, and Caputo–Fabrizio [52].

$$\begin{aligned} {}_0^C\mathscr{D}_t^\alpha [\mathbb{E}_p] &= \delta^\alpha (\mathbb{E}_p(0) - \mathbb{E}_p) - \gamma^\alpha \mathbb{E}_p \mathbb{F} \\ {}_0^C\mathscr{D}_t^\alpha [\mathbb{I}_p] &= \gamma^\alpha \mathbb{E}_p \mathbb{F} - \beta^\alpha \mathbb{I}_p \\ {}_0^C\mathscr{D}_t^\alpha [\mathbb{F}] &= \rho^\alpha \mathbb{I}_p - \omega^\alpha \mathbb{F}, \end{aligned} \qquad (3)$$

with initial conditions

$$\mathbb{E}_p(0) = \mathscr{K}_1 > 0, \mathbb{I}_p(0) = \mathscr{K}_2 \geq 0, \text{and,} \mathbb{F}(0) = \mathscr{K}_3 \geq 0. \qquad (4)$$

3. Basic Definitions and Theorems

Definition 1. *The Caputo fractional derivative of order α of $z : (0, \infty) \to R$ is defined as*

$$ {}_0^C\mathscr{D}_t^\alpha [z(t)] = \frac{1}{\Gamma(\mathscr{K} - \alpha)} \int_0^t (t - \zeta)^{\mathscr{K} - \alpha - 1} z^{(\mathscr{K})}(\zeta) d\zeta, $$

where $\alpha \in (\mathscr{K} - 1, \mathscr{K}]$, $\mathscr{K} = [\alpha] + 1$, and $[\alpha]$ represents the integer part of α.

Theorem 1 ([49]). *Let the equilibrium of the following non-autonomous fractional order system be $z = 0$.*

$$ {}_0^C\mathscr{D}_t^\alpha z(t) = f(t, z), \qquad z(t_0) = z_0. $$

Let $\psi \subseteq \mathbb{R}^n$ be a domain containing $z = 0$. Let $U(t, z) : [t_0, \infty] \times \psi \to \mathbb{R}$ be a continuously differentiable function such that $V_1(z) \leq U(t, z) \leq V_2(z)$ and

$$ {}_0^C\mathscr{D}_t^\alpha U(t, z) \leq -V_3(z), \quad \text{for} \quad t \geq 0, z \in \psi, $$

where $V_1(t, z), V_2(t, z)$ and $V_3(t, z)$ are continuous non-negative definite functions on ψ, and U is a Lipschitz continuous function (LCF), so $z = 0$ is globally asymptotically stable.

Lemma 1 ([39]). *Let function $z(t) \in \mathbb{R}$ be continuously differentiable. It follows that, for any time $t \geq 0$,*

$$ \frac{1}{2} {}_0^C\mathscr{D}_t^\alpha z^2(t) \leq {}_0^C\mathscr{D}_t^\alpha z(t), \qquad \forall \alpha \in (0, 1). $$

4. Existences and Uniqueness

Firstly, we discuss the uniqueness and existence of the solution to the proposed model. Applying the fractional integral as $({}_0^C\mathscr{D}_t^{-\alpha}){}_0^C\mathscr{D}_t^\alpha(\mathcal{H}(t)) = \mathcal{H}(t) - \mathcal{H}(0)$ to Equation (3), we obtain

$$\mathbb{E}_p(t) - \mathbb{E}_p(0) = \frac{1}{\Gamma(\alpha)} \int_0^t (1-\eta)^{\alpha-1}(\delta^\alpha(\mathbb{E}_p(0) - \mathbb{E}_p(t)) - \gamma^\alpha \mathbb{E}_p(t)\mathbb{F}(t))d\eta,$$

$$\mathbb{I}_p(t) - \mathbb{I}_p(0) = \frac{1}{\Gamma(\alpha)} \int_0^t (1-\eta)^{\alpha-1}(\gamma^\alpha \mathbb{E}_p(t)\mathcal{F}(t) - \beta^\alpha \mathbb{I}_p(t))d\eta, \qquad (5)$$

$$\mathbb{F}(t) - \mathbb{F}(0) = \frac{1}{\Gamma(\alpha)} \int_0^t (1-\eta)^{\alpha-1}(\rho^\alpha \mathbb{I}_p(t) - \omega^\alpha \mathbb{F}(t))d\eta.$$

Using the initial conditions, (5) becomes

$$\mathbb{E}_p(t) = \mathscr{K}_1 - \frac{1}{\Gamma(\alpha)} \int_0^t (t-\eta)^{\alpha-1}(\delta^\alpha(\mathbb{E}_p(0) - \mathbb{E}_p(\eta)) - \gamma^\alpha \mathbb{E}_p(\eta)\mathbb{F}(\eta))d\eta,$$

$$\mathbb{I}_p(t) = \mathscr{K}_2 - \frac{1}{\Gamma(\alpha)} \int_0^t (t-\eta)^{\alpha-1}(\gamma^\alpha \mathbb{E}_p(\eta)\mathbb{F}(\eta) - \beta^\alpha \mathbb{I}_p(\eta))d\eta, \qquad (6)$$

$$\mathbb{F}(t) = \mathscr{K}_3 - \frac{1}{\Gamma(\alpha)} \int_0^t (t-\eta)^{\alpha-1}(\rho^\alpha \mathbb{I}_p(\eta) - \omega^\alpha \mathbb{F}(\eta))d\eta.$$

We define the kernels in System (6) as

$$\begin{aligned}
Y_1(t, \mathbb{E}_p, \mathbb{I}_p, \mathbb{F}) &= (\delta^\alpha(\mathbb{E}_p(0) - \mathbb{E}_p(t)) - \gamma^\alpha \mathbb{E}_p(t)\mathbb{F}(t)) \\
Y_2(t, \mathbb{E}_p, \mathbb{I}_p, \mathbb{F}) &= (\gamma^\alpha \mathbb{E}_p(t)\mathbb{F}(t) - \beta^\alpha \mathbb{I}_p(t)) \\
Y_3(t, \mathbb{E}_p, \mathbb{I}_p, \mathbb{F}) &= (\rho^\alpha \mathbb{I}_p(t) - \omega^\alpha \mathbb{F}(t)).
\end{aligned} \qquad (7)$$

Therefore, by using (7), the system (3) becomes

$$\mathbb{E}_p(t) = \mathscr{K}_1 - \frac{1}{\Gamma(\alpha)} \int_0^t (t-\eta)^{\alpha-1} Y_1(\eta, \mathbb{E}_p, \mathbb{I}_p, \mathbb{F}) d\eta,$$

$$\mathbb{I}_p(t) = \mathscr{K}_2 - \frac{1}{\Gamma(\alpha)} \int_0^t (t-\eta)^{\alpha-1} Y_3(\eta, \mathbb{E}_p, \mathbb{I}_p, \mathbb{F}) d\eta, \qquad (8)$$

$$\mathbb{F}(t) = \mathscr{K}_3 - \frac{1}{\Gamma(\alpha)} \int_0^t (t-\eta)^{\alpha-1} Y_3(\eta, \mathbb{E}_p, \mathbb{I}_p, \mathbb{F}) d\eta.$$

Theorem 2. *The kernels of System (3) satisfy the Lipschitz continuity if there are finite and positive scalar constants $C_i, i = 1, 2, 3$, such that $C_1 = \left|\gamma^\alpha \max_{t\in[0,t^*]} \mathbb{F} - \delta^\alpha\right| \geq 0$, $C_2 = \beta^\alpha \geq 0$ and $C_3 = \omega^\alpha \geq 0$.*

Proof. By considering the kernels given in (3), we have

$$\begin{aligned}
\left|Y_1(t, \mathbb{E}_p, \mathbb{I}_p, \mathbb{F}) - Y_2(t, \mathbb{E}_p^*, \mathbb{I}_p, \mathbb{F})\right| &= \left|(\delta^\alpha(\mathbb{E}_p - \mathbb{E}_p(0)) - \gamma^\alpha \mathbb{E}_p \mathbb{F}) - (\delta^\alpha(\mathbb{E}_p^* - \mathbb{E}^*(0)) - \gamma^\alpha \mathbb{E}^*\mathbb{F})\right| \\
&= \left|\gamma^\alpha \mathbb{F}(\mathbb{E}_p - \mathbb{E}_p^*) - \delta^\alpha\left((\mathbb{E}_p(0) - \mathbb{E}^*(0)) + (\mathbb{E}_p - \mathbb{E}_p^*)\right)\right| \\
&\leq \left|(\gamma^\alpha \mathbb{F} - \delta^\alpha)(\mathbb{E}_p - \mathbb{E}_p^*)\right| \\
&\leq |\gamma^\alpha \mathbb{F} - \delta^\alpha|\|\mathbb{E}_p - \mathbb{E}_p^*\| \\
&\leq \left|\gamma^\alpha \max_{t\in[0,t^*]} \mathbb{F} - \delta^\alpha\right|\|\mathbb{E}_p - \mathbb{E}_p^*\| \\
&\leq C_1 \|\mathbb{E}_p - \mathbb{E}_p^*\|, \quad \left(C_1 = \left|\gamma^\alpha \max_{t\in[0,t^*]} \mathbb{F} - \delta^\alpha\right|\right),
\end{aligned}$$

$$\begin{aligned}
\left|Y_1(t,\mathbb{E}_p,\mathbb{I}_p,\mathbb{F}) - Y_2\left(t,\mathbb{E}_p,\mathbb{I}_p^*,\mathbb{F}\right)\right| &= \left|(\gamma^\alpha \mathbb{E}_p\mathbb{F} - \beta^\alpha \mathbb{I}_p) - (\gamma^\alpha \mathbb{E}\mathbb{F} - \beta^\alpha \mathbb{I}_p^*)\right| \\
&= \left|\beta^\alpha \left(I_p^* - I_p\right)\right| \\
&\leq |\beta^\alpha|\left\|\mathbb{I}_p^* - \mathbb{I}_p\right\| \\
&\leq C_2 \left\|\mathbb{I}_p^* - \mathbb{I}_p\right\|, \quad (C_2 = \beta^\alpha),
\end{aligned} \tag{9}$$

$$\begin{aligned}
\left|Y_1(t,E_p,I_p,\mathcal{F}) - Y_2(t,E_p,I_p,\mathbb{F}^*)\right| &= \left|(\rho^\alpha I_p - \omega^\alpha \mathbb{F}) - (\rho^\alpha I_p - \omega^\alpha \mathbb{F}^*)\right| \\
&= |\omega^\alpha (\mathbb{F}^* - \mathbb{F})| \\
&\leq |\omega^\alpha|\|\mathbb{F}^* - \mathbb{F}(t)\| \\
&\leq C_3\|\mathbb{F}^* - \mathbb{F}\|, \quad (C_3 = \omega^\alpha).
\end{aligned}$$

Hence, the proposed system satisfies the Lipschitz continuity. This means that the system is continuous and bounded. □

Theorem 3. *Let $\alpha \in (0,1)$, $J = [0,t^*] \subseteq \mathbb{R}$ and $l = \left|\mathbb{E}_p(t) - \mathbb{E}_p^*(t)\right| \leq \mathcal{A}_1$. Let the function $Y_1 : j \times l \to \mathbb{R}$ be continuous and bounded. $\exists M > 0$ such that $\left|Y_1(t,\mathbb{E}_p,\mathbb{I}_p,\mathbb{F})\right| \leq M_1$. We assume that v_1 satisfies the Lipschitz conditions. If $C_1\mathcal{A}_1 < M_1$, then there is a unique $Y_1(t,\mathbb{E}_p,\mathbb{I}_p,\mathbb{F}) \in C[0,t^*]$, such that $t^* = \min\left[t, \left(\frac{\mathcal{A}_1 \Gamma(\alpha+1)}{M1}\right)\right]$.*

Proof. If $F = \{\mathbb{E}_b \in C(0,t^*) : \|\mathbb{E}_b(t) - \mathbb{E}_b(0)\| \leq \mathcal{A}_1\}$, then F is a complete metric space since $F \subseteq \mathbb{R}$, and it is also a closed set. We now define the operator T in F as

$$T\mathbb{E}_p(t) = \mathbb{E}_p(0) + \frac{1}{\Gamma(\alpha)} \int_0^t (t-\eta)^{\alpha-1} Y_1(\eta,\mathbb{E}_p,\mathbb{I}_p,\mathbb{F}) d\eta.$$

We then have

$$\begin{aligned}
\left|T\mathbb{E}_p(t) - \mathbb{E}_p(0)\right| &= \left|\frac{1}{\Gamma(\alpha)} \int_0^t (t-\eta)^{\alpha-1} Y_1(\eta,\mathbb{E}_p,\mathbb{I}_p,\mathbb{F}) d\eta\right| \\
&\leq \frac{1}{\Gamma(\alpha)} \int_0^t (t-\eta)^{\alpha-1} \left|Y_1(\eta,E_p,I_p,\mathcal{F})\right| d\eta \\
&\leq \frac{1}{\Gamma(\alpha)} \int_0^t (t-\eta)^{\alpha-1} M_1 d\eta \\
&= \frac{M_1}{\Gamma(\alpha+1)} t^\alpha \\
&\leq \frac{M_1}{\Gamma(\alpha+1)} (t^*)^\alpha \\
&\leq \frac{M_1}{\Gamma(\alpha+1)} \frac{\mathcal{A}_1 \Gamma(\alpha+1)}{M1}) = \mathcal{A}_1.
\end{aligned}$$

Hence,

$$\left|T\mathbb{E}_p(t) - \mathbb{E}_p(0)\right| \leq \mathcal{A}_1.$$

Similarly, we easily show that

$$\left|T\mathbb{I}_p - \mathbb{I}_p(0)\right| \leq \mathcal{A}_2,$$

and

$$|T\mathbb{F} - \mathbb{F}(0)| \leq \mathcal{A}_3.$$

Finally, we need to show that T satisfies the contraction mapping theorem.

$$T\mathbb{E}_p - T\mathbb{E}_p^*(t) = \mathbb{E}_p(0) - \mathbb{E}_p^*(0) + \frac{1}{\Gamma(\alpha)} \int_0^t (t-\eta)^{\alpha-1} \Big(Y_1\big(\eta, \mathbb{E}_p(\eta), \mathbb{I}_p(\eta), \mathbb{F}(\eta)\big) - Y_1\big(\eta, \mathbb{E}_p^*(\eta), \mathbb{I}_p(\eta), \mathbb{F}(\eta)\big) \Big) d\eta.$$

Assuming that $\mathbb{E}_p(0) = \mathbb{E}_p^*(0)$,

$$\left| T\mathbb{E}_p - T\mathbb{E}_p^*(t) \right| = \left| \frac{1}{\Gamma(\alpha)} \int_0^t (t-\eta)^{\alpha-1} \Big(Y_1\big(\eta, \mathbb{E}_p(\eta), \mathbb{I}_p(\eta), \mathbb{F}(\eta)\big) - Y_1\big(\eta, \mathbb{E}_p^*(\eta), \mathbb{I}_p(\eta), \mathbb{F}(\eta)\big) \Big) d\eta \right|,$$

which implies that

$$\left| T\mathbb{E}_p - T\mathbb{E}_p^* \right| \leq \frac{1}{\Gamma(\alpha)} \int_0^t (t-\eta)^{\alpha-1} \left| \Big(Y_1\big(\eta, \mathbb{E}_p(\eta), \mathbb{I}_p(\eta), \mathbb{F}(\eta)\big) - Y_1\big(\eta, \mathbb{E}_p^*(\eta), \mathbb{I}_p(\eta), \mathbb{F}(\eta)\big) \Big) \right| d\eta.$$

By using the value of $|(Y_1(\eta, \mathbb{E}_p(\eta), \mathbb{I}_p(\eta), \mathbb{F}(\eta)) - Y_1(\eta, \mathbb{E}_p^*(\eta), \mathbb{I}_p(\eta), \mathbb{F}(\eta))| d\eta$, we obtain

$$\left| T\mathbb{E}_p - T\mathbb{E}_p^* \right| \leq \frac{1}{\Gamma(\alpha)} \int_0^t (t-\eta)^{\alpha-1} C_1 \left\| \mathbb{E}_p^* - \mathbb{E}_p \right\| d\eta$$

$$\leq \frac{C_1}{\Gamma(\alpha)} \left\| \mathbb{E}_p^* - \mathbb{E}_p \right\| \int_0^t (t-\eta)^{\alpha-1} d\eta$$

$$\leq \frac{C_1}{\Gamma(\alpha+1)} \left\| \mathbb{E}_p^* - \mathbb{E}_p \right\| t^\alpha$$

$$\leq \frac{C_1}{\Gamma(\alpha+1)} \left\| \mathbb{E}_p^* - \mathbb{E}_p \right\| (t^*)^\alpha$$

$$\leq \frac{C_1}{\Gamma(\alpha+1)} \left\| \mathbb{E}_p^* - \mathbb{E}_p \right\| \frac{A_1 \Gamma(\alpha+1)}{M_1}.$$

Hence,

$$\left| T\mathbb{E}_p - T\mathbb{E}_p^*(t) \right| \leq \frac{A_1 C_1}{M_1} \left\| \mathbb{E}_p^* - \mathbb{E}_p \right\|. \tag{10}$$

Since $\frac{A_1 C_1}{M_1} < 1$, one can conclude that T satisfies the contraction mapping theorem and it has a unique fixed point.

In the same procedure, we obtain

$$\left| TI_p - TI_p^* \right| \leq \frac{A_2 C_2}{M_2} \left\| \mathbb{I}_p^* - \mathbb{I}_p \right\|. \tag{11}$$

$$\left| T\mathbb{F} - T\mathbb{F}^* \right| \leq \frac{A_3 C_3}{M_3} \left\| \mathbb{F}^* - \mathbb{F} \right\|. \tag{12}$$

Thus, System (3) has a unique solution. □

5. Steady State and Derivation of Reproduction Number $\mathcal{R}_0$

Let E^0 be the disease-free equilibrium point, and from the equations in (3), we set the right-hand sides as equal to zero and solve for variables.

$$\delta^\alpha (\mathbb{E}_p - \mathbb{E}_p(0)) - \gamma^\alpha \mathbb{E}_p \mathbb{F} = 0, \tag{13}$$

$$\gamma^\alpha \mathbb{E}_p \mathbb{F} - \beta^\alpha \mathbb{I}_p = 0, \tag{14}$$

$$\rho^\alpha \mathbb{I}_p - \omega^\alpha \mathbb{F} = 0. \tag{15}$$

If $\mathbb{I}_p$ and $\mathbb{F}$ are equal to zero, we obtain the disease-free equilibrium as

$$E^0 = \left(\mathbb{E}_p^0, \mathbb{I}_p^0, \mathbb{F}^0 \right) = \left(\mathbb{E}_p(0), 0, 0 \right). \tag{16}$$

To find the endemic equilibrium $\mathbb{E}^* = \left(\mathbb{E}_p^*, \mathbb{I}_p^*, \mathbb{F}^*\right)$, we consider $\mathbb{E}_p(t) \neq 0, \mathbb{I}_p(t) \neq 0$, in Equations (13)–(15) as

$$\mathbb{E}_p^* = \frac{1}{\delta^\alpha}\left(-\beta^\alpha \mathbb{I}_p^* - \mathbb{E}_p(0)\right), \tag{17}$$

$$\mathbb{I}_p^* = \frac{\gamma^\alpha}{\beta^\alpha \delta^\alpha}\left(\frac{-\beta^\alpha \omega^\alpha}{\rho^\alpha}\mathbb{F}^* - \mathbb{E}_p(0)\right)\mathbb{F}^*, \tag{18}$$

$$\mathbb{F}^* = \frac{\omega^\alpha}{\rho^\alpha}\mathbb{I}^*. \tag{19}$$

Next, we want to derive the reproduction number $\mathcal{R}_0$. The reproduction number is a threshold quantity representing the total number of secondary illnesses caused by an infected individual in a fully susceptible population throughout the infectious period [53].

For this, we develop the next generation matrix approach. Let $M(\mathcal{S})$ represent the rate of new infections, and let $X(\mathcal{S})$ represent the transfer rate of individual. We then have $M(\mathcal{S}) = \begin{pmatrix} \gamma^\alpha \mathbb{E}_p(t)\mathbb{F}(t) \\ 0 \end{pmatrix}$ and $X(\mathcal{S}) = \begin{pmatrix} \beta^\alpha \mathbb{I}_p \\ \rho^\alpha \mathbb{I}_p - \omega^\alpha \mathbb{F} \end{pmatrix}$.

The Jacobian matrices $JM(\mathcal{S})$ and $JX(\mathcal{S})$ at the non-infected steady state (16) are

$$m = JM(\mathcal{S}) = \begin{pmatrix} 0 & \gamma^\alpha \mathbb{E}_p(0) \\ 0 & 0 \end{pmatrix}, \quad x = JX(\mathcal{S}) = \begin{pmatrix} \beta^\alpha & 0 \\ \rho^\alpha & -\omega^\alpha \end{pmatrix}.$$

$$x^{-1} = \frac{1}{-\omega^\alpha \beta^\alpha}\begin{pmatrix} -\omega^\alpha & 0 \\ -\rho^\alpha & \beta^\alpha \end{pmatrix}.$$

$$mx^{-1} = \frac{1}{-\omega^\alpha \beta^\alpha}\begin{pmatrix} 0 & \gamma^\alpha \mathbb{E}_p(0) \\ 0 & 0 \end{pmatrix}\begin{pmatrix} -\omega^\alpha & 0 \\ -\rho^\alpha & \beta^\alpha \end{pmatrix} = \begin{pmatrix} \frac{-\rho^\alpha \gamma^\alpha \mathbb{E}_p(0)}{-\omega^\alpha \beta^\alpha} & \frac{\beta^\alpha \gamma^\alpha \mathbb{E}_p(0)}{-\omega^\alpha \beta^\alpha} \\ 0 & 0 \end{pmatrix}.$$

The reproduction number is given by the spectral radius of the next generation matrix mx^{-1}. We then obtain $\lambda_1 = 0, \lambda_2 = \frac{\rho^\alpha \gamma^\alpha \mathbb{E}_p(0)}{\lambda^\alpha \beta^\alpha}$, from the absolute highest eigenvalues from mx^{-1}. Thus, from the model (3), we obtain the expression for $\mathcal{R}_0$ as

$$\mathcal{R}_0 = \frac{\rho^\alpha \gamma^\alpha \mathbb{E}_p(0)}{\lambda^\alpha \beta^\alpha}.$$

The following graphical representation describes the potential impact of introducing a new SARS-CoV-2 variant with high transmission rates. Figure 1 represents the effects of the basic reproduction number with respect to different parameters.

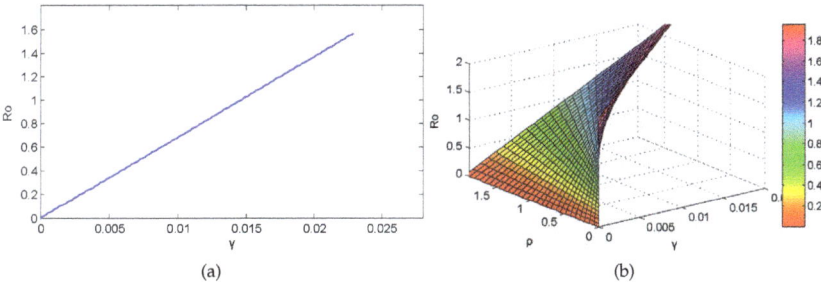

Figure 1. It is clear that, when $\mathcal{R}_0 < 1$, the model (3) has no endemic equilibrium and the disease-free equilibrium is stable. (**a**) Variation of R_0 with respect to the transmission rate γ. (**b**) Impact of γ and ρ on R_0.

6. Local Stability

In this part of the paper, we discuss the local stability of the steady-state point (16). For this need, we write the Jacobian matrix for the system (3) as

$$J = \begin{pmatrix} \delta^\alpha - \gamma^\alpha \mathbb{F} & 0 & -\gamma^\alpha \mathbb{E}_p \\ \gamma^\alpha \mathbb{F} & -\beta^\alpha & \gamma^\alpha \mathbb{E}_p \\ 0 & \rho^\alpha & -\omega^\alpha \end{pmatrix}. \tag{20}$$

Theorem 4. *The non-infected steady state E^0 is locally asymptotically stable when $\mathcal{R}_0 < 1$.*

Proof. The Jacobian matrix for the steady state (16) as □

$$J(E^0) = \begin{pmatrix} \delta^\alpha & 0 & -\gamma^\alpha \mathbb{E}_p(0) \\ 0 & -\beta^\alpha & \gamma^\alpha \mathbb{E}_p(0) \\ 0 & \rho^\alpha & -\omega^\alpha \end{pmatrix}. \tag{21}$$

According to the Routh–Hurwitz criteria [54], if all the real parts of the value of the real eigenvalues of the Jacobian matrix are negative, then E^0 is locally asymptotically stable. In order to show that, we have

$$\left| \lambda I - J E^0 \right| = \begin{vmatrix} \delta^\alpha - \lambda & 0 & -\gamma^\alpha \mathbb{E}_p(0) \\ 0 & -\beta^\alpha - \lambda & \gamma^\alpha \mathbb{E}_p(0) \\ 0 & \rho^\alpha & -\omega^\alpha - \lambda \end{vmatrix} = 0.$$

The characteristics equation of the above matrix is

$$(\delta^\alpha - \lambda)\left(\lambda^2 + \lambda(\omega^\alpha + \beta^\alpha) + \beta^\alpha \omega^\alpha - \rho^\alpha \gamma^\alpha \mathbb{E}_p(0)\right) = 0,$$

$$(\delta^\alpha - \lambda)\left(\lambda^2 + a_1 \lambda + a_2\right) = 0,$$

with $a_1 = \omega^\alpha + \beta^\alpha$, and $a_2 = \beta^\alpha \omega^\alpha - \rho^\alpha \gamma^\alpha \mathbb{E}_p(0)$.

Based on an equation, the eigenvalues $\lambda_1 = \delta^\alpha > 0$, and $a_1 = \omega^\alpha + \beta^\alpha > 0$ were obtained. According to Routh–Hurwitz stability criteria, $a_2 = \beta^\alpha \omega^\alpha - \rho^\alpha \gamma^\alpha \mathbb{E}_p(0) > 0 \Rightarrow \beta^\alpha \omega^\alpha > \rho^\alpha \gamma^\alpha \mathbb{E}_p(0) \Rightarrow 1 > \frac{\rho^\alpha \gamma^\alpha \mathbb{E}_p(0)}{\beta^\alpha \omega^\alpha} \Rightarrow \mathcal{R}_0 < 1$.

Therefore, if $\mathcal{R}_0 < 1$, then all the conditions of Routh–Hurwitz criteria are satisfied. Hence, the non-infected steady-state E^0 becomes locally asymptotically stable if $\mathcal{R}_0 < 1$ and unstable if $\mathcal{R}_0 > 1$.

7. Global Stability

In this part of the paper, we use the Lyapunov function approach to investigate the result for the model's globally asymptotically stability (GAS) in the disease-free state. For this, we have the following theorem.

Theorem 5. *When $\mathcal{R}_0 < 1$, the disease-free equilibrium E^0 is globally asymptotically stable; otherwise, it is unstable.*

Proof. For this, we derive the Lyapunov candidate function (LCF) for the fractional-order as in [38]. We then take the family of the Lyapunov function

$$L(e_1, e_2, \ldots, e_n) = \sum_{i=1}^{n} \frac{p_i}{2}(e_i(t) - e^*)^2.$$

LCF is defined as

$$L(\mathbb{E}_p, \mathbb{I}_p, \mathbb{F}) = \frac{1}{2}\left(\mathbb{E}_p - \mathbb{E}_p^*\right)^2 + \frac{1}{2}\left(\mathbb{I}_p - \mathbb{I}_p^*\right)^2 + \frac{1}{2}\left(\mathbb{F}_p - \mathbb{F}_p^*\right)^2. \tag{22}$$

Applying the Caputo fractional derivative and using its linearity property yields

$$_0^c\mathscr{D}_t^\alpha L(\mathbb{E}_p, \mathbb{I}_p, \mathbb{F}) = \frac{1}{2}\left[_0^c\mathscr{D}_t^\alpha\left(\mathbb{E}_p - \mathbb{E}_p^*\right)^2 + _0^c\mathscr{D}_t^\alpha\left(\mathbb{I}_p(t) - I_p^*\right)^2 + _0^c\mathscr{D}_t^\alpha\left(\mathbb{F}_p - \mathbb{F}_p^*\right)^2\right]. \tag{23}$$

Applying Lemma 2 of [38] to (23), we obtain

$$_0^c\mathscr{D}_t^\alpha L(\mathbb{E}_p, \mathbb{I}_p, \mathbb{F}(t)) \leq {}_0^c\mathscr{D}_t^\alpha\left(\mathbb{E}_p - \mathbb{E}_p^*\right)^2 + _0^c\mathscr{D}_t^\alpha\left(\mathbb{I}_p - \mathbb{I}_p^*\right)^2 + _0^c\mathscr{D}_t^\alpha\left(\mathbb{F}_p - \mathbb{F}_p^*\right)^2. \tag{24}$$

$$_0^c\mathscr{D}_t^\alpha L(\mathbb{E}_p, \mathbb{I}_p, \mathbb{F}(t)) = \frac{(1-(\delta^\alpha)^2)}{\delta^\alpha}\mathbb{E}_p(0) + \delta^\alpha \mathbb{E}_p + (\rho^\alpha - \beta^\alpha)\mathbb{I}_p - \left(\frac{\delta^\alpha \omega^\alpha - \beta^\alpha \rho^\alpha}{\delta^\alpha \rho^\alpha}\right)\mathbb{I}_p^* - \omega^\alpha \mathbb{F}$$
$$+ \left(\frac{\gamma^\alpha \omega^\alpha}{\delta^\alpha \rho^\alpha}\mathbb{F}^* + \frac{\gamma^\alpha}{\beta^\alpha \delta^\alpha}\mathbb{E}_p(0)\right)\mathbb{F}^*.$$

Substituting the disease-free equilibrium, we obtain

$$_0^c\mathcal{D}_t^\alpha L(\mathbb{E}_p, \mathbb{I}_p, \mathbb{F}) \leq \left(\frac{(1-(\delta^\alpha)^2)}{\delta^\alpha} + \delta^\alpha\right)\mathbb{E}_p(0) - (\beta^\alpha - \rho^\alpha)\mathbb{I}_p - \omega^\alpha \mathbb{F}, \tag{25}$$

so

$$_0^c\mathscr{D}_t^\alpha L(\mathbb{E}_p, \mathbb{I}_p, \mathbb{F}) \leq -Z(p), \tag{26}$$

where

$$Z(p) = (\beta^\alpha - \rho^\alpha)\mathbb{I}_p + \omega^\alpha \mathbb{F} - \left(\frac{(1-(\delta^\alpha)^2)}{\delta^\alpha} + \delta^\alpha\right)\mathbb{E}_p(0).$$

Hence, by Theorem 2 in [39], the disease-free equilibrium is globally asymptotically stable. □

The existence of equilibria of the model is shown for different values of $\mathcal{R}_0$. In plotting Figures 2 and 3, we have varied the value of infection rate γ. It is observed that the disease-free equilibrium E^0 is stable for low infection rates, corresponding to $\mathcal{R}_0 < 1$. It becomes unstable for high infection rates, corresponding to $\mathcal{R}_0 > 1$.

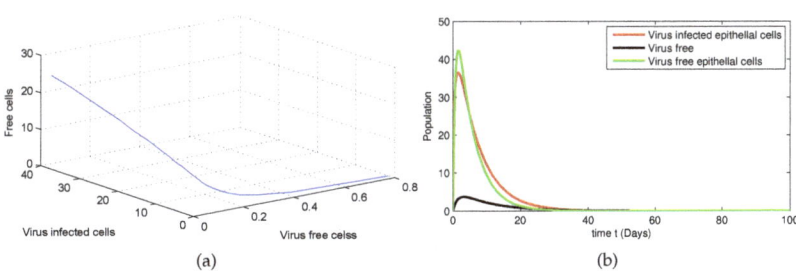

Figure 2. Simulation of the numbers of E_p, I_p, and F when $\mathcal{R}_0 < 1$ with (**a**) three-dimensional plot and (**b**) two-dimensional plot.

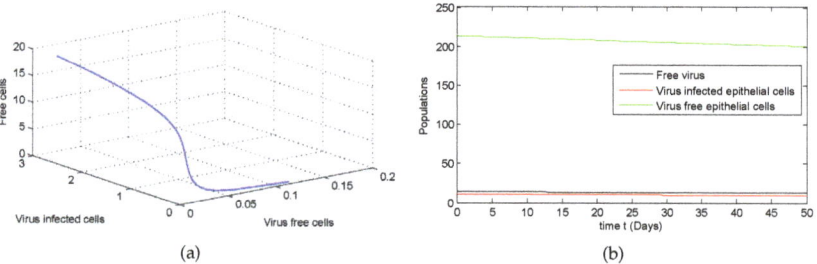

Figure 3. Dynamics of the numbers of virus-infected epithelial cells, SARS-CoV-2 virus and virus-free epithelial cells when $\mathcal{R}_0 > 1$ with (**a**) three-dimensional plot and (**b**) two-dimensional plot.

8. Algorithm for the Solution

In this part of the paper, we derive the general procedure for the approximate solution of the considered fractional-order model (3). For this, we extend the numerical Euler method [55].

Now, using (9), we write (3) as

$$\begin{cases} {}_0^c\mathcal{D}_t^\alpha[\mathbb{E}_p] = Y_1(t, \mathbb{E}_p, \mathbb{I}_p, \mathbb{F}), \\ {}_0^c\mathcal{D}_t^\alpha[\mathbb{I}_p] = Y_2(t, \mathbb{E}_p, \mathbb{I}_p, \mathbb{F}), \\ {}_0^c\mathcal{D}_t^\alpha[\mathbb{F}_p] = Y_3(t, \mathbb{E}_p, \mathbb{I}_p, \mathbb{F}). \end{cases} \quad (27)$$

Let $[0, T]$ be the interval where we want to find the solution of (27). For this, we divide the given interval into an i sub-interval $[t_i, t_{i+1}]$ of equal width $h = \frac{T}{i}$, using the nodes $t_i = ih$ for $i = 0, 1, 2, 3, ..., k - 1$. Here, we assume that $\mathbb{E}_p, {}_0^c\mathcal{D}_t^\alpha[\mathbb{E}_p]$, and ${}_0^c\mathcal{D}_t^{2\alpha}[\mathbb{E}_p]$ are continuous up to a higher order on $[0, T]$.

We take into account the modified Euler method (MEM) for $t = t_0 = 0$ to (27). The expression for t_1 is

$$\begin{cases} \mathbb{E}_p(t_1) = \mathbb{E}_p(t_0) + Y_1\big(\mathbb{E}_p(t_0), \mathbb{I}_p(t_0), \mathbb{F}(t_0)\big)\frac{t^\alpha}{\Gamma(\eta+1)} + {}_0^c\mathcal{D}_t^{2\alpha}\mathbb{E}_p(t)\frac{t^{2\alpha}}{\Gamma(2\eta+1)}, \\ \mathbb{I}_p(t_1) = \mathbb{I}_p(t_0) + Y_2\big(\mathbb{E}_p(t_0), \mathbb{I}_p(t_0), \mathbb{F}(t_0)\big)\frac{t^\alpha}{\Gamma(\eta+1)} + {}_0^c\mathcal{D}_t^{2\alpha}\mathbb{I}_p(t)\frac{t^{2\alpha}}{\Gamma(2\eta+1)}, \\ \mathbb{F}(t_1) = \mathbb{F}(t_0) + Y_3\big(\mathbb{E}_p(t_0), \mathbb{I}_p(t_0), \mathbb{F}(t_0)\big)\frac{t^\alpha}{\Gamma(\eta+1)} + {}_0^c\mathscr{D}_t^{2\alpha}\mathbb{F}(t)\frac{t^{2\alpha}}{\Gamma(2\eta+1)}. \end{cases} \quad (28)$$

In this procedure, we neglect the second-order involving $t^{2\alpha}$ because we the step size h is very small.

$$\begin{cases} \mathbb{E}_p(t_1) = \mathbb{E}_p(t_0) + Y_1\big(\mathbb{E}_p(t_0), \mathbb{I}_p(t_0), \mathbb{F}(t_0)\big)\frac{t^\alpha}{\Gamma(\eta+1)}, \\ \mathbb{I}_p(t_1) = \mathbb{I}_p(t_0) + Y_2\big(\mathbb{E}_p(t_0), \mathbb{I}_p(t_0), \mathbb{F}(t_0)\big)\frac{t^\alpha}{\Gamma(\eta+1)}, \\ \mathbb{F}(t_1) = \mathbb{F}(t_0) + Y_3\big(\mathbb{E}_p(t_0), \mathbb{I}_p(t_0), \mathbb{F}(t_0)\big)\frac{t^\alpha}{\Gamma(\eta+1)}. \end{cases} \quad (29)$$

The subsequent terms are

$$\begin{cases} \mathbb{E}_p(t_2) = \mathbb{E}_p(t_0) + Y_1\big(\mathbb{E}_p(t_1), \mathbb{I}_p(t_1), \mathbb{F}(t_1)\big)\frac{t^\alpha}{\Gamma(\eta+1)}, \\ \mathbb{I}_p(t_2) = \mathbb{I}_p(t_0) + Y_2\big(\mathbb{E}_p(t_1), \mathbb{I}_p(t_1), \mathbb{F}(t_1)\big)\frac{t^\alpha}{\Gamma(\eta+1)}, \\ \mathbb{F}(t_2) = \mathbb{F}(t_0) + Y_3\big(\mathbb{E}_p(t_1), \mathbb{I}_p(t_1), \mathbb{F}(t_1)\big)\frac{t^\alpha}{\Gamma(\eta+1)}. \end{cases} \quad (30)$$

In the above fashion, a general formula at $t_{i+1} = t_i + h$ is developed:

$$\begin{cases} \mathbb{E}_p(t_{i+1}) = \mathbb{E}_p(t_0) + Y_1\big(\mathbb{E}_p(t_i), \mathbb{I}_p(t_i), \mathbb{F}(t_i)\big)\frac{t^\alpha}{\Gamma(\eta+1)}, \\ \mathbb{I}_p(t_{i+1}) = \mathbb{I}_p(t_0) + Y_2\big(\mathbb{E}_p(t_i), \mathbb{I}_p(t_i), \mathbb{F}(t_i)\big)\frac{t^\alpha}{\Gamma(\eta+1)}, \\ \mathbb{F}(t_{i+1}) = \mathbb{F}(t_0) + Y_3\big(\mathbb{E}_p(t_i), \mathbb{I}_p(t_i), \mathbb{F}(t_i)\big)\frac{t^\alpha}{\Gamma(\eta+1)}, \end{cases} \quad (31)$$

where $i = 0, 1, 2, ..., k-1$.

9. Graphical Representations

In this section, we discuss the obtain approximate solutions of (31) graphically using the values of the parameters shown in Table 1 with different α values.

Table 1. Parameters and their values.

Symbol	Parameter Values	References
δ	0.09932	Assumed
β	0.229	Assumed
ω	0.0326	Assumed
γ	0.001	[5]
ρ	0.7492	[5]
$\mathbb{E}_p(0)$	80	Assumed
$\mathbb{I}(0)$	50	Assumed
$\mathbb{F}(0)$	5	Assumed

We conduct graphical representation to represent the solution effects of our model with different fractional-order α. By using MATLAB software, we set up an algorithm to simulate the results in Figure 4–9. For this, we consider some appropriate values used in the model for the parameters in Table 1. The parameter values of the model (3) have been estimated based on chest radiograph score data [5] using the Monte Carlo Markov Chain method. We utilize that parameter; more specifically, $\mathbb{E}_p(0) = 50$, $\mathbb{I}_p(0) = 50$, and $\mathbb{F}(0) = 100$.

In Figure 4, we take the fractional-order $\alpha = 0.9$, which is close to the integer-order $\alpha = 1$. For this model, the results obtained from the fractional-order model of SARS-CoV-2 are very similar to those of the integer-order model [5]. Further, Figure 5–9 show series plots of the approximate solutions (31) with the fractional orders slowly decreasing as follows: $\alpha = 0.90, 0.80, 0.70, 0.60, 0.50$. We observe from these graphs that the virus-infected, virus-free epithelial and the virus-free curves have approximately the same trend for different values of α. However, their convergence toward stability of the virus-infected epithelial is slightly changed. There is a notable difference in the graph at order 0.90 and 0.50. We also note that the equilibrium points are the same for the different fractional orders in Figure 4–9, but the equilibrium points of the virus-infected epithelial go to the fixed point over a longer period when the fractional-order increases.

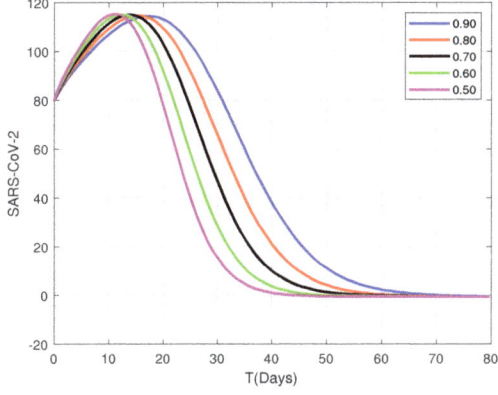

Figure 4. Graphical representation of the approximate solutions of the SARS-CoV-2 model for order $\alpha = 0.9, 0.8, 0.7, 0.6, 0.5$.

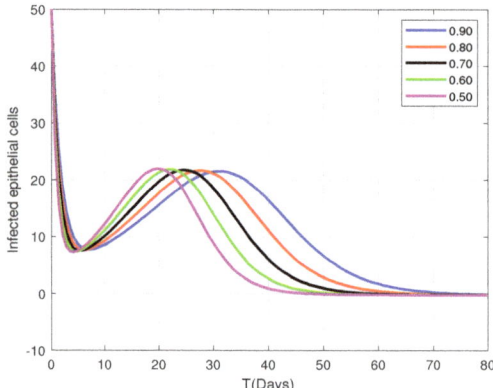

Figure 5. Graphical representation of the approximate solutions of the infected virus epithelial cells for fractional order $\alpha = 0.9, 0.8, 0.7, 0.6, 0.5$.

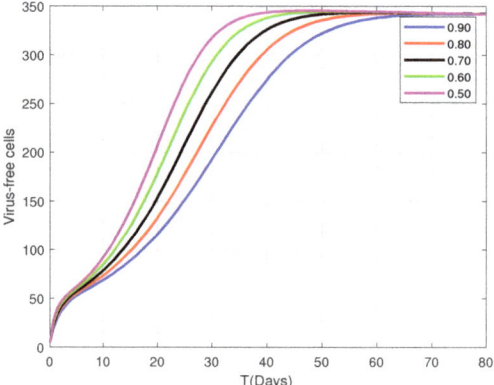

Figure 6. Graphical representation of the approximate solutions of the virus-free epithelial cells for fractional order $\alpha = 0.9, 0.8, 0.7, 0.6, 0.5$.

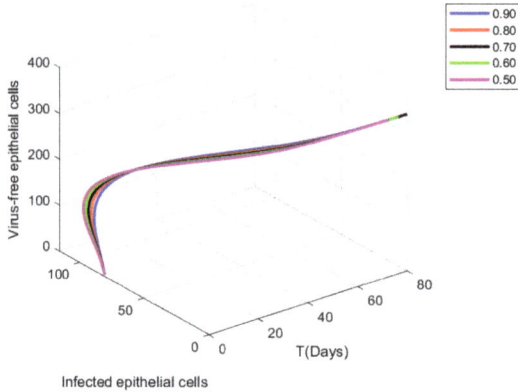

Figure 7. Graphical representation of the virus-infected epithelial cells and virus-free epithelial cells for fractional order $\alpha = 0.9, 0.8, 0.7, 0.6, 0.5$ when $\mathcal{R}_0 < 1$.

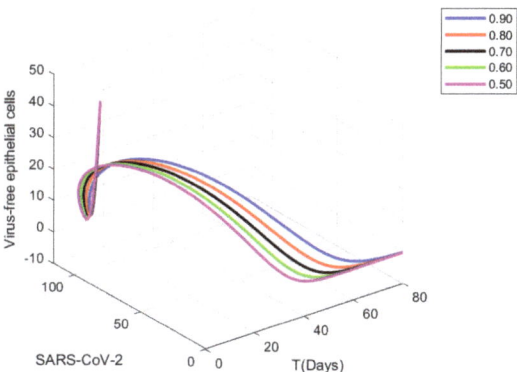

Figure 8. Graphical representation of the SARS-CoV-2 and virus-free epithelial cells for fractional order $\alpha = 0.9, 0.8, 0.7, 0.6, 0.5$ when $\mathcal{R}_0 < 1$.

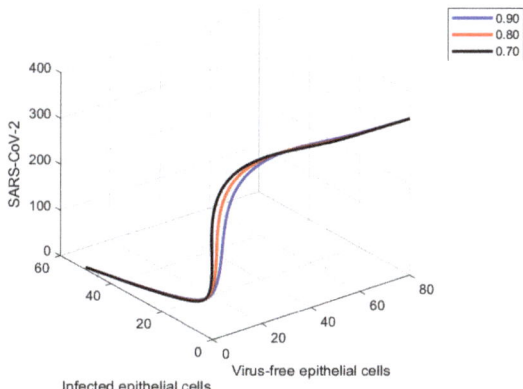

Figure 9. Graphical representation of the SARS-CoV-2, virus-infected epithelial cells, and virus-free epithelial cells of approximate solutions for fractional order $\alpha = 0.9, 0.8, 0.7$.

From the above plotting, we have concluded that the infection rate γ can be low. This is because, if we take the greater infection rate in such a way that $\mathcal{R}_0 > 1$, the infection prevails in the body since the virus cannot be controlled. However, if the infection rate γ is lower than $\mathcal{R}_0 < 1$, this leads to being controlled by the virus-infected epithelial cells rate in the body. Otherwise, the number of virus-free epithelial cells will decrease. Such infected virus epithelial cells and the virus-free cells will not stabilize very quickly in a body with time. In this case, the patient's condition will vitiate with time. We also conclude that the fractional derivative is the generalization of the integer-order derivative. We use fractional-order to obtain good accuracy and reduce the possible errors arising from the mistreated parameters in the distributed modeling system and the system with memory.

10. Conclusions

This article presents a Caputo fractional-order model for the within-host dynamics of SARS-CoV-2. First, we found the existence and uniqueness of the model's solution by using the fixed point theory. We obtained the disease-free and endemic equilibrium points. The critical parameter (reproduction number) $\mathcal{R}_0$ was determined using the next-generation matrix approach. Moreover, we developed the considered model's local and global stability conditions.

Further, we calculated the approximate solution to the model (3) via a powerful method due to Euler. Finally, graphical representations of the obtained approximate solutions were performed to verify the theoretical analysis using MATLAB. By biology, an infection will be cleaned from a human body when the basic reproduction number $\mathcal{R}_0 < 1$ is approached; otherwise, therapy must be used to minimize and eliminate the infection from the body. Additionally, it was shown that an infection will continue for any level of viral load in the host's body if the basic reproduction number is greater than one. For the eradication of the virus from an infected human body, our future work will include using various treatment strategies and control parameters in this model.

Author Contributions: Conceptualization, I.U.H.; methodology, I.U.H. and M.Y.; software, I.U.H.; validation, M.Y. and A.A.; investigation, I.U.H.; resources, A.A.; data curation, M.Y.; writing—original draft preparation, I.U.H. and N.A.; writing—review and editing, M.Y.; visualization, M.Y. and N.A.; supervision, N.A.; project administration, N.A. and A.A. All authors have read and agreed to the published version of the manuscript.

Funding: This research received no specific grant from any funding agency in the public, commercial, or not-for-profit sectors.

Acknowledgments: Authors are very much thankful for the anonymous reviewers and editors for their great efforts and comments that have improved the quality of the paper.

Conflicts of Interest: The authors declare that they have no conflict of interest.

References

1. Reusken, C.B.; Buiting, A.; Bleeker-Rovers, C.; Diederen, B.; Hooiveld, M.; Friesema, I.; Koopmans, M.; Kortbeek, T.; Lutgens, S.P.; Meijer, A.; et al. Rapid assessment of regional SARS-CoV-2 community transmission through a convenience sample of healthcare workers, the Netherlands, March 2020. *Eurosurveillance* **2020**, *25*, 2000334. [CrossRef]
2. Zhou, P.; Yang, X.L.; Wang, X.G.; Hu, B.; Zhang, L.; Zhang, W.; Si, H.R.; Zhu, Y.; Li, B.; Huang, C.L.; et al. Discovery of a novel coronavirus associated with the recent pneumonia outbreak in humans and its potential bat origin. *BioRxiv* **2020**, *22*, 914952.
3. Miron, V.D. COVID-19 in the pediatric population and parental perceptions. *Germs* **2020**, *10*, 294. [CrossRef] [PubMed]
4. Liang, K. Mathematical model of infection kinetics and its analysis for COVID-19, SARS and MERS. *Infect. Genet. Evol.* **2020**, *82*, 104306. [CrossRef] [PubMed]
5. Li, C.; Xu, J.; Liu, J.; Zhou, Y. The within-host viral kinetics of SARS-CoV-2. *bioRxiv* **2020**, *17*, 234. [CrossRef]
6. Mason, R.J. Pathogenesis of COVID-19 from a cell biology perspective. *Eur. Respir. J.* **2020**, *55*, 2000607. [CrossRef]
7. World Health Orgnization. Naming the Coronavirus Disease (COVID-19) and the Virus That Causes It. 2020. Available online: https://www.who.int/emergencies/diseases/novel-coronavirus-2019/technical-guidance/naming-the-coronavirus-disease-(covid-2019)-and-the-virus-that-causes-it (accessed on 22 September 2022).
8. Yang, C.; Wang, J. A mathematical model for the novel coronavirus epidemic in Wuhan, China. *Math. Biosci. Eng.* **2020**, *17*, 2853–2861. [CrossRef]
9. Sinan, M.; Leng, J.; Anjum, M.; Fiaz, M. Asymptotic behavior and semi-analytic solution of a novel compartmental biological model. *Math. Model. Numer. Simul. Appl.* **2022**, *2*, 88–107. [CrossRef]
10. Tang, B.; Bragazzi, N.L.; Li, Q.; Tang, S.; Xiao, Y.; Wu, J. An updated estimation of the risk of transmission of the novel coronavirus (2019-nCov). *Infect. Dis. Model.* **2020**, *5*, 248–255. [CrossRef]
11. Kochańczyk, M.; Grabowski, F.; Lipniacki, T. Dynamics of COVID-19 pandemic at constant and time-dependent contact rates. *Math. Model. Nat. Phenom.* **2020**, *15*, 28. [CrossRef]
12. Naik, P.A.; Yavuz, M.; Qureshi, S.; Zu, J.; Townley, S. Modeling and analysis of COVID-19 epidemics with treatment in fractional derivatives using real data from Pakistan. *Eur. Phys. J. Plus* **2020**, *135*, 1–42. [CrossRef]
13. Allegretti, S.; Bulai, I.M.; Marino, R.; Menandro, M.A.; Parisi, K. Vaccination effect conjoint to fraction of avoided contacts for a Sars-Cov-2 mathematical model. *Math. Model. Numer. Simul. Appl.* **2021**, *1*, 56–66. [CrossRef]
14. Özköse, F.; Yavuz, M.; Şenel, M.T.; Habbireeh, R. Fractional order modelling of omicron SARS-CoV-2 variant containing heart attack effect using real data from the United Kingdom. *Chaos Solitons Fractals* **2022**, *157*, 111954. [CrossRef]
15. Haq, I.U.; Ali, N.; Nisar, K.S. An optimal control strategy and Grünwald-Letnikov finite-difference numerical scheme for the fractional-order COVID-19 model. *Math. Model. Numer. Simul. Appl.* **2022**, *2*, 108–116. [CrossRef]
16. Özköse, F.; Yavuz, M. Investigation of interactions between COVID-19 and diabetes with hereditary traits using real data: A case study in Turkey. *Comput. Biol. Med.* **2022**, *141*, 105044. [CrossRef]
17. Ikram, R.; Khan, A.; Zahri, M.; Saeed, A.; Yavuz, M.; Kumam, P. Extinction and stationary distribution of a stochastic COVID-19 epidemic model with time-delay. *Comput. Biol. Med.* **2022**, *141*, 105115. [CrossRef]
18. Naik, P.A.; Eskandari, Z.; Yavuz, M.; Zu, J. Complex dynamics of a discrete-time Bazykin–Berezovskaya prey-predator model with a strong Allee effect. *J. Comput. Appl. Math.* **2022**, *413*, 114401. [CrossRef]

19. Moussouni, N.; Aliane, M. Optimal control of COVID-19. *Int. J. Optim. Control Theor. Appl.* **2021**, *11*, 114–122. [CrossRef]
20. Hamou, A.A.; Rasul, R.R.; Hammouch, Z.; Özdemir, N. Analysis and dynamics of a mathematical model to predict unreported cases of COVID-19 epidemic in Morocco. *Comput. Appl. Math.* **2022**, *41*, 1–33. [CrossRef]
21. Evirgen, F. Transmission of Nipah virus dynamics under Caputo fractional derivative. *J. Comput. Appl. Math.* **2023**, *418*, 114654. [CrossRef]
22. Du, S.Q.; Yuan, W. Mathematical modeling of interaction between innate and adaptive immune responses in COVID-19 and implications for viral pathogenesis. *J. Med. Virol.* **2020**, *92*, 1615–1628. [CrossRef]
23. Abuin, P.; Anderson, A.; Ferramosca, A.; Hernandez-Vargas, E.A.; Gonzalez, A.H. Characterization of SARS-CoV-2 dynamics in the host. *Annu. Rev. Control* **2020**, *50*, 457–468. [CrossRef]
24. Nath, B.J.; Dehingia, K.; Mishra, V.N.; Chu, Y.M.; Sarmah, H.K. Mathematical analysis of a within-host model of SARS-CoV-2. *Adv. Differ. Equ.* **2021**, *2021*, 1–11. [CrossRef]
25. Agarwal, P.; Deniz, S.; Jain, S.; Alderremy, A.A.; Aly, S. A new analysis of a partial differential equation arising in biology and population genetics via semi analytical techniques. *Phys. A Stat. Mech. Appl.* **2020**, *542*, 122769. [CrossRef]
26. Lei, S.; Jiang, F.; Su, W.; Chen, C.; Chen, J.; Mei, W.; Zhan, L.Y.; Jia, Y.; Zhang, L.; Liu, D.; et al. Clinical characteristics and outcomes of patients undergoing surgeries during the incubation period of COVID-19 infection. *EClinicalMedicine* **2020**, *21*, 100331. [CrossRef]
27. Wu, J.T.; Leung, K.; Leung, G.M. Nowcasting and forecasting the potential domestic and international spread of the 2019-nCoV outbreak originating in Wuhan, China: A modelling study. *Lancet* **2020**, *395*, 689–697. [CrossRef]
28. Chan, J.F.W.; Yuan, S.; Kok, K.H.; To, K.K.W.; Chu, H.; Yang, J.; Xing, F.; Liu, J.; Yip, C.C.Y.; Poon, R.W.S.; et al. A familial cluster of pneumonia associated with the 2019 novel coronavirus indicating person-to-person transmission: A study of a family cluster. *Lancet* **2020**, *395*, 514–523. [CrossRef]
29. Letko, M.; Munster, V. Functional assessment of cell entry and receptor usage for lineage B β-coronaviruses, including 2019-nCoV. *bioRxiv* **2020**. [CrossRef]
30. Liu, J.; Liao, X.; Qian, S.; Yuan, J.; Wang, F.; Liu, Y.; Wang, Z.; Wang, F.S.; Liu, L.; Zhang, Z. Community transmission of severe acute respiratory syndrome coronavirus 2, Shenzhen, China, 2020. *Emerg. Infect. Dis.* **2020**, *26*, 1320. [CrossRef]
31. Agarwal, P.; Nieto, J.J.; Ruzhansky, M.; Torres, D.F. *Analysis of Infectious Disease Problems (Covid-19) and Their Global Impact*; Springer: Berlin/Heidelberg, Germany, 2021.
32. Yavuz, M.; Coşar, F.Ö.; Günay, F.; Özdemir, F.N. A new mathematical modeling of the COVID-19 pandemic including the vaccination campaign. *J Model. Simul.* **2021**, *9*, 299–321. [CrossRef]
33. Tuite, A.R.; Fisman, D.N.; Greer, A.L. Mathematical modelling of COVID-19 transmission and mitigation strategies in the population of Ontario, Canada. *CMAJ* **2020**, *192*, E497–E505. [CrossRef] [PubMed]
34. Marovich, M.; Mascola, J.R.; Cohen, M.S. Monoclonal antibodies for prevention and treatment of COVID-19. *JAMA* **2020**, *324*, 131–132. [CrossRef] [PubMed]
35. Li, G.; Fan, Y.; Lai, Y.; Han, T.; Li, Z.; Zhou, P.; Pan, P.; Wang, W.; Hu, D.; Liu, X.; et al. Coronavirus infections and immune responses. *J. Med. Virol.* **2020**, *92*, 424–432. [CrossRef] [PubMed]
36. Harapan, H.; Itoh, N.; Yufika, A.; Winardi, W.; Keam, S.; Te, H.; Megawati, D.; Hayati, Z.; Wagner, A.L.; Mudatsir, M. Coronavirus disease 2019 (COVID-19): A literature review. *J. Infect. Public Health* **2020**, *13*, 667–673. [CrossRef]
37. Chen, T.M.; Rui, J.; Wang, Q.P.; Zhao, Z.Y.; Cui, J.A.; Yin, L. A mathematical model for simulating the phase-based transmissibility of a novel coronavirus. *Infect. Dis. Poverty* **2020**, *9*, 1–8. [CrossRef]
38. Ahmed, I.; Baba, I.A.; Yusuf, A.; Kumam, P.; Kumam, W. Analysis of Caputo fractional-order model for COVID-19 with lockdown. *Adv. Differ. Equ.* **2020**, *2020*, 1–14. [CrossRef]
39. Baba, I.A.; Nasidi, B.A. Fractional order model for the role of mild cases in the transmission of COVID-19. *Chaos Solitons Fractals* **2021**, *142*, 110374. [CrossRef]
40. Hamdan, N.; Kilicman, A. Analysis of the fractional order dengue transmission model: A case study in Malaysia. *Adv. Differ. Equ.* **2019**, *2019*, 1–13. [CrossRef]
41. Khan, M.; Khan, A.; Elsonbaty, A.; Elsadany, A. Modeling and simulation results of a fractional dengue model. *Eur. Phys. J. Plus* **2019**, *134*, 379. [CrossRef]
42. Hammouch, Z.; Yavuz, M.; Özdemir, N. Numerical solutions and synchronization of a variable-order fractional chaotic system. *Math. Model. Numer. Simul. Appl.* **2021**, *1*, 11–23. [CrossRef]
43. Din, A.; Abidin, M.Z. Analysis of fractional-order vaccinated Hepatitis-B epidemic model with Mittag-Leffler kernels. *Math. Model. Numer. Simul. Appl.* **2022**, *2*, 59–72. [CrossRef]
44. Kalidass, M.; Zeng, S.; Yavuz, M. Stability of Fractional-Order Quasi-Linear Impulsive Integro-Differential Systems with Multiple Delays. *Axioms* **2022**, *11*, 308. [CrossRef]
45. Caputo, M.; Fabrizio, M. A new definition of fractional derivative without singular kernel. *Prog. Fract. Differ. Appl.* **2015**, *1*, 73–85.
46. Atangana, A.; Baleanu, D. New fractional derivatives with nonlocal and non-singular kernel: Theory and application to heat transfer model. *arXiv* **2016**, arXiv:1602.03408.
47. Lee, H.Y.; Topham, D.J.; Park, S.Y.; Hollenbaugh, J.; Treanor, J.; Mosmann, T.R.; Jin, X.; Ward, B.M.; Miao, H.; Holden-Wiltse, J.; et al. Simulation and prediction of the adaptive immune response to influenza A virus infection. *J. Virol.* **2009**, *83*, 7151–7165. [CrossRef]

48. Higazy, M. Novel fractional order SIDARTHE mathematical model of COVID-19 pandemic. *Chaos Solitons Fractals* **2020**, *138*, 110007. [CrossRef]
49. Ahmad, S.; Ullah, A.; Al-Mdallal, Q.M.; Khan, H.; Shah, K.; Khan, A. *Fractional Order Mathematical Modeling of COVID-19 Transmission*; Elsevier: Amsterdam, The Netherlands, 2020; Volume 139, p. 110256.
50. Joshi, H.; Jha, B.K. Chaos of calcium diffusion in Parkinson's infectious disease model and treatment mechanism via Hilfer fractional derivative. *Math. Model. Numer. Simul. Appl.* **2021**, *1*, 84–94.
51. Yavuz, M.; Sene, N.; Yıldız, M. Analysis of the influences of parameters in the fractional second-grade fluid dynamics. *Mathematics* **2022**, *10*, 1125. [CrossRef]
52. Kilbas, A.; Trujillo, J. Differential equations of fractional order: Methods, results and problems. II. *Appl. Anal.* **2002**, *81*, 435–493. [CrossRef]
53. Diekmann, O.; Heesterbeek, J.; Roberts, M.G. The construction of next-generation matrices for compartmental epidemic models. *J. R. Soc. Interface* **2010**, *7*, 873–885. [CrossRef]
54. Ahmed, E.; Elgazzar, A. On fractional order differential equations model for nonlocal epidemics. *Phys. A Stat. Mech. Its Appl.* **2007**, *379*, 607–614. [CrossRef]
55. Ahmady, N.; Allahviranloo, T.; Ahmady, E. A modified Euler method for solving fuzzy differential equations under generalized differentiability. *Comput. Appl. Math.* **2020**, *39*, 1–21. [CrossRef]

Mathematical and Computational Applications

Article

Controllability Criteria for Nonlinear Impulsive Fractional Differential Systems with Distributed Delays in Controls

Amar Debbouche [1,*], Bhaskar Sundara Vadivoo [2], Vladimir E. Fedorov [3] and Valery Antonov [4]

[1] Department of Mathematics, Guelma University, Guelma 24000, Algeria
[2] Department of Mathematics, Alagappa University, Karaikudi 630 004, India
[3] Department of Mathematical Analysis, Chelyabinsk State University, 129 Kashirin Brothers St., 454001 Chelyabinsk, Russia
[4] Department of Mathematics, Peter the Great Saint Petersburg Polytechnic University, 195251 Saint Petersburg, Russia
* Correspondence: amar_debbouche@yahoo.fr

Abstract: We establish a class of nonlinear fractional differential systems with distributed time delays in the controls and impulse effects. We discuss the controllability criteria for both linear and nonlinear systems. The main results required a suitable Gramian matrix defined by the Mittag–Leffler function, using the standard Laplace transform and Schauder fixed-point techniques. Further, we provide an illustrative example supported by graphical representations to show the validity of the obtained abstract results.

Keywords: fractional differential equations; Caputo fractional derivative; discrete-delays; distributed-delays; impulses

MSC: 93B05; 34A37; 26A33; 33E12

Citation: Debbouche, A.; Vadivoo, B.S.; Fedorov, V.E.; Antonov, V. Controllability Criteria for Nonlinear Impulsive Fractional Differential Systems with Distributed Delays in Controls. *Math. Comput. Appl.* **2023**, *28*, 13. https://doi.org/10.3390/mca28010013

Academic Editors: Mehmet Yavuz and Ioannis Dassios

Received: 6 December 2022
Revised: 9 January 2023
Accepted: 12 January 2023
Published: 15 January 2023

Copyright: © 2023 by the authors. Licensee MDPI, Basel, Switzerland. This article is an open access article distributed under the terms and conditions of the Creative Commons Attribution (CC BY) license (https://creativecommons.org/licenses/by/4.0/).

1. Introduction

Fractional calculus has become a topic of growing interest in Applied Mathematics because of its potential to model many physical phenomena; in fact, it has become a subject of significant interest to many researchers, scientists and engineers, since it applies to a wide range of applications in physics, mathematics and engineering; see, for instance [1–11]. Concerning different applications and mathematical models, the literature contains, among many others, reaction–diffusion problems [12], neural networks [13], a COVID-19 model [14] and an anomalous transport model [15].

A delay differential equation is a differential equation where the time derivatives at the current time depend on the solution and possibly its derivatives at previous times. Instead of a simple initial condition, an initial history function needs to be specified. Fractional differential equations with delays have recently played a significant role in modelling in many areas of science. Appropriately, fractional differential equations are further considered to be alternative models to nonlinear differential equations. For more details, see the monographs of Kilbas et al. [16], Miller and Ross [17], and Podlubny [18]. Mathematical models for systems with distributed delays in the controls occur in the study of agricultural economics and population dynamics [19,20].

On the other hand, it is noted that controllability is one of the most important qualitative behaviours of a dynamical structure. Based on this fact, we can infer that it is possible to steer any initial state of the system to any final state in some finite time using an admissible control. Moreover, controllability outcomes can be acquired by using non-identical techniques, for which the fixed point theory is the most powerful tool [21]. Therefore, the fusion of fractional-order derivatives and integrals in control theory lead to better results than integer order approaches. Recently, Balachandran et al. [22] proved the relative controllability of fractional dynamical systems with distributed delays in the controls. In [23], the authors established some analysis for the stability and controllability of a fractional damped differential system with non-instantaneous impulses supported by numerical treatments. Furthermore, the dynamics of developing processes is frequently subjected to immediate changes such as shocks, harvesting or natural disasters, and so on. These types of short-term performances are regularly treated as having acted instantaneously or in the form of impulses. Zhang et al. [24] proved the controllability of an impulsive fractional differential equation with a state delay. Very recently, in [25], the authors proved in a relative controllability analysis fractional order differential equations with multiple time delays. For further works, the readers may refer to [26–29]. Motivated by the above statements and extending the results of [22,25], in this work, we are concerned with the problem of controllability of impulsive fractional differential systems with distributed delays in controls.

$$
\begin{aligned}
{}^C D^\alpha x(t) &= \mathfrak{A} x(t) + K x(t-\tau) + \int_{-h}^{0} d_\tau \mathfrak{B}(t,\tau) u(t+\tau) + f(t, x(t), x(t-h), u(t-\tau)), \\
& \quad t \in [0,T] - \{t_1, t_2, \ldots, t_k\}, \\
\Delta x(t_i) &= x(t_i^+) - x(t_i^-) = I_i(x(t_i)), i = 1,2,\ldots,k, \\
x(t) &= \varphi(t), t \in [-\tau, 0],
\end{aligned}
\quad (1)
$$

where ${}^C D^\alpha$ represents the Caputo fractional derivative of order α, $0 < \alpha < 1$ and $\mathfrak{A} \in \mathbb{R}^{n \times n}$ denotes a constant matrix, $x \in \mathbb{R}^n$ is the state variable and the third integral term is in the Lebesgue–Stieltjes sense with respect to τ. Let f, k and $h > 0$ be given. The control input $u : [-h, T] \to \mathbb{R}^m$ for all $t \in J$, and u_t denotes the function on $[-h, 0]$, defined by $u_t(s) = u(t+s)$ for $s \in [-h, 0)$. $\mathfrak{B}(t, \tau)$ is an $n \times m$ dimensional matrix continuous in t for fixed τ and is of bounded variation in τ on $[-h, 0)$ for each $t \in J$ and continuous from left in τ on the interval. $(-h, 0)$, $\varphi \in C([-\tau, 0], \mathbb{R}^n)$ is the initial state function, where $C([-\tau, 0], \mathbb{R}^n)$ denotes the space of all continuous functions mapping the interval $[-\tau, 0]$ into $\mathbb{R}^n$; $I_i : \mathbb{R}^n \to \mathbb{R}^n$ is continuous for $i = 1, 2, \ldots, k$, and

$$
\begin{aligned}
x(t_i^+) &= \lim_{\varepsilon \to 0^+} x(t_i + \varepsilon), \\
x(t_i^-) &= \lim_{\varepsilon \to 0^-} x(t_i + \varepsilon),
\end{aligned}
\quad (2)
$$

represent the right and left limits of $x(t)$ at $t = t_i$ and the discontinuous points

$$t_1 < t_2 < \cdots < t_i < \cdots < t_k,$$

where $0 = t_0 < \tau < t_1, t_k < t_{k+1} = T < +\infty$, and $x(t_i) = x(t_i^-)$, which implies that the solution of the system (1) is left continuous at t_i.

The notable contributions of our work is as follows:

- Nonlinear impulsive fractional differential systems with distributed delays in controls are considered.
- The solution representation is formulated via an unsymmetric Fubini's theorem.
- The controllability of the linear system is proved by using the controllability Gramian operator.
- The controllability of the nonlinear system is investigated by employing the Schauder fixed-point theorem.
- Numerical treatments are given using MATLAB.

Our paper is organized as follows. In Section 2, we present some basic definitions and preliminary facts, which will be used in order to obtain our desired results. In Section 3, we state and prove the main results of this work. In Section 4, an example is given to illustrate the effectiveness and validity of our controllability results. Finally, we conclude our results and suggest new directions in Section 5.

2. Preliminaries

Throughout the paper, $C_P([0,T], \mathbb{R}^n)$ denotes the space of all piecewise left-continuous functions mapping the interval $[0,T]$ into $\mathbb{R}^n$.

Definition 1 ([18]). *The Caputo fractional derivative of order $\alpha > 0$, $n-1 < \alpha < n$ is defined as*

$$(^C D_{0+}^\alpha f)(t) = \frac{1}{\Gamma(n-\alpha)} \int_0^t (t-s)^{n-\alpha-1} f^{(n)}(s) ds,$$

where the function $f(t)$ has absolutely continuous derivatives up to order $(n-1)$. If $0 < \alpha < 1$, then

$$(^C D_{0+}^\alpha f)(t) = \frac{1}{\Gamma(1-\alpha)} \int_0^t \frac{f'(s)}{(t-s)^\alpha} ds.$$

Definition 2 ([18]). *The Mittag–Leffler function in two parameters is defined as*

$$E_{\alpha,\beta}(z) = \sum_{k=0}^{\infty} \frac{z^k}{\Gamma(k\alpha + \beta)}, \text{ for } \alpha, \beta > 0,$$

so that $z \in \mathbb{C}$, $\mathbb{C}$ denotes the complex plane. The general Mittag–Leffler function satisfies

$$\int_0^\infty e^{-t} t^{\beta-1} E_{\alpha,\beta}(t^\alpha z) dt = \frac{1}{1-z}, \text{ for } |z| < 1.$$

The linear fractional delay differential system without impulses is considered as follows.

$$\begin{aligned}
^C D^\alpha x(t) &= \mathfrak{A} x(t) + K x(t-\tau) + \int_{-h}^{0} d_\tau \mathfrak{B}(t,\tau) u(t+\tau), \ t \in [0,T], \\
x(t) &= \varphi(t), t \in [-\tau, 0].
\end{aligned} \quad (3)$$

The nonlinear fractional delay differential system without impulses is considered as follows.

$$\begin{aligned}
^C D^\alpha x(t) &= \mathfrak{A} x(t) + K x(t-\tau) + \int_{-h}^{0} d_\tau \mathfrak{B}(t,\tau) u(t+\tau) + f(t, x(t), x(t-\tau), u(t)), \ t \in [0,T], \\
x(t) &= \varphi(t), t \in [-\tau, 0].
\end{aligned} \quad (4)$$

Lemma 1. *For $0 < \alpha < 1$, if $f : [0,T] \to \mathbb{R}^n$ is continuous and exponentially bounded, then the solution of the system (3) can be represented as*

$$\begin{aligned}
x(t) =\ & \phi(0) + \int_0^t (t-s)^{\alpha-1} E_{\alpha,\alpha}(\mathfrak{A}(t-s)^\alpha) [\mathfrak{A}\phi(0) + Kx(s-\tau)] ds \\
& + \int_{-h}^{0} d\mathfrak{B}_\tau [\int_\tau^0 (t-(s-\tau))^{\alpha-1} E_{\alpha,\alpha}(\mathfrak{A}(t-(s-\tau))^\alpha) \mathfrak{B}(s-\tau, \tau) u_0(s) ds] \\
& + \int_0^t [\int_{-h}^{0} (t-(s-\tau))^{\alpha-1} E_{\alpha,\alpha}(\mathfrak{A}(t-(s-\tau))^\alpha) d_\tau \mathfrak{B}_t(s-\tau, \tau) u(s) ds, \ t \in [0,T],
\end{aligned}$$

where $\mathfrak{B}_t(s,\tau) = \begin{cases} \mathfrak{B}(s,\tau), s \le t, \\ 0, \quad s > t, \end{cases}$

and $x(t) = \varphi(t), t \in [-\tau, 0]$.

Proof. Let $t \in [0,T]$, employing the Laplace transform with respect to t on both sides of system (3), the result is

$$s^\alpha L[x(t)] - s^{\alpha-1}\phi(0) = \mathfrak{A}L[x(t)] + L[Kx(t-\tau) + \int_{-h}^{0} d_\tau \mathfrak{B}(t,\tau)u(t+\tau)],$$

$$L[x(t)] = (s^\alpha I - \mathfrak{A})^{-1} s^{\alpha-1}\phi(0) + (s^\alpha I - \mathfrak{A})^{-1} L[Kx(t-\tau) + \int_{-h}^{0} d_\tau \mathfrak{B}(t,\tau)u(t+\tau)],$$

$$L[x(t)] = L[\phi(0)] + (s^\alpha I - \mathfrak{A})^{-1} L[\mathfrak{A}\phi(0) + Kx(t-\tau) + \int_{-h}^{0} d_\tau \mathfrak{B}(t,\tau)u(t+\tau)],$$

$$= L[\phi(0)] + L[t^{\alpha-1} E_{\alpha,\alpha}(\mathfrak{A}t^\alpha)] L[\mathfrak{A}\phi(0) + Kx(t-\tau)]$$
$$+ \int_{-h}^{0} d_\tau \mathfrak{B}(t,\tau)u(t+\tau)]. \quad (5)$$

Applying the convolution theorem of the Laplace transform to (5), we get

$$L[x(t)] = L[\phi(0)] + L[t^{\alpha-1} E_{\alpha,\alpha}(\mathfrak{A}t^\alpha)][\mathfrak{A}\phi(0) + Kx(t-\tau) + \int_{-h}^{0} d_\tau \mathfrak{B}(t,\tau)u(t+\tau)].$$

Employing the inverse Laplace transform, then we have

$$x(t) = \phi(0) + \int_0^t (t-s)^{\alpha-1} E_{\alpha,\alpha}[\mathfrak{A}(t-s)^\alpha][\mathfrak{A}\phi(0) + Kx(s-\tau)]ds$$
$$+ \int_0^t (t-s)^{\alpha-1} E_{\alpha,\alpha}[\mathfrak{A}(t-s)^\alpha][\int_{-h}^{0} d_\tau \mathfrak{B}(s,\tau)u(s+\tau)]ds.$$

Using the well-known result of the unsymmetric Fubini theorem [30] and the change of order of the integration to the last term, we have

$$x(t) = \phi(0) + \int_0^t (t-s)^{\alpha-1} E_{\alpha,\alpha}[\mathfrak{A}(t-s)^\alpha][\mathfrak{A}\phi(0) + Kx(s-\tau)]ds$$
$$+ \int_{-h}^{0} d\mathfrak{B}_\tau [\int_0^t (t-s)^{\alpha-1} E_{\alpha,\alpha}[\mathfrak{A}(t-s)^\alpha] u(s+\tau) \mathfrak{B}(s,\tau)ds]$$
$$= \phi(0) + \int_0^t (t-s)^{\alpha-1} E_{\alpha,\alpha}[\mathfrak{A}(t-s)^\alpha][\mathfrak{A}\phi(0) + Kx(s-\tau)]ds$$
$$+ \int_{-h}^{0} d\mathfrak{B}_\tau [\int_\tau^{0} (t-(s-\tau))^{\alpha-1} E_{\alpha,\alpha}[\mathfrak{A}(t-(s-\tau))^\alpha] \mathfrak{B}(s-\tau,\tau) u_0(s)ds]$$
$$+ \int_{-h}^{0} d\mathfrak{B}_\tau [\int_0^{t+\tau} (t-(s-\tau))^{\alpha-1} E_{\alpha,\alpha}[\mathfrak{A}(t-(s-\tau))^\alpha] \mathfrak{B}(s-\tau,\tau) u(s)ds]$$
$$= \phi(0) + \int_0^t (t-s)^{\alpha-1} E_{\alpha,\alpha}[\mathfrak{A}(t-s)^\alpha][\mathfrak{A}\phi(0) + Kx(s-\tau)]ds$$
$$+ \int_{-h}^{0} d\mathfrak{B}_\tau [\int_\tau^{0} (t-(s-\tau))^{\alpha-1} E_{\alpha,\alpha}[\mathfrak{A}(t-(s-\tau))^\alpha] \mathfrak{B}(s-\tau,\tau) u_0(s)ds]$$
$$+ \int_0^t [\int_{-h}^{0} (t-(s-\tau))^{\alpha-1} E_{\alpha,\alpha}[\mathfrak{A}(t-(s-\tau))^\alpha] d_\tau \mathfrak{B}_t(s-\tau,\tau)) u(s)ds,$$

where

$$\mathfrak{B}_t(s,\tau) = \begin{cases} \mathfrak{B}(s,\tau), & s \leq t, \\ 0, & s > t, \end{cases}$$

and $d\mathfrak{B}_\tau$ denotes the integration of the Lebesgue–Stieltjes sense with respect to the variable τ in the function $\mathfrak{B}(t,\tau)$, hence the proof. □

Lemma 2. *For $0 < \alpha < 1$, the solution representation of the nonlinear structure (4) is*

$$x(t) = \phi(0) + \int_0^t (t-s)^{\alpha-1} E_{\alpha,\alpha}(\mathfrak{A}(t-s)^\alpha)[\mathfrak{A}\phi(0) + Kx(s-\tau) + f(s,x(s),x(s-h),u(s))]ds,$$
$$+ \int_{-h}^0 d\mathfrak{B}_\tau [\int_\tau^0 (t-(s-\tau))^{\alpha-1} E_{\alpha,\alpha}(\mathfrak{A}(t-(s-\tau))^\alpha) \mathfrak{B}(s-\tau,\tau) u_0(s) ds],$$
$$+ \int_0^t [\int_{-h}^0 (t-(s-\tau))^{\alpha-1} E_{\alpha,\alpha}(\mathfrak{A}(t-(s-\tau))^\alpha) d_\tau \mathfrak{B}_t(s-\tau,\tau)] u(s) ds, \quad t \in [0,T], \tag{6}$$

where

$$\mathfrak{B}_t(s,\tau) = \begin{cases} \mathfrak{B}(s,\tau), & s \le t, \\ 0, & s > t, \end{cases}$$

and $x(t) = \varphi(t), t \in [-\tau, 0]$.

Proof. The proof is similar to Lemma 1. Hence, it is eliminated. □

Lemma 3. *Let $0 < \alpha < 1$ and $u \in C_p([0,T], \mathbb{R}^m)$ then the solution of structure (1) is as follows.*
For $t \in [-\tau, 0]$, $x(t) = \varphi(t)$,
For $t \in [0, t_1)$,

$$x(t) = \phi(0) + \int_0^t (t-s)^{\alpha-1} E_{\alpha,\alpha}[\mathfrak{A}(t-s)^\alpha][\mathfrak{A}\phi(0) + Kx(s-\tau)]ds,$$
$$+ \int_{-h}^0 d\mathfrak{B}_\tau [\int_\tau^0 (t-(s-\tau))^{\alpha-1} E_{\alpha,\alpha}[\mathfrak{A}(t-(s-\tau))^\alpha] \mathfrak{B}(s-\tau,\tau) u_0(s) ds],$$
$$+ \int_0^t [\int_{-h}^0 (t-(s-\tau))^{\alpha-1} E_{\alpha,\alpha}[\mathfrak{A}(t-(s-\tau))^\alpha] d_\tau \mathfrak{B}_t(s-\tau,\tau)) u(s) ds. \tag{7}$$

For $t \in (t_1, t_2)$,

$$x(t) = \phi(0) + I_1(x(t_1^-)) + \int_0^t (t-s)^{\alpha-1} E_{\alpha,\alpha}[\mathfrak{A}(t-s)^\alpha][\mathfrak{A}\phi(0) + Kx(s-\tau)]ds,$$
$$+ \int_{-h}^0 d\mathfrak{B}_\tau [\int_\tau^0 (t-(s-\tau))^{\alpha-1} E_{\alpha,\alpha}[\mathfrak{A}(t-(s-\tau))^\alpha] \mathfrak{B}(s-\tau,\tau) u_0(s) ds],$$
$$+ \int_0^t [\int_{-h}^0 (t-(s-\tau))^{\alpha-1} E_{\alpha,\alpha}[\mathfrak{A}(t-(s-\tau))^\alpha] d_\tau \mathfrak{B}_t(s-\tau,\tau)) u(s) ds. \tag{8}$$

For $t \in (t_i, T], i = 1, 2, \ldots, k$,

$$x(t) = \phi(0) + \sum_{j=1}^i I_j(x(t_j^-)) + \int_0^t (t-s)^{\alpha-1} E_{\alpha,\alpha}[\mathfrak{A}(t-s)^\alpha][\mathfrak{A}\phi(0) + Kx(s-\tau)]ds,$$
$$+ \int_{-h}^0 d\mathfrak{B}_\tau [\int_\tau^0 (t-(s-\tau))^{\alpha-1} E_{\alpha,\alpha}[\mathfrak{A}(t-(s-\tau))^\alpha] \mathfrak{B}(s-\tau,\tau) u_0(s) ds],$$
$$+ \int_0^t [\int_{-h}^0 (t-(s-\tau))^{\alpha-1} E_{\alpha,\alpha}[\mathfrak{A}(t-(s-\tau))^\alpha] d_\tau \mathfrak{B}_t(s-\tau,\tau)) u(s) ds. \tag{9}$$

Proof. For $t \in [-\tau, 0]$, the proof is obvious. For $t \in [0, t_1)$, by Lemma 2,

$$\begin{aligned}
x(t) &= \phi(0) + \int_0^t (t-s)^{\alpha-1} E_{\alpha,\alpha}[\mathfrak{A}(t-s)^\alpha][\mathfrak{A}\phi(0) + Kx(s-\tau)]ds \\
&+ \int_{-h}^0 d\mathfrak{B}_\tau [\int_\tau^0 (t-(s-\tau))^{\alpha-1} E_{\alpha,\alpha}[\mathfrak{A}(t-(s-\tau))^\alpha]\mathfrak{B}(s-\tau,\tau)u_0(s)ds] \\
&+ \int_0^t [\int_{-h}^0 (t-(s-\tau))^{\alpha-1} E_{\alpha,\alpha}[\mathfrak{A}(t-(s-\tau))^\alpha]d_\tau \mathfrak{B}_t(s-\tau,\tau))u(s)ds. \\
x(t_1) &= \phi(0) + \int_0^{t_1} (t_1-s)^{\alpha-1} E_{\alpha,\alpha}[\mathfrak{A}(t_1-s)^\alpha][\mathfrak{A}\phi(0) + Kx(s-\tau)]ds \\
&+ \int_{-h}^0 d\mathfrak{B}_\tau [\int_\tau^0 (t_1-(s-\tau))^{\alpha-1} E_{\alpha,\alpha}[\mathfrak{A}(t_1-(s-\tau))^\alpha]\mathfrak{B}(s-\tau,\tau)u_0(s)ds] \\
&+ \int_0^{t_1} [\int_{-h}^0 (t_1-(s-\tau))^{\alpha-1} E_{\alpha,\alpha}[\mathfrak{A}(t_1-(s-\tau))^\alpha]d_\tau \mathfrak{B}_{t_1}(s-\tau,\tau))u(s)ds.
\end{aligned}$$

If $t \in (t_1, t_2)$, using (7), we have

$$\begin{aligned}
x(t) &= x(t_1^+) - \int_0^{t_1} (t_1-s)^{\alpha-1} E_{\alpha,\alpha}[\mathfrak{A}(t_1-s)^\alpha][\mathfrak{A}\phi(0) + Kx(s-\tau)]ds \\
&+ \int_{-h}^0 d\mathfrak{B}_\tau [\int_\tau^0 (t_1-(s-\tau))^{\alpha-1} E_{\alpha,\alpha}[\mathfrak{A}(t_1-(s-\tau))^\alpha]\mathfrak{B}(s-\tau,\tau)u_0(s)ds] \\
&+ \int_0^{t_1} [\int_{-h}^0 (t_1-(s-\tau))^{\alpha-1} E_{\alpha,\alpha}[\mathfrak{A}(t_1-(s-\tau))^\alpha]d_\tau \mathfrak{B}_{t_1}(s-\tau,\tau))u(s)ds \\
&+ \int_0^t (t-s)^{\alpha-1} E_{\alpha,\alpha}[\mathfrak{A}(t-s)^\alpha][\mathfrak{A}\phi(0) + Kx(s-\tau)]ds + \int_{-h}^0 d\mathfrak{B}_\tau [\int_\tau^0 (t-(s-\tau))^{\alpha-1} \\
&\times E_{\alpha,\alpha}[\mathfrak{A}(t-(s-\tau))^\alpha]\mathfrak{B}(s-\tau,\tau)u_0(s)ds] + \int_0^t [\int_{-h}^0 (t-(s-\tau))^{\alpha-1} E_{\alpha,\alpha}[\mathfrak{A}(t-(s-\tau))^\alpha] \\
&\times d_\tau \mathfrak{B}_t(s-\tau,\tau))u(s)ds. \\
x(t) &= x(t_1^-) + I_1(x(t_1^-)) - \int_0^{t_1} (t_1-s)^{\alpha-1} E_{\alpha,\alpha}[\mathfrak{A}(t_1-s)^\alpha][\mathfrak{A}\phi(0) + Kx(s-\tau)]ds \\
&+ \int_{-h}^0 d\mathfrak{B}_\tau [\int_\tau^0 (t_1-(s-\tau))^{\alpha-1} E_{\alpha,\alpha}[\mathfrak{A}(t_1-(s-\tau))^\alpha]\mathfrak{B}(s-\tau,\tau)u_0(s)ds] \\
&+ \int_0^{t_1} [\int_{-h}^0 (t_1-(s-\tau))^{\alpha-1} E_{\alpha,\alpha}[\mathfrak{A}(t_1-(s-\tau))^\alpha]d_\tau \mathfrak{B}_{t_1}(s-\tau,\tau))u(s)ds \\
&+ \int_0^t (t-s)^{\alpha-1} E_{\alpha,\alpha}[\mathfrak{A}(t-s)^\alpha][\mathfrak{A}\phi(0) + Kx(s-\tau)]ds + \int_{-h}^0 d\mathfrak{B}_\tau [\int_\tau^0 (t-(s-\tau))^{\alpha-1} \\
&\times E_{\alpha,\alpha}[\mathfrak{A}(t-(s-\tau))^\alpha]\mathfrak{B}(s-\tau,\tau)u_0(s)ds] + \int_0^t [\int_{-h}^0 (t-(s-\tau))^{\alpha-1} E_{\alpha,\alpha}[\mathfrak{A}(t-(s-\tau))^\alpha] \\
&\times d_\tau \mathfrak{B}_t(s-\tau,\tau))u(s)ds \\
x(t) &= \phi(0) + I_1(x(t_1^-)) + \int_0^t (t-s)^{\alpha-1} E_{\alpha,\alpha}[\mathfrak{A}(t-s)^\alpha][\mathfrak{A}\phi(0) + Kx(s-\tau)]ds \\
&+ \int_{-h}^0 d\mathfrak{B}_\tau [\int_\tau^0 (t-(s-\tau))^{\alpha-1} E_{\alpha,\alpha}[\mathfrak{A}(t-(s-\tau))^\alpha]\mathfrak{B}(s-\tau,\tau)u_0(s)ds] \\
&+ \int_0^t [\int_{-h}^0 (t-(s-\tau))^{\alpha-1} E_{\alpha,\alpha}[\mathfrak{A}(t-(s-\tau))^\alpha]d_\tau \mathfrak{B}_t(s-\tau,\tau))u(s)ds.
\end{aligned}$$

If $t \in (t_2, t_3)$, then

$$\begin{aligned}
x(t) &= x(t_2^+) - \int_0^{t_2}(t_2-s)^{\alpha-1}E_{\alpha,\alpha}[\mathfrak{A}(t_2-s)^\alpha][\mathfrak{A}\phi(0)+Kx(s-\tau)]ds \\
&+ \int_{-h}^0 d\mathfrak{B}_\tau[\int_\tau^0(t_2-(s-\tau))^{\alpha-1}E_{\alpha,\alpha}[\mathfrak{A}(t_2-(s-\tau))^\alpha]\mathfrak{B}(s-\tau,\tau)u_0(s)ds] \\
&+ \int_0^{t_2}[\int_{-h}^0(t_2-(s-\tau))^{\alpha-1}E_{\alpha,\alpha}[\mathfrak{A}(t_2-(s-\tau))^\alpha]d_\tau\mathfrak{B}_{t_2}(s-\tau,\tau))u(s)ds \\
&+ \int_0^t(t-s)^{\alpha-1}E_{\alpha,\alpha}[\mathfrak{A}(t-s)^\alpha][\mathfrak{A}\phi(0)+Kx(s-\tau)]ds \\
&+ \int_{-h}^0 d\mathfrak{B}_\tau[\int_\tau^0(t-(s-\tau))^{\alpha-1}E_{\alpha,\alpha}[\mathfrak{A}(t-(s-\tau))^\alpha]\mathfrak{B}(s-\tau,\tau)u_0(s)ds] \\
&+ \int_0^t[\int_{-h}^0(t-(s-\tau))^{\alpha-1}E_{\alpha,\alpha}[\mathfrak{A}(t-(s-\tau))^\alpha]d_\tau\mathfrak{B}_t(s-\tau,\tau))u(s)ds.
\end{aligned}$$

$$\begin{aligned}
x(t) &= \phi(0) + \sum_{j=1}^2 I_j(x(t_j^-)) + \int_0^t(t-s)^{\alpha-1}E_{\alpha,\alpha}[\mathfrak{A}(t-s)^\alpha][\mathfrak{A}\phi(0)+Kx(s-\tau)]ds \\
&+ \int_{-h}^0 d\mathfrak{B}_\tau[\int_\tau^0(t-(s-\tau))^{\alpha-1}E_{\alpha,\alpha}[\mathfrak{A}(t-(s-\tau))^\alpha]\mathfrak{B}(s-\tau,\tau)u_0(s)ds] \\
&+ \int_0^t[\int_{-h}^0(t-(s-\tau))^{\alpha-1}E_{\alpha,\alpha}[\mathfrak{A}(t-(s-\tau))^\alpha]d_\tau\mathfrak{B}_t(s-\tau,\tau))u(s)ds.
\end{aligned}$$

If $t \in (t_i, T] (i = 1, 2, \ldots, k)$, using similar reasoning, we get

$$\begin{aligned}
x(t) &= \phi(0) + \sum_{j=1}^i I_j(x(t_j^-)) + \int_0^t(t-s)^{\alpha-1}E_{\alpha,\alpha}[\mathfrak{A}(t-s)^\alpha][\mathfrak{A}\phi(0)+Kx(s-\tau)]ds \\
&+ \int_{-h}^0 d\mathfrak{B}_\tau[\int_\tau^0(t-(s-\tau))^{\alpha-1}E_{\alpha,\alpha}[\mathfrak{A}(t-(s-\tau))^\alpha]\mathfrak{B}(s-\tau,\tau)u_0(s)ds] \\
&+ \int_0^t[\int_{-h}^0(t-(s-\tau))^{\alpha-1}E_{\alpha,\alpha}[\mathfrak{A}(t-(s-\tau))^\alpha]d_\tau\mathfrak{B}_t(s-\tau,\tau))u(s)ds.
\end{aligned}$$

The proof is complete. □

3. Controllability Results

In this section, we prove the controllability result of the labelled system.

Definition 3. *System (1) is called controllable on $[0, w] (w \in (0, T])$; for any initial function, $\varphi \in C([-\tau, 0], \mathbb{R}^n)$, and any state, $x_w \in \mathbb{R}^n$, there exists a control input $u(t) \in C_p([0, w], \mathbb{R}^m)$, so that the corresponding solution of (1) satisfies $x(w) = x_w$.*

Theorem 1. *Structure (1) is controllable on $[0, w]$ if and only if the Gramian matrix*

$$W_C[0, w] = \int_0^w G(w-s)G^*(w,s)ds, \tag{10}$$

is nonsingular for some $w \in [0, T]$, where

$$G(w,s) = \int_{-h}^0 (w-(s-\tau))^{\alpha-1}E_{\alpha,\alpha}[\mathfrak{A}(t-(s-\tau))^\alpha]d_\tau\mathfrak{B}_w(s-\tau,\tau)$$

and $*$ denotes the matrix transpose.

Proof. Assume that $W[0, w]$ is nonsingular, then $W^{-1}[0, w]$ is well defined. If $\varphi \in C([-\tau, 0], \mathbb{R}^n)$, let $w \in [0, t_1]$ the control function is

$$\begin{aligned} u(t) &= G^*(w, t) W^{-1}[0, w][x_w - \phi(0) - \int_0^w (w-s)^{\alpha-1} E_{\alpha,\alpha}(\mathfrak{A}(w-s)^{\alpha})[\mathfrak{A}\phi(0) + Kx(s-\tau)]ds, \\ &\quad - \int_{-h}^0 d\mathfrak{B}_\tau [\int_\tau^0 (w-(s-\tau))^{\alpha-1} E_{\alpha,\alpha} \mathfrak{A}(w-(s-\tau))^{\alpha} \mathfrak{B}(s-\tau, \tau) u_0(s) ds]]. \end{aligned} \tag{11}$$

By substituting $t = w$ in (7) and inserting (11), we get

$$\begin{aligned} x(w) &= \phi(0) + \int_0^w (w-s)^{\alpha-1} E_{\alpha,\alpha}[\mathfrak{A}(w-s)^{\alpha}][\mathfrak{A}\phi(0) + Kx(s-\tau))]ds \\ &\quad + \int_{-h}^0 d\mathfrak{B}_\tau [\int_\tau^0 (w-(s-\tau))^{\alpha-1} E_{\alpha,\alpha}[\mathfrak{A}(w-(s-\tau))^{\alpha}]\mathfrak{B}(s-\tau, \tau) u_0(s) ds] \\ &\quad + \int_0^w G(w,s) G^*(w,s) W^{-1}[0, w][x_w - \phi(0) - \int_0^w (w-s)^{\alpha-1} E_{\alpha,\alpha}(\mathfrak{A}(w-s)^{\alpha}) \\ &\quad \times [\mathfrak{A}\phi(0) + Kx(s-\tau)]ds - \int_{-h}^0 d\mathfrak{B}_\tau [\int_\tau^0 (w-(s-\tau))^{\alpha-1} E_{\alpha,\alpha} \mathfrak{A}(w-(s-\tau))^{\alpha} \\ &\quad \times \mathfrak{B}(s-\tau, \tau) u_0(s) ds]]d\tau. \end{aligned}$$

$$x(w) = x_w.$$

Thus, system (1) is controllable on $[0, w], w \in [0, t_1]$. For $w \in (t_1, t_2]$, we take the control function as

$$\begin{aligned} u(t) &= G^*(w, t) W^{-1}[0, w][x_w - \phi(0) - I_1(x(t_1^-)) - \int_0^w (w-s)^{\alpha-1} E_{\alpha,\alpha}(\mathfrak{A}(w-s)^{\alpha}) \\ &\quad \times [\mathfrak{A}\phi(0) + Kx(s-\tau)]ds - \int_{-h}^0 d\mathfrak{B}_\tau [\int_\tau^0 (w-(s-\tau))^{\alpha-1} E_{\alpha,\alpha} \mathfrak{A}(w-(s-\tau))^{\alpha} \\ &\quad \mathfrak{B}(s-\tau, \tau) u_0(s) ds]]. \end{aligned} \tag{12}$$

By substituting $t = w$ in (8) and inserting (12), we get

$$\begin{aligned} x(w) &= \phi(0) + I_1(x(t_1^-)) + \int_0^w (w-s)^{\alpha-1} E_{\alpha,\alpha}[\mathfrak{A}(w-s)^{\alpha}][\mathfrak{A}\phi(0) + Kx(s-\tau))]ds \\ &\quad + \int_{-h}^0 d\mathfrak{B}_\tau [\int_\tau^0 (w-(s-\tau))^{\alpha-1} E_{\alpha,\alpha}[\mathfrak{A}(w-(s-\tau))^{\alpha}]\mathfrak{B}(s-\tau, \tau) u_0(s) ds] \\ &\quad + \int_0^w G(w,s) G^*(w,s) W^{-1}[0, w][x_w - \phi(0) - \int_0^w (w-s)^{\alpha-1} E_{\alpha,\alpha}(\mathfrak{A}(w-s)^{\alpha}) \\ &\quad [\mathfrak{A}\phi(0) + Kx(s-\tau)]ds - \int_{-h}^0 d\mathfrak{B}_\tau [\int_\tau^0 (w-(s-\tau))^{\alpha-1} E_{\alpha,\alpha} \mathfrak{A}(w-(s-\tau))^{\alpha} \\ &\quad \times \mathfrak{B}(s-\tau, \tau) u_0(s) ds]]d\tau. \end{aligned}$$

$x(w) = x_w.$

Hence, system (1) is controllable on $[0, w], w \in [t_1, t_2]$. For $w \in (t_i, t_{i+1}], i = 1, 2, \ldots, k$, the control function, u, is defined by

$$\begin{aligned} u(t) &= G^*(w, t) W^{-1}[0, w][x_w - \phi(0) - \sum_{j=1}^i I_j(x(t_j^-)) - \int_0^w (w-s)^{\alpha-1} E_{\alpha,\alpha}(\mathfrak{A}(w-s)^{\alpha}) \\ &\quad \times [\mathfrak{A}\phi(0) + Kx(s-\tau)]ds - \int_{-h}^0 d\mathfrak{B}_\tau [\int_\tau^0 (w-(s-\tau))^{\alpha-1} E_{\alpha,\alpha} \\ &\quad \times \mathfrak{A}(w-(s-\tau))^{\alpha} \mathfrak{B}(s-\tau, \tau) u_0(s) ds]]. \end{aligned} \tag{13}$$

By substituting $t = w$ in (9) and installing the result in (13), similar reasoning gives $x(w) = x_w$. Hence, structure (1) is controllable on $[0, w]$.

Conversely, assume that $W[0, w]$ is singular, If $w \in (t_i, t_{i+1}), i = 1, 2, \ldots, k$, there is a vector $z_0 \neq 0$, such that $z_0^* W[0, w] z_0 = 0$. That is,

$$z_0^* \int_0^w G(w, s) G^*(W, s) z_0 ds = 0,$$
$$z_0^* G(w, s) = 0, \quad on [0, w].$$

Because structure (1) is controllable, there exist control inputs, $u_1(t)$ and $u_2(t)$, so that

$$\begin{aligned} x(w) &= \phi(0) + \sum_{j=1}^{i} I_j(x(t_j^-)) + \int_0^w (w-s)^{\alpha-1} E_{\alpha,\alpha}[\mathfrak{A}(w-s)^\alpha][\mathfrak{A}\phi(0) + Kx(s-\tau)]ds \\ &+ \int_{-h}^0 d\mathfrak{B}_\tau [\int_\tau^0 (w-(s-\tau))^{\alpha-1} E_{\alpha,\alpha}[\mathfrak{A}(w-(s-\tau))^\alpha]\mathfrak{B}(s-\tau,\tau) u_0(s) ds] \\ &+ \int_0^w [\int_{-h}^0 (w-(s-\tau))^{\alpha-1} E_{\alpha,\alpha}[\mathfrak{A}(w-(s-\tau))^\alpha] d_\tau \mathfrak{B}_w(s-\tau,\tau)) u_1(s) ds. \end{aligned} \tag{14}$$

$$\begin{aligned} z_0 &= \phi(0) + \sum_{j=1}^{i} I_j(x(t_j^-)) + \int_0^w (w-s)^{\alpha-1} E_{\alpha,\alpha}[\mathfrak{A}(w-s)^\alpha][\mathfrak{A}\phi(0) + Kx(s-\tau)]ds \\ &+ \int_{-h}^0 d\mathfrak{B}_\tau [\int_\tau^0 (w-(s-\tau))^{\alpha-1} E_{\alpha,\alpha}[\mathfrak{A}(w-(s-\tau))^\alpha]\mathfrak{B}(s-\tau,\tau) u_0(s) ds] \\ &+ \int_0^w [\int_{-h}^0 (w-(s-\tau))^{\alpha-1} E_{\alpha,\alpha}[\mathfrak{A}(w-(s-\tau))^\alpha] d_\tau \mathfrak{B}_w(s-\tau,\tau)) u_2(s) ds. \end{aligned} \tag{15}$$

By combining (14) and (15), we get

$$z_0 - \int_0^w [\int_{-h}^0 (w-(s-\tau))^{\alpha-1} E_{\alpha,\alpha}[\mathfrak{A}(w-(s-\tau))^\alpha] d_\tau \mathfrak{B}_w(s-\tau,\tau))(u_2(s)-u_1(s)) ds = 0. \tag{16}$$

By multiplying z_0^* on both sides of (16), we get

$$z_0^* z_0 - \int_0^w z_0^* G(w, s)[u_2(s) - u_1(s)] ds = 0.$$

According to $z_0^* G(w, s) = 0$, we have $z_0^* z_0 = 0$. Thus, $z_0 = 0$. This is a contradiction to $z_0 \neq 0$, hence the proof. □

Definition 4. *Systems (3) or (4) are said to be completely controllable on $[0, w](w \in [0, T])$; for any initial function, $\varphi \in C([-\tau, 0], \mathbb{R}^n)$, and any state, $x_w \in \mathbb{R}^n$, there exists a control input $u(t)$, so that the corresponding solutions of (3) or (4) satisfy $x(w) = x_w$.*

Theorem 2. *System (3) is completely controllable on $[0, w]$ if and only if W is nonsingular for some $w \in [0, T]$.*

Proof. Assume that W is nonsingular. Let $\phi(t)$ be continuous on $[-\tau, 0]$, and let $x_w \in \mathbb{R}^n$. The control function u can be taken as

$$\begin{aligned} u(t) &= G^*(w, t) W^{-1}[0, w][x_w - \phi(0) - \int_0^w (w-s)^{\alpha-1} E_{\alpha,\alpha}(\mathfrak{A}(w-s)^\alpha)[\mathfrak{A}\phi(0) + Kx(s-\tau)]ds \\ &- \int_{-h}^0 d\mathfrak{B}_\tau [\int_\tau^0 (w-(s-\tau))^{\alpha-1} E_{\alpha,\alpha} \mathfrak{A}(w-(s-\tau))^\alpha \mathfrak{B}(s-\tau,\tau) u_0(s) ds]], \end{aligned} \tag{17}$$

where

$$G(w, s) = \int_{-h}^0 (w-(s-\tau))^{\alpha-1} E_{\alpha,\alpha}[\mathfrak{A}(t-(s-\tau))^\alpha] d_\tau \mathfrak{B}_w(s-\tau,\tau).$$

By substituting $t = w$ in the solution of (7), we get

$$\begin{aligned}
x(w) &= \phi(0) + \int_0^w (w-s)^{\alpha-1} E_{\alpha,\alpha}(\mathfrak{A}(w-s)^\alpha)[\mathfrak{A}\phi(0) + Kx(s-\tau)]ds \\
&+ \int_{-h}^0 d\mathfrak{B}_\tau [\int_\tau^0 (w-(s-\tau))^{\alpha-1} E_{\alpha,\alpha}(A(w-(s-\tau))^\alpha) \mathfrak{B}(s-\tau,\tau)u_0(s)ds] \\
&+ \int_0^w [\int_{-h}^0 (w-(s-\tau))^{\alpha-1} E_{\alpha,\alpha}(\mathfrak{A}(w-(s-\tau))^\alpha) d_\tau \mathfrak{B}_w(s-\tau,\tau)]u(s)ds.
\end{aligned} \quad (18)$$

and, using (17) in (18), we have

$$\begin{aligned}
x(w) &= \phi(0) + \int_0^w (w-s)^{\alpha-1} E_{\alpha,\alpha}(\mathfrak{A}(w-s)^\alpha)[\mathfrak{A}\phi(0) + Kx(s-\tau)]ds \\
&+ \int_{-h}^0 d\mathfrak{B}_\tau [\int_\tau^0 (w-(s-\tau))^{\alpha-1} E_{\alpha,\alpha}(\mathfrak{A}(w-(s-\tau))^\alpha) \mathfrak{B}(s-\tau,\tau)u_0(s)ds] \\
&+ \int_0^w G(w,s) G^*(w,s) W^{-1}[0,w][x_w - \phi(0) - \int_0^w (w-s)^{\alpha-1} E_{\alpha,\alpha}(\mathfrak{A}(w-s)^\alpha) \\
&\times [\mathfrak{A}\phi(0) + Kx(s-\tau)]ds - \int_{-h}^0 d\mathfrak{B}_\tau [\int_\tau^0 (w-(s-\tau))^{\alpha-1} E_{\alpha,\alpha} \\
&\times \mathfrak{A}(w-(s-\tau))^\alpha \mathfrak{B}(s-\tau,\tau)u_0(s)ds]]d\tau.
\end{aligned}$$

$$x(w) = x_w.$$

Now, we assume that W is singular. There exists a non-zero, z, so that $z^* W z = 0$. That is, $Z^* \int_0^w G(w,s) G^*(w,s) z ds = 0$. $z^* G(w,s) = 0$ on $[0, w], w \in [0, T]$. Take $\phi = 0$ and the terminal point, $x_w = z$. Since the system is controllable, there exists a control, $u(t)$, on J that steers the response to $x_w = z$ at $t = w$, that is, $x(w) = z$. From $\phi = 0, x(w, \phi) = 0$, and $z^* z \neq 0$ for $z \neq 0$. On the other hand,

$$\begin{aligned}
z &= x(w) = \phi(0) + \int_0^w (w-s)^{\alpha-1} E_{\alpha,\alpha}(\mathfrak{A}(w-s)^\alpha)[\mathfrak{A}\phi(0) + Kx(s-\tau)]ds \\
&+ \int_{-h}^0 d\mathfrak{B}_\tau [\int_\tau^0 (w-(s-\tau))^{\alpha-1} E_{\alpha,\alpha}(\mathfrak{A}(w-(s-\tau))^\alpha) \mathfrak{B}(s-\tau,\tau)u_0(s)ds] \\
&+ \int_0^w [\int_{-h}^0 (w-(s-\tau))^{\alpha-1} E_{\alpha,\alpha}(\mathfrak{A}(w-(s-\tau))^\alpha) d_\tau \mathfrak{B}_w(s-\tau,\tau)]u(s)ds,
\end{aligned}$$

hence

$$\begin{aligned}
z^* z &= \int_0^w z^* G(w,s) u(s) ds + z^* \int_{-h}^0 d\mathfrak{B}_\tau [\int_\tau^0 (w-(s-\tau))^{\alpha-1} \\
&\times E_{\alpha,\alpha}(\mathfrak{A}(w-(s-\tau))^\alpha) \mathfrak{B}(s-\tau,\tau)u_0(s)ds].
\end{aligned}$$

Therefore, $z^* z = 0$, which yields a contradiction that $z \neq 0$. Hence, W is nonsingular, hence the proof. □

Theorem 3. *Let the continuous function, f, satisfy the condition $\lim |p| \to \infty \frac{|f(t,p)|}{|p|} = 0$ uniformly in $t \in J$, and suppose that the system, (3), is completely controllable on J. Then, the system (4) is completely controllable on J. Here $p = (x, z, u) \in \mathbb{R}^n \times \mathbb{R}^n \times \mathbb{R}^m$, and let $|p| = |x| + |z| + |u|$.*

Proof. Let $\phi(t)$ be continuous on $[-\tau, 0]$, and let $x_w \in \mathbb{R}^n$. Let Q be the Banach space of all the continuous functions $(x, u) : [-\tau, w] \times [-\tau, w] \to \mathbb{R}^n \times \mathbb{R}^m$, with the norm $\|(x, u)\| = \|x\| + \|u\|$, where $\|x(t)\| = \{\sup |x(t)| \text{ for } t \in [-\tau, w]\}$ and $\|u\| = \{\sup |u(t)| \text{ for } t \in [0, w]\}$. The operator $\Psi : Q \to Q$ is defined by $\Psi(x, u) = (z, v)$, where

$$v(t) = G^*(w,t)W^{-1}[0,w][x_w - \phi(0) - \int_0^w (w-s)^{\alpha-1} E_{\alpha,\alpha}(\mathfrak{A}(w-s)^\alpha)[\mathfrak{A}\phi(0) + Kx(s-\tau)]ds$$
$$- \int_{-h}^0 d\mathfrak{B}_\tau [\int_\tau^0 (w-(s-\tau))^{\alpha-1} E_{\alpha,\alpha} \mathfrak{A}(w-(s-\tau))^\alpha \mathfrak{B}(s-\tau,\tau) u_0(s) ds]].$$

$$z(t) = \phi(0) + \int_0^w (w-s)^{\alpha-1} E_{\alpha,\alpha}(\mathfrak{A}(w-s)^\alpha)[\mathfrak{A}\phi(0) + Kx(s-\tau)]ds$$
$$+ \int_{-h}^0 d\mathfrak{B}_\tau [\int_\tau^0 (w-(s-\tau))^{\alpha-1} E_{\alpha,\alpha}(\mathfrak{A}(w-(s-\tau))^\alpha) \mathfrak{B}(s-\tau,\tau) u_0(s) ds]$$
$$+ \int_0^w [\int_{-h}^0 (w-(s-\tau))^{\alpha-1} E_{\alpha,\alpha}(\mathfrak{A}(w-(s-\tau))^\alpha) d_\tau \mathfrak{B}_w(s-\tau,\tau)] u(s) ds,$$

for $t \in J$ and $z(t) = \phi(t), t \in [-\tau, 0]$. Let

$$a_1 = \sup \|\phi(0)\|, \quad a_2 = \sup \|Kx(s-\tau)\|,$$
$$a_3 = \sup \|E_{\alpha,\alpha}(\mathfrak{A}(w-s)^\alpha)\|, \quad a_4 = \sup \|E_{\alpha,\alpha}(\mathfrak{A}(w-(s-\tau))^\alpha)\|,$$
$$a_5 = \|\int_\tau^0 (w-(s-\tau))^{\alpha-1} E_{\alpha,\alpha} \mathfrak{A}(w-(s-\tau))^\alpha \mathfrak{B}(s-\tau,\tau) u_0(s) ds\|,$$
$$a_6 = \sup \|G^*(w,t)\|, \quad a_7 = W^{-1}[0,w],$$
$$a = \max\{a_4 w \|G(w,s)\|, 1\}, \quad d_1 = a_6 a_7 [|x_w + a_1 + a_5|], \quad d_2 = 8(a_1 + a_5),$$
$$c_1 = 8a_3 a_6 a_7 w^\alpha \alpha^{-1}(a_1 + a_2), \quad c_2 = 8a_3(a_1 + a_2) w^\alpha \alpha^{-1}$$

$$e_1 = 8a_3 a_6 a_7 w^\alpha \alpha^{-1}, \quad e_2 = 8a_3 w^\alpha \alpha^{-1},$$
$$c = \max\{c_1, c_2\}, \quad d = \max\{d_1, d_2\}, \quad e = \max\{e_1, e_2\},$$
$$\sup |f| = \sup s \in J\{|f(s, x(s), x(s-\tau), u(s))|\}.$$

Then,

$$|v(t)| \leq \|G^*(w,t)\| \|W^{-1}[0,w]\|[x_w + a_1 + a_5] + \|G^*(w,t)\| \|W^{-1}[0,w]\| a_3 w^\alpha \alpha^{-1}[a_1 + a_2]$$
$$+ \|G^*(w,t)\| \|W^{-1}[0,w]\| a_3 w^\alpha \alpha^{-1} \sup |f|.$$

$$|u(t)| \leq \frac{d_1}{8a} + \frac{c_1}{8a} + \frac{e_1}{8a} \sup |f|$$
$$\leq \frac{1}{8a}(d + c + e \sup |f|).$$

$$|z(t)| \leq (a_1 + a_5) + a_4 \int_0^t \|G(t,s)\| \|u(s)\| ds + a_3 \int_0^t (t-s)^{\alpha-1} \sup |f| ds$$
$$+ a_3 \int_0^t (t-s)^{\alpha-1}(a_1 + a_2) ds$$
$$\leq \frac{d}{8} + \frac{1}{8}[d + c + e \sup |f|] + \frac{e}{8} \sup |f|$$
$$\leq \frac{d}{4} + \frac{c}{8} + \frac{e}{4} \sup |f|.$$

We make the following assumption about the function f, as in [31]. Letting c and d be each pair of the positive constants, there exists a positive constant, r, so that, if $|(x, u)| \leq r$, then

$$c|f(t,p)| + d \leq r, \text{ for all } t \in J, \tag{19}$$

then, any r_1, as long as $r < r_1$, will also satisfy (19). Let r be chosen so that (19) is satisfied and $\sup_{-1 \leq t \leq 0} |\phi(t)| \leq \frac{r}{4}$. Therefore, if $\| x \| \leq \frac{r}{4}$ and $\| u \| \leq \frac{r}{4}$, then $|x(s)| + |x(s-h)| + |u(s)| \leq r, s \in J$. It follows that $d + c + e \sup |f| \leq r$, for $s \in J$. Therefore, $|v(t)| \leq \frac{r}{8a}$ for all $t \in J$ and, hence, $\| v(t) \| \leq \frac{r}{8a}$, we have $\| z \| \leq \frac{r}{4}$. Thus, if $Q(r) = \{(x, v) \in Q : \| x \| \leq \frac{r}{4}$ and $\| u \| \leq \frac{r}{4}\}$, then Ψ maps $Q(r)$ into itself. The operator Ψ is continuous since f is continuous. Let M_0 be a bounded subset of Q. Consider a sequence, (z_j, v_j), contained in $\Psi(M)$; let $(z_j, v_j) = \Psi(x_j, u_j)$, for some $(x_j, u_j) \in M_0$, for $j = 1, 2, \ldots$. Hence, $v_j(t)$ is an equicontinuous and uniformly bounded sequence on $[0, w]$. $\Psi(M_0)$ is sequentially compact; hence, the closure is sequentially compact. Thus, Ψ is completely continuous. Since $Q(r)$ is closed, bounded and convex, using the Schauder fixed-point theorem, Ψ has a fixed point $(x, u) \in Q(r)$, so that $(z, v) = \Psi(x, u) = (x, u)$. Therefore,

$$x(t) = \phi(0) + \int_0^t (t-s)^{\alpha-1} E_{\alpha,\alpha}(\mathfrak{A}(t-s)^\alpha)[\mathfrak{A}\phi(0) + Kx(s-\tau) + f(s, x(s), x(s-h), u(s))]ds$$
$$+ \int_{-h}^0 d\mathfrak{B}_\tau [\int_\tau^0 (t-(s-\tau))^{\alpha-1} E_{\alpha,\alpha}(\mathfrak{A}(t-(s-\tau))^\alpha) \mathfrak{B}(s-\tau,\tau) u_0(s) ds]$$
$$+ \int_0^t [\int_{-h}^0 (t-(s-\tau))^{\alpha-1} E_{\alpha,\alpha}(\mathfrak{A}(t-(s-\tau))^\alpha) d_\tau \mathfrak{B}_t(s-\tau,\tau) u(s) ds, \ t \in [0, T] = J,$$

where

$$\mathfrak{B}_t(s, \tau) = \begin{cases} \mathfrak{B}(s, \tau), & s \leq t, \\ 0, & s > t, \end{cases}$$

$$x(t) = \varphi(t), t \in [-\tau, 0].$$

Therefore, $x(t)$ is the solution to the system, and

$$x(w) = \phi(0) + \int_0^w (w-s)^{\alpha-1} E_{\alpha,\alpha}(\mathfrak{A}(w-s)^\alpha)[\mathfrak{A}\phi(0) + Kx(s-\tau)]ds$$
$$+ \int_{-h}^0 d\mathfrak{B}_\tau [\int_\tau^0 (w-(s-\tau))^{\alpha-1} E_{\alpha,\alpha}(\mathfrak{A}(w-(s-\tau))^\alpha) \mathfrak{B}(s-\tau,\tau) u_0(s) ds]$$
$$+ \int_0^w G(w,s) G^*(w,s) W^{-1}[0,w][x_w - \phi(0) - \int_0^w (w-s)^{\alpha-1}$$
$$\times E_{\alpha,\alpha}(\mathfrak{A}(w-s)^\alpha)[\mathfrak{A}\phi(0) + Kx(s-\tau)]ds - \int_{-h}^0 d\mathfrak{B}_\tau [\int_\tau^0 (w-(s-\tau))^{\alpha-1}$$
$$\times E_{\alpha,\alpha} \mathfrak{A}(w-(s-\tau))^\alpha \mathfrak{B}(s-\tau,\tau) u_0(s) ds]] d\tau.$$
$$x(w) = x_w.$$

Hence, the system (4) is completely controllable. □

4. Example

Consider the following linear fractional dynamical system:

$$^C D^{\frac{1}{2}} x_1(t) = x_2(t) + \int_{-1}^0 e^\tau [\sin t u_1(t+\tau) + \cos t u_2(t+\tau)] d\tau,$$
$$^C D^{\frac{1}{2}} x_2(t) = -x_1(t) + \int_{-1}^0 e^\tau [-\cos t u_1(t+\tau) + \sin t u_2(t+\tau)] d\tau,$$
$$x(t) = 1, \ -1 \leq t \leq 0, \tag{20}$$

for $t \in [0, 3]$ and $\alpha = \frac{1}{2}$. Here,

$$\mathfrak{A} = \begin{pmatrix} 0 & 1 \\ -1 & 0 \end{pmatrix}, \mathfrak{B}(t, \tau) = \begin{pmatrix} e^\tau \sin t & e^\tau \cos t \\ -e^\tau \cos t & e^\tau \sin t \end{pmatrix}, x(t) = \begin{pmatrix} x_1(t) \\ x_2(t) \end{pmatrix}$$

and

$$E_{\frac{1}{2}}(\mathfrak{A}t^{\frac{1}{2}}) = \begin{pmatrix} \sum_{j=0}^{\infty} \frac{(-1)^j t^j}{\Gamma(1+j)} & \sum_{j=0}^{\infty} \frac{(-1)^j t^{(2j+1)/2}}{\Gamma(1+(2j+1)/2)} \\ \sum_{j=0}^{\infty} \frac{(-1)^j t^{(2j+1)/2}}{\Gamma(1+(2j+1)/2)} & \sum_{j=0}^{\infty} \frac{(-1)^j t^j}{\Gamma(1+j)} \end{pmatrix}.$$

Further,

$$E_{\frac{1}{2},\frac{1}{2}}(\mathfrak{A}(3-(s-\tau))^{\frac{1}{2}}) = \begin{pmatrix} \sum_{j=0}^{\infty} \frac{(-1)^j (3-(s-\tau))^j}{\Gamma(1+j)} & \sum_{j=0}^{\infty} \frac{(-1)^j (3-(s-\tau))^{(2j+1)/2}}{\Gamma[1+(2j+1)/2]} \\ -\sum_{j=0}^{\infty} \frac{(-1)^j (3-(s-\tau))^{(2j+1)/2}}{\Gamma[1+(2j+1)/2]} & \sum_{j=0}^{\infty} \frac{(-1)^j (3-(s-\tau))^j}{\Gamma(1+j)} \end{pmatrix}$$

and

$$(3-(s-\tau))^{-\frac{1}{2}} E_{\frac{1}{2},\frac{1}{2}}(\mathfrak{A}(3-(s-\tau))^{\frac{1}{2}}) = \begin{pmatrix} \sin_{\frac{1}{2}}(t) & \cos_{\frac{1}{2}}(t) \\ -\cos_{\frac{1}{2}}(t) & \sin_{\frac{1}{2}}(t) \end{pmatrix},$$

where

$$\cos_{\frac{1}{2}}(t) = \sum_{j=0}^{\infty} \frac{(-1)^j (3-(s-\tau))^{-(2j+1)/2}}{\Gamma[(2j+1)/2]},$$

$$\sin_{\frac{1}{2}}(t) = \sum_{j=0}^{\infty} \frac{(-1)^j (3-(s-\tau))^{(j+1)-1}}{\Gamma(j+1)}.$$

Also,

$$G(3,s) = \int_{-1}^{0} (3-(s-\tau))^{-\frac{1}{2}} E_{\frac{1}{2},\frac{1}{2}}(\mathfrak{A}(3-(s-\tau))^{\frac{1}{2}}) d\tau \mathfrak{B}_3(s-\tau,\tau)$$

$$= \begin{pmatrix} p(s) & q(s) \\ -q(s) & p(s) \end{pmatrix},$$

such that,

$$p(s) = \int_{-1}^{0} e^{\tau}[\sin_{\alpha}(3-(s-\tau))\sin(s-\tau) - \cos_{\frac{1}{2}}(3-(s-\tau))\cos(s-\tau)]d\tau,$$

$$q(s) = \int_{-1}^{0} e^{\tau}[\cos_{\frac{1}{2}}(3-(s-\tau))\sin(s-\tau) - \sin_{\frac{1}{2}}(3-(s-\tau))\cos(s-\tau)]d\tau.$$

Using matrix calculation,

$$W(0,3) = \int_{0}^{3} G(3,s) G^*(3,s) ds$$

$$= \int_{0}^{3} [p^2(s) + q^2(s)] \begin{pmatrix} 1 & 0 \\ 0 & 1 \end{pmatrix} ds$$

$$= \begin{pmatrix} 84.6306 & 40.9686 \\ 200.6702 & 84.6306 \end{pmatrix},$$

$$W^{-1}(0,3) = \begin{pmatrix} -0.0799 & 0.0387 \\ 0.1895 & -0.0799 \end{pmatrix}.$$

Hence, by Theorem 2, the fractional system (20) is completely controllable on $[0,3]$. Based on our chosen values, we have drawn diagrams for the state function with control Figure 1, the state function without control Figure 2 and the steering control function Figure 3 respectively.

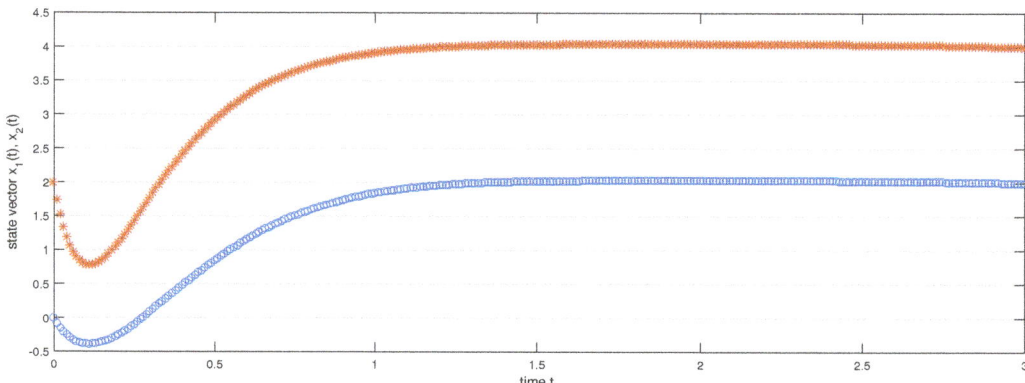

Figure 1. State with control function steers initial state $x(0) = (0, 2)^T$ to final state $x(2) = (2, 4)^T$.

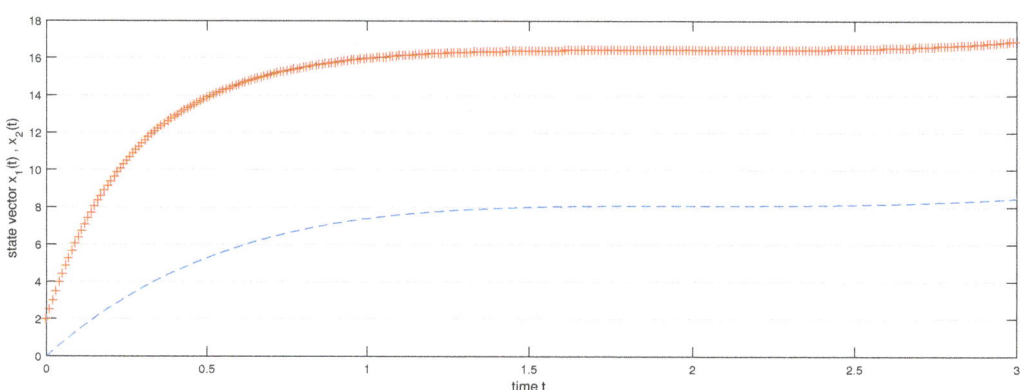

Figure 2. State vectors without control function.

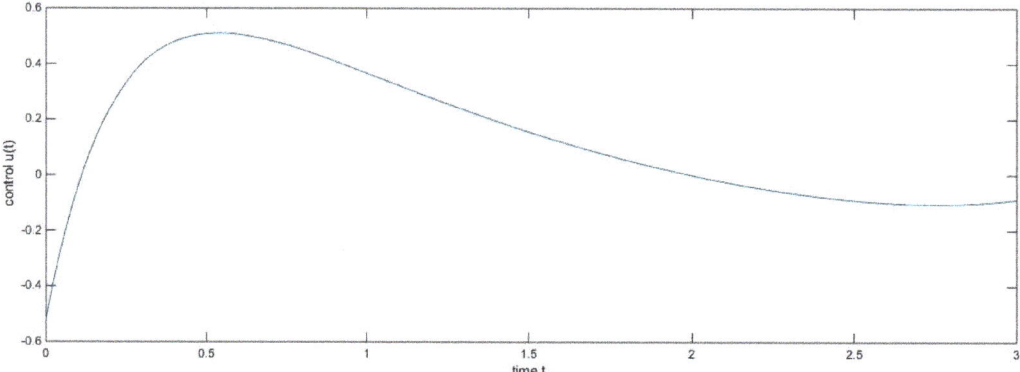

Figure 3. The steering control function.

Remark 1. Consider the following nonlinear impulsive fractional dynamical system

$$
\begin{aligned}
{}^C D^{\frac{2}{3}} x_1(t) &= x_2(t) + \int_{-1}^{0} e^{\tau}[\sin t u_1(t+\tau) + \cos t u_2(t+\tau)]d\tau + \frac{10 x_1(t)}{1 + x_1^2(t) + x_2^2(t)}, \\
{}^C D^{\frac{2}{3}} x_2(t) &= -x_1(t) + \int_{-1}^{0} e^{\tau}[-\cos t u_1(t+\tau) + \sin t u_2(t+\tau)]d\tau + \frac{x_2(t)}{1 + x_1^2(t) + t}, \\
\Delta x|_{t=\frac{1}{2}} &= \frac{|x(\frac{1}{2}^{-})|}{8 + |x(\frac{1}{2}^{-})|}, \\
x(t) &= 1, \quad -1 \le t \le 0.
\end{aligned} \quad (21)
$$

Under appropriate choices and by following the previous techniques, Theorem 3 can be applied to guarantee the controllability result of the fractional system (21), and hence the diagrams can be also associated.

5. Conclusions

We investigated the concept of controllability criteria for nonlinear fractional differential systems with state delays and distributed delays in the controls with impulsive perturbations. We used the unsymmetric Fubini's theorem with the change of order of integration, and also, by effecting the notion of Mittag–Leffler's matrix function, we find the solution representation for the considered system. Further, by applying the controllability Gramian matrix, we studied the controllability results for the system addressed in the preliminary section. Moreover, we have given a numerical example that justifies the exactness of the obtained theoretical results in our main results. As further directions to be considered in our future projects, we intend to combine the above analysis with the topics of differential inclusion, fractional discreet calculus and variable order derivatives.

Author Contributions: Conceptualization, B.S.V.; methodology, B.S.V.; validation, A.D. and V.E.F.; formal analysis, V.A.; investigation, A.D. and V.E.F.; writing–original draft preparation, B.S.V.; writing–review and editing, A.D. and V.A.; supervision, A.D.; project administration, V.A. All authors have read and agreed to the published version of the manuscript.

Funding: The second author was supported by RUSA-Phase 2.0 grant sanctioned vide letter No.F 24-51/2014-U, Policy (TN Multi-Gen), Dept. of Edn. Govt. of India, Dt.09.10.2018; and the third author was supported by the Russian Science Foundation, project number 22-21-20095.

Conflicts of Interest: The authors declare no conflict of interest.

References

1. Jahanshahi, H.; Munoz-Pacheco, J.M.; Bekiros, S.; Alotaibi, N.D. A fractional-order SIRD model with time-dependent memory indexes for encompassing the multi-fractional characteristics of the COVID-19. *Chaos Solitons Fractals* **2021**, *143*, 110632. [CrossRef] [PubMed]
2. Hendy, A.S.; Taha, T.R.; Suragan, D.; Zaky, M.A. An energy-preserving computational approach for the semilinear space fractional damped Klein–Gordon equation with a generalized scalar potential. *Appl. Math. Model.* **2022**, *108*, 512–530. [CrossRef]
3. Jumarie, J. An approach via fractional analysis to non-linearity induced by coarse-graining in space. *Nonlinear Anal. Real World Appl.* **2010**, *11*, 535–546. [CrossRef]
4. Rehman, A.U.; Riaz, M.B.; Rehman, W.; Awrejcewicz, J.; Baleanu, D. Fractional Modeling of Viscous Fluid over a Moveable Inclined Plate Subject to Exponential Heating with Singular and Non-Singular Kernels. *Math. Comput. Appl.* **2022**, *27*, 8. [CrossRef]
5. Luchko, Y.F; Rivero, M.; Trujillo, J.J.; Velasco, M.P. Fractional models, non-locality, and complex systems. *Comput. Math. Appl.* **2010**, *59*, 1048–1056. [CrossRef]
6. Manimaran, J.; Shangerganesh, L.; Debbouche, A.; Cortés, J.C. A time-fractional HIV infection model with nonlinear diffusion. *Results Phys.* **2021**, *25*, 104293. [CrossRef]
7. Guo, T.L.; Jiang, W. Impulsive fractional functional differential equations. *Comput. Math. Appl.* **2012**, *64*, 3414–3424. [CrossRef]
8. Sivasankar, S.; Udhayakumar, R.; Subramanian, V.; AlNemer, G.; Elshenhab, A.M. Existence of Hilfer Fractional Stochastic Differential Equations with Nonlocal Conditions and Delay via Almost Sectorial Operators. *Mathematics* **2022**, *10*, 4392. [CrossRef]
9. Fang, H.; Song, M. Existence results for fractional order impulsive functional differential equations with multiple delays. *Adv. Differ. Equ.* **2018**, *2018*, 139. [CrossRef]

10. Al-Sawalha, M.M.; Ababneh, O.Y.; Shah, R.; Khan, A.; Nonlaopon, K. Numerical analysis of fractional-order Whitham–Broer–Kaup equations with non-singular kernel operators. *AIMS Math.* **2023**, *8*, 2308–2336. [CrossRef]
11. Al-Sawalha, M.M.; Shah, R.; Nonlaopon, K.; Khan, I.; Ababneh, O.Y. Fractional evaluation of Kaup–Kupershmidt equation with the exponential-decay kernel. *AIMS Math.* **2023**, *8*, 3730–3746. [CrossRef]
12. Gafiychuk, V.; Datsun, B.; Meleshko, V. Mathematical modelling of time fractional reaction-diffusion systems. *J. Comput. Appl. Math.* **2008**, *220*, 215–225. [CrossRef]
13. Udhayakumar, K.; Rihan, F.A.; Rakkiyappan, R.; Cao, J. Fractional-order discontinuous systems with indefinite LKFs: An application to fractional-order neural networks with time delays. *Neural Netw.* **2022**, *145*, 319–330. [CrossRef]
14. Kumar, P.; Erturk, V.S.; Murillo-Arcila, M. A new fractional mathematical modelling of COVID-19 with the availability of vaccine. *Results Phys.* **2021**, *24*, 104213. [CrossRef] [PubMed]
15. Metzler, R.; Klafter, J. The restaurant at the end of the random walk: Recent developments in the description of anomalous transport by fractional dynamics. *J. Phys. A Math. Gen.* **2004**, *37*, 161–208. [CrossRef]
16. Kilbas, A.A.; Srivastava, H.M.; Trujillo, J.J. *Theory and Applications of Fractional Differential Equations*; North-Holland Mathematics Studies 204; Elsevier Science B.V.: Amsterdam, The Netherlands, 2006.
17. Miller, K.S.; Ross, B. *An Introduction to the Fractional Calculus and Fractional Differential Equations*; Wiley: New York, NY, USA, 1993.
18. Podlubny, I. *Fractional Differential Equations, Volume 198 of Mathematics in Science and Engineering*; Technical University of Kosice: Kosice, Slovak Republic, 1999.
19. Artstein, Z. Linear systems with delayed controls: A reduction. *IEEE Trans. Autom. Control.* **1982**, *27*, 869–879. [CrossRef]
20. Artstein, Z.; Tadmor, G. Linear systems with indirect controls: The underlying measures. *SIAM J. Control. Optim.* **1982**, *20*, 96–111. [CrossRef]
21. Balachandran, K.; Dauer, J.P. Controllability of nonlinear systems via fixed point theorems. *J. Optim. Theory Appl.* **1987**, *53*, 345–352. [CrossRef]
22. Balachandran, K.; Zhou, Y.; Kokila, J. Relative controllability of fractional dynamical systems with distributed delays in control. *Comput. Math. Appl.* **2012**, *64*, 3201–3209. [CrossRef]
23. Kumar, V.; Malik, M.; Debbouche, A. Stability and controllability analysis of fractional damped differential system with non-instantaneous impulses. *Appl. Math. Comput.* **2021**, *391*, 125633. [CrossRef]
24. Zhang, H.; Cao, J.; Jiang, W. Controllability criteria for linear fractional differential systems with state delay and impulses. *J. Appl. Math.* **2013**, *2013*, 146010. [CrossRef]
25. Vadivoo, B.S.; Jothilakshmi, G.; Almalki, Y.; Debbouche, A.; Lavanya, M. Relative controllability analysis of fractional order differential equations with multiple time delays. *Appl. Math. Comput.* **2022**, *28*, 127192. [CrossRef]
26. He, B.B.; Zhou, H.C.; Kou, C.H. The controllability of fractional damped dynamical systems with control delay. *Commun. Nonlinear Sci. Numer. Simul.* **2016**, *32*, 190–198. [CrossRef]
27. Guo, T.L. Controllability and observability of impulsive fractional linear time-invariant system. *Comput. Math. Appl.* **2012**, *64*, 3171–3182. [CrossRef]
28. Jiang, W.; Song, W.Z. Controllability of singular systems with control delay. *Automatica* **2001**, *37*, 1873–1877.
29. Wei, J. The controllability of fractional control systems with control delay. *Comput. Math. Appl.* **2012**, *64*, 3153–3159. [CrossRef]
30. Cameron, R.H.; Martin, W.T. An unsymmetric Fubini theorem. *Bull. Am. Math. Lett.* **2011**, *24*, 2019–2023. [CrossRef]
31. Dauer, J.P. Nonlinear perturbations of quasi-linear control systems. *J. Math. Anal. Appl.* **1976**, *54*, 717–725. [CrossRef]

Disclaimer/Publisher's Note: The statements, opinions and data contained in all publications are solely those of the individual author(s) and contributor(s) and not of MDPI and/or the editor(s). MDPI and/or the editor(s) disclaim responsibility for any injury to people or property resulting from any ideas, methods, instructions or products referred to in the content.

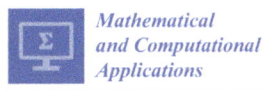

Article

Numerical Computation of Ag/Al₂O₃ Nanofluid over a Riga Plate with Heat Sink/Source and Non-Fourier Heat Flux Model

S. Divya [1], S. Eswaramoorthi [1,*] and Karuppusamy Loganathan [2,*]

[1] Department of Mathematics, Dr. N.G.P. Arts and Science College, Coimbatore 641035, Tamil Nadu, India
[2] Department of Mathematics and Statistics, Manipal University Jaipur, Jaipur 303007, Rajasthan, India
* Correspondence: eswaran.bharathiar@gmail.com (S.E.); loganathankaruppusamy304@gmail.com (K.L.)

Abstract: The main goal of the current research is to investigate the numerical computation of Ag/Al₂O₃ nanofluid over a Riga plate with injection/suction. The energy equation is formulated using the Cattaneo–Christov heat flux, non-linear thermal radiation, and heat sink/source. The leading equations are non-dimensionalized by employing the suitable transformations, and the numerical results are achieved by using the MATLAB bvp4c technique. The fluctuations of fluid flow and heat transfer on porosity, Forchheimer number, radiation, suction/injection, velocity slip, and nanoparticle volume fraction are investigated. Furthermore, the local skin friction coefficient (SFC), and local Nusselt number (LNN) are also addressed. Compared to previously reported studies, our computational results exactly coincided with the outcomes of the previous reports. We noticed that the Forchheimer number, suction/injection, slip, and nanoparticle volume fraction factors slow the velocity profile. We also noted that with improving rates of thermal radiation and convective heating, the heat transfer gradient decreases. The 40% presence of the Hartmann number leads to improved drag force by 14% and heat transfer gradient by 0.5%. The 20% presence of nanoparticle volume fraction leads to a decrement in heat transfer gradient for 21% of Ag nanoparticles and 18% of Al₂O₃ nanoparticles.

Keywords: nanofluid; riga plate; heat source/sink; non-linear thermal radiation; Cattaneo–Christov heat flux

Citation: Divya, S.; Eswaramoorthi, S.; Loganathan, K. Numerical Computation of Ag/Al₂O₃ Nanofluid over a Riga Plate with Heat Sink/Source and Non-Fourier Heat Flux Model. *Math. Comput. Appl.* **2023**, *28*, 20. https://doi.org/10.3390/mca28010020

Academic Editors: Mehmet Yavuz and Ioannis Dassios

Received: 21 December 2022
Revised: 29 January 2023
Accepted: 1 February 2023
Published: 3 February 2023

Copyright: © 2023 by the authors. Licensee MDPI, Basel, Switzerland. This article is an open access article distributed under the terms and conditions of the Creative Commons Attribution (CC BY) license (https://creativecommons.org/licenses/by/4.0/).

1. Introduction

The importance of nanofluids has piqued the interest of many industrial researchers. Nanofluid combines base fluids and nanoparticles (1–100 nm). Nanoparticles typically have better thermal distribution properties than convectional heat distribution liquids. Various researchers have been drawn to nanofluid in the last decade, with Choi and Eastman [1] being the first person to come up with the word nanofluid. Martin et al. [2] combined and analyzed a porous medium with nanofluids to increase heat transmission around a vertical finned cylindrical antenna. They detected that the nanoparticle volume fraction is enhanced when mounting the porosity parameter. Uddin et al. [3] examined a single-phase CuO–water nanofluid flow through an isosceles triangular geometry. They observed that the heat transmission is enhanced when the nanoparticle volume fraction increases. The copper-water nanofluid flow over a rotating disk was examined by Nayak et al. [4]. The heat transfer analysis of a nanofluid on a non-linearly stretching plate was scrutinized by Adem and Kishan [5]. The consequences of surface waves on heat transmission and flow were studied by Uddin et al. [6]. They observed that the nanofluids with a lower nanoparticle volume fraction have higher flow configurations. Verma et al. [7] investigated the copper-water nanofluid over a porous medium. They found that the velocity declines when enriching the nanoparticle volume fraction. The MHD flow of a Casson–Williamson nanofluid over a porous medium was examined by Yousef et al. [8]. Mohamed et al. [9] scrutinized the heat transfer flow of Ag–Al₂O₃/water-hybrid nanofluid over a stretching sheet. They found that the SFC increased due to a rise in the nanoparticle volume fraction.

Shahzad et al. [10] investigated the heat transfer of copper-nanofluid slip flow over a convective heated sheet. They noted that the SFC decreases when increasing the volume fraction parameter.

The Riga plate plays a vital role in enhancing the electrical conductivity. This plate consists of electrodes and magnets that are arranged alternatively. Gailitis and Lielausis [11] were the first to commence the Riga plate, which generates a Lorentz force parallel to the flow-controlling wall. The mixed convective flow of nanofluid flow on a Riga plate was initiated by Vaidya et al. [12]. They revealed that the warmness of the fluid downturns when improving the modified Hartmann number. Shah et al. [13] inspected the flow of Maxwell fluid through a Riga plate with the generalized Fourier's law. Rizwana and Nadeem [14] analyzed the unsteady MHD flow of copper-water nanofluid past a Riga plate. They found that the MBL thickens when escalating the modified Hartmann number. The Maxwell fluid flow passing through a Riga plate was analyzed by Ramesh et al. [15]. Abbas et al. [16] scrutinized the nanofluid flow over a Riga plate with entropy generation. The hyperbolic nanofluid flow over a Riga plate was numerically studied by Waqas et al. [17]. Eswaramoorthi et al. [18] implemented the double stratification of a Darcy–Forchheimer flow over a Riga plate. They revealed that increasing the modified Hartmann number causes a significant increase in wall shear stress. The microorganisms swimming in the Sutterby nanofluid, passed through a Riga plate, was inspected by Faizan et al. [19]. They proved that the fluid speed is able to enhance the modified Hartmann number. Karthik et al. [20] explored the swimming microorganisms of zero and non-zero mass flux over a Riga plate. They revealed that the fluid speed declines when it strengthens the modified Hartmann number. Parvine and Alam [21] examined the MHD nanofluid flows across a Riga plate. Computational study of a micropolar nanofluid moving in a stratified pattern over a Riga plate was investigated by Rafique et al. [22].

Generally, two types of internal heat generation/consumption occur. The first type of internal heat sink/source depends on the warmth of the fluid. The second type is a non-uniform heat sink/source that depends on warmth and space. Recently, many researchers have been working on heat sinks and sources. An even more intriguing debate on the effects of a non-uniform heat sink/source was dealt with by Madhukesh et al. [23]. It is found that the warmness of the fluid increases when raising the heat sink/source parameter. Oke et al. [24] identified the water nanoparticles of 47-nm alumina over a heat sink/source. They proved that the LNN is proportional when the heat transfer rate amplifies. The heat sink/source of Jeffrey fluid over a heat and mass transfer was scrutinized by Qasim [25]. He identified that when the heat sink parameter is raised, the temperature drops. The effects of Darcy–Forchheimer flow in an unsteady MHD viscous fluid over a non-uniform heat sink/source was investigated by Sharma and Gandhi [26]. Vieru et al. [27] explored the impact of unsteady flow of viscous fluid with a heat sink/source. The non-uniform heat sink/source of Jeffry and Maxwell nanofluid using a stretching sheet was investigated by Sandeep and Sulochana [28]. They discovered that the thermal boundary layer thickness increases as the values of the non-uniform heat source or sink parameters are increased. Jena et al. [29] inspected the movement of a fluid with a high viscosity past a heat sink/source. The MHD-mixed convective flow of micropolar fluid past an SS with a non-uniform heat sink/source was studied by Sandeep and Sulochana [30]. Reddy and Rao [31] scrutinized the chemical reaction in the heat and mass transfer of nanofluids containing Al_2O_3-water and Ag-water through a vertical cone. They revealed that heat source/sink characteristics lead to improving the temperature profile. A few key researches on this perception have been gathered in Refs. ([32,33]).

Thermally radiative flow is typically encountered when there is a significant warmth difference between the free stream and the surface, and it is important in many industrial processes. Most of the research is based on the Rosseland approximation with linearization, however, this concept is most useful when the warmness difference between ambient and liquid is minuscule, and this difference is typically very significant in many industrial situations. A non-linearized Rosseland approximation is applicable for overcoming this constraint. Rashidi et al. [34] analyzed the buoyancy effect of MHD nanofluid flow with thermal radiation. They noted that the magnetic and radiation parameters affect the skin friction coefficient. The radiative nanofluid flow over an SS with convective boundary conditions was investigated by Kameswaran et al. [35]. Maleki et al. [36] investigated the radiation impact of a nanofluid flow over a porous plate. They noticed that the local Nusselt number declines when the radiation parameter is increased. The 3D radiative flow of carbon nanotubes in glycerin flown past a Riga plate was addressed by Eswaramoorthi et al. [37]. They proved that increasing the radiation parameter develops the entropy profile. The effect of thermal radiation of a Walters'-B nanofluid was depicted by Mahat et al. [38]. They proved that the temperature of the fluid upgrades to strengthen the thermal radiation. Mahanthesh et al. [39] examined the boundary layer flow of a melting plate with non-linear thermal radiation. The Darcy–Forchheimer flow of an Eyring–Powell nanofluid with non-linear thermal radiation was explored by Bhatti et al. [40]. The thermally radiative flow of Casson–Williamson nanofluid with binary chemical reaction was investigated by Eswaramoorthi et al. [41]. They noticed that when the radiation parameter is increased, the heat transfer gradient rises. Mahanta et al. [42] analyzed the 3D MHD nanofluid flow passing through an SS with non-linear radiation. They identified that the higher thermal radiation parameter leads to develop the Bejan number. The influence of radiation on a magnetohydrodynamic (MHD) three-dimensional stagnation-point flow of a graphene oxide nanofluid based on water and produced by a non-uniform heat source/sink over a horizontal plane surface was investigated by Waqas et al. [43]. They noticed that the temperature profile increased as the radiation parameter increased. A few cutting-edge research reports have have been gathered in Refs. ([44–46]).

According to study findings in the literature, as mentioned above, the majority of the researchers are working to discover the nature of the radiative flow of nanofluid with non-uniform heat sink/source and Cattaneo–Christov heat flux past an SS but have yet to be analyzed through a Riga plate with velocity slip. As a result, our primary objective is to fill this knowledge gap. Our research describes the consequence of non-linear thermal radiation, non-uniform heat sink/source, and Cattaneo–Christov of Darcy–Forchheimer flow of water-based (Ag and Al_2O_3) nanoparticles past a Riga plate with a slip condition, because the upshot of slip is more crucial when the particles' mean free path is tantamount or smaller than the problem's usual structure. In these situations, the continuance flow presumptions are limited. In such places, the slip boundary presumptions act a vital role in restraining the flow attributes (e.g., see Aldabesh et al. [47]). The primary goal of utilizing nanoparticles, such as Ag and Al_2O_3, is as nanofluid coolant for contemporary engines. This work will be useful for thermal engineers in developing models of thermal systems. The key takeaways of this study can be summed up as follows:

1. Modify the current mathematical model to include nanofluids based on Ag/Al_2O_3-water, Cattaneo–Christov heat flux, non-linear thermal radiation, and heat source/sink.
2. In what ways does it affect Darcy–Forchheimer flow on a Riga plate?
3. Exactly how do the Cattaneo–Christov heat flux phenomenon and non-linear thermal radiation influence heat transfer?
4. When convective heating conditions are applied, how does the heat transfer gradient respond?

2. Mathematical Formulation

We explored the 2D Darcy–Forchheimer flow of water-based Ag/Al_2O_3 nanoparticles past a heated Riga plate. We consider that the x-axis should be aligned in the same direction as the plate, but the y-axis should be perpendicular to it. The heat equation is constructed by non-linear thermal radiation, Cattaneo–Christov theory and a non-uniform heat sink/source. Let T_w and $T_\infty (\leq T_w)$ be the fluid temperature and free stream temperature, respectively. The bottom of the plate was heated by passing hot fluid with temperature T_f and this generate a heat transfer coefficient h_c. The sketch of the Riga plate and the flow model are shown in Figure 1a,b. The equations of mass, momentum, and energy with their associated constraints are shown below (e.g., Kameswaran et al. [35], Maleki et al. [36]).

$$\frac{\partial u}{\partial x} + \frac{\partial v}{\partial y} = 0, \tag{1}$$

$$u\frac{\partial u}{\partial x} + v\frac{\partial u}{\partial y} = \nu_{nf}\frac{\partial^2 u}{\partial y^2} - \frac{\nu_{nf}}{k_1^*}u - \frac{c_b}{\sqrt{k^*}}u^2 + \frac{\pi J_0 M}{8\rho_{nf}}Exp\left[-\frac{\pi}{a_1}y\right], \tag{2}$$

$$u\frac{\partial T}{\partial x} + v\frac{\partial T}{\partial y} = \frac{k_{nf}}{(\rho c_p)_{nf}}\frac{\partial^2 T}{\partial y^2} + \frac{16\sigma^*}{3k^*(\rho C_p)_{nf}}\frac{\partial}{\partial y}\left(T^3\frac{\partial T}{\partial y}\right) - \lambda\left[u^2\frac{\partial^2 T}{\partial x^2}\right.$$

$$+ v^2\frac{\partial^2 T}{\partial y^2} + 2uv\frac{\partial^2 T}{\partial x\partial y} + \left(u\frac{\partial u}{\partial x} + v\frac{\partial u}{\partial y}\right)\frac{\partial T}{\partial x} + \left(u\frac{\partial v}{\partial x} + v\frac{\partial v}{\partial y}\right)\frac{\partial T}{\partial y}\right]$$

$$+ \frac{1}{(\rho c_p)_{nf}}\frac{k_{nf}U_w}{x\nu_{nf}}[A^*(T_f - T_\infty)f' + B^*(T - T_\infty)]. \tag{3}$$

The corresponding boundary conditions, see Mahmood et al. [48] and Hayat et al. [49]:

$$u = U_w + \mu_{nf}\frac{\partial u}{\partial y}, \quad v = -V_w, \quad -k_{nf}T_y = h_c[T_f - T] \text{ at } y = 0$$

$$u \to 0, v \to 0, T \to T_\infty \text{ as } y \to \infty \tag{4}$$

In order to solve the governing system of PDEs (1)–(4), stream function ψ is introduced, as seen in Afify [50].

$$\psi = (a\nu_f)^{\frac{1}{2}}xf(\varsigma), \quad u = \frac{\partial \psi}{\partial y}, \quad v = -\frac{\partial \psi}{\partial x}. \tag{5}$$

Define the variables,

$$\varsigma = \sqrt{\frac{a}{\nu_f}}y, \quad u = axf'(\varsigma), \quad v = -\sqrt{a\nu_f}f(\varsigma), \quad \theta = \frac{T - T_\infty}{T_f - T_\infty}. \tag{6}$$

Considering the aforementioned changes, Equations (2) and (3) are written as follows:

$$\frac{1}{A_1A_2}f'''(\varsigma) + f(\varsigma)f''(\varsigma) - f'^2(\varsigma) - \frac{1}{A_1A_2}\lambda f'(\varsigma) - Frf'^2(\varsigma) + \frac{1}{A_2}HaExp[-\beta_R\varsigma] = 0, \tag{7}$$

$$f(\varsigma)\theta'(\varsigma) + \left[\frac{A_5}{A_3}\frac{1}{Pr}\right]\theta''(\varsigma) + \frac{A_1A_2A_5}{A_3}\frac{1}{Pr}[A^*f'(\varsigma) + B^*\theta(\varsigma)] - \Gamma_1\{f^2(\varsigma)\theta''(\varsigma)$$

$$+ f(\varsigma)f'(\varsigma)\theta'(\varsigma)\} + \frac{1}{Pr}\frac{1}{A_3}\frac{4}{3}Rd\left[(\theta_w - 1)^3\{3\theta^2(\varsigma)\theta'^2(\varsigma) + \theta^3(\varsigma)\theta''(\varsigma)\} + (\theta_w - 1)^2\right.$$

$$\{6\theta(\varsigma)\theta'^2(\varsigma) + 3\theta^2(\varsigma)\theta''(\varsigma)\} + (\theta_w - 1)\{3\theta'^2(\varsigma) + 3\theta(\varsigma)\theta''(\varsigma)\} + \theta''(\varsigma)\right] = 0. \tag{8}$$

The appropriate boundary conditions (4) are remodeled as follows,

$$f(0) = fw, \quad f'(0) = 1 + \frac{\Lambda}{A_1}f''(0), \quad f'(\infty) = 0,$$

$$\theta'(0) = -\frac{Bi}{A_5}[1 - \theta(0)], \quad \theta(\infty) = 0. \tag{9}$$

The skin friction coefficient and local Nusselt number can be expressed as follows,

$$C_f \sqrt{Re} = \frac{1}{A_1} f''(0),$$
$$\frac{Nu}{\sqrt{Re}} = -\left[A_5 + \frac{4}{3} Rd \{1 + \theta(0)(\theta_w - 1)\}^3\right] \theta'(0)$$

The nomenclature section specifies all the variables involved in the flow.

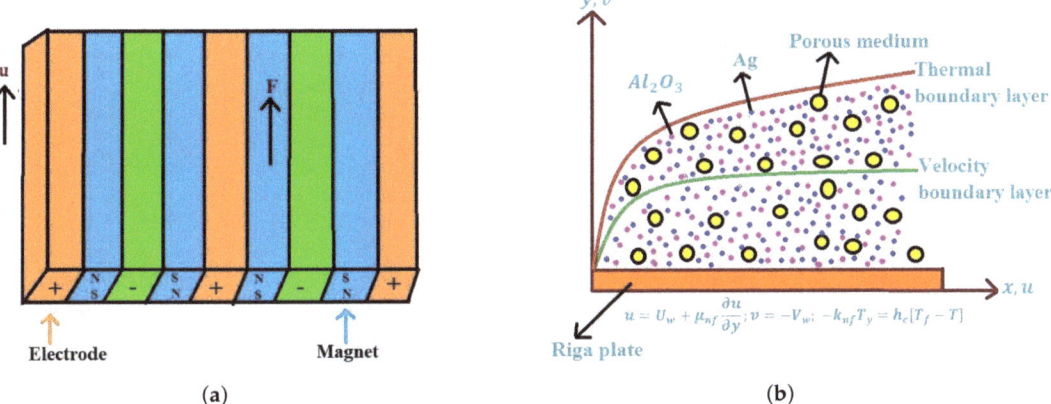

Figure 1. (**a**) Sketch of a Riga plate and (**b**) physical configuration of the flow model.

3. Numerical Solution

The MATLAB bvp4c technique is used to solve the remodeled ODEs (Equations (7) and (8)) and corresponding boundary conditions (9). In this case, the coupled non-linear PDEs and the boundary conditions can be transformed into five equivalent first-order ODEs and boundary conditions, respectively, see Asshaari et al. [51] and Shampine et al. [52]. To carry out this procedure, we must do the following:

$$f = K_1,\ f' = K_2,\ f'' = K_3,\ \theta = K_4,\ \theta' = K_5$$

The system of equations are

$$K_1' = K_2$$
$$K_2' = K_3$$
$$K_3' = A_1 A_2 \left[K_2^2 - K_1 K_3 + \frac{1}{A_1 A_2} \lambda K_2 + Fr K_2^2 - \frac{1}{A_2} Ha Exp[-\beta_R \varsigma]\right]$$
$$K_4' = K_5$$
$$K_5' = \frac{B_1}{B_2}$$

where

$$B_1 = -K_1 K_5 - \frac{A_1 A_2 A_5}{A_3} \frac{1}{Pr} [A^* K_2 + B^* K_4] + \Gamma_1 \{K_1 K_2 K_5\}$$
$$- \frac{1}{Pr} \frac{1}{A_3} \frac{4}{3} Rd \left[(\theta_w - 1)^3 \{3K_4^2 K_5^2\} + (\theta_w - 1)^2 \{6K_4 K_5^2\} + (\theta_w - 1)\{3K_5^2\}\right]$$
$$B_2 = \frac{A_5}{A_3 Pr} - \Gamma_1 (K_2^2) + \frac{1}{Pr} \frac{1}{A_3} \frac{4}{3} Rd \left[(\theta_w - 1)^3 \{K_4^3\} + (\theta_w - 1)^2 \{3K_4^2\} + (\theta_w - 1)\{3K_4\} + 1\right]$$

With the corresponding conditions

$$K_1(0) = fw, \quad K_2(0) = 1 + \frac{\Lambda}{A_1} K_3(0), \quad K_2(\infty) = 0,$$

$$K_5(0) = -\frac{Bi}{A_5}[1 - K_4(0)], \quad K_4(\infty) = 0$$

The advantage of this method is the ability to handle non-linear problems in simple domains more quickly. The technique is shown to be efficient and accurate in various boundary value scenarios, all described in Shampine et al. [53]. The process repeats itself further until a tolerance of 10^{-5} and a step size of 0.05 is reached.

4. Results and Discussion

The primary goal of this segment is to provide a clear understanding of the flow regime, specifically, the variations in the nanofluid velocity, nanofluid temperature, skin friction coefficient, and local Nusselt number for both nanoparticles (Ag and Al$_2$O$_3$) as a result of various regulatory flow parameters. Table 1 provides the physical properties of nanoparticles (Ag and Al$_2$O$_3$) and base fluid (H$_2$O). The nanofluid specifications are depicted in Table 2. Table 3 provides a comparison of $-f''(0)$ to Prabakaran et al. [54], Ibrahim and Shankar [55] for different values of fw with $\lambda = Fr = Ha = \phi = 0$ and observed that our numerical results corresponded perfectly with theirs. The fluctuations of Ag nanoparticle on SFC and LNN for different values of $\lambda, Fr, Ha, fw, \Lambda$, and ϕ are portrayed in Table 4. Table 5 represents the fluctuations of Al$_2$O$_3$ nanoparticles on SFC and LNN for different values of $\lambda, Fr, Ha, fw, \Lambda$, and ϕ. From Tables 4 and 5 it is detected that the surface drag force ($C_f Re^{1/2}$) decimates when augmenting the values of λ, Fr, fw, and ϕ and it augments for the larger quantities of Ha, and Λ. The heat transfer rate of ($NuRe^{-1/2}$) decreases when increasing the size of λ, Fr, Λ and ϕ and is enhanced for larger values of the modified Hartmann number and injection/suction parameter. Table 6 shows the consequence of A^*, B^*, Γ_1, Rd and Bi on LNN. It is observed that the LNN slumps when enhancing the values of A^* and B^* and it improves when increasing the quantity of Γ_1, Rd and Bi.

Table 1. The thermo-physical properties of the nanomaterials and water, see Roja and Gireesha [56].

Physical Properties	Silver (Ag)	Aluminium Oxide (Al$_2$O$_3$)	Water (H$_2$O)
$\rho/(\text{kg/m}^{-3})$	10,500	3970	997.1
$C_p/(\text{J.kg}^{-1}.\text{K}^{-1})$	235	765	4179
$\sigma/(\Omega.\text{m})^{-1}$	6.3×10^7	3.5×10^7	5.5×10^{-6}
$k/(\text{W.m}^{-1}.\text{K}^{-1})$	429	40	0.613

Table 2. Physical characteristics, see Sharma [26].

Properties	Nanofluid
Viscosity (μ)	$A_1 = \frac{\mu_f}{\mu_{nf}} = (1-\phi)^{2.5}$
Density (ρ)	$A_2 = \frac{\rho_{nf}}{\rho_f} = \left(1 - \phi + \phi \frac{\rho_s}{\rho_f}\right)$
Heat capacity (ρCp)	$A_3 = \frac{(\rho Cp)_{nf}}{(\rho Cp)_f} = \left(1 - \phi + \phi \frac{(\rho Cp)_s}{(\rho Cp)_f}\right)$
Electrical conductivity (σ)	$A_4 = \frac{\sigma_{nf}}{\sigma_f} = 1 + \frac{3\left(\frac{\sigma_s}{\sigma_f}-1\right)\phi}{\left(\frac{\sigma_s}{\sigma_f}+2\right)-\left(\frac{\sigma_s}{\sigma_f}-1\right)\phi}$
Thermal conductivity (k)	$A_5 = \frac{k_{nf}}{k_f} = \frac{k_s + (m-1)k_f - (m-1)\phi(k_f - k_s)}{k_s + (m-1)k_f + \phi(k_f - k_s)}$

Table 3. Comparison of $-f''(0)$ for disparate values of fw with $\lambda = Fr = Ha = \phi = 0$ to Prabakaran et al. [54], Ibrahim and Shankar [55].

fw	Present Study	Ref. [54]	Ref. [55]
0	1.000001	1.000000	1.0000
0.5	1.280776	1.280776	1.2808

Table 4. SFC & LNN comparison for diverse combo of $\lambda, Fr, Ha, fw, \Lambda, \phi$.

λ	Fr	Ha	fw	Λ	ϕ	Ag C_f	Ag Nu
0.2	0.4	0.3	0.5	1	0.05	−0.540406	0.722099
0.3						−0.549413	0.721707
0.4						−0.557932	0.721327
0.5						−0.566000	0.720961
0.6						−0.573647	0.720606
0.2	0.4	0.3	0.5	1	0.05	−0.540406	0.722099
	0.8					−0.553538	0.721507
	1.2					−0.565041	0.720977
	1.6					−0.575249	0.720498
	2					−0.584406	0.720062
0.2	0.4	0	0.5	1	0.05	−0.598291	0.719486
		0.1				−0.578264	0.720432
		0.2				−0.559002	0.721299
		0.3				−0.540406	0.722099
		0.4				−0.522401	0.722842
0.2	0.4	0.3	−0.6	1	0.05	−0.409777	0.139884
			−0.2			−0.453539	0.455283
			0			−0.477364	0.571358
			0.2			−0.502169	0.649742
			0.6			−0.553210	0.738959
0.2	0.4	0.3	0.5	0.2	0.05	−1.198806	0.730271
				0.4		−0.911637	0.727170
				0.6		−0.739594	0.725004
				0.8		−0.623925	0.723378
				1		−0.540406	0.722099
0.2	0.4	0.3	0.5	1	0	−0.474647	0.772332
					0.05	−0.540406	0.722099
					0.1	−0.590914	0.680030
					0.15	−0.632065	0.644168
					0.2	−0.666931	0.613247

Figure 2a–d portray the outcomes of λ, Fr, Ha and fw on the nanofluid velocity profile. The results show that a larger modified Hartmann number values increases the nanofluid flow speed, whereas a larger λ, Fr, and fw result in an opposite behavior. Physically, larger values of the modified Hartmann number produce larger electrical fields, which in turn produce larger values of the wall-parallel Lorentz force experienced by the body. Since this is the case, the fluid's speed increases. Further, the higher porosity enriches the fluid resistance during flow, which slows down fluid motion and makes the boundary layer thinner. The variations in the slip parameter and nanoparticle volume fraction on the nanofluid velocity profile are illustrated in Figure 3a,b. It is found that the increased availability of Λ and ϕ leads to a decay in the nanofluid velocity. Physically, the fluid deforms as the velocity slip parameter increases because of the low adhesive forces.

Table 5. SFC & LNN comparison for a diverse combination of λ, Fr, Ha, fw, Λ, ϕ.

λ	Fr	Ha	fw	Λ	ϕ	Al_2O_3 C_f	Nu
0.2	0.4	0.3	0.5	1	0.05	−0.507314	0.728057
0.3						−0.518302	0.727571
0.4						−0.528618	0.727103
0.5						−0.538316	0.726652
0.6						−0.547446	0.726219
0.2	0.4	0.3	0.5	1	0.05	−0.507314	0.728057
	0.8					−0.521096	0.727438
	1.2					−0.533185	0.726883
	1.6					−0.543925	0.726380
	2					−0.553570	0.725921
0.2	0.4	0	0.5	1	0.05	−0.569436	0.725170
		0.1				−0.548014	0.726214
		0.2				−0.527336	0.727172
		0.3				−0.507314	0.728057
		0.4				−0.487879	0.728880
0.2	0.4	0.3	−0.6	1	0.05	−0.393978	0.175973
			−0.2			−0.432415	0.479912
			0			−0.453043	0.587601
			0.2			−0.474401	0.660208
			0.6			−0.518389	0.744083
0.2	0.4	0.3	0.5	0.2	0.05	−1.074296	0.736057
				0.4		−0.833493	0.733090
				0.6		−0.684442	0.730967
				0.8		−0.582187	0.729347
				1		−0.507314	0.728057
0.2	0.4	0.3	0.5	1	0	−0.474647	0.772332
					0.05	−0.507314	0.728057
					0.1	−0.538018	0.690530
					0.15	−0.567324	0.658335
					0.2	−0.595710	0.630453

Figure 4a–d depict the transitions on the temperature distribution for various values of A^*, B^*, Rd and ϕ. It is demonstrated that the thickness of the TBL increased due to the increased presence of A^*, B^*, Rd, and ϕ. Physically, strengthening the thermal radiation causes increased energy transport between the particles and this causes an enrichment of the thermal boundary-layer thickness. Figure 5a–d delineates the changes in the temperature profile for disparate values of fw, Γ_1 and Bi. It is revealed that the fluid warmness declines when the values for convective cooling, injection/suction, and the thermal relaxation time parameter are enhanced, and it intensifies for larger values for the convective heating parameter. Physically, improving the convective heating parameter leads to a greater heat transfer coefficient, and this coefficient increases the fluid temperatures and thickens the thermal boundary layer. Also, Ag nanoparticles have a thicker thermal boundary layer compared to the Al_2O_3 nanoparticles. Generally, Ag nanoparticles have higher thermal conductivity than the Al_2O_3 nanoparticles. Figures 6a–d and 7a–d indicate the upshot of Fr, Ha, fw, λ and Λ on the SFC. It is observed that the surface drag force decreases when increasing the Fr, λ and fw values and it enlarges when heightening the values of Ha and Λ. The changes of LNN for various combinations of Ha, Rd, Γ_1, fw and λ are illustrated in Figure 8a–d. Based on these graphs, it can be seen that the LNN enlarges when enhancing the values of Ha, fw and Γ_1, and opposite reaction is observed for larger values of λ. Figure 9a,b shows the consequence of A^*, B^* and fw on LNN. It is explored that the LNN decays when enhancing the overall quantity of A^* and B^* and it enriches for larger values of fw.

Table 6. Variations of LNN for a diverse combination of A^*, B^*, Γ_1, Rd, Bi.

A^*	B^*	Γ_1	Rd	Bi	Ag	Al_2O_3
0	0.1	0.1	0.6	0.5	0.730125	0.734846
0.2					0.714032	0.721239
0.4					0.697778	0.707516
0.6					0.681362	0.693676
0.8					0.664781	0.679719
0.1	0	0.1	0.6	0.5	0.723775	0.729211
	0.2				0.720341	0.726864
	0.4				0.716550	0.724352
	0.6				0.712333	0.721652
	0.8				0.707854	0.718741
0.1	0.1	0	0.6	0.5	0.712420	0.718396
		0.1			0.722099	0.728057
		0.2			0.731930	0.737842
		0.3			0.741850	0.747699
		0.4			0.759113	0.757502
0.1	0.1	0.1	0	0.5	0.440869	0.442943
			1		0.898688	0.907764
			2		1.305605	1.323422
			3		1.675997	1.701921
			4		2.025144	2.057481
0.1	0.1	0.1	0.6	0.1	0.162427	0.163222
				0.3	0.459119	0.462158
				0.5	0.722099	0.728057
				0.7	0.955640	0.964981
				1	1.259007	1.273932

Figure 10a–d shows the slumping/growing percentage of the SFC for distinct quantities of λ, Fr, Ha and fw. In the case of the porosity parameter, the greatest diminishing percentage (2.30%) is collected in viscous fluid when λ is changed from 0.2 to 0.3 and the least diminishing percentage (1.35%) is obtained in Ag nanofluid when λ is changed from 0.5 to 0.6. In the case of Fr, the greatest diminishing percentage (3.05%) is observed in viscous fluid when Fr changed from 0.4 to 0.8, and the least diminishing percentage (1.59%) is observed in Ag nanofluid when Fr is changed from 1.6 to 2. In the case of the modified Hartmann number, the greatest improving percentage (4.33%) is collected in viscous fluid when Ha is changed from 0.3 to 0.4, and the least improving percentage (3.32%) is obtained in Ag nanofluid when Ha is changed from 0.2 to 0.3. In the case of the injection/suction parameter, the greatest diminishing percentage (2.59%) is collected in Ag nanofluid when fw is changed from -0.2 to -0.1 and the least diminishing percentage (2.35%) is obtained in Al_2O_3 nanofluid when fw is changed from -0.5 to -0.4. Figure 11a,b shows the declining SFC percentages for a distinct quantity of Λ and fw. In the case of the slip parameter, the greatest improving percentage (23.95%) is collected in Ag nanofluid when Λ is changed from 0.2 to 0.4, and the least improving percentage (12.35%) is obtained in viscous fluid when Λ is changed from 0.8 to 1. In the case of the injection/suction parameter, the greatest diminishing percentage (2.57%) is collected in Ag nanofluid when fw is changed from 0 to 0.1, and the least diminishing percentage (2.26%) is obtained in Al_2O_3 nanofluid when fw is changed from 0.3 to 0.4.

The improving/declining percentages of LNN on λ, Fr, Ha, Rd, A^*, B^*, Bi and Λ are illustrated in Figures 12a–d and 13a–d. In the case of the porosity parameter, the greatest diminishing percentage (0.066%) is collected in Al_2O_3 nanofluid when λ is changed from 0.2 to 0.3, and the least diminishing percentage (0.049%) is obtained in Ag nanofluid when λ is changed from 0.5 to 0.6. In the case of Fr, the greatest diminishing percentage (0.088%) is collected in viscous fluid when Fr is changed from 0.4 to 0.8 and the least diminishing percentage (0.060%) is observed in Ag nanofluid when Fr is changed from 1.6 to 2. In the case of the modified Hartmann number, the greatest improving percentage (0.151%)

is collected in viscous fluid when Ha is changed from 0 to 0.1, and the least improving percentage (0.102%) is observed in Ag nanofluid when Ha is changed from 0.3 to 0.4. In the case of non-linear radiation, the greatest improving percentage (119.56%) is collected in viscous fluid when Rd is changed from 0 to 1, and the least improving percentage (20.76%) is observed in viscous fluid when Rd is changed from 3 to 4. In the case of A^*, the greatest diminishing percentage (2.433%) is collected in Ag nanofluid when A^* is changed from 0.6 to 0.8, and the least diminishing percentage (1.619%) is observed in viscous fluid when A^* is changed from 0 to 0.2. In the case of B^*, the greatest diminishing percentage (0.628%) is collected in Ag nanofluid when B^* is changed from 0.6 to 0.8, and the least diminishing percentage (0.245%) is observed in viscous fluid when B^* is changed from 0 to 0.2. In the case of the Brinkmann number, the greatest improving percentage (183.14%) is collected in Al_2O_3 nanofluid when Bi is changed from 0.1 to 0.3, and the least improving percentage (31.74%) is observed in Ag nanofluid when Bi is changed from 0.7 to 1. In the case of the slip parameter, the greatest diminishing percentage (0.424%) is collected in Ag nanofluid when Λ is changed from 0.2 to 0.4, and the least diminishing percentage (0.173%) is observed in viscous fluid when Λ is changed from 0.8 to 1.

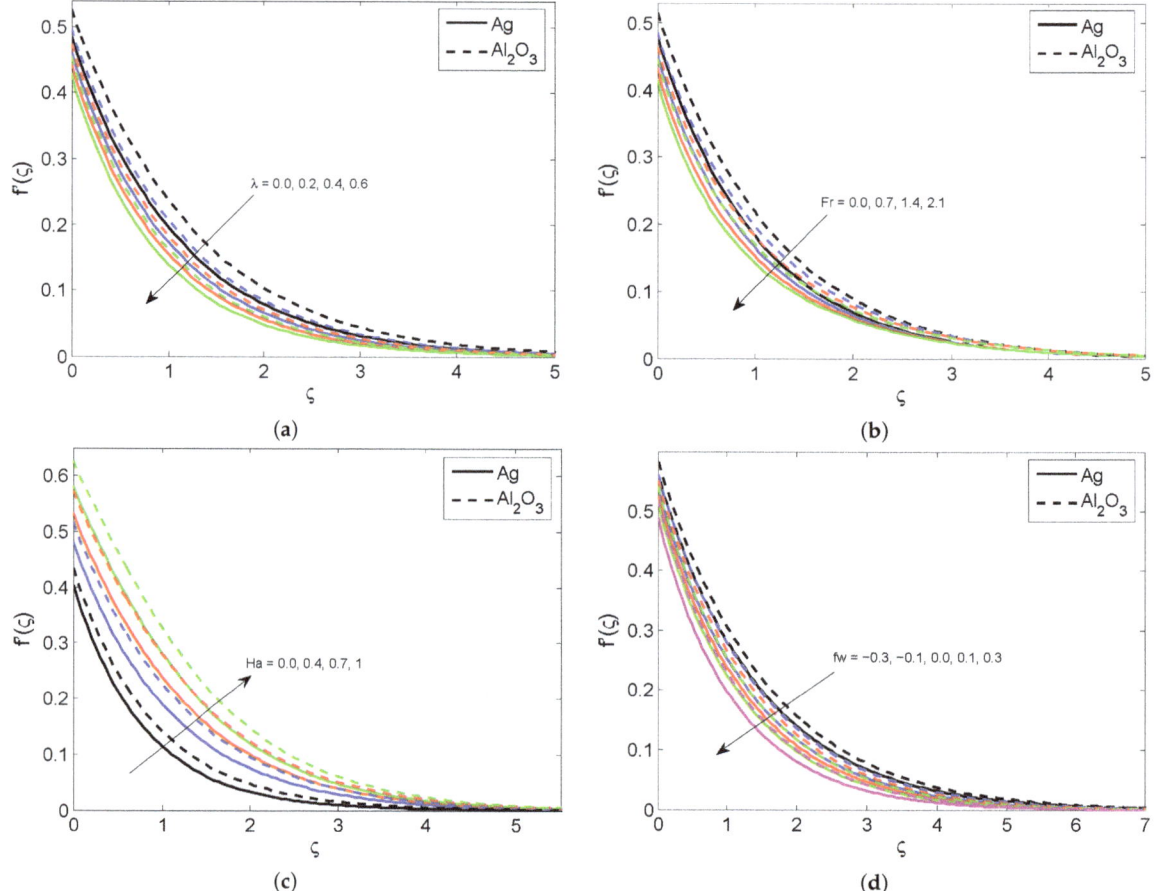

Figure 2. The variation of $f'(\varsigma)$ in relation to (**a**) λ, (**b**) Fr, (**c**) Ha and (**d**) fw.

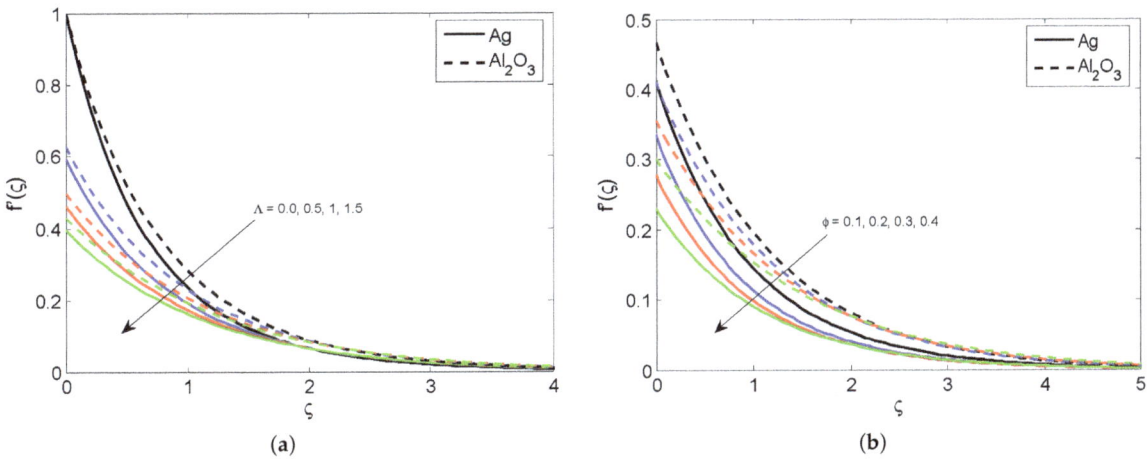

Figure 3. The variation of $f'(\varsigma)$ in relation to (**a**) Λ and (**b**) ϕ.

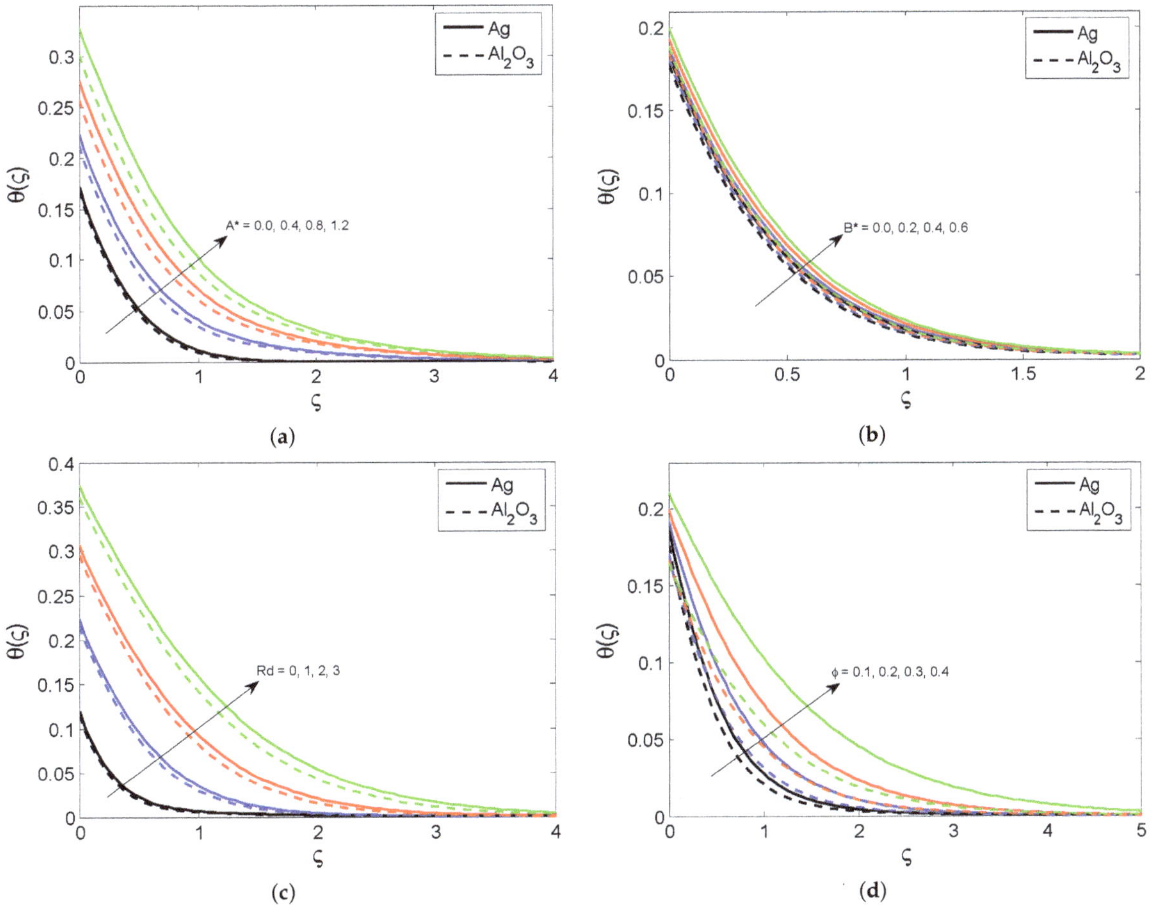

Figure 4. The variation of $\theta(\varsigma)$ in relation to (**a**) A^*, (**b**) B^*, (**c**) Rd and (**d**) ϕ.

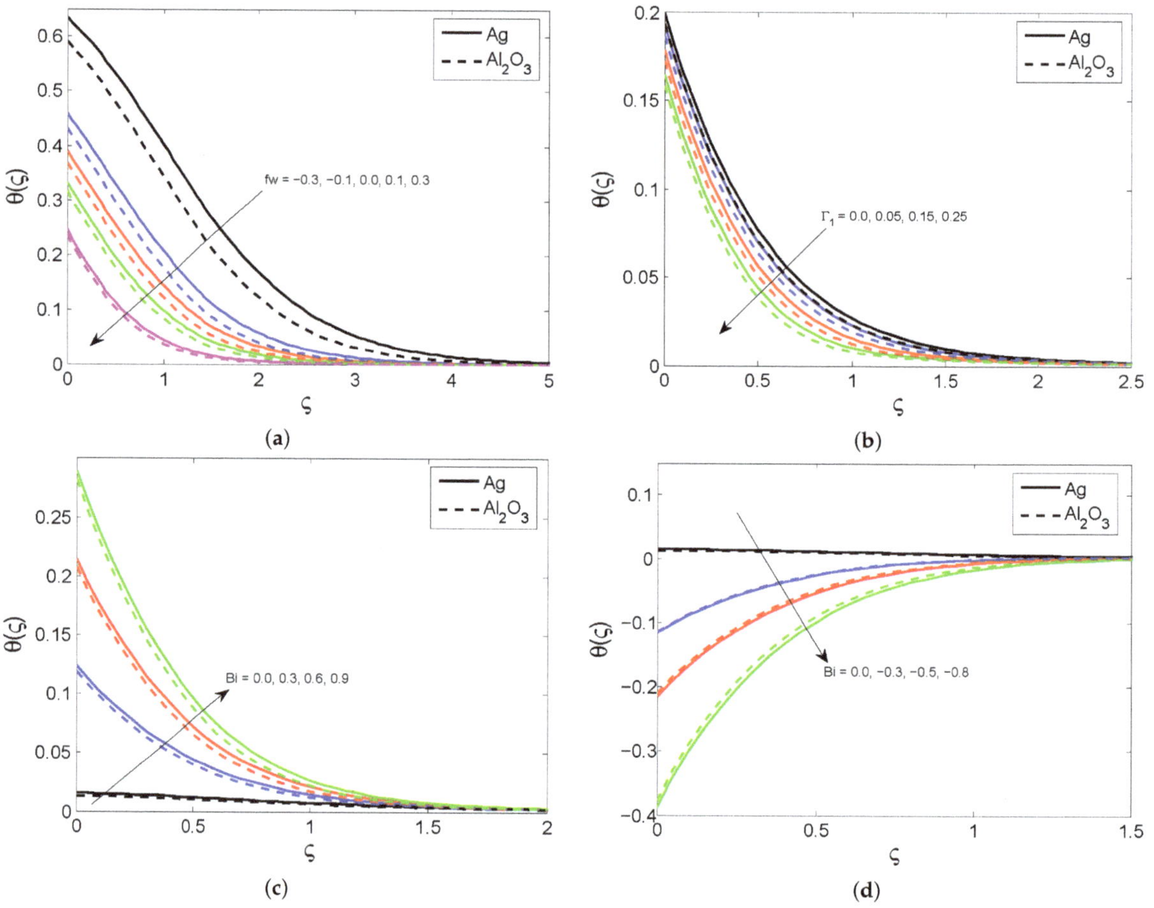

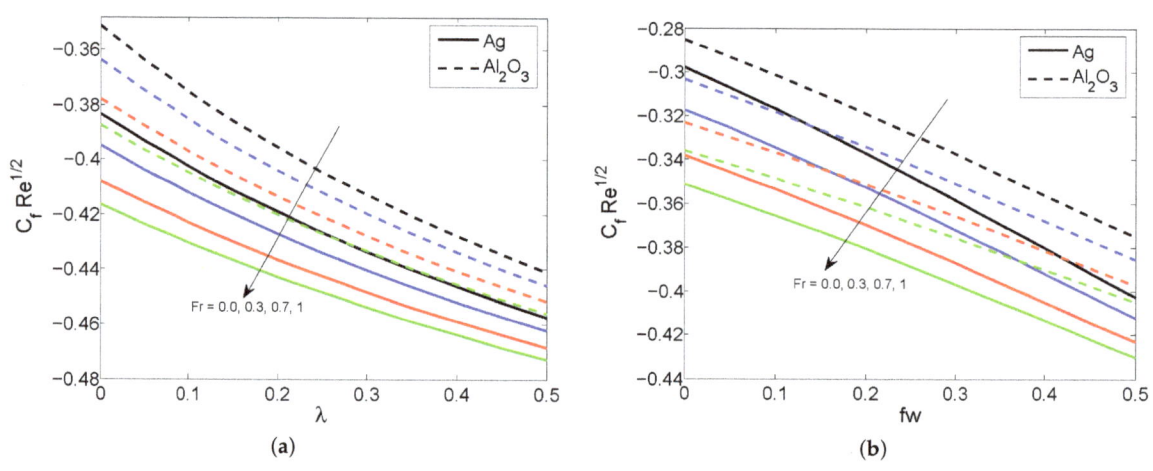

Figure 5. The variation of $\theta(\varsigma)$ in relation to (**a**) fw, (**b**) Γ_1, (**c**) Bi (convective heating) and (**d**) Bi (convective cooling).

Figure 6. Cont.

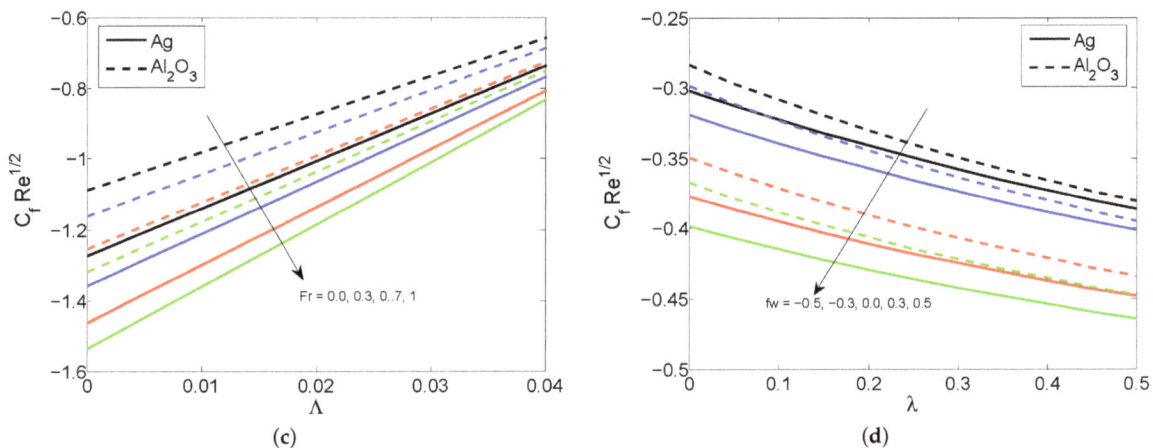

Figure 6. SFC variation for diverging values of (**a**) Fr & λ, (**b**) Fr & fw, (**c**) Fr & Λ and (**d**) fw & Λ.

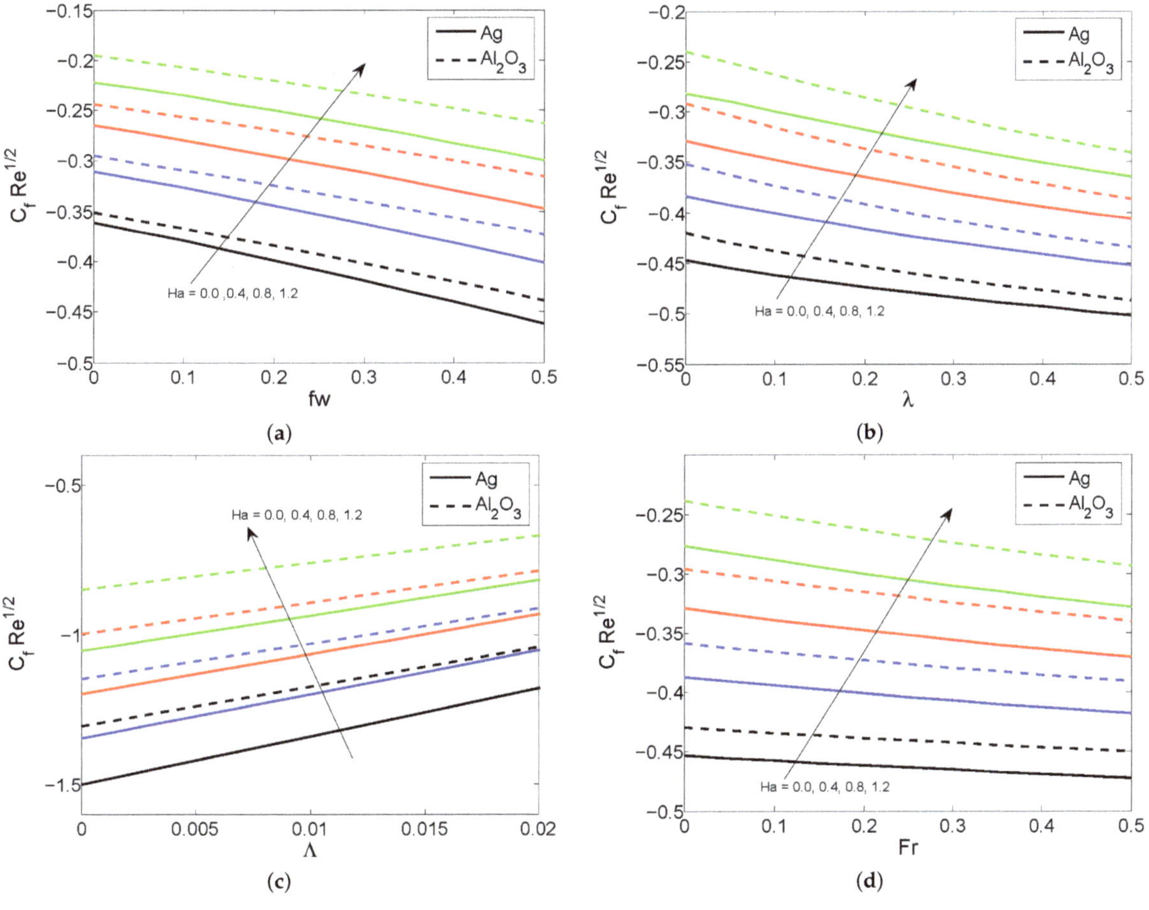

Figure 7. SFC variation for diverging values of (**a**) fw, (**b**) λ, (**c**) Λ and (**d**) Fr.

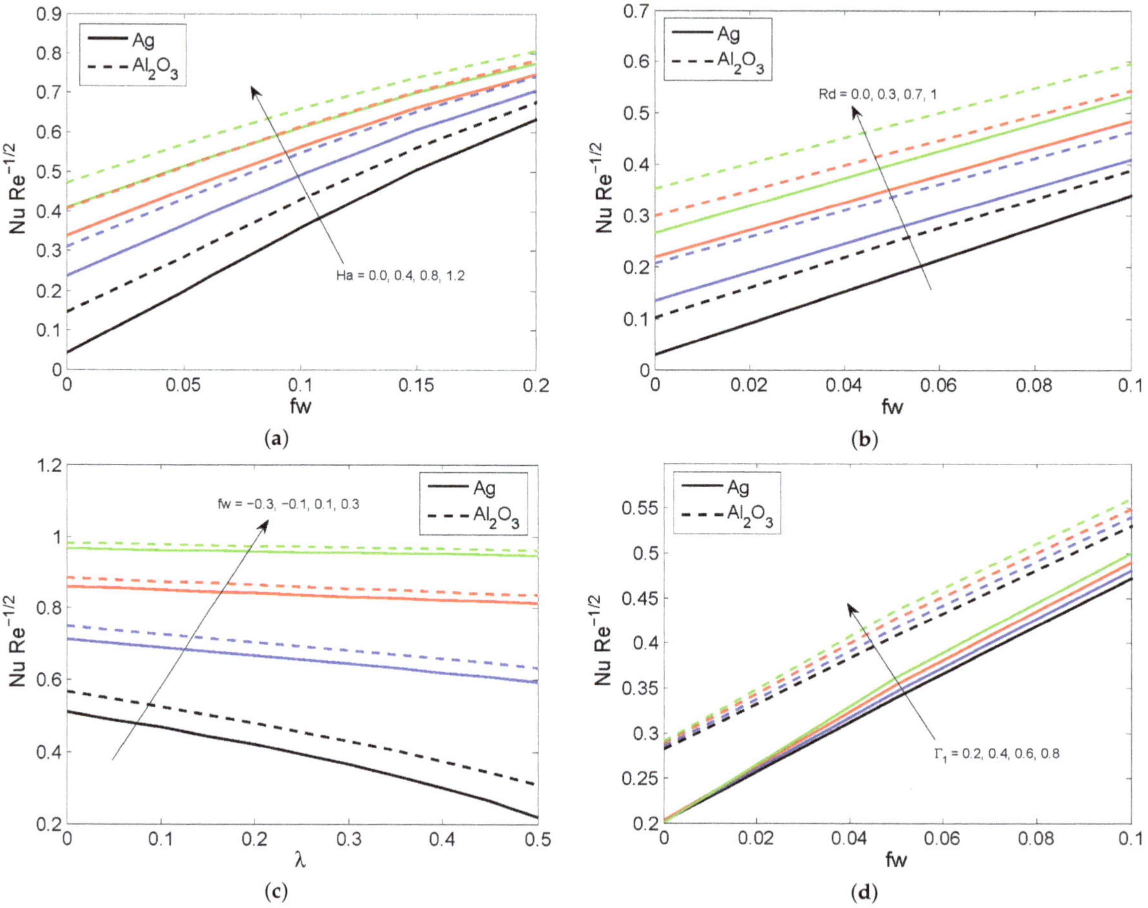

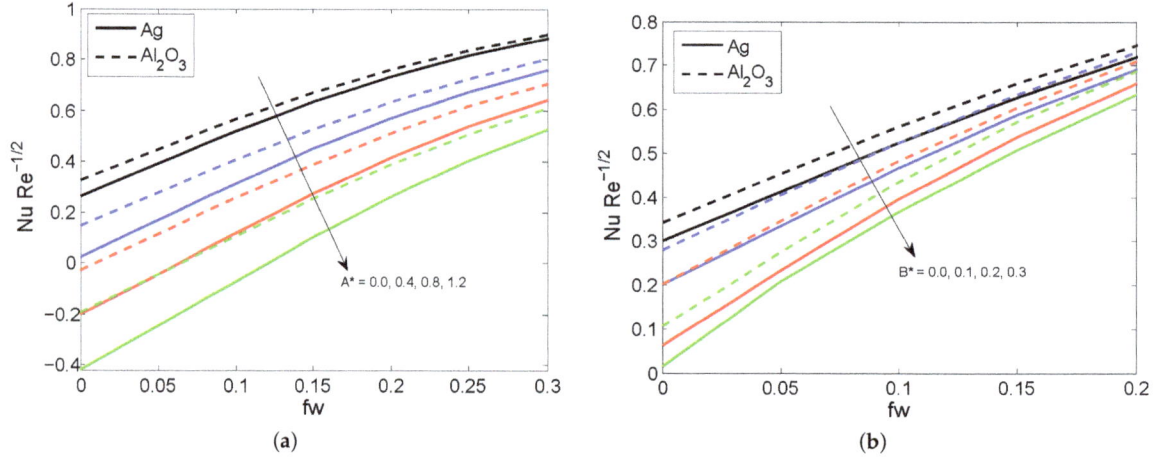

Figure 8. LNN variation for diverging values of (**a**) Ha, (**b**) Rd, (**c**) fw and (**d**) Γ_1.

Figure 9. LNN variation for diverging values of (**a**) A^* and (**b**) B^*.

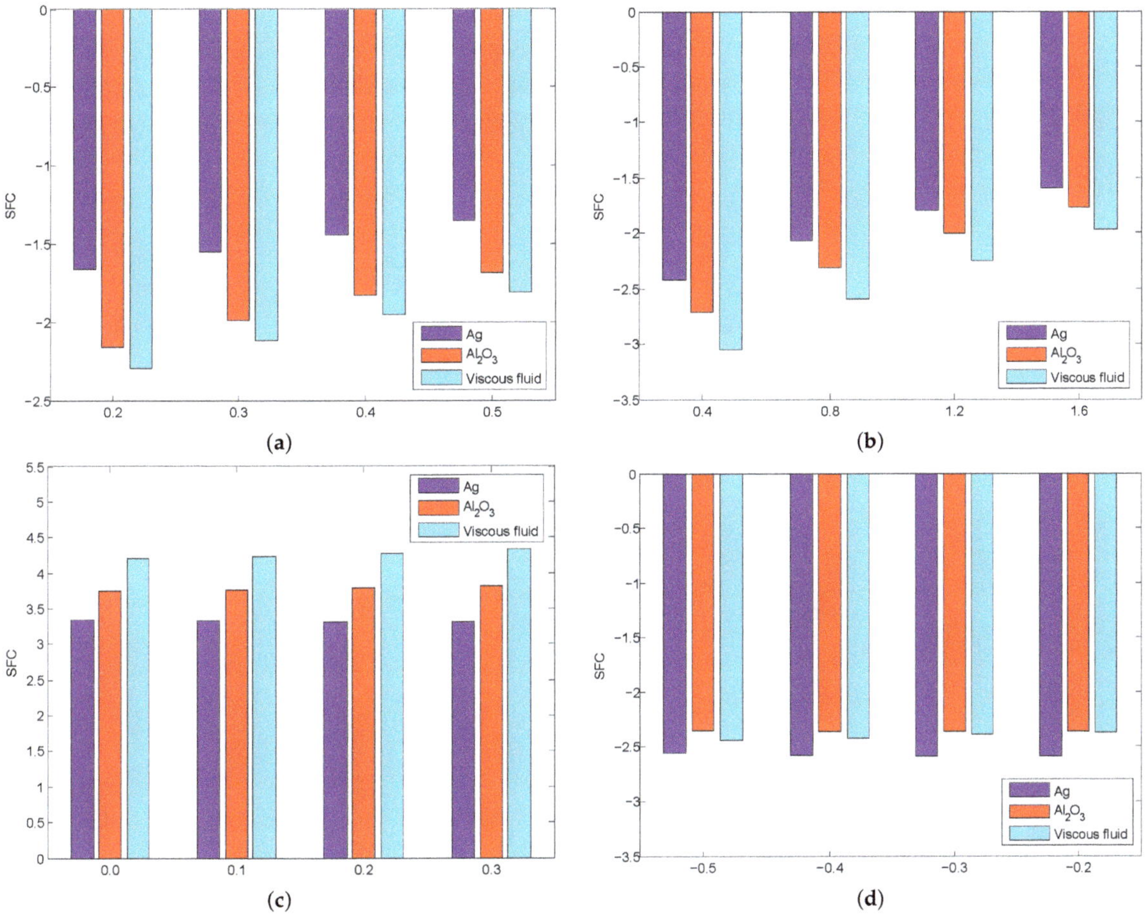

Figure 10. The increasing/declining percentage of SFC on (a) λ, (b) Fr, (c) Ha and (d) fw.

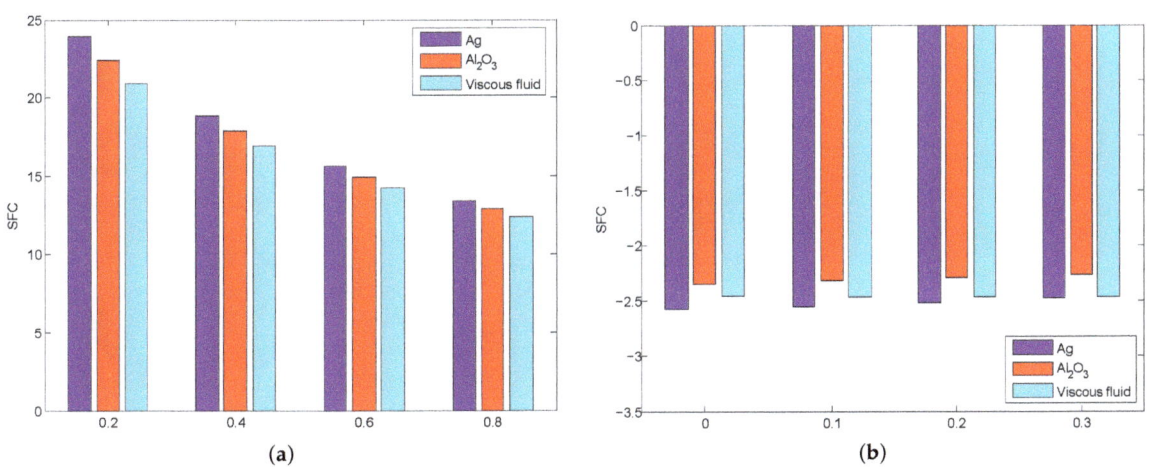

Figure 11. The increasing/declining percentage of SFC on (a) Λ and (b) fw.

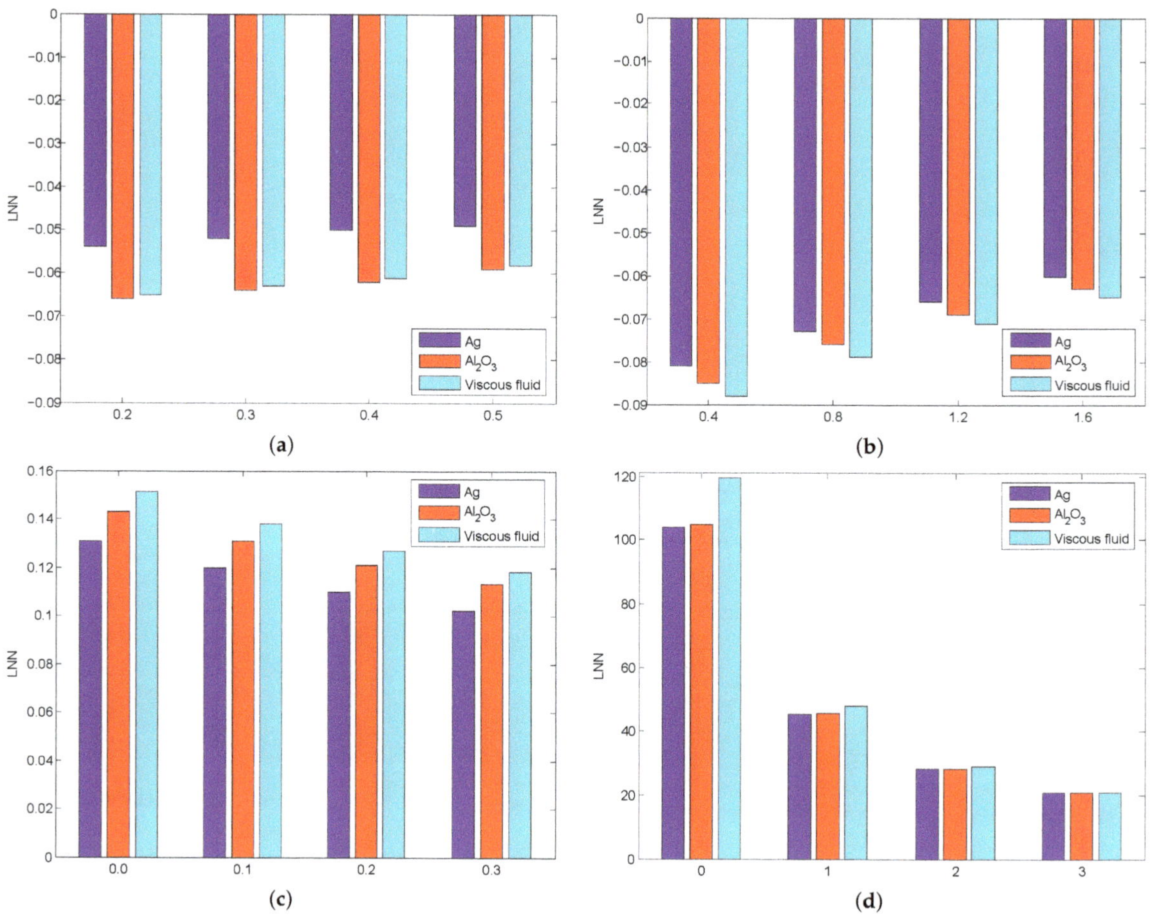

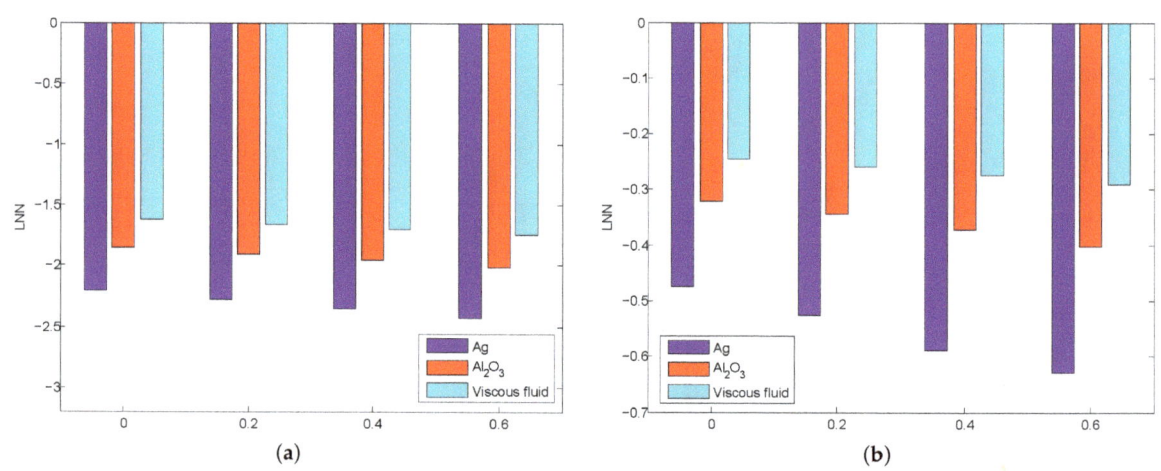

Figure 12. The increasing/declining percentage of LNN on (**a**) λ, (**b**) Fr, (**c**) Ha and (**d**) Rd.

Figure 13. *Cont.*

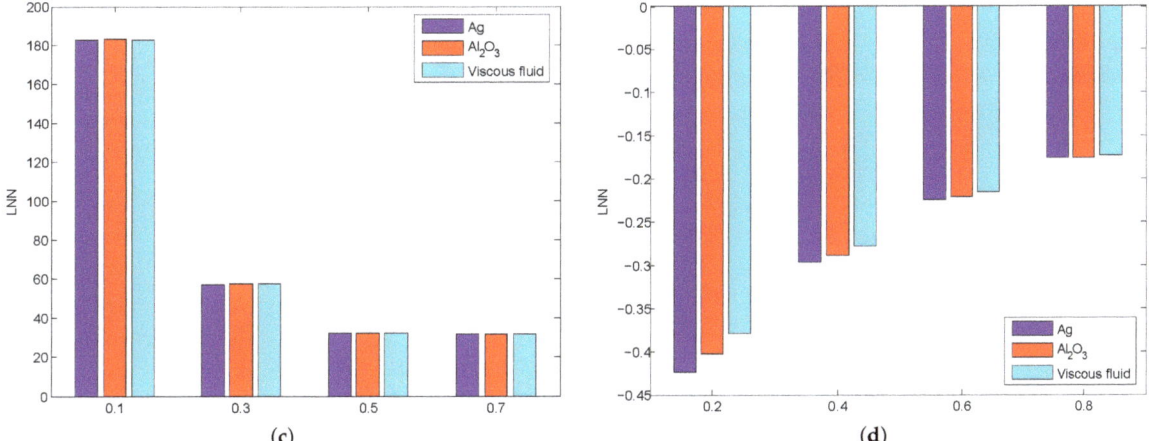

Figure 13. The increasing/declining percentage of LNN on (**a**) A^*, (**b**) B^*, (**c**) Bi and (**d**) Λ.

5. Conclusions

The main purpose of this research is to scrutinize the consequences of Darcy–Forchheimer flow in water-based Ag/Al_2O_3 nanofluid past a Riga plate. The energy equation is formed by including the Cattaneo–Christov heat flux, heat sink/source, and non-linear thermal radiation impacts. The governing models are re-framed by implementing suitable variables. The re-framed models are solved numerically by implementing the MATLAB bvp4c technique. The notable findings derived from the current study are as follows:

- The nanofluid velocity profile reduces for higher values of porosity, the Forchheimer number, the suction/injection parameter, and the slip parameter.
- The greater the thermal radiation, nanoparticle volume fraction, space and temperature dependent heat source parameter, the greater the nanofluid temperature profile.
- The nanofluid temperature declines for larger values of convection cooling, injection/suction and the thermal relaxation time parameter.
- The skin friction coefficient declines for increasing values of the Forchheimer number and suction/injection parameter, and increases when the modified Hartmann number increases.
- The heat transfer gradient increases with increasing values for the Hartmann number, radiation, suction/injection and the thermal relaxation time parameter, whereas it declines when the space and temperature dependent heat source parameter is increased.
- In future, we will expand this flow model by including hybrid and ternary hybrid nanofluids with different shape factors.

Author Contributions: Conceptualization, S.E. and K.L.; methodology, S.E.; software, K.L.; validation, S.E.; formal analysis, S.D.; investigation, K.L.; resources, S.D.; data curation, S.E.; writing—original draft preparation, S.D.; writing—review and editing, S.D. and S.E.; visualization, S.E.; supervision, S.E.; project administration, K.L.; funding acquisition, K.L. All authors have read and agreed to the published version of the manuscript.

Funding: This research received no external funding.

Conflicts of Interest: The authors declare no conflict of interest.

Nomenclature

Symbols	Description
a_1	positive constants
A^*	space-dependent heat source parameter
B^*	temperature-dependent heat source parameter
$Bi\left(=\frac{h_c}{k_f}\sqrt{\frac{v_f}{a}}\right)$	Biot number
C_p	specific heat capacity
c_b	drag coefficient
C_f	skin friction coefficient
f	subscript represent base fluid
$f_w\left(=\frac{V_w}{\sqrt{a(v)_f}}\right)$	suction/injection parameter
$Fr\left(=\frac{c_b}{\sqrt{k_1^*}}\right)$	Forchheimer number
h_c	heat transfer coefficient
$Ha\left(=\frac{\pi J_0 M x}{8(\rho)_f a^2}\right)$	modified Hartmann number
J_0	current density applied to the electrodes
k_1^*	permeability of porous medium
k^*	Rosseland absorption coefficient
M	magnetic field
nf	subscript represent nanoliquid
Nu	Nusselt number
$Pr\left(=\frac{\alpha_f}{v_f}\right)$	Prandtl number
$Rd\left(=\frac{4\sigma^* T_\infty^3}{k^*(k)_f}\right)$	radiation parameter
$Re\left(=\frac{ax^2}{v_f}\right)$	local Reynolds number
T	fluid temperature
T_f	temperature of the hot fluid
T_∞	ambient temperature
u, v	velocity components
x, y	Cartesian coordinates
U_w, V_w	surface stretching velocities
Greek Symbols	
ρ	density
μ	dynamic viscosity
ς	dimensionless variable
θ	dimensionless temperature
$\beta_R\left(=\frac{\pi}{a_1}\sqrt{\frac{v_f}{a}}\right)$	dimensionless parameter
$\theta_w\left(=\frac{T_f}{T_\infty}\right)$	heating variable
v	kinematic viscosity
$\lambda\left(=\frac{v_f}{k_1^* a}\right)$	local porosity parameter
ϕ	nanoparticle volume fraction
ψ	stream function
σ^*	Stefen-Boltzmann constant
Λ	slip parameter
α	thermal diffusivity
$\Gamma_1\left(=\lambda a\right)$	thermal relaxation time parameter
Abbreviations	
LNN	local Nusselt number
MHD	magnetohydrodynamics
ODEs	ordinary differential equations
PDEs	partial differential equations
SFC	skin friction coefficient
SS	stretching sheet
TBL	thermal boundary layer

References

1. Choi, S.U.; Eastman, J.A. *Enhancing Thermal Conductivity of Fluids with Nanoparticles.* (No. ANL/MSD/CP-84938; CONF-951135-29); Argonne National Lab. (ANL): Argonne, IL, USA, 1995.
2. Martin, E.; Sastre, F.; Velazquez, A.; Bairi, A. Heat transfer enhancement around a finned vertical antenna by means of porous media saturated with Water-Copper nanofluid. *Case Stud. Therm. Eng.* **2021**, *28*, 101555. [CrossRef]
3. Uddin, M.J.; Al-Balushi, J.; Mahatabuddin, S.; Rahman, M.M. Convective heat transport for copper oxide-water nanofluid in an isosceles triangular cavity with a rippled base wall in the presence of magnetic field. *Int. J. Thermofluid* **2022**, *16*, 100195. [CrossRef]
4. Nayak, M.K.; Shaw, S.; Khan, M.I.; Pandey, V.S.; Nazeer, M. Flow and thermal analysis on Darcy–Forchheimer flow of copper-water nanofluid due to a rotating disk: A static and dynamic approach. *J. Mater. Res. Technol.* **2020**, *9*, 7387–7408. [CrossRef]
5. Adem, G.A.; Kishan, N. Slip effects in a flow and heat transfer of a nanofluid over a nonlinearly stretching sheet using optimal homotopy asymptotic method. *Int. J. Eng. Manuf. Sci.* **2018**, *8*, 25–46.
6. Uddin, M.J.; Rasel, S.K.; Adewole, J.K.; Al Kalbani, K.S. Finite element simulation on the convective double diffusive water-based copper oxide nanofluid flow in a square cavity having vertical wavy surfaces in presence of hydro-magnetic field. *Results Eng.* **2022**, *13*, 100364. [CrossRef]
7. Verma, A.K.; Rajput, S.; Bhattacharyya, K.; Chamkha, A.J. Nanoparticle's radius effect on unsteady mixed convective copper-water nanofluid flow over an expanding sheet in porous medium with boundary slip. *J. Adv. Chem. Eng.* **2022**, *12*, 100366. [CrossRef]
8. Yousef, N.S.; Megahed, A.M.; Ghoneim, N.I.; Elsafi, M.; Fares, E. Chemical reaction impact on MHD dissipative Casson-Williamson nanofluid flow over a slippery stretching sheet through porous medium. *Alex. Eng. J.* **2022**, *61*, 10161–10170. [CrossRef]
9. Mohamed, M.K.A.; Ong, H.R.; Alkasasbeh, H.T.; Salleh, M.Z. Heat Transfer of $Ag - Al_2O_3$/Water Hybrid Nanofluid on a Stagnation Point Flow over a Stretching Sheet with Newtonian Heating. *J. Phys. Conf. Ser.* **2020**, *1529*, 042085. [CrossRef]
10. Shahzad, A.; Liaqat, F.; Ellahi, Z.; Sohail, M.; Ayub, M.; Ali, M.R. Thin film flow and heat transfer of Cu-nanofluids with slip and convective boundary condition over a stretching sheet. *Sci. Rep.* **2022**, *12*, 14254. [CrossRef]
11. Gailitis, A.; Lielausis, O. On a possibility to reduce the hydrodynamic resistance of a plate in an electrolyte. *Appl. Magnetohydrodyn.* **1961**, *12*, 143–146.
12. Vaidya, H.; Prasad, K.V.; Tlili, I.; Makinde, O.D.; Rajashekhar, C.; Khan, S.U.; Kumar, R.; Mahendra, D.L. Mixed convective nanofluid flow over a non linearly stretched Riga plate. *Case Stud. Therm. Eng.* **2021**, *24*, 100828. [CrossRef]
13. Shah, S.; Hussain, S.; Sagheer, M. Impacts of variable thermal conductivity on stagnation point boundary layer flow past a Riga plate with variable thickness using generalized Fourier's law. *Results Phys.* **2018**, *9*, 303–312. [CrossRef]
14. Rizwana, R.; Nadeem, S. Series solution of unsteady MHD oblique stagnation point flow of copper-water nanofluid flow towards Riga plate. *Heliyon* **2020**, *6*, e04689. [CrossRef]
15. Ramesh, G.K.; Roopa, G.S.; Gireesha, B.J.; Shehzad, S.A.; Abbasi, F.M. An electro-magneto-hydrodynamic flow Maxwell nanoliquid past a Riga plate: A numerical study. *J. Braz. Soc. Mech. Sci. Eng.* **2017**, *39*, 4547–4554. [CrossRef]
16. Abbas, T.; Ayub, M.; Bhatti, M.M.; Rashidi, M.M.; Ali, M.E.S. Entropy generation on nanofluid flow through a horizontal Riga plate. *Entropy* **2016**, *18*, 223. [CrossRef]
17. Waqas, H.; Kafait, A.; Muhammad, T.; Farooq, U. Numerical study for bio-convection flow of tangent hyperbolic nanofluid over a Riga plate with activation energy. *Alex. Eng. J.* **2022**, *61*, 1803–1814. [CrossRef]
18. Eswaramoorthi, S.; Alessa, N.; Sangeethavaanee, M.; Namgyel, N. Numerical and Analytical Investigation for Darcy–Forchheimer Flow of a Williamson Fluid over a Riga Plate with Double Stratification and Cattaneo–Christov Dual Flux. *Adv. Math. Phys.* **2021**, *2021*, 1867824. [CrossRef]
19. Faizan, M.; Ali, F.; Loganathan, K.; Zaib, A.; Reddy, C.A.; Abdelsalam, S.I. Entropy Analysis of Sutterby Nanofluid Flow over a Riga Sheet with Gyrotactic Microorganisms and Cattaneo–Christov Double Diffusion. *Mathematics* **2022**, *10*, 3157. [CrossRef]
20. Karthik, T.S.; Loganathan, K.; Shankar, A.N.; Carmichael, M.J.; Mohan, A.; Kaabar, M.K.; Kayikci, S. Zero and nonzero mass flux effects of bioconvective viscoelastic nanofluid over a 3D Riga surface with the swimming of gyrotactic microorganisms. *Adv. Math. Phys.* **2021**, *2021*, 9914134. [CrossRef]
21. Parvine, M.; Alam, M.M. Nano fluid flow along the Riga plate with electromagnetic field in a rotating system. *AIP Conf. Proc.* **2019**, *2121*, 070003.
22. Rafique, K.; Alotaibi, H.; Ibrar, N.; Khan, I. Stratified Flow of Micropolar Nanofluid over Riga Plate: Numerical Analysis. *Energies* **2022**, *15*, 316.
23. Madhukesh, J.K.; Ramesh, G.K.; Aly, E.H.; Chamkha, A.J. Dynamics of water conveying SWCNT nanoparticles and swimming microorganisms over a Riga plate subject to heat source/sink. *Alex. Eng. J.* **2022**, *61*, 2418–2429. [CrossRef]
24. Oke, A.S.; Animasaun, I.L.; Mutuku, W.N.; Kimathi, M.; Shah, N.A.; Saleem, S. Significance of Coriolis force, volume fraction, and heat source/sink on the dynamics of water conveying 47 nm alumina nanoparticles over a uniform surface. *Chin. J. Phys.* **2021**, *71*, 716–727. [CrossRef]
25. Qasim, M. Heat and mass transfer in a Jeffrey fluid over a stretching sheet with heat source/sink. *Alex. Eng. J.* **2013**, *52*, 571–575. [CrossRef]

26. Sharma, B.K.; Gandhi, R. Combined effects of Joule heating and non-uniform heat source/sink on unsteady MHD mixed convective flow over a vertical stretching surface embedded in a Darcy–Forchheimer porous medium. *Propuls. Power Res.* **2022**, *11*, 276–292. [CrossRef]
27. Vieru, D.; Fetecau, C.; Shah, N.A.; Yook, S.J. Unsteady natural convection flow due to fractional thermal transport and symmetric heat source/sink. *Alex. Eng. J.* **2022**, *64*, 761–770. [CrossRef]
28. Sandeep, N.; Sulochana, C. Momentum and heat transfer behaviour of Jeffrey, Maxwell and Oldroyd-B nanofluids past a stretching surface with non-uniform heat source/sink. *Ain Shams Eng. J.* **2018**, *9*, 517–524. [CrossRef]
29. Jena, S.; Dash, G.C.; Mishra, S.R. Chemical reaction effect on MHD viscoelastic fluid flow over a vertical stretching sheet with heat source/sink. *Ain Shams Eng. J.* **2018**, *9*, 1205–1213. [CrossRef]
30. Sandeep, N.; Sulochana, C. Dual solutions for unsteady mixed convection flow of MHD micropolar fluid over a stretching/shrinking sheet with non-uniform heat source/sink. *Eng. Sci. Technol. Int. J.* **2015**, *18*, 738–745. [CrossRef]
31. Reddy, P.S.; Rao, K.S. MHD natural convection heat and mass transfer of Al_2O_3-water and Ag-water nanofluids over a vertical cone with chemical reaction. *Procedia Eng.* **2015**, *127*, 476–484. [CrossRef]
32. Khan, U.; Zaib, A.; Ishak, A.; Alotaibi, A.M.; Eldin, S.M.; Akkurt, N.; Waini, I.; Madhukesh, J.K. Stability Analysis of Buoyancy Magneto Flow of Hybrid Nanofluid through a Stretchable/Shrinkable Vertical Sheet Induced by a Micropolar Fluid Subject to Nonlinear Heat Sink/Source. *Magnetochemistry* **2022**, *8*, 188. [CrossRef]
33. Yu, Y.; Khan, U.; Zaib, A.; Ishak, A.; Waini, I.; Raizah, Z.; Galal, A.M. Exploration of 3D stagnation-point flow induced by nanofluid through a horizontal plane surface saturated in a porous medium with generalized slip effects. *Ain Shams Eng. J.* **2023**, *14*, 101873. [CrossRef]
34. Rashidi, M.M.; Ganesh, N.V.; Hakeem, A.A.; Ganga, B. Buoyancy effect on MHD flow of nanofluid over a stretching sheet in the presence of thermal radiation. *J. Mol. Liq.* **2014**, *198*, 234–238. [CrossRef]
35. Kameswaran, P.K.; Sibanda, P.; Murti, A.S.N. Nanofluid flow over a permeable surface with convective boundary conditions and radiative heat transfer. *Math. Probl. Eng.* **2013**, *2013*, 201219. [CrossRef]
36. Maleki, H.; Alsarraf, J.; Moghanizadeh, A.; Hajabdollahi, H.; Safaei, M.R. Heat transfer and nanofluid flow over a porous plate with radiation and slip boundary conditions. *J. Cent. South Univ.* **2019**, *26*, 1099–1115. [CrossRef]
37. Eswaramoorthi, S.; Loganathan, K.; Jain, R.; Gyeltshen, S. Darcy–Forchheimer 3D Flow of Glycerin-Based Carbon Nanotubes on a Riga Plate with Nonlinear Thermal Radiation and Cattaneo–Christov Heat Flux. *J. Nanomater.* **2022**, *2022*, 5286921. [CrossRef]
38. Mahat, R.; Saqib, M.; Khan, I.; Shafie, S.; Noor, N.A.M. Thermal radiation effect on Viscoelastic Walters'-B nanofluid flow through a circular cylinder in convective and constant heat flux. *Case Stud. Therm. Eng.* **2022**, *39*, 102394. [CrossRef]
39. Mahanthesh, B.; Gireesha, B.J.; Animasaun, I.L. Exploration of non-linear thermal radiation and suspended nanoparticles effects on mixed convection boundary layer flow of nanoliquids on a melting vertical surface. *J. Nanofluids* **2018**, *7*, 833–843. [CrossRef]
40. Bhatti, M.M.; Al-Khaled, K.; Khan, S.U.; Chammam, W.; Awais, M. Darcy–Forchheimer higher-order slip flow of Eyring–Powell nanofluid with nonlinear thermal radiation and bioconvection phenomenon. *J. Dispers. Sci. Technol.* **2021**, 1–11. [CrossRef]
41. Eswaramoorthi, S.; Thamaraiselvi, S.; Loganathan, K. Exploration of Darcy–Forchheimer Flows of Non-Newtonian Casson and Williamson Conveying Tiny Particles Experiencing Binary Chemical Reaction and Thermal Radiation: Comparative Analysis. *Math. Comput. Appl.* **2022**, *27*, 52. [CrossRef]
42. Mahanta, G.; Das, M.; Nayak, M.K.; Shaw, S. Irreversibility analysis of 3D magnetohydrodynamic Casson nanofluid flow past through two bi-directional stretching surfaces with nonlinear radiation. *J. Nanofluids* **2021**, *10*, 316–326. [CrossRef]
43. Waqas, M.; Khan, U.; Zaib, A.; Ishak, A.; Albaqami, M.D.; Waini, I.; Alotabi, R.G.; Pop, I. Radiation effect on MHD three-dimensional stagnation-point flow comprising water-based graphene oxide nanofluid induced by a nonuniform heat source/sink over a horizontal plane surface. *Int. J. Mod. Phys. B* **2022**, *2022*, 2350146. [CrossRef]
44. Jha, B.K.; Samaila, G. The role of thermal radiation on the boundary layer past a stationary flat plate with constant surface boundary condition. *J. Nat.* **2022**, *2*, 7–11. [CrossRef]
45. Eswaramoorthi, S.; Divya, S.; Faisal, M.; Namgyel, N. Entropy and heat transfer analysis for MHD flow of-water-based nanofluid on a heated 3D plate with nonlinear radiation. *Math. Probl. Eng.* **2022**, *2022*, 7319988.
46. Alzahrani, H.A.; Alsaiari, A.; Madhukesh, J.K.; Naveen Kumar, R.; Prasanna, B.M. Effect of thermal radiation on heat transfer in plane wall jet flow of Casson nanofluid with suction subject to a slip boundary condition. *Waves Random Complex Media* **2022**, 1–18. [CrossRef]
47. Aldabesh, A.; Khan, S.U.; Habib, D.; Waqas, H.; Tlili, I.; Khan, M.I.; Khan, W.A. Unsteady transient slip flow of Williamson nanofluid containing gyrotactic microorganism and activation energy. *Alex. Eng. J.* **2020**, *59*, 4315–4328. [CrossRef]
48. Mahmood, A.; Jamshed, W.; Aziz, A. Entropy and heat transfer analysis using Cattaneo–Christov heat flux model for a boundary layer flow of Casson nanoliquid. *Results Phys.* **2018**, *10*, 640–649. [CrossRef]
49. Hayat, T.; Khan, M.I.; Khan, T.A.; Khan, M.I.; Ahmad, S.; Alsaedi, A. Entropy generation in Darcy–Forchheimer bidirectional flow of water-based carbon nanotubes with convective boundary condition. *J. Mol. Liq.* **2018**, *265*, 629–638. [CrossRef]
50. Afify, A.A. The influence of slip boundary condition on Casson nanofluid flow over a stretching sheet in the presence of viscous dissipation and chemical reaction. *Math. Probl. Eng.* **2017**, *2017*, 3804751. [CrossRef]

51. Asshaari, I.; Jedi, A.; Abdullah, S. Brownian Motion and Thermophoresis Effects in co-Flowing Carbon Nanotubes towards a Moving Plate. *Results Phys.* **2022**, *44*, 106165. [CrossRef]
52. Shampine, L.F.; Kierzenka, J.; Reichelt, M.W. Solving boundary value problems for ordinary differential equations in MATLAB with bvp4c. *World J. Mech.* **2013**, *3*, 1–27.
53. Shampine, L.F.; Gladwell, I.; Thompson, I. *Solving ODEs with MATLAB*, 1st ed.; Cambridge University Press: Cambridge, UK, 2003.
54. Prabakaran, R.; Eswaramoorthi, S.; Loganathan, K.; Gyeltshen, S. Thermal Radiation and Viscous Dissipation Impacts of Water and Kerosene-Based Carbon Nanotubes over a Heated Riga Sheet. *J. Nanomater.* **2022**, *2022*, 1865763.
55. Ibrahim, W.; Shankar, B. MHD boundary layer flow and heat transfer of a nanofluid past a permeable stretching sheet with velocity, thermal and solutal slip boundary conditions. *Comput. Fluids* **2013**, *75*, 1–10.
56. Roja, A.; Gireesha, B.J. Impact of Hall and Ion effects on MHD couple stress nanofluid flow through an inclined channel subjected to convective, hydraulic slip, heat generation, and thermal radiation. *Heat Transf.* **2020**, *49*, 3314–3333.

Disclaimer/Publisher's Note: The statements, opinions and data contained in all publications are solely those of the individual author(s) and contributor(s) and not of MDPI and/or the editor(s). MDPI and/or the editor(s) disclaim responsibility for any injury to people or property resulting from any ideas, methods, instructions or products referred to in the content.

Article

Preconditioning Technique for an Image Deblurring Problem with the Total Fractional-Order Variation Model

Adel M. Al-Mahdi [1,2]

[1] PYP-Math, King Fahd University of Petroleum & Minerals, Dhahran 31261, Saudi Arabia; almahdi@kfupm.edu.sa

[2] The Interdisciplinary Research Center in Construction and Building Materials, King Fahd University of Petroleum & Minerals, Dhahran 31261, Saudi Arabia

Abstract: Total fractional-order variation (TFOV) in image deblurring problems can reduce/remove the staircase problems observed with the image deblurring technique by using the standard total variation (TV) model. However, the discretization of the Euler–Lagrange equations associated with the TFOV model generates a saddle point system of equations where the coefficient matrix of this system is dense and ill conditioned (it has a huge condition number). The ill-conditioned property leads to slowing of the convergence of any iterative method, such as Krylov subspace methods. One treatment for the slowness property is to apply the preconditioning technique. In this paper, we propose a block triangular preconditioner because we know that using the exact triangular preconditioner leads to a preconditioned matrix with exactly two distinct eigenvalues. This means that we need at most two iterations to converge to the exact solution. However, we cannot use the exact preconditioner because the Shur complement of our system is of the form $S = K^*K + \lambda L_\alpha$ which is a huge and dense matrix. The first matrix, K^*K, comes from the blurred operator, while the second one is from the TFOV regularization model. To overcome this difficulty, we propose two preconditioners based on the circulant and standard TV matrices. In our algorithm, we use the flexible preconditioned GMRES method for the outer iterations, the preconditioned conjugate gradient (PCG) method for the inner iterations, and the fixed point iteration (FPI) method to handle the nonlinearity. Fast convergence was found in the numerical results by using the proposed preconditioners.

Keywords: preconditioning technique; image deblurring; Krylov subspace methods; fractional derivatives; Toeplitz and circulant matrices

Citation: Al-Mahdi, A.M. Preconditioning Technique for an Image Deblurring Problem with the Total Fractional-Order Variation Model. *Math. Comput. Appl.* **2023**, *28*, 97. https://doi.org/10.3390/mca28050097

Academic Editor: Christian Gout

Received: 2 August 2023
Revised: 12 September 2023
Accepted: 18 September 2023
Published: 22 September 2023

Copyright: © 2023 by the authors. Licensee MDPI, Basel, Switzerland. This article is an open access article distributed under the terms and conditions of the Creative Commons Attribution (CC BY) license (https://creativecommons.org/licenses/by/4.0/).

1. Introduction

Although TV regularization is a commonly employed technique in image deblurring problems [1–4], one significant drawback is the appearance of the "staircase effect", wherein edges are depicted as a sequence of steps rather than smooth transitions. This phenomenon arises because TV regularization encourages the creation of piecewise constant regions, which leads to the appearance of blocks around edges rather than accurately capturing their continuous nature. As a result, researchers are actively investigating and advancing alternative regularization techniques and algorithms to remove or reduce these "staircase effects" and enhance the overall quality of image deblurring methods. An alternative regularization approach is the TFOV model [5–8]. TFOV regularization presents a robust method for enhancing image deblurring, offering a combination of benefits such as edge preservation, flexibility, noise resilience, and reduction in staircase effects. Its effectiveness has been substantiated in numerous studies, significantly contributing to the progression of image deblurring techniques. However, when it comes to discretizing the Euler–Lagrange equations of the TFOV-based model, a substantial nonlinear and ill-conditioned system emerges. Efficiently solving such systems poses a considerable challenge for numerical methods, even with the application of potent numerical algorithms like Krylov subspace methods, such as the generalized minimal residual (GMRES) and conjugate gradient (CG). These methods tend to exhibit slow convergence in this context. One potential remedy to address this slow convergence is the use of preconditioning techniques. Preconditioning is a technique used to transform a linear system of the form $Ax = b$ into another system to improve the spectral properties of the system matrix. A preconditioner is a matrix P that is easy to invert and the preconditioned matrix $P^{-1}A$ shows good clustering behavior for the eigenvalues. This is because rapid convergence is often associated with a clustered spectrum of $P^{-1}A$. In the preconditioning technique, we solve $P^{-1}Ax = P^{-1}b$ instead of solving the original $Ax = b$ because the new system $P^{-1}Ax = P^{-1}b$ converges rapidly when we use a suitable preconditioner. To apply the preconditioner matrix P within a Krylov subspace method, we need to compute the multiplication of a matrix by a vector of the form $z = Pr$ at each iteration. Hence, evaluating this product must be cheap. In the literature, several preconditioners are developed in [9] for a special linear system, such as block preconditioners and constraint preconditioners. For diagonal preconditioners, we can refer to Silvester and Wathen [10] and Wathen and Silvester [11]. For the block triangular preconditioners, we can refer to Bramble and Pasciak [12] and [13–16], as well as the references therein. For constraint preconditioners, see, for example, Axelsson and Neytcheva [17]. Other preconditioners based on Hermitian/skew-Hermitian splitting are studied in [18–20]. Recently, several new preconditioners for Krylov subspace methods have been introduced. For example, Cao et al. [21] derived two block triangular Schur complement preconditioners from a splitting of the (1, 1)-block of the two-by-two block matrix. Chen and Ma [22] proposed a generalized shift-splitting preconditioner for saddle point problems with a symmetric positive definite (1, 1)-block. Salkuyeh et al. [23] proposed a modified generalized shift-splitting preconditioner where the (1, 1)-block is symmetric positive definite and the (2, 2)-block matrix is symmetric positive semidefinite (not zero). Very recently, block diagonal and block triangular splitting preconditioners were studded by Beik et al. [24], and the authors introduced new variants of the splitting preconditioners and obtained new results for the convergence of the associated stationary iterations and new bounds for the eigenvalues of the corresponding preconditioned matrices. Moreover, they considered inexact versions as preconditioners for flexible Krylov subspace methods. A good survey of preconditioning techniques for general linear systems can be found in [9,25,26].

In our paper, we consider the following two-by-two block nonlinear system of equations:

$$\underbrace{\begin{bmatrix} I_n & K_h \\ -K_h^* & \lambda L_h^\alpha(U_h) \end{bmatrix}}_{A} \underbrace{\begin{bmatrix} V_h \\ U_h \end{bmatrix}}_{x} = \underbrace{\begin{bmatrix} Z_h \\ 0 \end{bmatrix}}_{b}. \qquad (1)$$

This system is obtained by discretizing the Euler-Lagrange equations associated with TFOV in image deblurring problems, and the coefficient matrix of this system has a size of $2n$ by $2n$, where $n := N^2$ and N is the number of pixels in the image. The coefficient matrix of this system is non-symmetric, ill conditioned, dense, and huge. These properties complicate the development of an efficient numerical algorithm. We know that using direct methods for solving Equation (1) requires $O(N^3)$ and, hence, they are not applicable here. For this system, iterative methods, like Krylov subspace methods, are applicable. However, their convergence is too slow because they are sensitive to the condition numbers. Hence, preconditioning is needed to accelerate the convergence of the Krylov subspace methods. In this paper, we propose two block triangular preconditioners for Equation (1). In the literature, it has been shown that such preconditioners are among the most effective for solving problems of the saddle point type. Moreover, it is known that using the exact triangular preconditioner leads to a preconditioned matrix with exactly two distinct eigenvalues [25]. This means that we need at most two iterations to converge to the exact solution. Since the coefficient matrix A is not symmetric, the suitable outer iterative method is the GMRES method [27], and since the (2, 2)-block in the matrix A is symmetric positive definite, the suitable inner iterative method is the CG method. However, using the GMRES

Krylov subspace method as a preconditioner within a different Krylov subspace method (the CG method) may lead to a changing preconditioner. In such cases, the preconditioner matrix changes from step to step. For this reason, we use flexible GMRES (FGMRES) instead of GMRES [27]. The flexibility here means that FGMRES is designed to be flexible in terms of the choice of the inner Krylov subspace method and the choice of the preconditioner. This flexibility allows FGMRES to adapt to different Krylov subspace methods. FGMRES can be restarted after a certain number of iterations to control the memory usage and computational cost, especially when solving multiple linear systems with different right-hand sides. The main contributions of this work are follows:

- We propose two block triangular preconditioners and study the bounds of the eigenvalues of the preconditioned matrices. In addition, we demonstrate the effectiveness of our algorithm in the numerical results by starting with the fixed point iteration (FPI) Method as in [28] to linearize the nonlinear primal system $[K^T K + \lambda L_h^\alpha(U^m)]U^{m+1} = K^T Z$, $m = 0, 1, \ldots$, then we use the preconditioned conjugate gradient (PCG) method [29] for the inner iterations. After that, we use FGMRES method for the outer iterations. We illustrate the performance of our approach by calculating the peak signal-to-noise ratio (PSNR), CPU-time, residuals and the number of iterations. Finally, we calculate the PSNR for different values of the order of the fractional derivative, α, to show the impact of using the TFOV model.

The remainder of this paper is organized as follows: Section 2 presents the mathematical model of the image deblurring problem, different regularization models, three definitions of the fractional derivative, and the Euler–Lagrange equations associated with the TFOV model. System (1) is obtained at the end of this section. Section 3 presents all theoretical contributions of this paper. Section 4 reports some numerical results that show the efficiency of our preconditioners. Section 5 briefly states our conclusions.

2. Problem Setup

We know that blurring and noise affect the quality of the received image. To deblur an image, we need a mathematical model of how it was blurred. The recorded image z and the true (exact) image **u** are related by the equation

$$z = \mathbf{K}\mathbf{u} + \varepsilon, \qquad (2)$$

where **K** denotes the following blurring operator:

$$(\mathbf{K}\mathbf{u})(x) = \int_\Omega k(x, x')\mathbf{u}(x')dx', \qquad x \in \Omega \qquad (3)$$

with translation-invariant kernel, $k(x, x') = k(x - x')$, known as the point spread function (PSF). ε is the additive noise function. Ω will denote a square in $\mathcal{R}^2$ on which the image intensity is defined. When **K** is the identity operator, the problem (2) becomes image de-noising. In this paper, we focus on de-blurring problem. The PSF function must be known. However, if it is unknown, another technique named blind deconvolution can be used [30]. The operator **K** is compact, so the problem (2) is ill-posed [31], and then the resulting matrix systems from the discretization of this problem are highly ill-conditioned. In this case, directly solving this problem is difficult. The most popular approach to obtain a well-posed problem is to add a regularization term. Different regularization terms are used in the literature, for example:

1. Tikhonov regularization [32] is used to stabilize the problem (2) and also called as penalized least squares. In this case, the problem is then to find a u that minimize the functional

$$F(u) = \frac{1}{2} \parallel \mathbf{K}u - z \parallel^2 + \lambda J(u), \qquad (4)$$

with a small positive parameter λ called the regularization parameter that controls the trade-off between the data fitting term (the first term) and the regularization term (the second term). $\|\cdot\|$ denotes the norm in $\mathcal{L}^2(\Omega)$. The functional J has to be known. Common choices for the functional J are

$$J(u) = \int_\Omega u^2 dx, \tag{5}$$

the above functional gives what is known as Tikhonov regularization with the identity, and

$$J(u) = \int_\Omega |\nabla u|^2 \, dx, \tag{6}$$

where $|\cdot|$ denotes Euclidean norm, and $\nabla = \left(\frac{\partial}{\partial x}, \frac{\partial}{\partial y}\right)$. When u is discontinuous, the functional in (5) often induces either oscillations or ringing. However, in the functional (6), we need to assume that u is a smooth function. Although, this model is easy to use and simple to calculate, it cannot preserve image edges. Hence, both the above choices are unsuitable for image processing applications when we need to recover sharp contrasts modeled by discontinuities in u [28].

2. Total Variation (TV): One of the most commonly used regularization models is the TV. It was introduced for the first time [33] in edge-preserving image denoising by Rudin, Osher and Fatemi (ROF) and it has improved in recent years for image de-noising, de-blurring, in-painting, blind de-convolution, and processing [1–4,34–39]. When using the TV model, the problem is then to find a u that minimizes the functional

$$F(u) = \frac{1}{2} \| \mathbf{K}u - z \|^2 + \lambda J_{TV}(u), \tag{7}$$

where

$$J_{TV}(u) = \int_\Omega |\nabla u| \, dx. \tag{8}$$

Note that, we do not require the continuity of u. Hence, (8) is a good regularization in image processing. However, the Euclidean norm, $|\nabla u|$, is not differentiable at zero. Common modification is to add a small positive parameter β. The resulting is in the modified functional:

$$J_{TV\beta}(u) = \int_\Omega \sqrt{|\nabla u|^2 + \beta^2} dx. \tag{9}$$

The well-posedness of the above minimization problem (7) with the functional given in (9) is studied and analyzed in the literature, such as in [1]. The success of using TV regularization is that TV gives a balance between the ability to describe piecewise smooth images and the complexity of the resulting algorithms. Moreover, the TV regularization performs very well for removing noise/blur while preserving edges. Despite the good contributions of the TV regularization mentioned above, it favors a piecewise constant solution in the bounded variation (BV) space which often leads to the staircase effect. Thus, stair casing remains one of the drawbacks of the TV regularization. To remove the stair case effects, two modifications to the TV regularization model have been used in the literature. The first approach is to higher the order of the derivatives in the TV regularization term, such as the mean curvature or a nonlinear combination of the first and second derivatives [40–45]. These modifications remove/reduce the staircase effects and they are effective but they are computationally expensive due to the increasing the order of the derivatives or due to the nonlinearity terms. The second approach is to use the fractional-order derivatives in the TV regularization terms as shown in [46,47].

2.1. Fractional-Order Derivative in Image Deblurring

The most important advantage of using fractional differential equations is their nonlocal property. The integer order differential operator is a local operator but the fractional order differential operator is nonlocal. This means that the next state of a system depends not only on its current state but also upon all of its historical states. This is more realistic and it is one reason why fractional calculus has become more and more popular.

In image deblurring problems, the blurring is considered nonlocal in some cases and local in others depending on the cause of the blur. For example, if a body is moving while the background is stationary, then the blur is local and in case the camera is moving then the blur is nonlocal. The blurring operator is a convolution operator that depends on the definition of the kernel functions. In the case of a moving camera, the blurring operator involves each pixel in the image, which means that the blurring process is a nonlocal. The bulrring is nonlocal, in this case, so it is appropriate to choose a regularization operator with the same nonlocal property. This property is available in operators that contain fractional derivatives. Comparative studies have shown that fractional-order differentials are more reliable than the integer-order differentials for enhancing edges in image processing. A similar trend has been observed for the texture and area-preserving properties. Therefore, images processed by fractional differentials are clearer and have higher contrast [48]. This approach is widely used in image processing [5–8,49,50]. These works have shown that the fractional-order derivative performs well in achieving a satisfactory compromise between avoiding staircasing and preserving important fine-scale features such as edges and textures. In this paper, we compare the results of the usual TV model with the TFOV model for two image deblurring problems. From Figures 1–6, we can see that the TFOV shows better edge enhancement results than TV in some regions where we can observe that the PSNR at $\alpha = 1$ is lower than PSNR at $\alpha > 1$.

Example 1. *We used the exact Golden House image plotted in Figure 9, the deblurred Golden House image using the TV-model plotted in Figure 27, and the deblurred Golden House image using the TFOV-model plotted in Figure 29. We took a vertical line almost in the middle of these images and plotted the results of the cross sections in Figure 1. In Figure 1, we highlighted three corners (boxes). From Figures 1–6, we can clearly see that the TFOV-based image deblurring results are smoother than the TV-based image deblurring. Additionally, in each corner TV based image deblurring creates a higher error than TFOV. This shows that TFOV-based image deblurring is better and edge-preserving.*

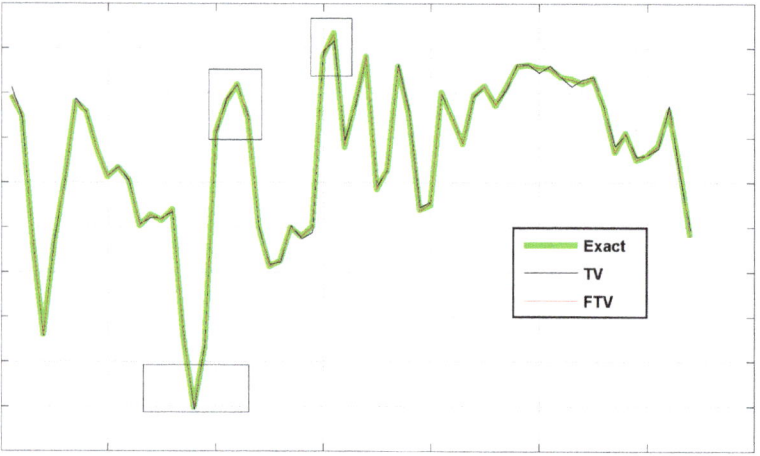

Figure 1. Cross sections.

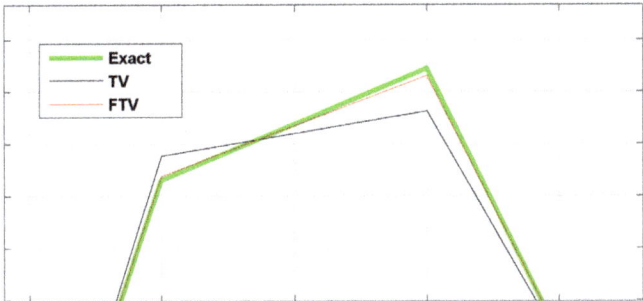

Figure 2. Right box.

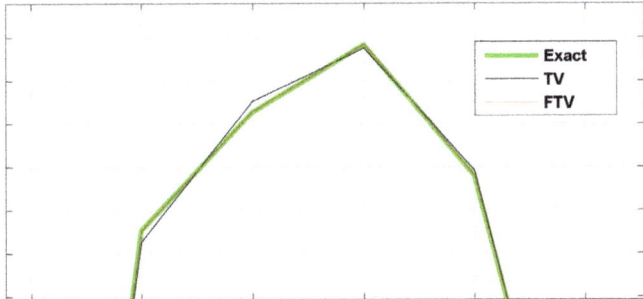

Figure 3. Middle box.

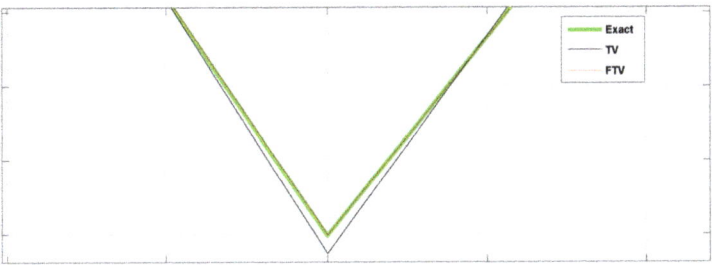

Figure 4. Left box.

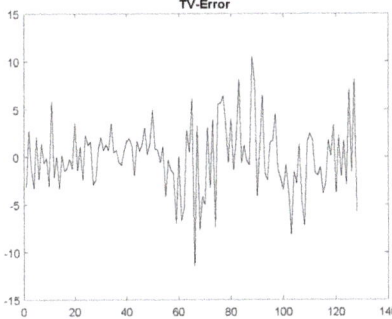

Figure 5. TV-error.

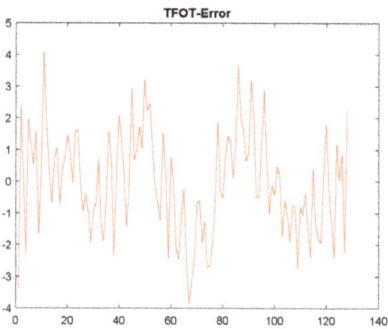

Figure 6. TFOV-error.

The numerical results in the above examples reflect good performance, and motivating us to use the TFOV model in our preconditioners.

2.2. The TFOV-Model

Let $BV^\alpha(\Omega)$ denotes the space of functions of α-bounded variation on Ω defined by

$$BV^\alpha(\Omega) := \left\{ u \in L^1(\Omega) | TV^\alpha(u) < +\infty \right\}.$$

with the BV^α norm $||u||_{BV^\alpha} = ||u||_{L^1} + \int_\Omega |\nabla^\alpha u| dx$. The parameter α represents the order of the fractional derivatives, the fractional-order total variation of u, TV^α is defined by

$$TV^\alpha(u) = \int_\Omega |\nabla^\alpha u| dx := \sup_{\phi \in T} \int_\Omega (-u \, div^\alpha \phi) dx,$$

and $div^\alpha \phi = \frac{\partial^\alpha \phi_1}{\partial x} + \frac{\partial^\alpha \phi_2}{\partial y}$, $\frac{\partial^\alpha \phi_1}{\partial x}$ and $\frac{\partial^\alpha \phi_2}{\partial y}$ denote the fractional-order derivative along the x and y directions respectively. The space T denotes the space of special test functions

$$T := \left\{ \phi \in C_0^\ell(\Omega, \mathbb{R}^2) | |\phi(x)| \leq 1, \quad \forall x \in \Omega \right\}$$

where $|\phi(x)| = \sqrt{\Sigma_{i=1}^2 \phi_i^2}$ and $C^\ell(\Omega, \mathbb{R}^2)$ denote the space of α-order continuously differentiable functions. Hence, when the TFOV- model is used, the problem is then to find a $u \in BV^\alpha(\Omega) \cap L^2(\Omega)$ that minimizes the functional

$$F^\alpha(u) = \frac{1}{2} \| \mathbf{K}u - z \|^2 + \lambda J_{TV\beta}^\alpha(u) \tag{10}$$

where $J_{TV\beta}^\alpha$ is called the modified total fractional-order variation and defined by

$$J_{TV\beta}^\alpha(u) = \int_\Omega \sqrt{|\nabla^\alpha u|^2 + \beta^2} dx, \tag{11}$$

where $|\nabla^\alpha u|^2 = (D_x^\alpha u)^2 + (D_y^\alpha u)^2$ where D_x^α, D_y^α are the fractional derivative operators along the x and y directions respectively. Existence and uniqueness of a minimizer to the above problem (10) with the functional (11) are studied and analyzed in the literature [8,51].

2.3. Fractional-Order Derivatives

Several definitions have been proposed for fractional-order derivatives [52–54]. We shall present some of them below. For a systematic presentation of mathematics, a fractional-order derivative is denoted as function operator $D^\alpha_{[a,x]}$, where a and x are the bounds of the integrals, and α is the order of the fractional derivative such that $0 < n - 1 < \alpha < n$ where $n = [\alpha] + 1$ and $[\cdot]$ is the greatest integer function.

1. **Riemann–Liouville (RL) definitions**: The left- and right-sided RL derivatives of order α of a function $f(x)$ are given as follows:

$$D^\alpha_{[a,x]} f(x) = \frac{1}{\Gamma(n-\alpha)} \left(\frac{d}{dx}\right)^n \int_a^x (x-t)^{n-\alpha-1} f(t) dt \tag{12}$$

and

$$D^\alpha_{[x,b]} f(x) = \frac{(-1)^n}{\Gamma(n-\alpha)} \left(\frac{d}{dx}\right)^n \int_x^b (t-x)^{n-\alpha-1} f(t) dt \tag{13}$$

where $\Gamma(\cdot)$ is the gamma function, defined by

$$\Gamma(z) = \int_0^\infty e^{-t} t^{z-1} dt.$$

2. **Grünwald–Letnikov (GL) definitions**: The left- and right-sided GL derivatives are defined by

$$^G D^\alpha_{[a,x]} f(x) = \lim_{h \to 0} \frac{\sum_{j=0}^{[\frac{x-a}{h}]} (-1)^j C_\alpha^j f(x-jh)}{h^\alpha} \tag{14}$$

and

$$^G D^\alpha_{[x,b]} f(x) = \lim_{h \to 0} \frac{\sum_{j=0}^{[\frac{b-x}{h}]} (-1)^j C_\alpha^j f(x+jh)}{h^\alpha} \tag{15}$$

where

$$C_\alpha^j = \frac{\alpha(\alpha-1)\dots(\alpha-j+1)}{j!}. \tag{16}$$

3. **Caputo (C) definitions**: The left- and right-sided Caputo derivatives are defined by

$$^C D^\alpha_{[a,x]} f(x) = \frac{1}{\Gamma(n-\alpha)} \int_a^x (x-t)^{n-\alpha-1} f^{(n)}(t) dt \tag{17}$$

and

$$^C D^\alpha_{[x,b]} f(x) = \frac{(-1)^n}{\Gamma(n-\alpha)} \int_x^b (t-x)^{n-\alpha-1} f^{(n)}(t) dt \tag{18}$$

where $f^{(n)}$ denotes the nth-order derivative of function $f(x)$.

2.4. Euler-Lagrange Equations

In this subsection, we present the Euler-Lagrange equations associated with the TFOV in image de-blurring problem.

Theorem 1. *If $\alpha \in (1,2)$, the Euler-Lagrange equations for the functional given in (10) are:*

$$K^*(Ku - z) + \lambda L_\alpha(u) u = 0, \text{ in } \Omega$$

$$D^{\alpha-2}\left(\frac{\nabla^\alpha u}{\sqrt{|\nabla^\alpha u|^2 + \beta^2}}\right) \cdot \vec{n} = 0, \quad D^{\alpha-1}\left(\frac{\nabla^\alpha u}{\sqrt{|\nabla^\alpha u|^2 + \beta^2}}\right) \cdot \vec{n} = 0, \text{ on } \partial\Omega, \tag{19}$$

where K^* is the adjoint operator of the integral operator K and the nonlinear deferential operator $L_\alpha(u)$ is given by:

$$L_\alpha(u) w = (-1)^n \nabla^\alpha \cdot \left(\frac{\nabla^\alpha w}{\sqrt{|\nabla^\alpha u|^2 + \beta^2}}\right). \tag{20}$$

Proof. Let $v \in W_1^\alpha(\Omega)$ be a function. Then for $u \in W_1^\alpha(\Omega) \subset BV^\alpha(\Omega)$, the first order Gateaux derivative of the functional $F^\alpha(u)$ of (10) in the direction of v is

$$\frac{\partial F^\alpha(u)v}{\partial v} = \lim_{t \to 0} \frac{F^\alpha(u+tv) - F^\alpha(u)}{t} \tag{21}$$

$$= \lim_{t \to 0} \frac{G_1(u+tv) - G_1(u)}{t} + \lim_{t \to 0} \frac{G_2(u+tv) - G_2(u)}{t},$$

where $G_1(u) = \frac{1}{2} \int_\Omega (Ku - z) dx$ and $G_2(u) = \lambda J_{TV\beta}^\alpha(u)$. By using the Taylor series in the direction of t, we have

$$\frac{\partial F^\alpha(u)v}{\partial v} = \int_\Omega \mathbf{K}^*(Ku - z) dx + \int_\Omega (\mathbf{W}.\nabla^\alpha v) dx, \tag{22}$$

where $\mathbf{W} = \lambda \frac{\nabla^\alpha u}{\sqrt{|\nabla^\alpha u|^2 + \beta^2}}$. Now consider,

$$\int_\Omega (\mathbf{W}.\nabla^\alpha v) dx = (-1)^n \int_\Omega (v^C div^\alpha \mathbf{W}) dx \tag{23}$$

$$-\sum_{j=0}^{n-1} (-1)^j \int_0^1 D_{[a,b]}^{\alpha+j-n} W_1 \frac{\partial^{n-j-1} v(x)}{\partial x_1^{n-j-1}}\Big|_{x_1=0}^{x_1=1} dx_2 - \sum_{j=0}^{n-1} (-1)^j \int_0^1 D_{[a,b]}^{\alpha+j-n} W_2 \frac{\partial^{n-j-1} v(x)}{\partial x_2^{n-j-1}}\Big|_{x_2=0}^{x_2=1} dx_1,$$

where we know that $n = 2$ for $1 < \alpha < 2$.

Case-I: If $u(x)\big|_{\partial\Omega} = b_1(x)$ and $\frac{\partial u(x)}{\partial n}\big|_{\partial\Omega} = b_2(x)$, so $\left(u(x) + tv(x)\right)\big|_{\partial\Omega} = b_1(x)$ and $\frac{\partial (u(x)+tv(x))}{\partial n}\big|_{\partial\Omega} = b_2(x)$. Then it suffices to take $v \in C_0^1(\Omega, \mathbb{R})$, this implies

$$\frac{\partial^i v(x)}{\partial n^i}\Big|_{\partial\Omega} = 0, \quad i = 0, 1,$$

$$\Rightarrow \frac{\partial^{n-j-1} v(x)}{\partial x_1^{n-j-1}}\Big|_{x_1=0,1} = \frac{\partial^{n-j-1} v(x)}{\partial x_2^{n-j-1}}\Big|_{x_2=0,1} = 0, \quad n-j-1 = 0, 1.$$

Hence (22) reduces to (19).

Case-II: If $v \in W_1^\alpha(\Omega)$, then

$$\frac{\partial^{n-j-1} v(x)}{\partial x_1^{n-j-1}}\Big|_{x_1=0,1} \neq 0, \quad \frac{\partial^{n-j-1} v(x)}{\partial x_2^{n-j-1}}\Big|_{x_2=0,1} \neq 0, \quad n-j-1 = 0, 1.$$

So boundary terms in (23) can only become zero if

$$D_{[a,b]}^{\alpha+j-n} W_1 \Big|_{x_1=0,1} = D_{[a,b]}^{\alpha+j-n} W_2 \Big|_{x_2=0,1} = 0$$

$$\Rightarrow D^{\alpha+j-n} \mathbf{W}.n = 0, \quad j = 0, 1.$$

This completes the proof. □

Note that (19) is a nonlinear integro-differential equation of elliptic type. Equation (19) can be expressed as a nonlinear first order system [55]:

$$\mathbf{K}^* Ku + \lambda \nabla^\alpha . \vec{v} = \mathbf{K}^* z, \tag{24}$$

$$-\nabla^\alpha u + \sqrt{|\nabla^\alpha u|^2 + \beta} \vec{v} = \vec{0}, \tag{25}$$

with the dual, or flux, variable

$$\vec{v} = \frac{\nabla^\alpha u}{\sqrt{|\nabla^\alpha u|^2 + \beta}}. \tag{26}$$

We apply the Galerkin method to (24)–(25) together with the midpoint quadrature for the integral term and cell-centered finite difference method for the derivative part.

2.5. Discretization of the Fractional Derivative

First, we divide the square domain $\Omega = (0,1) \times (0,1)$ into N^2 equal squares (cells) where N denotes the number of equispaced partitions in the x or y directions. Then, we follow the same discretization in [8,51]. We define a spatial partition (x_k, y_l) (for all $k, l = 0, 1, \ldots, N+1$) of image domain Ω. Assume u has a zero Dirichlet boundary condition, we consider the discretization of the α-order fractional derivative at the inner point (x_k, y_l) (for all $k, l = 0, 1, \ldots, N$) on Ω along the x-direction by using the shifted Grünwald approximation approach [56,57]

$$\begin{aligned} D^\alpha f(x_k, y_l) &= \frac{\delta_0^\alpha f(x_k, y_l)}{h^\alpha} + O(h) = \frac{1}{2}\left(\frac{\delta_-^\alpha f(x_k, y_l)}{h^\alpha} + \frac{\delta_+^\alpha f(x_k, y_l)}{h^\alpha}\right) + O(h) \\ &= \frac{1}{2h^\alpha}\left(\Sigma_{j=0}^{k+1} \omega_j^\alpha f_{k-j+1}^l + \Sigma_{j=0}^{N-k+2} \omega_j^\alpha f_{k+j-1}^l\right) + O(h) \end{aligned} \tag{27}$$

where $f_s^l = f_{s,l}$ and $\omega_j^\alpha = (-1)^j \binom{\alpha}{j} j = 0, 1, \ldots, N$ and $\omega_0^\alpha = 1$, $\omega_j^\alpha = (1 - \frac{1+\alpha}{j})\omega_{j-1}^\alpha$ for $j > 0$. Observe from (27) that the first order estimate of the α-order fractional derivative $D_{[a,b]}^\alpha f(x_k, y_l)$ along the x-direction at the point (x_k, y_l) with a fixed y_l is a linear combination of $N+2$ values $f_0^l, f_1^l, \ldots, f_N^l, f_{N+1}^l$. After incorporating the zero boundary condition in the matrix approximation of fractional derivative, all N equations of fractional derivatives along the x direction in (27) can be written simultaneously in the matrix form

$$\begin{bmatrix} \delta_0^\alpha f(x_1, y_l) \\ \delta_0^\alpha f(x_2, y_l) \\ \vdots \\ \vdots \\ \delta_0^\alpha f(x_N, y_l) \end{bmatrix} = \frac{1}{2h^\alpha} \underbrace{\begin{bmatrix} 2\omega_1^\alpha & \omega_0^\alpha + \omega_2^\alpha & \omega_3^\alpha & \cdots & \omega_N^\alpha \\ \omega_0^\alpha + \omega_2^\alpha & 2\omega_1^\alpha & \ddots & \ddots & \vdots \\ \omega_3^\alpha & \ddots & \ddots & \ddots & \omega_3^\alpha \\ \vdots & \ddots & \ddots & 2\omega_1^\alpha & \omega_0^\alpha + \omega_2^\alpha \\ \omega_N^\alpha & \cdots & \omega_3^\alpha & \omega_0^\alpha + \omega_2^\alpha & 2\omega_1^\alpha \end{bmatrix}}_{B_N^\alpha} \begin{bmatrix} f_1^l \\ f_2^l \\ \vdots \\ \vdots \\ f_N^l \end{bmatrix}.$$

From the definition of fractional-order derivative (27), for any $1 < \alpha < 2$, the coefficients ω_k^α have the following properties:

(1) $\omega_0^\alpha = 1$, $\omega_1^\alpha = -\alpha < 0$, $1 \geq \omega_2^\alpha \geq \omega_3^\alpha \geq \ldots \geq 0$.
(2) $\Sigma_{k=0}^\infty \omega_k^\alpha = 0$, $\Sigma_{k=0}^m \omega_k^\alpha \leq 0 (m \geq 1)$.

Hence by the Gershgorin circle theorem, we can derive that matrix B_N^α is a symmetric and negative definite Toeplitz matrix (i.e., $-B_N^\alpha$ is a positive definite Toeplitz matrix). Let $U \in \mathbb{R}^{N \times N}$ denote the solution matrix at all nodes $(khx; lhy), k, l = 1, \ldots, N$ corresponding to x-direction and y-direction spatial discretization nodes. Denote by $\vec{u} \in \mathbb{R}^{N^2 \times 1}$, the ordered solution vector of U. The direct and discrete analogue of differentiation of arbitrary α order derivative is

$$u_x^\alpha = (I_N \otimes B^\alpha{}_N)\vec{u} = B_x^\alpha \vec{u} \tag{28}$$

Similarly, all values of α-th order y-direction derivative of $u(x;y)$ at these nodes are approximated by

$$u_y^\alpha = (B^\alpha{}_N \otimes I_N)\vec{u} = B_y^\alpha \vec{u}, \tag{29}$$

where

$$u_x^\alpha = (u_{11}^\alpha, \ldots, u_{N1}^\alpha, u_{12}^\alpha, \ldots, u_{NN}^\alpha)^T, \quad u_y^\alpha = (u_{11}^\alpha, \ldots, u_{1N}^\alpha, u_{21}^\alpha, \ldots, u_{NN}^\alpha)^T, \tag{30}$$

$\vec{u} = u_{11}, u_{12}, \ldots, u_{NN}$ and $\otimes$ denotes the Kronecker product. For more details in the discretization, we refer to [54,58]. Now, using the cell center finite difference Method (CCFDM), the fractional discretization shown above, and using the fact that $[(-1)^n \nabla^\alpha \cdot]$ is the adjoint operator of the operator ∇^α, then (24)–(25) leads to the following system

$$\begin{aligned} V + K_h U &= Z, \\ K_h^* V - \lambda (L^\alpha{}_h U^m) U^{m+1} &= 0, \quad m = 0, 1, 2 \ldots N_F, \end{aligned} \tag{31}$$

where N_F is the number of Fixed-Point Iterations used to linearize the nonlinear term in the square root in (26). The matrix K_h is obtained form using the midpoint quadrature for the integral operator as follows:

$$(\mathbf{K}u)(x_i, y_j) \approx [K_h U]_{ij}, \quad i, j = 1, 2, \ldots, N. \tag{32}$$

with entries $[K_h U]_{ij,lm} = h^2 k(x_i - x_j, y_l - y_m)$. With using the lexicographical order, K_h is a block Toeplitz with Toeplitz block (BTTB) matrix. The need for BTTB property will be discussed later in the paper. The discrete scheme of the matrix $L^\alpha{}_h U$ is given by:

$$(L^\alpha(U^m))U^{m+1} = [B_N(D_1(U^m)) \circ (B_N U^{m+1})] + [(D_2(U^m) \circ (U^{m+1} B_M))]B_N \tag{33}$$

where $\circ$ is the point wise multiplication and m is the $m - th$ Fixed-Point Iteration. U is an $N \times N$-size reshaped matrix of the vector u and the matrices $D_1(U^m)$ and $D_2(U^m)$ are the diagonal of the Hadamard inverses of the non-zero matrices $B_x^\alpha(U^m)$ and $B_y^\alpha(U^m)$ respectively.

2.6. Difficulties in TFOV-Model Compared to TV-Model

In this subsection, we compare the TFOV-system (1):

$$\underbrace{\begin{bmatrix} I_n & K_h \\ -K_h^* & \lambda L_h^\alpha(U_h) \end{bmatrix}}_{A^\alpha} \underbrace{\begin{bmatrix} V_h \\ U_h \end{bmatrix}}_{x} = \underbrace{\begin{bmatrix} Z_h \\ 0 \end{bmatrix}}_{b},$$

and the following TV-system:

$$\underbrace{\begin{bmatrix} I_n & K_h \\ -K_h^* & \lambda L_h(U_h) \end{bmatrix}}_{A} \underbrace{\begin{bmatrix} V_h \\ U_h \end{bmatrix}}_{x} = \underbrace{\begin{bmatrix} Z_h \\ 0 \end{bmatrix}}_{b}. \tag{34}$$

In the TFOV system (1), the fractional matrix L_h^α is obtained from discretizing a fractional deferential operator and it is dense. The density property leads to an expensive matrix-vector multiplication. In this case, the coefficient matrix A^α in the system (1) contains three dense submatrices, while in TV system (34), the non-fractional matrix L_h is obtained from discretizing a non-fractional deferential operator and it is a sparse matrix, then the coefficient matrix A in the system (34) contains only two dense submatrices. Further, the Schur complement matrix associated with (1) is a sum of two dense matrices while the Schur complement matrix associated with (34) is a sum of one dense matrix and one sparse matrix.

3. Preconditioning Technique

In the literature, it has been shown that block triangular preconditioners are among the most effective preconditioners for solving saddle point problems. In this paper, we develop two block triangular preconditioners for solving (1). First, we present our main preconditioner matrix [12] and its inverse:

$$P = \begin{bmatrix} I_n & K \\ 0 & -S \end{bmatrix}, \quad P^{-1} = \begin{bmatrix} I_n & KS^{-1} \\ 0 & -S^{-1} \end{bmatrix}, \tag{35}$$

where $S = K^*K + \lambda L_\alpha$ is the Schur complement matrix. We notice that the Schur complement matrix contains the product (K^*K) which is not a BTTB matrix. We know that a BTTB matrix-vector product computation cost $O(N \log N)$ but using a BCCB extension. Since this extension is not an easy task in some cases, the idea of using a circulant matrix as a preconditioner for a Toeplitz matrix is needed. This idea was first proposed by Strang [59] and Olkin [60] and extended by others to block Toeplitz systems for example Chan et al. [61]. Many researchers use Toeplitz preconditioners and block Toeplitz preconditioners for Toeplitz systems. For instance, Chan et al. [62], and Lin and Fu-Rong [63]. Band Toeplitz preconditioner and band BTTB preconditioner are proposed by Chan and Raymond [64] and Serra and Stefano [65]. In Lin et al. [66], BTTB preconditioners for BTTB systems are discussed. Several kinds of circulant preconditioners have been proposed to be good preconditioners, see for instance [59,62,67–69]. Several kinds of circulant preconditioners have been proposed and proven to be good preconditioners. Therefore, the PCG methods with circulant preconditioners converge very fast when they are used to solve Toeplitz systems. Motivated by these papers, we propose the following two block triangular preconditioners:

$$P_1 = \begin{bmatrix} I_n & K \\ 0 & -S_1 \end{bmatrix}, \quad P_2 = \begin{bmatrix} I_n & K \\ 0 & -S_2 \end{bmatrix}, \tag{36}$$

where $S_1 = (I + \lambda L_{TV})$ and $S_2 = (C^*C + \lambda L_{TV})$. Where I is the denoising operator, the identity matrix is a circulant matrix, and L_{TV} comes from discretizing the TV model ($\alpha = 1$) which is a sparse matrix and C is the Strang circulant approximation of the matrix K [59]. These circulant approximations are very important to allow us to use the FFT and the convolution theorem. We know that all circulant matrices can be diagonalized by the Fourier matrix, see [70]. Also using FFT and the convolution theorem will reduce the cost of the computation from $O(N^2)$ into $O(N \log N)$. Moreover, all that is needed for computation is the first column or the first row of the circulant matrix, which decreases the amount of required storage. This reduction in the computations and storage leads to efficient solvers for our problem (1).

4. Preconditioned GMRES Algorithm

In this section, we give a detailed algorithms for using our preconditioner P (P_1 and P_2). In Algorithm 1, GMRES method is used to solve the linear system (1).

In Algorithm 1, in Steps 3 and 7, we need to solve a matrix times a vector of the form

$$\underbrace{\begin{bmatrix} I_n & K \\ 0 & -S \end{bmatrix}}_{P} \underbrace{\begin{bmatrix} x_1 \\ x_2 \end{bmatrix}}_{x} = \underbrace{\begin{bmatrix} b_1 \\ b_2 \end{bmatrix}}_{b}, \tag{37}$$

where $S = S_1$ or $S = S_2$. To do the above multiplications, we use the conjugate gradients method as in Algorithms 2 and 3:

Algorithm 1 Preconditioned GMRES Algorithm

1: Choose x^0 as the initial guess
2: Compute $\tilde{r}^0 = b - Ax^0$
3: Solve $P\, r^0 = \tilde{r}^0$
4: Let $\beta_0 = \|r^0\|$, and compute $v^{(1)} = r^0/\beta_0$
5: **for** $k = 1, 2, \ldots$ until $\beta_k < \tau\beta_0$ **do**
6:     $\tilde{w}_0^{(k+1)} = Av^{(k)}$
7:     Solve $P\, w_0^{(k+1)} = \tilde{w}_0^{(k+1)}$
8:     **for** $l = 1$ to k **do**
9:         $h_{lk} = \langle w_l^{(k+1)}, v^{(l)} \rangle$
10:        $w_l^{(k+1)} = w_l^{(k+1)} - h_{lk}v^{(l)}$
11:     **end for**
12:     $h_{k+1,k} = w_{k+1}^{(k+1)}/h_{k+1,k}$
13:     Compute $y^{(k)}$ such that $\beta_k = \|\beta_0 e_1 - \hat{H}_k y^{(k)}\|$ is minimized, where $\hat{H}_k = [h_{ij}]_{1 \le i \le k+1, 1 \le j \le k}$ and $e_1 = (1, 0, \ldots, 0)^T$
14: **end for**
15: $x^{(k)} = x^0 + V_k y^{(k)}$

Algorithm 2 P_1-Conjugate Gradient Method Algorithm.

1: $x_1 = x(1:n) = b(1:n) - Kx_2$;
2: $S_1 = P_1(n+1:2n, n+1:2n)$;
3: $b_2 = b(n+1:2n)$;
4: $x_2 = x(n+1:2n)$
5: Solve for x_2 in the system $-S_1 x_2 = b_2$ using conjugate gradient method.

Algorithm 3 P_2-Conjugate Gradient Method Algorithm.

1: $x_1 = x(1:n) = b(1:n) - Kx_2$;
2: $S_2 = P_2(n+1:2n, n+1:2n)$;
3: $b_2 = b(n+1:2n)$;
4: $x_2 = x(n+1:2n)$;
5: Solve for x_2 in the system $-S_2 x_2 = b_2$ using conjugate gradient method.

Eigenvalues Estimates

In this subsection, we need to study the eigenvalues of the exact preconditioned matrix $P^{-1}A$. Since $P^{-1}A$ and AP^{-1} are similar matrices, they have the same eigenvalues. Hence we study the eigenvalues of the matrix AP^{-1}.

Theorem 2. *If the linear system (1) is left preconditioned by the matrix P, then the preconditioned matrix is*

$$AP^{-1} = \begin{bmatrix} I_n & 0 \\ -K^* & -I_n \end{bmatrix}, \qquad (38)$$

and its minimal polynomial is $(\nu - 1)(\nu + 1)$ where ν is the eigenvalue of the matrix AP^{-1}.

Proof. Since AP^{-1} and $P^{-1}A$ are similar, it is easy to study the eigenvalues of AP^{-1} instead of $P^{-1}A$. From the form of AP^{-1}, we notice that the preconditioned matrix has only two distinct eigenvalues ± 1 and then we notice that a minimal polynomial of degree at most 2. Hence, when Krylov subspace methods like FGMRES is used, then it converges in 2 iterations or less, in exact arithmetic. This property is of practical use when inexpensive approximations of the Schur complement exist. However, when we approximate the Schur complement matrix S by the matrix S_1 or S_2, we have the following eigenvalue estimation. □

Theorem 3. If the linear system (1) is left preconditioned by the matrix P_1 or P_2, then the eigenvalues of the preconditioned matrices

$$A(P_1)^{-1} = \begin{bmatrix} I_n & 0 \\ -K^* & -SS_1^{-1} \end{bmatrix}, \text{ and } A(P_2)^{-1} = \begin{bmatrix} I_n & 0 \\ -K^* & -SS_2^{-1} \end{bmatrix} \quad (39)$$

are described as follows:

$$\nu_+ = \{1\}, \text{ and } \nu_- \in [\sigma_1, \sigma_n], \quad (40)$$

where σ_1 and σ_n are the minimum and the maximum eigenvalues of the matrix $(-SS_1^{-1})$ or $(-SS_2^{-1})$.

Example 2. In this example, our aim is to verify that the bounds given in the above theorem are matched. We take $N = 16$, i.e., $n = (16)^2 = 256$ and we fix $\alpha = 1.4$, $\beta = 0.1$, $\lambda = 0.001$. For this task, we use the preconditioner P_1 and we use the test image "Golden House". We notice that the positive eigenvalues are equal to one whereas the negatives are contained in the interval $[\sigma_1, \sigma_n]$ where σ_1 and σ_n are defined in the above theorem. In this example $\sigma_1 \cong -1.01$ and $\sigma_n \cong -1$. The results of this example are plotted and shown in Figures 7 and 8. Moreover, in this experiment, we find that the $\text{cond}(A) = 3.2915 \times 10^4$ and $\text{cond}((P_1)^{-1}A) = 1.6219$ which indicate that our preconditioner is effective.

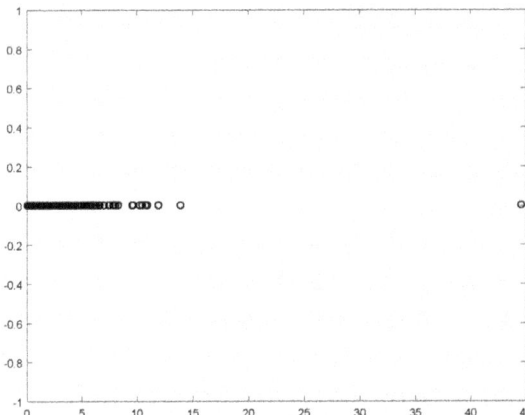

Figure 7. Eigenvalues of A.

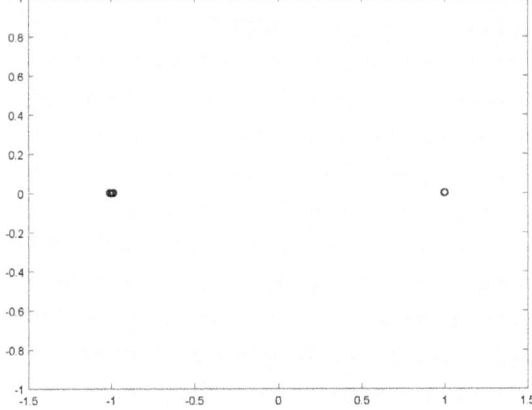

Figure 8. Eigenvalues of $(P_1)^{-1}A$.

From Figures 7 and 8, we notice that the preconditioned matrix has a good clustering behavior of the eigenvalues. The eigenvalues are clustering around 1 and -1. This clustering verifies the above theorem guarantees fast convergence of the FGMRES method.

5. Numerical Results

In this section, we experimentally study the performance of the FGMRES method with the proposed preconditioners P_1 and P_2. In the following numerical experiments, we implement Algorithms 1–3, and we take the zero vector to be the initial guess. We stopped the outer iterations (FGMRES) when the residuals satisfies $\|b - Ax^k\| < 10^{-7} \|b\|$ where $x^k = (v^k, u^k)$ is the solution vector in the $k-th$ iteration. We used only one iteration of the Fixed-Point Iteration method to linearize the nonlinear term and then we used the PCG for the inner iterations and it is stopped when the tolerance is 10^{-9}. No restarting is used for FGMRES algorithm. For this purpose, two famous 128×128 test images, called Retinal Image and Golden House are used in the experiments, as shown in Figures 9 and 10 and they are blurred by the motion kernel as shown in Figure 11.

Figure 9. Golden house image.

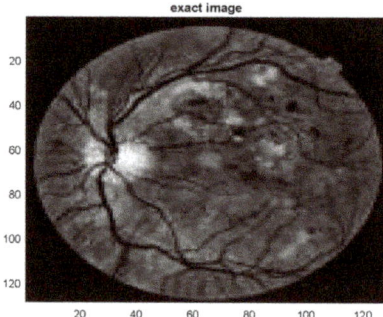

Figure 10. Retinal image.

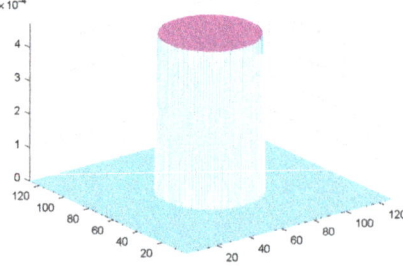

Figure 11. Shape of the kernel.

In order to show the performance of the proposed preconditioners, we need to calculate the PSNR which is commonly used in the signal processing field. It can be calculated by the following formula:

$$PSNR(u_e, u_d) = 10 \log \left(\frac{n \max_{1 \leq i,j \leq n} |u_e|}{\sum_{i=1}^{n_x} \sum_{j=1}^{n_x} \left(u_{eij} - u_{dij} \right)^2} \right) \quad (41)$$

where u_e and u_d are the exact and deblurred images, respectively. Bigger PSNR means better deblurring performance.

5.1. The Parameters β and λ Selecting

The value of the parameters β and λ also play a vital role in the performance of the numerical technique used for the image deblurring model. Small values of β affect the convergence rate of the iterations in the numerical technique but do not change the quality of the deblurred images. We have chosen $\beta = 1, \beta = 0.1$ and $\beta = 0.01$ which are commonly used in the literature [28]. We noticed no significant difference in the results between these values. Regarding the values of the regularization parameters λ, we have chosen λ small enough, 10^{-3}, 10^{-5} 10^{-6} and 10^{-8} to ensure the best deblurring performance of the corresponding deblurring model. These values are commonly used in the literature [28].

Example 3. *In this example, we show the impact of our preconditioners on the convergence speed of the FGMRES algorithm for the fractional-order image deblurring problem. We fix $N = 128$, $\beta = 0.1$, and the regularization parameter $\lambda = 0.001$. No restarting is used for the FGMRES algorithm and it is stopped when the tolerance is 10^{-7}. We use the test image "Golden House". In each FGMRES iteration, the logarithm of $\frac{||r^{(k)}||_2}{||r^{(0)}||_2}$ is calculated and then plotted for different values of the regularization parameter λ in Figures 12 and 13.*

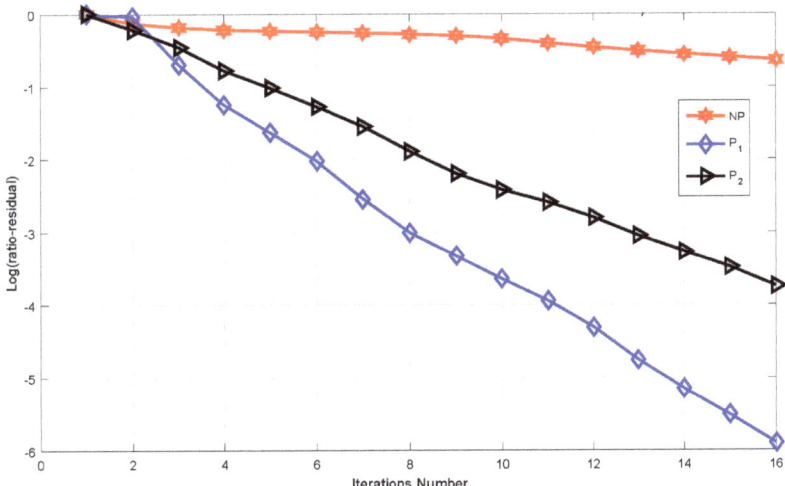

Figure 12. Residual versus iterations number when $\lambda = 1 \times 10^{-3}$.

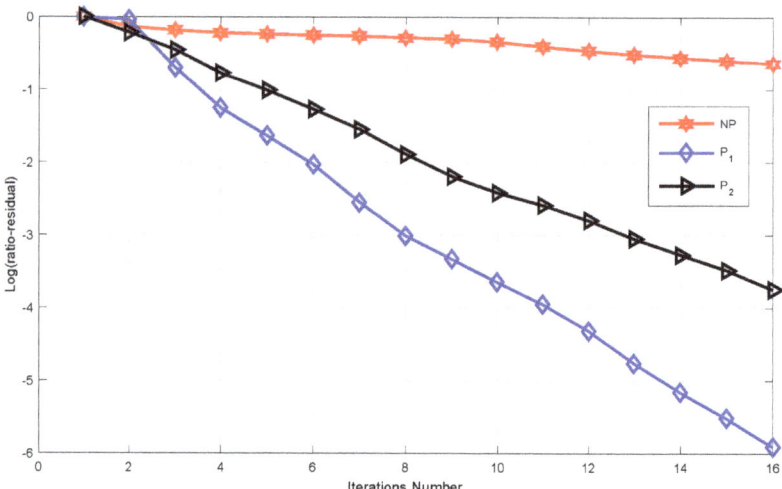

Figure 13. Residual versus iterations number when $\lambda = 1 \times 10^{-5}$.

In Figures 12 and 13, we show the algorithm of the ratio of the current residual norm to the initial residual norm, plotted against the number of FGMRES iteration, for different values of the regularization parameter λ. NP stands for FGMRES without preconditioners, P_1 stands for FGMRES with the preconditioner P_1 and P_2 stands for FGMRES with the preconditioner P_2. The results in Figures 12 and 13 show that our block triangular preconditioners P_1 and P_2 significantly accelerate the convergence of FGMRES, compared to FGMRES without preconditioners. Additionally, P_1 outperforms P_2.

Example 4. In this example, we show the effectiveness of our proposed preconditioners in deblurring images. We used two blurred images (of size 128×128) shown in Figures 14 and 15. We select the following parameters: $\alpha = 1.8$, $\beta = 1$, and $\lambda = 0.00001$. We used our preconditioners P_1 and P_2 to deblur the images and the results are shown in Figures 16–23.

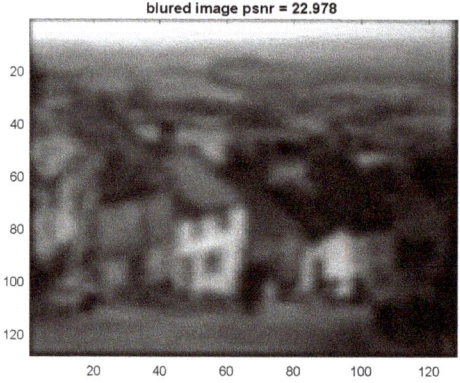

Figure 14. Golden house image (blurred).

From Figures 16–23, the results show that our preconditioners are effective in deblurring images, with significant improvement in the PSNR. For example, the PSNR of deblurred image in Figure 16 is 49.41, compared to the PSNR 22.978 for the blurred image in Figure 23.

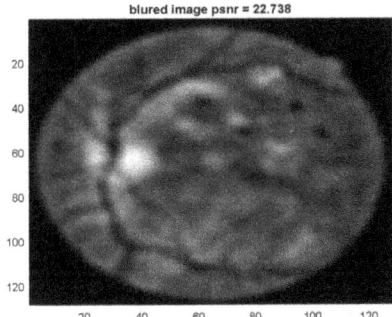

Figure 15. Retinal image (blurred).

Figure 16. Using P_1 with $\alpha = 1$.

Figure 17. Using P_2 with $\alpha = 1$.

Figure 18. Using P_1 with $\alpha = 1.8$.

Figure 19. Using P_2 with $\alpha = 1.8$.

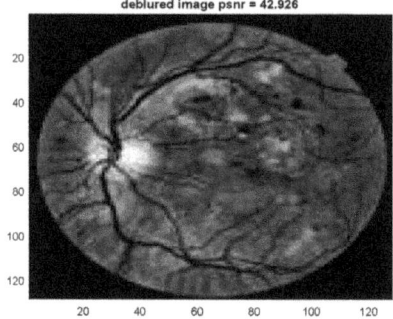

Figure 20. Using P_1 with $\alpha = 1$.

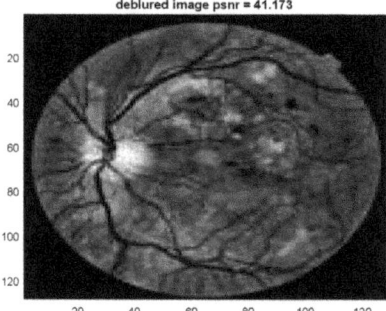

Figure 21. Using P_2 with $\alpha = 1$.

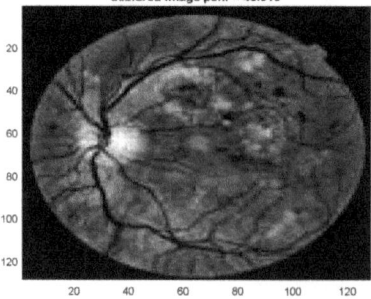

Figure 22. Using P_1 with $\alpha = 1.8$.

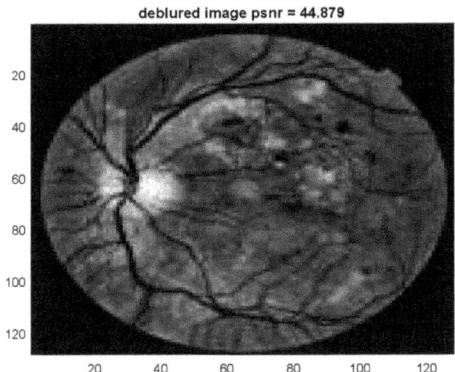

Figure 23. Using P_2 with $\alpha = 1.8$.

Example 5. *In this example, we compare the total CPU-time (in seconds) required for the convergence of the FGMRES with and without our proposed preconditioners P_1 and P_2. The results are shown in Table 1 for different $N, \alpha, \beta, \lambda$.*

Table 1. The CPU time comparison of GMRES and FGMRES.

Parameters				Iterations			CPU-Time		
N	α	λ	β	NP	P_1	P_2	NP	P_1	P_2
32	1.3	10^{-3}	1	53	30	32	3.44	1.88	1.98
64	1.8	10^{-8}	0.1	301	166	194	39.71	20.97	20.55
128	1.6	10^{-6}	0.01	178	68	91	76.64	35.86	38.22

From Table 1, the results show that both P_1 and P_2 can significantly reduce the CPU-time required for convergence, compared to FGMRES without preconditioners. For example, for $N = 128$, $\alpha = 1.6$, $\beta = 0.01$, and $\lambda = 10^{-6}$, the CPU-time for FGMRES without preconditioning is 76.64 s, while the CPU-time for FGMRES with P_1 is 35.86 s and the CPU-time for FGMRES with P_2 is 38.22. Overall, the results show our proposed preconditioners P_1 and P_2 are effective in accelerating the convergence of FGMRES for the fractional-order image deblurring problem. This can lead to significant reductions in CPU-time, which is important for practical applications.

5.2. GMRES versus FGMRES

In this experimental result, we compared the performance of GMRES and FGMRES with our preconditioner P_1 using the following parameters: $N = 64$, $\alpha = 1.4$, $\beta = 0.1$, and $\lambda = 10^{-5}$. We used the test image "Golden House". We used both GMRES and FGMRES. In this example, both GMRES and FGMRES were stopped when the tolerance was 10^{-7} and no restarting is used. The comparison results are shown in Figure 24, where P_1GM stand for $GMRES$ with P_1 and P_1FG stands for $FGMRES$ with P_1. As shown in the figure, FGMRES is performed slightly better than GMRES.

In the following numerical result, we show the comparison of our TFOV-based algorithm with TV-based algorithm [28].

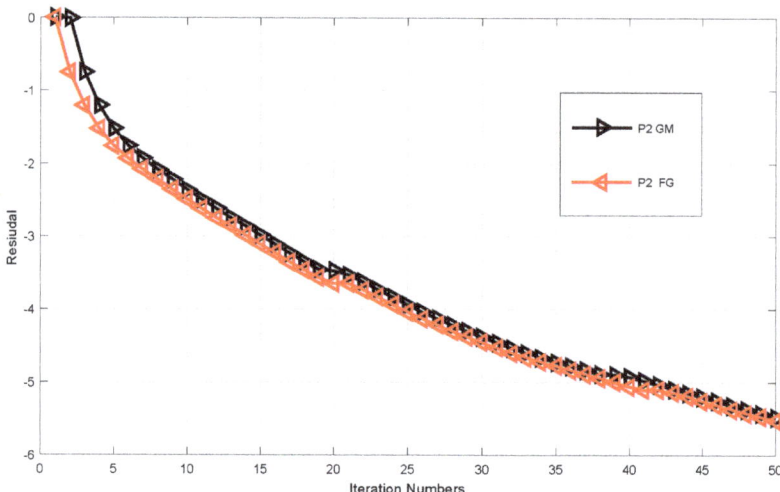

Figure 24. FGMRES vs. GMRES.

Example 6. *In this example, we compare our TFOV- based algorithm with the TV-based algorithm on the nontextured peppers image. We use a Gaussian kernel with standard deviation $\sigma = 1.5$. The results are shown in Figures 25–30. The size of each subfigure is 256×256. The subfigures are as follows: (a) exact image (b) blurry image (c) deblurred image by TV (d) deblurred image by NP (e) deblurred image by P_1 and (f) deblurred image P_2. For numerical calculations, we used the motion kernel. For the TV-based method we used $\beta = 1$ and λ varying from 10^{-2} to 10^{-4}, according to [28]. The parameters for TFOV-based method are listed in Table 2. For comparison we used three different values of N: 64, 128 and 256. Their corresponding blurred PSNRs are 20.1827, 20.1124 and 20.5531 respectively. For the stopping criteria of the numerical methods, we used tolerance $tol = 10^{-7}$.*

Remark 1.

1. Figures 27–30 are almost similar, indicating that all methods generate the same quality results.
2. From Figures 31–33, we can clearly see the effectiveness of preconditioning. For all values of N, the number of P_1 and P_2 iterations is much lower than the number of TFOV-based NP and TV-based P_1 iterations to reach the required accuracy $tol = 10^{-7}$. The later fixed-point iterations also have similar results.
3. From Table 2, we observed that the PSNR by the TFOV-based PGMRES method is almost the same as that of the ordinary TFOV-based GMRES method, but much higher than that of the TV-based P_1 method for all values of N. However, the P_1 and P_2 methods generate this better PSNR in much fewer iterations. For example, to achieve a better PSNR the P_1 method needs only 18 iterations, and the P_2 method needs only 20 iterations for $N = 64$. However, the NP method needs 120+ iterations to get the same PSNR. The TV-based P_1 method also takes 120+ iterations to get its lower PSNR. The same is the case for other values of N. This means that the TFOV-based FGMRES method is faster than the TFOV-based GMRES and TV-based P_1 methods.

Figure 25. Peppers image (exact).

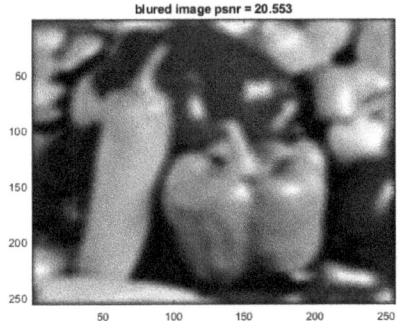

Figure 26. Peppers image (blurred).

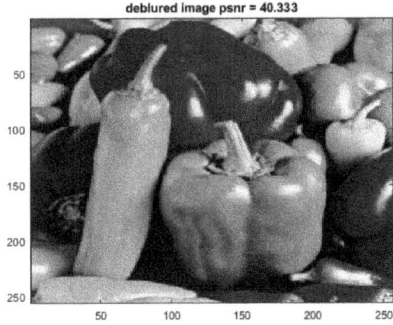

Figure 27. Using TV ($\alpha = 1$).

Figure 28. Using NP.

Figure 29. Using P_1 with $\alpha = 1.9$.

Figure 30. Using P_2 with $\alpha = 1.9$.

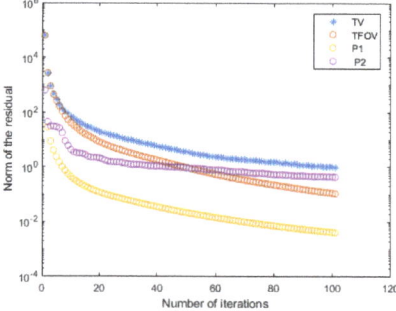

Figure 31. $N = 64$.

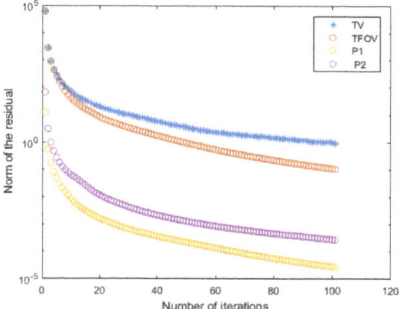

Figure 32. $N = 128$.

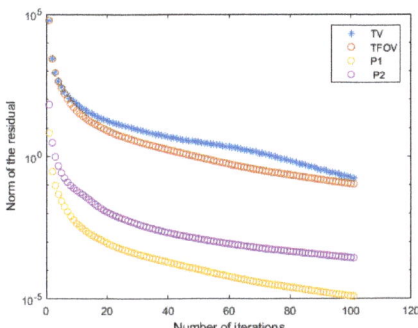

Figure 33. $N = 256$.

Table 2. The PSNR Comparison of TV, NP, P_1 and P_2.

Parameters				Iterations				Deblurred PSNR			
N	α	λ	β	TV ($\alpha = 1$)	NP	P_1	P_2	TV ($\alpha = 1$)	NP	P_1	P_2
64	1.6	10^{-4}	1	120+	120+	20	18	47.2230	48.6422	49.0131	48.9233
128	1.8	10^{-4}	1	120+	120+	40	22	45.2243	46.0352	46.8526	46.8957
256	1.9	10^{-7}	1	120+	120+	60	38	40.3331	44.1220	44.6277	44.6241

Example 7. *In this example, we utilized satellite images used by Chowdhury et al. [71]. The images underwent deliberate blurring and were corrupted by Poisson noise, resulting in the presence of blurring artifacts. To achieve the blurring, we applied a kernel with specific parameters, namely, we used the Gaussian build in kernel "$fspecial('gaussian', 9, sqrt(3))$". The introduction of Poisson noise to the image presents a substantial challenge for most deblurring techniques, as this type of noise frequently occurs in scenarios involving photon counting across various imaging methods. Simultaneously, blurring is an inevitable consequence due to the underlying physical principles of the imaging system, which can be thought of as the convolution of the image with a point spread function. For the sake of comparison, we chose to employ the non-blind fractional order TV-based algorithm (NFOV) proposed by Chaudhury et al. [71]. The restored satellite images can be seen in Figures 34–38, with each image sized at 128×128. We configured the parameters for the NFOV method as specified in the reference by Chowdhury et al. [71]. For comparison, we have used two different values of N. These are 64 and 128. Their corresponding blurred PSNR are 20.2985 and 20.4559 respectively. The computational technique's stopping criterion is determined by a tolerance value of $tol = 10^{-7}$. Additional details regarding this experiment can be located in Table 3.*

Remark 2. *Upon examining Figures 35–38 and Table 3, it becomes apparent that the results generated by all methods are virtually indistinguishable. Nevertheless, our proposed methods (GMRES and FGMRES) exhibit slightly higher PSNR values while demanding significantly less CPU time. This observation underscores the improved efficiency and speed of our suggested methods (GMRES and FGMRES) in comparison to the NFOV technique.*

Table 3. The PSNR Comparison of NFOV, NP, P_1 and P_2.

Parameters				Iterations				Deblurred PSNR			
N	α	λ	β	NFOV	NP	P_1	P_2	NFOV	NP	P_1	P_2
64	1.7	10^{-4}	1	120+	120+	41	26	25.9869	26.5625	26.7861	26.8283
128	1.9	10^{-7}	1	120+	120+	65	45	24.1417	25.1908	25.4312	25.6952

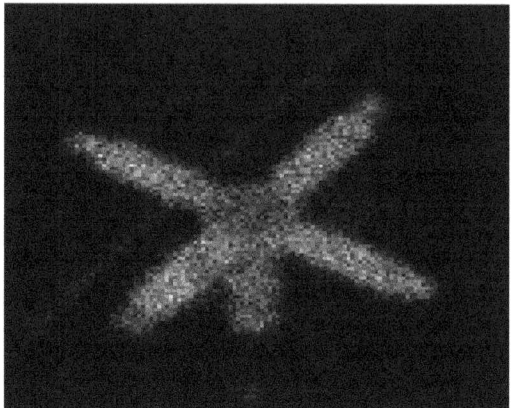

Figure 34. Satel image (blurred).

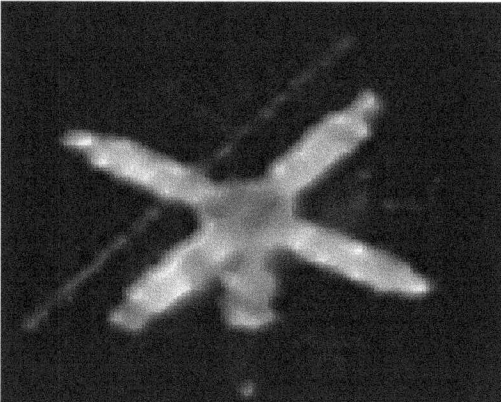

Figure 35. Using NFOV.

Figure 36. Using NP.

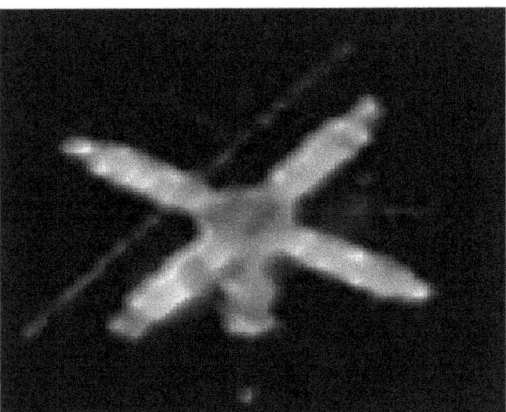

Figure 37. Using P_1 with $\alpha = 1.9$.

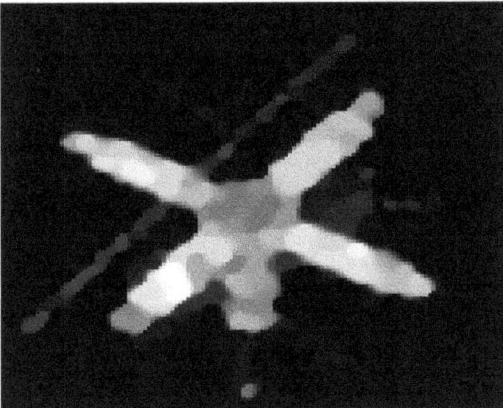

Figure 38. Using P_2 with $\alpha = 1.9$.

6. Conclusions

In this paper we have proposed two block triangular preconditioners for solving the generalized saddle point system which is derived from discretizing the Euler Lagrange equations associated with the TFOV in image de-blurring based problems. We have investigated the performance of the proposed preconditioners with the FGMRES method. We have tested this method on three types of digital images. We have also compared our algorithm with TV based algorithm. Our experiments show that the block triangular preconditioners are very effective. We have also shown that our technique improves the quality of the reconstruction images via calculation of the PSNR. We showed the performance of both GMRES and FGMRES with our proposed preconditioner and we concluded that FGMRES is slightly better than GMRES. Few iterations and CPU-time are needed to obtain a fast rate of convergence and good de-blurring performance. Circulant approximations are used in the first term of the Shur complement to reduce the cost of the computation from $O(N^2)$ into $O(N \log N)$ and reduce the storage. The spectrums of the preconditioned matrices are clustered around 1 and -1.

Funding: This research was funded by King Fahd University of Petroleum and Minerals (KFUPM-IRC-CBM) grant number INCB2315.

Data Availability Statement: No data were used to support this study.

Acknowledgments: The author would like to acknowledge the support provided by King Fahd University of Petroleum & Minerals (KFUPM), Saudi Arabia. The author also would like to thank the referees for their very careful reading and valuable comments. The support provided by the Interdisciplinary Research Center for Construction & Building Materials (IRC-CBM) at King Fahd University of Petroleum & Minerals (KFUPM), Saudi Arabia, for funding this work through Project No. INCB2315, is also greatly acknowledged.

Conflicts of Interest: The author declares that there is no conflict of interest.

References

1. Acar, R.; Vogel, C.R. Analysis of bounded variation penalty methods for ill-posed problems. *Inverse Probl.* **1994**, *10*, 1217. [CrossRef]
2. Agarwal, V.; Gribok, A.V.; Abidi, M.A. Image restoration using L_1 norm penalty function. *Inverse Probl. Sci. Eng.* **2007**, *15*, 785–809. [CrossRef]
3. Aujol, J.-F. Some first-order algorithms for total variation based image restoration. *J. Math. Imaging Vis.* **2009**, *34*, 307–327. [CrossRef]
4. Tai, X.-C.; Lie, K.-A.; Chan, T.F.; Osher, S. Image processing based on partial differential equations. In Proceedings of the International Conference on PDE-Based Image Processing and Related Inverse Problems, CMA, Oslo, Norway, 8–12 August 2005; Springer Science & Business Media: Berlin/Heidelberg, Germany, 2006.
5. Chen, D.; Chen, Y.; Xue, D. Fractional-order total variation image restoration based on primal-dual algorithm. In *Abstract and Applied Analysis*; Hindawi Publishing Corporation: London, UK, 2013; Volume 2013.
6. Williams, B.M.; Zhang, J.; Chen, K. A new image deconvolution method with fractional regularisation. *J. Algorithms Comput.* **2016**, *10*, 265–276. [CrossRef]
7. Chan, R.; Lanza, A.; Morigi, S.; Sgallari, F. An adaptive strategy for the restoration of textured images using fractional order regularization. *Numer. Math. Theory Methods Appl.* **2013**, *6*, 276–296. [CrossRef]
8. Zhang, J.; Chen, K. Variational image registration by a total fractional-order variation model. *J. Comput. Phys.* **2015**, *293*, 442–461. [CrossRef]
9. Benzi, M.; Golub, G.H.; Liesen, J. Numerical solution of saddle point problems. *Acta Numer.* **2005**, *14*, 1–137. [CrossRef]
10. Silvester, D.; Wathen, A. Fast iterative solution of stabilised Stokes systems. Part II: Using general block preconditioners. *SIAM J. Numer. Anal.* **1994**, *31*, 1352–1367. [CrossRef]
11. Wathen, A.; Silvester, D. Fast iterative solution of stabilised Stokes systems. Part I: Using simple diagonal preconditioners. *SIAM J. Numer. Anal.* **1993**, *30*, 630–649. [CrossRef]
12. Bramble, J.H.; Pasciak, J.E. A preconditioning technique for indefinite systems resulting from mixed approximations of elliptic problems. *Math. Comput.* **1988**, *50*, 1–17. [CrossRef]
13. Cao, Z.-H. Positive stable block triangular preconditioners for symmetric saddle point problems. *Appl. Numer. Math.* **2007**, *57*, 899–910. [CrossRef]
14. Klawonn, A. Block-triangular preconditioners for saddle point problems with a penalty term. *SIAM J. Sci. Comput.* **1998**, *19*, 172–184. [CrossRef]
15. Pestana, J. On the eigenvalues and eigenvectors of block triangular preconditioned block matrices. *SIAM J. Matrix Anal. Appl.* **2014**, *35*, 517–525. [CrossRef]
16. Simoncini, V. Block triangular preconditioners for symmetric saddle-point problems. *Appl. Numer. Math.* **2004**, *49*, 63–80. [CrossRef]
17. Axelsson, O.; Neytcheva, M. Preconditioning methods for linear systems arising in constrained optimization problems. *Numer. Linear Algebr. Appl.* **2003**, *10*, 3–31. [CrossRef]
18. Bai, Z.-Z.; Golub, G.H. Accelerated Hermitian and skew-Hermitian splitting iteration methods for saddle-point problems. *IMA J. Numer.* **2007**, *27*, 1–23. [CrossRef]
19. Benzi, M.; Ng, M.K. Preconditioned iterative methods for weighted Toeplitz least squares problems. *SIAM J. Matrix Anal. Appl.* **2006**, *27*, 1106–1124. [CrossRef]
20. Ng, M.K.; Pan, J. Weighted Toeplitz regularized least squares computation for image restoration. *SIAM J. Sci. Comput.* **2014**, *36*, B94–B121. [CrossRef]
21. Cao, Z.-H. Block triangular Schur complement preconditioners for saddle point problems and application to the Oseen equations. *Appl. Numer.* **2010**, *60*, 193–207. [CrossRef]
22. Chen, C.; Ma, C. A generalized shift-splitting preconditioner for saddle point problems. *Appl. Math. Lett.* **2015**, *43*, 49–55. [CrossRef]
23. Salkuyeh, D.K.; Masoudi, M.; Hezari, D. On the generalized shift-splitting preconditioner for saddle point problems. *Appl. Math.* **2015**, *48*, 55–61. [CrossRef]
24. Beik, F.P.A.; Benzi, M.; Chaparpordi, S.-H.A. On block diagonal and block triangular iterative schemes and preconditioners for stabilized saddle point problems. *J. Comput. Appl. Math.* **2017**, *326*, 15–30. [CrossRef]

25. Murphy, M.F.; Golub, G.H.; Wathen, A.J. A note on preconditioning for indefinite linear systems. *Siam J. Sci. Comput.* **2000**, *21*, 1969–1972. [CrossRef]
26. Benzi, M.; Golub, G.H. A preconditioner for generalized saddle point problems. *SIAM J. Matrix Anal. Appl.* **2004**, *26*, 20–41. [CrossRef]
27. Saad, Y. *Iterative Methods for Sparse Linear Systems*; SIAM: Philadelphia, PA, USA, 2003.
28. Vogel, C.R.; Oman, M.E. Fast, robust total variation-based reconstruction of noisy, blurred images. *IEEE Trans. Image Process.* **1998**, *7*, 813–824. [CrossRef] [PubMed]
29. Axelsson, O. *Iterative Solution Methods*; Cambridge University Press: Cambridge, UK, 1996.
30. Campisi, P.; Egiazarian, K. *Blind Image Deconvolution: Theory and Applications*; CRC Press: Boca Raton, FL, USA, 2016.
31. Groetsch, C.W.; Groetsch, C. *Inverse Problems in the Mathematical Sciences*; Springer: Berlin/Heidelberg, Germany, 1993; Volume 52.
32. Tikhonov, A.N. Regularization of incorrectly posed problems. *Sov. Math. Dokl.* **1963**, *4*, 1624–1627.
33. Rudin, L.I.; Osher, S.; Fatemi, E. Nonlinear total variation based noise removal algorithms. *Phys. D Nonlinear Phenom.* **1992**, *60*, 259–268. [CrossRef]
34. Osher, S.; Solé, A.; Vese, L. Image decomposition and restoration using total variation minimization and the h^1. *Multiscale Model. Simul.* **2003**, *1*, 349–370. [CrossRef]
35. Getreuer, P. Total variation inpainting using split Bregman. *Image Process. Line* **2012**, *2*, 147–157. [CrossRef]
36. Guo, W.; Qiao, L.-H. Inpainting based on total variation. In Proceedings of the 2007 International Conference on Wavelet Analysis and Pattern Recognition, Beijing, China, 2–4 November 2007; Volume 2, pp. 939–943.
37. Bresson, X.; Esedoglu, S.; Vandergheynst, P.; Thiran, J.-P.; Osher, S. Fast global minimization of the active contour/snake model. *J. Math. Imaging Vis.* **2007**, *28*, 151–167. [CrossRef]
38. Unger, M.; Pock, T.; Trobin, W.; Cremers, D.; Bischof, H. Tvseg-interactive total variation based image segmentation. *BMVC* **2008**, *31*, 44–46.
39. Yan, H.; Zhang, J.-X.; Zhang, X. Injected infrared and visible image fusion via $l\_\{1\}$ decomposition model and guided filtering. *IEEE Trans. Comput. Imaging* **2022**, *8*, 162–173. [CrossRef]
40. Chan, T.; Marquina, A.; Mulet, P. High-order total variation-based image restoration. *SIAM J. Sci. Comput.* **2000**, *22*, 503–516. [CrossRef]
41. Steidl, G.; Didas, S.; Neumann, J. Relations between higher order TV regularization and support vector regression. In *International Conference on Scale-Space Theories in Computer Vision*; Springer: Berlin/Heidelberg, Germany, 2005; pp. 515–527.
42. Bredies, K.; Kunisch, K.; Pock, T. Total generalized variation. *SIAM J. Imaging Sci.* **2010**, *3*, 492–526. [CrossRef]
43. Zhu, W.; Chan, T. Image denoising using mean curvature of image surface. *SIAM J. Imaging Sci.* **2012**, *5*, 1–32. [CrossRef]
44. Lysaker, M.; Osher, S.; Tai, X.-C. Noise removal using smoothed normals and surface fitting. *IEEE Trans. Image Process.* **2004**, *13*, 1345–1357. [CrossRef]
45. Ahmad, S.; Al-Mahdi, A.M.; Ahmed, R. Two new preconditioners for mean curvature-based image deblurring problem. *AIMS Math.* **2021**, *6*, 13824–13844. [CrossRef]
46. Al-Mahdi, A.; Fairag, F. Block diagonal preconditioners for an image de-blurring problem with fractional total variation. *J. Phys. Conf. Ser.* **2018**, *1132*, 012063. [CrossRef]
47. Fairag, F.; Al-Mahdi, A.; Ahmad, S. Two-level method for the total fractional-order variation model in image deblurring problem. *Numer. Algorithms* **2020**, *85*, 931–950. [CrossRef]
48. Sohail, A.; Bég, O.; Li, Z.; Celik, S. Physics of fractional imaging in biomedicine. *Prog. Biophys. Mol. Biol.* **2018**, *140*, 13–20. [CrossRef]
49. Xu, K.-D.; Zhang, J.-X. Prescribed performance tracking control of lower-triangular systems with unknown fractional powers. *Fractal Fract.* **2023**, *7*, 594. [CrossRef]
50. Wang, Y.; Zhang, X.; Boutat, D.; Shi, P. Quadratic admissibility for a class of lti uncertain singular fractional-order systems with $0 < \alpha < 2$. *Fractal Fract.* **2022**, *7*, 1.
51. Zhang, J.; Chen, K. A total fractional-order variation model for image restoration with nonhomogeneous boundary conditions and its numerical solution. *SIAM J. Imaging Sci.* **2015**, *8*, 2487–2518. [CrossRef]
52. Miller, K.S.; Ross, B. *An Introduction to the Fractional Calculus and Fractional Differential Equations*; Wiley: Hoboken, NJ, USA, 1993.
53. Oldham, K.; Spanier, J. *The Fractional Calculus Theory and Applications of Differentiation and Integration to Arbitrary Order*; Elsevier: Amsterdam, The Netherlands, 1974; Volume 111.
54. Podlubny, I. *Fractional Differential Equations: An Introduction to Fractional Derivatives, Fractional Differential Equations, to Methods of Their Solution and Some of Their Applications*; Academic Press: Cambridge, MA, USA, 1998; Volume 198.
55. Chan, T.F.; Golub, G.H.; Mulet, P. A nonlinear primal-dual method for total variation-based image restoration. *SIAM J. Sci.* **1999**, *20*, 1964–1977. [CrossRef]
56. Meerschaert, M.M.; Tadjeran, C. Finite difference approximations for fractional advection–dispersion flow equations. *J. Comput. Appl. Math.* **2004**, *172*, 65–77. [CrossRef]
57. Meerschaert, M.M.; Tadjeran, C. Finite difference approximations for two-sided space-fractional partial differential equations. *Appl. Numer. Math.* **2006**, *56*, 80–90. [CrossRef]
58. Wang, H.; Du, N. Fast solution methods for space-fractional diffusion equations. *J. Comput. Appl. Math.* **2014**, *255*, 376–383. [CrossRef]

59. Strang, G. A proposal for Toeplitz matrix calculations. *Stud. Appl. Math.* **1986**, *74*, 171–176. [CrossRef]
60. Olkin, J.A. Linear and Nonlinear Deconvolution Problems (Optimization). Ph.D. Thesis, Rice University, Houston, TX, USA, 1986.
61. Chan, T.F.; Olkin, J.A. Circulant preconditioners for Toeplitz-block matrices. *Numer. Algorithms* **1994**, *6*, 89–101. [CrossRef]
62. Chan, R.H.; Ng, K.-P. Toeplitz preconditioners for Hermitian Toeplitz systems. *Linear Algebra Appl.* **1993**, *190*, 181–208. [CrossRef]
63. Lin, F.-R. Preconditioners for block Toeplitz systems based on circulant preconditioners. *Numer. Algorithms* **2001**, *26*, 365–379. [CrossRef]
64. Chan, R.H. Toeplitz preconditioners for Toeplitz systems with nonnegative generating functions. *IMA J. Numer. Anal.* **1991**, *11*, 333–345. [CrossRef]
65. Serra, S. Preconditioning strategies for asymptotically ill-conditioned block Toeplitz systems. *BIT Numer. Math.* **1994**, *34*, 579–594. [CrossRef]
66. Lin, F.-R.; Wang, C.-X. BTTB preconditioners for BTTB systems. *Numer. Algorithms* **2012**, *60*, 153–167. [CrossRef]
67. Chan, R.H.; Strang, G. Toeplitz equations by conjugate gradients with circulant preconditioner. *SIAM J. Sci. Stat.* **1989**, *10*, 104–119. [CrossRef]
68. Chan, R.H.; Yeung, M.-C. Circulant preconditioners constructed from kernels. *SIAM J. Numer. Anal.* **1992**, *29*, 1093–1103. [CrossRef]
69. Chan, T.F. An optimal circulant preconditioner for Toeplitz systems. *SIAM J. Sci. Stat. Comput.* **1988**, *9*, 766–771. [CrossRef]
70. Davis, P.J. *Circulant Matrices*; American Mathematical Soc.: New York, NY, USA, 2012.
71. Chowdhury, M.R.; Qin, J.; Lou, Y. Non-blind and blind deconvolution under Poisson noise using fractional-order total variation. *J. Math. Imaging Vis.* **2020**, *62*, 1238–1255. [CrossRef]

Disclaimer/Publisher's Note: The statements, opinions and data contained in all publications are solely those of the individual author(s) and contributor(s) and not of MDPI and/or the editor(s). MDPI and/or the editor(s) disclaim responsibility for any injury to people or property resulting from any ideas, methods, instructions or products referred to in the content.

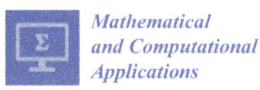

Article

Fractional Hermite–Hadamard-Type Inequalities for Differentiable Preinvex Mappings and Applications to Modified Bessel and q-Digamma Functions

Muhammad Tariq [1], Hijaz Ahmad [2,3,*], Asif Ali Shaikh [1,4], Sotiris K. Ntouyas [5], Evren Hınçal [4] and Sania Qureshi [1,2,4,*]

1. Department of Basic Sciences and Related Studies, Mehran University of Engineering and Technology, Jamshoro 76062, Pakistan; captaintariq2187@gmail.com (M.T.); asif.shaikh@faculty.muet.edu.pk (A.A.S.)
2. Department of Computer Science and Mathematics, Lebanese American University, Beirut 1102-2801, Lebanon
3. Operational Research Center in Healthcare, Near East University, Mersin 99138, Turkey
4. Department of Mathematics, Near East University, Mersin 99138, Turkey; evren.hincal@neu.edu.tr
5. Department of Mathematics, University of Ioannina, 45110 Ioannina, Greece; sntouyas@uoi.gr
* Correspondence: hijaz.ahmad@lau.edu.lb (H.A.); sania.qureshi@faculty.muet.edu.pk (S.Q.)

Abstract: The theory of convexity pertaining to fractional calculus is a well-established concept that has attracted significant attention in mathematics and various scientific disciplines for over a century. In the realm of applied mathematics, convexity, particularly in relation to fractional analysis, finds extensive and remarkable applications. In this manuscript, we establish new fractional identities. Employing these identities, some extensions of the fractional H-H type inequality via generalized preinvexities are explored. Finally, we discuss some applications to the q-digamma and Bessel functions via the established results. We believe that the methodologies and approaches presented in this work will intrigue and spark the researcher's interest even more.

Keywords: convex function; invex sets; preinvex functions; Hölder's inequality; power mean inequality

Citation: Tariq, M.; Ahmad, H.; Shaikh, A.A.; Ntouyas, S.K.; Hınçal, E.; Qureshi, S. Fractional Hermite–Hadamard-Type Inequalities for Differentiable Preinvex Mappings and Applications to Modified Bessel and q-Digamma Functions. *Math. Comput. Appl.* **2023**, *28*, 108. https://doi.org/10.3390/mca28060108

Received: 10 September 2023
Revised: 22 October 2023
Accepted: 7 November 2023
Published: 9 November 2023

Copyright: © 2023 by the authors. Licensee MDPI, Basel, Switzerland. This article is an open access article distributed under the terms and conditions of the Creative Commons Attribution (CC BY) license (https:// creativecommons.org/licenses/by/ 4.0/).

1. Introduction

Convex inequalities are mathematical inequalities involving convex functions. A convex inequality is similar to the definition of a convex function, but it applies to the inequalities formed by these functions. In order to design constraints that limit the viable region to convex sets, convex inequalities are crucial in optimization issues. Convexity is well known as playing a significant and critical role in a range of domains such as economics, finance, optimization, game theory, statistical theory, quality management, and numerous sciences. For the literature regarding convexity, see the references [1–14].

Inequalities are an amazing mathematical tool due to their importance in fractional calculus, traditional calculus, quantum calculus, stochastic, time-scale calculus, fractal sets, and other fields. The crucial mathematical tool that connects integrals and inequalities, integral inequalities provide insights into the behavior of functions over particular intervals. For the literature regarding inequalities, see the references [15–19].

Fractional calculus, which focuses on fractional integration across complex domains, has recently acquired popularity due to its practical applications and has piqued the curiosity of mathematicians. The research of well-known inequalities, such as Ostrowski, Simpson, and Hadamard, inspired the study of fractional integral inequality. Transform theory, engineering, modeling, finance, mathematical biology, fluid flow, natural phenomenon prediction, healthcare, and image processing are all domains where fractional calculus is used.

The goal of this article is to prove some integral inequalities for derivable mapping whose absolute values are preinvex. Next, we will review some concepts in invexity analysis that will be utilized throughout the paper (see [20–24] and references therein). The idea of convexity is a strong and magnificent tool for dealing with a huge range of applied and pure science problems. Many researchers have recently devoted themselves to researching the properties and inequalities associated with the topic of convexity in different areas, (see [25,26] and the references therein).

We constructed this manuscript in the following way: first, we explore some fundamental ideas and definitions in Section 2. In Section 3, we investigate and prove new integral identities. In Section 4, we investigate some applications involving modified Bessel functions and q-digamma functions. Lastly, in Section 5, future directions and conclusions of the newly discussed concept are elaborated.

2. Preliminaries

The main objective of this section is to remember and discuss specific related ideas and concepts that are pertinent to our analysis in later sections of this paper.

Jensen introduced the term convexity for the first time in the following manner:

Definition 1 ([27]). *A mapping $\Pi : \mathfrak{K} \subseteq \mathbb{R} \to \mathbb{R}$ is said to be convex if*
$$\Pi(\iota \tau_1 + (1-\iota)\tau_2) \leq \iota \Pi(\tau_1) + (1-\iota)\Pi(\tau_2),$$
for all $\tau_1, \tau_2 \in \mathfrak{K}$ and $\iota \in [0,1]$.

Definition 2 ([28]). *The term invexity (ξ-connected set) is defined on a set $\mathfrak{K} \subset \mathbb{R}^n$ with respect to $\xi(*,*)$, if $\tau_1, \tau_2 \in \mathfrak{K}$ and $\iota \in [0,1]$*
$$\tau_1 + \iota \xi(\tau_2, \tau_1) \in \mathfrak{K}.$$

It is self-evident that every convex set is invex in terms of $\xi(\tau_2, \tau_1) = \tau_2 - \tau_1$. However, there are invex sets that are not convex [20].

Definition 3 ([29]). *Let $\mathbb{I} \subseteq \mathbb{R}^n$, then $\mathbb{I}$ is m–invex w.r.t $\xi : \mathbb{I} \times \mathbb{I} \times (0,1] \to \mathbb{R}^n$, if*
$$m\tau_1 + \iota \xi(\tau_2, \tau_1, m) \in \mathbb{I},$$
for every $\tau_1, \tau_2 \in \mathbb{I}, m \in (0,1]$ and $\iota \in [0,1]$.

Example 1 ([29]). *Suppose $m = \frac{1}{4}$, $\mathbb{I} = [\frac{-\pi}{2}, 0) \cup (0, \frac{1}{2}]$ and*
$$\xi(\tau_2, \tau_1, m) = \begin{cases} m\cos(\tau_2 - \tau_1) & \text{if } \tau_1 \in (0, \frac{\pi}{2}], \tau_2 \in (0, \frac{\pi}{2}]; \\ -m\cos(\tau_2 - \tau_1) & \text{if } \tau_1 \in [\frac{-\pi}{2}, 0), \tau_2 \in [\frac{-\pi}{2}, 0); \\ m\cos(\tau_1) & \text{if } \tau_1 \in (0, \frac{\pi}{2}], \tau_2 \in [\frac{-\pi}{2}, 0); \\ -m\cos(\tau_1) & \text{if } \tau_1 \in [-\frac{\pi}{2}, 0), \tau_2 \in (0, \frac{\pi}{2}]. \end{cases}$$

Then, $\mathbb{I}$ is an m-invex set with respect to ξ for $\iota \in [0,1]$ and $m = \frac{1}{4}$. It is obvious that $\mathbb{I}$ is not a convex set.

In the year 1988, Mond and Weir [30] explored the idea of invex set to introduce the idea of preinvexity.

Definition 4 ([30]). *A function $\Pi : \mathfrak{K} \to \mathbb{R}^n$ is said to be preinvex with respect to ξ, if*
$$\Pi(\tau_1 + \iota \xi(\tau_2, \tau_1)) \leq (1-\iota)\Pi(\tau_1) + \iota \Pi(\tau_2), \quad \forall \tau_1, \tau_2 \in \mathfrak{K}, \ \iota \in [0,1].$$

It is very important to mark that every convex is a preinvex function, but the converse is not true [21]. For example, $\Pi(\iota) = -|\iota|$, $\forall \iota \in \mathbb{R}$, is preinvex but not convex with respect to

$$\xi(\tau_2, \tau_1) = \begin{cases} \tau_2 - \tau_1 & \text{if } \tau_1\tau_2 \geq 0 \\ \tau_1 - \tau_2 & \text{if } \tau_1\tau_2 < 0. \end{cases}$$

Recently, Deng [31] introduced m–preinvex function, which is defined as:

Definition 5. *A function $\Pi : \mathbb{I} \to \mathbb{R}$ is said to be generalized m–preinvex with respect to $\xi : \mathbb{I} \times \mathbb{I} \times (0, 1] \to \mathbb{R}^n$ for $m \in (0, 1]$, if*

$$\Pi(m\tau_1 + \iota\xi(\tau_2, \tau_1, m)) \leq m(1 - \iota)\Pi(\tau_1) + \iota\Pi(\tau_2), \tag{1}$$

for every $\tau_1, \tau_2 \in \mathbb{I}$, $\iota \in [0, 1]$.

The following condition C was explored and discussed for the first time by Mohan and Neogy [32].

Condition-C: Assume that $\mathfrak{K} \subset \mathbb{R}^n$ is an open invex subset with respect to $\xi : \mathfrak{K} \times \mathfrak{K} \to \mathbb{R}$. We say the ξ satisfies the condition C if for any $\tau_1, \tau_2 \in \mathfrak{K}$ and $\iota \in [0, 1]$,

$$\begin{aligned} \xi(\tau_2, \tau_2 + \iota\,\xi(\tau_1, \tau_2)) &= -\iota\,\xi(\tau_1, \tau_2) \\ \xi(\tau_1, \tau_2 + \iota\,\xi(\tau_1, \tau_2)) &= (1 - \iota)\,\xi(\tau_1, \tau_2). \end{aligned} \tag{2}$$

For any $\tau_1, \tau_2 \in \mathfrak{K}$ and $\iota_1, \iota_2 \in [0, 1]$ from condition C, we have

$$\xi(\tau_2 + \iota_2\,\xi(\tau_1, \tau_2), \tau_2 + \iota_1\,\xi(\tau_1, \tau_2)) = (\iota_2 - \iota_1)\xi(\tau_1, \tau_2).$$

If Π is a preinvex on $[\tau_1, \tau_1 + \xi(\tau_2, \tau_1)]$ and ξ satisfies condition C, then for each $\iota \in [0, 1]$, from above Equation (2), it yields

$$\begin{aligned} |\Pi(\tau_1 + \iota\xi(\tau_2, \tau_1))| &= |\Pi(\tau_1 + \xi(\tau_2, \tau_1)) + (1 - \iota)\xi(\tau_1, \tau_1 + \xi(\tau_2, \tau_1))| \\ &\leq \iota|\Pi(\tau_1 + \xi(\tau_2, \tau_1))| + (1 - \iota)|\Pi(\tau_1)| \end{aligned}$$

and

$$\begin{aligned} |\Pi(\tau_1 + (1 - \iota)\xi(\tau_2, \tau_1))| &= |\Pi(\tau_1 + \xi(\tau_2, \tau_1)) + \iota\xi(\tau_1, \tau_1 + \xi(\tau_2, \tau_1))| \\ &\leq (1 - \iota)|\Pi(\tau_1 + \xi(\tau_2, \tau_1))| + \iota|\Pi(\tau_1)|. \end{aligned}$$

The following generalized Condition C first time introduced by Du [33] in the aspect of m–preinvex.

Extended Condition-C: Assume that $\mathfrak{K} \subset \mathbb{R}^n$ be an open invex subset with respect to $\xi : \mathfrak{K} \times \mathfrak{K} \times (0, 1] \to \mathbb{R}$. We say the ξ satisfies the extended condition C, for any $\tau_1, \tau_2 \in \mathfrak{K}$, $\iota \in [0, 1]$ and $m \in (0, 1]$, if

$$\begin{aligned} \xi(\tau_1, m\tau_1 + \iota\xi(\tau_2, \tau_1, m), m) &= -\iota\,\xi(\tau_2, \tau_1, m), \\ \xi(\tau_2, m\tau_1 + \iota\,\xi(\tau_2, \tau_1, m), m) &= (1 - \iota)\,\xi(\tau_2, \tau_1, m), \\ \xi(\tau_2, \tau_1, m) &= -\xi(\tau_1, \tau_2, m). \end{aligned}$$

If Π is a m-preinvex on $[m\tau_1, m\tau_1 + \xi(\tau_2, \tau_1, m)]$ and ξ satisfies extended condition C, then for each $\iota \in [0, 1]$, from above equation, it yields

$$\begin{aligned} |\Pi(m\tau_1 + \iota\xi(\tau_2, \tau_1, m))| &= |\Pi(m\tau_1 + \xi(\tau_2, \tau_1, m)) + (1 - \iota)\xi(m\tau_1, m\tau_1 + \xi(\tau_2, \tau_1, m))| \\ &\leq \iota|\Pi(m\tau_1 + \xi(\tau_2, \tau_1, m))| + (1 - \iota)|\Pi(m\tau_1)| \end{aligned}$$

and

$$\begin{aligned}|\Pi(m\tau_1+(1-\iota)\xi(\tau_2,\tau_1,m))| &= |\Pi(m\tau_1+\xi(\tau_2,\tau_1,m))+\iota\xi(m\tau_1,m\tau_1+\xi(\tau_2,\tau_1,m))| \\ &\leq (1-\iota)|\Pi(m\tau_1+\xi(\tau_2,\tau_1,m))|+m\iota|\Pi(\tau_1)|.\end{aligned}$$

There are numerous vector functions that meet the condition C in [28], with trivial case $\xi(\tau_1,\tau_2)=\tau_1-\tau_2$.

For example, suppose $\mathfrak{K}=\mathbb{R}\backslash\{0\}$ and

$$\xi(\tau_2,\tau_1)=\begin{cases}\tau_2-\tau_1 & \text{if } \tau_1>0,\tau_2>0 \\ \tau_2-\tau_1 & \text{if } \tau_1<0,\tau_2<0 \\ -\tau_2, & \text{otherwise}\end{cases}$$

The set $\mathfrak{K}$ is invex set and the condition C is satisfied by ξ.

In Noor [34], the following H-H type inequalities were demonstrated.

Theorem 1. *Assume that function* $\Pi:\mathfrak{K}=[\tau_1,\tau_1+\xi(\tau_2,\tau_1)]\to(0,\infty)$ *is preinvex on* $\mathfrak{K}^0$ *with* $\xi(\tau_2,\tau_1)>0$. *Then:*

$$\Pi\left(\frac{2\tau_1+\xi(\tau_2,\tau_1)}{2}\right)\leq\frac{1}{\xi(\tau_2,\tau_1)}\int_{\tau_1}^{\tau_1+\xi(\tau_2,\tau_1)}\Pi(x)\,dx\leq\frac{\Pi(\tau_1)+\Pi(\tau_2)}{2}.$$

Definition 6 ([35]). *Suppose* $\Pi\in\mathcal{L}[\tau_1,\tau_2]$. *The left-sided and right-sided Riemann–Liouville fractional integrals of order* $\varrho>0$ *defined by*

$$J_{\tau_1}^{\varrho}\Pi(\tau)=\frac{1}{\Gamma(\varrho)}\int_{\tau_1}^{\tau}(\tau-\mu)^{\varrho-1}\Pi(\mu)d\mu,\quad\tau_1<\tau$$

and

$$J_{\tau_2}^{\varrho}\Pi(\tau)=\frac{1}{\Gamma(\varrho)}\int_{\tau}^{\tau_2}(\mu-\tau)^{\varrho-1}\Pi(\mu)d\mu,\quad\tau<\tau_2.$$

The gamma function is defined as $\Gamma(\varrho)=\int_0^{\infty}e^{-u}u^{\varrho-1}du$.

Note that $J_{\tau_1}^0 f(\tau)=J_{\tau_2}^0\Pi(\tau)=\Pi(\tau)$.

Throughout the paper, we will consider that $\Gamma(.)$ is the gamma function and $\varrho>0$.

3. Main Results

Lemma 1. *Let an open invex subset* $\mathfrak{K}\subseteq\mathbb{R}$ *with respect to* $\xi:\mathfrak{K}\times\mathfrak{K}\longrightarrow\mathbb{R}$ *and* $\tau_1,\tau_2\in\mathfrak{K}$ *with* $m\tau_1<m\tau_1+\xi(\tau_2,\tau_1,m)$. *Assume that* $\Pi:\mathfrak{K}\to\mathbb{R}$ *is differentiable function on* $\mathfrak{K}$ *such that* $\Pi'\in\mathcal{L}([m\tau_1,m\tau_1+\xi(\tau_2,\tau_1,m)])$. *Then:*

$$\frac{\Gamma(\varrho+1)}{[\xi(\tau_2,\tau_1,m)]^{\varrho}}J_{m\tau_1^+}^{\varrho}\Pi(m\tau_1+\xi(\tau_2,\tau_1,m))-\Pi\left(m\tau_1+\frac{\varrho}{\varrho+1}\xi(\tau_2,\tau_1,m)\right) \quad (3)$$
$$=\xi(\tau_2,\tau_1,m)\left[-\int_0^{\frac{\varrho}{\varrho+1}}\iota^{\varrho}\Pi'(m\tau_1+\iota\xi(\tau_2,\tau_1,m))d\iota+\int_{\frac{\varrho}{\varrho+1}}^1(1-\iota^{\varrho})\Pi'(m\tau_1+\iota\xi(\tau_2,\tau_1,m))d\iota\right].$$

Proof. By applying the integration by parts to the right hand side of (3), we obtain

$$\xi(\tau_2,\tau_1,m)\left[-\int_0^{\frac{\varrho}{\varrho+1}}\iota^{\varrho}\Pi'(m\tau_1+\iota\xi(\tau_2,\tau_1,m))d\iota+\int_{\frac{\varrho}{\varrho+1}}^1(1-\iota^{\varrho})\Pi'(m\tau_1+\iota\xi(\tau_2,\tau_1,m))d\iota\right]$$

$$=\xi(\tau_2,\tau_1,m)\left[-\int_0^1\iota^{\varrho}\Pi'(m\tau_1+\iota\xi(\tau_2,\tau_1,m))d\iota+\int_{\frac{\varrho}{\varrho+1}}^1\Pi'(m\tau_1+\iota\xi(\tau_2,\tau_1,m))d\iota\right]$$

$$= -\Pi(m\tau_1 + \xi(\tau_2,\tau_1,m)) + \varrho \int_0^1 \iota^{\varrho-1}\Pi(m\tau_1 + \iota\xi(\tau_2,\tau_1,m))d\iota + \Pi(m\tau_1 + \xi(\tau_2,\tau_1,m))$$
$$- \Pi\left(m\tau_1 + \frac{\varrho}{\varrho+1}\xi(\tau_2,\tau_1,m)\right)$$
$$= \frac{\Gamma(\varrho+1)}{[\xi(\tau_2,\tau_1,m)]^\varrho} J^\varrho_{m\tau_1^+}\Pi(m\tau_1 + \xi(\tau_2,\tau_1,m)) - \Pi\left(m\tau_1 + \frac{\varrho}{\varrho+1}\xi(\tau_2,\tau_1,m)\right).$$

This ends the proof. □

Lemma 2. *Let an open invex subset $\mathfrak{K} \subseteq \mathbb{R}$ with respect to $\xi : \mathfrak{K} \times \mathfrak{K} \longrightarrow \mathbb{R}$ and $\tau_1, \tau_2 \in \mathfrak{K}$ with $m\tau_1 < m\tau_1 + \xi(\tau_2,\tau_1,m)$. Assume that $\Pi : \mathfrak{K} \to \mathbb{R}$ is twice differentiable function on $\mathfrak{K}$ such that $\Pi'' \in \mathcal{L}([m\tau_1, m\tau_1 + \xi(\tau_2,\tau_1,m)])$. Then:*

$$\frac{\Gamma(\varrho+1)}{[\xi(\tau_2,\tau_1,m)]^{\varrho+1}}\left\{J^{\varrho-1}_{(m\tau_1 + \frac{1}{2}\xi(\tau_2,\tau_1,m))^-}\Pi(m\tau_1) + J^{\varrho-1}_{(m\tau_1 + \frac{1}{2}\xi(\tau_2,\tau_1,m))^+}\Pi(m\tau_1 + \xi(\tau_2,\tau_1,m))\right\} \quad (4)$$
$$- \frac{\varrho\,\Pi\left(m\tau_1 + \frac{1}{2}\xi(\tau_2,\tau_1,m)\right)}{2^{\varrho-2}[\xi(\tau_2,\tau_1,m)]^2}$$
$$= \int_0^{\frac{1}{2}} \iota^\varrho \Pi''(m\tau_1 + \iota\,\xi(\tau_2,\tau_1,m))\,d\iota + \int_{\frac{1}{2}}^1 (1-\iota)^\varrho \Pi''(m\tau_1 + \iota\,\xi(\tau_2,\tau_1,m))\,d\iota.$$

Proof. It suffices to write that

$$\begin{aligned}I &= \int_0^{\frac{1}{2}} \iota^\varrho \Pi''(m\tau_1 + \iota\,\xi(\tau_2,\tau_1,m))\,d\iota + \int_{\frac{1}{2}}^1 (1-\iota)^\varrho \Pi''(m\tau_1 + \iota\,\xi(\tau_2,\tau_1,m))\,d\iota\\ &= I_1 + I_2,\end{aligned} \quad (5)$$

where

$$\begin{aligned}I_1 &= \int_0^{\frac{1}{2}} \iota^\varrho \Pi''(m\tau_1 + \iota\,\xi(\tau_2,\tau_1,m))\,d\iota\\ &= \frac{\iota^\varrho \Pi'(m\tau_1 + \iota\,\xi(\tau_2,\tau_1,m))}{\xi(\tau_2,\tau_1,m)}\bigg|_0^{\frac{1}{2}} - \frac{\varrho}{\xi(\tau_2,\tau_1,m)}\int_0^{\frac{1}{2}} \iota^{\varrho-1}\Pi'(m\tau_1 + \iota\,\xi(\tau_2,\tau_1,m))\,d\iota\\ &= \frac{\Pi'\left(m\tau_1 + \frac{1}{2}\xi(\tau_2,\tau_1,m)\right)}{2^\varrho\,\xi(\tau_2,\tau_1,m)} - \frac{\varrho\,\Pi\left(m\tau_1 + \frac{1}{2}\xi(\tau_2,\tau_1,m)\right)}{2^{\varrho-1}[\xi(\tau_2,\tau_1,m)]^2}\\ &\quad + \frac{\Gamma(\varrho+1)}{[\xi(\tau_2,\tau_1,m)]^{\varrho+1}}J^{\varrho-1}_{(m\tau_1 + \frac{1}{2}\xi(\tau_2,\tau_1,m))^-}\Pi(m\tau_1)\end{aligned} \quad (6)$$

and

$$\begin{aligned}I_2 &= \int_{\frac{1}{2}}^1 (1-\iota)^\varrho \Pi''(m\tau_1 + \iota\,\xi(\tau_2,\tau_1,m))\,d\iota\\ &= \frac{(1-\iota)^\varrho \Pi'(m\tau_1 + \iota\,\xi(\tau_2,\tau_1,m))}{\xi(\tau_2,\tau_1,m)}\bigg|_{\frac{1}{2}}^1 + \frac{\varrho}{\xi(\tau_2,\tau_1,m)}\int_{\frac{1}{2}}^1 (1-\iota)^{\varrho-1}\Pi'(m\tau_1 + \iota\,\xi(\tau_2,\tau_1,m))\,d\iota\\ &= -\frac{\Pi'\left(m\tau_1 + \frac{1}{2}\xi(\tau_2,\tau_1,m)\right)}{2^\varrho\xi(\tau_2,\tau_1,m)} + \frac{\varrho}{\xi(\tau_2,\tau_1,m)}\int_{\frac{1}{2}}^1 (1-\iota)^{\varrho-1}\Pi'(m\tau_1 + \iota\,\xi(\tau_2,\tau_1,m))\,d\iota\end{aligned}$$

$$
\begin{aligned}
=\ & -\frac{\Pi'\left(m\tau_1+\frac{1}{2}\xi(\tau_2,\tau_1,m)\right)}{2^\varrho\,\xi(\tau_2,\tau_1,m)}-\frac{\varrho\,\Pi\left(m\tau_1+\frac{1}{2}\xi(\tau_2,\tau_1,m)\right)}{2^{\varrho-1}[\xi(\tau_2,\tau_1,m)]^2}\\
& +\frac{\Gamma(\varrho+1)}{[\xi(\tau_2,\tau_1,m)]^{\varrho+1}}\,J^{\varrho-1}_{(m\tau_1+\frac{1}{2}\xi(\tau_2,\tau_1,m))^+}\,\Pi(m\tau_1+\xi(\tau_2,\tau_1,m)).
\end{aligned}
\qquad(7)
$$

Combine Equations (6) and (7) with (5), and obtain Equation (4). □

Theorem 2. *Let all the conditions in Lemma 1 are satisfied. If $|\Pi'|$ is m-preinvex on $[m\tau_1,m\tau_1+\xi(\tau_2,\tau_1,m)]$, then, for fractional integrals, the following inequality with $\varrho>0$ holds:*

$$
\begin{aligned}
\Bigg|\frac{\Gamma(\varrho+1)}{[\xi(\tau_2,\tau_1,m)]^\varrho}\,J^\varrho_{m\tau_1^+}\Pi(m\tau_1+\xi(\tau_2,\tau_1,m))-\Pi\left(m\tau_1+\frac{\varrho}{\varrho+1}\xi(\tau_2,\tau_1,m)\right)\Bigg| \qquad(8)\\
\le \xi(\tau_2,\tau_1,m)\left[\frac{m\varrho}{2(\varrho+1)^2(\varrho+2)}|\Pi'(\tau_1)|+\frac{\varrho(-\varrho^{\varrho+1}+2\varrho^\varrho+(\varrho+1)^\varrho)}{2(\varrho+1)^{\varrho+2}(\varrho+2)}|\Pi'(\tau_2)|\right].
\end{aligned}
$$

Proof. From inequality (3) and the m-preinvexity of $|\Pi'|$, we have

$$
\begin{aligned}
& \Bigg|\frac{\Gamma(\varrho+1)}{[\xi(\tau_2,\tau_1,m)]^\varrho}\,J^\varrho_{m\tau_1^+}\Pi(m\tau_1+\xi(\tau_2,\tau_1,m))-\Pi\left(m\tau_1+\frac{\varrho}{\varrho+1}\xi(\tau_2,\tau_1,m)\right)\Bigg|\\
\le\ & \xi(\tau_2,\tau_1,m)\Bigg[\int_0^{\frac{\varrho}{\varrho+1}}\iota^\varrho|\Pi'(m\tau_1+\iota\xi(\tau_2,\tau_1,m))|\,d\iota\\
& +\int_{\frac{\varrho}{\varrho+1}}^1 (1-\iota^\varrho)|\Pi'(m\tau_1+\iota\xi(\tau_2,\tau_1,m))|\,d\iota\Bigg]\\
\le\ & \xi(\tau_2,\tau_1,m)\Bigg[\int_0^{\frac{\varrho}{\varrho+1}}\iota^\varrho\{m(1-\iota)|\Pi'(\tau_1)|+\iota|\Pi'(\tau_2)|\}\,d\iota\\
& +\int_{\frac{\varrho}{\varrho+1}}^1 (1-\iota^\varrho)\{m(1-\iota)|\Pi'(\tau_1)|+\iota|\Pi'(\tau_2)|\}\,d\iota\Bigg]\\
\le\ & \xi(\tau_2,\tau_1,m)\Bigg[m|\Pi'(\tau_1)|\int_0^{\frac{\varrho}{\varrho+1}}\iota^\varrho(1-\iota)\,d\iota+|\Pi'(\tau_2)|\int_0^{\frac{\varrho}{\varrho+1}}\iota^{\varrho+1}\,d\iota\\
& +m|\Pi'(\tau_1)|\int_{\frac{\varrho}{\varrho+1}}^1(1-\iota^\varrho)(1-\iota)\,d\iota+|\Pi'(\tau_2)|\int_{\frac{\varrho}{\varrho+1}}^1(1-\iota^\varrho)\iota\,d\iota\Bigg]\\
=\ & \xi(\tau_2,\tau_1,m)\left[\frac{m\varrho}{2(\varrho+1)^2(\varrho+2)}|\Pi'(\tau_1)|+\frac{\varrho(-\varrho^{\varrho+1}+2\varrho^\varrho+(\varrho+1)^\varrho)}{2(\varrho+1)^{\varrho+2}(\varrho+2)}|\Pi'(\tau_2)|\right],
\end{aligned}
$$

where

$$
\begin{aligned}
\int_0^{\frac{\varrho}{\varrho+1}}\iota^{\varrho+1}\,d\iota &= \frac{\varrho^{\varrho+2}}{(\varrho+1)^{\varrho+2}(\varrho+2)},\\
\int_0^{\frac{\varrho}{\varrho+1}}\left(\iota^\varrho-\iota^{\varrho+1}\right)d\iota &= \frac{2\varrho^{\varrho+1}}{(\varrho+1)^{\varrho+2}(\varrho+2)},\\
\int_{\frac{\varrho}{\varrho+1}}^1\left(\iota-\iota^{\varrho+1}\right)d\iota &= \frac{2\varrho^{\varrho+1}+\varrho(\varrho+1)^\varrho}{2(\varrho+1)^{\varrho+2}(\varrho+2)},\\
\int_{\frac{\varrho}{\varrho+1}}^1 (1-\iota^\varrho)(1-\iota)\,d\iota &= \frac{4\varrho^{\varrho+1}-\varrho(\varrho+1)^\varrho}{2(\varrho+1)^{\varrho+2}(\varrho+2)}.
\end{aligned}
$$

This ends the proof. □

Remark 1. In inequality (8), if we take $\xi(\tau_2, \tau_1, m) = \tau_2 - m\tau_1$ and $\varrho = m = 1$, then we get the inequality proven in [36], Theorem 2.2.

Corollary 1. In inequality (8), if we take $\xi(\tau_2, \tau_1, m) = \tau_2 - m\tau_1$, then

$$\left| \frac{\Gamma(\varrho+1)}{[(\tau_2 - m\tau_1)]^\varrho} J^\varrho_{m\tau_1^+} \Pi(\tau_2) - \Pi\left(\frac{m\tau_1 + \varrho\tau_2}{\varrho+1}\right) \right| \qquad (9)$$

$$\leq (\tau_2 - m\tau_1) \left[\frac{m\varrho}{2(\varrho+1)^2(\varrho+2)} |\Pi'(\tau_1)| + \frac{\varrho(-\varrho^{\varrho+1} + 2\varrho^\varrho + (\varrho+1)^\varrho)}{2(\varrho+1)^{\varrho+2}(\varrho+2)} |\Pi'(\tau_2)| \right].$$

Corollary 2. In inequality (8), if we take $\xi(\tau_2, \tau_1, m) = \tau_2 - m\tau_1$ and $m = 1$, then

$$\left| \frac{\Gamma(\varrho+1)}{[(\tau_2 - \tau_1)]^\varrho} J^\varrho_{\tau_1^+} \Pi(\tau_2) - \Pi\left(\frac{\tau_1 + \varrho\tau_2}{\varrho+1}\right) \right| \qquad (10)$$

$$\leq (\tau_2 - \tau_1) \left[\frac{\varrho}{2(\varrho+1)^2(\varrho+2)} |\Pi'(\tau_1)| + \frac{\varrho(-\varrho^{\varrho+1} + 2\varrho^\varrho + (\varrho+1)^\varrho)}{2(\varrho+1)^{\varrho+2}(\varrho+2)} |\Pi'(\tau_2)| \right].$$

Corollary 3. If ξ satisfies the extended condition C, then by definition of the m-preinvexity of $|\Pi'|$, we obtain

$$\begin{aligned}|\Pi'(m\tau_1 + \iota\xi(\tau_2, \tau_1, m))| &= |\Pi'(m\tau_1 + \xi(\tau_2, \tau_1, m)) + (1-\iota)\xi(m\tau_1, m\tau_1 + \xi(\tau_2, \tau_1, m))| \\ &\leq \iota |\Pi'(m\tau_1 + \xi(\tau_2, \tau_1, m))| + m(1-\iota)|\Pi'(\tau_1)|.\end{aligned} \qquad (11)$$

Using inequality (11) in the proof of Theorem 2, the inequality (8) becomes

$$\left| \frac{\Gamma(\varrho+1)}{[\xi(\tau_2, \tau_1, m)]^\varrho} J^\varrho_{m\tau_1^+} \Pi(m\tau_1 + \xi(\tau_2, \tau_1, m)) - \Pi\left(m\tau_1 + \frac{\varrho}{\varrho+1}\xi(\tau_2, \tau_1, m)\right) \right| \qquad (12)$$

$$\leq \xi(\tau_2, \tau_1, m)$$

$$\times \left[\frac{m\varrho}{2(\varrho+1)^2(\varrho+2)} |\Pi'(\tau_1)| + \frac{\varrho(-\varrho^{\varrho+1} + 2\varrho^\varrho + (\varrho+1)^\varrho)}{2(\varrho+1)^{\varrho+2}(\varrho+2)} |\Pi'(m\tau_1 + \xi(\tau_2, \tau_1, m))| \right].$$

We observe that, by employing the m-preinvexity of $|\Pi'|$, we have

$$|\Pi'(m\tau_1 + \xi(\tau_2, \tau_1, m))| \leq |\Pi'(\tau_2)|.$$

Therefore, inequality (12) is better than inequality (8).

Corollary 4. If ξ satisfies the condition C and $m = 1$, then by definition of the preinvexity of $|\Pi'|$, we obtain

$$\begin{aligned}|\Pi'(\tau_1 + \iota\xi(\tau_2, \tau_1))| &= |\Pi'(\tau_1 + \xi(\tau_2, \tau_1)) + (1-\iota)\xi(m\tau_1 + \xi(\tau_2, \tau_1))| \\ &\leq \iota |\Pi'(\tau_1 + \xi(\tau_2, \tau_1))| + (1-\iota)|\Pi'(\tau_1)|.\end{aligned} \qquad (13)$$

Using inequality (13) in proof of Theorem 2, inequality (8) becomes the following:

$$\left| \frac{\Gamma(\varrho+1)}{[\xi(\tau_2, \tau_1)]^\varrho} J^\varrho_{\tau_1^+} \Pi(\tau_1 + \xi(\tau_2, \tau_1)) - \Pi\left(\tau_1 + \frac{\varrho}{\varrho+1}\xi(\tau_2, \tau_1)\right) \right| \qquad (14)$$

$$\leq \xi(\tau_2, \tau_1)$$

$$\times \left[\frac{\varrho}{2(\varrho+1)^2(\varrho+2)} |\Pi'(\tau_1)| + \frac{\varrho(-\varrho^{\varrho+1} + 2\varrho^\varrho + (\varrho+1)^\varrho)}{2(\varrho+1)^{\varrho+2}(\varrho+2)} |\Pi'(\tau_1 + \xi(\tau_2, \tau_1))| \right].$$

We observe that, by employing the preinvexity of $|\Pi'|$, we have

$$|\Pi'(\tau_1 + \xi(\tau_2, \tau_1))| \leq |\Pi'(\tau_2)|.$$

Therefore, inequality (14) is better than inequality (8).

Theorem 3. *Let all conditions in Lemma 1 be satisfied. If $|\Pi'|^q$ is m-preinvex on $[m\tau_1, m\tau_1 + \xi(\tau_2, \tau_1, m)]$ for $y \geq 1$, then, for fractional integrals, the following inequality holds:*

$$\left| \frac{\Gamma(\varrho+1)}{[\xi(\tau_2,\tau_1,m)]^\varrho} J^\varrho_{m\tau_1^+} \Pi(m\tau_1 + \xi(\tau_2,\tau_1,m)) - \Pi\left(m\tau_1 + \frac{\varrho}{\varrho+1}\xi(\tau_2,\tau_1,m)\right) \right| \quad (15)$$

$$\leq \xi(\tau_2,\tau_1,m) \left(\frac{\varrho^{\varrho+1}}{(\varrho+1)^{\varrho+2}}\right)^{1-\frac{1}{y}}$$

$$\times \left\{ \left(\frac{2m\varrho^{\varrho+1}}{(\varrho+1)^{\varrho+2}(\varrho+2)} |\Pi'(\tau_1)|^y + \frac{\varrho^{\varrho+2}}{(\varrho+1)^{\varrho+2}(\varrho+2)} |\Pi'(\tau_2)|^y \right)^{\frac{1}{y}} \right.$$

$$\left. + \left(\frac{4\varrho^{\varrho+1} - \varrho(\varrho+1)^\varrho}{2(\varrho+1)^{\varrho+2}(\varrho+2)} m|\Pi'(\tau_1)|^y + \frac{2\varrho^{\varrho+1} + \varrho(\varrho+1)^\varrho}{2(\varrho+1)^{\varrho+2}(\varrho+2)} |\Pi'(\tau_2)|^y \right)^{\frac{1}{y}} \right\},$$

where $x^{-1} = 1 - y^{-1}$.

Proof. From inequality (3), by utilizing power-mean inequality and definition of m-preinvexity of $|\Pi'|^q$, we have

$$\left| \frac{\Gamma(\varrho+1)}{[\xi(\tau_2,\tau_1,m)]^\varrho} J^\varrho_{m\tau_1^+} \Pi(m\tau_1 + \xi(\tau_2,\tau_1,m)) - \Pi\left(m\tau_1 + \frac{\varrho}{\varrho+1}\xi(\tau_2,\tau_1,m)\right) \right|$$

$$\leq \xi(\tau_2,\tau_1,m) \left[\int_0^{\frac{\varrho}{\varrho+1}} \iota^\varrho \Pi'(m\tau_1 + \iota\xi(\tau_2,\tau_1,m)) d\iota + \int_{\frac{\varrho}{\varrho+1}}^1 (1-\iota^\varrho)\Pi'(m\tau_1 + \iota\xi(\tau_2,\tau_1,m)) d\iota \right]$$

$$\leq \xi(\tau_2,\tau_1,m) \left\{ \left(\int_0^{\frac{\varrho}{\varrho+1}} \iota^\varrho d\iota\right)^{1-\frac{1}{y}} \left(\int_0^{\frac{\varrho}{\varrho+1}} \iota^\varrho |\Pi'(m\tau_1 + \iota\xi(\tau_2,\tau_1,m))| d\iota\right)^{\frac{1}{y}} \right.$$

$$\left. + \left(\int_{\frac{\varrho}{\varrho+1}}^1 (1-\iota^\varrho) d\iota\right)^{1-\frac{1}{y}} \left(\int_{\frac{\varrho}{\varrho+1}}^1 (1-\iota^\varrho) |\Pi'(m\tau_1 + \iota\xi(\tau_2,\tau_1,m))| d\iota\right)^{\frac{1}{y}} \right\}$$

$$\leq \xi(\tau_2,\tau_1,m) \left(\frac{\varrho^{\varrho+1}}{(\varrho+1)^{\varrho+2}}\right)^{1-\frac{1}{y}} \left\{ \left(\int_0^{\frac{\varrho}{\varrho+1}} \iota^\varrho (m(1-\iota)|\Pi'(\tau_1)|^y + \iota|\Pi'(\tau_2)|^y) d\iota\right)^{\frac{1}{y}} \right.$$

$$\left. + \int_{\frac{\varrho}{\varrho+1}}^1 (1-\iota^\varrho)(m(1-\iota)|\Pi'(\tau_1)|^y + \iota|\Pi'(\tau_2)|^y) d\iota \right\}$$

$$= \xi(\tau_2,\tau_1,m) \left(\frac{\varrho^{\varrho+1}}{(\varrho+1)^{\varrho+2}}\right)^{1-\frac{1}{y}}$$

$$\times \left\{ \left(\frac{2m\varrho^{\varrho+1}}{(\varrho+1)^{\varrho+2}(\varrho+2)} |\Pi'(\tau_1)|^y + \frac{\varrho^{\varrho+2}}{(\varrho+1)^{\varrho+2}(\varrho+2)} |\Pi'(\tau_2)|^y \right)^{\frac{1}{y}} \right.$$

$$\left. + \left(\frac{4\varrho^{\varrho+1} - \varrho(\varrho+1)^\varrho}{2(\varrho+1)^{\varrho+2}(\varrho+2)} m|\Pi'(\tau_1)|^y + \frac{2\varrho^{\varrho+1} + \varrho(\varrho+1)^\varrho}{2(\varrho+1)^{\varrho+2}(\varrho+2)} |\Pi'(\tau_2)|^y \right)^{\frac{1}{y}} \right\}.$$

This ends the proof. □

Corollary 5. *In inequality (15), if we take* $\xi(\tau_2, \tau_1, m) = \tau_2 - m\tau_1$, *then*

$$\left| \frac{\Gamma(\varrho+1)}{[(\tau_2 - m\tau_1)]^\varrho} J^\varrho_{m\tau_1^+} \Pi(\tau_2) - \Pi\left(\frac{m\tau_1 + \varrho\tau_2}{\varrho+1}\right) \right|$$

$$\leq \xi(\tau_2 - m\tau_1) \left(\frac{\varrho^{\varrho+1}}{(\varrho+1)^{\varrho+2}}\right)^{1-\frac{1}{y}} \tag{16}$$

$$\times \left\{ \left(\frac{2m\varrho^{\varrho+1}}{(\varrho+1)^{\varrho+2}(\varrho+2)} |\Pi'(\tau_1)|^y + \frac{\varrho^{\varrho+2}}{(\varrho+1)^{\varrho+2}(\varrho+2)} |\Pi'(\tau_2)|^y \right)^{\frac{1}{y}} \right.$$

$$\left. + \left(\frac{4\varrho^{\varrho+1} - \varrho(\varrho+1)^\varrho}{2(\varrho+1)^{\varrho+2}(\varrho+2)} m|\Pi'(\tau_1)|^y + \frac{2\varrho^{\varrho+1} + \varrho(\varrho+1)^\varrho}{2(\varrho+1)^{\varrho+2}(\varrho+2)} |\Pi'(\tau_2)|^y \right)^{\frac{1}{y}} \right\}.$$

Corollary 6. *In inequality (15), if we take* $\xi(\tau_2, \tau_1, m) = \tau_2 - m\tau_1$ *and* $m = 1$, *then*

$$\left| \frac{\Gamma(\varrho+1)}{[(\tau_2 - \tau_1)]^\varrho} J^\varrho_{\tau_1^+} \Pi(\tau_2) - \Pi\left(\frac{\tau_1 + \varrho\tau_2}{\varrho+1}\right) \right|$$

$$\leq \xi(\tau_2 - \tau_1) \left(\frac{\varrho^{\varrho+1}}{(\varrho+1)^{\varrho+2}}\right)^{1-\frac{1}{y}} \tag{17}$$

$$\times \left\{ \left(\frac{2\varrho^{\varrho+1}}{(\varrho+1)^{\varrho+2}(\varrho+2)} |\Pi'(\tau_1)|^y + \frac{\varrho^{\varrho+2}}{(\varrho+1)^{\varrho+2}(\varrho+2)} |\Pi'(\tau_2)|^y \right)^{\frac{1}{y}} \right.$$

$$\left. + \left(\frac{4\varrho^{\varrho+1} - \varrho(\varrho+1)^\varrho}{2(\varrho+1)^{\varrho+2}(\varrho+2)} |\Pi'(\tau_1)|^y + \frac{2\varrho^{\varrho+1} + \varrho(\varrho+1)^\varrho}{2(\varrho+1)^{\varrho+2}(\varrho+2)} |\Pi'(\tau_2)|^y \right)^{\frac{1}{y}} \right\}.$$

Corollary 7. *In inequality (15), if we set* $\xi(\tau_2, \tau_1, m) = \tau_2 - m\tau_1$ *and* $\varrho = 1$, *then we obtain the following midpoint-type inequality:*

$$\left| \frac{1}{\tau_2 - m\tau_1} \int_{m\tau_1}^{\tau_2} \Pi(x) dx - \Pi\left(\frac{\tau_1 + \tau_2}{2}\right) \right| \tag{18}$$

$$\leq \frac{\tau_2 - m\tau_1}{8} \left\{ \left(\frac{m|\Pi'(\tau_1)|^y + 2|\Pi'(\tau_2)|^y}{3}\right)^{\frac{1}{y}} + \left(\frac{2m|\Pi'(\tau_1)|^y + |\Pi'(\tau_2)|^y}{3}\right)^{\frac{1}{y}} \right\}.$$

Corollary 8. *In inequality (15), if we set* $\xi(\tau_2, \tau_1) = \tau_2 - \tau_1$, $m = 1$ *and* $\varrho = 1$, *then we obtain the following midpoint-type inequality*

$$\left| \frac{1}{\tau_2 - \tau_1} \int_{\tau_1}^{\tau_2} \Pi(x) dx - \Pi\left(\frac{\tau_1 + \tau_2}{2}\right) \right| \tag{19}$$

$$\leq \frac{\tau_2 - \tau_1}{8} \left\{ \left(\frac{|\Pi'(\tau_1)|^y + 2|\Pi'(\tau_2)|^y}{3}\right)^{\frac{1}{y}} + \left(\frac{2|\Pi'(\tau_1)|^y + |\Pi'(\tau_2)|^y}{3}\right)^{\frac{1}{y}} \right\}.$$

Corollary 9. *In inequality (15), considering that ξ meets the extended condition C and using inequality (3), we obtain*

$$\left| \frac{\Gamma(\varrho+1)}{[\xi(\tau_2, \tau_1, m)]^\varrho} J^\varrho_{m\tau_1^+} \Pi(m\tau_1 + \xi(\tau_2, \tau_1, m)) - \Pi\left(m\tau_1 + \frac{\varrho}{\varrho+1}\xi(\tau_2, \tau_1, m)\right) \right|$$

$$\leq \xi(\tau_2,\tau_1,m)\left(\frac{\varrho^{\varrho+1}}{(\varrho+1)^{\varrho+2}}\right)^{1-\frac{1}{y}}$$

$$\times\left\{\left(\frac{2m\varrho^{\varrho+1}}{(\varrho+1)^{\varrho+2}(\varrho+2)}|\Pi'(\tau_1)|^y + \frac{\varrho^{\varrho+2}}{(\varrho+1)^{\varrho+2}(\varrho+2)}|\Pi'(m\tau_1+\xi(\tau_2,\tau_1,m))|^y\right)^{\frac{1}{y}}\right.$$

$$\left. + \left(\frac{4\varrho^{\varrho+1}-\varrho(\varrho+1)^\varrho}{2(\varrho+1)^{\varrho+2}(\varrho+2)}m|\Pi'(\tau_1)|^y + \frac{2\varrho^{\varrho+1}+\varrho(\varrho+1)^\varrho}{2(\varrho+1)^{\varrho+2}(\varrho+2)}|\Pi'(m\tau_1+\xi(\tau_2,\tau_1,m))|^y\right)^{\frac{1}{y}}\right\}.$$

Corollary 10. *In inequality (15), considering that ξ meets the extended condition C, $m=1$ and using inequality (3), we obtain*

$$\left|\frac{\Gamma(\varrho+1)}{[\xi(\tau_2,\tau_1,m)]^\varrho}J^\varrho_{\tau_1^+}\Pi(\tau_1+\xi(\tau_2,\tau_1)) - \Pi\left(\tau_1+\frac{\varrho}{\varrho+1}\xi(\tau_2,\tau_1)\right)\right|$$

$$\leq \xi(\tau_2,\tau_1)\left(\frac{\varrho^{\varrho+1}}{(\varrho+1)^{\varrho+2}}\right)^{1-\frac{1}{y}}$$

$$\times\left\{\left(\frac{2\varrho^{\varrho+1}}{(\varrho+1)^{\varrho+2}(\varrho+2)}|\Pi'(\tau_1)|^y + \frac{\varrho^{\varrho+2}}{(\varrho+1)^{\varrho+2}(\varrho+2)}|\Pi'(\tau_1+\xi(\tau_2,\tau_1))|^y\right)^{\frac{1}{y}}\right.$$

$$\left. + \left(\frac{4\varrho^{\varrho+1}-\varrho(\varrho+1)^\varrho}{2(\varrho+1)^{\varrho+2}(\varrho+2)}|\Pi'(\tau_1)|^y + \frac{2\varrho^{\varrho+1}+\varrho(\varrho+1)^\varrho}{2(\varrho+1)^{\varrho+2}(\varrho+2)}|\Pi'(\tau_1+\xi(\tau_2,\tau_1))|^y\right)^{\frac{1}{y}}\right\}.$$

Theorem 4. *Let all conditions in Lemma 1 be satisfied. If $|\Pi'|^q$ is m-preinvex on $[m\tau_1, m\tau_1 + \xi(\tau_2,\tau_1,m)]$ for $y > 1$, then, for fractional integrals, the following inequality holds:*

$$\left|\frac{\Gamma(\varrho+1)}{[\xi(\tau_2,\tau_1,m)]^\varrho}J^\varrho_{m\tau_1^+}\Pi(m\tau_1+\xi(\tau_2,\tau_1,m)) - \Pi\left(m\tau_1+\frac{\varrho}{\varrho+1}\xi(\tau_2,\tau_1,m)\right)\right|$$

$$\leq \xi(\tau_2,\tau_1,m)\left\{\left(M(\varrho,x)\right)^{\frac{1}{x}}\left(\frac{\varrho^2+2\varrho}{2(\varrho+1)^2}m|\Pi'(\tau_1)|^y + \frac{\varrho^2}{2(\varrho+1)^2}|\Pi'(\tau_2)|^y\right)^{\frac{1}{y}}\right.$$

$$\left. + \left(N(\varrho,x)\right)^{\frac{1}{x}}\left(\frac{m}{2(\varrho+1)^2}|\Pi'(\tau_1)|^y + \frac{2\varrho+1}{2(\varrho+1)^2}|\Pi'(\tau_2)|^y\right)^{\frac{1}{y}}\right\}, \qquad (20)$$

where

$$M(\varrho,x) = \int_0^{\frac{\varrho}{\varrho+1}} \iota^{\varrho x}d\iota,$$

$$N(\varrho,x) = \int_{\frac{\varrho}{\varrho+1}}^1 (1-\iota^\varrho)^x d\iota,$$

where $x^{-1}+y^{-1}=1$.

Proof. From inequality (3), from the Hölder integral inequality and the m-preinvexity of $|\Pi'|^q$, we have

$$\left|\frac{\Gamma(\varrho+1)}{[\xi(\tau_2,\tau_1,m)]^\varrho}J^\varrho_{\tau_1^+}\Pi(m\tau_1+\xi(\tau_2,\tau_1,m)) - \Pi\left(m\tau_1+\frac{\varrho}{\varrho+1}\xi(\tau_2,\tau_1,m)\right)\right|$$

$$\leq \xi(\tau_2,\tau_1,m)\left[\int_0^{\frac{\varrho}{\varrho+1}}\iota^\varrho|\Pi'(\tau_1+\iota\xi(\tau_2,\tau_1,m))|d\iota\right.$$

$$\left. + \int_{\frac{\varrho}{\varrho+1}}^1 (1-\iota^\varrho)|\Pi'(m\tau_1+\iota\xi(\tau_2,\tau_1,m))|d\iota\right]$$

$$\leq \xi(\tau_2,\tau_1,m)\left\{\left(\int_0^{\frac{\varrho}{\varrho+1}} \iota^{\varrho x}d\iota\right)^{\frac{1}{x}}\left(\int_0^{\frac{\varrho}{\varrho+1}}|\Pi'(m\tau_1+\iota\xi(\tau_2,\tau_1,m))|^y d\iota\right)^{\frac{1}{y}}\right.$$

$$\left.+\left(\int_{\frac{\varrho}{\varrho+1}}^1 (1-\iota^\varrho)^x d\wp\right)^{\frac{1}{x}}\left(\int_{\frac{\varrho}{\varrho+1}}^1 |\Pi'(m\tau_1+\iota\xi(\tau_2,\tau_1,m))|^y d\iota\right)^{\frac{1}{y}}\right\}$$

$$\leq \xi(\tau_2,\tau_1,m)\left\{\left(\int_0^{\frac{\varrho}{\varrho+1}} \iota^{\varrho x}d\iota\right)^{\frac{1}{x}}\left(\int_0^{\frac{\varrho}{\varrho+1}}\{m(1-\iota)|\Pi'(\tau_1)|^y + \iota|\Pi'(\tau_2)|^y\}d\iota\right)^{\frac{1}{y}}\right.$$

$$\left.+\left(\int_{\frac{\varrho}{\varrho+1}}^1 (1-\iota^\varrho)^x d\iota\right)^{\frac{1}{x}}\left(\int_{\frac{\varrho}{\varrho+1}}^1 \{m(1-\iota)|\Pi'(\tau_1)|^y + \iota|\Pi'(\tau_2)|^y\}d\iota\right)^{\frac{1}{y}}\right\}$$

$$= \xi(\tau_2,\tau_1,m)\left\{\left(M(\varrho,x)\right)^{\frac{1}{x}}\left(\frac{\varrho^2+2\varrho}{2(\varrho+1)^2}m|\Pi'(\tau_1)|^y - \frac{\varrho^2}{2(\varrho+1)^2}|\Pi'(\tau_2)|^y\right)^{\frac{1}{y}}\right.$$

$$\left.+\left(N(\varrho,x)\right)^{\frac{1}{x}}\left(\frac{m}{2(\varrho+1)^2}|\Pi'(\tau_1)|^y + \frac{2\varrho+1}{2(\varrho+1)^2}|\Pi'(\tau_2)|^y\right)^{\frac{1}{y}}\right\}.$$

This ends the proof. □

Remark 2. *In inequality (20), if we take $\xi(\tau_2,\tau_1,m) = \tau_2 - m\tau_1$ and $\varrho = 1$, then we obtain the inequality proved in [36], Theorem 2.3.*

Corollary 11. *In inequality (20), if we take $\xi(\tau_2,\tau_1,m) = \tau_2 - m\tau_1$, then*

$$\left|\frac{\Gamma(\varrho+1)}{[(\tau_2-m\tau_1)]^\varrho} J^\varrho_{m\tau_1^+}\Pi(\tau_2) - \Pi\left(\frac{m\tau_1+\varrho\tau_2}{\varrho+1}\right)\right|$$

$$\leq (\tau_2 - m\tau_1)\left\{\left(M(\varrho,x)\right)^{\frac{1}{x}}\left(\frac{\varrho^2+2\varrho}{2(\varrho+1)^2}m|\Pi'(\tau_1)|^y + \frac{\varrho^2}{2(\varrho+1)^2}|\Pi'(\tau_2)|^y\right)^{\frac{1}{y}}\right.$$

$$\left.+\left(N(\varrho,x)\right)^{\frac{1}{x}}\left(\frac{m}{2(\varrho+1)^2}|\Pi'(\tau_1)|^y + \frac{2\varrho+1}{2(\varrho+1)^2}|\Pi'(\tau_2)|^y\right)^{\frac{1}{y}}\right\}.$$

Corollary 12. *In inequality (20), if we take $\xi(\tau_2,\tau_1) = \tau_2 - \tau_1$ and $m = 1$, then*

$$\left|\frac{\Gamma(\varrho+1)}{[(\tau_2-\tau_1)]^\varrho} J^\varrho_{\tau_1^+}\Pi(\tau_2) - \Pi\left(\frac{\tau_1+\varrho\tau_2}{\varrho+1}\right)\right|$$

$$\leq (\tau_2 - \tau_1)\left\{\left(M(\varrho,x)\right)^{\frac{1}{x}}\left(\frac{\varrho^2+2\varrho}{2(\varrho+1)^2}|\Pi'(\tau_1)|^y + \frac{\varrho^2}{2(\varrho+1)^2}|\Pi'(\tau_2)|^y\right)^{\frac{1}{y}}\right.$$

$$\left.+\left(N(\varrho,x)\right)^{\frac{1}{x}}\left(\frac{1}{2(\varrho+1)^2}|\Pi'(\tau_1)|^y + \frac{2\varrho+1}{2(\varrho+1)^2}|\Pi'(\tau_2)|^y\right)^{\frac{1}{y}}\right\}.$$

Corollary 13. *In inequality (20), considering that ξ meets the extended condition C and using inequality (3), we obtain*

$$\left|\frac{\Gamma(\varrho+1)}{[\xi(\tau_2,\tau_1,m)]^\varrho} J^\varrho_{m\tau_1^+}\Pi(m\tau_1+\xi(\tau_2,\tau_1,m)) - \Pi\left(m\tau_1 + \frac{\varrho}{\varrho+1}\xi(\tau_2,\tau_1,m)\right)\right|$$

$$\leq \xi(\tau_2,\tau_1,m)$$

$$\times\left\{\left(M(\varrho,x)\right)^{\frac{1}{x}}\left(\frac{\varrho^2+2\varrho}{2(\varrho+1)^2}m|\Pi'(\tau_1)|^y + \frac{\varrho^2}{2(\varrho+1)^2}|\Pi'(m\tau_1+\xi(\tau_2,\tau_1,m))|^y\right)^{\frac{1}{y}}\right.$$

$$+\left(N(\varrho,x)\right)^{\frac{1}{x}}\left(\frac{m}{2(\varrho+1)^2}|\Pi'(\tau_1)|^y+\frac{2\varrho+1}{2(\varrho+1)^2}|\Pi'(m\tau_1+\xi(\tau_2,\tau_1,m))|^y\right)^{\frac{1}{y}}\right\}.$$

Corollary 14. *In inequality (20), considering that ξ meets the extended condition C, $m=1$ and using inequality (3), we obtain*

$$\left|\frac{\Gamma(\varrho+1)}{[\xi(\tau_2,\tau_1)]^\varrho}J^\varrho_{\tau_1^+}\Pi(\tau_1+\xi(\tau_2,\tau_1))-\Pi\left(\tau_1+\frac{\varrho}{\varrho+1}\xi(\tau_2,\tau_1)\right)\right|$$
$$\leq \xi(\tau_2,\tau_1)\left\{\left(M(\varrho,x)\right)^{\frac{1}{x}}\left(\frac{\varrho^2+2\varrho}{2(\varrho+1)^2}|\Pi'(\tau_1)|^y+\frac{\varrho^2}{2(\varrho+1)^2}|\Pi'(\tau_1+\xi(\tau_2,\tau_1))|^y\right)^{\frac{1}{y}}\right.$$
$$\left.+\left(N(\varrho,x)\right)^{\frac{1}{x}}\left(\frac{1}{2(\varrho+1)^2}|\Pi'(\tau_1)|^y+\frac{2\varrho+1}{2(\varrho+1)^2}|\Pi'(\tau_1+\xi(\tau_2,\tau_1))|^y\right)^{\frac{1}{y}}\right\}.$$

Theorem 5. *Let all conditions in Lemma 2 be satisfied. If $|\Pi''|^q$ is m-preinvex on $[m\tau_1, m\tau_1+\xi(\tau_2,\tau_1,m)]$ for $y>1$, then, for fractional integrals, the following inequality holds:*

$$\left|\frac{\Gamma(\varrho+1)}{[\xi(\tau_2,\tau_1,m)]^{\varrho+1}}\left\{J^{\varrho-1}_{(m\tau_1+\frac{1}{2}\xi(\tau_2,\tau_1,m))^-}\Pi(m\tau_1)+J^{\varrho-1}_{(m\tau_1+\frac{1}{2}\xi(\tau_2,\tau_1,m))^+}\Pi(m\tau_1+\xi(\tau_2,\tau_1,m))\right\}\right.$$
$$\left.-\frac{\varrho\Pi\left(m\tau_1+\frac{1}{2}\xi(\tau_2,\tau_1,m)\right)}{2^{\varrho-2}[\xi(\tau_2,\tau_1,m)]^2}\right|$$
$$\leq \left(\frac{2^{-\varrho-1}}{\varrho+1}\right)^{\frac{1}{x}}\times\left\{\left[m|\Pi''(\tau_1)|^y\left(\frac{(\varrho+3)2^{-\varrho-2}}{(\varrho+1)(\varrho+2)}\right)+|\Pi''(\tau_2)|^y\left(\frac{2^{-\varrho-2}}{\varrho+2}\right)\right]^{\frac{1}{q}}\right.$$
$$\left.+\left[m|\Pi''(\tau_1)|^y(\frac{2^{-\varrho-2}}{\varrho+2})+|\Pi''(\tau_2)|^y\left(\frac{4-(\varrho+3)2^{-\varrho}}{4(\varrho+1)(\varrho+2)}\right)\right]^{\frac{1}{y}}\right\}, \qquad (21)$$

where $x^{-1}+y^{-1}=1$.

Proof. From inequality (4) and Hölder's integral inequality, we have

$$\left|\frac{\Gamma(\varrho+1)}{[\xi(\tau_2,\tau_1,m)]^{\varrho+1}}\left\{J^{\varrho-1}_{(m\tau_1+\frac{1}{2}\xi(\tau_2,\tau_1,m))^-}\Pi(m\tau_1)+J^{\varrho-1}_{(m\tau_1+\frac{1}{2}\xi(\tau_2,\tau_1,m))^+}\Pi(m\tau_1+\xi(\tau_2,\tau_1,m))\right\}\right.$$
$$\left.-\frac{\varrho\Pi\left(m\tau_1+\frac{1}{2}\xi(\tau_2,\tau_1,m)\right)}{2^{\varrho-2}[\xi(\tau_2,\tau_1,m)]^2}\right|$$
$$\leq \int_0^{\frac{1}{2}}\iota^\varrho|\Pi''(m\tau_1+\iota\xi(\tau_2,\tau_1,m))|\,d\iota+\int_{\frac{1}{2}}^1(1-\iota)^\varrho|\Pi''(m\tau_1+\iota\xi(\tau_2,\tau_1,m))|\,d\iota$$
$$\leq \left(\int_0^{\frac{1}{2}}\iota^\varrho\,d\iota\right)^{\frac{1}{x}}\left(\int_0^{\frac{1}{2}}\iota^\varrho|\Pi''(m\tau_1+\iota\xi(\tau_2,\tau_1,m))|^y\,d\iota\right)^{\frac{1}{y}}$$
$$+\left(\int_0^{\frac{1}{2}}(1-\iota)^\varrho\,d\iota\right)^{\frac{1}{x}}\left(\int_0^{\frac{1}{2}}(1-\iota)^\varrho|\Pi''(m\tau_1+\iota\xi(\tau_2,\tau_1,m))|^y\,d\iota\right)^{\frac{1}{y}}. \qquad (22)$$

Since $|\Pi''|^q$ is m-preinvex function on $[m\tau_1, m\tau_1+\xi(\tau_2,\tau_1,m)]$, we have

$$\int_0^{\frac{1}{2}}\iota^\varrho|\Pi''(m\tau_1+\iota\xi(\tau_2,\tau_1,m))|^y\,d\iota\leq\int_0^{\frac{1}{2}}\iota^\varrho\left\{m(1-\iota)|\Pi''(\tau_1)|^y+\iota|\Pi''(\tau_2)|^y\right\}d\iota \qquad (23)$$

$$\leq m|\Pi''(\tau_1)|^y \left(\frac{(\varrho+3)2^{-\varrho-2}}{(\varrho+1)(\varrho+2)}\right) + |\Pi''(\tau_2)|^y \left(\frac{2^{-\varrho-2}}{\varrho+2}\right)$$

and

$$\int_{\frac{1}{2}}^{1} (1-\iota)^{\varrho} |\Pi''(m\tau_1 + \iota\,\xi(\tau_2,\tau_1,m))|^y \, d\iota \leq \int_{\frac{1}{2}}^{1} (1-\iota)^{\varrho} \left\{m(1-\iota)|\Pi''(\tau_1)|^y + \iota |\Pi''(\tau_2)|^y\right\} d\iota$$

$$\leq m|\Pi''(\tau_1)|^y \left(\frac{2^{-\varrho-2}}{\varrho+2}\right) + |\Pi''(\tau_2)|^y \left(\frac{4-(\varrho+3)2^{-\varrho}}{4(\varrho+1)(\varrho+2)}\right). \tag{24}$$

Using Equations (23) and (24) in (22) and obtaining the result of (21) completes the proof. □

Corollary 15. *In inequality (21), if we take $\xi(\tau_2,\tau_1) = \tau_2 - m\tau_1$, then*

$$\left|\frac{\Gamma(\varrho+1)}{(\tau_2 - m\tau_1)^{\varrho+1}} \left\{J^{\varrho-1}_{\left(\frac{m\tau_1+\tau_2}{2}\right)^{-}} \Pi(m\tau_1) + J^{\varrho-1}_{\left(\frac{m\tau_1+\tau_2}{2}\right)^{+}} \Pi(\tau_2)\right\} - \frac{\varrho\Pi\left(\frac{m\tau_1+\tau_2}{2}\right)}{2^{\varrho-2}(\tau_2-m\tau_1)^2}\right|$$

$$\leq \left(\frac{2^{-\varrho-1}}{\varrho+1}\right)^{\frac{1}{x}} \times \left\{\left[m|\Pi''(\tau_1)|^y \left(\frac{(\varrho+3)2^{-\varrho-2}}{(\varrho+1)(\varrho+2)}\right) + |\Pi''(\tau_2)|^y \left(\frac{2^{-\varrho-2}}{\varrho+2}\right)\right]^{\frac{1}{y}} \right.$$
$$\left. + \left[m|\Pi''(\tau_1)|^y \left(\frac{2^{-\varrho-2}}{\varrho+2}\right) + |\Pi''(\tau_2)|^y \left(\frac{4-(\varrho+3)2^{-\varrho}}{4(\varrho+1)(\varrho+2)}\right)\right]^{\frac{1}{y}}\right\}.$$

Corollary 16. *In inequality (21), if we take $\xi(\tau_2,\tau_1) = \tau_2 - m\tau_1$ and $m=1$, then*

$$\left|\frac{\Gamma(\varrho+1)}{(\tau_2 - \tau_1)^{\varrho+1}} \left\{J^{\varrho-1}_{\left(\frac{\tau_1+\tau_2}{2}\right)^{-}} \Pi(\tau_1) + J^{\varrho-1}_{\left(\frac{\tau_1+\tau_2}{2}\right)^{+}} \Pi(\tau_2)\right\} - \frac{\varrho\Pi\left(\frac{\tau_1+\tau_2}{2}\right)}{2^{\varrho-2}(\tau_2-\tau_1)^2}\right|$$

$$\leq \left(\frac{2^{-\varrho-1}}{\varrho+1}\right)^{\frac{1}{x}} \times \left\{\left[|\Pi''(\tau_1)|^y \left(\frac{(\varrho+3)2^{-\varrho-2}}{(\varrho+1)(\varrho+2)}\right) + |\Pi''(\tau_2)|^y \left(\frac{2^{-\varrho-2}}{\varrho+2}\right)\right]^{\frac{1}{y}} \right.$$
$$\left. + \left[|\Pi''(\tau_1)|^y \left(\frac{2^{-\varrho-2}}{\varrho+2}\right) + |\Pi''(\tau_2)|^y \left(\frac{4-(\varrho+3)2^{-\varrho}}{4(\varrho+1)(\varrho+2)}\right)\right]^{\frac{1}{y}}\right\}.$$

Corollary 17. *In inequality (21), considering that ξ meets the extended condition C and using inequality (4), we obtain*

$$\left|\frac{\Gamma(\varrho+1)}{[\xi(\tau_2,\tau_1,m)]^{\varrho+1}} \left\{J^{\varrho-1}_{\left(m\tau_1+\frac{1}{2}\xi(\tau_2,\tau_1,m)\right)^{-}} \Pi(\tau_1) + J^{\varrho-1}_{\left(m\tau_1+\frac{1}{2}\xi(\tau_2,\tau_1,m)\right)^{+}} \Pi(m\tau_1+\xi(\tau_2,\tau_1,m))\right\}\right.$$
$$\left. - \frac{\varrho\Pi\left(m\tau_1+\frac{1}{2}\xi(\tau_2,\tau_1,m)\right)}{2^{\varrho-2}[\xi(\tau_2,\tau_1,m)]^2}\right|$$

$$\leq \left(\frac{2^{-\varrho-1}}{\varrho+1}\right)^{\frac{1}{x}} \times \left\{\left[m|\Pi''(\tau_1)|^y \left(\frac{(\varrho+3)2^{-\varrho-2}}{(\varrho+1)(\varrho+2)}\right) + |\Pi''(m\tau_1+\xi(\tau_2,\tau_1,m))|^y \left(\frac{2^{-\varrho-2}}{\varrho+2}\right)\right]^{\frac{1}{y}} \right.$$
$$\left. + \left[m|\Pi''(\tau_1)|^y \left(\frac{2^{-\varrho-2}}{\varrho+2}\right) + |\Pi''(m\tau_1+\xi(\tau_2,\tau_1,m))|^y \left(\frac{4-(\varrho+3)2^{-\varrho}}{4(\varrho+1)(\varrho+2)}\right)\right]^{\frac{1}{y}}\right\}.$$

Corollary 18. *In inequality (21), considering that ξ meets the extended condition C, $m = 1$ and using inequality (4), we obtain*

$$\left| \frac{\Gamma(\varrho+1)}{[\xi(\tau_2,\tau_1)]^{\varrho+1}} \left\{ J^{\varrho-1}_{(\tau_1+\frac{1}{2}\xi(\tau_2,\tau_1))^-} \Pi(\tau_1) + J^{\varrho-1}_{(\tau_1+\frac{1}{2}\xi(\tau_2,\tau_1))^+} \Pi(\tau_1+\xi(\tau_2,\tau_1)) \right\} \right.$$
$$\left. - \frac{\varrho \Pi\left(\tau_1+\frac{1}{2}\xi(\tau_2,\tau_1)\right)}{2^{\varrho-2}[\xi(\tau_2,\tau_1)]^2} \right|$$
$$\leq \left(\frac{2^{-\varrho-1}}{\varrho+1}\right)^{\frac{1}{x}} \times \left\{ \left[|\Pi''(\tau_1)|^y \left(\frac{(\varrho+3)2^{-\varrho-2}}{(\varrho+1)(\varrho+2)}\right) + |\Pi''(\tau_1+\xi(\tau_2,\tau_1))|^y \left(\frac{2^{-\varrho-2}}{\varrho+2}\right) \right]^{\frac{1}{y}} \right.$$
$$\left. + \left[|\Pi''(\tau_1)|^y \left(\frac{2^{-\varrho-2}}{\varrho+2}\right) + |\Pi''(\tau_1+\xi(\tau_2,\tau_1))|^y \left(\frac{4-(\varrho+3)2^{-\varrho}}{4(\varrho+1)(\varrho+2)}\right) \right]^{\frac{1}{y}} \right\}.$$

Theorem 6. *Let all the conditions in Lemma 2 be satisfied. If $|\Pi''|^q$ is m-preinvex function on $[m\tau_1, m\tau_1 + \xi(\tau_2, \tau_1, m)]$ for $y > 1$, $y \geq r$, $s \geq 0$. Then, for fractional integrals, the following inequality is satisfied:*

$$\left| \frac{\Gamma(\varrho+1)}{[\xi(\tau_2,\tau_1,m)]^{\varrho+1}} \left\{ J^{\varrho-1}_{(m\tau_1+\frac{1}{2}\xi(\tau_2,\tau_1,m))^-} \Pi(m\tau_1) + J^{\varrho-1}_{(m\tau_1+\frac{1}{2}\xi(\tau_2,\tau_1,m))^+} \Pi(m\tau_1+\xi(\tau_2,\tau_1,m)) \right\} \right.$$
$$\left. - \frac{\varrho \Pi\left(m\tau_1+\frac{1}{2}\xi(\tau_2,\tau_1,m)\right)}{2^{\varrho-2}[\xi(\tau_2,\tau_1,m)]^2} \right|$$
$$\leq \left(\frac{1}{2^{\varrho\left(\frac{y-r}{y-1}\right)+1} \cdot \varrho\left(\frac{y-r}{y-1}\right)+1}\right)^{1-\frac{1}{y}} \left\{ \left[m|\Pi''(\tau_1)|^y \left(\frac{(\varrho r+3)2^{-\varrho r-2}}{(\varrho r+1)(\varrho r+2)}\right) + |\Pi''(\tau_2)|^y \left(\frac{2^{-\varrho r-2}}{\varrho r+2}\right)\right]^{\frac{1}{y}} \right\}$$
$$+ \left(\frac{1}{2^{\varrho\left(\frac{y-s}{y-1}\right)+1} \cdot \varrho\left(\frac{y-s}{y-1}\right)+1}\right)^{1-\frac{1}{y}} \left\{ \left[m|\Pi''(\tau_1)|^y \left(\frac{2^{-\varrho s-2}}{\varrho s+2}\right) + |\Pi''(\tau_2)|^y \left(\frac{(\varrho s+3)e^{-\ln(2)\varrho s}}{4(\varrho s+1)(\varrho s+2)}\right)\right]^{\frac{1}{y}} \right\}. \quad (25)$$

where $x^{-1} + y^{-1} = 1$.

Proof. From inequality (4) and Hölder's integral inequality, we have

$$\left| \frac{\Gamma(\varrho+1)}{[\xi(\tau_2,\tau_1,m)]^{\varrho+1}} \left\{ J^{\varrho-1}_{(m\tau_1+\frac{1}{2}\xi(\tau_2,\tau_1,m))^-} \Pi(m\tau_1) + J^{\varrho-1}_{(\tau_1+\frac{1}{2}\xi(\tau_2,\tau_1,m))^+} \Pi(m\tau_1+\xi(\tau_2,\tau_1,m)) \right\} \right.$$
$$\left. - \frac{\varrho \Pi\left(m\tau_1+\frac{1}{2}\xi(\tau_2,\tau_1,m)\right)}{2^{\varrho-2}[\xi(\tau_2,\tau_1,m)]^2} \right|$$
$$\leq \left\{ \left(\int_0^{\frac{1}{2}} \iota^{\varrho\left(\frac{y-r}{y-1}\right)} d\iota\right)^{1-\frac{1}{y}} \left(\int_0^{\frac{1}{2}} \varrho^{\varrho r} |\Pi''(m\tau_1+\varrho\,\xi(\tau_2,\tau_1,m))|^y d\iota\right)^{\frac{1}{y}} \right.$$
$$\left. + \left(\int_{\frac{1}{2}}^1 (1-\iota)^{\varrho\left(\frac{y-s}{y-1}\right)} d\iota\right)^{1-\frac{1}{y}} \left(\int_{\frac{1}{2}}^1 (1-\varrho)^{\varrho s} |\Pi''(m\tau_1+\varrho\,\xi(\tau_2,\tau_1,m))|^y d\iota\right)^{\frac{1}{y}} \right\}. \quad (26)$$

Since $|\Pi''|^y$ is m-preinvex function on $[m\tau_1, m\tau_1 + \xi(\tau_2, \tau_1, m)]$ we have

$$\int_0^{\frac{1}{2}} \iota^{\varrho r} |\Pi''(m\tau_1+\iota\,\xi(\tau_2,\tau_1,m))|^y d\iota \leq \int_0^{\frac{1}{2}} \iota^{\varrho r} \left\{ m(1-\varrho)|\Pi''(\tau_1)|^y + \iota|\Pi''(\tau_2)|^y \right\} d\iota$$
$$\leq m|\Pi''(\tau_1)|^y \left(\frac{(\varrho r+3)2^{-\varrho r-2}}{(\varrho r+1)(\varrho r+2)}\right) + |\Pi''(\tau_2)|^y \left(\frac{2^{-\varrho r-2}}{\varrho r+2}\right) \quad (27)$$

and

$$\int_{\frac{1}{2}}^{1} (1-\iota)^{\varrho s} \left|\Pi''(m\tau_1 + \iota\,\xi(\tau_2,\tau_1,m))\right|^y d\iota$$
$$\leq \int_{\frac{1}{2}}^{1} (1-\iota)^{\varrho s} \left\{ m(1-\iota)\left|\Pi''(\tau_1)\right|^y + \iota\left|\Pi''(\tau_2)\right|^y \right\} d\iota$$
$$\leq m\left|\Pi''(\tau_1)\right|^y \left(\frac{2^{-\varrho s-2}}{\varrho s + 2}\right) + \left|\Pi''(\tau_2)\right|^y \left(\frac{(\varrho s+3)e^{-\ln(2)\varrho s}}{4(\varrho s+1)(\varrho s+2)}\right). \quad (28)$$

Use Equations (27) and (28) in (26) and obtain (25). This ends the proof. □

Corollary 19. *In inequality (25), if we take $\xi(\tau_2,\tau_1) = \tau_2 - m\tau_1$, then*

$$\left|\frac{\Gamma(\varrho+1)}{(\tau_2 - m\tau_1)^{\varrho+1}} \left\{ J^{\varrho-1}_{\left(\frac{m\tau_1+\tau_2}{2}\right)^-}\Pi(m\tau_1) + J^{\varrho-1}_{\left(\frac{m\tau_1+\tau_2}{2}\right)^+}\Pi(\tau_2) \right\} - \frac{\varrho \Pi\left(\frac{m\tau_1+\tau_2}{2}\right)}{2^{\varrho-2}(\tau_2 - m\tau_1)^2}\right|$$
$$\leq \left(\frac{1}{2^{\varrho\left(\frac{y-r}{y-1}\right)+1} \cdot \varrho\left(\frac{y-r}{y-1}\right)+1}\right)^{1-\frac{1}{y}} \left\{ \left[m\left|\Pi''(\tau_1)\right|^y \left(\frac{(\varrho r+3)2^{-\varrho r-2}}{(\varrho r+1)(\varrho r+2)}\right) + \left|\Pi''(\tau_2)\right|^y \left(\frac{2^{-\varrho r-2}}{\varrho r+2}\right) \right]^{\frac{1}{y}} \right\}$$
$$+ \left(\frac{1}{2^{\varrho\left(\frac{y-s}{y-1}\right)+1} \cdot \varrho\left(\frac{y-s}{y-1}\right)+1}\right)^{1-\frac{1}{y}} \left\{ \left[m\left|\Pi''(\tau_1)\right|^y \left(\frac{2^{-\varrho s-2}}{\varrho s+2}\right) + \left|\Pi''(\tau_2)\right|^y \left(\frac{(\varrho s+3)e^{-\ln(2)\varrho s}}{4(\varrho s+1)(\varrho s+2)}\right) \right]^{\frac{1}{y}} \right\}.$$

Corollary 20. *In inequality (25), if we take $\xi(\tau_2,\tau_1) = \tau_2 - m\tau_1$ and $m = 1$, then*

$$\left|\frac{\Gamma(\varrho+1)}{(\tau_2 - \tau_1)^{\varrho+1}} \left\{ J^{\varrho-1}_{\left(\frac{\tau_1+\tau_2}{2}\right)^-}\Pi(\tau_1) + J^{\varrho-1}_{\left(\frac{\tau_1+\tau_2}{2}\right)^+}\Pi(\tau_2) \right\} - \frac{\varrho \Pi\left(\frac{\tau_1+\tau_2}{2}\right)}{2^{\varrho-2}(\tau_2 - \tau_1)^2}\right|$$
$$\leq \left(\frac{1}{2^{\varrho\left(\frac{y-r}{y-1}\right)+1} \cdot \varrho\left(\frac{y-r}{y-1}\right)+1}\right)^{1-\frac{1}{y}} \left\{ \left[\left|\Pi''(\tau_1)\right|^y \left(\frac{(\varrho r+3)2^{-\varrho r-2}}{(\varrho r+1)(\varrho r+2)}\right) + \left|\Pi''(\tau_2)\right|^y \left(\frac{2^{-\varrho r-2}}{\varrho r+2}\right) \right]^{\frac{1}{y}} \right\}$$
$$+ \left(\frac{1}{2^{\varrho\left(\frac{y-s}{y-1}\right)+1} \cdot \varrho\left(\frac{y-s}{y-1}\right)+1}\right)^{1-\frac{1}{y}} \left\{ \left[\left|\Pi''(\tau_1)\right|^y \left(\frac{2^{-\varrho s-2}}{\varrho s+2}\right) + \left|\Pi''(\tau_2)\right|^y \left(\frac{(\varrho s+3)e^{-\ln(2)\varrho s}}{4(\varrho s+1)(\varrho s+2)}\right) \right]^{\frac{1}{y}} \right\}.$$

Corollary 21. *In inequality (25), considering that ξ meets the extended condition C and using inequality (4), we obtain*

$$\left|\frac{\Gamma(\varrho+1)}{[\xi(\tau_2,\tau_1,m)]^{\varrho+1}} \left\{ J^{\varrho-1}_{\left(m\tau_1+\frac{1}{2}\xi(\tau_2,\tau_1,m)\right)^-}\Pi(m\tau_1) + J^{\varrho-1}_{\left(m\tau_1+\frac{1}{2}\xi(\tau_2,\tau_1,m)\right)^+}\Pi(m\tau_1 + \xi(\tau_2,\tau_1,m)) \right\}\right.$$
$$\left. - \frac{\varrho \Pi\left(m\tau_1 + \frac{1}{2}\xi(\tau_2,\tau_1,m)\right)}{2^{\varrho-2}[\xi(\tau_2,\tau_1,m)]^2}\right|$$
$$\leq \left(\frac{1}{2^{\varrho\left(\frac{y-r}{y-1}\right)+1} \cdot \varrho\left(\frac{y-r}{y-1}\right)+1}\right)^{1-\frac{1}{y}}$$
$$\times \left\{ \left[m\left|\Pi''(\tau_1)\right|^y \left(\frac{(\varrho r+3)2^{-\varrho r-2}}{(\varrho r+1)(\varrho r+2)}\right) + \left|\Pi''(m\tau_1 + \xi(\tau_2,\tau_1,m))\right|^y \left(\frac{2^{-\varrho r-2}}{\varrho r+2}\right) \right]^{\frac{1}{y}} \right\}$$
$$+ \left(\frac{1}{2^{\varrho\left(\frac{y-s}{y-1}\right)+1} \cdot \varrho\left(\frac{y-s}{y-1}\right)+1}\right)^{1-\frac{1}{y}}$$

$$\times \left\{ \left[m|\Pi''(\tau_1)|^y \left(\frac{2^{-\varrho s-2}}{\varrho s+2}\right) + |\Pi''(m\tau_1 + \xi(\tau_2,\tau_1,m))|^y \left(\frac{(\varrho s+3)e^{-\ln(2)\varrho s}}{4(\varrho s+1)(\varrho s+2)}\right) \right]^{\frac{1}{y}} \right\}.$$

Corollary 22. *In inequality (25), considering that ξ meets the extended condition C, $m=1$ and using inequality (4), we obtain*

$$\left| \frac{\Gamma(\varrho+1)}{[\xi(\tau_2,\tau_1)]^{\varrho+1}} \left\{ J^{\varrho-1}_{(\tau_1+\frac{1}{2}\xi(\tau_2,\tau_1))^-} \Pi(\tau_1) + J^{\varrho-1}_{(\tau_1+\frac{1}{2}\xi(\tau_2,\tau_1))^+} \Pi(\tau_1+\xi(\tau_2,\tau_1)) \right\} \right.$$
$$\left. - \frac{\varrho \Pi\left(\tau_1 + \frac{1}{2}\xi(\tau_2,\tau_1)\right)}{2^{\varrho-2}[\xi(\tau_2,\tau_1)]^2} \right|$$
$$\leq \left(\frac{1}{2^{\varrho\left(\frac{y-r}{y-1}\right)+1} \cdot \varrho\left(\frac{y-r}{y-1}\right)+1} \right)^{1-\frac{1}{y}}$$
$$\times \left\{ \left[|\Pi''(\tau_1)|^y \left(\frac{(\varrho r+3)2^{-\varrho r-2}}{(\varrho r+1)(\varrho r+2)}\right) + |\Pi''(\tau_1+\xi(\tau_2,\tau_1))|^y \left(\frac{2^{-\varrho r-2}}{\varrho r+2}\right) \right]^{\frac{1}{y}} \right\}$$
$$+ \left(\frac{1}{2^{\varrho\left(\frac{y-s}{y-1}\right)+1} \cdot \varrho\left(\frac{y-s}{y-1}\right)+1} \right)^{1-\frac{1}{y}}$$
$$\times \left\{ \left[|\Pi''(\tau_1)|^y \left(\frac{2^{-\varrho s-2}}{\varrho s+2}\right) + |\Pi''(\tau_1+\xi(\tau_2,\tau_1))|^y \left(\frac{(\varrho s+3)e^{-\ln(2)\varrho s}}{4(\varrho s+1)(\varrho s+2)}\right) \right]^{\frac{1}{y}} \right\}.$$

Corollary 23. *In inequality (25), when $r=s$, we have*

$$\left| \frac{\Gamma(\varrho+1)}{[\xi(\tau_2,\tau_1,m)]^{\varrho+1}} \left\{ J^{\varrho-1}_{(m\tau_1+\frac{1}{2}\xi(\tau_2,\tau_1,m))^-} \Pi(m\tau_1) + J^{\varrho-1}_{(m\tau_1+\frac{1}{2}\xi(\tau_2,\tau_1,m))^+} \Pi(m\tau_1+\xi(\tau_2,\tau_1,m)) \right\} \right.$$
$$\left. - \frac{\varrho \Pi\left(m\tau_1+\frac{1}{2}\xi(\tau_2,\tau_1,m)\right)}{2^{\varrho-2}[\xi(\tau_2,\tau_1,m)]^2} \right|$$
$$\leq \left(\frac{1}{2^{\varrho\left(\frac{y-r}{y-1}\right)+1} \varrho\left(\frac{y-r}{y-1}\right)+1} \right)^{1-\frac{1}{y}} \times \left\{ \left\{ \left[m|\Pi''(\tau_1)|^y \left(\frac{(\varrho r+3)2^{-\varrho r-2}}{(\varrho r+1)(\varrho r+2)}\right) + |\Pi''(\tau_2)|^y \left(\frac{2^{-\varrho r-2}}{\varrho r+2}\right) \right]^{\frac{1}{y}} \right\} \right.$$
$$\left. + \left\{ \left[m|\Pi''(\tau_1)|^y \left(\frac{2^{-\varrho r-2}}{\varrho r+2}\right) + |\Pi''(\tau_2)|^y \left(\frac{(\varrho r+3)e^{-\ln(2)\varrho r}}{4(\varrho r+1)(\varrho r+2)}\right) \right]^{\frac{1}{y}} \right\} \right\}.$$

Corollary 24. *In inequality (25), when $r=s$ and $m=1$, we have*

$$\left| \frac{\Gamma(\varrho+1)}{[\xi(\tau_2,\tau_1)]^{\varrho+1}} \left\{ J^{\varrho-1}_{(\tau_1+\frac{1}{2}\xi(\tau_2,\tau_1))^-} \Pi(\tau_1) + J^{\varrho-1}_{(\tau_1+\frac{1}{2}\xi(\tau_2,\tau_1))^+} \Pi(\tau_1+\xi(\tau_2,\tau_1)) \right\} \right.$$
$$\left. - \frac{\varrho \Pi\left(\tau_1+\frac{1}{2}\xi(\tau_2,\tau_1)\right)}{2^{\varrho-2}[\xi(\tau_2,\tau_1)]^2} \right|$$
$$\leq \left(\frac{1}{2^{\varrho\left(\frac{y-r}{y-1}\right)+1} \varrho\left(\frac{y-r}{y-1}\right)+1} \right)^{1-\frac{1}{y}} \times \left\{ \left\{ \left[|\Pi''(\tau_1)|^y \left(\frac{(\varrho r+3)2^{-\varrho r-2}}{(\varrho r+1)(\varrho r+2)}\right) + |\Pi''(\tau_2)|^y \left(\frac{2^{-\varrho r-2}}{\varrho r+2}\right) \right]^{\frac{1}{y}} \right\} \right.$$
$$\left. + \left\{ \left[|\Pi''(\tau_1)|^y \left(\frac{2^{-\varrho r-2}}{\varrho r+2}\right) + |\Pi''(\tau_2)|^y \left(\frac{(\varrho r+3)e^{-\ln(2)\varrho r}}{4(\varrho r+1)(\varrho r+2)}\right) \right]^{\frac{1}{y}} \right\} \right\}.$$

Corollary 25. In inequality (25), when $r = 0 = s$, we have

$$\left| \frac{\Gamma(\varrho+1)}{[\xi(\tau_2,\tau_1,m)]^{\varrho+1}} \left\{ J^{\varrho-1}_{(m\tau_1+\frac{1}{2}\xi(\tau_2,\tau_1,m))^-} \Pi(m\tau_1) + J^{\varrho-1}_{(m\tau_1+\frac{1}{2}\xi(\tau_2,\tau_1,m))^+} \Pi(m\tau_1+\xi(\tau_2,\tau_1,m)) \right\} \right.$$
$$\left. - \frac{\varrho \Pi\left(m\tau_1+\frac{1}{2}\xi(\tau_2,\tau_1,m)\right)}{2^{\varrho-2}[\xi(\tau_2,\tau_1,m)]^2} \right|$$
$$\leq \left(\frac{1}{2^{\varrho\left(\frac{y}{y-1}\right)+1} \cdot \varrho\left(\frac{y}{y-1}\right)+1} \right)^{1-\frac{1}{y}}$$
$$\times \left\{ \left(m|\Pi''(\tau_1)|^y \frac{3}{8} + |\Pi''(\tau_2)|^y \frac{1}{8} \right)^{\frac{1}{y}} + \left(m|\Pi''(\tau_1)|^y \frac{1}{8} + |\Pi''(\tau_2)|^y \frac{3}{8} \right)^{\frac{1}{y}} \right\}.$$

Corollary 26. In inequality (25), when $r = 0 = s$ and $m = 1$, we have

$$\left| \frac{\Gamma(\varrho+1)}{[\xi(\tau_2,\tau_1)]^{\varrho+1}} \left\{ J^{\varrho-1}_{(\tau_1+\frac{1}{2}\xi(\tau_2,\tau_1))^-} \Pi(\tau_1) + J^{\varrho-1}_{(\tau_1+\frac{1}{2}\xi(\tau_2,\tau_1))^+} \Pi(\tau_1+\xi(\tau_2,\tau_1)) \right\} \right.$$
$$\left. - \frac{\varrho \Pi\left(\tau_1+\frac{1}{2}\xi(\tau_2,\tau_1)\right)}{2^{\varrho-2}[\xi(\tau_2,\tau_1)]^2} \right|$$
$$\leq \left(\frac{1}{2^{\varrho\left(\frac{y}{y-1}\right)+1} \cdot \varrho\left(\frac{y}{y-1}\right)+1} \right)^{1-\frac{1}{y}}$$
$$\times \left\{ \left(|\Pi''(\tau_1)|^y \frac{3}{8} + |\Pi''(\tau_2)|^y \frac{1}{8} \right)^{\frac{1}{y}} + \left(|\Pi''(\tau_1)|^y \frac{1}{8} + |\Pi''(\tau_2)|^y \frac{3}{8} \right)^{\frac{1}{y}} \right\}.$$

Corollary 27. In inequality (25), when $r = s = y$, we have

$$\left| \frac{\Gamma(\varrho+1)}{[\xi(\tau_2,\tau_1)]^{\varrho+1}} \left\{ J^{\varrho-1}_{(m\tau_1+\frac{1}{2}\xi(\tau_2,\tau_1,m))^-} \Pi(m\tau_1) + J^{\varrho-1}_{(m\tau_1+\frac{1}{2}\xi(\tau_2,\tau_1,m))^+} \Pi(m\tau_1+\xi(\tau_2,\tau_1,m)) \right\} \right.$$
$$\left. - \frac{\varrho \Pi\left(m\tau_1+\frac{1}{2}\xi(\tau_2,\tau_1,m)\right)}{2^{\varrho-2}[\xi(\tau_2,\tau_1,m)]^2} \right|$$
$$\leq \left(\frac{1}{2}\right)^{1-\frac{1}{y}} \times \left\{ \left(m|\Pi''(\tau_1)|^y \left(\frac{(\varrho y+3)2^{-\varrho y-2}}{(\varrho y+1)(\varrho y+2)} \right) + |\Pi''(\tau_2)|^y \left(\frac{2^{-\varrho y-2}}{(\varrho y+2)} \right) \right)^{\frac{1}{y}} \right.$$
$$\left. + \left(m|\Pi''(\tau_1)|^y \left(\frac{2^{-\varrho y-2}}{(\varrho y+2)} \right) + |\Pi''(\tau_2)|^y \left(\frac{(\varrho y+3)e^{-\ln(2)\varrho y}}{4(\varrho y+1)(\varrho y+2)} \right) \right)^{\frac{1}{y}} \right\}.$$

Corollary 28. In inequality (25), when $r = s = y$ and $m = 1$, we have

$$\left| \frac{\Gamma(\varrho+1)}{[\xi(\tau_2,\tau_1)]^{\varrho+1}} \left\{ J^{\varrho-1}_{(\tau_1+\frac{1}{2}\xi(\tau_2,\tau_1))^-} \Pi(\tau_1) + J^{\varrho-1}_{(\tau_1+\frac{1}{2}\xi(\tau_2,\tau_1))^+} \Pi(\tau_1+\xi(\tau_2,\tau_1)) \right\} \right.$$
$$\left. - \frac{\varrho \Pi\left(\tau_1+\frac{1}{2}\xi(\tau_2,\tau_1)\right)}{2^{\varrho-2}[\xi(\tau_2,\tau_1)]^2} \right|$$
$$\leq \left(\frac{1}{2}\right)^{1-\frac{1}{y}} \times \left\{ \left(|\Pi''(\tau_1)|^y \left(\frac{(\varrho y+3)2^{-\varrho y-2}}{(\varrho y+1)(\varrho y+2)} \right) + |\Pi''(\tau_2)|^y \left(\frac{2^{-\varrho y-2}}{(\varrho y+2)} \right) \right)^{\frac{1}{y}} \right.$$

$$+ \left(|\Pi''(\tau_1)|^y \left(\frac{2^{-\varrho y-2}}{(\varrho y+2)} \right) + |\Pi''(\tau_2)|^y \left(\frac{(\varrho y+3)e^{-\ln(2)\varrho y}}{4(\varrho y+1)(\varrho y+2)} \right) \right)^{\frac{1}{y}} \right\}.$$

4. Applications to Some Special Functions

4.1. q-Digamma Function

Let $0 < \mathbf{q} < 1$, the mathematically **q**-digamma function $\varphi_\mathbf{q}$ (see [37,38]), which is given as:

$$\varphi_\mathbf{q} = -\ln(1-\mathbf{q}) + \ln \mathbf{q} \sum_{k=0}^{\infty} \frac{\mathbf{q}^{k+\zeta}}{1-\mathbf{q}^{k+\zeta}}$$

$$= -\ln(1-\mathbf{q}) + \ln \mathbf{q} \sum_{k=0}^{\infty} \frac{\mathbf{q}^{k\zeta}}{1-\mathbf{q}^{k\zeta}}.$$

For $\mathbf{q} > 1$ and $\zeta > 0$, **q**-digamma function $\varphi_\mathbf{q}$ can be given as:

$$\varphi_\mathbf{q} = -\ln(\mathbf{q}-1) + \ln \mathbf{q} \left[\zeta - \frac{1}{2} - \sum_{k=0}^{\infty} \frac{\mathbf{q}^{-(k+\zeta)}}{1-\mathbf{q}^{-(k+\zeta)}} \right]$$

$$= -\ln(\mathbf{q}-1) + \ln \mathbf{q} \left[\zeta - \frac{1}{2} - \sum_{k=0}^{\infty} \frac{\mathbf{q}^{-k\zeta}}{1-\mathbf{q}^{-k\zeta}} \right].$$

Proposition 1. *Assume that $\tau_1, \tau_2 \in R$ such that $0 < \tau_1 < \tau_2$ and $0 < q < 1$. Then:*

$$\left| \frac{1}{\tau_2 - \tau_1} \int_{\tau_1}^{\tau_2} \varphi_q(\varepsilon) \, d\varepsilon - \varphi_q \left(\frac{\tau_1 + \tau_2}{2} \right) \right| \leq \left(\frac{\tau_2 - \tau_1}{8} \right) \left\{ \left(\frac{\left| \varphi_q^{(1)}(\tau_1) \right|^y + 2 \left| \varphi_q^{(1)}(\tau_2) \right|^y}{3} \right)^{\frac{1}{y}} \right. \quad (29)$$

$$\left. + \left(\frac{2 \left| \varphi_q^{(1)}(\tau_1) \right|^y + \left| \varphi_q^{(1)}(\tau_2) \right|^y}{3} \right)^{\frac{1}{y}} \right\}.$$

Proof. The assertion can be obtained immediately by inequality (18), when $m = 1$, $\Pi(\varepsilon) = \varphi_\mathbf{q}(\varepsilon)$ and $\varepsilon > 0$, since $\Pi'(\varepsilon) = \varphi'_\mathbf{q}(\varepsilon)$ is convex on $(0, +\infty)$. □

4.2. Modified Bessel Function

This section contains multiple uses related to the prediction of a few special functions, specifically modified Bessel functions. Such functions can be observed in statistical mechanics, non-uniform beams, transmission line studies, and statistical treatment of relativistic gas. First, we add the mathematical form of modified Bessel function $\Im_\rho$, in the first sense, which is given by (see [37], p. 77)

$$\Im_\rho(\zeta) = \Sigma_{n\geq 0} \frac{\left(\frac{\zeta}{2} \right)^{\rho+2n}}{n!\Gamma(\rho+n+1)}.$$

where $\zeta \in \mathbb{R}$ and $\rho > -1$, while the mathematical form of modified Bessel function $\mathfrak{K}_\rho$ in the second sense (see [37], p. 78) is usually explored as

$$\mathfrak{K}_\rho(\zeta) = \frac{\pi}{2} \frac{\Im_{-\rho}(\zeta) - \Im_\rho(\zeta)}{\sin \rho \pi}.$$

Consider the function $\Omega_\rho(\zeta) : \mathbb{R} \to [1, \infty)$ defined by

$$\Omega_\rho(\zeta) = 2^\rho \Gamma(\rho+1) \zeta^{-\rho} \Im_\rho(\zeta).$$

The first order derivative formula of $\Omega_\rho(\zeta)$ is given by [37]:

$$\Omega'_\rho(\zeta) = \frac{\zeta}{2(\rho+1)} \Omega_{\rho+1}(\zeta), \tag{30}$$

and the second derivative can be attained easily from (30) to be

$$\Omega''_\rho(\zeta) = \frac{\zeta^2 \Omega_{\rho+2}(\zeta)}{4(\rho+1)(\rho+2)} + \frac{\Omega_{\rho+1}(\zeta)}{2(\rho+1)}. \tag{31}$$

Proposition 2. *Suppose that $\rho > -1$ and $0 < \tau_1 < \tau_2$. Then, we have*

$$\left| \frac{\tau_1 + \tau_2}{4(\rho+1)} \Omega_{\rho+1}\left(\frac{\tau_1+\tau_2}{8}\right) - \frac{\Omega_\rho(\tau_2) - \Omega_\rho(\tau_1)}{\tau_2 - \tau_1} \right|$$
$$\leq \frac{\tau_2 - \tau_1}{8} \left[\frac{1}{3} \left\{ \left(\frac{\tau_1^2 \Omega_{\rho+2}(\tau_1)}{4(\rho+1)(\rho+2)} + \frac{\Omega_{\rho+1}(\tau_1)}{2(\rho+1)} \right)^q + 2\left(\frac{\tau_2^2 \Omega_{\rho+2}(\tau_2)}{4(\rho+1)(\rho+2)} + \frac{\Omega_{\rho+1}(\tau_2)}{2(\rho+1)} \right)^q \right\}^{\frac{1}{q}} \right.$$
$$\left. + \frac{1}{3} \left\{ 2\left(\frac{\tau_1^2 \Omega_{\rho+2}(\tau_1)}{4(\rho+1)(\rho+2)} + \frac{\Omega_{\rho+1}(\tau_1)}{2(\rho+1)} \right)^q + \left(\frac{\tau_2^2 \Omega_{\rho+2}(\tau_2)}{4(\rho+1)(\rho+2)} + \frac{\Omega_{\rho+1}(\tau_2)}{2(\rho+1)} \right)^q \right\}^{\frac{1}{q}} \right].$$

Proof. Applying the inequality (18) to the mapping $\Pi(\zeta) = \Omega'_\rho(\zeta)$, $\zeta > 0$, $m = 1$ and the identities (30) and (31) we have the result. (Note that all assumptions are satisfied). □

5. Conclusions

The work on integral inequalities associated with fractional operators has proven to be an abundant source of inspiration for numerous researchers in a variety of fields. Improvements and generalizations achieved with the concept of preinvexity result in better and sharper bounds when compared to convex functions. First, in this work, we established a few fractional identities. Employing these new notations and identities, we derived some Hermite–Hadamard-type inequalities applicable to the R-L fractional integrals. Furthermore, various examples are provided to demonstrate the accuracy of the results. With the help of power mean and Hölder inequality, we derived the generalizations of H-H inequality that brought the work more aesthetic appeal. Our findings provide improvements and modifications to prior investigations, encouraging additional investigation.

Author Contributions: Conceptualization, M.T., S.K.N. and A.A.S.; methodology, H.A., S.Q. and E.H.; software, M.T. and S.Q.; validation, M.T., E.H. and S.Q.; formal analysis, M.T., S.K.N. and S.Q.; investigation, H.A.; resources, M.T.; data curation, A.A.S.; writing—original draft preparation, M.T., H.A. and S.Q.; writing—review and editing, M.T., H.A. and S.K.N.; visualization, H.A.; supervision, S.K.N. All authors have read and agreed to the published version of the manuscript.

Funding: This research received no external funding.

Conflicts of Interest: The authors declare no conflict of interest.

References

1. Breaz, D.; Yildiz, C.; Cotirla, L.; Rahman, G.; Yergöz, B. New Hadamard type inequalities for modified h-convex functions. *Fractal Fract.* **2023**, *7*, 216. [CrossRef]
2. Khan, M.B.; Noor, M.A.; Noor, K.I.; Chu, Y.M. New Hermite–Hadamard-type inequalities for-convex fuzzy-interval-valued functions. *Adv. Differ. Equ.* **2021**, *2021*, 149. [CrossRef]
3. Noor, M.A.; Noor, K.I.; Awan, M.U. Generalized convexity and integral inequalities. *Appl. Math. Inf. Sci.* **2015**, *9*, 233–243. [CrossRef]
4. Kadakal, M.; İşcan, İ.; Kadakal, H.; Bekar, K. On improvements of some integral inequalities. *Honam Math. J.* **2021**, *43*, 441–452. [CrossRef]
5. Noor, M.A.; Noor, K.I.; Awan, M.U. Geometrically relative convex functions. *Appl. Math. Inf. Sci.* **2014**, *8*, 607. [CrossRef]
6. Noor, M.A.; Noor, K.I. Higher order strongly generalized convex functions. *Appl. Math. Inf. Sci.* **2020**, *14*, 133–139. [CrossRef]
7. İşcan, İ. A new generalization of some integral inequalities for (α, m)-convex functions. *Math. Sci.* **2013**, *7*, 22. [CrossRef]

8. Wu, S.; Awan, M.U.; Noor, M.A.; Noor, K.I.; Iftikhar, S. On a new class of convex functions and integral inequalities. *J. Inequal. Appl.* **2019**, *2019*, 131. [CrossRef]
9. Sahoo, S.K.; Ahmad, H.; Tariq, M.; Kodamasingh, B.; Aydi, H.; De la Sen, M. Hermite-Hadamard type inequalities involving k-fractional operator for (h, m)-convex functions. *Symmetry* **2021**, *13*, 1686. [CrossRef]
10. Butt, S.I.; Nadeem, M.; Farid, G. On Caputo fractional derivatives via exponential s-convex functions. *Turk. J. Sci.* **2020**, *5*, 140–146.
11. Butt, S.I.; Yousaf, S.; Akdemir, A.O.; Dokuyucu, M.A. New Hadamard-type integral inequalities via a general form of fractional integral operators. *Chaos Soliton Fract.* **2021**, *148*, 111025. [CrossRef]
12. Set, E.; Butt, S.I.; Akdemir, A.O.; Karaoglan, A.; Abdeljawad, T. New integral inequalities for differentiable convex functions via Atangana-Baleanu fractional integral operators. *Chaos Solitons Fractals* **2021**, *143*, 110554. [CrossRef]
13. Tariq, M.; Ahmad, H.; Sahoo, S.K. The Hermite-Hadamard type inequality and its estimations via generalized convex functions of Raina type. *Math. Model. Numer. Simul. Appl.* **2021**, *1*, 32–43. [CrossRef]
14. Tariq, M.; Sahoo, S.K.; Ahmad, H.; Shaikh, A.A.; Kodamasingh, B.; Khan, D. Some integral inequalities via new family of preinvex functions. *Math. Model. Numer. Simul. Appl.* **2022**, *2*, 117–126. [CrossRef]
15. Butt, S.I.; Horváth, L.; Pečarić, D.; Pečarić, J. *Cyclic Improvements of Jensen's Inequalities: Cyclic Inequalities in Information Theory*; Element: Zagreb, Croatia, 2020.
16. Rasheed, T.; Butt, S.I.; Pečarić, D.; Pečarić, J. Generalized cyclic Jensen and information inequalities. *Chaos Solitons Fractals* **2022**, *163*, 112602. [CrossRef]
17. Butt, S.I.; Pečarić, D.; Pečarić, J. Several Jensen–Gruss inequalities with applications in information theory. *Ukrain. Mate. Zhurnal.* **2023**, *74*, 1654–1672. [CrossRef]
18. Mehmood, N.; Butt, S.I.; Pečarić, D.; Pečarić, J. Generalizations of cyclic refinements of Jensen's inequality by Lidstone's polynomial with applications in Information Theory. *J. Math. Inequal.* **2019**, *14*, 249–271. [CrossRef]
19. Özdemir, M.E.; Butt, S.I.; Bayraktar, B.; Nasir, J. Several integral inequalities for (α, s, m)-convex functions. *AIMS Math.* **2020**, *5*, 3906–3921. [CrossRef]
20. Antczak, T. Mean value in invexity analysis. *Nonlinear Anal.* **2005**, *60*, 1473–1484. [CrossRef]
21. Mishra, S.K.; Giorgi, G. *Invexity and Optimization*; Springer: Berlin/Heidelberg, Germany, 2008.
22. Yang, X.M.; Li, D. On properties of preinvex functions. *J. Math. Anal. Appl.* **2001**, *256*, 229–241. [CrossRef]
23. Pini, R. Invexity and generalized convexity. *Optimization* **1991**, *22*, 513–525. [CrossRef]
24. Noor, M.A. Hermite-Hadamard integral inequalities for log-preinvex functions. *J. Math. Anal. Approx. Theory* **2007**, *2*, 126–131.
25. Budak, H.; Ali, M.A.; Tarhanaci, M. Some new quantum Hermite–Hadamard like inequalities for coordinated convex functions. *J. Optim. Theory Appl.* **2020**, *186*, 899–910. [CrossRef]
26. Budak, H.; Tunc, T.; Sarikaya, M.Z. Fractional Hermite–Hadamard type inequalities for interval valued functions. *Proc. Amer. Math. Soc.* **2020**, *148*, 705–718. [CrossRef]
27. Işcan, I. Some new Hermite Hadamard type inequalities for geometrically convex functions. *Math. Stat.* **2013**, *1*, 86–91. [CrossRef]
28. Barani, A.; Ghazanfari, G.; Dragomir, S.S. Hermite-Hadamard inequality for functions whose derivatives absolute values are preinvex. *J. Inequal. Appl.* **2012**, *2012*, 247. [CrossRef]
29. Du, T.T.; Liao, J.G.; Li, Y.J. Properties and integral inequalities of Hadamard–Simpson type for the generalized (s, m)-preinvex functions. *J. Nonlinear Sci. Appl.* **2016**, *9*, 3112–3126. [CrossRef]
30. Weir, T.; Mond, B. Pre-inven functions in multiple objective optimization. *J. Math. Anal. Appl.* **1988**, *136*, 29–38. [CrossRef]
31. Deng, Y.; Kalsoom, H.; Wu, S. Some new Quantum Hermite–Hadamard-type estimates within a class of generalized (s, m)-preinvex functions. *Symmetry* **2019**, *11*, 1283. [CrossRef]
32. Mohan, S.R.; Neogy, S.K. On invex sets and preinvex functions. *J. Math. Anal. Appl.* **1995**, *189*, 901–908. [CrossRef]
33. Du, T.S.; Liao, J.G.; Chen, L.G.; Awan, M.U. Properties and Riemann–Liouville fractional Hermite–Hadamard inequalities for the generalized (α, m)–preinvex functions. *J. Inequal. Appl.* **2016**, *2016*, 306. [CrossRef]
34. Noor, M.A. Hadamard integral inequalities for product of two preinvex function. *Nonl. Anal. Forum.* **2009**, *14*, 167–173.
35. Gorenflo, R.; Mainardi, F. *Fractional Calculus Integral and Differential Equations of Fractional Order*; Springer: New York, NY, USA, 1997; pp. 223–276.
36. Kirmaci, U.S. Inequalities for differentiable mappings and applications to special means of real numbers and to midpoint formula. *Appl. Math. Comput.* **2004**, *147*, 137–146. [CrossRef]
37. Watson, G.N. *A Treatise on the Theory of Bessel Functions*; Cambridge University Press: Cambridge, UK, 1995.
38. Jain, S.; Mehrez, K.; Baleanu, D.; Agarwal, P. Certain Hermite–Hadamard inequalities for logarithmically convex functions with applications. *Mathematics* **2019**, *7*, 163. [CrossRef]

Disclaimer/Publisher's Note: The statements, opinions and data contained in all publications are solely those of the individual author(s) and contributor(s) and not of MDPI and/or the editor(s). MDPI and/or the editor(s) disclaim responsibility for any injury to people or property resulting from any ideas, methods, instructions or products referred to in the content.

MDPI AG
Grosspeteranlage 5
4052 Basel
Switzerland
Tel.: +41 61 683 77 34

Mathematical and Computational Applications Editorial Office
E-mail: mca@mdpi.com
www.mdpi.com/journal/mca

Disclaimer/Publisher's Note: The statements, opinions and data contained in all publications are solely those of the individual author(s) and contributor(s) and not of MDPI and/or the editor(s). MDPI and/or the editor(s) disclaim responsibility for any injury to people or property resulting from any ideas, methods, instructions or products referred to in the content.

www.ingramcontent.com/pod-product-compliance
Lightning Source LLC
LaVergne TN
LVHW070443100526
838202LV00014B/1654